Prentice Hall LITERATURE

PENGUIN  EDITION

Reader's Notebook

English Learner's Version

Grade Eleven

PEARSON

Upper Saddle River, New Jersey
Boston, Massachusetts
Chandler, Arizona
Glenview, Illinois
Shoreview, Minnesota

ISBN: 978-0-13-366721-9

1 2 3 4 5 6 7 8 9 10   17 16 15 14 13 12 11 10 09 08

ACKNOWLEDGMENTS

Grateful acknowledgment is made to the following for copyrighted material:

Sandra Dijkstra Literary Agency
"Mother Tongue" by Amy Tan from *The Joy Luck Club*. Copyright © 1989 by Amy Tan. Copyright © 1989 by Amy Tan. First appeared in *Threepenny Review*.

Farrar, Straus & Giroux, LLC
"The First Seven Years" by Bernard Malamud from *The Magic Barrel*. Copyright © 1950, 1958 and copyright renewed 1977, 1986 by Bernard Malamud.

Florida Master Site File
"Archaeological Short Form" from *http://www. flheritage.com*.

Georgia State University
"Georgia State University's Web Accessibility Policy". Copyright © Georgia State University.

Harcourt, Inc.
"Everyday Use" by Alice Walker from *In Love & Trouble: Stories of Black Women,* copyright © 1973 by Alice Walker. "A Worn Path" by Eudora Welty from *A Curtain of Green and Other Stories,* copyright 1941 and renewed in 1969 by Eudora Welty. This material may not be reproduced in any form or by any means without the prior written permission of the publisher.

The Landmark Project
"Son of Citation Machine and Landmarks Son of Citation Machine Masthead" from http://

citationmachine.net/ Copyright © 2006 by David Warlick & The Landmark Project.

League of Women Voters
"How to Watch a Debate" from *www.lwv.org*. The material in this publication on "How to Watch a Debate" was excerpted from a League of Women Voters of the United States (LWVUS) online document of the same title, located at www.lwv. org. Secondary users must request permission directly from the LWVUS, the copyright owner. Copyright © 2007 League of Women Voters. All rights reserved.

New York Times Agency
"Rock of the Modern Age, Arthur Miller is Everywhere" by Mel Gussow from diversityjobmarket.com

Princeton University Press
From "Walden" by Henry David Thoreau. Copyright © 1971 by Princeton University Press, 1999 renewed PUP, 1989 paperback edition.

Scribner, an imprint of Simon & Schuster
"In Another Country" by Ernest Hemingway from *Men Without Woman*. Copyright 1927 by Charles Scribner's Sons. Copyright renewed 1955 by Ernest Hemingway.

(Acknowledgments continue on page V68)

CONTENTS

PART 1

UNIT 1 A Gathering of Voices (Beginnings to 1800)

The Earth on Turtle's Back • When Grizzlies Walked Upright •
from **The Navajo Origin Legend**

The Earth on Turtle's Back from the Onondaga

Before You Read 1

Making Connections 2

When Grizzlies Walked Upright from the Modoc

Before You Read 3

Making Connections 4

from **The Navajo Origin Legend from the Navajo**

Before You Read 5

Making Connections 6

After You Read 7

Vocabulary Skill Review 8

from **The Iroquois Constitution from the Iroquois**

Before You Read 9

Making Connections 10

Selection 11

After You Read 14

Vocabulary Skill Review 15

A Journey Through Texas • Boulders Taller Than the Great Tower of Seville

A Journey Through Texas by Alvar Núñez Cabeza de Vaca

Before You Read 16

Making Connections 17

Boulders Taller Than the Great Tower of Seville by García López de Cárdenas

Before You Read 18

Making Connections 19

After You Read 20

Vocabulary Skill Review 21

CONTENTS

from **Of Plymouth Plantation** by William Bradford

Before You Read 22

Making Connections 23

After You Read 24

Vocabulary Skill Review 25

To My Dear and Loving Husband by Anne Bradstreet

Before You Read 26

Making Connections 27

After You Read 28

Vocabulary Skill Review 29

Huswifery by Edward Taylor

Before You Read 30

Making Connections 31

After You Read 32

Vocabulary Skill Review 33

from **Sinners in the Hands of an Angry God** by Jonathan Edwards

Before You Read 34

Making Connections 35

Selection 36

After You Read 40

Vocabulary Skill Review 41

Speech in the Virginia Convention • Speech in the Convention

Speech in the Virginia Convention by Patrick Henry

Before You Read 42

Making Connections 43

Selection 44

Speech in the Convention by Benjamin Franklin

Before You Read 47

Making Connections 48

After You Read 49

Vocabulary Skill Review 50

CONTENTS

The Declaration of Independence • *from* The Crisis, Number 1

The Declaration of Independence by Thomas Jefferson

Before You Read 51

Making Connections 52

from **The Crisis, Number 1 by Thomas Paine**

Before You Read 53

Making Connections 54

Selection 55

After You Read 58

Vocabulary Skill Review 59

To His Excellency, General Washington by Phyllis Wheatley

Before You Read 60

Making Connections 61

After You Read 62

Vocabulary Skill Review 63

INFORMATIONAL TEXTS

Instructional Manuals

Making Connections 64

Selection 65

After You Read 68

from **The Autobiography • *from* Poor Richard's Almanack**

from **The Autobiography by Benjamin Franklin**

Before You Read 69

Making Connections 70

Selection 71

from **Poor Richard's Almanack by Benjamin Franklin**

Before You Read 76

Making Connections 77

After You Read 78

Vocabulary Skill Review 79

from **The Interesting Narrative of the Life of Olaudah Equiano by Olaudah Equiano**

Before You Read 80

Making Connections 81

Selection 82

CONTENTS

After You Read 85

Vocabulary Skill Review 86

Unit 1 Vocabulary Review 87

UNIT 2 A Growing Nation: The American Renaissance (1800–1870)

The Devil and Tom Walker by Washington Irving

Before You Read 89

Making Connections 90

Selection 91

After You Read 97

Vocabulary Skill Review 98

Song of Hiawatha by Henry Wadsworth Longfellow • **The Tide Rises, The Tide Falls** by Henry Wadsworth Longfellow • **Thanatopsis** by William Cullen Bryant • **Old Ironsides** by Oliver Wendell Holmes

Before You Read 99

Making Connections 100

After You Read 101

Vocabulary Skill Review 102

The Minister's Black Veil by Nathaniel Hawthorne

Before You Read 103

Making Connections 104

After You Read 105

Vocabulary Skill Review 106

The Fall of the House of Usher • The Raven

The Fall of the House of Usher by Edgar Allen Poe

Before You Read 107

Making Connections 108

The Raven by Edgar Allen Poe

Before You Read 109

Making Connections 110

Selection 111

After You Read 116
Vocabulary Skill Review 117

from **Moby-Dick** by Herman Melville

Before You Read 118
Making Connections 119
After You Read 120
Vocabulary Skill Review 121

from **Nature** • *from* **Self-Reliance** • **Concord Hymn**

from **Nature** by Ralph Waldo Emerson

Before You Read 122
Making Connections 123

from **Self-Reliance** by Ralph Waldo Emerson

Before You Read 124
Making Connections 125

Concord Hymn by Ralph Waldo Emerson

Before You Read 126
Making Connections 127
After You Read 128
Vocabulary Skill Review 129

from **Walden** • *from* **Civil Disobedience**

from **Walden** by Henry David Thoreau

Before You Read 130
Making Connections 131
Selection 132

from **Civil Disobedience** by Henry David Thoreau

Before You Read 138
Making Connections 139
After You Read 140
Vocabulary Skill Review 141

INFORMATIONAL TEXTS

Government Publications

Making Connections 142
Selection 143
After You Read 145

CONTENTS

Because I could not stop for Death • I heard a Fly buzz—when I died • There's a certain Slant of light • My life closed twice before its close • The Soul selects her own Society • The Brain— is wider than the Sky • There is a solitude of space • Water, is taught by thirst by Emily Dickinson

Before You Read 146
Making Connections 147
After You Read 148
Vocabulary Skill Review 149

***from* Preface to the 1855 Edition of Leaves of Grass • *from* Song of Myself • When I Heard the Learn'd Astronomer • By the Bivouac's Fitful Flame • I Hear America Singing • A Noiseless Patient Spider** by Walt Whitman

Before You Read 150
Making Connections 151
After You Read 152
Vocabulary Skill Review 153

Unit 2 Vocabulary Review 154

UNIT 3 Division, Reconciliation, and Expansion: The Civil War Era (1850–1914)

An Occurrence at Owl Creek Bridge by Ambrose Bierce

Before You Read 156
Making Connections 157
After You Read 158
Vocabulary Skill Review 159

An Episode of War by Stephen Crane

Before You Read 160
Making Connections 161
Selection 162
After You Read 166
Vocabulary Skill Review 167

CONTENTS

from My Bondage and My Freedom by Frederick Douglass

Before You Read 168
Making Connections 169
Selection 170
After You Read 175
Vocabulary Skill Review 176

Go Down, Moses • Swing Low, Sweet Chariot

Before You Read 177
Making Connections 178
After You Read 179
Vocabulary Skill Review 180

**The Gettysburg Address by Abraham Lincoln •
Letter to His Son by Robert E. Lee**

Before You Read 181
Making Connections 182
After You Read 183
Vocabulary Skill Review 184

**An Account of an Experience With Discrimination
by Sojourner Truth**

Before You Read 185
Making Connections 186
After You Read 187
Vocabulary Skill Review 188

INFORMATIONAL TEXTS

Magazine Article Abstract

Making Connections 189
Selection 190
After You Read 192

**The Boys' Ambition _from_ Life on the Mississippi • The Notorious
Jumping Frog of Calaveras County by Mark Twain**

Before You Read 193
Making Connections 194
Selection 195

CONTENTS

After You Read 199
Vocabulary Skill Review 200

To Build a Fire by Jack London
Before You Read 201
Making Connections 202
After You Read 203
Vocabulary Skill Review 204

The Story of an Hour by Kate Chopin
Before You Read 205
Making Connections 206
Selection 207
After You Read 210
Vocabulary Skill Review 211

Douglass • We Wear the Mask by Paul Laurence Dunbar
Before You Read 212
Making Connections 213
After You Read 214
Vocabulary Skill Review 215

Luke Havergal • Richard Cory by Edwin Arlington Robinson •
Lucinda Matlock • Richard Bone by Edgar Lee Masters
Before You Read 216
Making Connections 217
After You Read 218
Vocabulary Skill Review 219

A Wagner Matinée by Willa Cather
Before You Read 220
Making Connections 221
After You Read 222
Vocabulary Skill Review 223

Unit 3 Vocabulary Review 224

UNIT 4 Disillusion, Defiance, and Discontent: The Modern Age (1914–1945)

The Love Song of J. Alfred Prufrock by T.S. Eliot

Before You Read 226

Making Connections 227

After You Read 228

Vocabulary Skill Review 229

A Few Don'ts • In a Station of the Metro by Ezra Pound •
The Red Wheelbarrow • This Is Just to Say • The Great Figure
by William Carlos Williams • **Pear Tree** by H.D.

Before You Read 230

Making Connections 231

After You Read 232

Vocabulary Skill Review 233

Winter Dreams by F. Scott Fitzgerald

Before You Read 234

Making Connections 235

After You Read 236

Vocabulary Skill Review 237

The Turtle *from* **The Grapes of Wrath** by John Steinbeck

Before You Read 238

Making Connections 239

Selection 240

After You Read 243

Vocabulary Skill Review 244

The Unknown Citizen by W.H. Auden

Before You Read 245

Making Connections 246

After You Read 247

Vocabulary Skill Review 248

CONTENTS

old age sticks • anyone lived in a pretty how town
by E.E. Cummings

Before You Read	249
Making Connections	250
After You Read	251
Vocabulary Skill Review	252

Of Modern Poetry by Wallace Stevens • **Ars Poetica**
by Archibald MacLeish • **Poetry** by Marianne Moore

Before You Read	253
Making Connections	254
After You Read	255
Vocabulary Skill Review	256

In Another Country by Ernest Hemingway

Before You Read	257
Making Connections	258
Selection	259
After You Read	264
Vocabulary Skill Review	265

A Rose For Emily • Nobel Prize Acceptance Speech

A Rose for Emily by William Faulkner

Before You Read	266
Making Connections	267

Nobel Prize Acceptance Speech by William Faulkner

Before You Read	268
Making Connections	269
After You Read	270
Vocabulary Skill Review	271

The Jilting of Granny Weatherall by Katherine Anne Porter

Before You Read	272
Making Connections	273
After You Read	274
Vocabulary Skill Review	275

CONTENTS

A Worn Path by Eudora Welty

Before You Read 276

Making Connections 277

Selection 278

After You Read 285

Vocabulary Skill Review 286

The Night the Ghost Got In by James Thurber

Before You Read 287

Making Connections 288

After You Read 289

Vocabulary Skill Review 290

Chicago • Grass by Carl Sandburg

Before You Read 291

Making Connections 292

After You Read 293

Vocabulary Skill Review 294

Birches • Stopping by Woods on a Snowy Evening • Mending Wall • "Out, Out—" • The Gift Outright • Acquainted With the Night by Robert Frost

Before You Read 295

Making Connections 296

After You Read 297

Vocabulary Skill Review 298

The Negro Speaks of Rivers • I, Too • Dream Variations • Refugee in America by Langston Hughes

Before You Read 299

Making Connections 300

After You Read 301

Vocabulary Skill Review 302

The Tropics in New York by Claude McKay • **From the Dark Tower** by Countee Cullen • **A Black Man Talks of Reaping** by Arna Bontemps

Before You Read 303

Making Connections 304

CONTENTS

After You Read 305
Vocabulary Skill Review 306

from **Dust Tracks on a Road** by Zora Neale Hurston

Before You Read 307
Making Connections 308
After You Read 309
Vocabulary Skill Review 310

INFORMATIONAL TEXTS
Digital Tools

Making Connections 311
Selection 312
After You Read 314

Unit 4 Vocabulary Review 315

UNIT 5 Prosperity and Protest: Literature of the Post-War Era (1945–1970)

from **Hiroshima** • **The Death of the Ball Turret Gunner**
from **Hiroshima** by John Hersey

Before You Read 317
Making Connections 318

The Death of the Ball Turret Gunner by Randall Jarrell

Before You Read 319
Making Connections 320
After You Read 321
Vocabulary Skill Review 322

The Life You Save May Be Your Own by Flannery O'Connor

Before You Read 323
Making Connections 324
After You Read 325
Vocabulary Skill Review 326

The First Seven Years by Bernard Malamud

Before You Read 327
Making Connections 328

CONTENTS

Selection 329
After You Read 337
Vocabulary Skill Review 338

Constantly Risking Absurdity by Lawrence Ferlinghetti

Before You Read 339
Making Connections 340
After You Read 341
Vocabulary Skill Review 342

Mirror by Sylvia Plath • **Courage** by Anne Sexton

Before You Read 343
Making Connections 344
After You Read 345
Vocabulary Skill Review 346

Cuttings • **Cuttings** (*later*) by Theodore Roethke

Before You Read 347
Making Connections 348
After You Read 349
Vocabulary Skill Review 350

The Explorer by Gwendolyn Brooks • **Frederick Douglass** by Robert Hayden

Before You Read 351
Making Connections 352
After You Read 353
Vocabulary Skill Review 354

One Art • **The Filling Station** by Elizabeth Bishop

Before You Read 355
Making Connections 356
After You Read 357
Vocabulary Skill Review 358

The Rockpile by James Baldwin

Before You Read 359
Making Connections 360

CONTENTS

Selection 361
After You Read 367
Vocabulary Skill Review 368

from On James Baldwin by Toni Morrison
Before You Read 369
Making Connections 370
Selection 371
After You Read 374
Vocabulary Skill Review 375

Inaugural Address • _from_ Letter from Birmingham City Jail
Inaugural Address by John F. Kennedy
Before You Read 376
Making Connections 377
from Letter from Birmingham City Jail by Martin Luther King, Jr.
Before You Read 378
Making Connections 379
After You Read 380
Vocabulary Skill Review 381

The Crucible by Arthur Miller, Act I
Before You Read 382
Making Connections 383
After You Read 384
Vocabulary Skill Review 385

The Crucible by Arthur Miller, Act II
Before You Read 386
Making Connections 387
After You Read 388
Vocabulary Skill Review 389

The Crucible by Arthur Miller, Act III
Before You Read 390
Making Connections 391
After You Read 392
Vocabulary Skill Review 393

CONTENTS

The Crucible by Arthur Miller, Act IV

Before You Read	394
Making Connections	395
After You Read	396
Vocabulary Skill Review	397

INFORMATIONAL TEXTS

Feature Articles

Making Connections	398
Selection	399
After You Read	401

Unit 5 Vocabulary Review ... 402

UNIT 6 The Contemporary World (1970–Present)

Antojos by Julia Alvarez

Before You Read	404
Making Connections	405
After You Read	406
Vocabulary Skill Review	407

Everyday Use by Alice Walker

Before You Read	408
Making Connections	409
Selection	410
After You Read	417
Vocabulary Skill Review	418

Everything Stuck to Him by Raymond Carver

Before You Read	419
Making Connections	420
After You Read	421
Vocabulary Skill Review	422

Traveling Through the Dark by William Stafford • **The Secret** by Denise Levertov • **The Gift** by Gill-Li-Yonglee

Before You Read	423
Making Connections	424

CONTENTS

After You Read 425
Vocabulary Skill Review 426

Who Burns for the Perfection of Paper • Camouflaging the Chimera • Streets

Who Burns for the Perfection of Paper by Martín Espada

Before You Read 427
Making Connections 428
Selection 429

Camouflaging the Chimera by Yusef Komunyakaa •
Streets by Naomi Shihab Nye

Before You Read 430
Making Connections 431
After You Read 432
Vocabulary Skill Review 433

Halley's Comet by Stanley Kunitz

Before You Read 434
Making Connections 435
After You Read 436
Vocabulary Skill Review 437

The Latin Deli by Judith Ortiz Cofer

Before You Read 438
Making Connections 439
After You Read 440
Vocabulary Skill Review 441

Onomotapoeia by William Safire

Before You Read 442
Making Connections 443
After You Read 444
Vocabulary Skill Review 445

Coyote v. Acme by Ian Frazier

Before You Read 446
Making Connections 447

After You Read 448
Vocabulary Skill Review 449

One Day, Now Broken in Two by Anna Quindlen
Before You Read 450
Making Connections 451
After You Read 452
Vocabulary Skill Review 453

Mother Tongue • For the Love of Books
Mother Tongue by Amy Tan
Before You Read 454
Making Connections 455
Selection 456
For the Love of Books by Rita Dove
Before You Read 462
Making Connections 463
After You Read 464
Vocabulary Skill Review 465

***from* The Woman Warrior • *from* The Names**
***from* The Woman Warrior** by Maxine Hong Kingston
Before You Read 466
Making Connections 467
***from* The Names** by N. Scott Momaday
Before You Read 468
Making Connections 469
After You Read 470
Vocabulary Skill Review 471

INFORMATIONAL TEXTS
Public Documents
Making Connections 472
Selection 473
After You Read 475

Unit 6 Vocabulary Review 476

CONTENTS

PART 2 Summary Translations

Unit 1 A Gathering of Voices (Beginnings to 1800)

The Earth on Turtle's Back T2

When Grizzlies Walked Upright T4

from The Navajo Origin Legend T6

from The Iroquois Constitution T7

A Journey Through Texas T9

Boulders Taller Than the Great Tower of Seville T11

from Of Plymouth Plantation T13

To My Dear and Loving Husband T15

Huswifery T15

from Sinners in the Hands of an Angry God T17

Speech in the Virginia Convention T19

Speech in the Convention T21

The Declaration of Independence T23

from The Crisis, Number 1 . . . . T25

To His Excellency, General Washington T27

from The Autobiography T28

from Poor Richard's Almanack T30

from The Interesting Narrative of the Life of Olaudah Equiano T32

UNIT 2 A Growing Nation: The American Renaissance (1800–1870)

The Devil and Tom Walker T34

Song of Hiawatha T36

The Tide Rises, The Tide Falls T36

Thanatopsis T36

Old Ironsides T36

The Minister's Black Veil T38

The Fall of the House of Usher T40

The Raven T42

from Moby-Dick T44

from Nature T46

from Self-Reliance T47

Concord Hymn . . . . .T48 *from* Walden T49

from Civil Disobedience. T51

Because I could not stop for Death T53

I heard a Fly buzz—when I died T53

There's a certain Slant of light T53

My life closed twice before its close T53

The Soul selects her own Society T53

The Brain—is wider than the Sky T53

There is a solitude of space T53

Water, is taught by thirst T53

from Preface to the 1855 Edition of Leaves of Grass T55

from Song of Myself T55

When I Heard the Learn'd Astronomer T55

By the Bivouac's Fitful Flame. T55

I Hear America Singing. T55

A Noiseless Patient Spider T55

UNIT 3 Division, Reconciliation, and Expansion: The Civil War Era (1850–1914)

An Occurrence at Owl Creek Bridge T57

An Episode of War. T59

Go Down, Moses T61

Swing Low, Sweet Chariot T61

The Gettysburg Address T63

Letter to His Son T63

An Account of an Experience With Discrimination T65

The Boys' Ambition *from* Life on the Mississippi T66

The Notorious Jumping Frog of Calaveras County T66

To Build a Fire T68

The Story of an Hour T70

Douglass T72

We Wear the Mask T72

Luke Havergal T74

Richard Cory T74

Lucinda Matlock T74

Richard Bone T74

A Wagner Matinée. T76

CONTENTS

UNIT 4 Disillusion, Defiance, and Discontent: The Modern Age (1914–1945)

The Love Song of J. Alfred Prufrock T78

A Few Don'ts T80

In a Station of the Metro T80

The Red Wheelbarrow T80

This Is Just to Say T80

The Great Figure T80

Pear Tree T80

Winter Dreams T82

The Turtle *from* The Grapes of Wrath T84

The Unknown Citizen T86

old age sticks T87

anyone lived in a pretty how town T87

Of Modern Poetry T89

Ars Poetica T89

Poetry T89

In Another Country T91

A Rose For Emily T93

Nobel Prize Acceptance Speech T95

The Jilting of Granny Weatherall T97

A Worn Path T99

The Night the Ghost Got In T100

Chicago T101

Grass T101

Birches T103

Stopping by Woods on a Snowy Evening T103

Mending Wall T103

"Out, Out—" T103

The Gift Outright T103

Acquainted With the Night T103

The Negro Speaks of Rivers T105

I, Too T105

Dream Variations T105

Refugee in America T105

The Tropics in New York T107

From the Dark Tower T107

A Black Man Talks of Reaping T107
from Dust Tracks on a Road T109

UNIT 5 Prosperity and Protest: Literature of the Post-War Era (1945–1970)

from Hiroshima T111
The Death of the Ball Turret Gunner T113
The Life You Save May Be Your Own T114
The First Seven Years T116
Constantly Risking Absurdity T118
Mirror T119
Courage T119
Cuttings T121
Cuttings *(later)* T121
The Explorer T123
Frederick Douglass T133
One Art T125
The Filling Station T125
The Rockpile T126
from On James Baldwin T128
Inaugural Address T130
from Letter from Birmingham City Jail T132
The Crucible, Act I T134
The Crucible, Act II T136
The Crucible, Act III T138
The Crucible, Act IV T140

UNIT 6 The Contemporary World (1970–Present)

Antojos T142
Everyday Use T144
Everything Stuck to Him T146
Traveling Through the Dark T147
The Secret T147
The Gift T147
Who Burns for the Perfection of Paper T149
Camouflaging the Chimera T150
Streets T150
Halley's Comet T151

The Latin Deli T152

Onomotapoeia. T154

Coyote v. Acme T156

One Day, Now Broken in Two T158

Mother Tongue. T159

For the Love of Books T161

from The Woman Warrior. T163

from The Names. T165

PART 3 Turbo Vocabulary

Prefixes V2

Word Roots V4

Suffixes V6

Learning About Etymologies V8

How to Use a Dictionary V12

Academic Words V14

Word Attack Skills: Phonics and Word Patterns V16

Vocabulary and the SAT® V18

Communication Guide: Diction and Etiquette. V22

Words in Other Subjects V26

Vocabulary Flash Cards V27

Vocabulary Fold-a-List. V33

Commonly Misspelled Words V39

Personal Thesaurus V41

As you read your hardcover student edition of *Prentice Hall Literature* use the **Reader's Notebook** to guide you in learning and practicing the skills presented. In addition, many selections in your student edition are presented here in an interactive format. The notes and instruction will guide you in applying reading and literary skills and in thinking about the selection. The examples on these pages show you how to use the notes as a companion when you read.

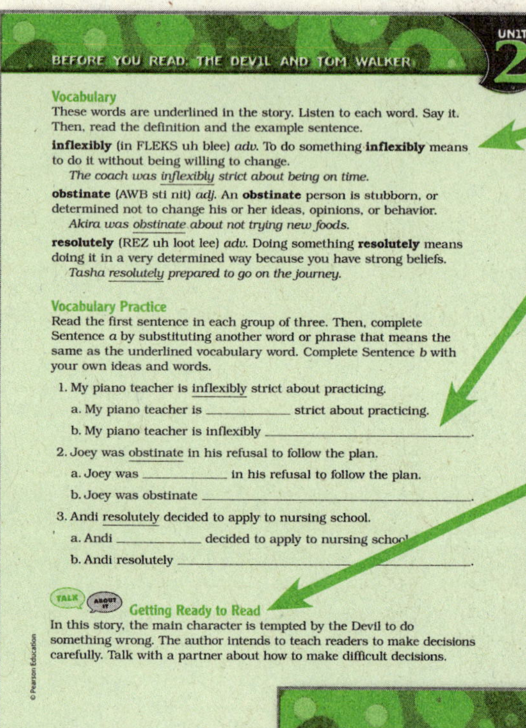

Build Your Vocabulary

Use the *Before You Read* page to learn vocabulary that you will read in the selection. To practice using the words, you can write on the lines in the practice sentences.

Get Ready to Read

This paragraph gives you more information about the selection. Before you read, you can discuss your thoughts and ideas with classmates.

Get the Big Idea

The *Making Connections* page presents a selection summary, which lets you know what the selection is about before you read.

Be an Active Reader

A *Note-taking Guide* helps you organize the main ideas of the selection. Complete the guide as you read to track your understanding.

secure what would make them wealthy for life. However Tom might have felt **disposed** to sell himself to the Devil, he was determined not to do so to **oblige** his wife; so he flatly refused out of the mere spirit of **contradiction.** Many and bitter were the **quarrels** they had on the subject. . . .

At length she determined to drive the bargain on her own account, and if she succeeded, to keep all the gain to herself. Being of the same fearless temper as her husband, she set off for the old Indian fort at the close of a summer's day.

* * *

To bargain with the Devil, Tom's wife takes the household silverware and other valuables, tying them up in her apron. She is never heard from again. According to one story, Tom goes hunting for her and finds nothing but her apron, with a heart and liver inside! Whatever happened, Tom seems more upset about losing his property than losing his wife. In fact, he decides that the Devil might have done him a favor. Soon he is again bargaining with the Devil to obtain the pirate's treasure.

* * *

There was one condition which need not be mentioned, being generally understood in all cases where the Devil grants favors; but there were others about which, though of less importance, he was inflexibly obstinate. He insisted that money

TAKE NOTES

Regular Verbs The past tense of a regular verb is formed by adding -ed or -d to the present form of the verb. List three regular past-tense verbs in the bracketed text.

Vocabulary Builder

Possessive Nouns Circle the word Tom's in this paragraph. The 's at the end of Tom makes it possessive. This means that it shows possession or ownership. Tom's wife means "the wife of Tom." Circle two more possessive nouns on this page. What do the nouns mean?

Comprehension Builder

Given what you have read about Tom, predict what he will do next. Will he make a bargain, or deal, with the Devil?

Everyday Words

secure (si KYOOR) v. make certain about; guarantee
disposed (dis POHZD) adj. inclined; prone to
oblige (o BLYDG) v. do what someone else wants; please
contradiction (kahn truh DIK shuhn) n. a difference between two statements, beliefs, or ideas about something that means both cannot be true
quarrels (KWAHR uhlz) n. angry arguments or disagreements

The Devil and Tom Walker **93**

Read the Text

Text set in a wider margin provides the author's actual words.

Text set in a narrow margin provides a summary of selection events or details.

Mark the Text

Use write-on lines to answer questions in the side column. You may also want to use the lines for your own notes.

When you see a pencil, you should underline, circle, or mark the text as indicated.

Take Notes

Side-column questions accompany the selections that appear in the Reader's Notebooks. These questions are a built-in tutor to help you practice the skills and understand what you read.

Check Your Understanding

Questions after every selection help you think about the selection. You can use the write-on lines and charts to answer the questions. Then, share your ideas in discussions and writing activities.

AFTER YOU READ

Thinking About the Selection

1. Several of Tom's actions reveal his characteristics. In the chart below, the left column lists Tom's characteristics. Complete the chart by describing what Tom does that demonstrates each characteristic. The first one has been done for you.

Characteristic	Action that Reveals the Characteristic
Tom has a spirit of contradiction.	Tom refuses his wife's request to bargain with the Devil, even though he may have wanted to.
Tom has a conscience.	

...is ______

...a partner, take turns reading aloud ...Walker and the Devil. Have each ...uss what motivates Tom to make the

...Question

...eflect society? Judging from the ...think Washington Irving might say ...iety?

The Devil and Tom Walker **97**

VOCABULARY SKILL REVIEW

Multiple-Meaning Words

Many words have several meanings, depending on the way a word is used in a sentence. Often, the only way to determine the particular meaning of a word is to understand a word's context.

Examples

Word	Meanings
find: verb	• discover something by chance
	• have a particular feeling about someone or something
matter: noun	• a subject or situation
	• the material that everything in the universe is made of
hot: adjective	• having a high temperature
	• very popular or fashionable

Now You Do It

Complete the sentences with words from the chart. Then, write the meaning of the word on the lines provided.

He called a meeting to discuss a very serious ______

She was surprised to ______ a wallet lying on the sidewalk.

The pot of water on the stove was ______ and bubbling.

Solids, liquids, and gases are forms of ______

First to Speak Select one of the words from this page. Think of and say a sentence that uses one of its meanings. Then, have a partner use the other meaning in a sentence.

Flash Test On flashcards, write sentences that use the multiple-meaning words from this page. Show a partner the cards. Ask your partner to define each multiple-meaning word.

350 English Learner's Notebook

Learn Vocabulary Skills

The *Vocabulary Skill Review* page provides more instruction in vocabulary skills. Practice what you learn in oral and writing activities.

Vocabulary

Listen to each word. Say it. Then, read the definition and the example sentence.

sacred (SAY krid) *adj.* Something **sacred** is very important or respected, often because it relates to a god or religion.
> *The children were taught to read from a sacred book.*

unconscious (uhn KAHN shuhs) *adj.* **Unconscious** describes being unable to see, move, or feel in the normal way because you are not conscious, or awake and aware.
> *When Marion fell, she hit her head and was knocked unconscious.*

depths (DEPTHS) *n.* The **depths** of something is the part that is farthest away and most difficult to reach.
> *Lionel finally returned from the depths of the basement.*

Vocabulary Practice

Read the first sentence in each group of three. Then, complete Sentence *a* by substituting another word or phrase that means the same as the underlined vocabulary word. Complete Sentence *b* with your own ideas and words.

1. An ancient <u>sacred</u> temple was discovered recently.

   a. An ancient _______________ temple was discovered recently.

   b. An ancient sacred temple _________________________________.

2. Julian remained <u>unconscious</u> for days after the car accident.

   a. Julian remained _______________ for days after the car accident.

   b. Julian remained unconscious _________________________________.

3. The divers searched the <u>depths</u> of the ocean for pearls.

   a. The divers searched the _______________ of the ocean for pearls.

   b. The divers searched the depths _________________________________.

Getting Ready to Read

Origin myths explain many things in nature. What myths and legends do you know? Share your stories with a partner.

The Earth on Turtle's Back
from the Onondaga

Summary The Onondaga are one of the Iroquois tribes of the Northeast woodlands. They tell about a time before Earth was above water. A brave muskrat brings a tiny piece of earth out of the water to help a woman who falls from the sky. A turtle's back then becomes the base for Earth. Then, life on Earth begins. A story such as this helps the reader understand the beliefs and thinking of the Onondaga people.

Note-taking Guide

Use this diagram to record the events in the order in which they happen in this story.

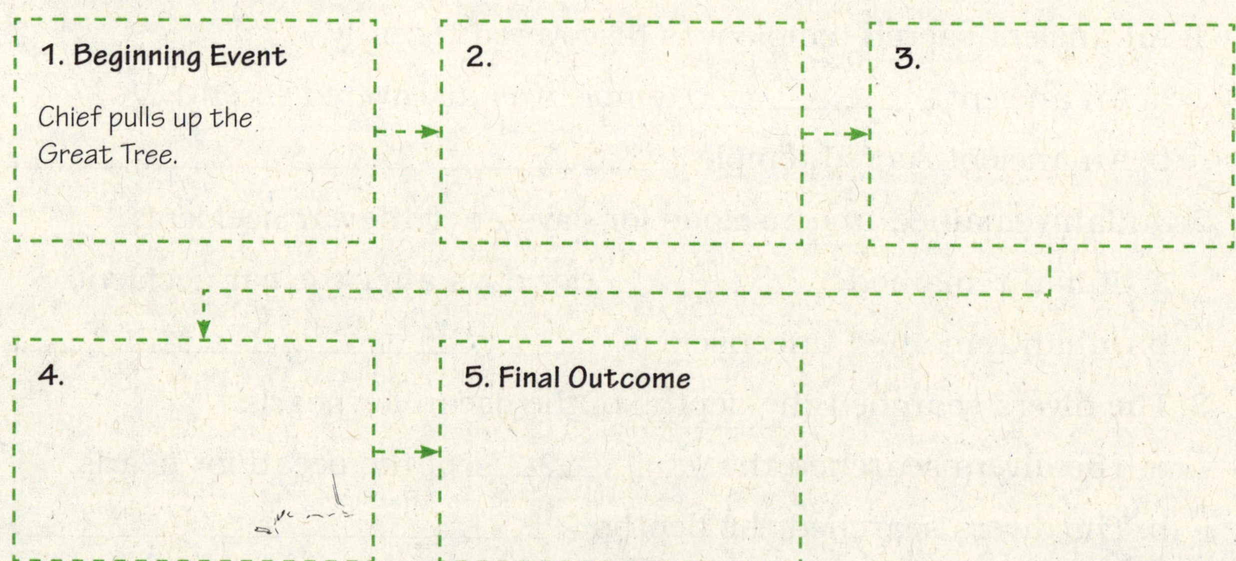

Vocabulary

Listen to each word. Say it. Then, read the definition and the example sentence.

sternly (STERN lee) *adv.* Something done **sternly** is done in a serious way that shows disapproval.

Gail sternly told her daughter to pick up the pieces of the broken clock.

promptly (PROMPT lee) *adv.* Something done **promptly** is done quickly or immediately.

Elsu did his homework promptly after finishing his dinner.

ancestors (AN ses terz) *n.* **Ancestors** are members of your family who lived a long time ago.

Giovanni's ancestors moved to New York almost 100 years ago.

Vocabulary Practice

Read the first sentence in each group of three. Then, complete Sentence *a* by substituting another word or phrase that means the same as the underlined vocabulary word. Complete Sentence *b* with your own ideas and words.

1. Han's brother looked at her sternly when she spilled juice.

   a. Han's brother looked at her _______________ when she spilled juice.

   b. Han's brother looked at her sternly _______________________________.

2. Kito rose promptly when he heard the alarm clock.

   a. Kito rose _______________ when he heard the alarm clock.

   b. Kito rose promptly _______________________________.

3. Mei Ling taught the children to respect their ancestors.

   a. Mei Ling taught the children to respect their _______________.

   b. Mei Ling _______________________________ their ancestors.

Getting Ready to Read

Grizzly bears are large brown bears found in North America. They eat fish and small mammals. What else do you know about grizzlies or other types of bears? Share your knowledge in a small group.

When Grizzlies Walked Upright
from the Modoc

Summary The Modoc lived in areas that became part of the western United States. They tell a story that explains where the first Native Americans come from. A daughter of the Chief of the Sky Spirits comes to Earth and marries a grizzly bear. Their children become the first Native Americans.

Note-taking Guide

Use this diagram to record the events in the order in which they happen in this story.

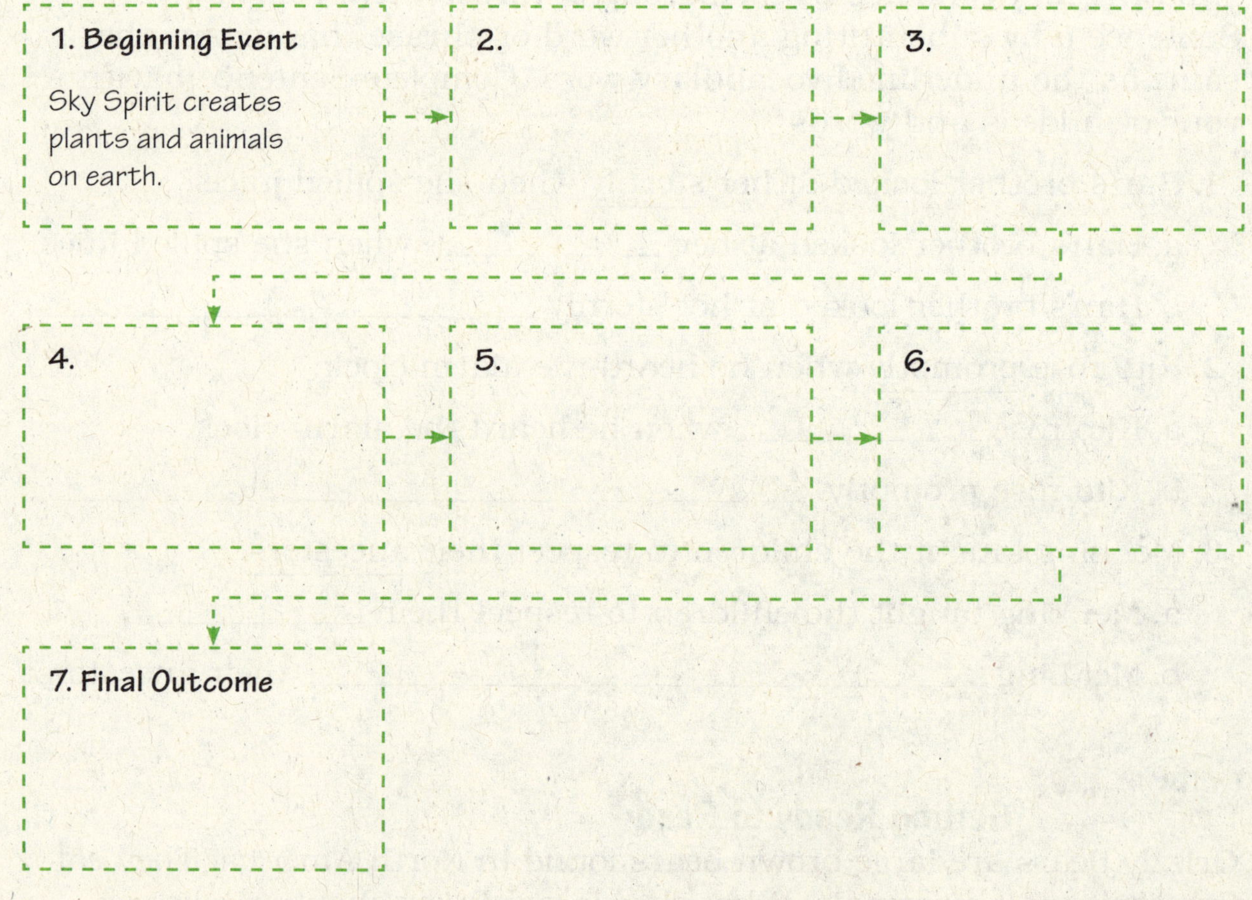

Vocabulary

Listen to each word. Say it. Then, read the definition and the example sentence.

protruded (proh TROOD id) *v.* Something that has **protruded** sticks out from somewhere.
Brandon cut his leg on a piece of wire that <u>protruded</u> from the fence.

ceases (SEES iz) *v.* When something **ceases,** it stops happening.
The rain <u>ceases</u>, and we run outside to play in the puddles.

directed (duh REKT id) *v.* When someone has **directed** another to do something, he or she has told that person to do it.
Kira <u>directed</u> the other servers to set clean silverware on the tables.

Vocabulary Practice

Read the first sentence in each group of three. Then, complete Sentence *a* by substituting another word or phrase that means the same as the underlined vocabulary word. Complete Sentence *b* with your own ideas and words.

1. I tore my coat on a sharp branch that <u>protruded</u> from a bush.

   a. I tore my coat on a sharp branch that _______________ from a bush.

   b. _______________________________________ protruded from a bush.

2. Bosco <u>ceases</u> his barking when I give him a bone.

   a. Bosco _______________ his barking when I give him a bone.

   b. Bosco ceases ____.

3. Elias <u>directed</u> us to stack the boxes in the corner.

   a. Elias _______________ us to stack the boxes in the corner.

   b. Elias directed ____.

Getting Ready to Read

Corn, also known as maize, was an important crop for the Navajo and other Native Americans. What else do you know about the Navajo or other Native Americans? Share your thoughts with a partner.

from The Navajo Origin Legend

Summary This part of the Navajo legend tells how the wind breathes life into corn to create the First Man and First Woman. This creation myth shows how important nature, corn, animal skins, feathers, and the wind are to the Navajo.

Note-taking Guide

Use this diagram to record the events in the order in which they happen in this story.

1. Beginning Event

Gods appear carrying corn and buckskins.

2.

3.

4.

5. Final Outcome

Thinking About the Selections

1. In the chart below, list the major elements of each story.

Story	Main Characters	What Does It Explain?
"The Earth on Turtle's Back"		
"When Grizzlies Walked Upright"		
"from the Navajo Origin Legend"		

2. All three stories explain ____

____.

TALK ABOUT IT **Tell the Story** These Native American myths were not written down until very recently. They were meant to be spoken and passed down through many generations. Practice telling one of these stories, in your own words, to a partner. Then, have your partner tell your version of the story back to you. Discuss how the story changes when it is retold.

____

____

Writing About the Essential Question

What is the relationship between place and literature? What do the qualities these mythmakers saw in nature show about the human traits they valued?

____

____

Suffixes

A suffix is a group of letters that is added to the end of a word to form a new word. Suffixes change a word's meaning. They often change its part of speech as well.

Examples

The suffix *-ness* means "a state of being." Adding -ness changes an adjective to a noun. For most adjectives that have more than one syllable and end in *y*, change the *y* to an *i* before adding *-ness*.

Adjective		Suffix		Noun	Meaning
sad	+	-ness	=	sadness	the state of being sad
happy	+	-ness	=	happiness	the state of being happy

Now You Do It

Change the adjectives below to nouns by adding the suffix *-ness*. Then, write a definition for each new word.

weak + -ness = ___________________

____

good + -ness = ___________________

____

pretty + -ness = ___________________

____

soft + -ness = ___________________

____

thoughtful + -ness = ___________________

____

shy + -ness = ___________________

____

TALK ABOUT IT **Sentence Sharing** With a partner, read aloud the adjectives and nouns listed above. Then, take turns saying each noun in a sentence.

WRITE ABOUT IT **What Does the Loch Ness Monster Think?** Many people believe that a giant creature called the Loch Ness Monster lives in a lake in Scotland. Write a dialogue in which you ask it five questions. Make sure that the Loch Ness Monster uses a *-ness* word in each reply.

Vocabulary

These words are underlined in the story. Listen to each word. Say it.
Then, read the definition and the example sentence.

tempered (TEM perd) *v.* When something has been **tempered,** it has
been made less severe or extreme, especially by adding something that
has the opposite effect.

> *The vandal's punishment was tempered to three months of community
> service.*

deliberation (di lib uh RAY shuhn) *n.* **Deliberation** describes careful
thought about or discussion of something.

> *The council's deliberation of the matter was private.*

oblivion (uh BLIV ee uhn) *n.* **Oblivion** is the state of being completely
forgotten.

> *The actor slipped into oblivion after the TV show ended.*

Vocabulary Practice

Read the first sentence in each group of three. Then, complete
Sentence *a* by substituting another word or phrase that means the
same as the underlined vocabulary word. Complete Sentence *b* with
your own ideas and words.

1. The summer heat was tempered by a cool rain shower.

   a. The summer heat was ________________ by a cool rain shower.

   b. The summer heat was tempered by ________________________.

2. After much deliberation, we decided to move to a new city.

   a. After much ______________, we decided to move to a new city.

   b. After much deliberation, ________________________________.

3. Some historical events have been lost to oblivion.

   a. Some historical events have been lost to ______________.

   b. ____ oblivion.

Getting Ready to Read

Native Americans agreed on laws known as the Iroquois Constitution.
Why do we have laws? Discuss your ideas with a partner.

from The Iroquois Constitution
Translated by Arthur C. Parker

Red Jacket, George Catlin, The Thomas Gilcrease Institute of Art, Tulsa, Oklahoma

Summary This selection is an excerpt, or a section, from The Iroquois Constitution. Dekanawidah, who is an Iroquois prophet, speaks here of the Tree of Great Peace that gives shelter and protection to the Iroquois nations. He explains why and how the Five Nations, a group of five Iroquois tribes, should come together to form a union or confederacy for their common good.

Note-taking Guide
Use this chart to list details about the union of Iroquois nations. Then, write a main idea sentence about the purpose of the union.

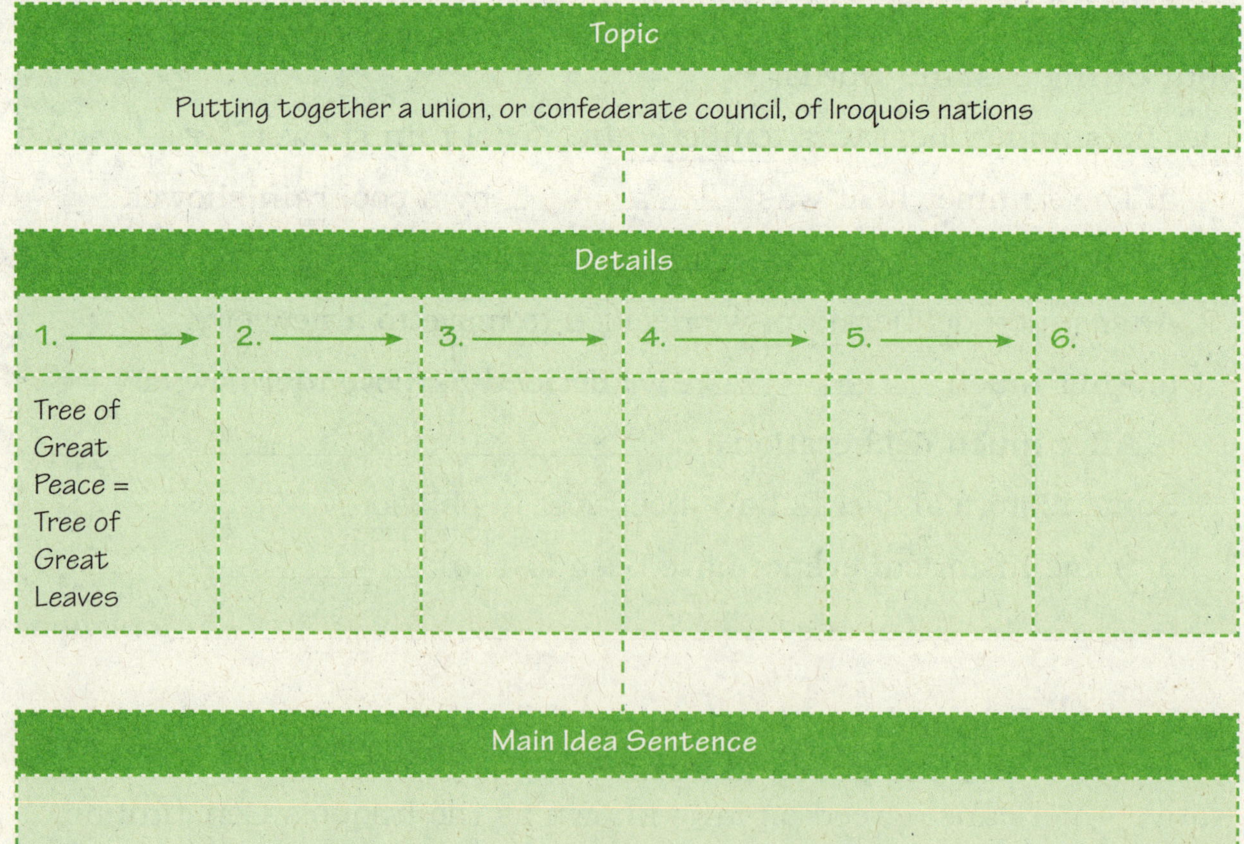

Topic					
Putting together a union, or confederate council, of Iroquois nations					

Details					
1. →	2. →	3. →	4. →	5. →	6.
Tree of Great Peace = Tree of Great Leaves					

Main Idea Sentence

from The Iroquois Constitution

Translated by Arthur C. Parker

I am Dekanawidah and with the Five Nations[1] confederate lords I plant the Tree of the Great Peace. I name the tree the Tree of the Great Long Leaves. Under the shade of this Tree of the Great Peace we spread the soft white feathery down of the globe thistle as seats for you, Adodarhoh, and your cousin lords.

We place you upon those seats, spread soft with the feathery down of the globe thistle, there beneath the shade of the spreading branches of the Tree of Peace. There shall you sit and watch the council fire of the confederacy of the Five Nations, and all the **affairs** of the Five Nations shall be transacted[2] at this place before you.

Roots have spread out from the Tree of the Great Peace, one to the north, one to the east, one to the south and one to the west. The name of these roots is the Great White Roots and their nature is peace and strength.

❖ ❖ ❖

Other nations wishing to speak with the Five Nations will **trace** the roots to the tree. Peaceful and **obedient** people will be welcomed.

❖ ❖ ❖

Everyday Words

affairs (uh FAYRZ) *n.* political events and activities

trace (TRAYS) *v.* find someone or something

obedient (oh BEE dee uhnt) *adj.* always doing what one is told to do or what the law says one must do

---

1. **Five Nations** the Mohawk, Oneida, Onondaga, Cayuga, and Seneca tribes. Together, these tribes formed the Iroquois Confederation.

2. **transacted** (trans ACT id) *v.* done

Vocabulary Builder 

Prefixes In English, the prefix *con-* means "with" or "together." A *constitution* is a set of basic laws set up by a group of people working together. A *confederacy* is a group of people who agree to work together for a common purpose. Complete these sentences, using each word:

The Five Nations of the Iroquois

formed a _______________.
Together, they wrote a

_______________________.

Vocabulary Builder 

Parts of Speech *Down* can be an adverb meaning "to or toward a lower place or position." It can also be a noun meaning "soft hair or feathers." Is *down* a noun or an adverb in the bracketed passage? With a partner, discuss how you know the answer.

____

Comprehension Builder 

In the text, *nature* means "the basic character of something." What is the nature of the Great White Roots?

____

What is the nature of the people whom the tree will welcome?

____

Vocabulary Builder

Prepositions A preposition is a word used before a noun or pronoun to show place, time, and direction. Prepositions include *above, below, at, on, during,* and *from.* List the prepositions in the first bracketed paragraph.

____

____

____

Vocabulary Builder

Multiple-Meaning Words *Hold* may mean "have something in one's hands or arms." It may also mean "regard or think about someone or something in a certain way." Which meaning does *hold* have in the second bracketed paragraph?

____

____

Vocabulary Builder

Parts of Speech *Pledge* may be a verb meaning "formally promise to do something." It may also be a noun meaning "something valuable offered as a sign of a promise." Is *pledge* a noun or a verb in the underlined sentence?

____

We place at the top of the Tree of the Long Leaves an eagle who is able to see afar. If he sees in the distance any evil approaching or danger threatening he will at once warn the people of the confederacy.

The smoke of the confederate council fire shall ever **ascend** and pierce the sky so that other nations who may be **allies** may see the council fire of the Great Peace . . .

◆　◆　◆

The Onondaga lords will open every council meeting by giving thanks to their cousin lords. They will also offer thanks to the earth, the waters, the crops, the trees, the animals, the sun, the moon, and the Great Creator.

◆　◆　◆

All lords of the Five Nations' Confederacy must be honest in all things . . . It shall be a serious wrong for anyone to lead a lord into trivial[3] affairs, for the people must ever hold their lords high in estimation[4] out of respect to their honorable positions.

◆　◆　◆

When a new lord joins the council, he must offer a pledge of four strings of shells. The speaker of the council will then welcome the new lord. The lords on the other side of the council fire will receive the pledge. Then they will speak these words to the new lord:

◆　◆　◆

Everyday Words

ascend (uh SEND) *v.* rise

allies (AL lyz) *n.* people who help and support one another, especially against others who oppose them

3. **trivial** (TRIV ee uhl) *adj.* unimportant

4. **estimation** (es ti MAY shuhn) *n.* opinion, judgment

"With endless patience you shall carry out your duty and your firmness shall be tempered with tenderness for your people. Neither anger nor fury shall find lodgement in your mind and all your words and actions shall be marked with calm deliberation. In all your deliberations in the confederate council, in your efforts at law making, in all your official acts, self-interest shall be cast into oblivion. Cast not over your shoulder behind you the warnings of the nephews and nieces should they chide[5] you for any error or wrong you may do, but return to the way of the Great Law which is just and right. Look and listen for the **welfare** of the whole people and have always in view not only the present but also the coming **generations,** even those whose faces are yet beneath the surface of the ground—the unborn of the future nation."

Everyday Words

welfare (WEL fayr) *n.* health and happiness

generations (jen uh RAY shuhnz) *n.* groups of all the people of about the same age

5. **chide** (CHY D) *v.* criticize

Vocabulary Builder

Multiple-Meaning Words The verb *cast* can mean "throw away." It can also mean "deposit a ballot when voting." Which meaning does *cast* have in the underlined sentence?

____

Fluency Builder 

Punctuation marks, such as commas (,) and dashes (—), separate ideas in sentences. When reading, you should pause briefly after each comma or dash. With a partner, take turns reading aloud the bracketed passage with expression. Discuss what the passage means.

Thinking About the Selection

1. In the graphic organizer, describe the main parts of the Iroquois Confederacy.

eagle:

Tree of the Great Peace:

council:

Great White Roots:

2. Dekanawidah believes that the confederacy should welcome

____

____.

TALK ABOUT IT **Planting a Tree** Dekanawidah describes a political arrangement as a great tree of peace. Why do you think he describes the confederacy as a tree with great roots that spread out in all directions? Why does he use this metaphor instead of speaking plainly? Discuss your thoughts in a small group.

Dekanawidah uses the metaphor of the tree because ______________

____.

Writing About the Essential Question

What is the relationship between place and literature? In what ways, both practical and spiritual, do the Iroquois rely on the natural world?

____

____

Synonyms

Synonyms are words that have the same or very similar meanings. Many times, a synonym can replace another word in a sentence without changing the meaning of the sentence.

Examples

violent *adj.* strong, angry, or involving actions that are intended to harm people	**harmful** *adj.* causing or likely to cause harm **destructive** *adj.* causing harm to people or things **fierce** *adj.* done with much energy and strong feelings, such as anger **wild** *adj.* behaving in an uncontrolled, somethimes angry or harmful way

Now You Do It

Write a sentence for each synonym for *violent* explained above.

1. **violent:** The woman became <u>violent</u> when the guards tried to stop her from leaving.

2. **harmful** ____

3. **destructive** ____

4. **fierce** ____

5. **wild** ____

TALK ABOUT IT

Swapping Synonyms With a partner, take turns reading aloud your sentences. Then, exchange sentences. Replace the underlined word in each sentence with another synonym. Read aloud the new sentences, and discuss how the synonyms change their meaning. Do all the sentences still make sense?

WRITE ABOUT IT

Make a Picture Book Write a picture book to teach younger children that violent actions do not solve problems. Use the synonyms above and pictures in your book. Suggest other ways to solve conflicts, such as asking an adult for help, or taking a break to calm down.

Vocabulary

Listen to each word. Say it. Then, read the definition and the example sentence.

entreated (in TREET id) *v.* If you have asked a person to do something, usually in an emotional way, then you have **entreated** him or her.
Lilian entreated her friend to help her study for the final exam.

feigned (FAYND) *v.* When someone has **feigned** something, he or she has pretended to have a particular feeling.
Kendra feigned interest in the football game.

advantageous (ad van TAY juhs) *adj.* Something that is **advantageous** is helpful and likely to make you successful.
The deal was advantageous for the growing company.

Vocabulary Practice

Read the first sentence in each group of three. Then, complete Sentence *a* by substituting another word or phrase that means the same as the underlined vocabulary word. Complete Sentence *b* with your own ideas and words.

1. Alonso entreated his coach to allow him to pitch.

   a. Alonso _______________ his coach to allow him to pitch.

   b. Alonso entreated ____.

2. Celia feigned enjoyment of the movie she disliked.

   a. Celia _______________ enjoyment of the movie she disliked

   b. Celia feigned ____.

3. The change in weather was advantageous for their wedding.

   a. The change in weather was _______________ for their wedding.

   b. The change in weather was advantageous _____________________.

Getting Ready to Read

Cabeza de Vaca was one of many explorers who wrote exploration narratives to describe the people and land that he encountered. He is best known for his journeys through what is now Texas. What do you know about European exploration in the Americas? Discuss your knowledge with a partner.

A Journey Through Texas
by Alvar Núñez Cabeza de Vaca

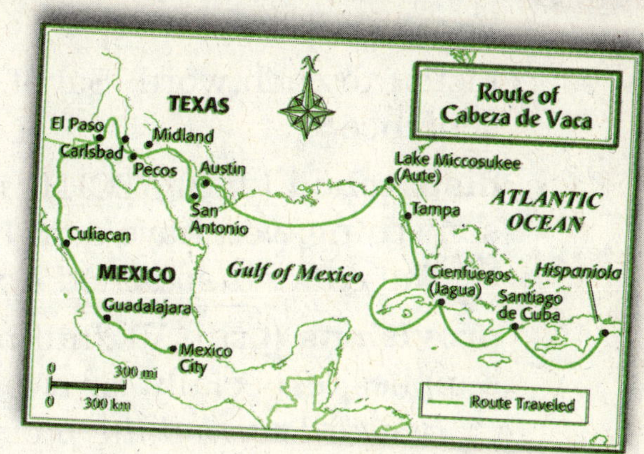

Summary In this narrative, the author describes his journey into what is now the state of Texas. There, he meets many Native Americans who help him on his journey. The Native Americans share food with him and help him find his way. The author learns to appreciate the different ways that people have found to live.

Note-taking Guide

Use this diagram to record details about the author's experiences.

Vocabulary

Listen to each word. Say it. Then, read the definition and the example sentence.

dispatched (di SPATCHT) *v.* When you have **dispatched** someone to do something, you have sent him or her on a specific assignment.
The editor dispatched two reporters to cover the earthquake.

provisions (pruh VI żhuhnz) *n.* **Provisions** are food and other supplies, especially for a long trip.
Bernard carried the provisions for the camping trip in his backpack.

obstacles (AHB stuh kuhlz) *n.* **Obstacles** make it difficult to achieve something.
Our team faced many obstacles to winning the national championship.

Vocabulary Practice

Read the first sentence in each group of three. Then, complete Sentence *a* by substituting another word or phrase that means the same as the underlined vocabulary word. Complete Sentence *b* with your own ideas and words.

1. Sheila <u>dispatched</u> her son to find the other children.

   a. Sheila _______________ her son to find the other children.

   b. Sheila dispatched ____.

2. We packed many <u>provisions</u> to help victims of the hurricane.

   a. We packed many _______________ to help victims of the hurricane.

   b. We packed many provisions _____________________________________.

3. The hero overcame many <u>obstacles</u> during the story.

   a. The hero overcame many _______________ during the story.

   b. The hero overcame many obstacles _______________________________.

Getting Ready to Read

Garcia López de Cárdenas and his men were the first Europeans to see the Grand Canyon. Would you like to discover an amazing place? Share your thoughts with a partner.

Boulders Taller Than the Great Tower of Seville

by García López de Cárdenas

Summary This narrative tells about the first time that Europeans come to the Grand Canyon. The author describes the canyon's vast size, difficult landscape, and cold weather. He explains what happens when his group tries to explore the canyon.

Note-taking Guide

Use this diagram to record details about the author's experiences.

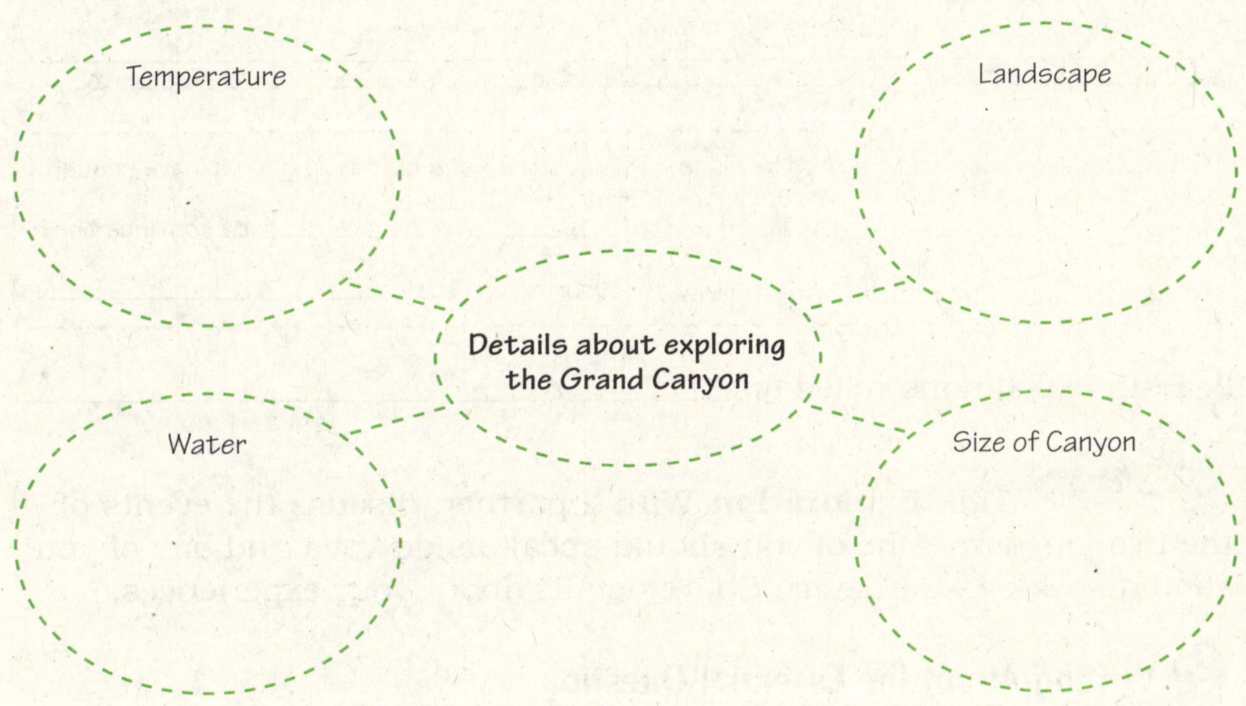

Thinking About the Selections

1. Use the sequence charts to fill in information about the travels of Cabeza de Vaca and Garcia López de Cárdenas. Complete the sentence in each box.

Cabeza de Vaca was traveling through ________________________.	Cárdenas led an expedition to explore ____________ about which they had heard.
In a Native American village, de Vaca learned ________________________.	They tried to find a way down to the river, but ____________________.
The Native Americans gave de Vaca ________________________.	Native Americans told them that ____________________.
Cabeza de Vaca decided to go to the place where ____________. His group went without ____________, but they survived.	Cardenas and his group did not have enough ____________ to continue their journey, so they ____________.

2. Both expeditions relied on ____.

TALK ABOUT IT **Talk Exploration** With a partner, discuss the events of the two journeys. One of you should speak as de Vaca and one of you should speak as Cárdenas. Share details about your experiences.

? Writing About the Essential Question

What is the relationship between place and literature? Judging from these accounts, what are some of the challenges Europeans faced in exploring—and understanding—the Americas?

____

____

____

Verb Tenses

The past tense form of a verb describes actions that took place in the past. Most English verbs form the past tense by adding *-ed* or *-d* to the present tense form of the verb. Some verbs, called irregular verbs, do not follow this rule.

Examples

Bring is one common irregular verb. Look at the chart below to learn about the form that *bring* takes in the past tense.

Present Tense: *Bring*	Past Tense: *Brought*
I *bring* a ball.	I *brought* a ball.
You *bring* a treat.	You *brought* a treat.
She *brings* a book.	He *brought* a book.
We *bring* our pets.	We *brought* our pets.
You two *bring* more photos.	You two *brought* more photos.
They *bring* us snacks every day.	They *brought* us snacks yesterday.

Now You Do It

Circle the correct tense of the verb bring in the following sentences.

He	**brings**	**brought**	us food all the time.
Last week I	**bring**	**brought**	that snack.
Tomas and Erik	**bring**	**brought**	the science project earlier today.
The moving van	**brings**	**brought**	my furniture yesterday morning.
He always	**brings**	**brought**	his camera with him.

TALK ABOUT IT **Choose the Correct Verb Tense** Write five new sentences, using the present or past tense of bring. Then, rewrite the sentences, leaving a blank line where the verb should be. Ask a partner to select the correct form and tense of the verb *bring* for each sentence.

WRITE ABOUT IT **What Did They Bring?** Write a news story about a canned food drive that has been going on. Describe the different things that people have brought and are still bringing for the project. Use the past tense of *bring* three times in your story and the present tense of *bring* two times.

Vocabulary

Listen to each word. Say it. Then, read the definition and the example sentence.

peril (PER uhl) *n.* **Peril** is great danger, especially of being harmed or killed.

The injured puppy was in peril when it slowly crossed the street.

calamity (kuh LAM uh tee) *n.* A **calamity** is a terrible and unexpected event that causes a great deal of damage or suffering.

The accident on the freeway was a calamity involving seven cars.

relent (ri LENT) *v.* To **relent** is to change your attitude and become less severe or cruel toward someone.

Samuel decided to relent and take his younger brother to the movies.

Vocabulary Practice

Read the first sentence in each group of three. Then, complete Sentence *a* by substituting another word or phrase that means the same as the underlined vocabulary word. Complete Sentence *b* with your own ideas and words.

1. Tara faced great peril standing at the cliff's edge.

   a. Tara faced great _______________ standing at the cliff's edge.

   b. Tara faced great peril _______________________________________.

2. The workers escaped the calamity of the fire in the factory.

   a. The workers escaped the _______________ of the fire in the factory.

   b. The workers escaped the calamity _______________________________.

3. Please relent and allow us to join you.

   a. Please _______________ and allow us to join you.

   b. Please relent ____.

Getting Ready to Read

William Bradford wrote about the Pilgrims' experiences in starting a new society in Plymouth during the first years of European settlement. What would it be like to start a colony in an unknown land? What challenges might you face? Discuss your answers in a small group.

from Of Plymouth Plantation

Summary This narrative account tells of the Puritans' first journey to the New World. The first part of the narrative describes their voyage. The second section describes the hardships of their first winter in Massachusetts. The third part tells how the Puritans received help from Native Americans and made a peace treaty with them.

The Coming of the Mayflower, N.C. Wyeth, from the Collection of Metropolitan Life Insurance Company, New York City, Photograph by Malcolm Varon

Note-taking Guide

Use this table to record how the settlers survived hardship and danger.

Section of text	Hardships the settlers faced	What the settlers did
Their Voyage		
The Starving Time		
Relations with Native Americans		

Thinking About the Selection

1. Complete the chart comparing the Pilgrims' attitude toward Native Americans before and after the Pilgrims met Samoset.

<table>
<tr><td>Before:</td><td>→</td><td>After:</td></tr>
</table>

2. The Pilgrims and Native Americans established rules about

____

____.

Why Did They Help? The Native Americans did not have to befriend and help the Pilgrims at Plymouth. Why do you think that they decided to help the survivors at Plymouth? Talk about your ideas with a partner.

I think that the Native Americans helped the Pilgrims because _______

____.

? Writing About the Essential Question

What makes American literature American? How are the Pilgrims' values and beliefs evident in the ways they respond to problems?

____

____

____

____

Word Families

Words that share the same base word make up a word family. Being able to identify words in the same word family can help a reader determine the meaning of unfamiliar or difficult words.

Examples

The verb *excite* means "make someone feel happy, eager or nervous."

Word	Part of Speech	Meaning
excitable	adjective	easily excited
unexciting	adjective	not making you feel happy or interested in something
excitement	noun	the feeling of being excited
excitedly	adverb	with a happy or hopeful attitude

Now You Do It

Draw a line from each sentence in the left column to the correct meaning of the underlined word in the right column. The first one has been done for you.

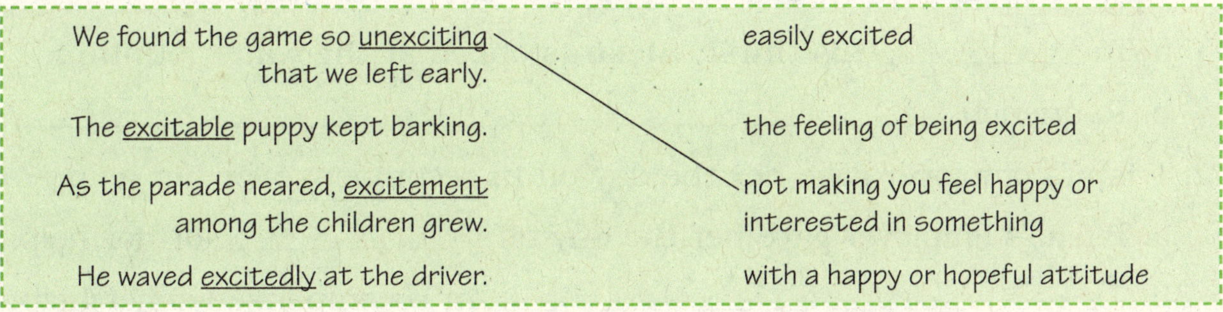

TALK ABOUT IT **That's So Exciting!** With a partner, take turns talking about school activities or events that excite you and those that do not.

WRITE ABOUT IT **What's So Exciting?** Choose one of the activities or events that you discussed about which to write an exciting review. Explain what you find so exciting about the activity, using at least four words from the same word family as *excite*.

Vocabulary

Listen to each word. Say it. Then, read the definition and the example sentence.

quench (KWEHNCH) *v.* To **quench** is to satisfy a feeling of wanting or needing something.

The new magazine will quench the public's thirst for information.

recompense (REK uhm pens) *n.* A **recompense** is something that you give to someone for trouble or losses that you have caused or as a reward for help.

Despite working all day, Tim received no recompense for his efforts.

persevere (per suh VEER) *v.* When you **persevere** to do something, you continue trying to do it in a very determined way, in spite of difficulties.

She encouraged John to persevere in his efforts to learn to swim.

Vocabulary Practice

Read the first sentence in each group of three. Then, complete Sentence *a* by substituting another word or phrase that means the same as the underlined vocabulary word. Complete Sentence *b* with your own ideas and words.

1. To quench his thirst, Stefan stopped at the water fountain.

   a. To ______________ his thirst, Stefan stopped at the water fountain.

   b. To quench ____.

2. Trisha's employer gave her the day off in recompense for her help.

   a. Trisha's employer gave her the day off in ____________ for her help.

   b. ____________________________________ in recompense for her help.

3. I tried to persevere in my work, but I became ill.

   a. I tried to ______________ in my work, but I became ill.

   b. I tried to persevere in my work, ____________________________.

Getting Ready to Read

As a Puritan, Anne Bradstreet cared for her home and eight children. She also wrote poems about her feelings and experiences. Why do you think she wrote poetry? Share your thoughts with a partner.

To My Dear and Loving Husband

Summary In Bradstreet's poem, the speaker addresses her husband. She expresses her deep love for him, and describes how happy they are together. She says that if they love each other well enough, their love will last even after their lives on Earth have ended.

Note-taking Guide

Use the chart to list three things that the speaker says about her love and her husband's love.

I prize thy love . . .	
My love is . . .	
Thy love is . . .	

Thinking About the Selection

1. Use the following chart to list elements of the poem.

The poet is speaking to	
Images in the poem include	
One religious reference in the poem includes	

2. Based on this poem, Bradstreet's marriage seems _________________
____.

TALK ABOUT IT **In Your Own Words** Bradstreet uses some difficult language to describe her feelings for her husband. With a partner, take turns explaining what each line in the poem means. Paraphrase each line in your own words.

Writing About the Essential Question

What makes American literature American? Which aspect of the speaker is more important in this poem—the private or the public self?

____

____

____

____

____

____

Vowel Sounds

A vowel is a sound in English represented by the letters *a, e, i, o,* or *u.*
Each letter has a short vowel sound and a long vowel sound, depending
on how it is combined with other letters. Two basic rules of pronunciation
are listed below.

Short Vowel Rule	Long Vowel Rule
When a syllable has only one vowel and the vowel comes between two consonants, the vowel is usually short.	When a syllable has two vowels, the first vowel is often long and the second is often silent. *Silent* means that you do not pronounce it.

Examples

Vowel	Short Vowel Sound		Long Vowel Sound	
a	hand, sack	A	brave, fate	AY
e	get, rest	E	feet, neat	EE
i	miss, pit	I	side, tried	Y
o	doll, frog	AW	goal, mode	OH
u	bus, dust	UH	clue, duped	OO

Now You Do It

For each word below, write the phonetic pronunciation on the line next
to it.

gave ______________   stone ______________

tent ______________   duck ______________

sprint ______________   blue ______________

TALK ABOUT IT **The Sound of Vowels** With a partner, take turns saying
sentences. In each sentence, use a pair of words that have a long vowel
sound and a short vowel sound for the same vowel.

WRITE ABOUT IT **Write a Poem** Use the words from this page to write a
short poem. Use at least one word for each long and short vowel sound.
Circle the words with short vowel sounds and underline the words
with long vowel sounds.

Vocabulary

Listen to each word. Say it. Then, read the definition and the example sentence.

affections (uh FEK shuhnz) *n.* **Affections** are gentle feelings of love and caring.

She realized that his affections were true when he sent her roses.

judgment (JUHJ muhnt) *n.* A **judgment** is an opinion that you form, especially after thinking carefully about something.

Matthew showed poor judgment when he decided to skip school.

apparel (uh PAR uhl) *n.* **Apparel** is another word for clothing, usually used by stores or the clothing industry.

The mall's second floor had men's and women's apparel only.

Vocabulary Practice

Read the first sentence in each group of three. Then, complete Sentence *a* by substituting another word or phrase that means the same as the underlined vocabulary word. Complete Sentence *b* with your own ideas and words.

1. The mother showed her affections by rocking the baby.

   a. The mother showed her ______________ by rocking the baby.

   b. The mother showed her affections ________________________________.

2. The coach made the final judgment about who would play.

   a. The coach made the final ______________ about who would play.

   b. The coach made the final judgment ________________________________.

3. The tailor displayed apparel in the store window.

   a. The tailor displayed ______________ in the store window.

   b. The tailor displayed apparel ________________________________.

Getting Ready to Read

Edward Taylor was a minister as well as a poet. Taylor addresses his poem "Huswifery" to God. Like many Christians, Taylor refers to the god in which he believes as "Lord." How do you think Taylor's role as a minister might shape his poetry? Talk about your ideas with a partner.

Huswifery

Summary Taylor's poem is addressed to God. The speaker in the poem compares himself to a spinning wheel that turns yarn into cloth. The speaker wants to be changed by God into a person who is worthy of being saved.

Note-taking Guide

Use the chart to list the ways in which the speaker wants God to change him.

The speaker asks the Lord to . . .
make the speaker
make the Lord's holy word
make the speaker's affections
make the speaker's soul
make the speaker's conversations
make the speaker

Thinking About the Selection

1. Taylor uses several examples of imagery in this poem. List five images that he creates. Then, identify to what Taylor compares each image. The first one has been done for you.

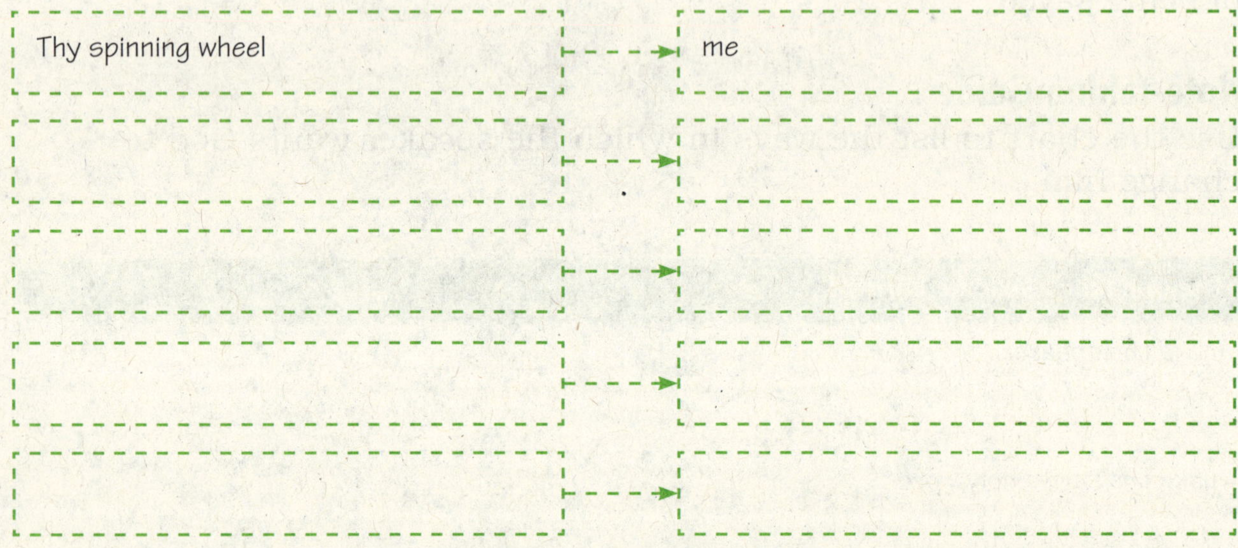

2. Taylor wants his understanding, will, affections, judgment, conscience, memory, words, and actions to _______________________

____ .

 **TALK ABOUT IT** **Think About Imagery** Taylor compares a woman making a beautiful garment to God making him into a better person. Do you think the comparison is appropriate and effective? Explain your answer to a partner, using examples from the poem to support your opinion.

I think it (is / is not) effective because _______________________

____ .

? Writing About the Essential Question

What makes American literature American? Do you think the Puritans would have considered this poem useful?

Antonyms

An antonym is a word that means the opposite of another word.
Writers may use antonyms to show contrasting ideas.

Examples

tame	wild
polite	rude
quiet	loud
calm	upset

Now You Do It

Read the sentences below. Then, rewrite each sentence, replacing the
underlined word with the appropriate antonym.

1. The dog was quite tame. _______________________________

   ____

2. My little brother was polite at the party. ________________

   ____

3. I like the park when it is quiet. ________________________

   ____

4. I felt quite calm when I heard the news. ________________

   ____

TALK ABOUT IT **Talk About Meanings** With a partner, take turns reading
aloud the sentences above. Then, combine each pair of sentences into
a new sentence. For example, *My dog was very tame, but your dog was
very wild.*

WRITE ABOUT IT **What's the Opposite World Like?** Write a short science
fiction story about a traveler who accidentally enters a world in which
everything is the opposite of what it should be. Use words from the
lesson in your writing.

Vocabulary

These words are underlined in the story. Listen to each word. Say it. Then, read the definition and the example sentence.

provoked (pruh VOHKT) *v.* When you have **provoked** someone, you have made him or her very angry, especially by annoying him or her.
Ian provoked David by teasing him for an entire period.

mediator (MEE dee ay tuhr) *n.* A **mediator** is someone who helps people end an argument and reach an agreement.
Pamela acted as a mediator when the two boys started arguing.

induce (in DOOS) *v.* When you **induce** someone, you make him or her decide to do something, especially something that does not seem wise.
Arnold tried to induce Jackie to sell her car for much less than it was worth.

Vocabulary Practice

Read the first sentence in each group of three. Then, complete Sentence *a* by substituting another word or phrase that means the same as the underlined vocabulary word. Complete Sentence *b* with your own ideas and words.

1. Kiesha provoked the dog by pulling his tail repeatedly.

   a. Kiesha ______________ the dog by pulling his tail repeatedly.

   b. Kiesha provoked ____.

2. The teacher acted as mediator between the angry students.

   a. The teacher ______________ between the angry students.

   b. The teacher acted as mediator ____________________________.

3. I was able to induce Karl to play longer.

   a. I was able to ______________ Karl to play longer.

   b. I was able to induce ________________________________.

Getting Ready to Read

During the 1700s, many preachers delivered emotional sermons to get people to change their lives for the better. What was and was not effective about a sermon or speech that you have heard? Share your thoughts with a partner.

from Sinners in the Hands of an Angry God

Jonathan Edwards

Summary Edwards's sermon tells about God's anger toward the sinners in his audience. He compares God's anger to floods and to a bow bent ready to shoot an arrow. The only thing that keeps God from dropping sinners into the fire is his mercy, according to Edwards. He tells the people that they can be reborn and save themselves from the anger.

Note-taking Guide

Use this chart to record details of what Edwards tells the sinners in his audience.

Purpose	Details to Achieve This Purpose
To motivate listeners to convert and save their souls	Only the power of God holds you up.

Cultural Understanding

Jonathan Edwards was a Christian preacher who lived more than a hundred years ago. Many Christians believe that sinners, or people who have done bad things and not asked forgiveness from their god, go to a place called Hell when they die. Hell is often described as a horrible, fiery place of punishment.

Comprehension Builder 

A *simile* compares two unlike things, using the words *like* or *as*. Circle three similes in the bracketed passage. What items are being compared in each simile?

____

____

____

Vocabulary Builder 

Multiple-Meaning Words
Executed may mean "killed someone." It may also mean "did something that has been carefully planned." Which meaning does *executed* have in the underlined text?

____

____

from Sinners in the Hands of an Angry God

Jonathan Edwards

The author, Jonathan Edwards, directs his **sermon** toward those with whom God is not pleased. He talks about a world of misery for them.

◆ ◆ ◆

There is the dreadful pit of the glowing flames of the **wrath** of God; there is Hell's wide gaping mouth open; and you have nothing to stand upon, nor anything to take hold of; there is nothing between you and Hell but the air; it is only the power and mere pleasure of God that holds you up.

◆ ◆ ◆

Sinners may think they are kept out of Hell by their own life and strength, but they are wrong. Sinners are like heavy weights of lead. If God chose to let them go, they would sink straight to Hell. God's anger is like a terrible storm, held back for the moment. God's wrath is like a stream that is dammed. The longer it is dammed, the stronger the waters will be once the dam is opened.

◆ ◆ ◆

It is true, that judgment against your evil works has not been executed hitherto;[1] the floods of God's vengeance have been withheld; but your guilt in the meantime is constantly increasing, and you are every day treasuring up more wrath; the waters are constantly rising, and **waxing** more and more mighty; and there is

Everyday Words
sermon (SER muhm) *n.* a talk given as part of a Christian church service, usually on a religious or moral subject
wrath (RATH) *n.* great anger
waxing (WAKS ing) *v.* increasing

1. **hitherto** (hi thuhr TOO) *adv.* up to now

nothing but the mere pleasure of God, that holds the waters back, that are unwilling to be stopped, and press hard to go forward.

◆　◆　◆

God's hand is holding the gate that controls the dam. If he should decide to move his hand, the flood of anger would be **inconceivable.** No human strength, or even the strength of the devil, could stop it.

◆　◆　◆

The bow of God's wrath is bent, and the arrow made ready on the string, and justice bends the arrow at your heart, and strains the bow, and it is nothing but the mere pleasure of God, and that of an angry God, without any promise or obligation at all, that keeps the arrow one moment from being made drunk with your blood.

◆　◆　◆

Everyone who does not **repent** risks being destroyed. Sinners may not believe that they are in danger now. There will come a time, though, when they will be convinced.

◆　◆　◆

The God that holds you over the pit of Hell, much as one holds a spider, or some loathsome[2] insect over the fire, **abhors** you, and is dreadfully provoked: his wrath towards you burns like fire; he looks upon you as worthy of nothing else, but to be cast into the fire; he is of purer eyes

---

Everyday Words

inconceivable (in kuhn SEEV uh buhl) *adj.* too strange or unusual to be thought of as possible

repent (ri PENT) *v.* be sorry for something and wish that you had not done it

abhors (uhb HOHRZ) *v.* hates a kind of behavior or way of thinking, especially because you think that it is morally wrong

---

2. **loathsome** (LOH<u>TH</u> suhm) *adj.* very unpleasant, unlikable, or cruel

---

Cultural Understanding

Many Christians believe in a being called *the devil.* In Christianity, the devil is a powerful evil spirit who tries to lead humans to commit sins, or evil acts. The devil lives in and rules over Hell.

Comprehension Builder 

Metaphors A metaphor describes one thing as something different. What is the metaphor for God's wrath in the bracketed paragraph?

____

Vocabulary Builder 

Multiple-Meaning Words
Cast may mean "choose which people will act certain parts in a play or other performance." It may also mean "throw." Which meaning does *cast* have in the underlined text?

____

Vocabulary Builder

Pronouns Pronouns are words—such as *I, you, they, me,* and *them*—that are used in place of nouns. To what noun do *they* and *them* in the bracketed paragraph refer?

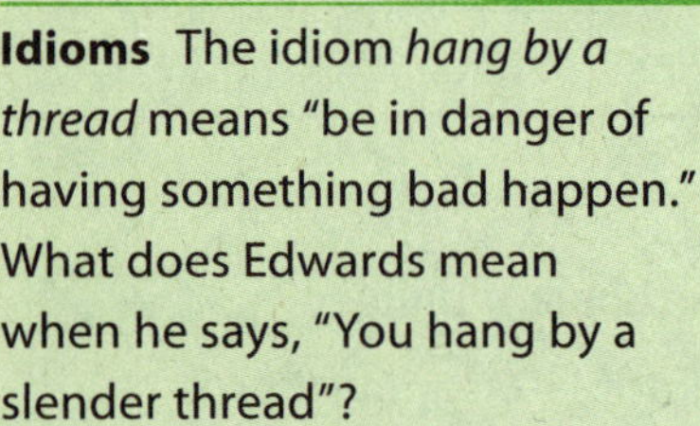

To what noun does *he* refer?

Vocabulary Builder

Idioms The idiom *hang by a thread* means "be in danger of having something bad happen." What does Edwards mean when he says, "You hang by a slender thread"?

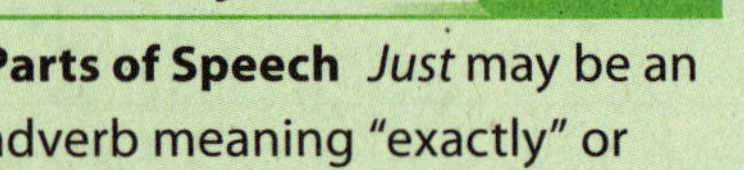

Vocabulary Builder

Parts of Speech *Just* may be an adverb meaning "exactly" or "only." It may also be an adjective meaning "right and fair." Is *just* an adjective or an adverb in the underlined sentence?

With a partner, discuss how you know the answer.

---

than to bear to have you in his sight; you are ten thousand times more **abominable** in his eyes, than the most hateful **venomous** serpent is in ours. . . .

◆ ◆ ◆

Edwards warns sinners that they are in great danger. God is as angry with them as he is with those already in Hell.

◆ ◆ ◆

You hang by a slender thread, with the flames of divine wrath flashing about it, and ready every moment to **singe** it, and burn it asunder;[3] and you have no interest in any mediator, and nothing to lay hold of to save yourself, nothing to keep off the flames of wrath, nothing of your own, nothing that you ever have done, nothing that you can do, to induce God to spare you one moment. . . .

◆ ◆ ◆

Edwards says that God will have no mercy on sinners who do not repent. However, the punishments of sinners will be just. If sinners repent now, God will show them mercy. If they refuse to repent, they will be tormented forever. Sinners who do not repent are in daily and hourly danger. Think of those who are now suffering endless misery in Hell. They have no more chances to obtain salvation.[4] But those who are still alive may still be saved.

Everyday Words

abominable (uh BAHM uh nuh buhl) *adj.* hateful, disgusting
venomous (VEN uh muhs) *adj.* poisonous
singe (SINJ) *v.* burn the surface of something slightly

3. **asunder** (uh SUN duhr) *v.* apart
4. **salvation** (sal VAY shuhn) *n.* in Christianity, the state of being saved from evil

Sinners now have a wonderful opportunity to gain forgiveness. They can save their souls from everlasting suffering. Many other sinners are flocking[5] to him and entering his kingdom. They are coming from everywhere. These sinners had been miserable, but now God has washed their sins away and they are **rejoicing.** It would be awful to be left behind and not join in this joyful celebration. Edwards says all sinners in his **congregation** should escape God's wrath and experience the saving grace of conversion.

◆ ◆ ◆

"Haste and escape for your lives, look not behind you, escape to the mountain, lest you be **consumed.**"[6]

Cultural Understanding

Grace has many meanings. In the bracketed paragraph, it means "God's kindness." The *saving grace* refers to the Christian idea that believing in the Christian God saves one's soul, or spirit, from eternal suffering.

Fluency Builder 

Preachers like Edwards often quote passages from the Bible in their sermons. The Bible is the holy book of Christianity. The passage that appears between quotation marks (" ") comes from a Bible story in which God destroys an evil city. In the story, God allows a few good people to escape. Read aloud the quoted passage with expression. Remember to pause briefly after each comma.

Everyday Words

rejoicing (ri JOYS ing) *v.* feeling or showing that you are very happy

congregation (kahng gruh GAY shuhn) *n.* members of a place of worship

consumed (kuhn SOOMD) *v.* destroyed completely

---

5. **flocking** (FLAHK ing) *v.* going somewhere in large numbers because something interesting or exciting is happening there

6. **"Haste . . . consumed"** from Genesis 19:17, the angels' warning to Lot, the only virtuous man in Sodom, to flee the city before they destroy it

Thinking About the Selection

1. Complete the sentences below to summarize the main points of Edwards's argument.

According to Edwards . . .

- Hell is a ____.

- Nothing stands between sinners and Hell but ______________________.

- Only ____________________________________ hold sinners up.

- Sinners are wrong to think that ____________________________________.

- God has withheld ____________________________________, but sinners' guilt and God's wrath ____________________________________.

- Sinners must ____________________________________ or be destroyed.

- God is as angry with sinners as with ____________________________________.

- God will show mercy to ____________________________________.

- God will ____________________________________ so that they can join the ____________ in his kingdom.

2. Edwards compares sinners to ____________ and ____________. He compares God's wrath and anger to ____________________________________, ____________________________________, and ____________________________________.

Think About Language Do you think Edwards's strong language is convincing and effective? In a small group, discuss why or why not.

? Writing About the Essential Question

How does literature shape or reflect society? This sermon played a significant role in reinvigorating Puritan faith during the 1740s. Why?

Food Idioms

Remember that an idiom is a group of words that have a special meaning together that is different from the ordinary meaning of the individual words. Many idioms relate to food items.

Examples

Idiom	Explanation
cool as a cucumber	very calm
apple of one's eye	one's favorite
half-baked	poorly thought out
in a nutshell	in summary
going bananas	becoming very emotional or angry

Now You Do It

Complete each sentence starter, using a different idiom from the chart above.

1. May's baby is the ___________________________.

2. During the debate, the politician was as ___________________________.

3. Milo had another ___________________________ plan to make money.

4. Lin explained ___________________________ what had happened.

5. Fritz was acting so strangely that I thought he must be

___________________________.

TALK ABOUT IT **Tell a Story** With a partner, plan and write a short detective story that uses the idioms on this page. Take turns making up sentences. For example, *Detective Sara Spade was always cool as a cucumber.*

WRITE ABOUT IT **Write an Interview** Imagine that you are a reporter sent to interview the detective in your story. Write a dialogue between you and the detective, using at least five of the idioms above.

Vocabulary

These words are underlined in the story. Listen to each word. Say it. Then, read the definition and the example sentence.

insidious (in SID ee uhs) *adj.* Something **insidious** is waiting for a chance to harm others.

His insidious plan would have destroyed the town.

privileges (PRIV lij iz) *n.* **Privileges** are special advantages or rights that are given to only one person or group.

My older sister has more privileges than I do.

vigilant (VIJ uh luhnt) *adj.* Someone who is **vigilant** is watchful.

The guard kept a vigilant eye on the candidate.

Vocabulary Practice

Read the first sentence in each group of three. Then, complete Sentence *a* by substituting another word or phrase that means the same as the underlined vocabulary word. Complete Sentence *b* with your own ideas and words.

1. The rebels had an insidious plan to overthrow the king.

   a. The rebels had a(n) _______________ plan to overthrow the king.

   b. The rebels had an insidious _________________________________.

2. The teacher awarded some students special privileges.

   a. The teacher awarded some students special _______________.

   b. _________________________________ special privileges.

3. The vigilant shepherds stayed close to their flock.

   a. The _______________ shepherds stayed close to their flock.

   b. The vigilant _________________________________.

Getting Ready to Read

Patrick Henry's fiery speeches helped persuade the American colonists to revolt against British rule. What else do you know about the American Revolution? Discuss your knowledge with a partner.

Speech in the Virginia Convention

Patrick Henry

Summary In this speech, Patrick Henry begins by saying that, without disrespect, he must disagree with the previous speeches. Judging by their conduct, he says, the British are preparing for war. We have tried discussing the problem. We are being ignored; there is no retreat except into slavery. The time for getting along peacefully is over. The war has already begun. "Give me liberty or give me death" is Henry's strong and well-known closing.

Note-taking Guide

Use this chart to compare the arguments for and against going to war.

Against	For
The colonists are too weak.	The colonists are as strong as they will ever be.

Vocabulary Builder

Idioms The idiom *see something in a different light* means "think about something in a different way." What does Henry mean when he says "see the same subject in different lights"?

____

____

Fluency Builder

Read aloud the underlined sentences. Then circle the words that tell how Patrick Henry judges the future.

Comprehension Builder

A metaphor describes one thing as something different. Circle the metaphor in the underlined sentence. What is being described as something else?

____

____

Speech in the Virginia Convention

Patrick Henry

Mr. President: No man thinks more highly than I do of the **patriotism,** as well as abilities, of the very worthy gentlemen who have just addressed the house. But different men often see the same subject in different lights . . . .

◆ ◆ ◆

Patrick Henry then says that the question before the house is very important. He cannot allow fear of offending someone to stop him from saying what he thinks.

He says it is natural for people to hold on to hope. But no matter how much it hurts, it is best to know the worst and to plan for it.

◆ ◆ ◆

I have but one lamp by which my feet are guided, and that is the lamp of experience. I know of no way of judging of the future but by the past. And judging by the past, I wish to know what there has been in the conduct of the British ministry for the last ten years to justify those hopes with which gentlemen have been pleased to **solace** themselves and the house? Is it that insidious smile with which our petition[1] has been lately received? Trust it not, sir; it will prove a **snare** to your feet. Suffer not yourselves to be betrayed with a kiss.[2]

◆ ◆ ◆

Everyday Words

patriotism (PAYT ree uh tizm) *n.* love for one's country and willingness to defend it

solace (SAHL uhs) *v.* comfort

snare (SNAYR) *n.* a trap

---

1. **petition** (puh TI shuhn) *n.* a written request signed by a lot of people, asking someone in authority to do something or change something

2. **betrayed with a kiss** In the Bible, Judas betrays Jesus with a kiss. This is a signal to the people who want to arrest Jesus.

He then says that the British are using the tools of war. What else can the display of British force mean? Does Britain have any enemies in this area of the world? No, she has none. So the navies and armies are here for one reason only.

◆ ◆ ◆

They are meant for us: they can be meant for no other. They are sent over to bind and rivet upon us those chains which the British ministry have been so long forging.

And what have we to oppose to them? Shall we try argument? Sir, we have been trying that for the last ten years. Have we anything new to offer upon the subject? Nothing. We have held the subject up in every light of which it is capable; but it has been all in vain.

◆ ◆ ◆

Henry says that the colonists' petitions have been ignored. Their protests have met more violence. Their pleas have been set aside. They have been insulted from the foot of the throne.

◆ ◆ ◆

There is no longer any room for hope. If we wish to be free, if we mean to **preserve** inviolate those inestimable privileges for which we have been so long contending, if we mean not basely to abandon the noble struggle in which we have been so long engaged, and which we have pledged ourselves never to abandon until the glorious object of our contest shall be obtained— we must fight! I repeat it, sir, we must fight! An appeal to arms and the God of Hosts is all that is left us!

They tell us, sir, that we are weak—unable to cope with so formidable an **adversary.** But

Everyday Words

preserve (pri SERV) *v.* make something continue without changing
adversary (AD ver sayr ee) *n.* enemy, opponent

TAKE NOTES

Vocabulary Builder

Parts of Speech *Bind* may be a noun meaning "a difficult situation" or a verb meaning "tie someone so that he or she cannot move." *Rivet* may be a noun meaning "a metal pin used to fasten pieces of metal together" or a verb meaning "fasten something together with metal pins." Are *bind* and *rivet* nouns or verbs in the second paragraph?

____

Vocabulary Builder

Idioms The idiom *has been in vain* means "has been without success or positive results despite one's efforts." Complete this sentence to practice using the idiom:

Henry says that argument with

the British ________________

_______________________.

Fluency Builder

An exclamation point signals strong emotions, such as excitement or anger. With a partner, read aloud the bracketed paragraph. Read with expression.

Vocabulary Builder

Suffixes The suffix *-ist* means "a person who does, makes, or practices." A *colony* is an area ruled by another country. What does the word *colonists* mean?

____

____

Vocabulary Builder

Parts of Speech *Base* can be a noun meaning "the lowest part or surface of something." It can also be an adjective meaning "not having good moral principles." What part of speech is *base* in the underlined sentence?

____

Comprehension Builder 

Why does Henry say that there is no peace? Underline the answer.

when shall we be stronger? Will it be the next week, or the next year? Will it be when we are totally disarmed, and when a British guard shall be stationed in every house?

◆　◆　◆

He continues by saying that the colonists are not weak. There are three million of them. They are "armed in the holy cause of liberty." They cannot be beaten by any force the enemy might send.

◆　◆　◆

The battle, sir, is not to the strong alone; it is to the vigilant, the active, the brave. Besides, sir, we have no election; if we were base enough to desire it, it is now too late to retire from the contest. There is no retreat but in submission and slavery! Our chains are forged! Their clanging may be heard on the plains of Boston! The war is **inevitable**—and let it come! I repeat it, sir, let it come!

It is vain, sir, to **extenuate** the matter. Gentlemen may cry "Peace, peace"—but there is no peace. The war is actually begun! The next gale[3] that sweeps from the north will bring to our ears the clash of resounding arms! Our brethren are already in the field! Why stand we here **idle?** What is it that gentlemen wish? What would they have? Is life so dear, or peace so sweet, as to be purchased at the price of chains and slavery? Forbid it, Almighty God! I know not what course others may take; but as for me, give me liberty or give me death!

Everyday Words

inevitable (in EV uh tuh buhl) *adj.* certain to happen and impossible to avoid
extenuate (ex TEN yoo ayt) *v.* to try to lessen how serious something is
idle (Y duhl) *adj.* not working or producing anything; lazy

---

3. **gale** (GAYL) *n.* a very strong wind

Vocabulary

Listen to each word. Say it. Then, read the definition and the example sentence.

sects (SEKTS) *n.* **Sects** are groups with particular beliefs and practices, especially those that have separated from a larger religious group.
Some religious <u>sects</u> differ from traditional practices.

despotism (DES puht iz uhm) *n.* **Despotism** is rule by someone who uses power in a cruel or unfair way.
The leader's <u>despotism</u> incited a rebellion.

unanimity (yoo nuh NIM uh tee) *n.* **Unanimity** is a state or situation of complete agreement among a group of people.
There is <u>unanimity</u> among the students that chocolate is the best ice cream flavor.

Vocabulary Practice

Read the first sentence in each group of three. Then, complete Sentence *a* by substituting another word or phrase that means the same as the underlined vocabulary word. Complete Sentence *b* with your own ideas and words.

1. Christianity includes different <u>sects</u> with specific beliefs.

   a. Christianity includes different _______________ with specific beliefs.

   b. _________________________________ sects with specific beliefs.

2. Students learned about <u>despotism</u> in history class.

   a. Students learned about _______________ in history class.

   b. Students learned about despotism _______________________.

3. The workers reached <u>unanimity</u> about their demands.

   a. The workers reached _______________ about their demands.

   b. The workers reached unanimity _______________________.

Getting Ready to Read

Benjamin Franklin worked hard to bring American leaders together to organize a new government. Franklin helped craft the United States Constitution of 1787. What do you know about the United States Constitution? Discuss your knowledge in a small group.

Speech in the Convention
Benjamin Franklin

Summary Benjamin Franklin expresses his doubts about the Constitution. However, he still approves of the document. He supports his opinions with several reasons. Franklin feels that this Constitution is the best document that imperfect men can offer. He also thinks that it is important to show complete support for the Constitution.

Note-taking Guide

Franklin suggests that a perfect Constitution will never be created. Use this web to list his reasons why the delegates should support it even though it is not perfect.

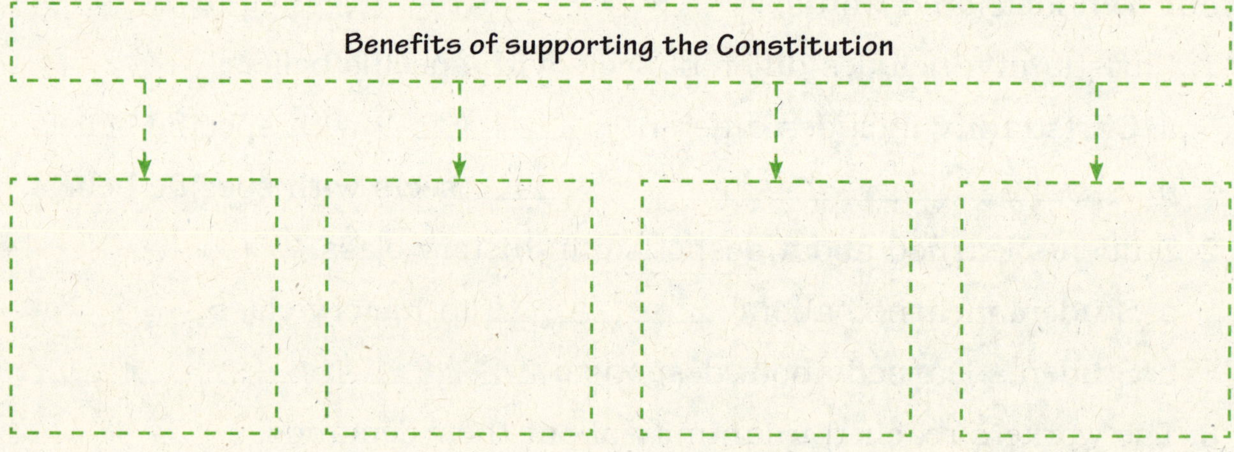

Thinking About the Selections

1. Both Henry and Franklin are trying to persuade their listeners to support their positions. List in this chart the major points made by Henry and Franklin in their arguments.

Henry wants people to support independence because . . .	Franklin wants people to support the new Constitution because . . .

2. Henry closes his speech with this statement: _______________

   ____

   Franklin closes his speech by asking the delegates to ___________

   ____

TALK **ABOUT IT** **Talk or Fight?** Henry says that talking to the British is useless and that the colonists must fight. Do you agree or disagree with Henry? Do you think that his speech is convincing? Discuss your thoughts with a partner.

I think Henry (is/is not) convincing because _____________________

   ____

   ____

Writing About the Essential Question

How does literature shape or reflect society? What connections do both Henry and Franklin make between the ability to face hard realities and ideas of loyalty to one's nation?

Present Progressive Tense

The present progressive tense describes an action that is currently happening. The action does not just happen and stop as in the simple present—*I read the letter.* It is ongoing—*I am reading the letter.* The present progressive tense can also describe an action that will occur in the future at a particular time—*I am writing a response letter tomorrow morning.*

The present progressive tense contains two parts: the appropriate form of the verb *to be* and the present participle of the verb showing the action. The present participle is formed by adding *-ing* to the end of the verb. When a verb ends in *e*, drop the *e* before adding *-ing*.

Examples

Verb Describing the Action	Subject Performing the Action	Present Progressive Tense
go	I	am going
talk	You	are talking
move	He/she/it	is moving
vote	We	are voting
play	They	are playing

Now You Do It

Write a sentence for each present progressive verb form listed above. Refer to a dictionary if you are unsure of any of the words' meanings.

TALK ABOUT IT **Making Future Plans** With a partner, take turns reading aloud your sentences. Then, revise each of your sentences to describe future actions that will take place at particular times. For example, *Tomorrow, Alexis is talking to the mayor about a community project.*

WRITE ABOUT IT **Dear Diary** Write a diary or journal entry about something that is happening in your life right now. Use at least four verbs in the present progressive tense to share your experiences.

Vocabulary

Listen to each word. Say it. Then, read the definition and the example sentence.

assent (uh SENT) *n.* When a person gives **assent,** he or she gives approval or agreement.

Congress refused to give its assent for war.

harass (huh RAS) *v.* When you **harass** someone, you annoy or threaten that person again and again.

Chris tried to harass Troy by continually stepping in front of him.

acquiesce (ak wee ES) *v.* To **acquiesce** is to unwillingly agree to do what someone wants without arguing or complaining.

The committee decided to acquiesce to the protestors' demands.

Vocabulary Practice

Read the first sentence in each group of three. Then, complete Sentence *a* by substituting another word or phrase that means the same as the underlined vocabulary word. Complete Sentence *b* with your own ideas and words.

1. Ms. Martin gave her <u>assent</u> to our proposed project.

   a. Ms. Martin gave her _______________ to our proposed project.

   b. Ms. Martin gave her assent _______________________________.

2. Tia's parents warned her not to <u>harass</u> the neighbor's dog.

   a. Tia's parents warned her not to _______________ the neighbor's dog.

   b. Tia's parents warned her not to harass _______________________.

3. I refused to <u>acquiesce</u> to my friend's demands.

   a. I refused to _______________ to my friend's demands.

   b. I refused to acquiesce _______________________________.

Getting Ready to Read

Thomas Jefferson was the main author of the Declaration of Independence. What do you know about the conflict between the American colonies and the British? Share your knowledge in a small group.

The Declaration of Independence
Thomas Jefferson

Summary Thomas Jefferson explains that it is important to state why America is separating from Britain. He claims certain basic rights for the colonists. He says that the English king abuses those rights. Based on these abuses, the colonies are independent of Britain and the colonists pledge their support of this declaration.

Note-taking Guide

Use this diagram to list Jefferson's main reasons for going to war with the British.

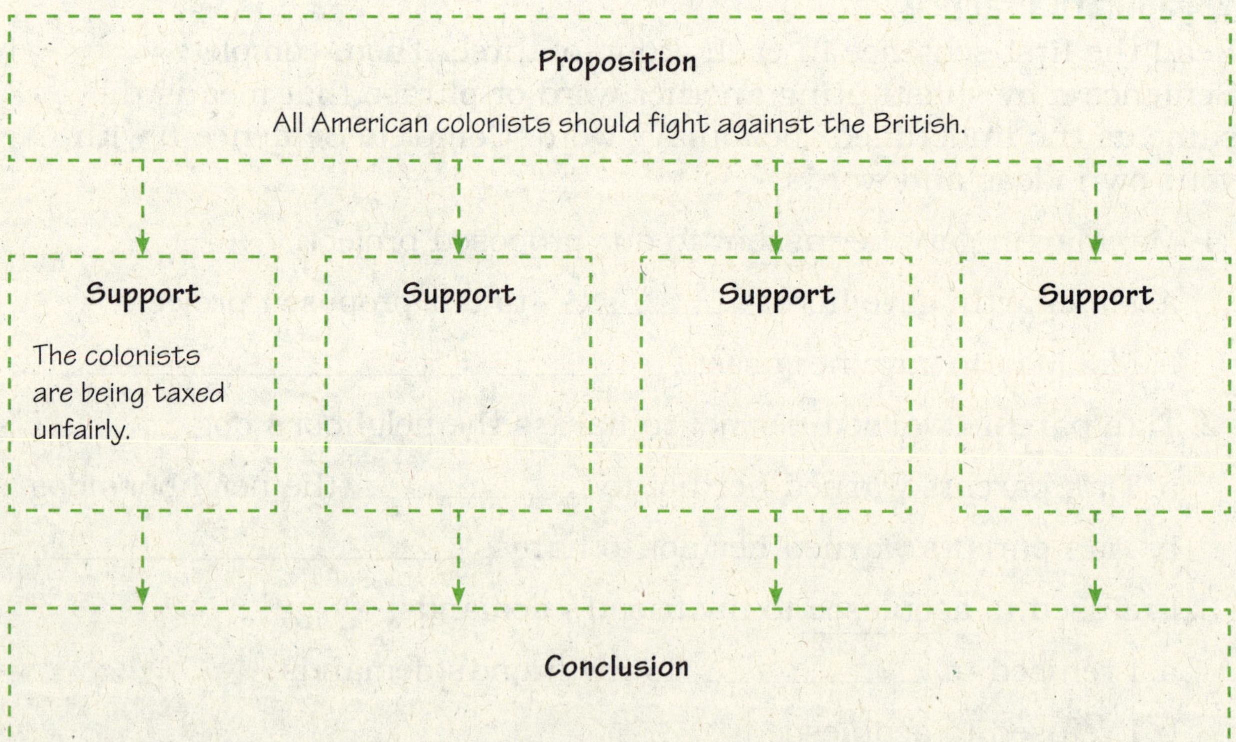

Vocabulary

These words are underlined in the story. Listen to each word. Say it. Then, read the definition and the example sentence.

consolation (kahn suh LAY shuhn) *n.* **Consolation** is something that makes you feel better, especially when you are sad or disappointed.

Wilson found consolation in reading books when he was sick.

esteem (es TEEM) *v.* When you **esteem** someone or something, you respect and admire that person or thing.

The students greatly esteem the band director's opinion.

prudent (PROO duhnt) *adj.* Someone who is **prudent** has a sensible and careful attitude and avoids unnecessary risks.

It is not prudent to go out in the cold without a jacket.

Vocabulary Practice

Read the first sentence in each group of three. Then, complete Sentence *a* by substituting another word or phrase that means the same as the underlined vocabulary word. Complete Sentence *b* with your own ideas and words.

1. Our team lost, but we took consolation in their efforts.

   a. Our team lost, but we took _______________ in their efforts.

   b. Our team lost, but we took consolation _____________________.

2. My parents esteem honesty and hard work.

   a. My parents _______________ honesty and hard work.

   b. My parents esteem _____________________.

3. Oni made the prudent decision not to hike in the dark.

   a. Oni made the _______________ decision not to hike in the dark.

   b. Oni made the prudent decision _____________________.

Getting Ready to Read

Thomas Paine wrote several pamphlets to oppose British taxes, laws, and other actions. What do you think were advantages and disadvantages of declaring independence from Britain? Discuss your ideas in a small group.

from The Crisis, Number 1
Thomas Paine

Summary Thomas Paine writes his essay to the American colonists. He wants to encourage them to fight against the British. Paine writes that God supports the American cause. He also argues that a good father will fight. If the fathers fight, their children may live in peace. Paine then asks Americans in every state to unite.

Note-taking Guide

Paine wants the colonists to agree that they should go to war. Use this chart to list evidence that Paine uses in his argument.

Evidence
Americans have already tried to avoid war in every way.

from The Crisis, Number 1

Thomas Paine

Paine says that these are difficult times. He says that those who fight against the British deserve thanks from everyone. He knows that the summer soldier and sunshine patriot[1] will not serve their country in this **crisis.**

◆ ◆ ◆

Tyranny, like hell, is not easily conquered; yet we have this consolation with us, that the harder the conflict, the more glorious the triumph. What we obtain too cheap, we esteem too lightly; 'tis dearness only that gives everything its value. Heaven knows how to put a proper price upon its goods. . . .

◆ ◆ ◆

Paine goes on to say that Britain has a big army to stand behind her tyranny. She has said that she will keep on taxing[2] the colonists and controlling them. Paine says this sounds like slavery. Britain has great power over America. Such power can belong only to God.

Paine believes that God Almighty will not give up on America. That is because America has tried so hard to avoid war. God would not give America up to the care of the devils. Paine says that the king of Britain is like a common murderer or robber. He has no grounds to look up to heaven for help against America.

Everyday Words

crisis (KRY sis) *n.* a situation in which many problems must be dealt with quickly so that the situation does not get worse or more dangerous

tyranny (TEER uh nee) *n.* oppressive or unfair power

---

1. **summer soldier and sunshine patriot** those who fight only when winning and those who are loyal only during good times

2. **taxing** (TAKS ing) *v.* charging a tax on something; A tax is an amount of money paid to the government according to one's income or property or based on the goods that one buys.

Vocabulary Builder

Contractions The apostrophe (') may show that a letter is missing in a contraction. The word *'tis* is not used much in modern English. In the past, it was used to mean "it is." The apostrophe stands for the missing letter *i*.

Vocabulary Builder

Idioms The idiom *stand behind* in the underlined sentence means "support or back up." What does Paine say that Britain has to stand behind her tyranny?

____

Vocabulary Builder

Multiple-Meaning Words *Grounds* may mean "the land or gardens around a building." It may also mean "a good reason for saying, doing, or believing something." Which meaning does *grounds* have in the bracketed paragraph?

____

____

Vocabulary Builder 

Homophones Words that are pronounced the same, but have different spellings and meanings are called *homophones*. The word *principals* means "leaders of schools." Circle the homophone for *principals* that means "moral rules or beliefs."

Vocabulary Builder 

Idioms The idiom *break out* means "start to happen." Complete this sentence, using the idiom:

Paine says that wars will continue

to ________________________

until America is free from

________________________ .

Vocabulary Builder 

Common Expressions When someone says that *there cannot be too much* of something, he or she means that there is a need for as much of that item as possible. What does Paine say that there cannot be too much of?

____

I once felt all that kind of anger, which a man ought to feel, against the mean principles that are held by the Tories;[3] a noted one, who kept a tavern at Amboy, was standing at his door, with as pretty a child in his hand, about eight or nine years old, as I ever saw, and after speaking his mind as freely as he thought was <u>prudent</u>, finished with this unfatherly **expression,** *"Well! give me peace in my day."*

◆　◆　◆

Paine says that a generous parent should have said, *"If there must be a war, let it be in my day. That way, my child can have peace."* America could be the happiest place on earth. She is located far from all the **wrangling** world. All she has to do is trade with the other countries. Paine is sure that America will not be happy until she gets clear of **foreign** control. Wars, with no endings, will break out until that time comes. America must be the winner in the end.

Paine appeals to Americans in all states to unite. He feels that there cannot be too much strength for such an important **mission.** He wants those in the future to know that when danger arrived, the Americans joined together to fight.

Paine explains that British control will affect them all, no matter who they are or where they live.

◆　◆　◆

Everyday Words

expression (ik SPRE shuhn) *n.* something that you say, write, or do that shows what you think or feel

wrangling (RANG gling) *n.* fighting, bickering, arguing

foreign (FOHR uhn) *adj.* from or relating to a country that is not your own

mission (MI shuhn) *n.* an important job; something that you feel you must do because you think that it is right

---

3. **Tories** colonists who were loyal to Britain

The heart that feels not now, is dead: the blood of his children will curse his **cowardice,** who shrinks back at a time when a little might have saved the whole, and made *them* happy. (I love the man that can smile at trouble; that can gather strength from **distress,** and grow brave by **reflection.**)

♦　♦　♦

Paine says that only those with little minds will shrink back. The strong of heart will fight unto death. He would not support an offensive[4] war for all the treasures in the world. Such a war is murder. Paine then asks an important question.

He wonders what the difference is between a thief breaking into his house and ordering him to obey and a king who orders him to obey. He finds no difference and feels that both deserve the same treatment.

♦　♦　♦

Everyday Words

cowardice (KOW uhr dis) *n.* lack of courage

distress (di STRES) *n.* suffering; extreme unhappiness

reflection (ri FLEK shuhn) *n.* careful thought

4. offensive (uh FEN siv) *adj.* used or intended for attacking

Fluency Builder 

Writers often use a colon (:) instead of a period (.) between two sentences that are closely related. When reading, you should pause briefly after a colon. Read aloud the bracketed paragraph with expression. Remember to pause after each colon and period. Pause more briefly after commas (,) and semicolons (;).

Comprehension Builder 

To what does Paine compare a king who orders him to obey?

____

____

Thinking About the Selection

1. The Declaration of Independence mentions things that the king had done to justify the colonies' separating from Britain. Thomas Paine wrote The Crisis in the early months of the revolution, when things were not going well for the Patriots. Use this chart to list the reasons for separation from Britain and the reasons for the Patriots to continue the fight.

The colonies should separate from Britain and form a new country because the king has . . .	The colonies should continue to fight for independence because . . .

2. The Declaration states that citizens can alter and abolish government when ____

____.

TALK ABOUT IT **The Value of Liberty** Paine states that people do not value the things that they win or obtain easily. Do you agree or disagree with this statement? What were the Patriots trying to win? Discuss your opinions with a partner.

Writing About the Essential Question

What makes American literature American? Are the ideals Jefferson and Paine defend in these writings still important to Americans? Explain.

Multiple-Meaning Words

Many words in English have several meanings. Context clues in the text around the word can help you determine a word's meaning.

Examples

Word	Meanings
stand, *noun*	• a piece of furniture that holds or supports something else • a table, booth, or other small structure used for showing and selling things • a position or an opinion that one state's firmly and publicly
take, *verb*	• move or go with someone or something from one place to another • study a particular subject in school or college • use a particular form of transport or a certain road or way to go somewhere

Now You Do It

Read each sentence below. Write the correct meaning of the underlined word.

1. Paulo adjusted the microphone <u>stand</u> while he sang.

____

2. Mr. Bukowski will <u>take</u> my mother to the airport.

____

3. The senator took a strong <u>stand</u> on the issue of healthcare.

____

4. I had to <u>take</u> a bus to reach Chicago.

____

TALK ABOUT IT **Guess the Meaning** With a partner, write sentences using *stand* and *take* in different ways. Then, exchange sentences with another pair. Guess the meanings of these words in each other's sentences.

WRITE ABOUT IT **Write Limericks** Write a humorous poem using one of the multiple-meaning words. Share your poem with a partner.

Vocabulary

Listen to each word. Say it. Then, read the definition and the example sentence.

propitious (proh PI shuhs) *adj.* Something that is **propitious** is good and is likely to bring good results.

> *The day that you get an assignment is the most propitious time to start it.*

implore (im PLOHR) *v.* When you **implore** someone for something, you ask for it in an emotional way.

> *Their mother will implore the two fighting siblings to get along.*

pensive (PEN siv) *adj.* When you are **pensive,** you are deeply or seriously thoughtful.

> *She listened intently, looking pensive.*

Vocabulary Practice

Read the first sentence in each group of three. Then, complete Sentence *a* by substituting another word or phrase that means the same as the underlined vocabulary word. Complete Sentence *b* with your own ideas and words.

1. The sunny afternoon was a <u>propitious</u> time for hiking.

    a. The sunny afternoon was a _____________ time for hiking.

    b. The sunny afternoon was a propitious time for _________________.

2. They often <u>implore</u> their parents for a bigger allowance.

    a. They often _____________ their parents for a bigger allowance.

    b. They often implore _________________________________.

3. My mother looked <u>pensive</u> as she studied her textbook.

    a. My mother looked _____________ as she studied her textbook.

    b. My mother looked pensive as she _____________________________.

Getting Ready to Read

Phillis Wheatley was enslaved, but learned to read and write English. Later, Phillis Wheatley gained her freedom and published poems about freedom, liberty, and virtue. How do you think her experiences affected her poetry and ideas? Share your thoughts with a partner.

To His Excellency, General Washington

Phillis Wheatley

Summaries "To His Excellency, General Washington" praises the revolutionary cause. The poem personifies America as the goddess Columbia. It also praises George Washington for his bravery and leadership.

Note-taking Guide

In the poem, Wheatley describes America (as the goddess Columbia) and George Washington. Use the chart to record details about America, or Columbia, and Washington.

America (Columbia)	Washington

Thinking About the Selection

1. Wheatley uses detailed language and imagery to describe the colonies, the British, and George Washington. Use this chart to identify the subject of each description.

Imagery	The colonies, the British, or George Washington?
freedom's cause her anxious breast alarms	
In bright array they seek the work of war	
Thee, first in peace and honors	
Fam'd for thy valor, for thy virtues more	
you, whoever dares disgrace	
The land of freedom's heaven-defended race	
Britannia droops the pensive head	
thy thirst of boundless power	
Proceed, great Chief	

2. Wheatley thinks that Washington is a great leader who has

____

____.

TALK ABOUT IT **Understanding Poetry** Wheatley's language can be difficult for modern readers to understand. With a partner, take turns reading the poem aloud. After each sentence, stop and discuss what you think that sentence means.

 **Writing About the Essential Question**

What makes American literature American? Do the qualities Wheatley attributes to Washington represent typical American values? Explain.

Prefixes

A prefix is a group of letters that is added to the beginning of a base word to form a new word with a different meaning.

Examples

The prefixes *in-* and *un-* mean "not" or "opposite of." Adding *in-* or *un-* to a base word forms a new word with the opposite meaning of the original word.

Prefix		Base Word		New Word	Meaning
in-	+	active	=	inactive	not active
un-	+	happy	=	unhappy	not happy

Now You Do It

Complete the chart below by adding each prefix to each base word. Then, write the meaning of each new word.

Prefix		Base Word		New Word	Meaning
in-	+	sensitive	=		
in-	+	frequent	=		
un-	+	popular	=		
un-	+	official	=		

TALK ABOUT IT **Using Opposites** With a partner, take turns using each pair of opposites from the chart above in a sentence. Each sentence should include the base word and the new word formed by adding the prefix. Check the meaning of words in a dictionary if you need help.

WRITE ABOUT IT **A Party for Your Unbirthday** Write a short story about a party held to celebrate your unbirthday—a day that is not your birthday. Describe the unusual celebration, including at least five words that have the prefix *in-* or *un-*.

Instructional Manuals

About Manuals

An **instructional manual** presents a step-by-step process for completing a certain task. The text explains how to perform a procedure, how to put something together, or how to use a product.

Most instructional manuals have these features:

- a specific result that the reader can accomplish by following the directions
- a series of steps explained in logical order
- a list of materials that are needed

Reading Skill

Text features organize and highlight important details in a manual. When you understand the way in which a manual is organized, you can **analyze and evaluate information from text features.** Text features include headings, bold and italic text, bulleted and numbered lists, and visual aids. Headings and subheadings identify main ideas presented in the manual. Text printed in bold or italic type draws your attention to important information. Lists provide details that support the main ideas or identify steps to be completed in a particular order. Visual aids, such as photographs and diagrams, may point out important details or provide additional information.

Basic Elements			Purpose
Headlines and subheads	Yes ☐	No ☐	
Boldfaced or italicized text	Yes ☐	No ☐	
Numbered or bulleted lists	Yes ☐	No ☐	
Photos or illustrations	Yes ☐	No ☐	

LEAGUE OF WOMEN VOTERS
MAKING DEMOCRACY WORK
HOW TO WATCH A DEBATE

STAY INFORMED

Sign up for the League's e-newsletter and get all the latest information delivered to your inbox.

HOW TO WATCH A DEBATE

Candidate debates have a long history in American politics. At every level of government—from city council to state legislature, from Congress to President of the United States—candidates participate in debates to help voters understand who and what they stand for. Watching debates is an important way for voters to learn more about the candidates and the issues before the election, so that they can cast an informed vote. At the same time, voters need to view debates with a careful eye to get the most information. Candidates rehearse thoroughly for debates, making it hard to get candid, spontaneous answers. Debates can emphasize form over substance, such as the candidates' appearance instead of their stands on the issues. You may watch a debate and still not get answers to the questions you have about the candidates and issues.

BEFORE THE DEBATE

It will help if you take some time before the debate to:

- Follow the campaign to learn about the candidates and their backgrounds;
- Find out what the important campaign issues are;
- Decide what issues are most important to you;
- Think about the questions you may have and the information you want to get from the debate to help you in your decision making;
- Open your mind to new opinions/impressions of the candidate regardless of party affiliation.

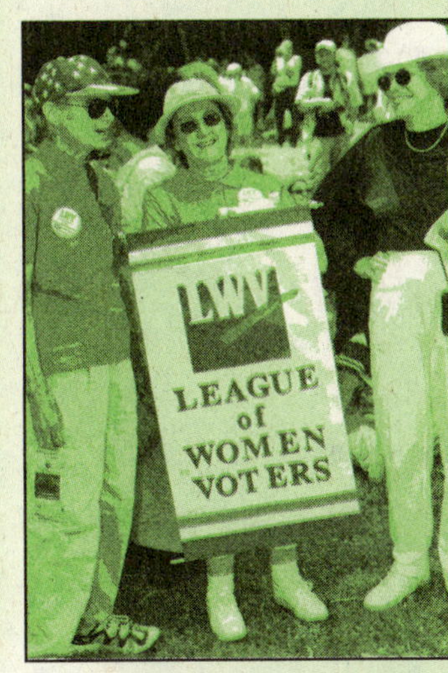

You may want to make plans to get together with friends or family to watch the debate. Watching the debate in a group and discussing it afterwards helps to clarify your thoughts about what was said in the debate and how the candidates performed.

A debate might not include all of the candidates for the office. Before the debate, note which candidates are included and which are not. If all candidates are not participating, try to find out why. Some debates include only candidates who have significant support, on the theory that the voters should be able to compare the candidates with a realistic chance of winning. Others invite all candidates who have qualified for the ballot. Sometimes candidates who are invited choose not to participate. Candidates with a strong lead might refuse to participate because they think there is no advantage to be gained by debating a lesser known opponent.

DURING THE DEBATE

When watching the debate, ask yourself questions like these to help you judge the fairness of the debate and the performance of the candidates:

The debate format and questions:

- Does the format give each candidate an equal opportunity to speak and respond to questions?
- Are the questions clear, fair, and equally tough on all candidates?
- Do the questions cover the issues that are important to you?
- Is the moderator in control of the debate? Does the moderator need to say less and let the candidates say more?

The candidates:

- Do they answer questions directly, or do they evade them or fail to answer the specific question?
- Do they give specifics about their stands on the issues, or do they speak in generalities? Do they support their positions and arguments with facts and figures?
- Do they talk about their own policies and positions, or do they mostly attack their opponents?
- Are their proposals realistic? Can they actually carry out the promises they are making?
- Do they appear sincere, confident and relaxed?
- Do they show how their backgrounds and experience qualify them to hold the office?
- Are their answers consistent with their previous positions, and if not, do they explain why?

- What image are they trying to create?
- Do their responses appear overly rehearsed or "canned"?

Media coverage:

- If you are watching the debate on television, are reaction shots or other techniques used to create a sense of drama or conflict?
- Are you being influenced by comments made by reporters and commentators immediately before and after the debate?

AFTER THE DEBATE

It will help clarify your thoughts about the candidates and the issues if you take some time after the debate to reflect on what you have just seen and heard. You can do this by:

- Comparing your impressions with others who watched the debate;
- Asking yourself, based on the information you got from watching the debate, which candidate appears most qualified for the office;
- Identifying the issues on which you agree with a candidate and those on which you disagree, and deciding whether that makes you more or less likely to vote for a particular candidate;
- Asking yourself if you learned something new about the issues or the candidate;
- Thinking about whether you have more questions about the issues or the candidates that you want to follow up;
- Getting more information about the candidates' positions from news reports, candidate Web sites and nonpartisan voter information Web sites.
- Watching later debates for more information or to confirm your current impressions of the candidates

CONCLUSION

Candidate debates give voters a chance to hear the candidates speak and respond to their opponents. They give candidates a chance to present their message directly to a wide audience. As a voter, asking yourself the right questions before, during, and after the debate can help you make the most of this opportunity to learn about the candidates and the issues.

Thinking About the Manual

1. Why does the League of Women Voters provide instructions for watching a debate?

   ____

2. What techniques or activities can the media use to influence the opinions of some voters?

   ____

Reading Skill

3. When should readers learn about candidates who participate in a debate? How do you know?

   ____

4. Why does the author use italic subheadings in the section DURING THE DEBATE?

   ____

WRITE ABOUT IT ▶ Timed Writing: Exposition (25 minutes)

Use the manual "How to Watch a Debate" to verify and clarify the following statement:

Watching debates is an important way for voters to learn about the candidates and the issues before an election.

Write a brief essay in support of the statement. Answer the questions below to help you organize your writing.

- What is the purpose of a debate?
- What should viewers do while watching a debate?
- How should viewers use what they have seen to decide which candidate to support?

Vocabulary

These words are underlined in the story. Listen to each word. Say it. Then, read the definition and the example sentence.

contrived (kuhn TRYVD) *v.* If you have **contrived** something, then you have made or invented it in a skillful way.

My father contrived a new way to print photographs.

deceit (di SEET) *n.* **Deceit** is misleading behavior that is meant to make someone believe something that is not true.

Gilian's deceit convinced Max to believe his sister's story.

incorrigible (in KOHR i juh buhl) *adj.* Someone who is **incorrigible** behaves badly or has bad habits that he or she does not change.

Shawn is an incorrigible liar, always doing what suits himself.

Vocabulary Practice

Read the first sentence in each group of three. Then, complete Sentence *a* by substituting another word or phrase that means the same as the underlined vocabulary word. Complete Sentence *b* with your own ideas and words.

1. Our team contrived a fantastic exhibit for the fair.

   a. Our team _______________ a fantastic exhibit for the fair.

   b. Our team contrived _________________________________.

2. After her deceit, Tanya's parents did not trust her.

   a. After her _______________, Tanya's parents did not trust her.

   b. After her deceit, _________________________________.

3. Sally was incorrigible about biting her fingernails.

   a. Sally was _______________ biting her fingernails.

   b. Sally was incorrigible _________________________________.

Getting Ready to Read

Franklin wrote his autobiography between 1771 and 1790. What strengths and weaknesses might an autobiography have, compared with a biography or another record of historical events? Discuss your thoughts with a partner.

from The Autobiography
Benjamin Franklin

Summary Franklin is working on a plan to reach moral perfection. He will work on thirteen virtues, or qualities. Franklin writes the virtues in a notebook to see how well he is doing. He makes a black mark beside a virtue every time he forgets to follow it. He works on a different virtue each week. Franklin thinks his plan is helpful but not completely successful.

Note-taking Guide

Use this chart to keep track of the different virtues that Franklin works on. List the virtues in order from most important to least important.

Virtues to Help Franklin Reach His Goal

- Temperance
-
-
-
-
-
-
-
-
-
-
-
-

from The Autobiography

Benjamin Franklin

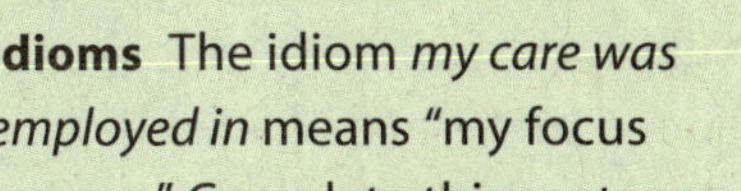

Franklin decides to take up a difficult project. He will try to live a perfect life. He knows, or thinks he knows, what is right and wrong. He does not see why he cannot always do the one and avoid the other.

◆ ◆ ◆

But I soon found I had undertaken a task of more difficulty than I had imagined. While my care was employed in guarding against one fault, I was often surprised by another. . . . I therefore <u>contrived</u> the following method.

◆ ◆ ◆

Franklin has read other people's lists of virtues in the past. These lists don't seem quite right to him. He writes his own list of thirteen virtues. He adds short notes. The notes explain what the virtue means to him. Here is his list.

◆ ◆ ◆

1. TEMPERANCE Eat not to dullness; drink not to elevation.
2. SILENCE Speak not but what may benefit others or yourself; avoid trifling conversation.
3. ORDER Let all your things have their places; let each part of your business have its time.
4. RESOLUTION Resolve to perform what you ought; perform without fail what you resolve.
5. FRUGALITY Make no expense but to do good to others or yourself; i.e., waste nothing.
6. INDUSTRY Lose no time; be always employed in something useful; cut off all unnecessary actions.
7. SINCERITY Use no hurtful <u>deceit</u>; think innocently and justly, and, if you speak, speak accordingly.

Vocabulary Builder 

Idioms The idiom *my care was employed in* means "my focus was on." Complete this sentence:

Franklin learned that while his

care was employed in

_______________________,

he was often surprised by

_______________________.

Vocabulary Builder

Word Families The noun *resolution* and the verb *resolve* are in the same word family. They have related meanings because they share the same root word. *Resolution* means "a definite or formal decision." What does *resolve* mean?

____

Comprehension Builder 

What is Franklin's attitude about wasting time? Circle the answer.

Vocabulary Builder

Suffixes A suffix is a word part added to the end of a word. It changes the part of speech of the word. The word *frugal* is used to describe a person who does not waste things. When you add the suffix *-ity,* it means "the quality of not being wasteful." The suffix *-ity* means "quality, state, or condition of." Find three other words in Franklin's list that end in *-ity.* Write them here:

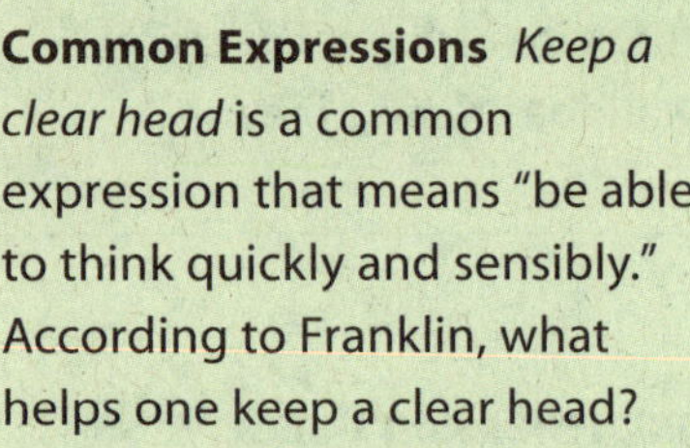

____

____

____

Vocabulary Builder

Common Expressions *Keep a clear head* is a common expression that means "be able to think quickly and sensibly." According to Franklin, what helps one keep a clear head?

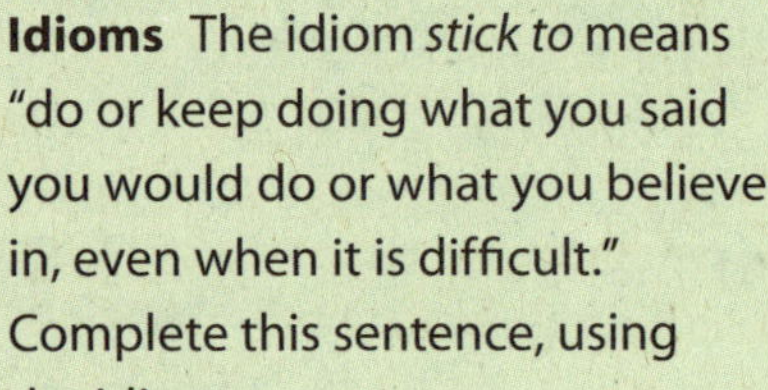

____

Vocabulary Builder

Idioms The idiom *stick to* means "do or keep doing what you said you would do or what you believe in, even when it is difficult." Complete this sentence, using the idiom:

Franklin wants to ______________

______________ his plan.

8. JUSTICE Wrong none by doing injuries, or omitting the benefits that are your duty.
9. MODERATION Avoid extremes; forebear[1] **resenting** injuries so much as you think they deserve.
10. CLEANLINESS Tolerate no uncleanliness in body, clothes, or habitation.[2]
11. TRANQUILITY Be not disturbed at trifles,[3] or at accidents common or unavoidable.
12. CHASTITY
13. HUMILITY Imitate Jesus and Socrates.

◆ ◆ ◆

Franklin's goal is to get into the habit of all these virtues. He tries one at a time, then goes on to the next. He thinks that some virtues might make other ones easier. That is why he lists *Temperance* first. Temperance helps you keep a clear head. A clear head helps you guard against bad habits. With the habit of temperance, *Silence* would be easier.

He also wants to gain knowledge. He knows that knowledge is obtained more by listening than by speaking. He gives *Silence* the second place. This virtue and the next, *Order,* would give him more time for his studies. *Resolution* is next. It will help Franklin stick to his plan. *Frugality* and *Industry* will help him pay all his debts. They will also help him add to his wealth. Then it will be easier to practice *Sincerity* and *Justice,* and so on. He decides to check his progress every day.

◆ ◆ ◆

I made a little book, in which I **allotted** a page for each of the virtues. I ruled each page with red ink, so as to have seven columns, one for each

Everyday Words

resenting (ri ZENT ing) *v.* feeling angry or upset about a situation or about something that someone has done

allotted (uh LOT ted) *v.* assigned, gave a part

1. **forebear** (fohr BAYR) *v.* stop doing something; spelled *forbear* today
2. **habitation** (hab uh TAY shuhn) *n.* a house or place to live in
3. **trifles** (TRY fuhlz) *n.* things that are unimportant or not valuable

day of the week, marking each column with a letter for the day. I crossed these columns with thirteen red lines, marking the beginning of each line with the first letter of one of the virtues, on which line and in its proper column I might mark, by a little black spot, every **fault** I found upon **examination** to have been committed respecting that virtue upon that day.

◆　◆　◆

He decides to spend a week on each virtue. In the first week, he practices Temperance. His goal the first week is to keep his first line, marked T, clear of spots. The next week, he might try the next virtue. He will try to keep both lines clear of spots. He can go through the whole list in thirteen weeks, and he repeats this process four times a year.

Franklin follows his plan for some time. One thing surprises him. He has more faults than he had imagined. But he is glad to see them become less and less. After a while, he goes through only one course in a year. Later, he goes through one in several years. At last, he stops doing it. He is too busy with trips and business in Europe. But he always carries his little book with him.

The virtue of Order gives him the most trouble. He just isn't used to putting papers and things in their places. He has a very good memory. He can always remember where he has left something.

◆　◆　◆

This article, therefore, cost me so much painful attention, and my faults in it **vexed** me so much, and I made so little progress in

---

Everyday Words

fault (FAHLT) *n.* a bad or weak part of one's character

examination (ig zam uh NAY shuhn) *n.* the process of looking at something carefully in order to see what it is like

vexed (VEKST) *v.* annoyed, bothered

Comprehension Builder 

Franklin has a plan for tracking his progress. Underline his plan. Predict what Franklin will learn from his chart. Will he have many faults, a few, or an average number?

____

____

Vocabulary Builder 

Multiple-Meaning Words
Course may mean "a class or a series of lessons in a certain subject." It may also mean "an action or series of actions that one takes in order to deal with a certain situation." Which meaning does *course* have in the bracketed paragraph?

____

____

Vocabulary Builder 

Idioms The idiom *used to* means "familiar with." What does Franklin mean when he says that he *isn't used to putting papers and things in their places?*

____

____

Vocabulary Builder

Homographs A homograph is a word that is spelled the same as another but has a different meaning and pronunciation. *Content,* when pronounced "KAHN tent," is a noun that means "the ideas, facts, or opinions contained in a speech, piece of writing, film, or material." Pronounced "kuhn TENT," it is an adjective that means "happy and satisfied." Which meaning and pronunciation does *content* have in the underlined text?

____

____

Vocabulary Builder

Parts of Speech *Struggle, envy,* and *hate* can be both nouns and verbs. Nouns are people, places, things, and ideas. Verbs describe actions, experiences, and states of being. What parts of speech are *struggle, envy,* and *hate* in the bracketed paragraph?

____

____

____

Vocabulary Builder

Pronouns An autobiography uses first-person pronouns, such as *I, me, my, we, us, mine, our,* and *ours,* to show that the story is about the author. These pronouns refer to the author of the story or book. Circle the first-person pronouns on this page that refer to Franklin.

amendment, and had such frequent **relapses,** that I was almost ready to give up the attempt, and content myself with a faulty character in that respect, like the man who, in buying an ax of a smith,[4] my neighbor, desired to have the whole of its surface as bright as the edge. The smith **consented** to grind it bright for him if he would turn the wheel; he turned, while the smith pressed the broad face of the ax hard and heavily on the stone, which made the turning of it very **fatiguing.** The man came every now and then from the wheel to see how the work went on, and at length would take his ax as it was, without farther grinding. "No," said the smith, "turn on, turn on; we shall have it bright by and by; as yet, it is only **speckled.**" "Yes," says the man, "*but I think I like a speckled ax best.*"

◆ ◆ ◆

Franklin believes that many people are like this man. Some people find it too difficult to form good habits. They just give up the struggle. They decide that "a speckled ax is best." Franklin is the same way about the virtue of Order. He thinks that other people might envy or hate him if he becomes perfect. He thinks that a good man should keep a few faults. This way, he can keep his friends.

◆ ◆ ◆

In truth, I found myself incorrigible with respect to Order; and now I am grown old, and

Everyday Words

amendment (uh MEND ment) *n.* improvement, correction
relapses (REE lap ses) *n.* slips back to a former state
consented (kuhn SENT id) *v.* agreed to do something
fatiguing (fuh TEEG ing) *adj.* tiring
speckled (SPEK uhld) *adj.* covered with small spots

4. **smith** (SMITH) *n.* a person who works in metals

my memory bad, I feel very sensibly the want of it. But, on the whole, though I never arrived at the perfection I had been so **ambitious** of obtaining, but fell far short of it, yet I was, by the **endeavor,** a better and a happier man than I otherwise should have been if I had not attempted it.

◆ ◆ ◆

Franklin wants his **descendants** to know about their **ancestor.** His list of virtues is important to him. In fact, he says he owes the constant happiness in his life to it. He is now seventy-nine years old. He owes his good health to *Temperance.* He owes his fortune to *Industry* and *Frugality.* To *Sincerity* and *Justice*, he owes the confidence his country has in him.

◆ ◆ ◆

. . . and to the joint influence of the whole mass of the virtues, even in the imperfect state he was able to acquire them, [their ancestor ascribes] all that evenness of temper, and that cheerfulness in conversation, which makes his company still sought for, and agreeable even to his younger acquaintance. I hope, therefore, that some of my descendants may follow the example and **reap** the benefit.

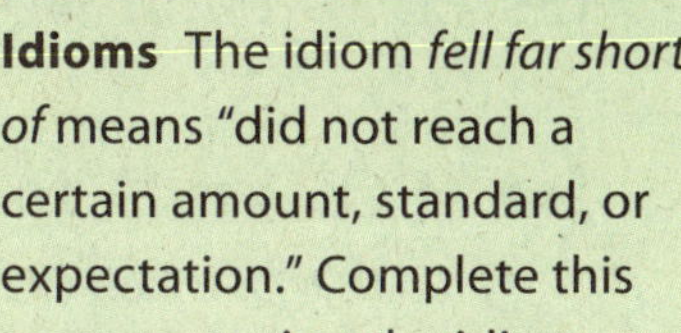

Vocabulary Builder

Idioms The idiom *fell far short of* means "did not reach a certain amount, standard, or expectation." Complete this sentence, using the idiom:

According to Franklin, he _______

____

perfection.

Comprehension Builder 

To what does Franklin say that he owes his good health?

____

To what does he owe the confidence that his country has in him?

____

Fluency Builder 

The underlined sentence is long and contains many phrases. Commas help separate the ideas in the sentence. Read the sentence silently, and circle all the commas. Then, read aloud the sentence, pausing briefly after each comma.

Everyday Words

ambitious (am BI shuhs) *adj.* greatly desiring to do something, especially something good

endeavor (en DEV er) *n.* try, attempt

descendants (dee SEN dents) *n.* people in one's family who come after

ancestor (AN ses ter) *n.* a person in one's family who came before

reap (REEP) *v.* get something, especially something good, as a result of what you have done

from The Autobiography   **75**

Vocabulary

Listen to each word. Say it. Then, read the definition and the example sentence.

foe (FOH) *n.* A **foe** is an enemy, or someone who opposes you.
Paulo prepared himself to fight his <u>foe</u> with strong words.

squander (SKWAHN der) *v.* When you **squander** something, you carelessly waste it on things that are not useful.
Neil worried that he would <u>squander</u> his paycheck on CDs.

haste (HAYST) *n.* **Haste** is great speed in doing something.
In my <u>haste</u> to get home, I left my jacket at school.

Vocabulary Practice

Read the first sentence in each group of three. Then, complete Sentence *a* by substituting another word or phrase that means the same as the underlined vocabulary word. Complete Sentence *b* with your own ideas and words.

1. They went out to meet the <u>foe</u> in battle.

   a. They went out to meet the _______________ in battle.

   b. They went out to meet the foe _________________________________.

2. We tried not to <u>squander</u> our food by eating all of it at once.

   a. We tried not to _______________ our food by eating all of it at once.

   b. We tried not to squander _________________________________.

3. Our <u>haste</u> caused us to make errors on the test.

   a. Our _______________ caused us to make errors on the test.

   b. Our haste _________________________________.

Getting Ready to Read

Benjamin Franklin wrote and published *Poor Richard's Almanack* from 1732 to 1758. Each book contained weather forecasts, humorous stories or poems, puzzles, and advice. He included aphorisms, or short sayings that have wise messages. Why do you think Franklin writes his ideas as aphorisms? Talk about your ideas with a partner.

from Poor Richard's Almanack
Benjamin Franklin

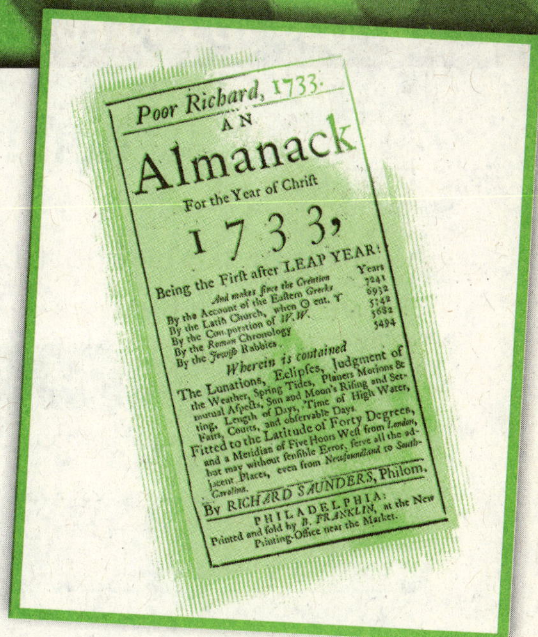

Summary Franklin gives advice about how people should behave. He presents his thoughts in **aphorisms,** or short sayings with a message. Many of his aphorisms come from traditional folk sayings. Sayings such as "Well done is better than well said" tell something about Franklin and what he values.

Note-taking Guide

Aphorisms can sometimes mean more than one thing. Use this chart to examine some of Franklin's sayings about friendship. Write down any second meanings.

Saying	Meaning
Be slow in choosing a friend, slower in changing.	Choose your friends carefully, and keep them.

Thinking About the Selections

1. Complete the chart below by paraphrasing some of the aphorisms in *Poor Richard's Almanack.*

Aphorism	Paraphrase
Keep thy shop, and thy shop will keep thee.	
Three may keep a secret if two of them are dead.	
A small leak will sink a great ship.	
No gains without pains.	
Well done is better than well said.	
Write injuries in dust, benefits in marble.	
Haste makes waste.	

2. In his autobiography, Benjamin Franklin explains that he tried to reach moral perfection by learning to follow the virtues of

____

____.

TALK ABOUT IT **The Virtue of Faults** Franklin decided that people could not and should not be morally perfect. He concluded that men and women needed to keep a few faults if they were going to be happy and have friends. Do you agree or disagree with Franklin's opinion? Discuss your ideas with a partner.

Writing About the Essential Question

What makes American literature American? In what ways do the goals Franklin sets for himself and the aphorisms that he wrote express values that are still widely held in America? Explain.

Word Families

Words that share the same base word make up a word family. Being able to identify words in the same word family can help you find the meanings of unfamiliar or difficult words.

Examples

Look at the chart below to see words in the same word family as *trust*.

trust	*noun*	a strong belief in the honesty or goodness of someone
trustee	*noun*	someone who has control of money or property for someone else
distrustful	*adjective*	not willing to trust someone or something
trusting	*adjective*	willing to believe that other people are good and honest
distrust	*verb*	not trust someone or something
trustworthy	*adjective*	able to be trusted and relied on

Now You Do It

Read the sentences below. Complete the sentences using a different word from the word family above in each.

1. The people were ___________ of their leaders' plans.

2. Angela is a very ___________ child.

3. ___________ is an important part of any friendship.

4. My father served as ___________ for his brother.

5. Voters sometimes ___________ election results.

6. Mario has proved that he is ___________ through his honesty.

TALK **ABOUT IT** **Earning Trust** Discuss ways that people can earn trust and ways that people can lose trust. Take turns using words in the word family in your discussion.

WRITE ABOUT IT **Who Do You Trust?** Think of someone you trust. Write two or three paragraphs to explain why you trust him or her. Include words in the trust family to describe the person's qualities.

Vocabulary

These words are underlined in the story. Listen to each word. Say it. Then, read the definition and the example sentence.

copious (KOH pee uhs) *adj.* Something that is **copious** exists or is produced in large quantities.

Rachel cried copious amounts of tears when she lost her necklace.

wretched (RETCH id) *adj.* Something that is **wretched** is extremely bad or unpleasant in a way that makes you feel upset.

The tornado left the town in wretched condition.

heightened (HYT uhnd) *v.* Something that is **heightened** is increased.

The campaign has heightened the public's awareness of the issues.

Vocabulary Practice

Read the first sentence in each group of three. Then, complete Sentence *a* by substituting another word or phrase that means the same as the underlined vocabulary word. Complete Sentence *b* with your own ideas and words.

1. Allison took copious notes for her book.

    a. Allison took ______________ notes for her book.

    b. Allison took copious ____.

2. The immigrants suffered because of the wretched conditions.

    a. The immigrants suffered because of the ______________ conditions.

    b. ____ the wretched conditions.

3. Matt's response only heightened Carlos's anger.

    a. Matt's response only ______________ Carlos's anger.

    b. Matt's response only heightened ____.

Getting Ready to Read

Olaudah Equiano was born in Africa and kidnapped into slavery as a young boy. Ships carried enslaved people from Africa to the Americas. Many people did not survive the journey. What else do you know about the African slave trade? Discuss your knowledge with a partner.

from The Interesting Narrative of the Life of Olaudah Equiano
Olaudah Equiano

Summary Olaudah Equiano tells what happened to him aboard a slave ship. He describes the crowded conditions and sickening smells. He also tells of the slaves' despair. He explains that the ship's crew chained, starved, and beat the slaves. Many people died during the terrible journey. Those who lived were examined and sold when they reached Barbados.

Note-taking Guide

Use this chart to describe the conditions on a slave ship.

Main Idea: Conditions on slave ships from Africa cause many slaves to die during the journey.		
The smell inside the ship is terrible.	The ship's crew is cruel.	Many slaves die.
	Slaves are chained.	

Fluency Builder 

The *subject* of a verb is the noun that takes the verb's action. Usually, a comma does not separate a subject from its verb. Read aloud the underlined sentence. Circle the verb that goes with the subject *ship*.

Vocabulary Builder 

Ship Terms A *vessel* is a ship or large boat. The *hold* of a ship is the part of the ship below the deck, where goods are often stored. The *deck* is the outside top level of a ship that you can walk and sit on. A ship's *cargo* is the goods that it is carrying. What is the cargo on the ship that Equiano describes?

____

____

Vocabulary Builder 

Idioms In colonial times, the phrase *necessary tubs* was a polite name for buckets used as toilets. Why do you think they were called "necessary tubs"? Write your answer on the lines below.

____

____

____

from The Interesting Narrative of the Life of Olaudah Equiano

Olaudah Equiano

At last when the ship we were in, had got in all her cargo, they made ready with many fearful noises, and we were all put under deck, so that we could not see how they managed the vessel. But this disappointment was the least of my sorrow. The **stench** of the hold while we were on the coast was so intolerably **loathsome,** that it was dangerous to remain there for any time, and some of us had been permitted to stay on the deck for the fresh air; but now that the whole ship's cargo were confined together, it became absolutely pestilential.[1] The closeness of the place, and the heat of the climate, added to the number in the ship, which was so crowded that each had **scarcely** room to turn himself, almost suffocated us. This produced copious perspirations, so that the air soon became unfit for respiration, from a variety of loathsome smells, and brought on a sickness among the slaves, of which many died—thus falling victims to the **improvident avarice,** as I may call it, of their purchasers. This wretched situation was again aggravated by the galling[2] of the chains, now become insupportable, and the filth of the necessary tubs, into which the children often fell, and were almost suffocated. The shrieks of the

---

Everyday Words

stench (STENCH) *n.* a very bad smell
loathsome (LOH<u>TH</u> suhm) *adj.* hateful
scarcely (SKAYRS lee) *adv.* almost none or almost none at all
improvident (im PRAH vuh duhnt) *adj.* shortsighted
avarice (AV uh ris) *n.* greed for riches

---

1. **pestilential** (pes ti LEN shuhl) *adj.* likely to cause disease
2. **galling** (GAWL ing) *n.* the creation of sores by rubbing or chafing

women, and the groans of the dying, rendered the whole a scene of horror almost inconceivable.

♦ ♦ ♦

Equiano envied the fish of the sea for their freedom. During the voyage, he grew more fearful of the white slavers' cruelty.

♦ ♦ ♦

One day they had taken a number of fishes; and when they had killed and satisfied themselves with as many as they thought fit, to our astonishment who were on deck, rather than give any of them to us to eat, as we expected, they tossed the remaining fish into the sea again, although we begged and prayed for some as well as we could, but in vain. . . .

♦ ♦ ♦

Some of the hungry slaves tried to get fish in secret. They were discovered and whipped. Then three desperate slaves jumped into the sea. The others were immediately put below deck. Two of the slaves drowned. The third was rescued and then beaten unmercifully.

♦ ♦ ♦

During our passage, I first saw flying fishes, which surprised me very much; they used frequently to fly across the ship, and many of them fell on the deck. I also now first saw the use of the quadrant;[3] I had often with astonishment seen the mariners make observations with it, and I could not think what it meant. They at last took notice of my surprise; and one of them, willing to increase it, as well as to gratify[4] my curiosity, made me one day look through it. The clouds appeared to me to be land, which disappeared as they passed along. This heightened my wonder; and I was now more

3. **quadrant** (KWAH druhnt) *n.* an instrument used by navigators to determine a ship's position
4. **gratify** (GRAT uh fy) *v.* satisfy

Comprehension Builder

Summarize the first bracketed section in your own words.

____

____

____

Vocabulary Builder

Word Parts The prefix *un-* means "not." The suffix *-fully* means "completely." The noun *mercy* means "forgiveness or kindness." What does the adverb *unmercifully* mean?

____

____

Fluency Builder

Read aloud the second bracketed passage with expression. Circle the two sights that attract Equiano's curiosity.

Cultural Understanding

The West Indies refers to the islands in the Caribbean Sea between the southeastern United States and northern South America. They were named the West Indies because the first European to reach them, Christopher Columbus, thought that he had sailed all the way around the world and reached India in southern Asia.

Comprehension Builder 

A simile compares two unlike things by using the words *like* or *as.* Underline the simile in the last paragraph. What two things are being compared?

____

____

persuaded than ever, that I was in another world, and that every thing about me was magic.

◆ ◆ ◆

The ship anchored off Bridgetown, the capital of the island of Barbados in the West Indies. Merchants and planters came on board to examine the slaves. The slaves on the ship were fearful, but some older slaves came from the land to reassure them. Finally, the slaves went ashore.

◆ ◆ ◆

We were **conducted** immediately to the merchant's yard, where we were all pent up together, like so many sheep in a fold, without regard to sex or age. . . . We were not many days in the merchant's **custody,** before we were sold after their usual manner, which is this: On a signal given (as the beat of a drum), the buyers rush at once into the yard where the slaves are confined, and make choice of that parcel[5] they like best. . . .

Everyday Words

conducted (kuhn DUHK tuhd) *v.* led
custody (KUHS tuh dee) *n.* keeping, possession

5. **parcel** (PAR suhl) *n.* a quantity of something offered for sale

Thinking About the Selection

1. Equiano creates a vivid image of the conditions in the hold of the slave ship. Use the following web to list some of the sights, sounds, and smells that he describes in the hold.

2. Equiano envies ____

____.

TALK ABOUT IT **Think About Descriptions** Equiano uses many descriptive words to portray life on the ship. Read aloud to a partner the first paragraph from Equiano's account. Pause to check each other's understanding of difficult words and descriptive phrases.

Writing About the Essential Question

How does literature shape or reflect society? What do you think the public of Equiano's day learned about the "accursed trade" of slavery that it may not have known before reading this narrative?

Parts of Speech

Many words have the same spelling and pronunciation but different meanings and parts of speech. Some words may be either a noun or a verb. Nouns name people, places, things, ideas, and events. Verbs show action and states of being.

Examples

Word	Pronunciation	Part of Speech/Meaning	Part of Speech/Meaning
bear	BAYR	*n.* a large strong animal with thick fur	*v.* bravely accept or deal with a painful or upsetting situation
plant	PLANT	*n.* a living thing that has leaves and roots and grows in soil	*v.* put plants or seeds in the ground to grow
watch	WAHCH	*n.* a small clock that you wear on your wrist or keep in your pocket	*v.* look at someone or something for a period of time

Now You Do It

In each sentence, identify the underlined word as a noun or a verb.

1. Anya did not think she could <u>bear</u> to take the test again. __________

2. My mother bought a spider <u>plant</u> to hang in the kitchen window. __________

3. Lin gave her <u>watch</u> to a friend as a gift. __________

TALK ABOUT IT **Changing Parts of Speech** With a partner, review the answers for the Now You Do It activity. Then, take turns using each pair of words from the chart in a single sentence. Continue until each of you has created a sentence for each pair.

WRITE ABOUT IT **In the News** Write a news article about a camping trip or other journey into the wilderness. Use each pair of words in your article, and be sure to write a fun headline.

Word Bank

community	heritage	splendor
doctrine	independence	terrors
govern	optimism	wilderness

A. Matching Draw a line to match each word in the left column to the correct definition in the right column. The first one has been done for you.

community	the traditional beliefs, values, and customs of a grooup of people
doctrine	officially control a country or another place and make all the decisions about laws, taxes, and public services
govern	a large area of land that has never been developed or farmed
heritage	the tendency to believe that good things will always happen
independence	the people who live in the same area or town
optimism	events or situations that make people feel extremely frightened, especially because they think that they may die
splendor	freedom from control by others, especially by the government of another country
terrors	impressive beauty, especially of a large building or place
wilderness	a set of beliefs that form an important part of a religion or system of ideas

B. **Syllables** A syllable is a part of a word that contains a vowel sound. Vowel sounds are usually represented by the letters *a, e, i, o, u.* Say each word in the word bank on page 87. If the word has two syllables, write it in the left column. If it has three syllables, write it in the middle column. If it has four or more syllables, write the word in the right column. *Optimism* has been done for you.

Two Syllables	Three Syllables	Four or More Syllables
		optimism

TALK ABOUT IT **Talking History** With a partner, discuss what you know about the settlement of the American colonies. Use these sentence starters and select a word from the word bank when indicated. Some words may need to be used in their plural form.

When Europeans came to the Americas, they found large stretches

of _______________. Many came to find new opportunities or to escape

persecution. They were impressed by the _______________ of the vast

continent. They hoped to use the land, water, and other resources

to build new _______________. Many early colonists were full of

_______________. Still, they faced many challenges as they learned to

live on the land and _______________ themselves.

WRITE ABOUT IT **Keep an Explorer's Log** Imagine that you are an explorer in the Americas. You keep a log of everything that you see so that you can report back to the colonists. Write three entries in your log, covering three days spent exploring. Use words from the word bank.

Vocabulary

These words are underlined in the story. Listen to each word. Say it. Then, read the definition and the example sentence.

inflexibly (in FLEKS uh blee) *adv.* To do something **inflexibly** means to do it without being willing to change.

The coach was inflexibly strict about being on time.

obstinate (AWB sti nit) *adj.* An **obstinate** person is stubborn, or determined not to change his or her ideas, opinions, or behavior.

Akira was obstinate about not trying new foods.

resolutely (REZ uh loot lee) *adv.* Doing something **resolutely** means doing it in a very determined way because you have strong beliefs.

Tasha resolutely prepared to go on the journey.

Vocabulary Practice

Read the first sentence in each group of three. Then, complete Sentence *a* by substituting another word or phrase that means the same as the underlined vocabulary word. Complete Sentence *b* with your own ideas and words.

1. My piano teacher is inflexibly strict about practicing.

   a. My piano teacher is _______________ strict about practicing.

   b. My piano teacher is inflexibly _________________________________.

2. Joey was obstinate in his refusal to follow the plan.

   a. Joey was _______________ in his refusal to follow the plan.

   b. Joey was obstinate _________________________________.

3. Andi resolutely decided to apply to nursing school.

   a. Andi _______________ decided to apply to nursing school.

   b. Andi resolutely _________________________________.

Getting Ready to Read

In this story, the main character is tempted by the Devil to do something wrong. The author intends to teach readers to make decisions carefully. Talk with a partner about how to make difficult decisions.

The Devil and Tom Walker
Washington Irving

Summary Tom Walker meets the Devil ("Old Scratch") in a swamp. The Devil offers Captain Kidd's pirate treasure to Tom on certain conditions. Tom's wife encourages him to accept, but Tom refuses. She leaves to find the Devil and make her own bargain. After her second try, she doesn't come back. Later, Tom finds her apron with a heart and liver in it. He assumes that the Devil has killed her. Tom looks for the Devil again. This time, he makes a deal. Tom will get Captain Kidd's treasure if he becomes a moneylender. Later, Tom regrets his deal and starts going to church often. But the Devil returns and sends Tom off on horseback into a storm. Tom never comes back, but his troubled spirit appears on stormy nights.

Note-taking Guide

Use this sequence chart to keep track of events in the story.

Event 1: Tom Walker takes a shortcut through the swamp and finds a skull.

Event 2:

Event 3:

Event 4:

Event 5:

Event 6:

Event 7:

Event 8:

Event 9:

Event 10:

The Devil and Tom Walker
Washington Irving

Outside Boston, Massachusetts, in about 1727, Tom Walker lives near a swampy forest. Captain Kidd supposedly buried his pirate treasure in this forest. Tom and his wife are very stingy—so stingy that they even cheat each other. One day, Tom takes a shortcut through the forest. At an old fort that Native Americans had once used in fighting the colonists, Tom meets a mysterious stranger. The stranger, who carries an ax on his shoulder, is not Native American or African American, but he is still very dark, as if covered in soot.

◆ ◆ ◆

"What are you doing on my grounds?" said the black man, with a hoarse growling voice.

"Your grounds!" said Tom with a sneer, "no more your grounds than mine; they belong to Deacon Peabody."

"Deacon Peabody be d____d," said the stranger, "as I flatter myself[1] he will be, if he does not look more to his own sins and less to those of his neighbors. Look yonder, and see how Deacon Peabody is faring."[2]

◆ ◆ ◆

Tom looks at a tree and sees carved into it the name of Deacon Peabody, a local churchman grown rich through clever land deals. Other trees bear the names of other wealthy members of the community. The trees all have ax marks, and one with the name Crowninshield is completely chopped down.

◆ ◆ ◆

1. **as I flatter myself** as I am delighted to think
2. **faring** (FAYR ing) *v.* doing

Cultural Understanding

In 1727, the United States had not yet been formed. Massachusetts was one of several colonies under British control in North America at the time. Native Americans still lived on much of the land that is now part of the United States.

Vocabulary Builder 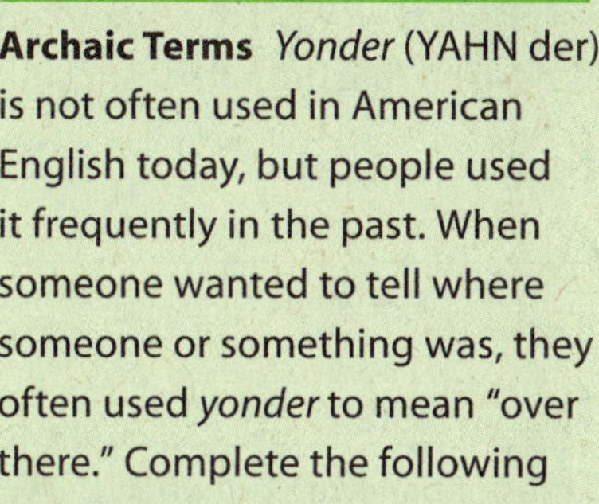

Archaic Terms *Yonder* (YAHN der) is not often used in American English today, but people used it frequently in the past. When someone wanted to tell where someone or something was, they often used *yonder* to mean "over there." Complete the following sentence:

To see how Deacon Peabody is faring, ___________________.

Vocabulary Builder 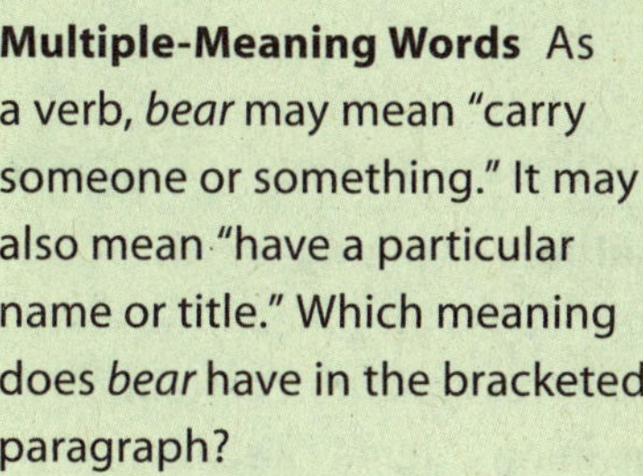

Multiple-Meaning Words As a verb, *bear* may mean "carry someone or something." It may also mean "have a particular name or title." Which meaning does *bear* have in the bracketed paragraph?

____

____

Vocabulary Builder 

Compound Words Firewood is a compound word formed by putting two smaller words together:

fire + wood = firewood

By studying the meanings of the smaller words, you can determine that *firewood* means "wood to burn for a fire." Circle another compound word in the bracketed passage. What does it mean?

____

____

Fluency Builder 

Lines of dialogue between the characters appear in quotation marks (" "). With a partner, read the lines of dialogue on this page. One of you should read Tom's lines; the other should read the black man's lines. Be sure to read with expression.

Vocabulary Builder

Multiple-Meaning Words The noun *terms* may mean "words or expressions with certain meanings." It may also mean "the conditions set for a contract or agreement." Which meaning does *terms* have in the underlined sentence?

____

____

"He's just ready for burning!" said the black man, with a growl of triumph. "You see I am likely to have a good stock of firewood for winter."

"But what right have you," said Tom, "to cut down Deacon Peabody's timber?"

"The right of a **prior** claim," said the other. "This woodland belonged to me long before one of your white-faced race put foot upon the soil."

"And pray, who are you, if I may be so bold?" said Tom.

"Oh, I go by various names. I am the wild huntsman in some countries; the black miner in others. In this neighborhood I am known by the name of the black woodsman. . . . "

"The upshot of all which is, that, if I mistake not," said Tom, sturdily, "you are he commonly called Old Scratch."

"The same, at your service," replied the black man, with a half-**civil** nod.

◆　◆　◆

The Devil offers Tom Captain Kidd's pirate treasure if Tom agrees to his terms. Tom makes no decision. Instead he asks for proof that the Devil is who he says he is. So the Devil presses his finger to Tom's forehead and then goes off. When Tom gets home, he finds a black thumbprint burned into his forehead. He also learns of the sudden death of Absalom Crowninshield. Convinced he has met the Devil, he tells his wife all about it.

◆　◆　◆

All her **avarice** was awakened at the mention of hidden gold, and she urged her husband to **comply** with the black man's terms and

Everyday Words

prior (PRY uhr) *adj.* previous; from before
civil (SIV uhl) *adj.* polite in a formal but not friendly way
avarice (AV uh ris) *adj.* greed
comply (kum PLY) *v.* go along with; agree to

secure what would make them wealthy for life. However Tom might have felt **disposed** to sell himself to the Devil, he was determined not to do so to **oblige** his wife; so he flatly refused out of the mere spirit of **contradiction.** Many and bitter were the **quarrels** they had on the subject. . . .

At length she determined to drive the bargain on her own account, and if she succeeded, to keep all the gain to herself. Being of the same fearless temper as her husband, she set off for the old Indian fort at the close of a summer's day.

◆　◆　◆

To bargain with the Devil, Tom's wife takes the household silverware and other valuables, tying them up in her apron. She is never heard from again. According to one story, Tom goes hunting for her and finds nothing but her apron, with a heart and liver inside! Whatever happened, Tom seems more upset about losing his property than losing his wife. In fact, he decides that the Devil might have done him a favor. Soon he is again bargaining with the Devil to obtain the pirate's treasure.

◆　◆　◆

There was one condition which need not be mentioned, being generally understood in all cases where the Devil grants favors; but there were others about which, though of less importance, he was <u>inflexibly</u> <u>obstinate</u>. He insisted that money

---

Everyday Words

secure (si KYOOR) *v.* make certain about; guarantee

disposed (dis POHZD) *adj.* inclined; prone to

oblige (u BLYDG) *v.* do what someone else wants; please

contradiction (kahn truh DIK shuhn) *n.* a difference between two statements, beliefs, or ideas about something that means both cannot be true

quarrels (KWAHR uhlz) *n.* angry arguments or disagreements

Vocabulary Builder

Regular Verbs The past tense of a regular verb is formed by adding *-ed* or *-d* to the present form of the verb. List three regular past-tense verbs in the bracketed text.

____

____

Vocabulary Builder 

Possessive Nouns Circle the word *Tom's* in this paragraph. The *'s* at the end of *Tom* makes it possessive. This means that it shows possession or ownership. *Tom's wife* means "the wife of Tom." Circle two more possessive nouns on this page. What do the nouns mean?

____

____

Comprehension Builder 

Given what you have read about Tom, predict what he will do next. Will he make a bargain, or deal, with the Devil?

____

____

____

Vocabulary Builder

Parts of Speech *Point* may be a noun meaning "a single fact, idea, or opinion that is part of an argument or discussion." It may also be a verb meaning "show something to someone by holding up one of your fingers or another object toward it." Which part of speech is *point* in the bracketed paragraph?

____

Vocabulary Builder

Idioms The idiom *struck a bargain* means "agreed to do something in exchange for something else." Use the idiom to complete this sentence:

Tom Walker ________________

________________ with the Devil.

Comprehension Builder 

Was your prediction about Tom correct? Explain.

____

____

____

____

found through his means should be employed in his service. He proposed, therefore, that Tom should employ it in the black traffic; that is to say, that he should fit out a slave ship. This, however, Tom resolutely refused: he was bad enough in all **conscience,** but the Devil himself could not tempt him to turn slave-trader.

Finding Tom so **squeamish** on this point, he did not insist upon it, but proposed, instead, that he should turn usurer.[3] . . . To this no objections were made, for it was just to Tom's taste.

"You shall open a broker's shop[4] in Boston next month," said the black man.

"I'll do it tomorrow, if you wish," said Tom Walker.

"You shall lend money at two per cent a month."

"Egad, I'll charge four!" replied Tom Walker. . . .

"Done!" said the Devil.

"Done!" said Tom Walker. So they shook hands and struck a bargain.

❖ ❖ ❖

So Tom becomes a cruel moneylender, charging his highest rates to his most **desperate** customers. He grows rich and powerful. He builds a large, showy house, though he is too stingy to furnish it well. He buys a fancy carriage but lets the horses nearly starve. Yet as he nears old age, he begins to worry.

❖ ❖ ❖

Everyday Words

conscience (KAHN shuhns) *n.* the part of your mind that tells you whether what you are doing is morally right or wrong

squeamish (SKWEEM ish) *adj.* easily shocked or upset

desperate (DES per it) *adj.* needing or wanting something very much

3. **usurer** (YOO zuhr uhr) *n.* a moneylender who charges high interest rates

4. **a broker's shop** a moneylending business

Having **secured** the good things of this world, he began to feel anxious about those of the next. He thought with regret on the bargain he had made with his black friend, and set his wits to work to cheat him out of the conditions. He became, therefore, all of a sudden, a violent churchgoer. . . . Tom was as **rigid** in religious as in money matters; he was a stern supervisor and censurer[5] of his neighbors, and seemed to think every sin entered up to their account became a credit on his own side of the page.

◆ ◆ ◆

Frightened of the Devil, Tom keeps a small Bible in his coat pocket and a large one on his desk at work. One hot afternoon, while still in his bathrobe, Tom goes down to his office to demand repayment of a loan. The man who has taken the loan is a land jobber, or speculator[6] who tried to make money by buying and selling land. In the past, Tom has acted as if this man were a good friend, but now Tom refuses to give him more time to repay his loan.

◆ ◆ ◆

"My family will be ruined and brought upon the parish," said the land jobber.

"Charity begins at home," replied Tom; "I must take care of myself in these hard times."

"You have made so much money out of me," said the speculator.

Tom lost his patience and his **piety**—"The Devil take me," said he, "if I have made a farthing!"[7]

Everyday Words

secured (si KYOORD) *v.* gotten or achieved something that will be permanent or long-lasting

rigid (RIJ id) *adj.* unwilling to change one's ideas or behavior

piety (PY uh tee) *n.* religious devotion

5. **censurer** (SEN sher er) *n.* someone who criticizes the behavior of others
6. **speculator** (SPEK yoo lay ter) *n.* someone who buys goods or property, hoping to make a large profit by reselling them
7. **farthing** (FAHR thing) *n.* a small coin of little value

Vocabulary Builder 

Verb Tenses The past perfect tense uses the helping verb *had* + the past participle of the main verb:

had lived   had done

It is used to show an action that happened before another action in the past. In the underlined text, label the verbs "2nd-past" and "1st-past perfect" to show which action came first.

Vocabulary Builder

Word Parts The noun *repayment* has three word parts. The prefix *re-* means "again" or "back to a former state." The base word *pay* means "give someone money for a product or service." The suffix *-ment* shows an action or the result of an action. What does *repayment* mean?

____

____

Cultural Understanding

"Charity begins at home" is a common proverb or saying in English. It means that a person should first help family or others in his or her own household before helping others.

Vocabulary Builder 

Prefixes The prefix *im-* is used before the letters *b, m,* or *p* instead of the prefix *in-*. *Im-* means "the opposite of or lack of something." Circle a word in the bracketed paragraph that contains the prefix *im-*. What does this word mean?

____

____

Vocabulary Builder 

Idioms The idiom *like mad* means "as quickly as possible." According to the author, what do the Devil and Tom do *like mad*?

____

____

Comprehension Builder 

What haunts the swamp and Indian fort? Underline the text that tells you.

Just then there were three loud knocks at the street door. He stepped out to see who was there. A black man was holding a black horse, which neighed and stamped with impatience.

"Tom, you're come for," said the black fellow, **gruffly.** Tom shrunk back, but too late. He had left his little Bible at the bottom of his coat pocket, and his big Bible on the desk . . . never was a sinner taken more unawares.[8]

♦   ♦   ♦

The Devil takes Tom up and rides off into a thunderstorm. They are said to have galloped like mad to the swamp by the old fort. Shortly afterward the forest is struck by lightning. The next day Tom's fancy new house catches fire and burns to the ground. Tom himself is never seen again. Those appointed to settle his affairs find nothing but ashes where his business papers should be and chests filled with worthless wood shavings instead of gold.

♦   ♦   ♦

Such was the end of Tom Walker and his ill-gotten wealth. Let all **griping** money brokers lay this story to heart. The truth of it is not to be doubted. The very hole under the oak trees, whence[9] he dug Kidd's money, is to be seen to this day; and the neighboring swamp and old Indian fort are often haunted in stormy nights by a figure on horseback, in morning gown and white cap, which is doubtless the troubled spirit of the usurer.

Everyday Words

gruffly (GRUHF lee) *adv.* abruptly
griping (GRYP ing) *adj.* complaining

8. **taken more unawares** If something takes you unawares, it happens when you are not expecting it and are unprepared.

9. **whence** (WENS) *prep.* from where

Thinking About the Selection

1. Several of Tom's actions reveal his characteristics. In the chart below, the left column lists Tom's characteristics. Complete the chart by describing what Tom does that demonstrates each characteristic. The first one has been done for you.

Characteristic	Action that Reveals the Characteristic
Tom has a spirit of contradiction.	Tom refuses his wife's request to bargain with the Devil, even though he may have wanted to.
Tom has a conscience.	
Tom is greedy.	
Tom is stingy.	
Tom is frightened.	

2. The moral lesson of this story is ________________________________

____.

TALK ABOUT IT   **Tell the Story** With a partner, take turns reading aloud the conversations between Tom Walker and the Devil. Have each person read a different role. Discuss what motivates Tom to make the deal with the Devil.

Writing About the Essential Question

How does literature shape or reflect society? Judging from the events of this story, what do you think Washington Irving might say about the effects of greed on society?

____

____

____

Suffixes

A suffix is a group of letters that is added to the end of a word to form a new word. Suffixes change a word's meaning. They often change its part of speech as well.

Examples

The suffix *-ion* means "the act, state, or process of doing something." Adding *-ion* to a verb changes it to a noun. For most verbs that end in *d*, you must change the *d* to an *s* before adding *-ion*. For most verbs that end in *e*, you must drop the *e* before adding *-ion*.

Verb		Suffix		Noun	Meaning
react	+	-ion	=	reaction	the act of reacting, or behaving in a certain way because of something that has happened
expand	+	-ion	=	expansion	the process of expanding, or increasing in size
regulate	+	-ion	=	regulation	the act of regulating, or controlling, an activity

Now You Do It

Change the verbs below to nouns by adding the suffix *-ion*. Then, write a definition for each new word.

act + -ion = _______________ ___________________________________

liberate + -ion = _______________ ___________________________________

imitate + -ion = _______________ ___________________________________

pollute + -ion = _______________ ___________________________________

express + -ion = _______________ ___________________________________

educate + -ion = _______________ ___________________________________

TALK ABOUT IT **Sentence Sharing** With a partner, read aloud the verbs and nouns listed above. Then, take turns using each noun in a sentence.

WRITE ABOUT IT **What Does the President Think?** Write a dialogue in which you interview the President of the United States. Ask him or her five questions. Have the President use an *-ion* word in each reply. Check a dictionary as needed.

Vocabulary

Listen to each word. Say it. Then, read the definition and the example sentence.

efface (i FAYS) *v.* When you **efface** something, you destroy or remove it.
Nothing can efface my memory of graduating from high school.

pensive (PEN siv) *adj.* When you are **pensive,** you are deeply or seriously thoughtful.
She listened carefully, looking pensive.

venerable (VEN uh ruh bul) *adj.* A **venerable** person is worthy of respect.
He asked for the advice of his venerable elders.

Vocabulary Practice

Read the first sentence in each group of three. Then, complete Sentence *a* by substituting another word or phrase that means the same as the underlined vocabulary word. Complete Sentence *b* with your own ideas and words.

1. Vandals tried to efface the painting on the wall.

   a. Vandals tried to ______________ the painting on the wall.

   b. Vandals tried to efface ______________________________.

2. The audience was pensive as they listened to the speech.

   a. The audience was ______________ as they listened to the speech.

   b. The audience was pensive ______________________________.

3. We held a parade to celebrate the venerable hero.

   a. We held a parade to celebrate the ______________ hero.

   b. ______________________________ the venerable hero.

Getting Ready to Read

"The Song of Hiawatha" is an epic poem that tells about the legends of the Ojibway people, especially the adventures of a great man named Hiawatha. What do you know about the Ojibway or other Native American groups? Talk about your knowledge with a partner.

from The Song of Hiawatha • The Tide Rises, The Tide Falls
Henry Wadsworth Longfellow

Thanatopsis
William Cullen Bryant

Old Ironsides
Oliver Wendell Holmes

Summaries The subjects of these poems connect to life in New England. Longfellow's **"The Song of Hiawatha"** explores the relationship between the Ojibway people and the lands of New England. His **"The Tide Rises, The Tide Falls"** compares the cycle of tides in the ocean to the cycle of life and death. In **"Thanatopsis,"** Bryant also explores the theme of death through images from nature, such as the earth and ocean. Holmes celebrates a ship's history at sea in **"Old Ironsides."**

Note-taking Guide

Use the chart below to record images of nature found in each of these poems.

from the Song of Hiawatha	The Tide Rises, The Tide Falls	Thanatopsis	Old Ironsides

Thinking About the Selections

1. Complete the graphic organizer to explain the main purpose of each of the four poems.

Poem	Purpose
"Song of Hiawatha"	to introduce the legend of Hiawatha
"The Tide Rises, The Tide Falls"	
"Thanatopsis"	
"Old Ironsides"	

2. Two of these poems deal in some way with ________________________.

TALK ABOUT IT **Talk About Poetry** These poems have some similarities and some differences. In a small group, discuss which poems you liked most and which you liked least. Explain your reasons.

I liked ________________________ *the best because* ________________
____

I liked ________________________ *the least because* ________________
____

Writing About the Essential Question

What makes American literature American? How is the subject matter of the poems in this grouping distinctly American?

____
____
____

Synonyms

Synonyms are words that have the same meaning or very similar meanings. Many times, a synonym can replace another word in a sentence without changing the meaning of the sentence. Other times, synonyms are not easily substituted for each other.

Examples

Synonyms	
awe *n.* a feeling of great respect and liking for someone or something	**admiration** *n.* a feeling of great respect and liking for something or someone **respect** *n.* a feeling of admiration for someone, especially because of his or her personal qualities, knowledge, or skills **amazement** *n.* a feeling of great surprise

Now You Do It

Write a sentence for each synonym. A sample sentence has been provided for *awe*. Underline the synonym of *awe* in each sentence.

awe: We gazed at the soldiers in <u>awe</u>.

admiration: ____

respect: ____

amazement: ____

TALK **ABOUT IT** **Thinking About Meaning** With a partner, take turns reading aloud your sentences. Then, talk about how the meanings of the synonyms are similar and different. Try swapping synonyms in some of your sentences. Do the sentences have the same meaning?

WRITE ABOUT IT **Make a Photo Collection** Use the Internet and library resources to collect photos that fill you with awe. Write a caption for each photo, using the synonyms above to describe the images.

Vocabulary

Listen to each word. Say it. Then, read the definition and the example sentence.

inanimate (in AN uh muht) *adj.* Something **inanimate** is not living.
The chair was inanimate, so it did not move on its own.

impertinent (im PER tuh nuhnt) *adj.* Someone **impertinent** is impolite and not respectful.
The impertinent teenager slammed the door on his mother.

obstinacy (AHB stuh nuh see) *n.* **Obstinacy** is stubbornness.
The child who refused to clean up was punished for her obstinacy.

Vocabulary Practice

Read the first sentence in each group of three. Then, complete Sentence *a* by substituting another word or phrase that means the same as the underlined vocabulary word. Complete Sentence *b* with your own ideas and words.

1. A rock is an <u>inanimate</u> object.

   a. A rock is a _______________ object.

   b. ____ is an inanimate object.

2. Mbutu's feelings were hurt by his brother's <u>impertinent</u> behavior.

   a. Mbutu's feelings were hurt by his brother's _______________ behavior.

   b. ____ impertinent behavior.

3. Kara's <u>obstinacy</u> delayed the completion of the project.

   a. Kara's _______________ delayed the completion of the project.

   b. Kara's obstinacy ____.

Getting Ready to Read

Nathaniel Hawthorne lived among the Puritans in the colonies of New England. Puritans were a group of Christians who had very strict rules, especially about behavior. Puritans were also very superstitious. With a partner, discuss what else you know about the Puritans and the New England region.

The Minister's Black Veil

Nathaniel Hawthorne

Summary The parson, Mr. Hooper, arrives at church wearing a black veil over his face. He wears the veil without explanation through his sermon, through the following sermon, and then through a funeral and a wedding. The congregation whispers among themselves. They fear the veil. Only Mr. Hooper's fiancée has the courage to ask him why he wears the veil. She does not understand the answer and leaves him. Mr. Hooper wears the veil for the rest of his life. In fact, he offers no other explanation for it until his death.

Note-taking Guide

Use this character wheel to record information about Reverend Hooper.

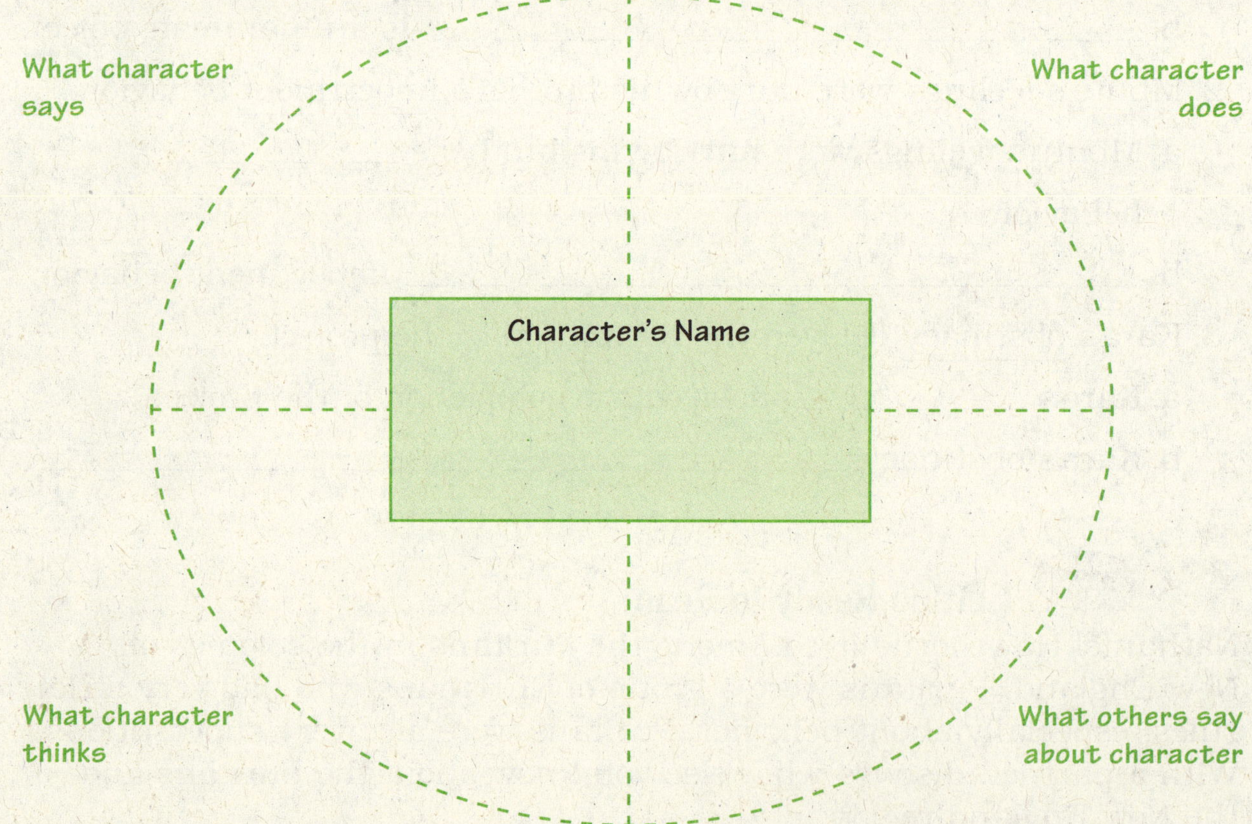

Thinking About the Selection

1. In this story, people react to something mysterious because they do not know what is causing it. Use the following chart to compare the reactions of the public to the veil and the real reasons that the minister wears it.

> The minister wears a black veil.

> The people first react by

> Then, they react by

> The real reson that the minister wears the veil is

2. The veil reminds people of ____

____.

TALK ABOUT IT **What Did They Learn?** The veil causes fear and upset among the people in the minister's community. In a small group, discuss what the minister wants the people to learn. Do you think the veil is as effective as the minister hoped it to be?

I (do/do not) think the veil is effective because ___________________

____.

? Writing About the Essential Question

What is the relationship between place and literature? Does the portrait this story paints of Puritan New England seem too sympathetic, too harsh, or simply accurate? Explain.

Homophones

Homophones are words that have the same pronunciation but different spellings and meanings.

Examples

		Pronunciation
plain: simple, without anything added or without decoration	*plane:* a vehicle that flies in the air and has wings and at least one engine	PLAYN
fare: the price you pay to travel somewhere by bus, plane, train, or another vehicle	*fair:* seeming reasonable, acceptable, and right	FAYR
flour: a powder made by crushing wheat or another grain	*flower:* the part of a plant or tree that produces its seeds or fruit	FLOW er
way: a road, path, or direction that you take to get to a particular place	*weigh:* have a particular weight	WAY

Now You Do It

Read the sentences below. Circle the correct word to complete each sentence.

1. I poured some *flour/flower* into the cake batter.

2. It was hard to find the *way/weigh* home through the dark forest.

3. Chan did not want to ride the *plain/plane* home.

4. I got on the bus and paid my *fare/fair*.

TALK ABOUT IT **Which Is Which?** With a partner, take turns using each of the homophones in a sentence. One partner should say a sentence, and the other partner should spell the homophone used.

WRITE ABOUT IT **Write a Funny Sketch** Use the homophones above to write a funny sketch in which two people confuse the word's meanings. Here is an Example

Character 1: I'm taking a plane!

Character 2: You're taking a plain what?

Character 1: No, I'm riding a *plane!* An airplane!

Vocabulary

Listen to each word. Say it. Then, read the definition and the example sentence.

munificent (myoo NIF uh suhnt) *adj.* Something **munificent** is very generous.

> *For my graduation, my grandparents gave me a munificent gift.*

equivocal (i KWIV uh kuhl) *adj.* Something **equivocal** has more than one possible interpretation or explanation.

> *Everyone had their own ideas about the equivocal poem.*

sentience (SEN shuhns) *n.* **Sentience** is the ability to feel both emotionally and physically.

> *Sentience is an important characteristic of being human.*

Vocabulary Practice

Read the first sentence in each group of three. Then, complete Sentence *a* by substituting another word or phrase that means the same as the underlined vocabulary word. Complete Sentence *b* with your own ideas and words.

1. A <u>munificent</u> donation funded the rebuilding of the museum.

   a. A _____________ donation funded the rebuilding of the museum.

   b. A munificent _____________________________________.

2. We debated the meaning of the politician's <u>equivocal</u> statement.

   a. We debated the meaning of the politician's _____________ statement.

   b. ____ equivocal statement.

3. Robots can do amazing things, but they lack <u>sentience</u>.

   a. Robots can do amazing things, but they lack _____________.

   b. ____ lack sentience.

Getting Ready to Read

Edgar Allan Poe led a troubled life marked by poverty and mental illness. Poe was skilled at using imagery and words to create fear, suspense, and other deep emotions in his readers. With a partner, talk about things you find frightening.

The Fall of the House of Usher

Edgar Allan Poe

Summary Roderick Usher has asked the narrator to stay with him while he is ill. The narrator answers his old friend's request and travels to Usher's gloomy mansion. There, he learns that Usher is not well physically or mentally. The narrator also finds out that Usher's twin sister, Madeline, is ill. One evening, Usher tells the narrator that his sister has died. Usher and the narrator take her coffin to a vault within the mansion. After they seal her inside, strange things begin to happen.

Note-taking Guide

Complete the following timeline with events from the story.

1. Narrator comes to Usher's mansion.

3.

5.

7.

2.

4.

6.

8.

Vocabulary

These words are underlined in the poem. Listen to each word. Say it. Then, read the definition and the example sentence.

craven (KRAYV uhn) *n.* A **craven** is a coward, or someone who lacks courage.

The craven ran from the fire, leaving his neighbors behind.

ungainly (uhn GAYN lee) *adj.* An **ungainly** person or thing is awkward or clumsy.

The ungainly horse needs much more practice before the race.

pallid (PAL uhd) *adj.* Something **pallid** is pale or white.

Clouds filled the pallid sky.

Vocabulary Practice

Read the first sentence in each group of three. Then, complete Sentence *a* by substituting another word or phrase that means the same as the underlined vocabulary word. Complete Sentence *b* with your own ideas and words.

1. The craven refused to stack sandbags against the flood.

   a. The _______________ refused to stack sandbags against the flood.

   b. The craven ____.

2. The ungainly girl had a hard time learning the new dance.

   a. The _______________ girl had a hard time learning the new dance.

   b. The ungainly ____.

3. Theo's pallid face showed how sick he was.

   a. Theo's _______________ face showed how sick he was.

   b. Theo's pallid ____.

Getting Ready to Read

The raven has long been a symbol of death. People around the world have feared the raven as an omen, or sign, of bad things to come. However, many people have also honored the cunning and courage of the raven. Why do you think the raven became a symbol of death or illness in so many cultures? Discuss your thoughts with a partner.

The Raven
Edgar Allan Poe

Summary The speaker in this poem sits alone reading at night. A mysterious raven comes knocking at his door. The speaker has been grieving for his lost love, Lenore. He begins to ask the raven questions, but the raven only has one response. Through the man's conversation with the raven, Poe explores a mind falling into madness.

Note-taking Guide
Complete the following chart by telling how the raven responds to the speaker.

What the speaker of the poem says	What the speaker hears the raven answer
• Excuse me, I was napping.	
• Lenore!	
• Tell me your name.	
• The bird will leave me tomorrow, as others have.	
• I need respite from my grief over Lenore.	
• "Is there balm in Gilead?"	
• Will I hold Lenore again?	

The Raven

Edgar Allan Poe

Once upon a midnight dreary, while I
pondered, weak and weary,
Over many a quaint and curious volume of
forgotten lore[1]—
While I nodded, nearly napping, suddenly there
came a tapping,
As of some one gently rapping, rapping at my
chamber door.
"'Tis some visitor," I muttered, "tapping at my
chamber door—
              Only this, and nothing more."
Ah, distinctly I remember it was in the bleak
December;
And each separate dying ember **wrought** its
ghost upon the floor.
Eagerly I wished the morrow;[2]—vainly I had
sought to borrow
From my books surcease of[3] sorrow—sorrow
for the lost Lenore—
For the rare and radiant maiden whom the
angels name Lenore—
              Nameless *here* for evermore.
And the silken, sad, uncertain rustling of each
purple curtain
Thrilled me—filled me with fantastic terrors
never felt before;
So that now, to still the beating of my heart, I
stood repeating
"'Tis some visitor entreating entrance at my
chamber door—

Everyday Words

pondered (PAHN derd) *v.* thought deeply

wrought (RAWT) *v.* formed

---

1. **quaint** (KWAYNT) **volume of forgotten lore** unusual book of forgotten knowledge

2. **the morrow** the next day

3. **surcease** (ser SEES) **of** relief from

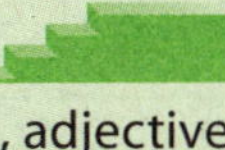

Vocabulary Builder

Adjectives In English, adjectives usually come before the nouns that they modify. In the first line, however, the adjective *dreary* comes after *midnight,* the noun that it modifies. The unusual order calls special attention to the words. Write *a midnight dreary* in standard English?

____

Fluency Builder 

In many poems, the words at the end of lines rhyme. In "The Raven," however, words in the middle of lines rhyme with words at the end of those lines. Underline the rhyming words in each line of the second stanza. Then, read the stanza aloud.

Vocabulary Builder 

Homographs *Entrance* is a homograph that has the same spelling as another word but a different meaning and pronunciation. Pronounced "in TRANS," *entrance* is a verb that means "capture and hold someone's attention." Pronounced "EN truhns," it is a noun that means "the act of entering." Which meaning and pronunciation does *entrance* have in the underlined line?

____

____

Comprehension Builder 

What does the speaker find when he opens the door? Circle your answer. What happens when he opens the window?

____

____

Vocabulary Builder 

Parts of Speech Poets often change parts of speech to fit the rhythm or rhyme of a line. The word *scarce* in the underlined line is written in its adjective form even though it serves as an adverb in the sentence. The adverb form is *scarcely*. Read aloud the line as it is written. Then, read aloud the line again, replacing *scarce* with *scarcely*. Notice how the rhythm of the line changes.

Fluency Builder 

The consonants *c* and *h* together often make the sound /ch/ as in *change* or *cheat*. Sometimes, however, *ch* has a hard /k/ sound, as in *echo*. Read aloud the bracketed paragraph, being sure to pronounce *echo* correctly.

Some late visitor entreating entrance at my
   chamber door;—
            This it is and nothing more."
Presently my soul grew stronger; hesitating
   then no longer,
"Sir," said I, "or Madam, truly your forgiveness
   I implore;
But the fact is I was napping, and so gently
   you came rapping,
And so faintly you came tapping, tapping at my
chamber door,
That I scarce was sure I heard you"—here I
   opened wide the door;—
          Darkness there and nothing more.

      ◆   ◆   ◆

The speaker searches the dark for the source of the knocking, but he sees nothing. When he calls out the name "Lenore," he hears only an echo. Then he hears the knocking again. This time he thinks it is someone at the window.

      ◆   ◆   ◆

Open here I flung the shutter, when, with
   many a flirt and flutter,
In there stepped a **stately** Raven of the
   saintly days of yore;[4]
Not the least obeisance[5] made he; not a
   minute stopped or stayed he;
But, with mien[6] of lord or lady, perched above
   my chamber door—
Perched upon a bust of Pallas[7] just above my
   chamber door—
        Perched, and sat, and nothing more.

Everyday Words

stately (STAYT lee) *adj.* elegant; dignified

4. **days of yore** (YAWR) olden days; days of long ago
5. **obeisance** (oh BAY suhns) *n.* show of respect, such as a bow or a curtsy
6. **mien** (MEEN) *n.* manner; way of conducting yourself
7. **bust of Pallas** (PAL is) sculpture of the head and shoulders of Pallas Athena (uh THEE nuh), the ancient Greek goddess of wisdom

Then this ebony bird beguiling my sad fancy[8]
    into smiling,
By the **grave** and stern decorum[9] of the
    countenance[10] it wore,
"Though thy crest be shorn and shaven,[11]
    thou," I said, "art sure no craven,
Ghastly grim and ancient Raven wandering
    from the Nightly shore—
Tell me what thy lordly name is on the Night's
    Plutonian[12] shore!"
            Quoth[13] the Raven, "Nevermore."

Much I marveled[14] this ungainly fowl to hear
    discourse[15] so plainly,
Though its answer little meaning—little
    relevancy bore;[16]
For we cannot help agreeing that no living
    human being
Ever yet was blessed with seeing bird above his
chamber door—
Bird or beast upon the sculptured bust above
    his chamber door,
            With such name as "Nevermore."

Everyday Words

grave (GRAYV) *adj.* very serious and worrying

ghastly (GAST lee) *adj.* extremely bad, shocking, or upsetting

grim (GRIM) *adj.* making you feel worried and unhappy

---

8. **ebony** (EB uh nee) **bird beguiling** (bi GYL ing) **my sad fancy** black bird charming my sad mood away

9. **decorum** (duh KAWR uhm) *n.* act of polite behavior

10. **countenance** (KOWN tuh nuns) *n.* face

11. **thy crest be shorn and shaven** The tuft of feathers on your head is clipped and shaved (by a previous owner).

12. **Plutonian** (ploo TOH nee uhn) *adj.* dark and evil; hellish (Pluto was the Roman god of the underworld.)

13. **quoth** (KWOHTH) *v.* quoted; recited; said

14. **marveled** (MAHR vuhld) *v.* found marvelous; felt awe or wonder about

15. **discourse** (dis KAWRS) *v.* speak; talk

16. **little relevancy** (REL uh vin see) **bore** had little meaning; did not make much sense

Vocabulary Builder

Archaic Terms Archaic terms were commonly used long ago but are not commonly used today. *Thy* is an archaic term for *your*. It shows possession. *Thou* is an archaic term for *you*. *Art* is also an archaic term, meaning "are." Rewrite the underlined line, replacing the archaic terms with standard English words.

____

____

Fluency Builder 

The second stanza on this page is one long sentence. Draw short lines between phrases to break the long sentence into manageable parts. Be sure to draw lines after punctuation marks. Punctuation marks separate phrases. Then, read the stanza aloud, pausing briefly after each punctuation mark.

Vocabulary Builder

Emphatic Past-Tense Verbs The past tense of *outpour*, a regular verb, is *outpoured*. However, for emphasis, English speakers often use the helping verb *do* with the base form of the verb. Change the *uttered* past-tense verb in the bracketed stanza to the emphatic past tense by combining the correct form of *do* with the verb. Write your answer below.

____

Vocabulary Builder 

Compound Words *Nevermore* is a compound word that combines *never* and *more*. It means "never again" or "no more." Circle another compound word in the bracketed stanza. Which words make up this word, and what does it mean?

____

____

Vocabulary Builder 

Verb Tenses The future tense combines the helping verb *will* with the base form of a verb. In poems and older texts, *shall* takes the place of *will*. Combine *shall* with the correct verb to complete this sentence:

The man wants to know whether

his soul _______________________

_______________________ a maiden named Lenore in heaven.

But the Raven, sitting lonely on the placid[17]
    bust, spoke only
That one word, as if his soul in that one word
    he did outpour.
Nothing farther then he uttered—not a feather
    then he fluttered—
Till I scarcely more than muttered, "Other
    friends have flown before—
On the morrow *he* will leave me, as my Hopes
    have flown before."
        Then the bird said, "Nevermore."

♦ ♦ ♦

The speaker worries about this "Nevermore." This time it sounds like a real answer to the question he asked. He tells himself that maybe the Raven knows just this one word. Yet he still keeps trying to find some meaning in the word. No matter what he asks the Raven, the bird says, "Nevermore." By now the speaker is angry.

♦ ♦ ♦

"**Prophet!**" said I, "thing of evil!—prophet still,
    if bird or devil!
By that Heaven that bends above us—by that
    God we both adore—
Tell this soul with sorrow laden[18] if, within the
    distant Aidenn,[19]
It shall **clasp** a sainted maiden whom the
    angels name Lenore—
Clasp a rare and radiant maiden whom the
    angels name Lenore."
        Quoth the Raven, "Nevermore."

Everyday Words

prophet (PRAHF it) *n.* someone who claims to know what will happen in the future

clasp (KLASP) *v.* close one's fingers or arms around someone or something

17. **placid** (PLA sid) *adj.* silent
18. **this soul with sorrow laden** (LAY duhn) the speaker's own sorrowful soul
19. **Aidenn** (AY den) Eden; heaven

"Be that word our sign of parting, bird or
    fiend!" I shrieked, upstarting[20] —
"Get thee back into the tempest and the Night's
    Plutonian shore!
Leave no black **plume** as a token[21] of that lie thy
    soul hath spoken!
Leave my loneliness unbroken!—quit the bust
    above my door!
Take thy beak from out my heart, and take thy
    form from off my door!"
                    Quoth the Raven, "Nevermore."

And the Raven, never **flitting,** still is sitting,
    still is sitting
On the pallid bust of Pallas just above my
    chamber door;
And his eyes have all the seeming of a demon's
    that is dreaming;
And the lamp-light o'er him streaming throws
    his shadow on the floor;
And my soul from out that shadow that lies
    floating on the floor
                    Shall be lifted—nevermore!

Everyday Words

fiend (FEEND) *n.* demon; devil
plume (PLOOM) *n.* feather
flitting (FLIT ing) *adj.* flying rapidly

---

20. **upstarting** starting up; standing; moving
21. **token** (TOH kin) *n.* something that represents a feeling, fact, or event

---

Vocabulary Builder

Multiple-Meaning Words The verb *quit* often means "stop doing something." It may also mean "leave a place." Which meaning does *quit* have in the underlined line?

____

____

Vocabulary Builder

Homonyms Homonyms have the same spelling and pronunciation but different meanings and are often different parts of speech. As a verb, *lie* may mean "be in a position that is flat on some surface," or it may mean "deliberately tell someone something that is not true." *Lie* may also be a noun meaning "something you say or write that you know is untrue." What are the meaning and part of speech of *lie* on this page?

____

____

Comprehension Builder

What is the situation at the end of the poem? Answer by completing this sentence:

The Raven is __________________

__________________________,

and the speaker is ____________

__________________________.

Thinking About the Selections

1. Use the chart to list details about the character, setting, and main events of "The Fall of the House of Usher" and "The Raven."

	Setting	Characters	Main Events
"The Fall of the House of Usher"			
"The Raven"			

2. In "The Raven," the speaker is grieving because _________________________

____.

TALK **ABOUT IT** **What's the Suspense?** Poe is a master of suspense. In a small group, discuss ways that Poe creates suspense in "The Fall of the House of Usher." Pay special attention to the words that he uses, the imagery, and the order of events.

? Writing About the Essential Question

What is the relationship between place and literature? Review your list of details that make Poe's settings seem dreamlike. Then, write a paragraph describing the power of Poe's landscapes.

Verb Tenses

The future tense of a verb describes actions that have not yet happened. They will happen in the future. Most verbs form the future tense by adding the word *will* before the infinitive form of the verb.

Examples

Present Tense: *run*	Future Tense: *will run, shall run*
I *run* in a race.	I *will run* in a race.
You *run* after me.	You *will run* after me.
She *runs* every day.	She *will run* tomorrow.
We *run* at recess	We *will run* at recess.
You two *run* home.	You two *will run* honme.
They *run* back to the bus.	They *will run* back to the bus.

Now You Do It

Change the following sentences into the future tense.

1. I <u>walk</u> with you. ___________________________________

2. You <u>go</u> to the library tomorrow. ___________________________

3. He <u>studies</u> for the test. ___________________________________

4. She <u>reads</u> the book tonight. _________________________________

5. We <u>take</u> out the trash on Friday. ______________________________

6. They <u>work</u> on their project. _________________________________

TALK ABOUT IT **Choose the Correct Verb Tense** Write five new sentences, using the present or future tense of the verbs above. Then, rewrite the sentences, leaving a blank line where the verb should be. Ask a partner to fill in the blanks.

WRITE ABOUT IT **What's Going to Happen?** Write a news story about a fund-raising event that will happen in the future. Use the future tense of at least five verbs in your story.

Vocabulary

Listen to each word. Say it. Then, read the definition and the example sentence.

inscrutable (in SKROO tuh buhl) *adj.* Something **inscrutable** is baffling and mysterious.

No one has ever figured out his <u>inscrutable</u> *personality.*

prescient (PRESH uhnt) *adj.* A **prescient** person is able to know what will happen in the future.

The <u>prescient</u> *fortune-teller played the lottery and won.*

impulsive (im PUHL siv) *adj.* Someone **impulsive** does things without considering the possible dangers or problems first.

Laurie just made an <u>impulsive</u> *decision to go rock climbing.*

Vocabulary Practice

Read the first sentence in each group of three. Then, complete Sentence *a* by substituting another word or phrase that means the same as the underlined vocabulary word. Complete Sentence *b* with your own ideas and words.

1. The captain's sudden decision to change course was <u>inscrutable</u>.

   a. The captain's sudden decision to change course was ______________.

   b. ____ was inscrutable.

2. Gran was <u>prescient</u> because she knew my cousin would visit.

   a. Gran was ______________ because she knew my cousin would visit.

   b. Gran was prescient because ________________________________.

3. The <u>impulsive</u> friends left suddenly on a trip to the city.

   a. The ______________ friends left suddenly on a trip to the city.

   b. The impulsive ____.

Getting Ready to Read

Moby Dick is believed to have been a sperm whale, which can grow up to 60 feet long. What else do you know about whales? Share your knowledge with a partner.

from Moby-Dick
Herman Melville

Summary Captain Ahab has led the crew of the *Pequod* on a whale hunt. In the first excerpt from *Moby-Dick*, Ahab explains that they are not hunting for business. Instead, Ahab is looking for revenge. He wants to hunt and kill the great white whale called Moby-Dick. He blames the whale for the loss of his leg. The second excerpt is the final chapter. Here, the narrator tells what happens when Ahab and his crew finally locate the whale.

Note-taking Guide

Put the events in order according to when they happen in the story. Write the letter for each event in the chart.

- **A** Moby-Dick is harpooned and attacks the ship.
- **B** Ahab tells the crew that they will hunt Moby-Dick.
- **C** Ahab's ship is destroyed and Ahab is lost at sea.
- **D** Ahab sets off in a whale boat to chase Moby-Dick.
- **E** Ahab paces the deck.
- **F** The ship's crew drinks together and swears to kill the whale.

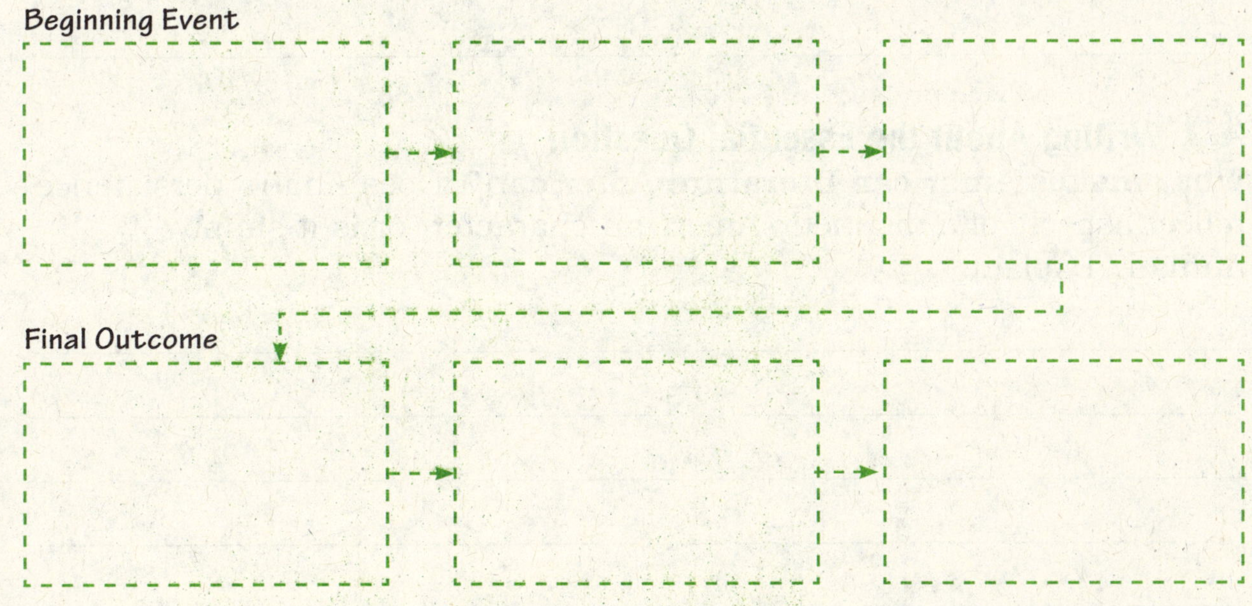

Thinking About the Selection

1. Complete the chart, contrasting the characters of Starbuck and
   Captain Ahab.

Starbuck:

Ahab:

2. At the end of the story, Ahab and most of his crew ________________,

   and Moby-Dick ____.

TALK ABOUT IT **Why Did They Go?** Many members of the crew realize
the danger that they are in. Why do you think they continue to follow
Ahab's orders? Talk about your ideas with a partner.

I think the crew members continue to follow Ahab's orders because

____.

Writing About the Essential Question

What makes American literature American? Does Ahab's persistence
reflect aspects of a distinctly American character, or is it simply
human? Explain.

____

____

____

____

____

Contractions

Shortened combinations of two or more words are called contractions. Many contractions use apostrophes (') to replace letters that have been dropped to combine the words.

Examples

To form contractions with the verbs *is* and *are*, add *'s* and *'re* to pronouns. To form a contraction with *am*, add *'m* to the pronoun *I*.

I + am = I'm	we + are = we're
it + is = it's	you + are = you're
she + is = she's	they + are = they're

Now You Do It

Form the correct contraction for the noun or pronoun with *am, is,* or *are* below. Then, write a sentence for each contraction.

1. it: ___________ ____

2. he: ___________ ____

3. they: ___________ ______________________________________

4. I: ___________ ____

5. you: ___________ _______________________________________

TALK ABOUT IT **Perform a Dialogue** Work with a partner to write and perform a dialogue between two friends who are planning a project to help the community. Use at least six contractions in your dialogue.

WRITE ABOUT IT **Formal and Informal** Contractions are used mainly in informal writing or when speaking. Write a formal letter asking someone to speak at your school. Then, write the same letter to a friend or family member, using contractions.

Dear Sir or Madam:

I am inviting you ____.

Dear ______________:

I'm inviting you ____.

Vocabulary

Listen to each word. Say it. Then, read the definition and the example sentence.

perpetual (puhr PE choo uhl) *adj.* Something that is **perpetual** is permanent, or continuing to exist for a long time or for all the time in the future

  The woods, far from town are in a state of perpetual peace.

decorum (di KAW ruhm) *n.* **Decorum** is behavior that is polite and correct for an occasion.

  The best man, lacking decorum, arrived late to the wedding.

occurrence (uh KER uhns) *n.* An **occurrence** is something happening.

  The rare occurrence of storms made the tornado shocking.

Vocabulary Practice

Read the first sentence in each group of three. Then, complete Sentence *a* by substituting another word or phrase that means the same as the underlined vocabulary word. Complete Sentence *b* with your own ideas and words.

1. The cave deep in the earth lies in <u>perpetual</u> darkness.

  a. The cave deep in the earth lies in _______________ darkness.

  b. ____ perpetual darkness.

2. Observing rules of <u>decorum</u>, Tim removed his hat.

  a. Observing rules of _______________, Tim removed his hat.

  b. Observing rules of decorum, _______________________________________.

3. Accidents on icy roads are a common <u>occurrence</u>.

  a. Accidents on icy roads are a common _______________.

  b. ____ a common occurrence.

Getting Ready to Read

Ralph Waldo Emerson believed that through contact with nature, humans could discover a connection among the universe, God, and every living thing. Have you ever felt moved by nature? Discuss your experiences with a partner.

from Nature
Ralph Waldo Emerson

Summary In this selection, Emerson writes about the harmony between himself and nature. He believes all living things are connected and reflect each other. Emerson describes how beauty, peace, and spirituality can be found in the natural world.

Note-taking Guide

Read the selection. Using the chart, rewrite complicated or long sentences in your own words.

from Nature:	In your own words:
"In the woods, too, a man casts off his years, as the snake his slough, and at what period soever of life is always a child."	
"I become a transparent eyeball; I am nothing; I see all; the currents of the Universal Being circulate through me; I am part or parcel of God."	

Vocabulary

Listen to each word. Say it. Then, read the definition and the example sentence.

conviction (kuhn VIK shuhn) *n.* **Conviction** is a strong belief.
It is her conviction that school is important.

aversion (uh VER zhuhn) *n.* An **aversion** a strong dislike of something or someone.
Hannah has a strong aversion to strawberries and will not eat them.

absolve (uhb ZAHLV) *v.* When you **absolve** someone of something, you publicly say that he or she is not guilty or responsible for it.
Oscar thought that moving would absolve him from having to pay his rent for that month.

Vocabulary Practice

Read the first sentence in each group of three. Then, complete Sentence *a* by substituting another word or phrase that means the same as the underlined vocabulary word. Complete Sentence *b* with your own ideas and words.

1. Jacob had the conviction that students should volunteer.

   a. Jacob had the _____________ that students should volunteer.

   b. Jacob had the conviction that _________________________________.

2. My aversion to getting sick makes me wash my hands often.

   a. My _____________ to getting sick makes me wash my hands often.

   b. My aversion to _________________________________.

3. He hoped that paying the fine would absolve him of guilt.

   a. He hoped that paying the fine would _____________ him of guilt.

   b. _________________________________ would absolve him of guilt.

Getting Ready to Read

Emerson greatly admired people in history who exhibited self-reliance and rejected conformity. How would you define self-reliance? Why do you think Emerson thought it was important? Share your thoughts with a partner.

from Self-Reliance
Ralph Waldo Emerson

Summary In this excerpt, Emerson speaks to the individual. He urges readers to avoid conforming to the standards of society. Instead, Emerson urges readers to think and act independently.

Note-taking Guide

Read the selection. Using the chart, rewrite complicated or long sentences in your own words.

from Self-Reliance:	In your own words:
"Trust thyself; every heart vibrates to that string"	
"Nothing is at last sacred but the integrity of your own mind. Absolve you to yourself, and you shall have the suffrage of the world . . ."	

Vocabulary

Listen to each word. Say it. Then, read the definition and the example sentence.

embattled (im BAT uhld) *adj.* Someone who is **embattled** is surrounded by enemies, especially in war or fighting.

The embattled city fought hard to keep out the enemy.

conqueror (KAHNG kuhr uhr) *n.* A **conqueror** is a person who defeats an enemy.

The conqueror led his army in the victory parade.

ruined (ROO ind) *adj.* Something that is **ruined** has been almost completely destroyed.

Broken glass and bricks surrounded the ruined building.

Vocabulary Practice

Read the first sentence in each group of three. Then, complete Sentence *a* by substituting another word or phrase that means the same as the underlined vocabulary word. Complete Sentence *b* with your own ideas and words.

1. The embattled army on the hill refused to give up the fight.

   a. The _______________ army on the hill refused to give up the fight.

   b. The embattled army ____ .

2. All of the treasure won in the attack went to the conqueror.

   a. All of the treasure won in the attack went to the _____________ .

   b. ______________________________________ went to the conqueror.

3. Visitors saw the old, ruined city walls still standing.

   a. Visitors could saw the old, _____________ city walls still standing.

   b. ______________________________________ still standing.

Getting Ready to Read

Emerson wrote "Concord Hymn" to honor the patriots of the American Revolution. Why are songs that honor the heroic actions of others important? Share your thoughts with a partner.

Concord Hymn
Ralph Waldo Emerson

Summary In this poem, Emerson celebrates the country. **"Concord Hymn"** honors the Minutemen who fought at Lexington and Concord during the American Revolution. The poem suggests that those who make great sacrifices for others should not be forgotten.

Note-taking Guide

Read each selection. Using the chart, rewrite complicated or long sentences in your own words.

Concord Hymn:	In your own words:
"On this green bank, by this soft stream, / We set today a votive stone; / That memory may their deed redeem, / When, like our sires, our sons are gone."	

Thinking About the Selections

1. Use the following chart to list the main ideas in each of Emerson's works.

"Nature"	Main idea:
"Self-Reliance"	Main idea:
"Concord Hymn"	Main idea:

2. Based on these poems, Emerson can be described as _______________.

____.

TALK ABOUT IT **Learn a Lesson** Emerson expresses important ideas in each selection. From his work, readers can learn valuable lessons about life. Which lesson did you find the most useful? Why? Discuss your ideas with a partner.

For me, the most useful of Emerson's writings was _______________

____.

? Writing About the Essential Question

How does literature shape or reflect society? Which passage in these essays best expresses belief in the importance of the individual? Explain the reasons for your choice.

____

____

____

____

Multiple-Meaning Words

Many English words have more than one meaning. Context clues in the text around a word can help you determine the word's meaning.

Examples

Word	Meanings
beat, *verb*	1. receive the most points or votes in a game, race, or other competition; win over someone else 2. mix ingredients together quickly with a fork or other kitchen utensil or machine
stir, *verb*	1. move a liquid or substance around with a spoon or other utensil or tool in order to mix it together 2. move slightly or make something else move slightly

Now You Do It

Read each sentence below. Then, write the number of the correct meaning from the chart above for the underlined word in each sentence.

_____ 1. Jessie did not want to <u>stir</u> the chemical mixture in class.

_____ 2. The recipe said to <u>beat</u> the eggs and milk together.

_____ 3. I finally <u>beat</u> my mother at Scrabble today.

_____ 4. Klaus and Monika hid in the closet and did not <u>stir</u> until the other children had gone past them.

TALK ABOUT IT **Look for Clues** With a partner, take turns reading aloud the sentences above. Circle the context clues in each sentence.

WRITE ABOUT IT **Write Your Own** With your partner, write *beat* or *stir* on the front of four note cards. On the back of each card, write two words—or context clues—to include in a sentence with the word. Then, exchange cards. Use the clues on the back of each card to write sentences. Then, share your sentences.

Vocabulary

These words are underlined in the selection. Listen to each word. Say it. Then, read the definition and the example sentence.

resignation (rez ig NAY shuhn) *n.* **Resignation** is the calm acceptance of a situation that cannot be changed, even though it is bad.
There was no solution, so he accepted the outcome with resignation.

discerns (di SERNZ) *v.* Someone **discerns** by recognizing separate ideas.
The child discerns the difference between work and play.

misgiving (mis GIV ing) *n.* **Misgiving** is a feeling of doubt or fear about what might happen or about whether something is right.
Viewing the old bridge with misgiving, she decided not to cross it.

Vocabulary Practice

Read the first sentence in each group of three. Then, complete Sentence *a* by substituting another word or phrase that means the same as the underlined vocabulary word. Complete Sentence *b* with your own ideas and words.

1. The team felt a sense of resignation about losing the game.

   a. The team felt a sense of _______________ about losing the game.

   b. The team felt a sense of resignation _______________________.

2. Although he is young, Victor discerns right from wrong.

   a. Although he is young, Victor _______________ right from wrong.

   b. Although he is young, Victor discerns _______________________.

3. Jamie entered the race with misgiving, due to his injury.

   a. Jamie entered the race with _______________, due to his injury.

   b. Jamie entered the race with misgiving, due to _______________.

Getting Ready to Read

Thoreau lived alone in a small cabin for two years. He believed that this separation from society would help him understand the meaning of life. What do you think it would be like to live apart from society for a long period of time? Share your thoughts with a partner.

from Walden
Henry David Thoreau

Summary For two years, Henry David Thoreau lived alone in a small cabin. He had built the cabin above Walden Pond. Seven years after he left the cabin, he used his journal to write *Walden.* In these selections, Thoreau shares his Transcendentalist vision. He believes human society has become too complex. He encourages people to simplify their lives, to slow down and do less, and to enjoy more.

Note-taking Guide

Use this table to keep track of Thoreau's statements and the details that support or clarify them.

Thoreau's Statement	Details
"The Holowell Farm has real attractions."	1. far from village 2. located on river

Cultural Understanding

July 4 celebrates the independence of the United States from Great Britain. People celebrated this holiday in Thoreau's time too.

Fluency Builder 

With a partner, take turns reading aloud the bracketed paragraph. The first sentence tells what Thoreau wanted to do. The second sentence tells what he did not want to do. Emphasize the words that show Thoreau's thoughts. Pause briefly after punctuation marks.

Comprehension Builder 

What did Thoreau want to do in the woods? Complete these sentences:

Thoreau went to the woods to

___________________. He

wanted to _______________
if it was wonderful. He wanted

to _______________ if it
was awful.

from Walden

Henry David Thoreau

When he was twenty-eight, Thoreau decided to leave the village of Concord, Massachusetts. He went to live several miles from town in the woods at Walden Pond. There he built a simple cabin that was little more than a shelter from the rain. He moved in on July 4, 1845—Independence Day. In a section of *Walden* called "Where I Lived and What I Lived For," he explains why he decided to live such a simple, rugged life, close to nature.

◆ ◆ ◆

I went to the woods because I wished to live **deliberately,** to front[1] only the **essential** facts of life, and see if I could not learn what it had to teach, and not, when I came to die, discover that I had not lived. I did not wish to live what was not life, living is so dear; nor did I wish to practice resignation, unless it was quite necessary.

◆ ◆ ◆

Thoreau went to the woods because he wanted to live life fully and find out what it was all about. If it was wonderful, he wanted to enjoy it. If it was awful, he wanted to face that too. He feels that too many people don't understand the meaning of life. Instead they live in a small way, like ants.

◆ ◆ ◆

Everyday Words

deliberately (di LIB rit lee) *adv.* with thought and care
essential (uh SEN shuhl) *adj.* vital; necessary

1. **front** confront; face

Our life is **frittered away** by detail. An honest man has hardly need to count more than his ten fingers, or in extreme cases he may add his ten toes, and lump the rest. Simplicity, simplicity, simplicity! I say, let your affairs be as two or three, and not a hundred or a thousand; instead of a million count half a dozen, and keep your accounts on your thumbnail. In the midst of this chopping sea of **civilized** life, such are the clouds and storms and quicksands and thousand-and-one items to be allowed for, that a man has to live, if he would not founder[2] and go to the bottom and not make his port at all, by dead reckoning.[3] Simplify, simplify. Instead of three meals a day, if it be necessary eat but one; instead of a hundred dishes, five; and reduce other things in **proportion.**

◆ ◆ ◆

Thoreau complains that there is too much stress on business and commerce in the young American nation. To him, the focus on material things is shallow. It takes people away from the more important spiritual side of life. Instead of wasting time working on new inventions, like the telegraph and the railroad, Thoreau thinks people should work on their souls. He sees no need to travel farther and faster on the railroad. He thinks people should not be in such a hurry to get nowhere different in their lives.

◆ ◆ ◆

Vocabulary Builder 

Word Family The verb *simplify* is in the same word family as the adjective *simple*. To *simplify* means "to make something simple, or easier and less complicated." Circle another related word in the bracketed paragraph. It ends with the suffix *-ity*, which means "the state of being a certain quality." What does the whole word mean?

____

____

Vocabulary Builder 

Multiple-Meaning Words The noun *stress* may mean "continuous feelings of worry." It may also mean "special attention or importance given to an activity or idea." What does *stress* mean in the underlined sentence?

____

____

Everyday Words

frittered (FRIT erd) **away** wasted, bit by bit

civilized (SIV uh lyzd) *adj.* organized and developed

proportion (pruh POHR shuhn) *n.* the relationship between two things in size, amount, or importance

2. **founder** (FOWN der) *v.* fill up with water and sink

3. **dead reckoning** (REK uhn ing) sailing without using the stars to guide you

Vocabulary Builder 

Dialect Using *a-* before an *-ing* verb form is not standard English, but it occurs in nonstandard spoken English:

Standard: I'm *going* now.
Nonstandard: I'm *a-going* now.

Circle the nonstandard word in the bracketed paragraph. How would it be written in standard English?

____

____

Comprehension Builder 

A metaphor describes one thing as something else; for example, *The eyes are a mirror to the soul.* What do the two metaphors in the bracketed paragraph compare?

____

____

____

____

Vocabulary Builder 

Multiple-Meaning Words The verb *wore* may mean "had something such as clothes or shoes on one's body." It may also mean "made something thinner, smoother, or flatter through continuous use." Which meaning does *wore* have in the underlined sentence?

____

____

Time is but the stream I go a-fishing in. I drink at it; but while I drink I see the sandy bottom and detect how shallow it is. Its thin current slides away, but eternity remains. I would drink deeper; fish in the sky, whose bottom is pebbly with stars. I cannot count one. I know not the first letter of the alphabet. I have always been regretting that I was not as wise as the day I was born. The intellect is a **cleaver;** it discerns and rifts[4] its way into the secret of things. I do not wish to be any more busy with my hands than is necessary. My head is hands and feet. I feel all my best **faculties** concentrated in it.

◆ ◆ ◆

Thoreau explains why he leaves his cabin on Walden Pond and returns to civilization.

◆ ◆ ◆

I left the woods for as good a reason as I went there. Perhaps it seemed to me that I had several more lives to live, and could not spare any more time for that one. It is remarkable how easily and insensibly[5] we fall into a particular **route,** and make a beaten track for ourselves. I had not lived there a week before my feet wore a path from my door to the pondside; and though it is five or six years since I trod[6] it, it is still quite **distinct.** It is true, I fear that others may have fallen into it, and so helped to keep it open. The surface of the

---

Everyday Words

cleaver (KLEE ver) *n.* a tool for cutting.
faculties (FAK uhl teez) *n.* powers; abilities
route (ROWT) *n.* a way from one place to another
distinct (di STINKT) *adj.* able to be seen clearly

---

4. **rifts** cuts through; divides
5. **insensibly** (in SEN suh blee) *adv.* without noticing
6. **trod** walked

earth is soft and impressible by the feet of men; and so with the paths which the mind travels. How worn and dusty, then, must be the highways of the world, how deep the ruts of tradition and **conformity!**

◆ ◆ ◆

Thoreau explains the things he learned from living in the woods. First, if a person follows his or her dreams, he or she will be rewarded in unexpected ways. Second, the more simply a person lives, the more rewarding his or her life will be. And last, there is no need to try to be like everyone else.

◆ ◆ ◆

Why should we be in such desperate **haste** to succeed, and in such desperate **enterprises?** If a man does not keep **pace** with his companions, perhaps it is because he hears a different drummer. Let him step to the music which he hears, however measured[7] or far away.

◆ ◆ ◆

To Thoreau, being alone is not the same as being lonely. And being poor does not stop you from enjoying the important things in life.

◆ ◆ ◆

However **mean** your life is, meet it and live it; do not **shun** it and call it hard names. It is not so bad as you are. It looks poorest when you are richest. The faultfinder will find faults even in paradise. Love your life, poor as it is. You may

---

Everyday Words

conformity (kuhn FOHR mi tee) *n.* behavior that obeys the accepted rules of society or a certain group and is the same as that of most other people

haste (HAYST) *n.* speed

enterprises (EN ter pry ziz) *n.* projects; undertakings

pace (PAYS) *n.* step

mean (MEEN) *adj.* low; petty

shun (SHUN) *v.* avoid

7. **measured** slow and steady

Fluency Builder 

Circle the punctuation mark that tells you to pronounce the underlined sentence with strong feeling. Then, read it aloud with expression.

Vocabulary Builder

Idioms Thoreau first used the idiom *hears a different drummer.* Today, the expression is often said as *marches to a different drummer.* The idiom means "is different from or behaves in a different way from other people." Complete the following sentence:

People who hear a different

drummer _____________________

_____________________________ .

Vocabulary Builder 

Adjectives *Poorest* is the superlative form of the adjective *poor.* The superlative compares more than two people, groups, or things:

• They are *poor.*
• They are the *poorest* people in town.

Short adjectives usually add *-est* to form the superlative. Longer adjectives usually use *most:*

• Of all the people in Concord, Thoreau was the *most unusual.*

Circle another superlative adjective on the page.

Vocabulary Builder 

Prefixes The prefix *dis-* means "not" or "the opposite of." *Disreputable* means "not considered reputable, or good, by society." Circle another word that begins with the prefix *dis-*. What does it mean?

____

____

Comprehension Builder 

What does Thoreau think is more important than clothes? Answer by circling a word in the underlined passage.

Vocabulary Builder 

Compound Adjectives The compound adjective *sixty-year-old* combines the words *sixty, years,* and *old.* Hyphens (-) connect the words. Complete this sentence by separating the words in the compound adjective:

They have a table that is

_______________________ .

perhaps have some pleasant, thrilling, glorious hours, even in a poorhouse. The setting sun is reflected from the windows of the almshouse[8] as brightly as from the rich man's abode;[9] the snow melts before its door as early in the spring. I do not see but a quiet mind may live as **contentedly** there, and have as cheering thoughts, as in a palace. The town's poor seem to me often to live the most independent lives of any. Maybe they are simply great enough to receive without misgiving. Most think that they are above being supported by the town; but it oftener happens that they are not above supporting themselves by dishonest means, which should be more **disreputable. Cultivate poverty** like a garden herb, like sage. Do not trouble yourself much to get new things, whether clothes or friends. Turn the old;[10] return to them. Things do not change; we change. Sell your clothes and keep your thoughts.

◆ ◆ ◆

Thoreau concludes with a story about a local farm family. They have a sixty-year-old kitchen table made from the wood of an apple tree. One day the family hears odd sounds from deep inside the table. Then, after several weeks, out comes a strong,

---

Everyday Words

contentedly (kuhn TEN tid lee) *adv.* with happy satisfaction

disreputable (dis REP yuh tuh buhl) *adj.* having a bad reputation; considered bad by society

cultivate (KUL tuh vayt) *v.* grow; encourage

poverty (PAHV er tee) *n.* the situation or experience of being poor

---

8. **almshouse** (AHMZ HOWS) *n.* a homeless shelter for the poor

9. **abode** (uh BOHD) *n.* home; residence

10. **Turn the old** turn worn old clothes inside out so that you can keep wearing them

beautiful bug. It hatched from an egg that had apparently been laid in the apple tree when it was still alive, sixty years before.

◆　◆　◆

Who knows what beautiful and winged life, whose egg has been buried for ages under many **concentric** layers of woodenness in the dead dry life of society, deposited at first in the alburnum[11] of the green and living tree, which has been gradually **converted** into the semblance of its well-seasoned tomb[12]—heard perchance[13] **gnawing** out now for years by the astonished family of man, as they sat round the festive board[14]—may unexpectedly come forth from amidst society's most **trivial** and handselled[15] furniture, to enjoy its perfect summer life at last!

I do not say that John or Jonathan[16] will realize all this; but such is the character of that morrow[17] which mere lapse of time can never make to dawn. The light which puts out our eyes is darkness to us. Only that day dawns to which we are awake. There is more day to dawn. The sun is but a morning star.

Everyday Words

concentric (kuhn SEN trik) *adj.* with one circle inside another

converted (kuhn VER tid) *v.* changed

gnawing (NAW ing) *adj.* chewing

trivial (TRIV ee uhl) *adj.* not serious, important, or valuable

---

11. **alburnum** (al BUR nuhm) *n.* the soft wood between the bark and the core of the tree
12. **the semblance** (SEM bluhns) **of its well-seasoned tomb** what seems like an aged tomb, or burial place
13. **perchance** (puhr CHANS) *adv.* perhaps
14. **festive** (FES tiv) **board** table
15. **handselled** (HAN suhld) adj. handmade
16. **John or Jonathan** average person
17. **the morrow** (MAHR oh) the next day

TAKE NOTES

Comprehension Builder 

The bracketed paragraph is one long sentence. With a partner, break it into shorter sentences, paraphrasing as necessary, so that its meaning is clearer. Then, summarize what Thoreau means.

____

____

____

____

Fluency Builder 

Read the last paragraph on this page silently. Notice the punctuation marks that signal pauses. Then, with a partner, take turns reading the paragraph aloud with expression.

Vocabulary

Listen to each word. Say it. Then, read the definition and the example sentence.

expedient (ik SPEE dee uhnt) *n.* An **expedient** is a resource that deals with a problem quickly and effectively.

Valerie avoided the other car by the expedient of switching lanes.

din (DIN) *n.* A **din** is a loud, unpleasant noise.

We could not hear each other over the din of the crowd.

alacrity (uh LAK ruh tee) *n.* **Alacrity** is speed and eagerness.

Jason cleaned his room with alacrity so that he could go to the game.

Vocabulary Practice

Read the first sentence in each group of three. Then, complete Sentence *a* by substituting another word or phrase that means the same as the underlined vocabulary word. Complete Sentence *b* with your own ideas and words.

1. The soldier's helmet was a useful expedient for holding water.

    a. The soldier's helmet was a useful ____________ for holding water.

    b. The soldier's helmet was a useful expedient for ________________.

2. The din of the engines hurt our ears.

    a. The ____________ of the engines hurt our ears.

    b. The din of the sirens _________________________________.

3. Gisele liked her work and did her job with alacrity.

    a. Gisele liked her work and did her job with ____________.

    b. ________________________________ with alacrity.

Getting Ready to Read

Thoreau urged people to try to make government be the best that it could be. This meant sometimes carrying out civil disobedience, the intentional breaking of laws in order to get governments to change. In what situations might a person be justified in breaking the law as an act of civil disobedience? Discuss this subject in a small group.

from Civil Disobedience
Henry David Thoreau

Summary In 1846, Henry David Thoreau spent a night in jail. He had refused to pay his taxes because he believed that the tax money would support the war against Mexico. He opposed the war. After he was released, he wrote "Civil Disobedience." In this essay, Thoreau argues that people should oppose laws that violate their principles. In this excerpt, he explains his views on government.

Note-taking Guide

Use this chart to keep track of Thoreau's comments about the government.

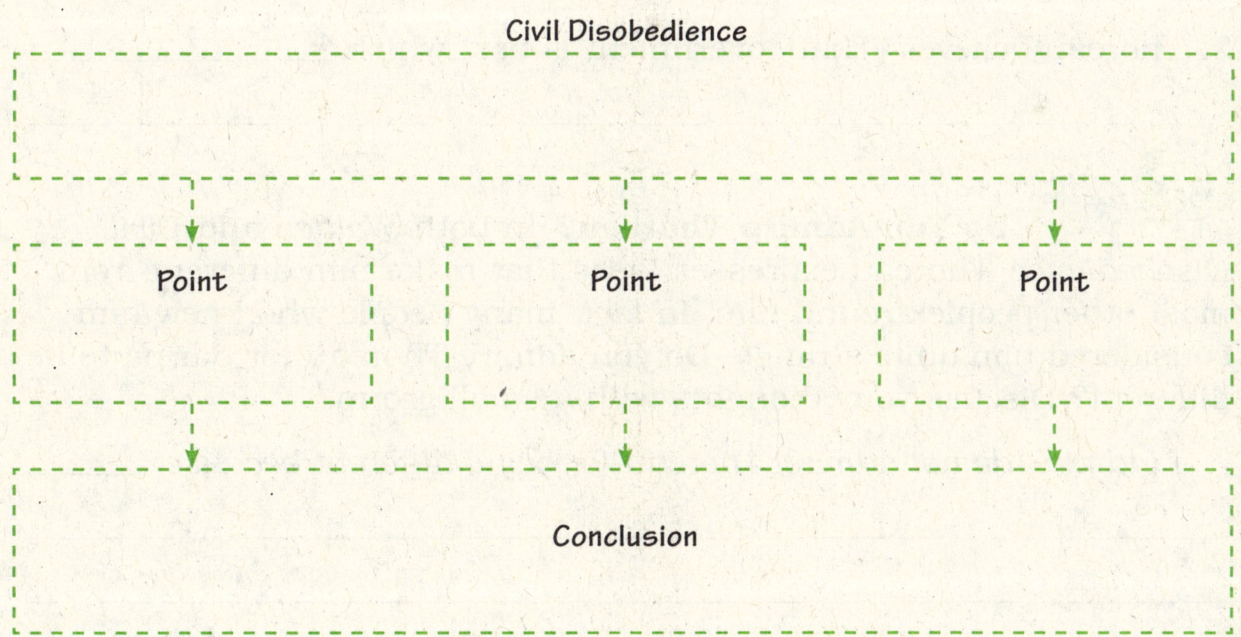

Thinking About the Selections

1. In *Walden,* Thoreau makes comparisons between individuals and society, and in *Civil Disobedience,* he makes comparisons between individuals and government. Use the following chart to list these comparisons.

Individuals:	vs.	Society:
Individuals:	vs.	Government:

2. Thoreau believes "That government is best which _________________________________."

TALK ABOUT IT **Do You Admire Thoreau?** In both *Walden* and *Civil Disobedience,* Thoreau expresses ideas that make him different from most other people around him. In fact, many people who knew him considered him quite strange. Do you admire Thoreau for daring to be different? Discuss your thoughts with a small group.

I (admire/do not admire) Thoreau for being different because _________

____.

 **Writing About the Essential Question**

How does literature shape or reflect society? Do you find it surprising that the goals Thoreau tried to achieve have influenced generations of people around the world? Explain.

Prefixes

A prefix is a group of letters added to a base word to form a new word with a new meaning.

Examples

The prefix *in-* means "not" or "opposite of." The prefix *im-* is used in place of *in-* when added to words that begin with the letters *b, m,* or *p.*

Prefix		Base Word		New word		Meaning
in-	+	accurate	=	inaccurate		not accurate
in-	+	sane	=	insane		not sane
im-	+	patient	=	impatient		not patient
im-	+	mobile	=	immobile		not mobile

Now You Do It

Form a new word meaning the opposite of each base word by adding *im-* or *in-*.

1. _____ + complete = _____________________

2. _____ + perfect = _____________________

3. _____ + direct = _____________________

4. _____ + mature = _____________________

5. _____ + balance = _____________________

6. _____ + appropriate = _____________________

TALK ABOUT IT **Quiz Time** With a partner, look up the meanings of the base words and their opposites above. Write each word on the front of a note card and its meaning on the back of the card. Then, take turns quizzing each other on the meaning of each word.

WRITE ABOUT IT **Is/Is Not** Using each word in Now You Do It, write an example of someone or something that fits each word and its opposite. For example, *My brother is patient, but I am impatient.*

Government Publications

About Government Publications

Citizens read **government publications** to find reliable information about issues that affect them. **Consumer guides** are a specific type of government publication. They provide information about products and services that people use, such as the drinking water that comes into their homes. Consumer guides present facts in ways that most people can understand. These facts help consumers make decisions about the products and services that they use and buy.

Reading Skill

Consumer guides may include graphs and charts that provide information in a visual way, making the information easier to understand. Graphs and charts often summarize information or provide additional details to support ideas in the text. When consumers **analyze and evaluate information from graphs and charts,** they gain a better understanding of the products and services that they use. To analyze and evaluate information in graphs and charts, ask yourself these questions:

1. What is the purpose of the graph or chart?

2. How do the different pieces of information in the chart relate to one another?

3. Does the information show cause and effect, comparison, or a process?

4. How does the information support or clarify information in the text?

Basic Elements			Purpose	Effectiveness
Titles and headings	Yes ❑	No ❑		
Charts or graphs	Yes ❑	No ❑		
Photos, maps, or illustrations	Yes ❑	No ❑		
Labels or captions	Yes ❑	No ❑		
Color-coding	Yes ❑	No ❑		
Issue dates	Yes ❑	No ❑		

EPA
United States
Environmental Protection
Agency

WATER ON TAP
what you need to know

Where Does My Drinking Water Come From And How Is It Treated?

Your drinking water comes from **surface water** or **ground water**. The water that systems pump and treat from sources open to the atmosphere, such as rivers, lakes, and reservoirs is known as surface water. Water pumped from wells drilled into underground **aquifers**, geologic formations containing water, is called ground water. The quantity of water produced by a well depends on the nature of the rock, sand, or soil in the aquifer from which the water is drawn. Drinking water wells may be shallow (50 feet or less) or deep (more than 1,000 feet). More water systems have ground water than surface water as a source (approx. 147,000 v. 14,500), but more people drink from a surface water system (195 million v. 101,400). Large-scale water supply systems tend to rely on surface water resources, while smaller water systems tend to use ground water. Your water utility or public works department can tell you the source of your public water supply.

How Does Water Get To My Faucet?

An underground network of pipes typically delivers drinking water to the homes and businesses served by the water system. Small

systems serving just a handful of households may be relatively simple, while large metropolitan systems can be extremely complex—sometimes consisting of thousands of miles of pipes serving millions of people. Drinking water must meet required health standards when it leaves the treatment plant. After treated water leaves the plant, it is monitored within the distribution system to identify and remedy any problems such as water main breaks, pressure variations, or growth of microorganisms.

The headings anticipate questions readers may have.

How Is My Water Treated To Make It Safe?

Water utilities treat nearly 34 billion gallons of water every day.[1] The amount and type of treatment applied varies with the source and quality of the water. Generally, surface water systems require more treatment than ground water systems because they are directly exposed to the atmosphere and runoff from rain and melting snow.Water suppliers use a variety of treatment processes to remove **contaminants** from drinking water. These individual processes can be arranged in a "treatment train" (a series of processes applied in a sequence). The most commonly used processes include coagulation (flocculation and sedimentation), filtration, and disinfection. Some water systems also use ion exchange and adsorption. Water utilities select the treatment combination most appropriate to treat the contaminants found in the source water of that particular system.

Coagulation (Flocculation & Sedimentation):

Flocculation: This step removes dirt and other particles suspended in the water. Alum and iron salts or synthetic organic polymers are added to the water to form tiny sticky particles called "floc," which attract the dirt particles.

All sources of drinking water contain some naturally occurring contaminants. At low levels, these contaminants generally are not harmful in our drinking water. Removing all contaminants would be extremely expensive, and in most cases, would not provide increased protection of public health. A few naturally occurring minerals may actually improve the taste of drinking water and may even have nutritional value at low levels.

Sedimentation: The flocculated particles then settle naturally out of the water.

Filtration:

Many water treatment facilities use filtration to remove all particles from the water. Those particles include clays and silts, natural organic matter, precipitates from other treatment processes in the facility, iron and manganese, and microorganisms. Filtration clarifies the water and enhances the effectiveness of disinfection.

Disinfection:

Disinfection of drinking water is considered to be one of the major public health advances of the 20th century. Water is often disinfected before it enters the distribution system to ensure that dangerous microbial contaminants are killed. Chlorine, chlorinates, or chlorine dioxides are most often used because they are very effective **disinfectants**, and residual concentrations can be maintained in the water system.

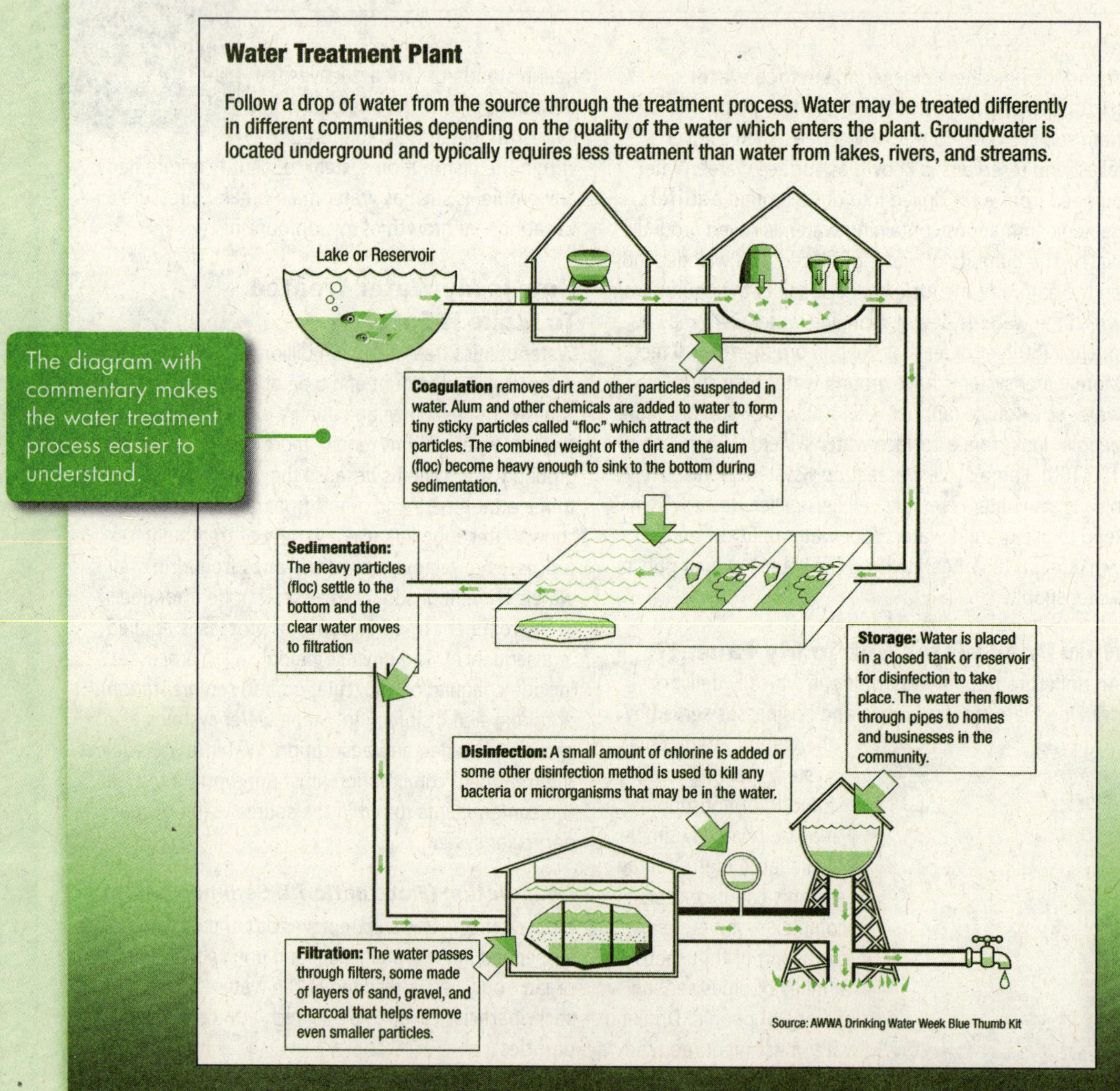

The diagram with commentary makes the water treatment process easier to understand.

Thinking About Government Publications

1. To what government agency would you go to find information about the source of your water?

   ____

2. Why might the government publish a guide about water sources and water treatment?

   ____

   ____

Reading Skill

3. Which step comes first in the "treatment train"—filtration or disinfection?

   ____

4. Where is water kept before it is used in the community?

   ____

WRITE ABOUT IT Timed Writing: Summarize (25 minutes)

Explain the following statement by summarizing the water treatment process. Describe where water comes from, how water is made safe to drink, and how it reaches your community.

Consumers may safely drink the water that comes into their homes.

____

____

____

____

Vocabulary

Listen to each word. Say it. Then, read the definition and the example sentence.

surmised (suhr MYZD) *v.* When something is **surmised,** it is guessed or inferred without evidence.

He held a bat, so she surmised that he was going to play baseball.

oppresses (uh PRES uhs) *v.* Something that **oppresses** others makes them feel uncomfortable, worried, or unhappy.

The dreary weather oppresses me in the winter.

affliction (uh FLIK shuhn) *n.* An **affliction** is something, usually a medical condition, that causes pain or unhappiness.

Mr. Innes suffers from an affliction of the stomach.

Vocabulary Practice

Read the first sentence in each group of three. Then, complete Sentence *a* by substituting another word or phrase that means the same as the underlined vocabulary word. Complete Sentence *b* with your own ideas and words.

1. When he didn't look up, she <u>surmised</u> that he was upset.

   a. When he didn't look up, she ______________ that he was upset.

   b. ______________________________ surmised that he was upset.

2. The gloom in the basement <u>oppresses</u> Keira.

   a. The gloom in the basement ______________ Keira.

   b. ______________________________ oppresses Keira.

3. Frostbite is an <u>affliction</u> that affects people during winter.

   a. Frostbite is a(n) ______________ that affects people during winter.

   b. Frostbite is an affliction that ______________________________.

Getting Ready to Read

Emily Dickinson rarely showed her poetry to anyone. In fact, of the 1,775 poems she wrote, only seven were published during her lifetime. Today, she is recognized as one of America's greatest poets. Why might someone hide such a gift? Share your thoughts with a partner.

Emily Dickinson's Poetry

Summaries In **"Because I could not stop for Death,"** the poet imagines that a carriage takes her to her grave after she dies. The poet also writes about her own death in **"I heard a fly buzz— when I died."** **"There's a certain Slant of light"** tells about the sad afternoon light of winter. In **"My life closed twice before its close,"** the poet thinks about enduring a terrible event. The poet speaks of the soul's tendency to prefer one person over all others in **"The Soul selects her own Society."** **"The Brain—is wider than the sky—"** is a poem that claims that all of nature and even God can be contained in the mind. In **"There is a solitude of space,"** the soul offers more solitude than any earthly place. The poet suggests that things can only be known through their opposites in **"Water, is taught by thirst."**

Note-taking Guide

Record references to nature found in Dickinson's poems in the diagram.

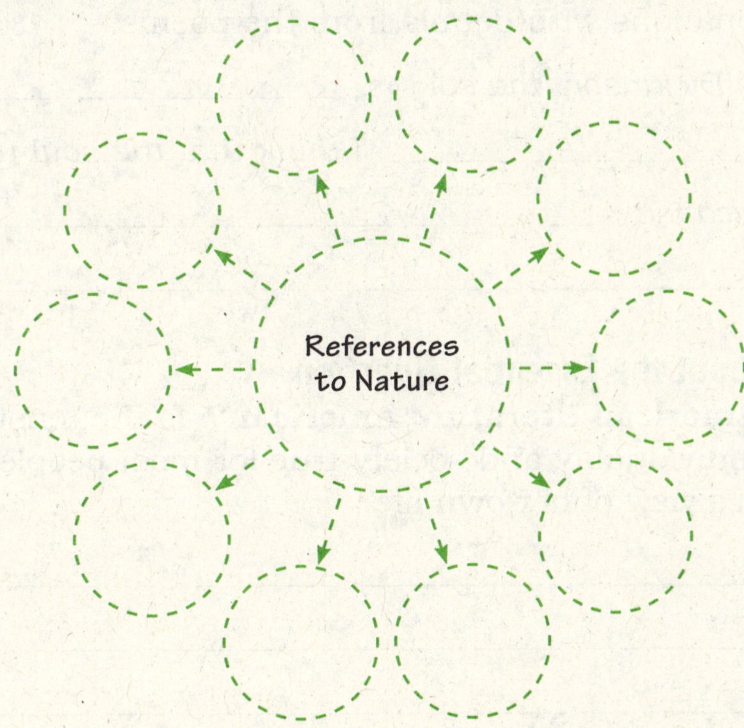

Thinking About the Selections

1. The topic of death appears in many of Dickinson's poems. Complete the chart with Dickinson's descriptions of death in the three poems listed below.

Poem	Death
"Because I could not stop for Death"	
"I heard a Fly buzz—when I died"	
"My life closed twice before its close"	

2. In Dickinson's poem "Water, is taught by thirst," peace is taught

by ________________________.

TALK ABOUT IT **Importance of the Soul** Many people believe the soul is the part of a person that is not physical and that contains the person's character, thoughts, and feelings. Dickinson talks about the soul in many of her poems. How does Dickinson view the soul? Why is it so important to her? Discuss your thoughts with a partner. Be sure to support your opinions with details from the poems.

According to Dickinson, the soul is ________________________________

________________________________. *I think that the soul was important*

to Dickinson because ________________________________

________________________________.

? Writing About the Essential Question

What makes American literature American? Is the tension Dickinson sees between individuality and society true for most people, or is it simply the poet's view of her own life?

____

____

____

____

Idioms

Remember that an idiom is a word or phrase that has a special meaning that is different from the ordinary meaning of the individual words. Many idioms relate to feet.

Examples

Idiom	Explanation
foot the bill	pay for something that one does not want to pay for
think on your feet	think of ideas and make decisions very quickly
put your best foot forward	make a good impression

Now You Do It

Complete each sentence starter with a different idiom from the chart above.

1. I _________________________ by wearing my new suit at the meeting.

2. In an emergency, you have to be able to _________________________.

3. Because no one else brought money, Simone had to

   _________________________.

TALK ABOUT IT **Guide to Improvement** With a partner, use the idioms to perform a radio commercial about getting a new job.

WRITE ABOUT IT **Write a Pamphlet** Imagine that your friend wants to attend a certain college, but he or she is afraid of being turned down by the school. Write a letter to your friend, using the idioms on this page, in which you encourage him or her to apply to the college.

Vocabulary

Listen to each word. Say it. Then, read the definition and the example sentence.

abeyance (uh BAY uhns) *n.* Something such as a custom, rule, or system that is in **abeyance** is not being used at the present time.
The rule about cell phones in school is in abeyance until the principal makes a decision.

effuse (i FYOOZ) *v.* To **effuse** something is to pour it out.
Robyn will effuse the liquid into the container without losing any of it.

robust (roh BUST) *adj.* A **robust** person is strong and healthy.
The football star was a robust fellow.

Vocabulary Practice

Read the first sentence in each group of three. Then, complete Sentence *a* by substituting another word or phrase that means the same as the underlined vocabulary word. Complete Sentence *b* with your own ideas and words.

1. Soccer practices were in abeyance until next season.

   a. Soccer practices were in _______________ until next season.

   b. Soccer practices were in abeyance _________________________________.

2. Water began to effuse from the crack in the dam.

   a. Water began to _______________ from the crack in the dam.

   b. Water began to effuse _________________________________.

3. The tall, robust man could lift the heavy log.

   a. The tall, _______________ man could lift the heavy log.

   b. The tall, robust man _________________________________.

Getting Ready to Read

Many of Walt Whitman's poems celebrate democratic ideas and the spirit of America. What other poems have you read or what songs have you heard that celebrate the good qualities of the United States? Share your experiences with a small group.

Walt Whitman's Poetry

Summaries In the Preface to the 1855 Edition of *Leaves of Grass*, the speaker says that the United States is a great poem. In **"Song of Myself,"** he describes himself. Then, he considers the grass as a symbol of immortality. The speaker leaves a lecture on the stars to view the heavens in "perfect silence" in **"When I Heard the Learn'd Astronomer." "By the Bivouac's Fitful Flame"** is a poem that considers the army, life, and death. The speaker tells about carpenters, masons, and other workers in **"I Hear America Singing."** In **"A Noiseless Patient Spider,"** the speaker compares a spider's work to that of a soul trying to become attached to something.

Note-taking Guide

Write the main idea of each poem in this chart.

Poem	Main Idea
from Preface to the 1855 Edition of Leaves of Grass	
from Song of Myself	
When I Heard the Learn'd Astronomer	
By the Bivouac's Fitful Frame	
I Hear America Singing	
A Noiseless Patient Spider	

Thinking About the Selections

1. Whitman wrote many of his poems to celebrate a particular event, occasion, or idea. Complete the chart below to list what each poem celebrates.

Poem	What the Speaker Celebrates
"Song of Myself"	
"When I Heard the Learn'd Astronomer"	
"I Hear America Singing"	
"A Noiseless Patient Spider"	

2. In "By the Bivouac's Fitful Flame," the speaker is a ______________.

TALK ABOUT IT **America Today** Whitman was deeply proud of his country. In many of his works, he describes great things about America. Do you think that these qualities are still true today? Why or why not? Share your ideas with a partner. Be sure to support your ideas with details from the selections.

I think these qualities (are/are not) still true because ______________

____

____.

Writing About the Essential Question

What makes American literature American? What characteristics of America and the American spirit can you find in all the poems presented here?

Word Families

Words that share the same base word make up a word family. Being able to identify words in the same word family can help a reader determine the meaning of unfamiliar or difficult words.

Examples

The word *similar* means "almost the same."

Words That Share the Base Word	Part of Speech	Meaning
similar	*adjective*	almost the same
similarity	*noun*	the quality of being similar
similarly	*adverb*	in a similar way
dissimilar	*adjective*	not the same

Now You Do It

Read the sentences below. Complete each sentence with a different word from the word family above.

1. I noticed the _______________ between the brothers.

2. One person must have written both letters because the handwriting both was quite _______________.

3. He is always well behaved for his mother, and he behaves _______________ with the babysitter.

4. They are sisters, but they have _______________ interests.

TALK ABOUT IT **Discussion Similarities** Read aloud the sentences that you completed with a partner. Then, talk about the ways in which you and your partner are similar. Use words in the word family.

WRITE ABOUT IT **Write a Review** Imagine that you write car reviews for a newspaper. Write a review in which you describe a new model of a popular car. This new model has many of the same features that made the older model so popular, but it also has some improvements. In your review, use all four words from the *similar* word family.

Word Bank

awe	grandeur	rights
expansion	personal	self-reliant
fantastic	prosperity	technology

A. Matching Complete the chart by drawing a line between a sentence starter and its completion. Follow the language of each sentence so that all the sentences make sense. The first one has been done for you.

When you are in **awe** of someone,	extremely good or enjoyable.
A country's **expansion** is	machines, tools, and other mechanical means of doing and making things.
Something **fantastic** is	one particular person, rather than to another person or to a group of people.
The **grandeur** of something refers to	things that they are morally or legally allowed to have or do.
Something **personal** belongs or relates to	you have great respect and admiration for that person.
People who have **prosperity** have	its impressive size, beauty, or power.
People's **rights** are	able to do or decide things without depending on the help of others.
Someone **self-reliant** is	its increase in size or power.
Technology includes	enough money to live what they consider to be a good life.

B. **Parts of Speech** Nouns are words for peoples, places, things, and ideas. Adjectives modify—or describe—nouns. Say aloud each word in the word bank on page 154. If the word is a noun, write it in the first column. If the word is an adjective, write it in the second column.

Noun	Adjective

Let's Talk About Society A society is a group of people, often in a country or other geographic area, who share common laws, traditions, and other ways of life. With a partner, talk about the society in which you now live, here in the United States. Complete these sentence starters with your own words or with words from the word bank when indicated.

People in the United States have many _______________ and liberties, which they need because they are _______________ people. I am in _______________ of the _______________ that some people in the United States have achieved. The _______________ of the nation has encouraged many people to come here. I believe that the greatest assets of the United States are _______________. One thing that makes the country a fantastic place to live is _______________, but I also think that people in America should come together to _______________.

Write a New Verse Read a copy or listen to a version of the folk song "This Land Is Your Land" by Woody Guthrie. With a partner, write a new verse for the song, sharing what the country means to you or what you think the country should be for its people.

Vocabulary

Listen to each word. Say it. Then, read the definition and the example sentence.

dictum (DIK tuhm) *n.* A **dictum** is a formal statement by someone who is respected or has authority.

The manager's dictum was well received by the staff.

summarily (sum AYR uh lee) *adv.* Doing something **summarily** is doing it immediately, without the usual processes or rules.

Justin summarily crossed the street and was nearly hit by a car.

apprised (uh PRYZD) *v.* When you have **apprised** someone of something, you have informed or told him about it.

The teacher apprised her students that there would be a test today.

Vocabulary Practice

Read the first sentence in each group of three. Then, complete Sentence *a* by substituting another word or phrase that means the same as the underlined vocabulary word. Complete Sentence *b* with your own ideas and words.

1. The judge delivered a dictum about civil rights.

   a. The judge delivered a ______________ about civil rights.

   b. The judge delivered a dictum about ______________________________.

2. The teacher summarily punished the misbehaving student.

   a. The teacher ______________ punished the misbehaving student.

   b. The teacher summarily punished ______________________________.

3. The boss apprised the workers of the holiday schedule.

   a. The boss ______________ the workers of the holiday schedule.

   b. The coach apprised the players of ______________________________.

Getting Ready to Read

The narrator of this story describes the thoughts of a southern plantation owner as Union soldiers hang the man from a bridge. The hanging happens quickly, but the man imagines that it continues for hours. Tell a partner about an experience you have had in which a short amount of time seemed a great deal longer.

An Occurrence at Owl Creek Bridge

Ambrose Bierce

Summary A southern plantation owner is about to be hanged. He stands at the edge of the Owl Creek Bridge. Union soldiers prepare to put him to death for trying to burn down the bridge. A sergeant releases the plank that supports the plantation owner, and the author describes what happens as the man falls.

Note-taking Guide

Make a story map by completing the chart below. Record your responses in the second column.

Setting	
Characters	
Main Events	
High Point of Story	
Conclusion	

Thinking About the Selection

1. The events of the story are listed in the chart below. Put a check mark in the column labeled **Real** if the event actually happens. Put a check mark in the column labeled **Imagined** if the event occurs only in Farquhar's imagination.

Events	Real	Imagined
Peyton Farquhar attempts to burn Owl Creek Bridge.		
Peyton Farquhar is caught and hung from the bridge.		
The rope snaps, and Peyton Farquhar falls into the water.		
Peyton Farquhar swims away from the bridge and finds his way home.		
Peyton Farquhar dies from hanging.		

2. Peyton Farquhar wants to destroy Owl Creek Bridge because _______

____

____.

TALK ABOUT IT **Discuss the Style** Bierce tricks readers into thinking that Peyton Farquhar escapes. At the end of the story, Farquhar's death is a surprise. With a partner, find two clues that hint at the ending of the story. Use the sentence starters below to help your discussion.

One clue is that _______________________________________.

Another clue is that _______________________________________.

Writing About the Essential Question

What is the relationship between place and literature? How does the contrast between the ordinary settings and the awful events of this story add to its power? Explain.

____

____

Prefixes

A prefix is a word part added to the beginning of a base word. A prefix changes the meaning of the base word. The prefix *re-* means "again" or "back to a former state."

Examples

Prefix + Base Word	Definition
re- + join = rejoin	The verb *rejoin* means "go back to a group of people or organization that you were with before."
re- + view = review	The verb *review* means "look again at something you have studied, such as notes or reports."
re- + arrange = rearrange	The verb *rearrange* means "change the postion or order of things."

Now You Do It

Make new words by adding the prefix *re-* to each word below. Write a definition for each new word. You may consult a dictionary for additional help.

do ____

play ____

write ____

TALK ABOUT IT **Do It Again** Have a partner state a task that he or she has recently done. Ask your partner to do the task again, using one of the words from this lesson. For example, your partner may say, "I wrote the essay last night." You may respond, "Please rewrite the essay and include the changes the teacher suggested." Repeat this exercise several times, switching roles with your partner each time.

WRITE ABOUT IT **One More Time** Write a descriptive paragraph about a task that you must do again or an experience that you would like to have again. Use at least two words from this lesson.

Vocabulary

These words are underlined in the story. Listen to each word. Say it. Then, read the definition and the example sentence.

commotion (kuh MOH shuhn) *n.* A **commotion** is sudden noisy activity or arguing.

> *The police tried to control the commotion that erupted after the party.*

interminable (in TUR mi nuh bul) *adj.* An **interminable** event is long and boring.

> *The interminable speech seemed as though it would never end.*

disdainfully (dis DAYN ful lee) *adv.* When you behave **disdainfully,** you act as though someone or something is beneath you.

> *The spoiled child acted disdainfully toward the other children.*

Vocabulary Practice

Read the first sentence in each group of three. Then, complete Sentence *a* by substituting another word or phrase that means the same as the underlined vocabulary word. Complete Sentence *b* with your own ideas and words.

1. The parade created a commotion in the street.

   a. The parade created a _______________ in the street.

   b. _______________________ created a commotion in the street.

2. The interminable airline delay caused Paolo to miss a meeting.

   a. The _______________ airline delay caused Paolo to miss a meeting.

   b. The interminable airline delay caused Paolo _______________.

3. The selfish king treated others disdainfully.

   a. The selfish king treated others _______________.

   b. _______________________ treated others disdainfully.

Getting Ready to Read

In "An Episode of War," a Civil War soldier is shot in the arm. The doctor amputates, or removes, the soldier's arm. The soldier sees the war as harsh and difficult. Discuss with a partner the reasons that a person's view of the world might change after a serious injury.

An Episode of War
Stephen Crane

Summary A soldier fighting in the Civil War prepares the day's portions of coffee for his squad. As he measures the coffee, a bullet strikes him in the arm and changes his life. This story follows the soldier as he confronts the tragedy of war.

Note-taking Guide

Use this chart to record what happens to the lieutenant.

Beginning Event

A lieutenant is shot in the arm while measuring coffee for his squad.

Final Outcome

Cultural Understanding

Stephen Crane mentions different ranks of soldiers in the military. Corporals and sergeants are enlisted persons who are lower in rank than officers. A sergeant has a higher rank than a corporal. A lieutenant is the lowest rank of officer and is usually responsible for a small group of enlisted men.

Comprehension Builder 

Why is there blood on the lieutenant's sleeve? What has happened?

____

____

Vocabulary Builder 

Adverbs Many adverbs end with the suffix -*ly*. Adding -*ly* to an adjective changes the adjective to an adverb. The suffix -*ly* means "in a particular way." Circle two adverbs in the bracketed paragraph that end in -*ly*. What do the adverbs mean?

____

____

An Episode of War
Stephen Crane

The lieutenant's rubber blanket lay on the ground, and upon it he had poured the company's supply of coffee. Corporals and other representatives of the grimy and hot-throated men who lined the breast-work[1] had come for each squad's portion.

The lieutenant was frowning and serious at this task of division. His lips pursed as he drew with his sword various crevices in the heap, until brown squares of coffee, **astoundingly** equal in size, appeared on the blanket. He was on the verge of a great triumph in mathematics, and the corporals were thronging forward, each to reap a little square, when suddenly the lieutenant cried out and looked quickly at a man near him as if he suspected it was a case of personal assault. The others cried out also when they saw blood upon the lieutenant's sleeve.

◆　◆　◆

The lieutenant stares at the forest in the distance. He sees little puffs of smoke from the gunfire. The lieutenant holds his sword in his left hand. He struggles to put it in its scabbard, or holder. An orderly-sergeant helps him. The men stare thoughtfully at the wounded lieutenant.

◆　◆　◆

There were others who **proffered** assistance. One timidly presented his shoulder and asked the lieutenant if he cared to lean upon it, but the latter[2] waved him away mournfully.

Everyday Words
astoundingly (uh STOWN ding lee) *adv.* amazingly
proffered (PRAH ferd) *v.* offered

1. **breast-work** low wall put up quickly as a defense in battle
2. **the latter** the second in a list of two people or things; here, "the latter" refers to the lieutenant.

He wore the look of one who knows he is the victim of a terrible disease and understands his helplessness. He again stared over the breast-work at the forest, and then, turning, went slowly rearward. He held his right wrist **tenderly** in his left hand as if the wounded arm was made of very **brittle** glass.

And the men in silence stared at the wood, then at the departing lieutenant: then at the wood, then at the lieutenant.

As the wounded officer passed from the line of battle, he was enabled to see many things which as a participant in the fight were unknown to him. He saw a general on a black horse gazing over the lines of blue infantry at the green woods which veiled his problems. An aide galloped furiously, dragged his horse suddenly to a halt, saluted, and presented a paper. It was, for a wonder, precisely like a historical painting.

◆ ◆ ◆

The lieutenant observes the swirling movement of a crew of men with heavy guns. The shooting crackles like brush-fires. The lieutenant comes across some **stragglers**. They tell him how to find the field hospital. At the roadside, an officer uses his handkerchief to bandage the lieutenant's wound.

◆ ◆ ◆

The low white tents of the hospital were grouped around an old schoolhouse. There was here a singular[3] commotion.

Everyday Words

tenderly (TEN der lee) *adv.* gently; carefully

brittle (BRIT tuhl) *adj.* stiff and easily broken

stragglers (STRAG lerz) *n.* people who are moving more slowly and are behind others in a group

---

3. singular (SING gyuh ler) *adj.* remarkable, noticeable

Vocabulary Builder

Multiple-Meaning Words The word *wood* can mean "small forest" or "material that trees are made of." What does *wood* mean in the first bracketed paragraph? How do you know?

____

____

Fluency Builder

Read silently the second bracketed paragraph. Notice that the last sentence contains a series, or a list separated by commas. Now, read the paragraph aloud, pausing after each comma.

Comprehension Builder

What building serves as the center of the army field hospital? Circle the correct word in the last paragraph on this page.

Vocabulary Builder

Prefixes The prefix *inter-* means "involving or occurring between two or more things." The verb *locked* can mean "became fixed in one position and unable to move." Paraphrase the underlined sentence, replacing the verb *interlocked* with your own words.

____

____

____

Vocabulary Builder

Slang The word *mutton-head,* meaning "stupid person" or "fool," is an example of slang or informal English. Mutton is sheep meat.

Vocabulary Builder

Parts of Speech *Scorn* may be a noun meaning "the feeling that someone or something is stupid." It may also be a verb meaning "show that you think that someone or something is stupid or unreasonable." Which part of speech is *scorn* in the bracketed paragraph?

____

In the foreground two ambulances interlocked wheels in the deep mud. The drivers were tossing the blame of it back and forth, gesticulating[4] and berating,[5] while from the ambulances, both **crammed** with wounded, there came an occasional groan. An interminable crowd of bandaged men were coming and going. Great numbers sat under the trees nursing heads or arms or legs. There was a **dispute** of some kind raging on the steps of the schoolhouse. Sitting with his back against a tree a man with a face as grey as a new army blanket was **serenely** smoking a corncob pipe. The lieutenant wished to rush forward and inform him that he was dying.

◆　◆　◆

A doctor greets the lieutenant and notices his wounded arm. The doctor looks at the wound.

◆　◆　◆

The doctor cried out impatiently, "What mutton-head had tied it up that way anyhow?" The lieutenant answered, "Oh, a man."

When the wound was disclosed the doctor fingered it disdainfully. "Humph," he said. "You come along with me and I'll 'tend to you." His voice contained the same scorn as if he were saying: "You will have to go to jail."

Everyday Words

crammed (KRAMD) *adj.* completely full of things or people
dispute (dis PYOOT) *n.* disagreement
serenely (suh REEN lee) *adv.* calmly

---

4. **gesticulating** (jes TIK yoo layt ing) *v.* making vigorous gestures
5. **berating** (bee RAYT ing) *v.* criticizing harshly

The lieutenant had been very **meek,** but now his face was flushed, and he looked into the doctor's eyes. "I guess I won't have it **amputated,**" he said.

"Nonsense, man! Nonsense! Nonsense!" cried the doctor. "Come along, now. I won't amputate it. Come along. Don't be a baby."

"Let go of me," said the lieutenant, holding back **wrathfully,** his glance fixed upon the door of the old schoolhouse, as **sinister** to him as the portals[6] of death.

And this is the story of how the lieutenant lost his arm. When he reached home, his sisters, his mother, his wife, sobbed for a long time at the sight of the flat sleeve. "Oh, well," he said, standing shamefaced in the midst of these tears, "I don't suppose it matters so much as all that."

Everyday Words

meek (MEEK) *adj.* humble, mild-mannered

amputated (AMP yoo tay tuhd) *v.* cut off

wrathfully (RATH fuh lee) *adv.* angrily

sinister (SIN uhs ter) *adj.* making you feel that something bad, dangerous, or illegal is happening or is about to happen

6. **portals** (PORT uhlz) *n.* doors

Vocabulary Builder 

Parts of Speech *Flushed* may be a verb meaning "made water go through a toilet or pipe in order to clean it." It may also be an adjective meaning "red in the face." Which part of speech is *flushed* in the bracketed paragraph?

____

Fluency Builder 

Lines of dialogue—or the words that the characters say—appear in quotation marks (" "). With a partner, read aloud the dialogue between the lieutenant and the doctor. One of you should read the lieutenant's lines and the other should read the doctor's lines. Read with expression, in the way the characters would say the words.

Comprehension Builder 

Summarize the events in this story.

____

____

____

____

____

Thinking About the Selection

1. The lieutenant's wound changes his understanding of the world. In the chart below, describe the lieutenant's attitude before he is wounded and his attitude after he is wounded.

Before the wound	After the wound

2. When the lieutenant returns to his family, his mother, sisters, and wife cry ____

____.

TALK ABOUT IT **Locate Sensory Language** Crane uses descriptive writing to show a change in the lieutenant. With a partner, find examples of words or phrases in the story that appeal to the senses.

These words or phrases appeal to sight: _________________________

____

These words or phrases appeal to hearing: _____________________

____

These words or phrases appeal to touch: _______________________

____

 **Writing About the Essential Question**

How does literature shape or reflect society? In your view, does society benefit from frank portrayals of suffering?

____

____

Idioms

An idiom is a word or phrase that has a special meaning different from the ordinary meaning of the words. The following idioms all contain references to cats or dogs.

Examples

Idiom	Special Meaning
fight like cats and dogs	fight viciously
let the cat out of the bag	reveal secret information
look like something the cat dragged in	broken or ragged in appearance
let sleeping dogs lie	leave a subject alone

Now You Do It

Write a sentence for each idiom.

1. fight like cats and dogs ________________________________

____

2. let the cat out of the bag ________________________________

____

3. look like something the cat dragged in ________________________

____

4. let sleeping dogs lie ________________________________

____

TALK ABOUT IT **Have a Conversation** Have a conversation with a partner in which each of you uses at least two idioms from the chart above.

WRITE ABOUT IT **Draw a Comic Strip** Create a comic strip in which two characters have a dialogue. Use at least two of the idioms from this lesson in the dialogue or in captions below the comic strip.

Vocabulary

These words are underlined in the story. Listen to each word. Say it. Then, read the definition and the example sentence.

congenial (kuhn JEE nee uhl) *adj.* Something that is **congenial** is pleasant in a way that is comfortable or relaxing.
The congenial conversation made everyone feel at ease.

benevolent (buh NEV uh lent) *adj.* A **benevolent** person is kind.
The benevolent family took in the injured puppy and cared for it.

incompatible (in kum PAT uh bul) *adj.* Things that are **incompatible** cannot exist or be accepted together.
Slavery is incompatible with the ideas of liberty and justice.

Vocabulary Practice

Read the first sentence in each group of three. Then, complete Sentence *a* by substituting another word or phrase that means the same as the underlined vocabulary word. Complete Sentence *b* with your own ideas and words.

1. The congenial welcome encouraged the new student.

   a. The _______________ welcome encouraged the new student.

   b. The congenial welcome _______________________________.

2. The benevolent man bought lunch for the hungry children.

   a. The _______________ man bought lunch for the hungry children.

   b. The benevolent man _______________________________.

3. The dog and cat were incompatible and had to be separated.

   a. The dog and cat were _______________ and had to be separated.

   b. The dog and cat were incompatible and _________________________.

Getting Ready to Read

During the period of American slavery, it was illegal in most states to teach slaves to read and write. Slave owners believed that these skills would make it difficult to control the slaves. What are your first memories of learning to read? Discuss your ideas with a partner.

from My Bondage and My Freedom
Frederick Douglass

Summary Frederick Douglass learns to read from his mistress. As he reads, he learns that he has the same abilities and the same rights to freedom as white children. Soon, his mistress begins to act differently toward Douglass. The change in his mistress teaches Douglass that slavery makes both slaves and slave-owners less human. His autobiography tells about his struggle to gain knowledge and freedom.

Note-taking Guide

As you read, use this diagram to keep track of the events that occur in this section of Douglass's autobiography.

Mrs. Auld begins teaching Douglass to read.

Vocabulary Builder

Multiple-Meaning Words
The noun *design* may mean "a drawing" or "a pattern." It may also mean "a scheme" or "a plan." What does *design* mean in the first paragraph?

____

____

Comprehension Builder 

Paraphrase the underlined sentence by rewriting it in your own words.

____

____

____

Vocabulary Builder 

Synonyms *Happiness* and *contentment* are synonyms. They have similar meanings. Both words mean "the state of being happy." What does Douglass use these words to describe?

____

____

from My Bondage and My Freedom
Frederick Douglass

I lived in the family of Master Hugh, at Baltimore, seven years, during which time—as the almanac makers say of the weather—my condition was variable. The most interesting feature of my history here, was my learning to read and write, under somewhat marked disadvantages. In attaining this knowledge, I was compelled to **resort** to indirections by no means congenial to my nature, and which were really humiliating to me. My mistress—who had begun to teach me—was suddenly checked[1] in her benevolent design, by the strong advice of her husband. In faithful compliance with this advice, the good lady had not only ceased to instruct me, herself, but had set her face as a flint against my learning to read by any means.

◆　◆　◆

Douglass says that nature does not prepare people to be either slaves or slaveholders. At first, Mrs. Auld treats Douglass well. It takes a struggle inside her own soul to make her treat him as less than human.

◆　◆　◆

When I went into their family, it was the **abode** of happiness and contentment. The mistress of the house was a model of affection and tenderness. Her **fervent piety** and watchful

---

1. **checked** stopped, prevented

uprightness made it impossible to see her without thinking and feeling—"that woman is a Christian." There was no sorrow nor suffering for which she had not a tear, and there was no innocent joy for which she did not [have] a smile. She had bread for the hungry, clothes for the naked, and comfort for every mourner that came within her reach. Slavery soon proved its ability to divest[2] her of these excellent qualities, and her home of its early happiness.

◆ ◆ ◆

Mrs. Auld stops teaching Douglass. Then she becomes even more opposed than her husband to his learning to read. She angrily snatches a book or a newspaper from his hand.

◆ ◆ ◆

Mrs. Auld was an apt[3] woman, and the advice of her husband, and her own experience, soon demonstrated, to her entire satisfaction, that education and slavery are incompatible with each other. When this **conviction** was **thoroughly** established, I was most narrowly watched in all my movements. If I remained in a separate room from the family for any considerable length of time, I was sure to be suspected of having a book, and was at once called upon to give an account of myself.

◆ ◆ ◆

However, these efforts come too late to stop Douglass from learning to read.

◆ ◆ ◆

Everyday Words

conviction (kuhn VIK shuhn) *n.* a very strong belief or opinion

thoroughly (THOR uh lee) *adv.* completely

2. **divest** (duh VEST) *v.* strip, remove from.

3. **apt** (APT) *adj.* quick to learn

TAKE NOTES

Vocabulary Builder

Double Negatives In English, two negative words cancel each other out, producing a positive. Rewrite the underlined sentence without using the words *no, nor,* or *not.* Be sure that your sentence has the same meaning as the original sentence.

____

____

____

Vocabulary Builder 

Pronouns Pronouns, such as *I, he, she,* and *your,* are used in place of nouns. Circle the pronouns in the first bracketed paragraph. To whom does each pronoun refer?

____

____

____

Vocabulary Builder 

Multiple-Meaning Words The noun *account* may mean "a description of events, or an explanation of what you are doing or what is happening." It may also refer to an arrangement in which a bank keeps your money safe for you. Which meaning does *account* have in the second bracketed paragraph?

____

____

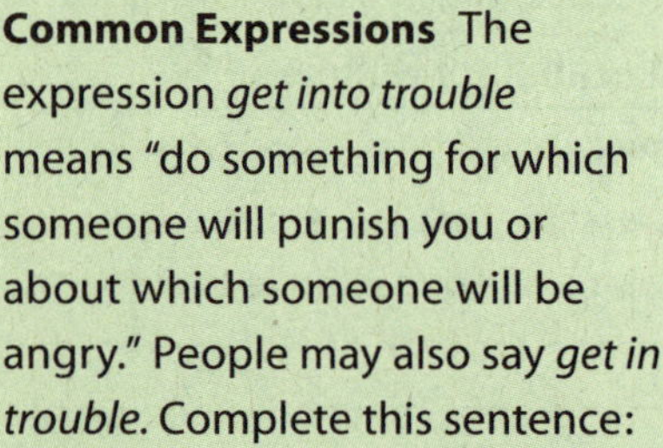

Vocabulary Builder

Idioms The idiom *hit upon* does not mean that Douglass slapped or punched something. It means that he discovered something unintentionally. Use the idiom to complete the following sentence:

Douglass ___________________

many ways to learn ____________.

Vocabulary Builder

Common Expressions The expression *get into trouble* means "do something for which someone will punish you or about which someone will be angry." People may also say *get in trouble.* Complete this sentence:

Douglass will not identify his teachers because he thinks that

they might ____________________.

Comprehension Builder 

How do human beings react by nature to slavery? Underline the phrase that gives Douglass's opinion.

Seized with a determination to learn to read, at any cost, I hit upon many expedients[4] to accomplish the desired end. The plea which I mainly adopted, and the one by which I was most successful, was that of using my young white playmates, with whom I met in the street, as teachers. I used to carry, almost constantly, a copy of Webster's spelling book in my pocket; and, when sent on errands, or when play time was allowed me, I would step, with my young friends, aside, and take a lesson in spelling. I generally paid my *tuition fee* to the boys, with bread, which I also carried in my pocket.

◆ ◆ ◆

Douglass feels grateful to the boys, but he does not want to identify his teachers by name. They might get into trouble for helping him.

◆ ◆ ◆

Although slavery was a delicate subject, and very cautiously talked about among grownup people in Maryland, I frequently talked about it—and that very freely—with the white boys. I would, sometimes, say to them, while seated on a curbstone or a cellar door, "I wish I could be free, as you will be when you get to be men." "You will be free, you know, as soon as you are twenty-one, and can go where you like, but I am a slave for life. Have I not as good a right to be free as you have?" Words like these, I observed, always troubled them; and I had no small satisfaction in wringing from the boys, occasionally, that fresh and bitter **condemnation** of slavery, that springs from nature, unseared and unperverted.[5]

◆ ◆ ◆

Everyday Words

condemnation (kahn duhm NAY shuhn) *n.* an expression of very strong disapproval of something

4. **expedients** (ek SPEE dee uhnts) *n.* ways of getting things done
5. **unperverted** (un puhr VERT id) *adj.* uncorrupted, pure

Douglass never meets a boy who defends slavery. His love of liberty grows steadily. By age thirteen, he has learned to read. He buys a schoolbook. But the praise of liberty in what he reads makes him feel unhappy and depressed. He cannot bear the idea that he will be a slave all his life.

◆ ◆ ◆

Once awakened by the silver trump[6] of knowledge, my spirit was roused to eternal wakefulness. Liberty! the inestimable[7] birthright of every man, had, for me, converted every object into an asserter of this great right. It was heard in every sound, and beheld in every object. It was ever present, to torment me with a sense of my wretched condition. The more beautiful and charming were the smiles of nature, the more horrible and desolate was my condition. I saw nothing without seeing it, and I heard nothing without hearing it. I do not exaggerate, when I say, that it looked from every star, smiled in every calm, breathed in every wind, and moved in every storm.

◆ ◆ ◆

Douglass has no doubt that Mrs. Auld notices his attitude. While nature has made them friends, slavery has made them enemies. Douglass is not cruelly treated, but he still hates the condition of slavery.

◆ ◆ ◆

I had been cheated. I saw through the attempt to keep me in **ignorance** . . . The feeding and clothing me well, could not **atone** for taking my liberty from me. The smiles of my mistress could

Everyday Words

ignorance (IG nuh ruhns) *n.* lack of knowledge or information about something

atone (uh TOHN) *v.* make up for

6. **trump** trumpet

7. **inestimable** (in ES tuh muh buhl) *adj.* priceless

Vocabulary Builder

Common Expression The expression *cannot bear something* means "cannot accept something or cannot let something happen because it is too difficult or unpleasant." What is it that Douglass cannot bear?

____

____

Fluency Builder 

With a partner, alternate reading aloud each sentence in the bracketed paragraph. Douglass reveals deep feelings. Read the sentences with expression, as though you were Douglass expressing your longing for freedom.

Vocabulary Builder

Idioms The idiom *saw through* means "understood." It usually means that someone has understood something negative, such as a plot to do something bad or a lie. Use the idiom to complete this sentence:

Mrs. Auld tried to keep Douglass from learning to read, but he

____

her plan.

Comprehension Builder 

How does Douglass describe both himself and Mrs. Auld?

____

____

Vocabulary Builder 

Prepositions The underlined phrase is a shortened form of the phrase *I speak nothing but the truth*. The word *nothing* is understood but not written. *But* is a preposition that, in this phrase, means *except*. Rewrite the phrase on the lines below, replacing *but* with *except*.

____

____

____

not remove the deep sorrow that dwelt in my young bosom. Indeed, these, in time, came only to deepen my sorrow. She had changed; and the reader will see that I had changed, too. We were both victims of the same **overshadowing** evil—*she*, as mistress, *I*, as slave. I will not **censure** her harshly; she cannot censure me, for she knows I speak but the truth, and have acted in my **opposition** to slavery, just as she herself would have acted, in a reverse of circumstances.

◆ ◆ ◆

Everyday Words

overshadowing (oh ver SHAD oh ing) *adj.* seeming more important than something else; overwhelming

censure (SEN shuhr) *v.* condemn as wrong

opposition (ahp uh ZI shuhn) *n.* strong disagreement with, or protest against, something

Thinking About the Selection

1. One way to think about someone's life is as a series of causes and effects. Douglass's reading lessons and the end of these lessons had several effects on his life. Identify the effect of each cause listed below.

Cause		Effect
Mrs. Auld decides that she does not want Douglass to continue learning to read.	_	
Douglass uses his white playmates as teachers.	_	
Douglass discusses slavery with his friends and becomes aware of the restrictions of slavery.	_	

2. Douglass draws the conclusion that slavery _________________________
   ____.

TALK **ABOUT IT** **Agree or Disagree?** Douglass says that education and slavery are incompatible. With a partner, discuss whether you agree or disagree with this statement and why. Use this sentence starter.

I agree (or disagree) that education and slavery are incompatible

because ____.

Writing About the Essential Question

How does literature shape or reflect society? What personal qualities do you think helped Douglass become an effective champion of human rights?

____

____

Parts of Speech

A noun is a person, a place, a thing, an activity, a quality, or an idea. A verb describes an action, an experience, or a state of being. Some words can function as both nouns and verbs. Use the position in the sentence and the context to determine the correct part of speech.

Examples

Word	Noun	Verb
flood	a very large amount of water that covers an area that is usually dry	cover a place with water
park	a large open area with grass and trees	put a car or other vehicle in a perticular place for a period of time
round	one of the parts of a competition that you have to finish or win before you can go on to the next part	go around something, such as a bend or the corner of a building

Now You Do It

Read the sentences below. Determine whether the underlined word in each sentence is a noun or a verb.

1. a) _________ The <u>flood</u> destroyed homes.

   b) _________ The water will <u>flood</u> the basement.

2. a) _________ Please <u>park</u> the car near the store.

   b) _________ The young children played baseball in the <u>park</u>.

3. a) _________ The runners will <u>round</u> the bend in a few minutes.

   b) _________ She will play in the final <u>round</u> of the game.

TALK ABOUT IT **Have a Conversation** With a partner, have a conversation that includes the words *park* and *round* as both nouns and verbs.

WRITE ABOUT IT **Noun and Verb** Write three sentences that include the words from this lesson. Select one word to appear in each sentence, and use the word as both parts of speech.

Vocabulary

Listen to each word. Say it. Then, read the definition and the example sentence.

chariot (CHAR ee uht) *n.* A **chariot** is a vehicle with two wheels pulled by a horse and was used in ancient times in battles and races.
The chariot raced ahead of the marching soldiers.

oppressed (uh PREST) *v.* Someone who is **oppressed** is kept down by a cruel or unjust power.
The dictator oppressed his people to maintain control over them.

smite (SMYT) *v.* When you **smite** someone, you kill him with a powerful blow.
The little boy was going to smite the ants with a rock.

Vocabulary Practice

Read the first sentence in each group of three. Then, complete Sentence *a* by substituting another word or phrase that means the same as the underlined vocabulary word. Complete Sentence *b* with your own ideas and words.

1. The carpenter built a model of an ancient chariot.

   a. The carpenter built a model of an ancient ________________.

   b. ________________________________ a model of an ancient chariot.

2. Unfair voting laws oppressed women's interests.

   a. Unfair voting laws ______________ women's interests.

   b. ________________________________ oppressed women's interests.

3. The soldier planned to smite his enemy.

   a. The soldier planned to ______________ his enemy.

   b. The soldier planned to smite ________________________________.

Getting Ready to Read

Spirituals bring comfort and hope to people. These songs remind people of their beliefs and provide a sense of community. When you feel sad, what songs or music do you listen to? Tell a partner why you listen to this music.

Go Down, Moses • Swing Low, Sweet Chariot

Summaries In **"Go Down, Moses,"** the singer tells the story of Moses following God's command to free the Israelites from Egypt. Moses tells the Pharaoh to "let my people go!" or God will punish the Egyptians. In the spiritual **"Swing Low, Sweet Chariot,"** the chorus describes a chariot coming to take the singer home to heaven. The singer also describes crossing the river Jordan with a band of angels. If listeners get to heaven first, they are encouraged to tell everyone that the singer is on the way.

Note-taking Guide

Write down the **symbols** that you see in these spirituals. Symbols are words that stand for something else. Write a brief phrase that explains what you think the symbol stands for. Use your prior knowledge of slavery in the American South.

Symbols	Possible Meaning
chariot	way to escape from slavery; Underground Railroad

Thinking About the Selections

1. These two spirituals share many common features. Fill in the chart below with information from the songs.

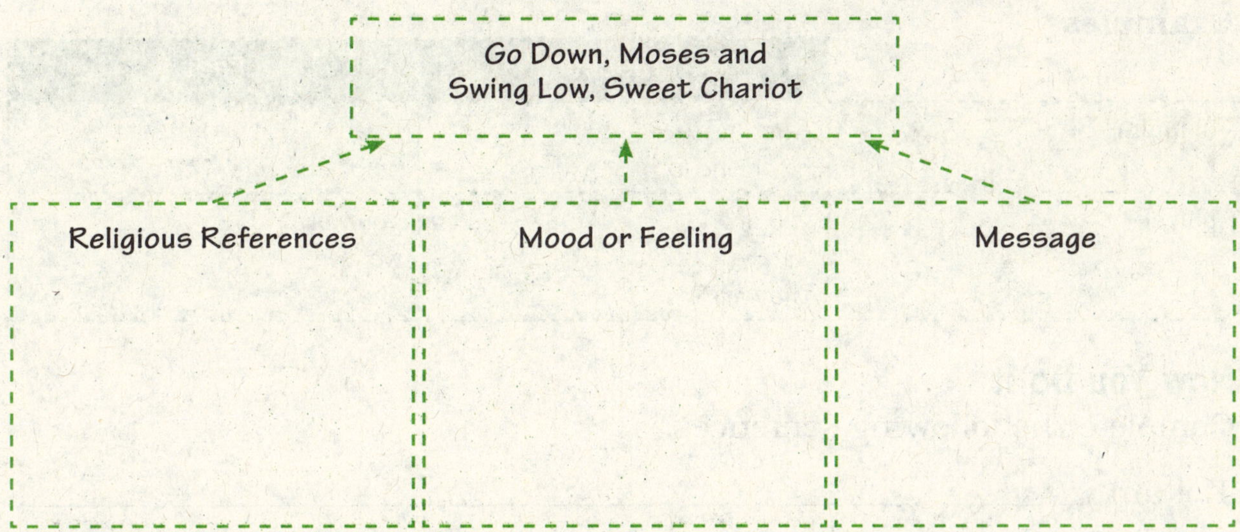

2. Both songs tell listeners that the singers are ________________________

____.

TALK ABOUT IT **Understand Symbols** American slaves were not allowed to talk openly about their desires for freedom. Many spirituals contain symbols or references that represent something other than what they say. For example, the Pharaoh is a character from the Bible. He may also represent slave holders. What other symbols do these songs contain? Discuss some of the songs' other symbols with a partner.

Writing About the Essential Question

What is the relationship between place and literature? What qualities do the places described in these songs have? How do they compare to the actual places inhabited by the slaves?

____

____

Irregular Verbs

To form the past and past participle of a regular verb, add the suffix *-d* or *-ed* to the base word *(call, called)*. Irregular verbs do not follow this pattern, and past and past participle forms are created in other ways. The verb *to be* is irregular.

Examples

	Present	Past
singular	I am he or she is	I was he or she was
plural	you are we are they are	you were we were they were

Now You Do It

Complete the following sentences.

1. I am ____.

2. We are ____.

3. She was ____.

4. They were ______________________________________.

TALK ABOUT IT **Conduct an Interview** Interview a partner about what he or she did last weekend. Ask questions such as "What were your plans for the weekend?" or "Were you happy with the weekend?" Use the different forms of the verb *to be* in both questions and answers.

WRITE ABOUT IT **Write a Summary** Use the information from the interview to write a summary of your partner's weekend. Use complete sentences to describe the weekend. Include present and past-tense forms of the verb *to be*. When you have completed your description, exchange it with a partner. Review and correct your partner's work.

____

____

____

Vocabulary

Listen to each word. Say it. Then, read the definition and the example sentence.

consecrate (KON suh krayt) *v.* To **consecrate** something means to state in a religious ceremony that something is holy and can be used for religious purposes.

The reverend will consecrate the new church this Sunday.

anarchy (AN ar kee) *n.* **Anarchy** is a situation in which there is no order, and people are not obeying the rules.

Anarchy erupted when the teacher left the classroom.

redress (ree DRES) *n.* **Redress** is money that someone pays you because he or she has caused you harm or damaged property.

The owner sought redress from the vandals in court.

Vocabulary Practice

Read the first sentence in each group of three. Then, complete Sentence *a* by substituting another word or phrase that means the same as the underlined vocabulary word. Complete Sentence *b* with your own ideas and words.

1. The president plans to <u>consecrate</u> the famous battlefield.

   a. The president plans to _______________ the famous battlefield.

   b. The president plans to consecrate _____________________________.

2. There was <u>anarchy</u> after the team won the game.

   a. There was _______________ after the team won the game.

   b. There was anarchy after _____________________________.

3. Oppressed groups sought <u>redress</u> from the government.

   a. Oppressed groups sought _______________ from the government.

   b. Oppressed groups sought redress _____________________________.

Getting Ready to Read

In thinking about the American Civil War, both Lincoln and Lee seem aware that they are involved in making history. Which current events do you think will be written about in history books? Why? Discuss your ideas with a partner.

The Gettysburg Address
Abraham Lincoln

Letter to His Son
Robert E. Lee

Summaries Lincoln delivers a brief speech to honor those who died at the battle of Gettysburg, Pennsylvania. In **"The Gettysburg Address,"** he calls on people to continue fighting to preserve the Union.

Robert E. Lee writes this **"Letter to His Son"** shortly before the Civil War starts. Lee discusses the conflict he feels over his belief in the Union and his commitment to his home state of Virginia.

Note-taking Guide

Use this chart to write down the main points from the selections.

	The Gettysburg Address	Letter to His Son
Point 1	The nation was formed around the idea that all men are created equal.	Washington would be sad to see what had happened to the nation he fought hard to form.
Point 2		
Point 3		
Point 4		

Thinking About the Selections

1. Use the chart below to compare and contrast the ideas of Lincoln and Lee. Write differences in the columns labeled *Lincoln* and *Lee*. Write similarities in the center column.

Lincoln	Similarities	Lee
1. feels obligated to the dead soldiers	1. references to founding fathers	1. believes that the Southern states deserve redress
2.	2.	2.
3.	3.	3.

2. Lee has an internal conflict regarding his loyalties to _______________

____.

TALK ABOUT IT **Identify Ideals** What ideals or principles of the United States do you believe are most important? Are there any ideals that you would fight for? Why? Use these sentence starters to discuss your ideas with a partner.

I believe that _____________________ is important because _________

____.

I believe that _____________________ is worth fighting for because

____.

? Writing About the Essential Question

How does literature shape or reflect society? Based on these selections, how do you think both Lincoln and Lee define American patriotism?

Word Families

Groups of words that share the same base word are called word families. A base word can stand alone or serve as the basis of new words. Often, new words are formed by adding affixes—such as prefixes, suffixes, verb endings, and other words—to the base word.

Examples

Base Word	Words in the Word Family	Definition
inform: *v.* officially tell someone about something or provide information	information	*n.* facts or details that tell you about something
	informative	*adj.* providing many useful facts or ideas
	uninformed	*adj.* not having enough knowledge or information
	informer	*n.* someone who tells the police or other officials about criminal activities, especially for money

Now You Do It

In each sentence below, add the missing letters to the base word *inform* so that the sentence makes sense. Some words may need only a prefix or only a suffix.

1. Someone who is ____inform____ does not have enough information to make a considered decision.

2. The ____inform____ told police about the gang.

3. The magazine was very ____inform____ and contained many facts about the event.

4. The manual provided a great deal of ____inform____ about the operation of the electric mixer.

TALK ABOUT IT **Talk About Research** Tell a partner about a research project that you have done. What information did you gather? Which sources were informative? What was the effect of being informed about this topic? What consequences do uninformed people suffer?

WRITE ABOUT IT **Write Research Tips** Write five tips or suggestions for other researchers. Use words that belong to the *inform* word family in your tips. Post your tips as a classroom resource.

Vocabulary

Listen to each word. Say it. Then, read the definition and the example sentence.

dismissed (dis MIST) *v.* When someone is **dismissed,** he or she is fired, or removed from a job.

The manager dismissed the employee who was frequently late.

ascended (uh SEND id) *v.* When something has **ascended,** it has moved up through the air.

The plane ascended rapidly during takeoff.

assault (uh SAWLT) *n.* **Assault** is the crime of attacking someone.

Many birds will assault an invader to protect their nests.

Vocabulary Practice

Read the first sentence in each group of three. Then, complete Sentence *a* by substituting another word or phrase that means the same as the underlined vocabulary word. Complete Sentence *b* with your own ideas and words.

1. The boss dismissed employees who did not follow policy.

   a. The boss _______________ employees who did not follow policy.

   b. The boss dismissed ____ .

2. The women ascended the mountain with courage.

   a. The women _______________ the mountain with courage.

   b. The women ascended the mountain _____________________________ .

3. My cats assault rabbits in the yard.

   a. My cats _______________ rabbits in the yard.

   b. My cats assault ____ .

TALK ABOUT IT ## Getting Ready to Read

After the Civil War ended, Congress passed laws that ended slavery and assured civil rights. However, legislation often does not change people's thinking or their behavior. Discuss how society can change people's thinking or behavior with regard to discrimination.

An Account of an Experience with Discrimination
Sejourner Truth

Summary In **"An Account of an Experience With Discrimination,"** Sojourner Truth tells about the discrimination that she experiences six months after the end of the Civil War.

Note-taking Guide
Use this chart to record the events of the selection.

Truth tries to hail a streetcar, but it will not stop for her.

Thinking About the Selection

1. Sojourner Truth files a legal action against a streetcar conductor. In a court, one must present evidence to support a claim. Fill in the graphic organizer by recording evidence of discrimination against Sojourner Truth.

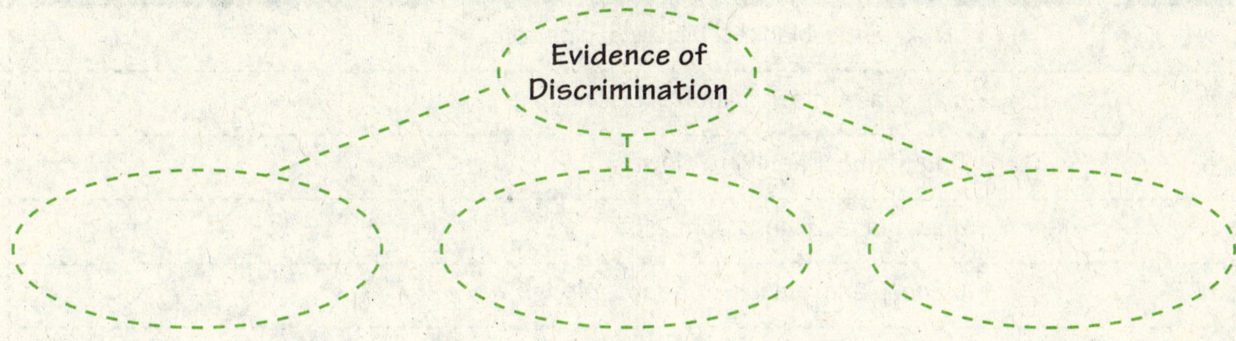

2. According to Truth, "the old slaveholding spirit" ________________________

____.

TALK ABOUT IT **Assess Social Change** Truth says that the thinking that leads to discrimination must end. She makes this statement in 1865. It is now the twenty-first century. Has this thinking ended, or is it still present? Discuss your opinion with a partner. Use this sentence frame.

Today, the thinking that leads to discrimination has (or has not)

ended. I believe it has (or has not) ended because ________________

____.

Writing About the Essential Question

What makes American Literature American? What does Truth's account suggest about the individual's responsibility to act with courage to promote positive social change?

____

____

Consonant *-l* Blends

In a consonant blend, two or three consonants blend to make a single sound. The consonant blends *bl-*, *cl-*, *fl-*, *gl-*, *pl-*, and *sl-* are called initial consonant blends because they appear at the beginnings of words.

Examples

Blend	Examples
bl-	black, blade, blanket, blizzard, blossom
cl-	clap, class, clean, climate, clothing
fl-	flag, flame, flashlight, flower, fluid
gl-	glad, glass, glide, gloom, glue
pl-	place, plane, player, pleasant, pledge
sl-	sled, sleep, slice, slipper, slowly

Now You Do It

Write the correct consonant blend to begin each word below. Refer to the chart above for help. After you have completed the word, say it aloud to practice the consonant blends.

_____ack   _____ace   _____ower   _____ad   _____imate

_____ag   _____anket   _____ean   _____ed   _____easant

TALK ABOUT IT **Ask and Answer Questions** Use words from the chart to ask a partner three questions. For example, "What color is the blanket?" Your partner should answer by repeating words from the question. For example, "The blanket is black." After you have asked three questions, answer three questions from your partner.

WRITE ABOUT IT **Write Silly Sentences** Use all five words for each blend to write silly sentences. For example, "The black blanket kept me warm during a blizzard while I waited for blade blossoms to bloom." Read each sentence aloud two or three times.

Magazine Articles

About Magazine Articles

A **magazine article** is a piece of writing that provides information about a topic. Magazines may be printed or on the Internet. Students may use magazine articles to research subjects that interest them. An abstract is a summary of an article's main ideas and important details. Sometimes it includes illustrations. Abstracts are available for some articles, either at the beginning of the article or in a separate publication. By reading the abstract first, researchers can determine whether a magazine article will provide the information that they need.

Reading Skill

Magazine articles and abstracts use text features, words, and illustrations to present information in a logical and pleasing way. An article's text format is the placement of text around design elements. Text features include headings, captions, and bold and italic print. Design elements include pictures and maps. The text format makes important information stand out. When you **evaluate text format,** you examine text and design features to determine the importance of the information.

Use the graphic organizer below to guide you as you read "A Community's Roots."

Note-Taking Strategy	When to Use
Anecdotal Scripting (highlighting texts and making marginal notes)	When first surveying a source (only on a personal copy or photocopy)
Outlining	When you want to extract key points or trace a line of reasoning
Making an Annotated Bibliography	When you want to keep track of information in a wide variety of sources
Concept Mapping	When many concepts are linked

ARCHAEOLOGY

A Publication of the Archaeological Institute of America

abstracts

Volume 59 Number 6, November/December 2006

The title, date, volume, and number of the source magazine for this article are clearly identified.

A Community's Roots

by Samir S. Patel

With Frederick Douglass's help, the past and present come together on a Maryland plantation.

The first section of the abstract includes an element from the article.

In Talbot County, Eastern Shore, State of Maryland, near Easton, the county town, there is a small district of country, thinly populated, and remarkable for nothing that I know of more than for the worn-out, sandy, desert-like appearance of its soil, the general dilapidation of its farms and fences, the indigent and spiritless character of its inhabitants, and the prevalence of ague and fever. It was in this dull, flat, and unthrifty district or neighborhood, bordered by the Choptank river, among the laziest and muddiest of streams surrounded by a white population of the lowest order, indolent and drunken to a proverb, and among slaves who, in point of ignorance and indolence, were fully in accord with their surroundings, that I, without any fault of my own, was born, and spent the first years of my childhood.

—Frederick Douglass,
 Life and Times of Frederick Douglass (1881)

(National Portrait Gallery, Smithsonian Institution/Art Resource)

The summary of the full article begins here.

Under the boughs of a huge tulip poplar, buried among clumps of roots and piles of oyster shells, is the brick foundation of a building, a remnant of a once-thriving slave community. For 18 months in the early nineteenth century, it was home to a young Frederick Douglass, the future African-American statesman, diplomat, orator, and author. Here, at the age of seven or eight, a shoeless, pantless, precocious Douglass first saw whippings and petty cruelties. Here, he first realized he was a slave. "A lot of the horror that comes through his autobiographies is grounded in those months that he was there," says James Oakes, a historian at the City University of New York who is working on a book about Douglass's relationship with Abraham Lincoln. The modest excavation at Wye House Farm,

Archaeologist Mark Leone and site supervisor Jenn Babiarz show the site to Derek Lloyd, an engineer at Howard University who may be descended from slaves who lived on the farm. (Samir S. Patel)

Photographs and captions from the actual article make this a particularly useful abstract.

a 350-year-old estate on Maryland's Eastern Shore, has yielded sherds, buttons, pipe stems, beads, and precious knowledge about everyday slave life, and is allowing the descendants of that slave community, many of whom live in the nearby rural African-American town of Unionville, to reclaim a lost cultural heritage.

A team of archaeologists and students started digging here in 2005 after archaeologist Lisa Kraus proposed the dig, on the basis of Douglass's descriptions of the site, to Mark Leone, director of the urban archaeology field school at the University of Maryland. Before beginning the excavation, Leone approached St. Stephen's African Methodist Episcopal Church, the social and religious center of Unionville, to ask what the people of the community wanted to learn from the archaeology. "You should ask the people who think it's their heritage what they want to know about it," Leone says. "The answers automatically dissolve the difference between then and now." This, he adds, is the heart of social archaeology, working with descendant communities and understanding that the past and present inform one another. The people of Unionville wanted to know about slave spirituality, what remained of African life, how the owner of the slaves did or did not support freedom, and how slaves found the strength to survive. They are questions a single dig is unlikely to answer, but they have opened an avenue of dialogue between the archaeologists and the people to whom their work matters most.

Pete Quantock, a University of Maryland student, profiles the site of a workshop, where slaves probably both slept and worked. (Samir S. Patel)

Samir S. Patel is an associate editor at ARCHAEOLOGY.
© 2006 by the Archaeological Institute of America

Thinking About the Magazine Article Abstract

1. Whose home is being excavated on Maryland's Eastern Shore?

   ____

2. Why did the archeologists talk with community members before starting the dig?

   ____

   ____

TALK ABOUT IT Reading Skill

3. How useful will the article "A Community's Roots" be to someone who needs information on recent archeological digs? How do you know?

   ____

   ____

4. How can a reader use the photographs to evaluate the usefulness of the article to someone who wants information about trees? How do you know?

   ____

   ____

WRITE ABOUT IT Timed Writing: Persuasive Essay (25 minutes)

Use the Periodical Abstract and the Government Form to write a persuasive essay about the importance of archeology and the need to keep records of history. Take a position about the types of information historians should strive to preserve, making references to the information in both documents. Allow approximately five minutes for prewriting and planning, ten minutes for drafting, and ten minutes for revising and editing.

Vocabulary

These words appear in the stories. Listen to each word. Say it. Then, read the definition and the example sentence.

transient (TRAN zee ent) *adj.* Something that is **transient** continues only for a short time.

He had transient dreams of being a fire fighter and a police officer.

prodigious (pruh DI jus) *adj.* Something that is **prodigious** is of great size or power.

The runner made a prodigious effort just before the finish line.

afflicted (uh FLIKT id) *adj.* Someone who is **afflicted** is suffering or affected by something in an unpleasant way.

The doctors spent days trying to find a cure for the afflicted patient.

Vocabulary Practice

Read the first sentence in each group of three. Then, complete Sentence *a* by substituting another word or phrase that means the same as the underlined vocabulary word. Complete Sentence *b* with your own ideas and words.

1. The boy's <u>transient</u> success was replaced by poor grades.

    a. The boy's _______________ success was replaced by poor grades.

    b. The boy's transient success _________________________________.

2. The <u>prodigious</u> protest resulted in changes in government.

    a. The _______________ protest resulted in changes in government.

    b. The prodigious protest _________________________________.

3. The <u>afflicted</u> horse made moaning sounds.

    a. The _______________ horse made moaning sounds.

    b. The afflicted horse _________________________________.

Getting Ready to Read

The first steamboat made its way along the Mississippi River in 1811. A river culture soon developed. Twain and his friends longed to become steamboatsmen because this culture was part of their childhoods. Tell a classmate what job you hope to have when you are grown and why.

The Boys' Ambition *from* Life on the Mississippi • The Notorious Jumping Frog of Calaveras County

Mark Twain

Summaries In **"The Boys' Ambition,"** a boy dreams of becoming a steamboat captain. This selection comes from the book *Life on the Mississippi.* In that book Mark Twain shares the thoughts and hopes of a young boy who grows up along the Mississippi River. **"The Notorious Jumping Frog of Calaveras County"** is a humorous tale about a betting man and his frog.

Note-taking Guide

As you read, use this chart to explore Twain's purposes, or reasons, for writing in each selection.

The Boys' Ambition

Author's Purpose	Examples From Text
To inform	
To entertain	
To persuade	
To reflect	

The Notorious Jumping Frog of Calaveras County

Author's Purpose	Examples From Text
To inform	
To entertain	
To persuade	
To reflect	

The Notorious Jumping Frog of Calaveras County

Mark Twain

A friend of the narrator's asks him to call on talkative old Simon Wheeler. The friend says he wants news of his friend Reverend Leonidas W. Smiley. Instead, Wheeler tells the narrator a **long-drawn-out** story about Jim Smiley. As he tells the story, Wheeler never smiles, and he never frowns.

◆ ◆ ◆

"Rev. Leonidas W. H'm, Reverend Le—well, there was a feller here once by the name of Jim Smiley, in the winter of '49—or maybe it was the spring of '50—I don't **recollect** exactly, somehow, though what makes me think it was one or the other is because I remember the big flume[1] warn't finished when he first come to the camp; but anyway, he was the curiousest man about always betting on anything that turned up you ever see, if he could get anybody to bet on the other side; and if he couldn't he'd change sides.

◆ ◆ ◆

Wheeler says Smiley was lucky. He almost always won his bets. He'd bet on horse races, dog fights, cat fights, and chicken fights. If he saw two birds sitting on a fence, he'd bet on which bird would fly first. He had several animals he'd bet on: a mare, a small bull-pup named Andrew Jackson, and lots of others. One day he caught a frog, taught him to catch flies, and named him Dan'l Webster.

◆ ◆ ◆

Everyday Words

long-drawn-out (lawng drawn OWT) *adj.* continuing for a longer time than is wanted or necessary

recollect (rek uh LEKT) *v.* remember

---

1. **flume** (FLOOM) *n.* artificial channel for carrying water to provide power and transport objects

---

TAKE NOTES

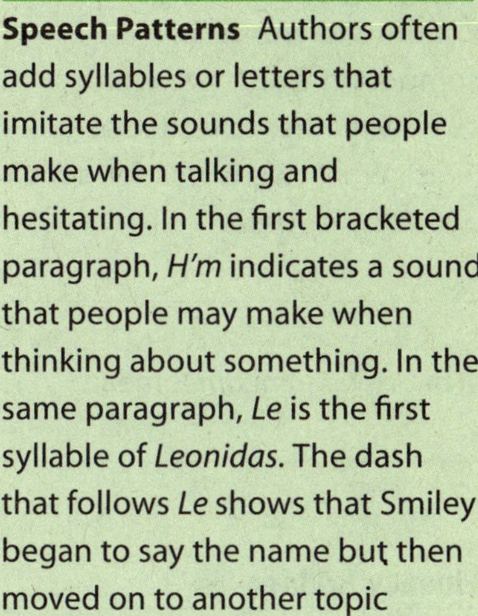

Vocabulary Builder

Speech Patterns Authors often add syllables or letters that imitate the sounds that people make when talking and hesitating. In the first bracketed paragraph, *H'm* indicates a sound that people may make when thinking about something. In the same paragraph, *Le* is the first syllable of *Leonidas*. The dash that follows *Le* shows that Smiley began to say the name but then moved on to another topic without saying the entire name.

Cultural Understanding

This story contains many examples of dialect, which Twain uses to imitate characters' ways of speaking. Some examples are *warn't* for *wasn't*, *feller* for *fellow*, *acrost* for *across*, *sorter* for *sort of*, *resk* for *risk*, *kinder* for *kind of*, *hisself* for *himself*, *ketched* for *caught*, and *better'n* for *better than*.

Vocabulary Builder 

Parts of Speech As a noun, *bet* means "an agreement to risk money on the result of a game, race, or other event." As a verb, it means "risk money on the result of a game, race, or other event." In the second bracketed paragraph, circle each *bet* or *bets* that is used as a noun, and draw a box around each *bet* or *bets* that is used as a verb.

Vocabulary Builder 

Compound Words In a compound word, two words come together to form one word. What two words form the word *sometimes?*

____

What does *sometimes* mean?

____

Fluency Builder

Lines of dialogue appear between quotation marks. With a partner, read aloud the dialogue in the bracketed passage. One person should read Smiley's lines, and the other should read the feller's lines. Be sure to speak slowly and with expression. Try to imitate the characters' tone and dialect.

Vocabulary Builder 

Nonstandard English The nonstandard contraction *ain't* can mean "am not," "is not," "are not," "do not," or "does not." It is considered incorrect, although it is often used in spoken English. Rewrite the underlined sentence, changing the expression *ain't got no* to standard English.

____

____

____

Well Smiley kep' the beast in a little lattice box and he used to fetch him **downtown** sometimes and lay for a bet. One day a feller—a stranger in the camp, he was—come acrost him with his box, and says:

"What might it be that you've got in the box?"

And Smiley says, sorter **indifferent**-like, "It might be a parrot, or it might be a canary, maybe, but it ain't—it's only just a frog."

And the feller took it, and looked at it careful, and turned it round this way and that, and says, "H'm—so 'tis. Well, what's *he* good for?"

"Well," Smiley says, easy and careless, "he's good enough for *one* thing, I should judge—he can outjump any frog in Calaveras county."

The feller took the box again, and took another long, particular look, and gave it back to Smiley, and says, very **deliberate,** "Well," he says, "I don't see no p'ints[2] about that frog that's any better'n any other frog."

"Maybe you don't," Smiley says. "Maybe you understand frogs and maybe you don't understand 'em; maybe you've had experience, and maybe you ain't only a amature,[3] as it were. Anyways, I've got *my* opinion, and I'll resk forty dollars that he can outjump any frog in Calaveras county."

And the feller studied a minute, and then says, kinder sad like, "Well, I'm only a stranger here, and I ain't got no frog; but if I had a frog, I'd bet you."

◆　◆　◆

Everyday Words

downtown (down TOWN) *n.* to or in the center or main business area of a town or city

indifferent (in DIF er uhnt) *adj.* not at all interested in someone or something

deliberate (di LIB rit) *adj.* carefully thought out

---

2. **p'ints** dialect for *points,* meaning fine points or advantages

3. **amature** dialect for *amateur* (AM uh chuhr) *n.* someone you think is not very skilled at something

Smiley offers to get the stranger a frog. Smiley leaves his own frog with the stranger while he looks for another frog. The stranger waits.

◆   ◆   ◆

So he set there a good while thinking and thinking to hisself, and then he got the frog out and prized[4] his mouth open and took a teaspoon and filled him full of quailshot[5]—filled him pretty near up to his chin—and set him on the floor. Smiley he went to the swamp and slopped around in the mud for a long time, and finally he ketched a frog, and fetched him in, and give him to this feller, and says:

"Now, if you're ready, set him alongside of Dan'l, with his forepaws just even with Dan'l's, and I'll give the word." Then he says, "One—two—three—*git!*" and him and the feller touched up the frogs from behind, and the new frog hopped off lively, but Dan'l give a heave, and hysted[6] up his shoulders—so—like a Frenchman, but it warn't no use—he couldn't budge; he was planted as solid as a church, and he couldn't no more stir than if he was anchored out. Smiley was a good deal surprised, and he was disgusted too, but he didn't have no idea what the matter was, of course.

The feller took the money and started away, and when he was going out at the door, he sorter jerked his thumb over his shoulder—so—at Dan'l, and says again, very deliberate, "Well," he says, "I don't see no p'ints about that frog that's any better'n any other frog."

Smiley he stood scratching his head and looking down at Dan'l a long time, and at last he says, "I do wonder what in the nation that frog throw'd off for—I wonder if there ain't something the matter with him—he 'pears to

---

4. **prized** (PRYZD) *v.* pried or forced something open

5. **quailshot** small lead pellets used for shooting quail

6. **hysted** dialect for *hoisted,* meaning raised

Comprehension Builder 

Smiley goes to get the stranger a frog so they can race. Predict what will happen next in the story.

____

____

____

Vocabulary Builder 

Multiple-Meaning Words The verb *stir* may mean "move." It may also mean "mix." What does *stir* mean in the underlined sentence? How do you know?

____

____

Vocabulary Builder

Idioms The idiom *what in the nation* expresses surprise or confusion. More familiar idioms, such as *what on earth* and *what in the world,* also express surprise and confusion. About what is Smiley so surprised?

____

____

Vocabulary Builder

Parts of Speech *Pound* can be a noun meaning "a unit for measuring weight." It can also be a verb meaning "hit something very hard several times and make a great deal of noise." Is *pound* a noun or a verb in the first paragraph on this page?

____

Comprehension Builder 

The narrator says that Smiley could *see how it was*. This means that he understood why Dan'l could not move and lost the race. Why couldn't Dan'l move?

____

____

Vocabulary Builder

Common Expressions The expression *took my leave* means "said goodbye and left." Read aloud the last paragraph as it is written. Then, read it again, replacing *took my leave* with another phrase that means the same thing.

look mighty baggy, somehow." And he ketched Dan'l by the nap of the neck, and hefted him, and says, "Why blame my cats if he don't weigh five pound!" and turned him upside down and he **belched** out a double handful of shot. And then he see how it was, and he was the maddest man—he set the frog down and took out after that feller, but he never ketched him. And—

◆　◆　◆

At this point someone calls Wheeler from the front yard. The narrator knows that Wheeler has no information about the Rev. Leonidas W. Smiley, so he starts to leave. He meets Wheeler at the door, and Wheeler says:

◆　◆　◆

"Well, thish-yer Smiley had a yaller[7] one-eyed cow that didn't have no tail, only just a short stump like a bannanner,[8] and—"

However, lacking both time and **inclination,** I did not wait to hear about the afflicted cow, but took my leave.

---

belched (BELCHD) *v.* let air from your stomach come out loudly through your mouth

inclination (in kluh NAY shuhn) *n.* liking or preference

---

7. **yaller** *adj.* dialect for *yellow*

8. **bannanner** *n.* dialect for *banana*

Thinking About the Selections

1. The narrator of "The Boys' Ambition" includes many details that reveal his admiration for the steamboats and the Mississippi River. In the chart below, list some of the details that show the narrator's admiration for the boats and the river.

Admiration for Steamboats and the Mississippi River
1. "Mississippi river shone in the sunshine, contrasting the darkness of the forest."
2.
3.
4.
5.

2. Simon Wheeler tells a long story about Jim Smiley, a man who

____

____.

TALK ABOUT IT **Exaggerate the Truth** Mark Twain is famous for his use of exaggeration. He describes people, items, and events in terms that suggest they are far larger or better than they actually are. Think about an activity or task that you do well. Describe this activity or task to a partner, but do so in terms that exaggerate how well you do it. Use the sentence starter below to begin your description.

I can ___________________________ better than anyone in the world.

Writing About the Essential Question

How does literature shape or reflect society? What image of America do both the excerpt from Twain's memoir and this comic story paint? Consider the sense of place, character, and event.

____

____

Comparative and Superlative Adjectives

A comparative adjective shows an increase in size, quality, or degree between two things. The suffix *-er* is added to most adjectives to make the comparative form. A superlative adjective shows which of several items exhibits a particular characteristic most strongly. The suffix *-est* is used to form superlative adjectives.

Examples

Base Word	Comparative Adjective	Superlative Adjective
small	smaller	smallest
The puppy is small.	The white puppy is smaller than the brown puppy.	The gray puppy is the smallest puppy in the litter.

Now You Do It

Add the suffixes *-er* and *-est* to the base word below. Then, write three sentences using each form of the word.

Base Word	Comparative Adjective	Superlative Adjective
fast		

1. Base word ____

2. Comparative adjective ______________________________________

3. Superlative adjective ______________________________________

TALK ABOUT IT **Classroom Comparison** With a partner, locate items in the classroom that can be compared, such as pencils, erasers, or books. Use the suffixes *-er* and *-est* to make statements of comparison regarding the objects. For example, "The yellow pencil is taller than the blue pencil. The green pencil is the tallest pencil in the cup."

WRITE ABOUT IT **Write a Comparison** Identify two or three activities, such as sports or hobbies, that you can compare. Write a paragraph comparing these activities. Use comparative and superlative adjectives in your comparison. For example, you might write "Soccer moves faster than baseball. Lacrosse is the fastest sport."

Vocabulary

Listen to each word. Say it. Then, read the definition and the example sentence.

conjectural (kuhn JEK cher uhl) *adj.* Something that is **conjectural** is based on guesswork.

His conjectural answer showed that he did not do his homework.

conflagration (kawn fluh GRAY shuhn) *n.* A **conflagration** is a very large fire over a large area that destroys many things.

The conflagration destroyed several hundred acres of the forest.

peremptorily (puh REMP tuh ri lee) *adv.* A person who acts **peremptorily** is not polite and does not want to be argued with.

She decided the plans peremptorily with no input from her friends.

Vocabulary Practice

Read the first sentence in each group of three. Then, complete Sentence *a* by substituting another word or phrase that means the same as the underlined vocabulary word. Complete Sentence *b* with your own ideas and words.

1. The scientist's theory was only <u>conjectural</u>.

   a. The scientist's theory was only _______________.

   b. _________________________________ was only conjectural.

2. The <u>conflagration</u> destroyed a whole city block.

   a. The _______________ destroyed a whole city block.

   b. The conflagration destroyed _________________________________.

3. The boss ended the meeting <u>peremptorily</u> when he walked out.

   a. The boss ended the meeting _______________ when he walked out.

   b. The boss ended the meeting peremptorily _________________________.

Getting Ready to Read

If the outdoor temperature is less than 40 degrees Fahrenheit, a body without extra protection cannot produce enough heat to replace the heat lost to nature. Think about a time when you were cold. What did you do to warm your body? Share your experiences with a partner.

To Build a Fire
Jack London

Summary This story focuses on a man who has been searching for gold in the Yukon, a frozen wilderness in Alaska. The man and his dog are walking toward a camp. The man does not recognize the danger of his journey. He does not realize that the temperature is far too cold for him to be traveling alone. Then, he builds his fire in the wrong place. The man's terrible mistakes turn out to be deadly.

Note-taking Guide

Writers use sensory language to help readers experience a story. Sensory language includes details that relate to the five senses—sight, sound, smell, taste, and touch. Use this diagram to show how London uses sensory language in "To Build a Fire."

Sights	Sounds	Smells	Tastes	Feelings

Thinking About the Selection

1. The man in the story makes a series of poor choices that result in his death. The chart below identifies these choices. In the column labeled Consequence, write the result of each choice. The first has been completed for you.

Choice	Consequence
1. travels alone in extreme cold	has no help when he gets in trouble
2. takes off his mittens to start a fire	
3. builds a fire beneath a snow-filled tree	
4. sits still in the snow and allows himself to fall asleep	

2. The dog obeys the man and stays with him because ________________

____ .

TALK ABOUT IT **Animal Tales** Have you ever had a pet or known someone else's pet? Have you ever visited a zoo? Did you observe loving and loyal behavior in these animals? Did you observe indifferent behavior? Discuss your experience or observations to a partner.

? Writing About the Essential Question

What is the relationship between place and literature? What does London suggest about human strength in the face of nature's power?

____

____

____

____

Multiple-Meaning Words

Many words have several different meanings, depending on their use in a sentence. You can determine the particular meaning of a word by understanding the word's context, or the other words in the sentence or surrounding sentences that provide clues to the meaning of the word.

Examples

Word	Meanings
degree	1. (noun) unit for measuring temperature 2. (noun) certification from an educational institution
hot	1. (adj) high in terperature 2. (adj) difficult or dangerous

Now You Do It

Complete the sentences with words from the chart. Make sure that the word fits the context of the sentence. Then, write the number of the definition shown in the chart.

1. Gretchen earned her college ____________ in four years. ______

2. As the rain began to fill the ditch, Eduard felt that the situation was getting a little ____________. ______

3. The sun is out, and I am feeling ____________. ______

4. When the barbecue started, the temperature had risen several ____________. ______

TALK ABOUT IT **Match the Meaning** Say aloud a sentence that includes one of the words from the lesson. Ask a partner to identify which meaning of the word you used in the sentence. Then, switch roles with your partner.

WRITE ABOUT IT **Write a Dialogue** Use the words from the chart to write a funny dialogue. Use the words to cause misunderstandings. Underline the multiple-meaning words in your dialogue.

Vocabulary

These words are underlined in the story. Listen to each word. Say it. Then, read the definition and the example sentence.

forestall (for STAHL) *v.* When you **forestall** an action or situation, you prevent it from happening by doing something else first.

    The National Guard was sent in to forestall any trouble.

exalted (ig ZAWLT uhd) *adj.* When a person feels **exalted,** he or she is filled with great joy.

    The team was exalted after the championship win.

perception (per SEP shuhn) *n.* **Perception** refers to the way you think about something and your idea of what it is like.

    Her perception of Tom changed when he opened his own business.

Vocabulary Practice

Read the first sentence in each group of three. Then, complete Sentence *a* by substituting another word or phrase that means the same as the underlined vocabulary word. Complete Sentence *b* with your own ideas and words.

1. The mayor tried to forestall the vote by giving a speech.

    a. The mayor tried to ______________ the vote by giving a speech.

    b. The mayor tried to forestall ________________________________.

2. The hard-working student felt exalted at his graduation.

    a. The hard-working student felt ______________ at his graduation.

    b. The hard-working student felt exalted ______________________.

3. The stranger's kindness changed Mary's perception of the city.

    a. The stranger's kindness changed Mary's ______________ of the city.

    b. The stranger's kindness changed Mary's perception ____________.

TALK ABOUT IT ## Getting Ready to Read

Kate Chopin began writing after the death of her husband in 1883. At the time, much of her work was criticized because it challenged people's beliefs regarding women. With a partner, talk about other authors who challenged people's beliefs about women.

The Story of an Hour
Kate Chopin

Summary Mrs. Mallard has just learned that her husband has died in a train accident. She goes to her room, sits in a comfortable armchair, and looks out her window. She feels something she does not understand. She cries for her lost husband but she feels something else she has never felt before—freedom.

Note-taking Guide

Use this chart to make notes about the character of Mrs. Mallard.

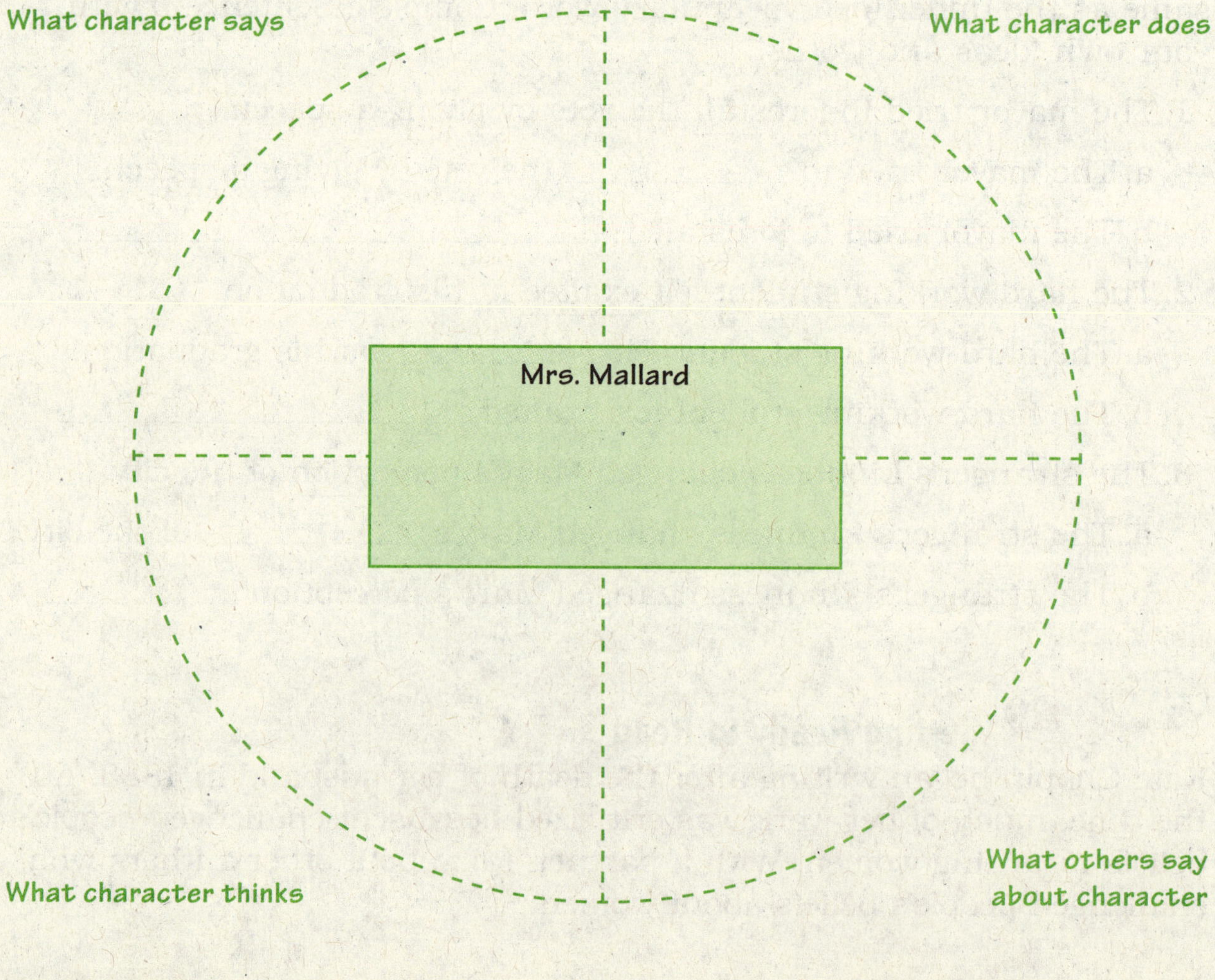

What character says

What character does

Mrs. Mallard

What character thinks

What others say about character

The Story of an Hour
Kate Chopin

Knowing that Mrs. Mallard was afflicted[1] with a heart trouble, great care was taken to break to her as gently as possible the news of her husband's death.

It was her sister Josephine who told her, in broken sentences; veiled[2] hints that revealed in half **concealing.** Her husband's friend Richards was there too, near her. It was he who had been in the newspaper office when intelligence of the railroad disaster was received, with Brently Mallard's name leading the list of "killed." He had only taken the time to **assure** himself of its truth by a second telegram, and had hastened to forestall any less careful, less tender friend in bearing the sad message.

◆ ◆ ◆

Mrs. Mallard bursts out weeping in her sister's arms. She goes to her room alone. There she sits in a chair facing the open window.

◆ ◆ ◆

She could see in the open square before her house the tops of trees that were all aquiver with the new spring life. The delicious breath of rain was in the air. In the street below a peddler was crying his wares.[3] The notes of a distant song which someone was singing reached her faintly, and countless sparrows were twittering in the eaves.

Everyday Words

concealing (kuhn SEEL ing) *n.* hiding something carefully

assure (uh SHYOOR) *v.* check that something is correct or true

---

1. **afflicted** (uh FLIK ted) *adj.* suffering from

2. **veiled** (VAYLD) *adj.* expressed so that something's exact meaning is hidden or unclear

3. **wares** (WAYRZ) *n.* merchandise

Vocabulary Builder

Multiple-Meaning Words The word *intelligence* may mean either "mental ability" or "news." Which meaning is used in the underlined sentence?

____

Vocabulary Builder 

Possessive Nouns An apostrophe and *s ('s)* following a noun indicates possession, or ownership. Circle three possessive nouns in the bracketed paragraphs. Explain what each "possesses."

____

____

____

Comprehension Builder 

Why is Mrs. Mallard crying? What has happened?

____

____

____

Vocabulary Builder

Plural Nouns In English, the most common way to form a plural noun is to add *-s* to the singular form. A noun adds *-es* to form the plural if it ends in *s, x, ch,* or *sh,* as in *patches.*

Fluency Builder

With a partner, take turns reading aloud the two bracketed paragraphs. Read with expression, remembering that Mrs. Mallard has just learned of her husband's death. Be sure to pay attention to punctuation marks.

Vocabulary Builder

Multiple-Meaning Words The noun *will* may refer to a legal document that names those to whom you give your money and property after you have died. It may also mean "what someone wants to happen." In the underlined sentence, *will* means "what someone wants to happen." To say that no one can bend Mrs. Mallard's will or impose his will on her means that no one can tell Mrs. Mallard what to do. Complete this sentence:

Mrs. Mallard realizes that

_______________ will decide how to live the rest of her life.

There were patches of blue sky showing here and there through the clouds that had met and piled one above the other in the west facing her window.

◆ ◆ ◆

Mrs. Mallard still sobs occasionally. She stares dully at the sky. Then, she senses a new emotion coming over her. She tries to fight her new feelings, but her effort is not successful.

◆ ◆ ◆

When she abandoned herself,[4] a little whispered word escaped her slightly parted lips. She said it over and over under her breath: "free, free, free!" The vacant stare and the look of terror that had followed it went from her eyes. They stayed keen and bright. Her pulses beat fast, and the coursing blood warmed and relaxed every inch of her body.

She did not stop to ask if it were or were not a monstrous joy that held her. A clear and exalted perception enabled her to dismiss the suggestion as **trivial.**

She knew that she would weep again when she saw the kind, tender hands folded in death; the face that had never looked save with love upon her, fixed and gray and dead. But she saw beyond that bitter moment a long procession of years to come that would belong to her absolutely. And she opened and spread her arms out to them in welcome.

There would be no one to live for her during those coming years; she would live for herself. There would be no powerful will bending hers in that blind persistence with which men and women believe they have a right to impose a private will upon a fellow creature.

◆ ◆ ◆

Everyday Words

trivial (TRIV i uhl) *adj.* unimportant

4. **abandoned herself** surrendered or gave herself up

Mrs. Mallard reflects on her new-found freedom. Compared to the future, the past matters little. Suddenly she hears her sister Josephine begging her to open the door. Mrs. Mallard dreams of her future life a little longer. She prays for a long life. Then, she opens the door and puts her arm around her sister. They go down the stairs together. At the bottom, Richards stands waiting for them.

◆ ◆ ◆

Someone was opening the front door with a latchkey. It was Brently Mallard who entered, a little travel-stained, composedly[5] carrying his gripsack[6] and umbrella. He had been far from the scene of the accident, and did not know there had been one. He stood amazed at Josephine's **piercing** cry; at Richards's quick motion to **screen** him from the view of his wife.

But Richards was too late.

When the doctors came they said she had died of heart disease—of joy that kills.

Everyday Words

piercing (PEERS ing) *adj.* high, sharp, and unpleasant

screen (SKREEN) *v.* hide, often by getting in front of something

---

5. **composedly** (kum POHZ uhd lee) *adj.* calmly

6. **gripsack** (GRIP sak) *n.* small bag for holding clothes

Vocabulary Builder

Multiple-Meaning Words

The verb *reflects* is often used to say that a surface such as a mirror shows an image of a particular person or thing. The verb may also mean "thinks about something." What does *reflects* mean in the bracketed paragraph?

____

____

Comprehension Builder 

This story has a surprise ending. Summarize what happens as Mrs. Mallard goes down the stairs.

____

____

____

____

____

____

____

Thinking About the Selection

1. Contrast your expectations of Mrs. Mallard's reactions to the actual reactions she has in the story. How did you expect Mrs. Mallard to react to the news that her husband had died? How does she react?

Expected Reaction	Actual Reaction
When Mrs. Mallard learns that her husband is dead, I expect that she will	When Mrs. Mallard learns that her husband is dead, she

2. When Mrs. Mallard learns that Mr. Mallard is not dead, she

____.

TALK ABOUT IT **Find Personal Freedom** When Mrs. Mallard learns of her husband's death, she whispers the word *free*. What does this reaction tell you about the life Mr. and Mrs. Mallard have led together? What do you imagine their marriage to have been like? Discuss your ideas with a partner. Use these sentence starters.

Mrs. Mallard does not feel free in her marriage because ___________.

Mrs. Mallard feels free after her husband's death because _________.

Writing About the Essential Question

How does literature shape or reflect society? How does Chopin emphasize differences between Mrs. Mallard's true self and the ways in which she is perceived?

____

____

____

Irregular Verbs

The past and past participle of a regular verb is formed by adding the suffix *-d* or *-ed* to the base *(play, played, has played)*. The past participle is preceded by another verb, such as *has.* Irregular verbs do not follow this pattern. The past and past participle forms are created in other ways. The verb *to do* is irregular.

Example

Present	Past	Past Participle
I *do*	I *did*	I *have done*
he/she *does*	he/she *did*	he/she *has done*
they *do*	they *did*	they *have done*
we *do*	we *did*	we *have done*
you *do*	you *did*	you *have done*

Now You Do It

Draft a sentence for each tense of the verb. Use the pronoun listed as the subject of the sentence.

1. *(present)* I ____.

2. *(past)* She ____.

3. *(past participle)* They _______________________________.

TALK ABOUT IT   **Ask and Answer** Ask a partner whether he or she has done a particular activity. Your partner should respond using the verb *to do* in the tense that reflects whether he or she has done it, did it once or at a specific time, or does it at the present time. For example, you may ask, "Do you do jumping jacks?" Your partner may answer, "I have done jumping jacks during gym class." Change roles with your partner and answer his or her questions.

WRITE ABOUT IT   **Write an Observational Report** Imagine that you are observing someone in action. For example, you might imagine an athlete at practice, someone cooking a meal, or someone dancing. Consider how he or she moves and what his or her expression looks like. Write a brief description of the person doing the activity. Use each tense of the verb *to do* at least once in your description.

Vocabulary

Listen to each word. Say it. Then, read the definition and the example sentence.

salient (SAY lee uhnt) *adj.* The **salient** points or features of something are the most important or most noticeable parts of it.

Visual aids made the salient points in her presentation stand out.

guile (GYL) *n.* **Guile** is the use of smart but dishonest methods to deceive someone.

The thief's guile allowed him to mystify detectives for several years.

myriad (MEER ee uhd) *adj.* When there is a **myriad** of something, there are many.

The maze has myriad turns.

Vocabulary Practice

Read the first sentence in each group of three. Then, complete Sentence *a* by substituting another word or phrase that means the same as the underlined vocabulary word. Complete Sentence *b* with your own ideas and words.

1. The teacher repeated the salient points of her lecture.

   a. The teacher repeated the _______________ points of her lecture.

   b. The teacher repeated the salient points _______________________.

2. The criminal's guile frustrated the officers.

   a. The criminal's _______________ frustrated the officers.

   b. The criminal's guile _________________________________.

3. The child was enchanted by the myriad toys in the store.

   a. The child was enchanted by the _______________ toys in the store.

   b. The child was enchanted by the myriad _______________________.

Getting Ready to Read

A metaphor is a comparison between two unlike items. A metaphor encourages readers to think about familiar topics in new ways. With a partner, create a metaphor for a problem that exists in your community or in society in general.

Douglass • We Wear the Mask

Paul Laurence Dunbar

Summaries In **"Douglass,"** Dunbar appeals to Frederick Douglass. Douglass was a nineteenth-century abolitionist known for his strong speeches and writing. He worked to gain equal rights for African Americans. In his sonnet to Douglass, Dunbar writes that the fight for equality is not over.

In **"We Wear the Mask,"** Dunbar describes the daily struggles of African Americans. He suggests that African Americans may appear content, but they are not. Dunbar describes how African Americans hide their despair from the eyes of white America.

Note-taking Guide

Use this chart to record the main ideas from each poem and the lines that support those ideas.

"Douglass" Main Idea	Lines that support the main idea

"We Wear the Mask" Main Idea	Lines that support the main idea

Thinking About the Selections

1. In "We Wear the Mask," Dunbar suggests that African Americans show faces to the outside world that hide their true thoughts and feelings. Write details from the poem that describe the mask and details that describe true thoughts and feelings.

Mask	True Thoughts and Feelings
• grins and lies	• torn and bleeding hearts
•	•
•	•
•	•
•	•

2. In "Douglass," the speaker longs for the return of Frederick

   Douglass because ____

   ____.

TALK ABOUT IT **Provide Comfort** In the two poems, the speaker suggests things that provide comfort for African Americans during the difficult fight for civil rights. With a partner, discuss the things in your life that provide comfort when you feel frustrated or sad.

   When I feel frustrated or sad, I ______________________________.

   This provides me with comfort because ____________________.

? Writing About the Essential Question

How does literature shape or reflect society? Based on your reading of these poems, how do you think the expression of personal emotion might lead to social change?

____

____

Idioms

Remember that an idiom is a word or phrase that has a special meaning different from the ordinary meaning of the words. The following idioms contain references to animals.

Examples

Idiom	Meaning	Example sentence
kill two birds with one stone	accomplish two goals or tasks with a single action	I *killed two birds with one stone* by buying stamps and milk at the grocery store.
have butterflies in one's stomach	feel nervous	Gina had *butterflies in her stomach* before the important test.
a wild goose chase	a search for something that one cannot get or achieve	Check that the library has the book so that you don't go on *a wild goose chase*.

Now You Do It

Write a sentence for each idiom.

1. kill two birds with one stone _______________________________

   ____

2. have butterflies in one's stomach ___________________________

   ____

3. a wild goose chase ____

   ____

TALK ABOUT IT   **Back and Forth** Have a conversation with a partner in which you use the idioms that appear in the chart above. Use an idiom in every comment or question to your partner and in every response.

WRITE ABOUT IT   **Where Did It Come From?** Choose one idiom from the chart. Write a fictional explanation of how the idiom came into being. For example, you might write that the phrase *wild goose chase* comes from ancient contests in which athletes tried to outrun wild geese.

____

____

Vocabulary

These words are underlined in the story. Listen to each word. Say it. Then, read the definition and the example sentence.

degenerate (di JEN uh ruht) *adj.* Someone who is **degenerate** has very low standards or moral behavior.

> *The degenerate criminal stole the little girl's piggy bank.*

epitaph (EP uh taf) *n.* An **epitaph** is a short piece of writing on the stone over someone's grave.

> *The epitaph was still clear over two hundred years later.*

chronicles (KRON i kuhlz) *n.* **Chronicles** are records of a series of events written in the order in which they happened.

> *Olivia kept chronicles of her trip around Europe.*

Vocabulary Practice

Read the first sentence in each group of three. Then, complete Sentence *a* by substituting another word or phrase that means the same as the underlined vocabulary word. Complete Sentence *b* with your own ideas and words.

1. The degenerate mayor stole tax dollars to pay for a vacation.

    a. The ______________ mayor stole tax dollars to pay for a vacation.

    b. The degenerate mayor ____.

2. The epitaph included a date of birth and a date of death.

    a. The ______________ included a date of birth and a date of death.

    b. The epitaph included ____.

3. The students read the chronicles of an explorer.

    a. The students read the ______________ of an explorer.

    b. The students read the chronicles ______________________________.

Getting Ready to Read

The poems "Luke Havergal," "Richard Cory," "Lucinda Matlock," and "Richard Bone," have first-person speakers. The speakers are characters in the stories of the poems, and they use the pronouns *I, me, we,* and *us.* Tell a partner a first-person story about life or death.

Luke Havergal • Richard Cory • Lucinda Matlock • Richard Bone

Edwin Arlington Robinson
Edgar Lee Masters

Summaries The two poems by Robinson focus on the pain of loss. In **"Luke Havergal,"** the speaker describes how Luke Havergal is grieving for his beloved. Havergal questions whether he can go on living. In contrast, **"Richard Cory"** describes a whole town in shock and grief over the suicide of a wealthy man.

The two poems by Masters describe characters who have the ability to face life in a changing world. From the grave, both characters speak about their lives. **"Lucinda Matlock"** died when she was ninety-six after a hard but fullfilling life. She does not listen to the complaints of young people who she thinks do not embrace life. **"Richard Bone"** tells the story of the man who carves messages on tombstones.

Note-taking Guide
Use this chart to describe the title character in each poem.

	What character does	Key character trait
Luke Havergal		
Richard Cory		prestige and charm
Lucinda Matlock		
Richard Bone	carves tombstones	

Thinking About the Selections

1. Each of these poems focuses on a character and his or her experiences with life and death. In the chart below, list what you know about each character.

Luke Havergal	Richard Cory	Lucinda Matlock	Richard Bone
1. Luke has lost a love.	1. Richard is well-dressed.	1. Lucinda is dead.	1. Richard is dead.
2.	2.	2.	2.
3.	3.	3.	3.

2. Lucinda Matlock criticizes younger generations for ____.

TALK ABOUT IT **From the Dead** With a partner, identify a famous historical figure with whom you are both familiar. Discuss what this person might say to modern people from his or her grave. Use these sentence starters.

If (name of person) could talk to us from the grave, he (or she)

might say ____.

He (or she) might say these words because ________________________.

Writing About the Essential Question

What is the relationship between place and literature? What image of life in small-town America do these poems project?

____

____

____

Word Families

You will recall that groups of words that share the same base word are called word families. Remember that a base word may stand alone or serve as a basis for new words. New words are formed by changing or adding prefixes and/or suffixes to the base word.

Examples

Base Word	Words in the Word Family	Definition
visible: *adj.* able to be seen	invisible	*adj.* unable to be seen
	visibility	*n.* the distance it is possible to see, especially when this is affected by weather
	visibly	*adv.* in a way that is easy to see or notice

Now You Do It

For each word below, identify whether a prefix or a suffix has been changed or added to the base word to form the new word.

1. invisible ____________

2. visibility ____________

3. visibly ____________

TALK ABOUT IT **Talk About Sight** With a partner, discuss and make lists of things that are *visible* and things that are *invisible*. For example, a ball is visible. Air is invisible. Then, make a list of types of weather that may affect *visibility*.

WRITE ABOUT IT **Write a Character Description** What does someone look like when he or she is visibly upset or happy? Use words from the *visible* word family to write a description of someone who shows a *visible* emotion.

____

____

____

Vocabulary

These words are underlined in the story. Listen to each word. Say it. Then, read the definition and the example sentence.

tremulously (TREM yoo luhs lee) *adv.* When you do something **tremulously,** you are shaking slightly, especially if you are nervous.

Fiona spoke tremulously in front of the large crowd.

inert (i NERT) *adj.* Something that is **inert** is not moving or not having the strength or power to move.

The lion lay inert in the grass, watching its prey.

jocularity (jahk yuh LAR uh tee) *n.* When there is **jocularity** in a situation, there is joking good humor.

The play's jocularity had the audience laughing and applauding.

Vocabulary Practice

Read the first sentence in each group of three. Then, complete Sentence *a* by substituting another word or phrase that means the same as the underlined vocabulary word. Complete Sentence *b* with your own ideas and words.

1. Jade sang tremulously at her first choir practice.

    a. Jade sang ____________ at her first choir practice.

    b. Jade sang tremulously ________________________________.

2. The sick patient lay inert in the hospital bed.

    a. The sick patient lay ____________ in the hospital bed.

    b. The sick patient lay inert ________________________________.

3. The students' jocularity helped them finish the difficult project.

    a. The students' ____________ helped them finish the difficult project.

    b. The students' jocularity ________________________________.

Getting Ready to Read

In his operas, composer Richard Wagner tried to combine music and drama. Discuss with a partner a song or a piece of music that causes strong feelings in you. Explain why the music affects you the way it does.

A Wagner Matinée
Willa Cather

Summary Aunt Georgiana was a music teacher who lived in Boston. She met her husband and moved to the Nebraska Territory. She returns to Boston many years later. The narrator meets her at the train station. He remembers his early years with her in Nebraska. He wants to share something special with her, so he takes her to hear a performance of an opera by Wagner. The narrator is surprised by the effect that the music has on his aunt.

Note-taking Guide

Use this chart to take notes about two important places in this story.

Details about Boston	Details about Nebraska

Thinking About the Selection

1. The narrator helps readers know Aunt Georgiana by describing how she looks when she arrives, giving details about what she does and says, and providing background information about her. In the chart below, write notes about Aunt Georgiana's appearance, actions, and background.

Aunt Georgiana

How She Looks	What She Does and Says	Background Information
1. Yellow skin	1. Voices concerns about forgotten instructions	1. Taught music
2.	2.	2.
3.	3.	3.
4.	4.	4.

2. These three words describe Aunt Georgiana: __________________________

__________________________.

TALK ABOUT IT **Discuss Caretakers** Aunt Georgiana makes sacrifices in her life that allow the narrator to have the life he has. Discuss with a small group a person who has made sacrifices for you. What sacrifices has this person made?

? Writing About the Essential Question

What is the relationship between place and literature? What do you think Cather would say about the importance of artistic and cultural outlets to the health of a community? Do you agree or disagree? Explain.

____

____

Consonant Digraphs

A consonant digraph is a grouping of letters that represent a single sound. For example, the letters -*ch* and -*tch* represent the sound /ch/ at the ends of words. To make the /ch/ sound, try blending the sounds /t/ and /sh/.

Examples

Digraph	Examples
-*ch*	beach, couch, each, lunch, much
-*tch*	catch, ditch, match, scratch, watch

Now You Do It

Use the words from the chart to answer the questions below.

___________ 1. Which word has the same ending sound as *ditch* and refers to a small clock that you can wear on your wrist?

___________ 2. Which words from the list rhyme with *catch*?

___________ 3. Which word has the same ending sound as *much* and refers to a piece of furniture you sit on?

___________ 4. Which word from the list rhymes with *each*?

TALK ABOUT IT **Interview a Partner** Use words from the chart to ask a partner three questions. For example, "What do you catch at the beach?" Your partner should answer by repeating words from the question. For example, "I catch a ball at the beach." Exchange roles. This time, your partner will ask the questions, and you will answer.

WRITE ABOUT IT **Write a Short Poem** Write a short poem that includes at least three words from the chart. For example,

I scratch a match
To watch for owls
In the dark.

Read your poem aloud to a small group of students.

Word Bank

escape	industry	realistic
fortune	lament	skyscraper
heredity	plantation	urban

A. Matching Draw an arrow from each word to its definition in the chart below.

Words	Definition
escape	*n.* the process by which mental and physical qualities are passed from a parent to a child before the child is born
fortune	*adj.* relating to towns and cities
heredity	*n.* a very large amount of money
industry	*n.* a large estate or farm where crops such as cotton are grown
lament	*v.* get away from a place or a dangerous situation
plantation	*n.* the large-scale production of goods or of substances such as coal and steel
realistic	*v.* express feelings of great sadness about something
skyscraper	*n.* a very tall modern city building
urban	*adj.* judging and dealing with situations in a practical way, according to what is actually possible

B. **True or False** Complete the chart by indicating whether each
statement is true or false.

Statement	True or False?
People may travel by horse on a plantation.	
You are likely to find a skyscraper on a farm.	
A wagon is an urban vehicle.	
A person who laments may cry.	
Factories are signs of industry.	
A person may try to escape from a concert.	
Heredity could be responsible for a person's natural hair color.	
If you see a situation in a realistic way, you see things as they are.	
A person who does not work hard is likely to earn a fortune.	

TALK ABOUT IT **Notice Change** American history is about vision and
change. It includes changes to the landscape. People replaced the
wilderness with farms, urban cities, and industry. It also includes
social changes. Women and people of color tried to escape unfair
laws by asking the government to change these laws. With a partner,
discuss any changes that you have noticed in the communities where
you live. Use the vocabulary words in your discussion.

WRITE ABOUT IT **Write About Change** Write a "before-and-after"
description of one of the changes you discussed above. Explain what
your community was like before the change and after it. Be sure to
explain the effects of the change on the community. For example, if
someone added a park to your neighborhood, the effect may be that
people spend more time outdoors exercising. Use the vocabulary words
in your description.

Vocabulary

Listen to each word. Say it. Then, read the definition and the example sentence.

malingers (muh LING gerz) *v.* When you **malinger,** you avoid work by pretending to be sick.

> *Walter sometimes <u>malingers</u> so that he can go out with his friends instead of going to work.*

meticulous (muh TIK yoo luhs) *adj.* Someone who is **meticulous** is extremely careful about details.

> *She was very <u>meticulous</u> when she applied her makeup.*

obtuse (uhb TOOS) *adj.* Someone who is **obtuse** is slow to understand or perceive something.

> *Franklin was <u>obtuse</u> when it came to driving a car for the first time.*

Vocabulary Practice

Read the first sentence in each group of three. Then, complete Sentence *a* by substituting another word or phrase that means the same as the underlined vocabulary word. Complete Sentence *b* with your own ideas and words.

1. The student <u>malingers</u> so that he can stay home from school.

   a. The student ______________ so that he can stay home from school.

   b. The student malingers ________________________________.

2. The <u>meticulous</u> secretary organized both supply closets.

   a. The ______________ secretary organized both supply closets.

   b. The meticulous secretary ________________________________.

3. Ann was not <u>obtuse</u>; she just needed to reread the story.

   a. Ann was not ______________; she just needed to reread the story.

   b. Ann was not obtuse; she just needed ________________________.

Getting Ready to Read

T. S. Eliot is recognized as a great modern poet. In "The Love Song of J. Alfred Prufrock," Eliot writes about pain and loneliness. What situations might make a person feel this way? Share your ideas with a partner.

The Love Song of J. Alfred Prufrock
T. S. Eliot

Summary J. Alfred Prufrock invites someone to go for a walk in a city at evening. The city he describes is gloomy and sad. Then, Prufrock asks some questions about himself: Could he have done more with his life? Can he express love for a woman? Is he able to do anything important? Do the answers to his questions even matter? Prufrock sees himself and others as drowning in a sea of troubles.

Note-taking Guide

Use this chart to record details about the poem.

Question	Your Answer	Detail from the Poem that Tells You
Who is the speaker?		
At what time of day does the poem take place?		
Where does the speaker go?		
What question does the speaker ask?		
What does the speaker seem to feel about himself?		

Thinking About the Selection

1. In this poem, the speaker, J. Alfred Prufrock, asks himself several questions. Three of these questions appear in the column on the left. In the column on the right, explain what this question reveals about Prufrock or his thoughts about himself.

Questions	What the Question Reveals
Do I dare Disturb the universe?	
Is it perfume from a dress That makes me so digress?	
Shall I part my hair behind?	

2. Prufrock asks many questions in the poem because _______________

____

____.

TALK ABOUT IT **Role Play** When Prufrock says that he is not Prince Hamlet, he means that he is not a hero. Instead, he says that he plays the role of the fool. What characteristics of a fool does he describe? What are some other characteristics that you believe a fool might possess? Discuss your ideas with a partner.

I believe that a fool is _______________ because _______________

____.

Writing About the Essential Question

How does literature shape or reflect society? Do you think the poem is simply a portrait of one man, or does it represent something deeper in modern society?

____

____

Prefixes

A prefix is a word part added to the beginning of a base word. A prefix changes the meaning of the base word. The prefixes *en-* and *em-* mean "make someone or something be in a particular state or have a particular quality." The prefix *em-* appears at the start of words that begin with the letter *b, m,* or *p.*

Examples

en + joy = enjoy   If you *enjoy* something, that item or activity makes you feel happy.

em + bitter = embitter   If you *embitter* someone, you cause him or her to have feelings of bitterness, or disappointment.

Now You Do It

Make new words by adding the prefix *en-* or *em-* to each word below. Write a definition for each new word. Consult a dictionary if necessary.

danger ________________ ____

courage ________________ ____

power ________________ ____

TALK ABOUT IT **Offer Encouragement** Ask a partner to identify a situation in which he or she might need encouragement. For example, a partner might need encouragement before playing in an important basketball game. Respond by offering your partner an encouraging pep talk, or short speech intended to give someone confidence. Use at least two of the words from this lesson in your pep talk. Then switch roles, and repeat the exercise.

WRITE ABOUT IT **Write a Dialogue** Using ideas from the previous activity, write a dialogue in which one friend encourages another to do something that he or she may be nervous about attempting. Use at least four of the words from this lesson in your dialogue.

____

____

____

Vocabulary

Listen to each word. Say it. Then, read the definition and the example sentence.

voluminous (vuh LOO muh nuhs) *adj.* **Voluminous** books and documents are very long and contain a lot of detail.

The voluminous textbook helped Troy study for the final exam.

dogma (DAHG muh) *n.* **Dogma** is a particular belief or set of beliefs that people are expected to accept without questioning them.

The country followed the dictator's dogma strictly.

apparition (ap uh RISH uhn) *n.* **Apparition** is the act of appearing or becoming visible.

The apparition of the clouds signaled the approaching storm.

Vocabulary Practice

Read the first sentence in each group of three. Then, complete Sentence *a* by substituting another word or phrase that means the same as the underlined vocabulary word. Complete Sentence *b* with your own ideas and words.

1. The library contained many <u>voluminous</u> books.

   a. The library contained many _______________ books.

   b. _______________________________ contained many voluminous books.

2. The king punished anyone who disagreed with his <u>dogma</u>.

   a. The king punished anyone who disagreed with his _______________.

   b. _______________________ anyone who disagreed with his dogma.

3. The magician's sudden <u>apparition</u> startled the audience.

   a. The magician's sudden _______________ startled the audience.

   b. The magician's sudden apparition _______________________________.

Getting Ready to Read

A poet creates an image in the mind of readers by using descriptive words that appeal to the five senses. Describe an object to a partner, but do not name it. Explain how it looks, sounds, smells, feels, and, if appropriate, tastes. Ask your partner to guess the object.

The Imagist Poets

Summaries In the essay **"A Few Don'ts by an Imagiste,"** Ezra Pound talks about rules for writing Imagist poetry. He says it is important to use few words and to make sure they are strong and specific.

In **"In a Station of the Metro,"** the speaker compares faces in a crowded subway station to flower petals on a tree branch.

In **"The Red Wheelbarrow,"** the speaker describes a wheelbarrow and some chickens.

"This Is Just to Say" is in the style of a personal note. The speaker is sorry for eating plums someone left in the refrigerator.

In **"The Great Figure,"** the speaker describes a moving fire truck.

In **"Pear Tree,"** the speaker describes a tree in bloom.

Note-taking Guide

Use this chart to record the sensory details in each poem.

Poem	Sensory Details
"In a Station of the Metro"	
"The Red Wheelbarrow"	
"This is Just to Say"	
"The Great Figure"	
"Pear Tree"	

Thinking About the Selections

1. The Imagist poets used specific sensory details to describe a single image, or just a few images, in their poems. In the chart below, note the central image that each poem depicts.

Poem	Central Image
"In a Station of the Metro"	
"The Red Wheelbarrow"	
"This is Just to Say"	
"The Great Figure"	
"Pear Tree"	

2. The poem _______________________________ is a good example of the ideas of Ezra Pound's essay "A Few Don'ts" because

____ .

TALK ABOUT IT **Writing with a Purpose** Writers write for different purposes: to inform, to persuade, to describe or explain, or to entertain. Discuss with a partner the purpose of an Imagist poem. Use this sentence frame.

The purpose of an Imagist poem is ______________________

____ .

Writing About the Essential Question

What is the relationship between place and literature? What larger portrait of the American landscape emerges from the common, everyday images in these poems?

____

____

____

Consonant -*r* Blends

In a consonant blend, two or three consonants blend to make a single sound. The consonant blends *br-*, *cr-*, *dr-*, *fr-*, *gr-*, *pr-*, and *tr-* are called initial consonant blends because they appear at the beginnings of words.

Blend	Examples
br-	brain, branch, bread, bring, brush
cr-	crash, crazy, crowd, crunch, crust
dr-	draft, drank, dream, drink, drum
fr-	frame, fresh, friend, from, frozen
gr-	grace, graph, grease, green, ground
pr-	practice, prepare, price, probably, prune
tr-	track, trash, trick, trumpet, truth

Now You Do It

Complete each word by writing the missing consonant blend. After you write each word, say it aloud.

_____aph   _____uth   _____ame   _____ust

_____anch   _____owd   _____actice   _____ice

TALK ABOUT IT   **Question Blender** In a small group, choose a consonant blend to work with. Ask another member of your group a question that uses a word containing that consonant blend. For example, you may select the blend *br-* and ask, "What kind of bread do you like?" The responding student should include in his or her answer as many words as possible that share the consonant blend. For example, "I like brown bread brushed with butter." Have another student select a consonant blend and continue the questions.

WRITE ABOUT IT   **Funny Sentences** Use all five words for each blend to write funny sentences. For example, "Please bring your brain, a branch, some bread, and a brush to breakfast." Read each sentence aloud two or three times.

Vocabulary

Listen to each word. Say it. Then, read the definition and the example sentence.

fortuitous (for TOO i tuhs) *adj.* Something that is **fortuitous** is lucky and happens by chance.

Sanford's day has been fortuitous; he found a $100 bill on the ground.

sinuous (SIN yoo uhs) *adj.* Something that is **sinuous** curves and twists smoothly, like the movements of a snake.

The road up the mountain was sinuous.

mundane (mun DAYN) *n.* Something that is **mundane** is ordinary and not interesting or exciting.

Lionel found his chores mundane, so he decided not to do them.

Vocabulary Practice

Read the first sentence in each group of three. Then, complete Sentence *a* by substituting another word or phrase that means the same as the underlined vocabulary word. Complete Sentence *b* with your own ideas and words.

1. Through <u>fortuitous</u> circumstances, he found the lost dog.

    a. Through ______________ circumstances, he found the lost dog.

    b. Through fortuitous circumstances, he ______________________.

2. The <u>sinuous</u> river curved through the canyon.

    a. The ______________ river curved through the canyon.

    b. The sinuous river ________________________________.

3. Phoebe abandoned her <u>mundane</u> assignment for a movie.

    a. Phoebe abandoned her ______________ assignment for a movie.

    b. Phoebe abandoned her mundane assignment ______________________.

Getting Ready to Read

F. Scott Fitzgerald called the 1920s the "Jazz Age"—a period of wealth, social change, and jazz music. Fitzgerald wrote of the waste and loneliness that lay beneath the excitement. With a partner, discuss both the positive and negative aspects of the present time in America.

Winter Dreams

Summary Dexter Green is the son of a grocer in a small Minnesota town. He loves Judy Jones, the daughter of a wealthy local family. Dexter and Judy meet at a country club when he is fourteen and she is eleven. He is attracted to her and quits his caddying job to avoid the humiliation of carrying her clubs. After college they meet again and begin a serious romance for one summer. Judy, however, does not want a commitment and dates other men. Dexter decides to marry the more sensible Irene Scheerer. On the eve of the engagement, Judy returns. She renews the relationship with Dexter, which causes Dexter to lose Irene. Judy then leaves Dexter once more. Years later, Dexter learns that Judy is now trapped in an unhappy marriage and has lost her beauty.

Note-taking Guide

Use this story map to record the main elements of the story.

Characters	
Setting	
Problem or Conflict	Dexter falls hopelessly in love with Judy, who is a big flirt.
Main Events	1. Dexter meets Judy and dates her. 2. 3. 4. 5.
Ending	

Thinking About the Selection

1. For Dexter Green, Judy Jones is a symbol, or a person who represents something greater than herself. Complete the chart by identifying the different ideas that Judy Jones represents for Dexter Green.

Judy Jones is a symbol of . . .
1. wealth
2. _______________________________
3. _______________________________
4. _______________________________
5. _______________________________

2. Dexter feels some relief when he becomes a soldier because

____

____.

TALK ABOUT IT **Discussing Loss** When Dexter learns that Judy Jones is married and that her beauty has faded, he cries. Why do you think he reacts so emotionally to this news? What does he mean when he says, "that thing is gone"? Discuss your ideas with a partner.

Writing About the Essential Question

How does literature shape or reflect society? Explain what material success did for Dexter and what it did not do. Based on this story, what observations can you make about a materialistic culture? Explain.

____

____

____

____

Idioms

An idiom is a word or phrase that has a special meaning different from the ordinary meaning of the words. The following idioms contain references to the face. Many of these idioms are based on an understanding of the face as a symbol for feelings or identity.

Examples

Idiom	Meaning
face the music	accept the negative consequences for something one has done
lose face	feel embarrassment
save face	protect one's feelings or reputation
put a brave face on something	behave in a way that makes people believe that one is happy or confident when one is not

Now You Do It

Write a sentence for each idiom.

1. face the music

____

____

2. lose face

____

____

3. save face

____

____

4. put a brave face on something

____

____

TALK ABOUT IT **Face the Situation** Generate a list of situations in which someone might have to face the music, in which someone might lose face or save face, and in which someone might have to put a brave face on something. Share your list with a small group, explaining your reasons for selecting each situation.

WRITE ABOUT IT **Facing It** Write a paragraph about a time when you had to face something unpleasant, such as admitting a mistake. Include in your paragraph at least two idioms from the lesson.

Vocabulary

These words are underlined in the story. Listen to each word. Say it. Then, read the definition and the example sentence.

threshed (THRESHT) *v.* If a person has **threshed** plants, he or she has separated the grains or seeds from the rest of the plant.

In the early autumn, the farmer threshed the corn for days.

embankment (im BANGK muhnt) *n.* An **embankment** is a wide wall of earth or stones built to stop water from flooding an area or to support a road or railroad.

Workers built an embankment on the river for protection.

swerved (SWERVD) *v.* Something that **swerved** made a sudden sideways movement while moving forwards.

The cyclist swerved to avoid hitting the rock in the road.

Vocabulary Practice

Read the first sentence in each group of three. Then, complete Sentence *a* by substituting another word or phrase that means the same as the underlined vocabulary word. Complete Sentence *b* with your own ideas and words.

1. The farmer threshed the corn with a special machine.

   a. The farmer ______________ the corn with a special machine.

   b. The farmer threshed ____.

2. Rocks from the embankment sometimes roll onto the train tracks.

   a. Rocks from the ______________ sometimes roll onto the train tracks.

   b. Rocks from the embankment ________________________________.

3. The skateboarder swerved to avoid a crack in the sidewalk.

   a. The skateboarder ______________ to avoid a crack in the sidewalk.

   b. The skateboarder swerved to avoid ______________________________.

Getting Ready to Read

Today many species of turtles are threatened with extinction. In this story, the turtle barely survives an encounter with a truck. Tell a partner about a conflict between humans and nature that you saw or read about.

The Turtle *from* The Grapes of Wrath

John Steinbeck

Summary A turtle crawls over some grass toward a highway. As he moves, some wild oat seeds become attached to the turtle's legs. With great effort, the turtle gets onto the highway. One car nearly hits the turtle. Another vehicle does hit the turtle, and it rolls off the highway onto its shell. After some time, the turtle rolls itself over. As it rolls, the wild oat seeds fall onto the ground. As the turtle moves, it drags dirt over the seeds.

Note-taking Guide

Complete the following sequence chart.

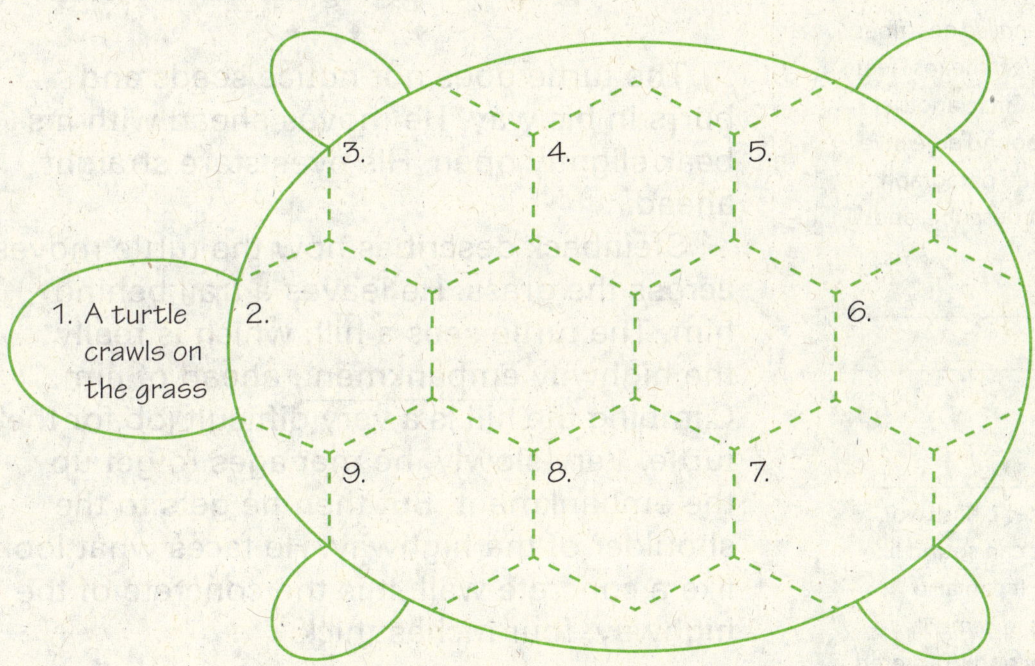

Cultural Understanding

John Steinbeck wrote *The Grapes of Wrath* in the 1930s during the Great Depression. The Great Depression was a time of hardship for many Americans. People lost jobs and homes, and they often did not have enough money to buy food and clothing. In the Midwest, drought made matters worse. Drought is a long period of dry weather when there is not enough water for plants and animals to live.

Vocabulary Builder 

Compound Words *Yellow-nailed* is a compound adjective. The two words that form a compound adjective are often joined by a hyphen (-). *Yellow-nailed* describes *feet. Yellow-nailed feet* means "feet with yellow nails." Circle another hyphenated compound adjective in the first bracketed paragraph. What noun does it describe, and what does it mean?

____

____

Fluency Builder 

In English, the letter *c* has two pronunciations. It can sound like a *k*, as in *concrete*. It can also sound like an *s*, as in *cement*. Read aloud the second bracketed passage. What sound does *c* have in each of these words from this page? Write *k* or *s*.

__ notice   __ across   __ climbing

__ carried   __ faces   __ covered

The Turtle *from* The Grapes of Wrath

John Steinbeck

Steinbeck opens by describing the land at the edge of a concrete highway. It is covered with a mat of dry grass full of **various** kinds of seeds. The seeds are waiting to be picked up by passing animals or to be carried by the wind.

Steinbeck continues by saying that the sun warms the grass. In the shade of the grass, many insects live.

◆ ◆ ◆

And over the grass at the roadside a land turtle crawled, turning aside for nothing, dragging his high-domed shell over the grass. His hard legs and yellow-nailed feet threshed slowly through the grass, not really walking, but **boosting** and dragging his shell along.

◆ ◆ ◆

The turtle does not notice seeds and burrs in his way. He moves ahead with his beak slightly open. His eyes stare straight ahead.

Steinbeck describes how the turtle moves across the grass. He leaves a trail behind him. The turtle sees a hill, which is really the highway embankment, ahead of him. Climbing the hill is a very difficult job for the turtle. Very slowly, he manages to get up the embankment. But then he gets to the shoulder of the highway. He faces what looks like a concrete wall. It is the concrete of the highway, four inches thick.

◆ ◆ ◆

Everyday Words

various (VER ee uhs) *adj.* several different types of something
boosting (BOOST ing) *v.* lifting or pushing

As though they worked independently the **hind** legs pushed the shell against the wall. The head upraised and **peered** over the wall to the broad smooth plain of cement.

◆ ◆ ◆

After much straining, the turtle lifts itself on the edge of the wall. As the turtle rests, a red ant runs into the turtle's shell. The turtle crushes it between its body and legs.

Steinbeck describes how some wild oat seeds are brought into the shell by the turtle's front leg. The turtle lies still for a moment. Then his head, legs, and tail come out of the shell. The turtle begins straining to reach the top of the cement. The hind legs slowly boost the rest of the turtle's body up. At last he gets to the top. The wild oat seeds are still attached around the turtle's front legs.

Movement is easy for the turtle now. The turtle begins to cross the highway.

◆ ◆ ◆

A **sedan** driven by a forty-year-old woman approached. She saw the turtle and swung to the right, off the highway, the wheels screamed and a cloud of dust boiled up.

◆ ◆ ◆

The car tips with the sudden swerve. After regaining control, the woman drives on slowly. The turtle had hidden in its shell in fear. But now the turtle hurries across the road.

◆ ◆ ◆

Everyday Words

hind (HYND) *adj.* back

peered (PEERD) *v.* looked very closely at something

sedan (si DAN) *n.* a hard-top car big enough for four to seven people

TAKE NOTES

Vocabulary Builder 

Multiple-Meaning Words The noun *plain* may mean "a large area of flat, often treeless land." It may also mean "a large flat expanse of something." Which meaning does *plain* have in the first paragraph?

____

____

Vocabulary Builder 

Parts of Speech *Straining* may be a verb meaning "trying very hard to do something, using all one's strength and ability." It may also be a gerund, a verb form ending in *ing* that can function as a noun. The gerund *straining* means "the effort or process of trying very hard to do something." Circle *straining* when it is used as a noun in the bracketed passage. Draw a box around *straining* when it is used as a verb.

Comprehension Builder 

Make a prediction about what will happen to the turtle.

____

____

____

Vocabulary Builder

Multiple-Meaning Words The verb *manages* may mean "directs or controls a business and the people, equipment, and money involved in it." It may also mean "succeeds in doing something difficult." What does *manages* mean in the bracketed paragraph?

____

____

Comprehension Builder 

Summarize what happens to the turtle and the wild oat seeds.

____

____

____

____

____

Vocabulary Builder 

Multiple-Meaning Words The adjective *humorous* may mean "funny and enjoyable." It may also mean "damp or moist." What does *humorous* mean in the last paragraph?

____

And now a light truck approached, and as it came near, the driver saw the turtle and swerved to hit it.

◆ ◆ ◆

The front wheel of the truck hits the turtle. The turtle flips over and rolls off the highway.

Steinbeck describes how the turtle lies on its back. Its body is drawn into its shell. Finally, the legs come out and start waving around in the air. The turtle is looking for something to grab onto. At last its front foot gets hold of a piece of quartz.[1] Very slowly, the turtle manages to pull itself over. At this point, the wild oat seeds fall out and get stuck in the ground.

As the turtle moves along, its shell buries the seeds with dirt.

◆ ◆ ◆

The turtle entered a dust road and **jerked** itself along, drawing a wavy shallow **trench** with its shell. The old humorous eyes looked ahead, and the horny beak opened a little. His yellow toe nails slipped a **fraction** in the dust.

Everyday Words

jerked (JERKD) *v.* moved with a quick sudden movement
trench (TRENCH) *n.* a deep ditch dug in the ground
fraction (FRAK shuhn) *n.* a very small amount

1. **quartz** (KWORTS) *n.* a type of rock or hard mineral

Thinking About the Selection

1. One way to think about nature is to consider it a series of causes and effects. The turtle's movement causes several things to happen. Record four effects in the chart below.

Effects

1. Wild oat seeds become caught in the turtle's shell.

2. _______________________

3. _______________________

4. _______________________

5. _______________________

Causes

The turtle moves across a road.

2. In this story, humans interact with nature by _______________________

____

____.

TALK ABOUT IT

Debate Do you think that it is possible for human society to progress without harming nature? Can humans expand buildings and roads without taking over natural landscapes? Discuss your ideas and opinions with a partner. Use this sentence starter.

I think that human society (can or cannot) progress without

harming nature because _______________________.

Writing About the Essential Question

How does literature shape or reflect society? What does the portrayal of the turtle lead you to expect about Steinbeck's portrayal of the Joads in *The Grapes of Wrath*? Explain.

____

____

____

Connotation

A synonym is a word that has almost the same meaning as another word. Although synonyms may have similar meanings, they often have different connotations. Connotations are the feelings and thoughts that readers connect with a word. Writers choose words on the basis of both literal meanings and connotations. Each word in the chart below is a synonym for *intelligent*.

Word: *Intelligent* means "having a high level of mental ability."

Synonym	Connotation
clever	able to use one's intelligence to get what one wants
bright	intelligent and able to learn things quickly; often refers to students
sharp	not easily deceived

Now You Do It

For each word, write a sentence that conveys the connotation of the synonym.

1. intelligent: The intelligent writer drew several new conclusions from her research.

2. clever: ____

3. bright: ____

4. sharp: ____

TALK ABOUT IT **Substitute a Synonym** Ask a partner a question that contains one of the synonyms in the chart. Your partner should answer the question, using the meaning of the synoym. Continue taking turns, using all the words.

WRITE ABOUT IT **Match Game** For each synonym, choose a famous person or literary character whom the word describes. Then, use the word to write a sentence about the person. For example, *Tom Sawyer was so clever that he persuaded others to do his chores.*

Vocabulary

Listen to each word. Say it. Then, read the definition and the example sentence.

conduct (CAHN dukt) *n.* **Conduct** is the way a person behaves.

Arnold's <u>conduct</u> in class was very different from the way he behaved at home.

sensible (SEN suh buhl) *adj.* Someone who is **sensible** is logical and practical.

She was <u>sensible</u> enough to save her money for college.

psychology (sy KAHL uh jee) *n.* **Psychology** is the study of the mind and how it works.

The study of <u>psychology</u> has been very useful to Mr. Torres as he tries to understand his students' behavior.

Vocabulary Practice

Read the first sentence in each group of three. Then, complete Sentence *a* by substituting another word or phrase that means the same as the underlined vocabulary word. Complete Sentence *b* with your own ideas and words.

1. He demonstrated poor <u>conduct</u> by interrupting her.

   a. He demonstrated poor _____________ by interrupting her.

   b. He demonstrated poor conduct by _____________________.

2. The <u>sensible</u> child wore rain boots on the stormy day.

   a. The _____________ child wore rain boots on the stormy day.

   b. The sensible child _________________________________.

3. Dr. Lee used her knowledge of <u>psychology</u> to help him relax.

   a. Dr. Lee used her knowledge of _____________ to help him relax.

   b. Dr. Lee used her knowledge of psychology _____________________.

Getting Ready to Read

A census is an official count of people and their characteristics. With a partner, list the types of information that a government might gather about citizens such as date of birth, home address, and so on.

The Unknown Citizen
W.H. Auden

Summary **"The Unknown Citizen"** honors a model citizen of his society. The speaker calls this man a saint because he serves the Greater Community. He works and pays his dues, and he owns the things that a citizen should own. He seems to live a proper and adequate life. However, no one knows anything about his true life experiences.

Note-taking Guide

Use this chart to record details about the Unknown Citizen.

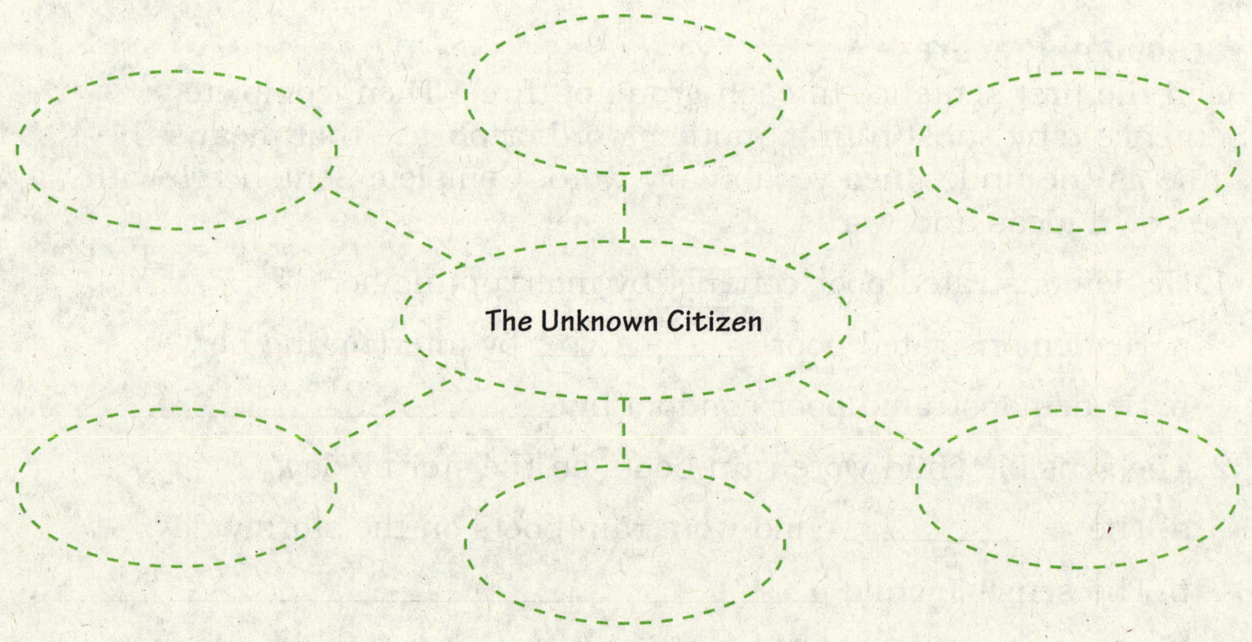

Thinking About the Selection

1. Different types of information may be used to describe a person. Fill in the chart below with the information that you know about the unknown citizen.

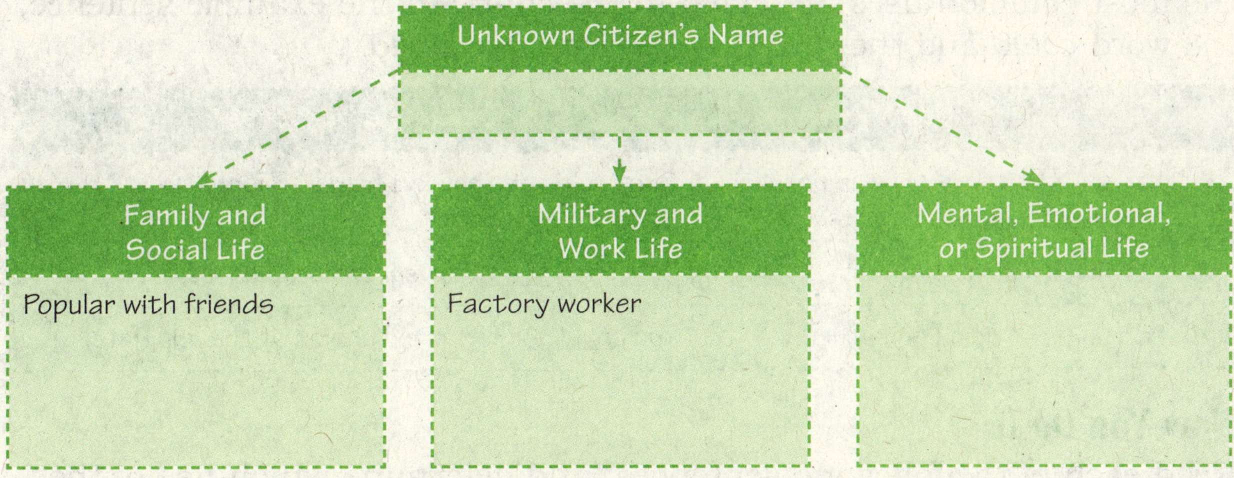

2. According to the speaker of the poem, the unknown citizen is a saint because ____

____.

TALK ABOUT IT **Evaluate Character** In many literary works, the main character is a hero of some kind—a person who is admired for bravery or courage. Is the unknown citizen a hero? Discuss your ideas with a partner. Use this sentence frame.

The unknown citizen is (is not) a hero because ___________________

____.

? **Writing About the Essential Question**

How does literature shape or reflect society? What view of individuals in the modern world does Auden express in this poem?

____

____

____

Helping Verbs

A helping verb assists a primary verb in telling about an action. The words *could, should,* and *would* are helping verbs.

Example

The helping verb **could** has several uses in the present tense. Three of the most common uses are listed in the chart. In the example sentence, the word *could* and the verb it helps are underlined.

	Use	Example Sentence
A	to say that something is possible or might happen	She <u>could see</u> the skyscrapers from a great distance.
B	to make a polite request	<u>Could</u> you <u>pass</u> the vegetables, please?
C	to suggest doing something	You <u>could ask</u> for an extension of the due date.

Now You Do It

Read each of the following sentences, and determine which use of the helping verb *could* appears in each sentence. Write the appropriate letter, **A, B,** or **C,** on the line beside the sentence.

_____ 1. I could lend you a pencil.

_____ 2. Pete, you could ask Sidney to the dance.

_____ 3. Could you turn to page 5 in your books?

_____ 4. You could park behind the field if the other lot is full.

_____ 5. Enzo could join the team if we need another player.

_____ 6. Could you answer the door, Kaelin?

TALK ABOUT IT **Sentence Rounds** Work with a partner to practice the different uses of the helping verb *could.* Have your partner identify one of the uses of the helping verb *could.* Say a sentence that contains the helping verb used in that way. Then, switch roles with your partner and continue the exercise.

WRITE ABOUT IT **Be a Superhero** Use the helping verb *could* to write a paragraph that describes what you could do if you had a superpower. Use *could* in at least two different ways in your paragraph.

Vocabulary

Listen to each word. Say it. Then, read the definition and the example sentence.

scolds (SKOHLDZ) *v.* When a person **scolds** someone, he or she angrily criticizes a person for something that person has done.
The grandfather scolds the child for making a mess..

sowed (SOHD) *v.* When you have **sowed** something, you have planted or scattered seeds on it.
They sowed the field with pumpkin seeds.

reaped (REEPT) *v.* When you have **reaped** something, you have received something as a result of what you have done.
Nancy reaped the benefits of studying hard when she got an A.

Vocabulary Practice

Read the first sentence in each group of three. Then, complete Sentence *a* by substituting another word or phrase that means the same as the underlined vocabulary word. Complete Sentence *b* with your own ideas and words.

1. The father <u>scolds</u> his misbehaving daughter.

   a. The father ______________ his misbehaving daughter.

   b. The father scolds ________________________________.

2. My grandmother <u>sowed</u> vegetable seeds in the garden.

   a. My grandmother ______________ vegetable seeds in the garden.

   b. My grandmother sowed ________________________________.

3. Lee <u>reaped</u> the benefits of hard work when he was promoted.

   a. Lee ______________ the benefits of hard work when he was promoted.

   b. Lee reaped ________________________________.

Getting Ready to Read

In his poetry, E. E. Cummings often ignores standard rules of English. Write a sentence, and then rewrite it in a nonstandard way. Exchange sentences with a partner to see whether both have the same meaning.

old age sticks • anyone lived in a pretty how town
E. E. Cummings

Summaries In **"old age sticks,"** the speaker says that the young ignore the warnings of the elderly. He suggests that although the young tear down warning "signs," one day they will be posting such "signs" themselves. In **"anyone lived in a pretty how town,"** the speaker tells about an anonymous town in which people live routine and ordinary lives. The main characters, "anyone" and "noone," do nothing special and are basically unnoticed by other people in the town.

Note-taking Guide

As you read each poem, consider who is the subject of each poem and what happens. Use this chart to keep track of your information.

old age sticks
Who is the subject?
What happens?

anyone lived in a pretty how town
Who is the subject?
What happens?

Thinking About the Selections

1. E. E. Cummings uses English grammar and usage in nontraditional ways to add meaning to his poems. Nevertheless, his poems have a clear message or make a clear statement. Summarize the message of each poem in the chart below.

	old age sticks	anyone lived in a pretty how town
Main Message		

2. Cummings's poems suggest that the lives of most people ___________

____

____.

TALK **ABOUT IT** **The Age Divide** What things do you see older people in your life do that you are sure you will never do? Perhaps you are sure that you will never care about having a garden. Perhaps you are sure that you will never worry about money. Discuss your ideas with a partner.

? Writing About the Essential Question

How does literature shape or reflect society? Do you think the emergence of new approaches to an art form, such as the experimental verse Cummings wrote, reflect larger changes in a society? Explain.

____

____

____

____

Word Families

Groups of words that share the same base word are called word families. A base word can stand alone or serve as the basis of new words. Often, new words are formed by adding prefixes, suffixes, verb endings, and other words to a base word.

Example

Base Word	Words That Share the Base Word
adapt: *v.* to change something to make it suitable for a different purpose	adaptable: *adj.* able to change in order to be successful in new and different situations
	adaptation: *n.* the process of changing something to make it suitable for a new situation
	adapted: *adj.* having changed in order to be successful in a new situation or environment

Now You Do It

Choose the word from the list below that best completes each sentence.

adapt   adaptable   adaptation   adapted

1. The small bird is well _________________ to its jungle environment.

2. A special _________________ enables the fish to live in deep water.

3. If she cannot _________________ to her new classes, she will have to attend summer school.

4. Scientists have found that certain types of insects are extremely

_________________.

TALK ABOUT IT **Talk About Adaptation** Tell a partner about an animal that has adapted to its environment. How has this animal demonstrated adaptability? What adaptations has this animal made? What would happen to this animal if it were inadaptable?

WRITE ABOUT IT **New Circumstances** Consider ways in which people must adapt to new situations and circumstances. Write a paragraph describing a situation or circumstance in which you have had to adapt. Include in your paragraph at least three words from this lesson.

Vocabulary

Listen to each word. Say it. Then, read the definition and the example sentence.

suffice (suh FYS) *v.* If something will **suffice,** it will be enough.
   Five tables will suffice for a party of this size.

insatiable (in SAY shuh buhl) *adj.* Someone who is **insatiable** always wants more of something.
   The athlete's insatiable appetite made buying groceries very expensive.

palpable (PAL puh bul) *adj.* Something that is **palpable** is able to be felt, touched, or handled.
   The tension during the exam was palpable.

Vocabulary Practice

Read the first sentence in each group of three. Then, complete Sentence *a* by substituting another word or phrase that means the same as the underlined vocabulary word. Complete Sentence *b* with your own ideas and words.

1. Chips and dip will <u>suffice</u> for a small number of guests.

   a. Chips and dip will ______________ for a small number of guests.

   b. ______________________ will suffice for a small number of guests.

2. The scientist had an <u>insatiable</u> desire to learn about the world.

   a. The scientist had an ______________ desire to learn about the world.

   b. The scientist had an insatiable ________________________.

3. The anxiety was <u>palpable</u> during the exam.

   a. The anxiety was ______________ during the exam.

   b. The anxiety was palpable ________________________.

Getting Ready to Read

Different poets have different ideas about what a poem should be and do. You may have your own ideas in regard to a definition for poetry. What is a poem? Discuss your ideas with a partner.

Of Modern Poetry
Wallace Stevens

Ars Poetica
Archibald MacLeish

Poetry
Marianne Moore

Summaries These poems are about poems. Each poet says what he or she thinks a poem is or should be. They say what they like or do not like about poems. Sometimes, they say things directly. Sometimes, they use images to give you a feeling about what they mean. In **"Of Modern Poetry,"** the speaker says that a poem must use the language of its own time. In **"Ars Poetica,"** the speaker compares a poem to several other things. He says that the image is the most important part of a poem. The meaning of the poem does not matter as much. In **"Poetry,"** the speaker feels sad for those who do not like poems. She thinks poems should be written so that readers can understand them.

Note-taking Guide

Use this chart to write down words and phrases from each poem that tell you what the poet likes about poetry or about some poems. Then, write down words and phrases that tell you what the poet does not like about poetry or about some poems.

Poem	Likes	Dislikes
Of Modern Poetry		
Ars Poetica		
Poetry		

Thinking About the Selections

1. Consider the different ideas about poetry that Stevens and MacLeish present. Complete the chart below by identifying the lines from each poem that you find most meaningful. Then, explain how these lines contribute to the meaning of the poem.

	Of Modern Poetry	Ars Poetica
Meaningful Lines		
Explanation of Lines		

2. The speaker in "Of Modern Poetry" states that unlike poetry of the past, modern poetry must be ____

____.

TALK ABOUT IT **Choose a Position** Which poem, "Of Modern Poetry" or "Ars Poetica," agrees more with your ideas about poetry? Explain which poem offers the better definition of poetry, and provide reasons to support your opinion.

Writing About the Essential Question

How does literature shape or reflect society? Based on the ideas these poets express, do you think poets have a significant role to play in today's world?

____

____

____

____

Suffixes

A suffix is a word part added to the end of a base word. Sometimes a suffix changes the meaning of the word. Sometimes it changes the word's part of speech. The suffixes *-ance* and *-ence* mean "the action, state, or quality of doing something or of being something." They are used to form nouns. Sometimes the spelling of the base word changes when these suffixes are added.

Examples

Base Word	Resulting Noun	Meaning
repent + -ance	repentance	state of feeling sorry for something that you have done
violent + -ence	violence	state of behavior that is intended to hurt other people physically

Now You Do It

Add the suffixes *-ance* or *-ence* to the following words. Use a dictionary to check the spelling of the new word. Then, use each noun in a sentence.

annoy	
resist	
differ	

TALK ABOUT IT **Share a Scenario** Choose one of the words from the charts above and tell a partner about a time when you felt resistance, annoyance, or repentance. Provide details to describe the situation effectively.

WRITE ABOUT IT **Write About Your Scenario** Now, write about the scenario you shared with your partner. Use descriptive words as well as words that have the suffix *-ance* or *-ence.*

Vocabulary

These words are underlined in the story. Listen to each word. Say it.
Then, read the definition and the example sentence.

detached (di TACHT) *adj.* Someone who is **detached** does not react or
become involved in something in an emotional way.

> *Jillian felt detached when she learned her family was going to move
> for the fifth time in two years.*

disgrace (dis GRAYS) *n.* A **disgrace** is someone or something that is
so bad, wrong, or unacceptable that people feel ashamed or upset.

> *The company that used child laborers was a disgrace.*

resign (ree ZYN) *v.* When you **resign** yourself to something, you make
yourself accept something that you do not like but cannot change.

> *Zachary will have to resign himself to the long walk home from school.*

Vocabulary Practice

Read the first sentence in each group of three. Then, complete
Sentence *a* by substituting another word or phrase that means the
same as the underlined vocabulary word. Complete Sentence *b* with
your own ideas and words.

1. The boy looked detached and gave no sign of his feelings.

   a. The boy looked _______________ and gave no sign of his feelings.

   b. The boy looked detached and _________________________________.

2. The poor football season was a disgrace to the coach.

   a. The poor football season was a _______________ to the coach.

   b. The poor football season was a disgrace _____________________.

3. Jesse must resign himself to a set of daily chores.

   a. Jesse must _______________ a set of daily chores.

   b. Jesse must resign himself _________________________________.

Getting Ready to Read

In this story, the narrator befriends other soldiers, yet he is never really
a part of the group. Tell a partner about a time when you felt that you
were an outsider.

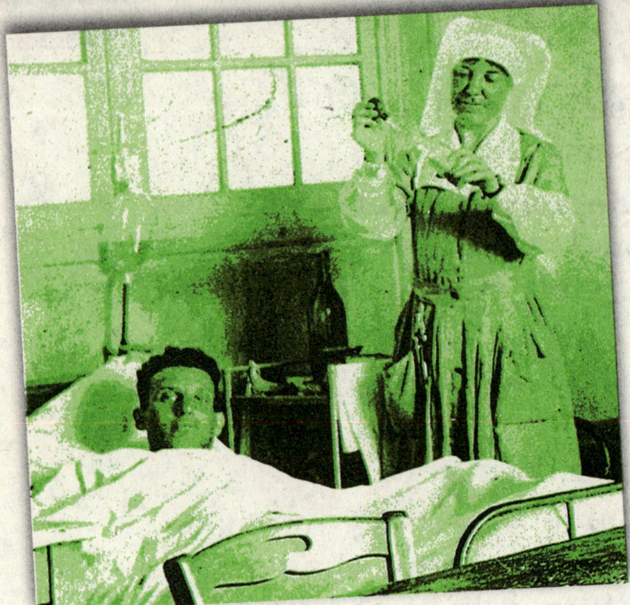

In Another Country
Ernest Hemingway

Summary In "In Another Country," an American officer recovering from a war injury meets three young Italian officers and an older major. All of the men are wounded. The major helps the American with his Italian grammar, advises him not to marry, and mourns the death of his own wife.

Note-taking Guide

Use this chart to record information about Hemingway's story "In Another Country."

Setting	Characters	Problem	Resolution

In Another Country

Ernest Hemingway

The story opens in Milan, Italy, during World War I. The narrator has been injured in the war. He and the other wounded men do not go to the front anymore. Instead, they go to a hospital for treatment every afternoon. There, they are treated with new machines that are supposed to help them heal.

The doctor approaches the narrator and asks him what he did before the war.

◆ ◆ ◆

Did you practice a sport?"

I said: "Yes, football."

"Good," he said. "You will be able to play football again better than ever."

◆ ◆ ◆

The narrator tells about another patient, a major. The major's hand is being treated in a machine. Before the war, the man had been the greatest fencer[1] in Italy. The doctor shows the major a picture of a hand that had been almost as small as the major's. He also shows him a picture of the same hand after treatment. In the second picture, the hand is a little larger.

The major asks if the hand in the picture had been wounded.

◆ ◆ ◆

"An **industrial** accident," the doctor said.

"Very interesting, very interesting," the major said, and handed it back to the doctor.

"You have **confidence?**"

"No," said the major.

◆ ◆ ◆

Everyday Words

industrial (in DUHS tree uhl) *adj.* relating to industry, or the large-scale production of goods

confidence (KAHN fuh duhns) *n.* being sure, being certain

---

1. **fencer** (FENS er) *n.* someone who fights with a long thin sword as a sport

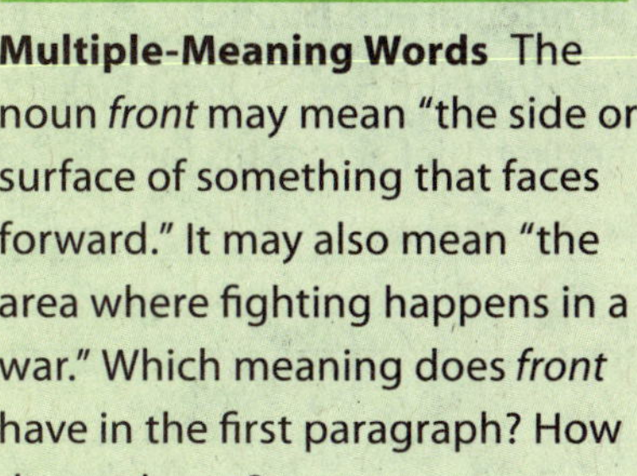

TAKE NOTES

Vocabulary Builder

Multiple-Meaning Words The noun *front* may mean "the side or surface of something that faces forward." It may also mean "the area where fighting happens in a war." Which meaning does *front* have in the first paragraph? How do you know?

____

____

____

Vocabulary Builder 

Parts of Speech *Patient* may be a noun meaning "someone who receives medical treatment from a doctor or a hospital." It may also be an adjective meaning "able to wait calmly for a long time or to accept difficulties without becoming angry." Is *patient* a noun or an adjective in the underlined sentence?

____

Fluency Builder 

In English, quotation marks are used to show the exact words of a speaker. Circle the quotation marks that are around the major's words in the bracketed passage. Then, with a partner, read aloud the dialogue between the doctor and the major.

Comprehension Builder

Why does the boy wear a black handkerchief across his face?

____

____

____

____

Vocabulary Builder

Common Expressions The expression *to deal with something* means "to succeed in controlling one's feelings about something so that it does not affect the rest of one's life." What were the boys in the hospital dealing with?

____

Vocabulary Builder

In English, the ending *n* or *an* added to the name of a country can form a noun or an adjective that tells where a person is from. For example, an American is from America, and an Italian is from Italy. Sometimes different endings are used. For example, a Spaniard is from Spain, an Iraqi is from Iraq, and a Chinese person is from China.

Other patients include three boys from Milan. Sometimes, when they are done with the machines, they walk to a nearby café. They are sometimes joined by another boy. He wears a black silk **handkerchief** across his face because he has no nose. He was injured within an hour of going to the front line for the first time.

He doesn't have any medals because he hasn't been in the service long enough. One boy, who was to be a lawyer, has three medals because he had a dangerous job. The rest of the boys and the narrator each have one medal. They are all dealing with death.

◆　◆　◆

We were all a little <u>detached</u>, and there was nothing that held us <u>together</u> except that we met every afternoon at the hospital.

◆　◆　◆

The narrator says that the boys once asked him what he had done to get his medals. He shows them the papers, which were full of pretty words. But all they really say was that he had gotten the medals because he was an American. After that, the boys act differently toward the narrator. He is still their friend, especially against outsiders. But he is never really one of them after that. It was different with the three Italian boys. They had really **earned** their medals.

Everyday Words

handkerchief (HANG ker chif) *n.* a piece of cloth that you use for drying your nose or eyes

earned (ERND) *v.* did something or had qualities that caused you to deserve something else

The narrator had been wounded but agrees that it was an accident.

◆   ◆   ◆

I was never **ashamed** of the ribbons, though, and sometimes, after the cocktail hour, I would imagine myself having done all the things they had done to get their medals; but walking home at night through the empty streets with the cold wind and all the shops closed, trying to keep near the street lights, I knew that I would never have done such things, and I was very much afraid to die, and often lay in bed at night by myself, afraid to die and wondering how I would be when I went back to the front again.

◆   ◆   ◆

The major, the former fencer, does not believe in bravery. He spends a lot of time correcting the narrator's Italian grammar as they sit in the machines. The narrator had once said that Italian seemed like such an easy language. But then the major starts helping him with the grammar. <u>Soon Italian seems so hard that the narrator is afraid to speak until he has the grammar straight in his mind.</u>

The major comes to the hospital every day. He doesn't believe in the machines but feels that they must be tested.

◆   ◆   ◆

It was an idiotic idea, he said, "a **theory,** like another." I had not learned my grammar, and he said I was a stupid impossible <u>disgrace</u>, and he was a **fool** to have bothered with me.

◆   ◆   ◆

TAKE NOTES

Cultural Understanding

A cocktail is an alcoholic drink made by mixing liquor with soda or fruit juice. The cocktail hour is a time when many people gather, often in restaurants or bars, and have drinks and talk together. In Italy, the cocktail hour is late in the evening, around 7 or 8 o'clock at night.

Vocabulary Builder

Multiple-Meaning Words The adjective *straight* may mean "not bending or curving." It may also mean "clear or understood." What does *straight* mean in the underlined sentence?

____

____

Vocabulary Builder

Synonyms The adjectives *idiotic* and *stupid* are synonyms. Both words mean "showing bad judgment or a lack of intelligence." Read aloud the bracketed paragraph as it is written. Then, read it again, replacing *idiotic* with *stupid* and *stupid* with *idiotic*.

Comprehension Builder 

What does the major tell the narrator that a man should not do? Underline the sentence that tells you.

Vocabulary Builder 

Suffixes The suffix *-ment* means "the act of." It is added to verbs to form nouns that show actions or the results of actions. The verb *treat* means "try to cure an illness or injury." What does the noun *treatment* mean?

____

____

Vocabulary Builder 

Multiple-Meaning Words
The adjective *sick* may mean "suffering from a disease or illness." It may also mean "upset or unhappy." What does *sick* mean in the bracketed dialogue?

____

____

The narrator and the major then start talking. The major asks if the narrator is married. The narrator says no, but he hopes to be. The major says that a man must not marry. When asked to explain, he says that a man should not place himself in a position to lose. Instead, he should find things he cannot lose. He speaks with anger and **bitterness**. The narrator speaks up.

♦ ♦ ♦

"But why should he necessarily lose it?"

"He'll lose it," the major said. He was looking at the wall. Then he looked down at the machine and jerked his little hand out from between the straps and slapped it hard against his thigh. "He'll lose it," he almost shouted. "Don't argue with me!"

♦ ♦ ♦

The major then asks the attendant to turn off the machine. He goes to the other room for more treatment. Then he asks the doctor if he can use the phone. When he returns, he comes toward the narrator and puts his arm on his shoulder.

♦ ♦ ♦

"I am so sorry," he said, and patted me on the shoulder with his good hand. "I would not be **rude.** My wife has just died. You must forgive me."

"Oh—" I said, feeling sick for him. "I am so sorry."

He stood there biting his lower lip. "It is very difficult," he said. "I cannot resign myself."

Everyday Words

bitterness (BIT er nes) *n.* a feeling of anger or jealousy, especially because you think you have been treated unfairly

rude (ROOD) *adj.* speaking or behaving in a way that is not polite and is likely to offend or annoy people

He looked straight past me and out through the window. Then he began to cry. "I am **utterly** unable to resign myself," he said and choked. And then crying, his head up looking at nothing, carrying himself straight and soldierly, with tears on both his cheeks and biting his lips, he walked past the machines and out the door.

◆ ◆ ◆

The doctor tells the narrator that the major's young wife had died of pneumonia. She had been sick for only a few days. No one thought she would die. The major stays away from the hospital for three days. When he comes back, he is wearing a black band on his sleeve.[2] Now there are large photographs on the wall of before-and-after pictures of wounds cured by the machines. There are three photographs of hands like the major's, completely cured.

◆ ◆ ◆

I do not know where the doctor got them. I always understood we were the first to use the machines. The photographs did not make much difference to the major because he only looked out of the window.

Everyday Words

utterly (UT er lee) *adv.* completely

2. **a black band on his sleeve** a sign of mourning

Vocabulary Builder 

Prefixes The prefix *un-* means "not." What does *unable* mean?

____

Comprehension Builder

What happened to the major's wife? How long had she been sick?

____

____

____

Vocabulary Builder 

Idioms The idiom *make much difference* means "have much of an effect." What does not have much of an effect on the major?

____

____

Thinking About the Selection

1. The narrator is acutely aware of the differences between himself and the Italian soldiers. Complete this chart. Note the similarities in the center column and the differences in the outer columns.

American Soldier	Similarities	Italian Soldiers
1. football player	1. wounded	1. fencing
2. ___________	2. ___________	2. ___________
3. ___________	3. ___________	3. ___________
4. ___________	4. ___________	4. ___________
5. ___________	5. ___________	

2. The narrator feels detached because ___________________________________
____
____.

TALK ABOUT IT **Group Identity** At the café, the narrator says that he supports the Italian soldiers against outsiders but that he is not really a member of the group. An outsider is someone who is not accepted as a member of a particular group. With a partner, discuss some of the different social groups in your school or community. Discuss reasons why social groups are important to people.

Writing About the Essential Question

What makes American literature American? Do you think Hemingway presents a typically American view of war in this story? Explain.

____
____
____
____

Multiple-Meaning Words

Many words have several different meanings. Use context clues to determine which meaning a writer intends. Context clues include synonyms, antonyms, explanations, examples, or restatements.

Examples

Word	Meanings
level	• (noun) particular standard of skill or ability • (noun) height of something
save	• (verb) make someone or something safe from danger • (verb) keep money in a bank for future use

Now You Do It

The sentences below contain underlined words from the chart. Examine the context that each sentence provides. Then, write the meaning of the underlined word on the lines provided.

Pelé reached a high level of excellence in soccer.

____

____

The animal expert knows how to save cats trapped in trees.

____

____

I will save my money by opening an account at the bank.

____

____

The top of the tree is at the same level as the building's roof.

____

____

TALK ABOUT IT **Give Advice** Advise a partner on how to improve his or her level of skill in a particular task or on how to save money. Use different meanings of the words *level* and *save* in your discussion. If possible, use both meanings of the word *catch* as well.

WRITE ABOUT IT **Sentence Sets** Write two sentences for each word in this lesson. Use a different meaning of the word in each sentence.

Vocabulary

Listen to each word. Say it. Then, read the definition and the example sentence.

encroached (in KROHCHT) *v.* When something is **encroached** upon, it is gradually covered or used so that it is affected or threatened.

The flood encroached upon the farmland and destroyed crops.

vindicated (VIN duh kay tuhd) *v.* When you have **vindicated** someone, you have proven that a person blamed for something is not guilty.

The surveillance video vindicated Quentin from vandalism charges.

inextricable (in ek STRIK uh bul) *adj.* Two or more things that are **inextricable** cannot be separated.

When the plastic melted into the metal, the two became inextricable.

Vocabulary Practice

Read the first sentence in each group of three. Then, complete Sentence *a* by substituting another word or phrase that means the same as the underlined vocabulary word. Complete Sentence *b* with your own ideas and words.

1. The rabbits <u>encroached</u> on the vegetable garden.

    a. The rabbits _______________ on the vegetable garden.

    b. The rabbits encroached _________________________________.

2. The defendant was <u>vindicated</u> by the witness's testimony.

    a. The defendant was _______________ by the witness's testimony.

    b. The defendant was vindicated _________________________________.

3. The noodles and melted cheese were <u>inextricable</u>.

    a. The noodles and melted cheese were _______________.

    b. _________________________________ were inextricable.

Getting Ready to Read

There is a gap between what Emily and her family once were and what she has become. With a partner, discuss the different ways people may react to changes in their lives.

A Rose for Emily
William Faulkner

Summary Emily Grierson is a woman in a small Southern town. She lives under the watchful eyes of the community. Because she is secretive and private, the townspeople believe that she may be crazy. When Emily shows interest in a man from another town, people wonder whether she will marry him. When the man disappears from town, Emily begins keeping to herself again. After her death, people find something shocking in her bedroom.

Note-taking Guide

Faulkner tells this story in five sections. These sections do not occur in time order. To make sense of the story, analyze what happens in each section. Use the following chart to record your observations:

Section I
What happens: Officials confront Emily about taxes.

Section II
What happens:

Section III
What happens:

Section IV
What happens:

Section V
What happens:

Vocabulary

Listen to each word. Say it. Then, read the definition and the example sentence.

commensurate (kuh MEN suh rit) *adj.* Something **commensurate** matches something else in size, quality, or length of time.

Her starting salary is commensurate with her experience.

pinnacle (PIN uh kuhl) *n.* The **pinnacle** is the top of a mountain.

The mountain climbers reached the pinnacle at dusk.

ephemeral (i FEM uh ruhl) *adj.* If something is **ephemeral,** it exists for only a short time.

The ephemeral fog was gone by noon.

Vocabulary Practice

Read the first sentence in each group of three. Then, complete Sentence *a* by substituting another word or phrase that means the same as the underlined vocabulary word. Complete Sentence *b* with your own ideas and words.

1. The banker's income is <u>commensurate</u> with his style of living.

   a. The banker's income is ________________ with his style of living.

   b. The banker's income is commensurate ________________________.

2. The view from the <u>pinnacle</u> was breathtaking.

   a. The view from the ______________ was breathtaking.

   b. The view from the pinnacle _________________________________.

3. The popularity of the rock song was <u>ephemeral</u>.

   a. The popularity of the rock song was ______________.

   b. The popularity ________________________________ was ephemeral.

Getting Ready to Read

The Cold War refers to a period of time between the end of World War II and the end of the 1980s. During this time, tension existed between democratic and communist countries. The threat of nuclear attack worried many people. Talk with a partner about ways to overcome this type of fear.

Nobel Prize Acceptance Speech

William Faulkner

Summary William Faulkner received the Nobel Prize for literature in 1950. In his acceptance speech, Faulkner presents his opinions about world affairs. He also talks about the role of literature in helping people make sense of the world. Faulkner tells young writers to set aside their fear of world destruction and address the basic problems of love, honor, and caring for others. He explains that it is the writer's duty to help people carry on. Writers can do this by reminding people of the glory of their past.

Note-taking Guide

In the chart, record the main idea of each paragraph of Faulkner's speech.

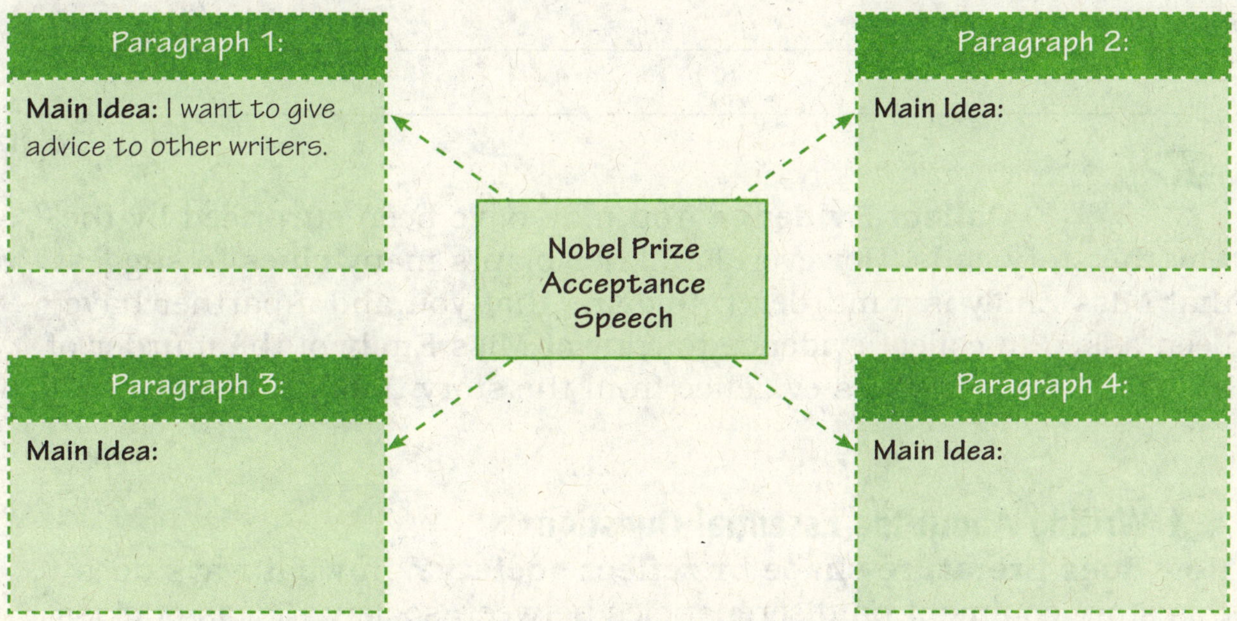

Thinking About the Selections

1. In "A Rose for Emily," a gap exists between what the townspeople believe about Miss Emily and the truth about her. Complete the chart below with details from the story.

What People Believe About Miss Emily	The Truth About Miss Emily
1. She doesn't have to follow the law.	1. Her life and home are decayed.
2.	2.
3.	3.
4.	4.

2. "A Rose for Emily" is an example of the kind of story that Faulkner discusses in his Nobel Prize acceptance speech because ____________

____

____.

TALK ABOUT IT **Collect Evidence** You may have been surprised by the way the story ends. However, Faulkner plants many clues to suggest that Miss Emily is a murderer. Imagine that you and a partner have been asked to collect evidence to convict Miss Emily of the murder of Homer Barron. Discuss evidence from the story that you might use to convict her.

Writing About the Essential Question

How does literature shape or reflect society? In what ways does this story comment on discrepancies between society's ideas of class, privilege, and respectability and the darker sides of human nature?

____

____

Helping Verbs

A helping verb assists a primary verb in telling about an action. The words *may, might,* and *must* are helping verbs.

Examples

may: indicates that something could be true, or could have happened, or will possibly happen in the future	• She may have hidden the key under a rock. • I may make spaghetti for dinner. • I may be smart, but I do make mistakes.
might: indicates the possibility that something is true or will happen in the future	• Mary might be late for dinner. • You might find the answer online. • There might be a recount after the close of the election.
must: indicates that something has to be done because it is necessary or important or because of a law or an order	• All students must turn in their assignments. • You must have been thrilled at the news. • Teenagers must be sixteen years old to obtain a license.

Now You Do It

Complete the following sentences.

1. I may ____.

2. She might ____.

3. The students must ____.

TALK ABOUT IT   **Fill In the Blank** Work with a partner. State a sentence with a missing helping verb. For example, you might say, *Carl _____ walk the dog before he can come with us.* Ask your partner to fill in the blank with the correct helping verb. *(must)* Take turns making statements and filling in the blanks.

WRITE ABOUT IT   **You Must Help Me with My Story** Now, write a short story containing the helping verbs *may, might,* and *must.* Leave a blank for each of these helping verbs. For example, you might write *David thought that he _____ cut down the oak tree in the backyard. He _____ need to buy an ax.* When you are done, ask a partner to fill in the blanks.

Vocabulary

Listen to each word. Say it. Then, read the definition and the example sentence.

dyspepsia (dis PEP see uh) *n.* **Dyspepsia** is a problem that your body has digesting the food you eat.
Brian's <u>dyspepsia</u> prevented him from eating junk food.

piety (PY uh tee) *n.* **Piety** is loyalty and devotion to family, the divine, or some other object of respect.
Her elders were pleased by her <u>piety</u>.

tactful (TAKT fuhl) *adj.* Someone who is **tactful** is careful not to say or do anything that will upset or embarrass others.
Because the teacher was <u>tactful</u>, she posted the grades anonymously.

Vocabulary Practice

Read the first sentence in each group of three. Then, complete Sentence *a* by substituting another word or phrase that means the same as the underlined vocabulary word. Complete Sentence *b* with your own ideas and words.

1. Bertha's <u>dyspepsia</u> caused her discomfort after meals.

   a. Bertha's _____________ caused her discomfort after meals.

   b. Bertha's dyspepsia caused her _________________________.

2. The priest demonstrated his <u>piety</u> through kind deeds.

   a. The priest demonstrated his _____________ through kind deeds.

   b. The priest demonstrated his piety _________________________.

3. The teacher is <u>tactful</u> when she critiques students' essays.

   a. The teacher is _____________ when she critiques students' essays.

   b. The teacher is tactful when she _________________________.

Getting Ready to Read

To feel *regret* means "to feel sadness about something that you wish had not happened." As Granny Weatherall dies, the joys and accomplishments in her life are overshadowed by one overwhelming regret. Tell a partner about something that you regret.

The Jilting of Granny Weatherall

Katherine Anne Porter

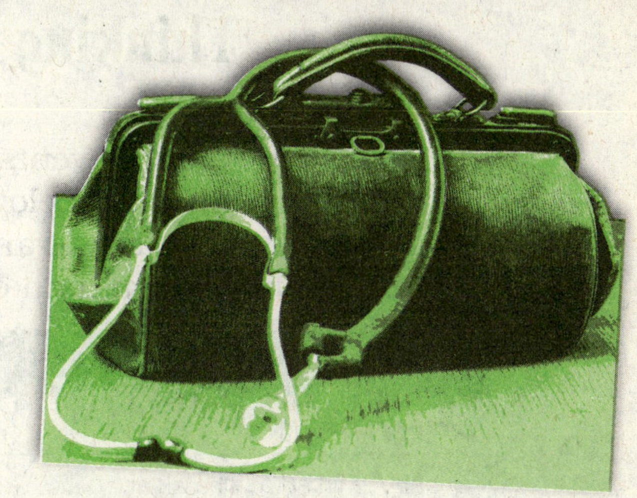

Summary Ellen Weatherall is on her deathbed. Her thoughts drift between moments in the present and memories of the past. She receives visits from her daughter, her doctor, and her priest. She recalls the people and events that filled her life. Her thoughts wander freely among the good and the bad memories.

Note-taking Guide

Use this chart to put the events of Granny's life in order.

Event 1	Event 2	Event 3	Event 4	Event 5	Event 6
George leaves Ellen standing at the altar on their wedding day.					

Thinking About the Selection

1. Some of the story's events occur in the past, and others occur in the present. In the chart below, put a check mark in the Past column if an event occurred in Granny Weatherall's past. Put a check mark in the Present column if an event occurs in the story's present.

Event	Past	Present
Granny is dying.		
Granny is jilted at the altar.		
Jimmy drops in to discuss business.		
Granny sits up with sick children and horses.		
The children and the priest visit Granny.		
Lydia drives eighty miles to ask Granny for advice.		
Cornelia takes care of Granny.		

2. On her deathbed, Granny wishes that she could find George, her first bridegroom, and tell him that ________________________

________________________ .

TALK ABOUT IT **Forgive and Forget** Granny's life and her death are marred by her inability to forgive and forget the bridegroom who jilted her. With a partner, discuss the advice you would give Granny about forgiving the bridegroom. Why is it important that she forgive him? How might she accomplish this task?

Writing About the Essential Question

How does literature shape or reflect society? Whose criteria do you think Granny uses to judge her life? Is her assessment of her life accurate or fair?

____

____

____

Idioms

Remember that an idiom is a word or phrase that has a special meaning different from the ordinary meaning of the words. The following idioms contain references to the head.

Examples

Idiom	Special Meaning
1. have something hanging over one's head	something that bothers one or that one has to do
2. keep one's head	remain calm
3. off the top of one's head	a first thought
4. put their heads together	join with others to think about a situation
5. over one's head	too difficult or complex.

Now You Do It

Write a sentence for each idiom.

1. ____
2. ____
3. ____
4. ____
5. ____

TALK ABOUT IT **Converse** Have a conversation with a partner in which you use the idioms that appear in the chart above. Make sure that the context of the conversation relates to the meanings of the idioms.

WRITE ABOUT IT **Write a Folktale** Choose one idiom and write a folktale that explains the origin of the expression. For example, "hanging over one's head" might come from the tale of a mythological character whom the gods punished for having selfish thoughts. Perhaps the gods made the thoughts visible by hanging them over the character's head.

Vocabulary

These words are underlined in the story. Listen to each word. Say it. Then, read the definition and the example sentence.

ravine (ruh VEEN) *n.* A **ravine** is a small, narrow valley with steep sides.

> *They could see a stream winding along the bottom of the ravine.*

utterly (UT er lee) *adv.* When a person does or feels something **utterly,** he or she does or feels it completely.

> *Gemma was utterly exhausted by the long hike through the woods.*

obstinate (AHB stuh nuht) *adj.* When you are **obstinate,** you are determined not to change your opinions, ideas, or behavior.

> *The obstinate man debated his thoughts at the assembly.*

Vocabulary Practice

Read the first sentence in each group of three. Then, complete Sentence *a* by substituting another word or phrase that means the same as the underlined vocabulary word. Complete Sentence *b* with your own ideas and words.

1. The hikers made their way across the ravine.

   a. The hikers made their way across the _______________.

   b. ____ across the ravine.

2. I am utterly impressed by your good behavior.

   a. I am _______________ impressed by your good behavior.

   b. I am utterly impressed by _________________________________.

3. The obstinate child would not eat his green beans.

   a. The _______________ child would not eat his green beans.

   b. The obstinate child ____.

Getting Ready to Read

In this story, Phoenix Jackson proves her determination and strength by walking a long distance, often with no path, to get medicine for her grandson. Have you ever done something difficult in order to help someone else? Discuss your experience with a partner.

A Worn Path
Eudora Welty

Summary In "A Worn Path," an old woman makes her way along a country path. Once in town, she goes to a doctor's office to get medicine for her grandson. She has been taking care of him since he swallowed lye some years before.

Note-taking Guide

Use this diagram to record information about Phoenix Jackson's journey in "A Worn Path."

Sequence of Events			
1.	2.	3.	4.
In December, Phoenix Jackson walks through the pine woods.			

5.	6.	7.

Vocabulary Builder 

Suffix The suffix *-ness* means "the state or condition of being a particular way." When added to an adjective, it changes the adjective into a noun. Circle two nouns in the first bracketed paragraph that end in *-ness*. What does each word mean?

____

____

____

____

Fluency Builder 

The words that Old Phoenix speaks appear between quotation marks. With a partner, take turns reading aloud the second bracketed paragraph. Read with expression, paying attention to punctuation marks. Remember that an ellipsis (. . .) may show a pause, and an exclamation point (!) may show that a person is speaking loudly or with great emotion.

Comprehension Builder 

How does Old Phoenix experience the walk along the path? Circle a phrase that describes the day. Underline three sentences that describe the way in which Old Phoenix walks.

A Worn Path
Eudora Welty

An old Negro woman named Phoenix Jackson leaves home on a cold December morning. She walks along a country path.

♦ ♦ ♦

She was very old and small and she walked slowly in the dark pine shadows, moving a little from side to side in her steps, with the balanced heaviness and lightness of a **pendulum** in a grandfather clock.

♦ ♦ ♦

The woman carries a cane that she taps as she walks.

Welty tells us that Phoenix's eyes are blue with age. Her skin is quite wrinkled. Her hair comes down in ringlets from under the red rag.

The woman notices some movement in the bushes.

♦ ♦ ♦

Old Phoenix said, "Out of my way, all you foxes, owls, beetles, jack rabbits, coons and wild animals! . . . Keep out from under these feet, little bobwhites. . . . Keep the big wild hogs out of my path. Don't let none of those come running my direction. I got a long way."

♦ ♦ ♦

Phoenix comes to a hill. She climbs up one side of the hill and down the other. On the way, a bush catches her dress. It takes her a long time to get her dress free. She crosses a creek by walking across a log with her eyes closed.

Everyday Words

pendulum (PEN dyoo luhm) *n.* a weight hanging from a fixed point so as to swing freely under the action of gravity

Phoenix is pleased with herself. She sits down to get comfortable and rest.

◆　◆　◆

Up above her was a tree in a pearly cloud of **mistletoe.** She did not dare to close her eyes, and when a little boy brought her a plate with a slice of marble cake on it she spoke to him. "That would be acceptable," she said. But when she went to take it there was just her own hand in the air.

◆　◆　◆

Phoenix keeps on walking. She has to go through a barbed-wire fence. She is very careful. She finally gets through the barbed-wire fence safely. Then, she sees a buzzard.[1] She asks him who he's watching. She comes to an old cotton field and then to a field of dead corn. There is no path here. Then, she sees something in front of her. It is tall, black, and thin. It is moving.

She sees what she thinks is a man but then is confused by the figure's silence.

◆　◆　◆

"Ghost," she said sharply, "who be you the ghost of? For I have heard of **nary** death close by."

◆　◆　◆

The figure moves in the wind but does not answer. She touches its clothes and realizes there is nothing **underneath.**

◆　◆　◆

Vocabulary Builder

Parts of Speech *Dare* may be a verb meaning "be brave enough to do something that is risky or that you are afraid to do." It may also be a noun meaning "something dangerous that you have challenged or tried to persuade someone else to do." Is *dare* a noun or a verb in the bracketed paragraph?

____

Cultural Understanding

Barbed-wire fences are common on farms and ranches. They are made of wire that has sharp points sticking out. The sharp points are designed to keep farm animals from getting out and to keep wild animals from getting in.

Comprehension Builder 

Phoenix sees something in front of her. What does she think it is?

____

____

____

____

Everyday Words

mistletoe (MIS uhl toh) *n.* a green plant that lives on other plants

nary (NAIR ee) *adj.* not one

underneath (un der NEETH) *prep.* directly under another object or covered by it

---

1. **sees a buzzard** (BUZ erd) A buzzard is a bird that waits for its prey to die, rather than killing it. Buzzards commonly circle dying prey, so they are seen as a sign of death.

Cultural Understanding

Scarecrows are like big, stuffed, life-size dolls. They are placed in fields where crops are growing. Their purpose is to scare crows and other birds who might eat the crops. The hope is that the birds will think a human being is in the field.

Vocabulary Builder

Parts of Speech *Past* may be a noun, meaning "the time that existed before the present," or a preposition, meaning "up to and beyond a particular person or place, without stopping." Identify the word's part of speech as it is used in the bracketed paragraph.

____

Vocabulary Builder

Multiple-Meaning Words The noun *spring* may mean "the season between winter and summer when leaves and flowers appear." It may also mean "a place where water comes up naturally from the ground." Which meaning does *spring* have in the second bracketed paragraph?

____

____

With a partner, discuss how you know the answer.

"You scarecrow," she said. Her face lighted. "I ought to be shut up[2] for good," she said with laughter. "My **senses** is gone. I too old. I the oldest people I ever know. Dance, old scarecrow," she said, "while I dancing with you."

♦　♦　♦

Phoenix keeps walking through the corn field. She gets to a wagon track. This is the easy part of the walk. She follows the track. She goes past bare fields, past some trees, past some old cabins. The doors and windows are all boarded. They remind Phoenix of old women who are under a spell, just sitting there.

♦　♦　♦

In a ravine she went where a spring was silently flowing through a **hollow** log. Old Phoenix bent and drank. "Sweet gum[3] makes the water sweet," she said, and drank more. "Nobody know who made this well, for it was here when I was born."

♦　♦　♦

As she walks along the path near a swamp, Phoenix speaks to the alligators. Then, she crosses a road that is shaded by oak trees.

A black dog comes up to Phoenix. He knocks her down, and she falls into a ditch. She cannot get out of it. A young white hunter comes along. He has a dog with him.

Everyday Words

senses (SENS iz) *n.* the five natural powers of sight, hearing, feeling, taste, and smell, which give us information about the things around us

hollow (HAWL oh) *adj.* having an empty space inside

2. **be shut up** be kept in a particular place and prevented from leaving, in this case for one's safety

3. **sweet gum** *n.* a tree that has a sweet-smelling juice

He asks Phoenix what she is doing. She jokes that she is pretending to be an **upside-down** bug. She needs his help to get up.

◆ ◆ ◆

He lifted her up, gave her a swing in the air, and set her down. "Anything broken, Granny?" "No sir, them old dead weeds is springy enough," said Phoenix, when she had got her breath. "I thank you for your trouble."

◆ ◆ ◆

The man asks Phoenix where she lives and where she's going. She tells him she's on her way to town. He tells her that's too far. He says she should just go back home.

Phoenix doesn't move.

◆ ◆ ◆

The deep lines in her face went into a **fierce** and different **radiation.** Without warning, she had seen with her own eyes a flashing nickel fall out of the man's pocket onto the ground.

◆ ◆ ◆

Phoenix distracts the man. She cries and claps her hands. She tells the black dog to get away. She whispers, "Sic him!"[4] The man tells Phoenix to watch how he gets rid of the dog. He tells his own dog, "Sic him!" The man runs and throws sticks at the black dog. Phoenix uses this time to pick up the nickel. She slowly bends down.

◆ ◆ ◆

Everyday Words

upside-down (UP syd DOWN) *adj.* in a position with the top at the bottom and the bottom at the top

fierce (FEERS) *adj.* showing a lot of energy or strong emotion

radiation (ray dee AY shuhn) *n.* arrangement from the center to the sides

4. **"Sic him!"** a command given to a dog to attack

Cultural Understanding

Granny is an English word that is used for a *grandmother*. Other words include *Grandma*, *Gran*, and *Nana*.

Comprehension Builder 

The man tells Old Phoenix that she should go back home because the town is too far away for her to walk to. Predict what Old Phoenix will do.

____

____

____

Vocabulary Builder 

Idioms The idiom *get rid of* means "make someone leave because the person is causing problems or because you do not like the person" or "take action so that you no longer have something unpleasant that you do not want." Use the idiom to complete these sentences:

The man says that he will

______________________ the dog. Old Phoenix probably wants to

______________________ the man.

Fluency Builder 

Underline the words in the bracketed paragraph that Old Phoenix says. Then, read aloud the bracketed paragraph with expression.

Vocabulary Builder 

Idioms The idiom *go off* means "explode or fire." When someone says that a gun goes off, he or she means that the gun fires, or shoots. Complete this sentence:

Old Phoenix has often seen a

gun ______________________ .

Cultural Understanding

Christmas, December 25, is a holiday in the United States. It is the time when Christians celebrate the birth of Christ, an important person in the Christian religion. Many Americans who are not Christian celebrate Christmas as well. During the holiday, people gather with family and friends and exchange gifts. Some may go to church, sing special songs, and hang decorations and lights on their homes and businesses.

Her chin was lowered almost to her knees. The yellow palm of her hand came out from the fold of her apron. Her fingers slid down and along the ground under the piece of money with the **grace** and care they would have in lifting an egg from under a setting hen. Then she slowly straightened up, she stood **erect,** and the nickel was in her apron pocket. A bird flew by. Her lips moved. "God watching me the whole time. I come to stealing."

◆　◆　◆

The man comes back. He tells Phoenix that he scared the dog off. Then, he points the gun at Phoenix. She just stands straight, facing him. He asks her if the gun scares her.

◆　◆　◆

"No, sir, I seen plenty go off closer by, in my day, and for less than what I done," she said, holding utterly still.

◆　◆　◆

The man admires her bravery. He would give her some money if he had any. He **advises** her to stay home to be safe. She tells him she has to continue her journey.

The man and Phoenix go in different directions. Phoenix keeps walking. At last she gets to Natchez.[5] The city is decorated for Christmas. Phoenix sees a lady who is carrying an armful of wrapped gifts. Phoenix asks the woman to tie her shoelaces. She says that

Everyday Words

grace (GRAYS) *n.* a smooth way of moving that looks natural and relaxed
erect (i REKT) *adj.* in a straight, upright position
advises (uhd VYZ iz) *v.* tells someone what you think he or she should do

5. **Natchez** (NACH iz) a town in southern Mississippi

untied shoes are fine for the country. But they don't look right in a big building. Phoenix goes into a big building. She says "Here I be" to the woman at the counter. The woman asks Phoenix for her name, but Phoenix does not answer. The woman asks if Phoenix is **deaf.** Then, the nurse comes in.

◆　◆　◆

"Oh, that's just old Aunt Phoenix," she said. "She doesn't come for herself—she has a little grandson. She makes these trips just as regular as clockwork. She lives away back off the Old Natchez Trace."[6] She bent down. "Well, Aunt Phoenix, why don't you just take a seat? We won't keep you standing after your long trip."

◆　◆　◆

Phoenix sits down. The nurse asks her about her grandson. She wants to know if his throat is any better. At first, Phoenix does not answer. The nurse asks if the boy is dead. At last, Phoenix answers. She tells the nurse that her memory had left her. She had forgotten why she had come. The nurse wonders how she could forget, after coming so far.

◆　◆　◆

"Throat never heals, does it?" said the nurse, speaking in a loud, sure voice to old Phoenix. By now she had a card with something written on it, a little list. "Yes. Swallowed **lye.** When was it?—January—two-three years ago—"

Phoenix spoke unasked now. "No, missy, he not dead, he just the same. Every little while his throat begin to close up again, and he not able to swallow. He not get his breath. He not able to

Vocabulary Builder

Dialect Old Phoenix does not use standard English when she says, "Here I be." She is speaking in dialect, or a form of the language spoken by a particular group of people or in a particular area. What form of the verb *to be* would Old Phoenix use if she were speaking standard English? Rewrite her statement in standard English.

____

Vocabulary Builder

Idioms The idiom *as regular as clockwork* means "happening at the same time and in the same way every time." What happens as regular as clockwork, according to the nurse?

____

____

Comprehension Builder 

What is wrong with Phoenix's grandson? Circle the passages in the bracketed section that answer the question.

Everyday Words

deaf (DEF) *adj.* physically unable to hear anything or unable to hear well

lye (LY) *n.* a strong chemical used in making soap

6. **the Old Natchez Trace** A trace is an old path or trail left by people, animals, or vehicles.

Vocabulary Builder 

Contractions A contraction is a shortened form of two words. In contractions, an apostrophe (') replaces one or more letters that are dropped. *It's* is a contraction of *it is.* Underline the sentence in which *it's* appears. Read aloud the sentence as it is written. Then, read it again, this time replacing *it's* with *it is.*

Vocabulary Builder 

Parts of Speech *Last* may be a noun meaning "the person or thing that comes after all the others in a group." It may also be a verb meaning "continue to exist or live for a long time." Which part of speech is *last* in the bracketed paragraph?

____

Cultural Understanding

A paper windmill is a toy. Curved pieces of paper are attached to one end of a stick. The paper pieces turn or spin when the wind blows on them. In the United States, paper windmills are called pinwheels, and often they are made of plastic.

help himself. So the time come around, and I go on another trip for the **soothing** medicine."

"All right. The doctor said as long as you came to get it, you could have it," said the nurse. "But it's an <u>obstinate</u> case."

◆ ◆ ◆

Phoenix talks about her grandson. She says that they are the only two left in the world. The boy **suffers,** but he is going to last. He is a sweet boy. The nurse then gives Phoenix the medicine. She says **"Charity"** as she makes a mark in a book. The nurse gives Phoenix a nickel out of her purse for Christmas. Phoenix takes the other nickel out of her pocket and looks at both of them.

She taps her cane to announce her plan. She is going to buy a paper windmill for her grandson. He has never seen one.

◆ ◆ ◆

She lifted her free hand, gave a little nod, turned around, and walked out of the doctor's office. Then her slow step began on the stairs, going down.

Everyday Words

soothing (SOO thing) *adj.* comforting
suffers (SUH fers) *v.* experiences physical or mental pain
charity (CHAR uh tee) *n.* money or other things given to help people who are poor or sick

Thinking About the Selection

1. As Phoenix Jackson walks to town to get medicine for her grandson, she has many interactions with people and animals. Summarize these interactions in the chart below.

Phoenix Jackson's Interactions	
With Nature	With People
talks to the animals	talks to and dances with scarecrow

2. Phoenix's interactions with nature are different from her interactions with people because ___________________________________

____.

TALK ABOUT IT **Making Sacrifices** Phoenix Jackson makes many sacrifices and endures many hardships to get medicine for her grandson. Discuss with a partner why Phoenix continues to make this trip. Use this sentence frame:

Phoenix Jackson continues to make the trip to town because

____.

Writing About the Essential Question

What is the relationship between place and literature? Does Phoenix seem more "at home" in the natural landscape or in the social landscape of Depression-era Mississippi? Explain.

____

____

____

Word Families

You will recall that groups of words that share the same base word are called word families. Remember that a base word may stand alone or serve as a basis for forming new words. New words are formed by adding prefixes, suffixes, verb endings and other words to the base word.

Example

Base Word	Words That Share the Base Word
change: *v.* to become different; to cause to become different	changeable: *adj.* likely to change; changing often
	changed: *adj.* having become different as a result of an important experience
	changeless: *adj.* without change
	unchangeable: *adj.* refusing to change; unable to be changed

Now You Do It

Complete each sentence with a word from the chart above.

1. Carter was a _____________ person after his trip.

2. The mountains seemed to be a place of _____________ beauty.

3. The young child's mood was as _____________ as the weather.

4. The teacher had an _____________ attitude about lateness.

5. Could you _____________ the station on the radio?

TALK ABOUT IT **Talk About Change** With a partner, discuss changes in your life. What has changed in your life since you were a small child? What remains changeless or unchangeable? What aspects of your life are changeable? How do you expect your life to change in the future?

WRITE ABOUT IT **Statements of Past and Present** Some people say that change is the only thing that you can expect in life. Write a statement that explains how one aspect of your life has changed. Use words from the *change* family in your statement.

Vocabulary

Listen to each word. Say it. Then, read the definition and the example sentence.

despondent (di SPAHN duhnt) *adj.* Someone who is **despondent** is extremely unhappy and without hope.

The news that the trip was cancelled made Penelope despondent.

intervene (in ter VEEN) *v.* When you **intervene,** you become involved in an argument or fight in order to change what happens.

It's not wise to intervene when dogs are fighting.

intuitively (in TOO i tiv lee) *adv.* When you do something **intuitively,** you do it based on feelings rather than on knowledge or facts.

Keith intuitively completed the test, having not studied for it.

Vocabulary Practice

Read the first sentence in each group of three. Then, complete Sentence *a* by substituting another word or phrase that means the same as the underlined vocabulary word. Complete Sentence *b* with your own ideas and words.

1. The man was <u>despondent</u> over the loss of his job.

   a. The man was _____________ over the loss of his job.

   b. The man was despondent over _________________________.

2. The mother chose to <u>intervene</u> in the children's argument.

   a. The mother chose to _____________ in the children's argument.

   b. The mother chose to intervene _________________________.

3. He reacted <u>intuitively</u> when he sensed danger.

   a. He reacted _____________ when he sensed danger.

   b. He reacted intuitively when _________________________.

Getting Ready to Read

The narrator thinks that unfamiliar sounds in the house may be a ghost. With a partner, discuss whether you believe that ghosts exist. Is there always a scientific explanation for all events?

The Night the Ghost Got In
James Thurber

Summary One night, the narrator hears footsteps. He wakes up his family. All of the confusion makes the narrator's crazy grandfather angry.

Note-taking Guide

As you read, use the chart to identify the topic, or the main idea, of each paragraph. An example is provided below.

Paragraph	Topic/Main Idea of the Paragraph
1	A ghost got into the house on November 17, 1915, and caused a great deal of confusion.
2	
3	
4	
5	
6	
7	
8	
9	
10	
11	
12	
13	
14	

Thinking About the Selection

1. James Thurber's work is filled with humor. Sometimes a detail is funny because it is surprising or unexpected. At other times, a detail is funny because of the situation or context. In the chart below, list examples of humor from the story.

Surprise	Situation
1. Mother throws a shoe through the window to wake the neighbors.	1. Grandfather calls the police officers cowards for running away from the war.
2.	2.
3.	3.

2. Without collecting evidence of any kind, the narrator speculates

   that the pacing is coming from a _____________________________,

   a _____________________________, or a _____________________________.

TALK ABOUT IT **Family Time** Tell a partner a funny story about your family. Use surprise and situation to create humor.

Writing About the Essential Question

What makes American literature American? This essay describes an event that took place in 1915. Do you think modern readers can still enjoy it? Has the American sense of humor changed since that time? Explain.

Silent Letters

The letters *g* and *k* are sometimes silent. These letters may be silent as a result of word origins or of pronunciation changes over time.

Letter	When It Is Silent	Sample Words
g	before *m* or *n*	gnarl gnaw assign sign phlegm
k	before the *n* at the beginning of a word	knew knife knight knock know

Now You Do It

In each word listed below, underline the silent letter.

gnarl	gnaw
knew	sign
assign	know

TALK ABOUT IT **Silent Talk** Take turns with a partner saying aloud each of the words from the chart. After you have said the word, use it in a sentence.

WRITE ABOUT IT **Silent Write** Use words from the chart to write a note to a partner. For example, you might write, "I wish I *knew* what homework we have tonight. What did the teacher *assign?*" Tell your partner to respond in writing. Exchange notes at least twice, and use at least one word from the chart in each note.

Vocabulary

Listen to each word. Say it. Then, read the definition and the example sentence.

brutal (BROO tl) *adj.* Someone who is **brutal** is cruel and often violent.
The brutal guards abused the prisoners.

wanton (WAHN tuhn) *adj.* Something that is **wanton** is deliberately harmful or damaging for no reason.
The factory's wanton disregard for the workers made them strike.

cunning (KUN ing) *adj.* Someone who is **cunning** is skillful in cheating or tricking.
Her cunning plan took everyone by surprise.

Vocabulary Practice

Read the first sentence in each group of three. Then, complete Sentence *a* by substituting another word or phrase that means the same as the underlined vocabulary word. Complete Sentence *b* with your own ideas and words.

1. The brutal criminal was imprisoned for his violent crimes.

   a. The ______________ criminal was imprisoned for his violent crimes.

   b. The brutal criminal ____.

2. The captain showed wanton disregard for his crew's safety.

   a. The captain showed ______________ disregard for his crew's safety.

   b. The captain showed wanton disregard ______________________.

3. The cunning lawyer won by producing a surprise witness.

   a. The ______________ lawyer won by producing a surprise witness.

   b. The cunning lawyer ____.

Getting Ready to Read

The growth of cities, factories, and technology has both positive and negative effects. With a partner, discuss those positive and negative aspects of the community in which you live.

Chicago • Grass
Carl Sandburg

Summaries In **"Chicago,"** Sandburg uses simple words to express his love and admiration for the city of Chicago. He challenges the reader to find a city with more life. In **"Grass,"** the grass explains that there is only grass where once important battles between great armies took place. The calmness of nature hides the horror and senselessness of war.

Note-taking Guide

Use the following chart to help you keep track of what each speaker talks about.

Chicago	
To whom is the speaker talking?	
What does the speaker talk about?	
What descriptions does the speaker use?	
Grass	
Who is the speaker?	
What does the speaker talk about?	
What does the speaker claim to do?	

Thinking About the Selections

1. In "Chicago," the speaker describes the positive and negative aspects of the city. List some of these items in the columns below. Include both references to industry and the adjectives that the speaker uses to describe the city.

Positive Aspects	Negative Aspects
1. food production (pork, wheat)	1. prostitution
2.	2.
3.	3.

2. In "Grass," Sandburg describes the power of nature to ______________

____

____ .

TALK ABOUT IT **Create Epithets** In "Chicago," Sandburg creates epithets, or phrases of characterization, to describe Chicago. For example, he calls Chicago "City of the Big Shoulders" and "Player with Railroads." With a partner, create three epithets that might describe the city or town in which you live. To generate some ideas, you might create similes or comparisons. Use this sentence frame:

______________ is like ______________ because ______________ .

Writing About the Essential Question

How does literature shape or reflect society? What do these poems suggest about the value of industry and labor to a society?

____

____

____

____

Prefixes

You will recall that a prefix is a word part added to the beginning of a base word. Generally, a prefix changes the meaning or part of speech of the base word. The prefix *ex-* means "former."

Example

ex- + president = ex-president

The new word *ex-president* means "former president."

Now You Do It

Make new words by adding the prefix *ex-* to each word below. Consult a dictionary and write a definition for each new word.

______mayor ____

______student ____

______teacher ____

______athlete ____

TALK ABOUT IT **Roles and Positions** With a partner, discuss different roles or positions that a person may have and then leave. After you have identified such a role or position, name it by using the *ex-* prefix. For example, you may note that a person could be an ex-sheriff after retiring from the position of sheriff.

WRITE ABOUT IT **Write a Letter** Choose one of the *ex-* roles or positions you identified in your discussion, and write a letter from that person's point of view. Address the letter to someone who might want to have that role or position, and offer advice to this person. In your letter, include at least two words that have the *ex-* prefix.

Vocabulary

Listen to each word. Say it. Then, read the definition and the example sentence.

poise (POYZ) *n.* **Poise** is a calm, confident way of behaving and the ability to control your feelings or reactions in difficult situations.
>*The jurors noticed the defendant's <u>poise</u> throughout the trial.*

rueful (ROO ful) *adj.* Someone who is **rueful** is feeling sorrow or regret.
>*Her thoughtless comment soon made her <u>rueful</u>.*

luminary (LOO muh nayr ee) *adj.* Something that is **luminary** gives off light. This is an uncommon variant of the word luminous.
>*The <u>luminary</u> moon reflected off the water.*

Vocabulary Practice

Read the first sentence in each group of three. Then, complete Sentence *a* by substituting another word or phrase that means the same as the underlined vocabulary word. Complete Sentence *b* with your own ideas and words.

1. The speaker showed <u>poise</u> as she answered questions.

   a. The speaker showed ________________ as she answered questions.

   b. The speaker showed poise as she ________________________________.

2. The boy was <u>rueful</u> after arguing with his mother.

   a. The boy was ________________ after arguing with his mother.

   b. The boy was rueful ________________________________.

3. The <u>luminary</u> candle shone in the dark window.

   a. The ________________ candle shone in the dark window.

   b. The luminary candle ________________________________.

Getting Ready to Read

Human beings look to nature for inspiration, but they sometimes view nature as something to conquer. The poetry of Robert Frost explores this relationship between human beings and nature. Tell a partner about times when you found inspiration in nature.

Robert Frost's Poetry

Summaries In **"Birches,"** the speaker recalls the pleasure of swinging from birch trees as a child. **"Stopping by Woods on a Snowy Evening"** describes a man tempted to linger in the peaceful woods. In **"Mending Wall,"** the speaker and his neighbor meet to repair breaks in the wall that separates their fields. The speaker wonders about the purpose of the wall and the forces of nature that continually pull it down. **"Out, Out—"** tells the harsh story of a young farm boy who loses control of his power saw while cutting wood. **"The Gift Outright"** examines the colonial spirit that struggled to tame a new land and form a nation. In **"Acquainted With the Night,"** the speaker admits to moments of loneliness in his life.

Note-taking Guide

Use this chart to record the main idea and an important detail from each of Frost's poems.

Poem	Main Idea	Important Detail
Birches		
Stopping by Woods on a Snowy Evening		
Mending Wall		
"Out, Out—"		
The Gift Outright		
Aquainted With the Night		

Thinking About the Selections

1. Frost uses images of nature to communicate about the human condition. Complete the chart with information from the poems.

Poem	Images of Nature	Comment on the Human Condition
Birches	birch trees	Youth is carefree; adulthood is burdensome.
Stopping by Woods on a Snowy Evening		
Mending Wall		
"Out, Out—"		
The Gift Outright	American landscape	
Aquainted With the Night	night and rain	

2. The speaker in "Out, Out—" wishes that the boy's family had let him have a half-hour to play because ____

____.

TALK ABOUT IT **Childhood Pastime** In "Birches," Frost writes about the simple joy of swinging in birch trees. Tell a partner about an activity that gave you joy as a child and that you no longer do.

? Writing About the Essential Question

What is the relationship between place and literature? What understanding of rural New England and America as a whole do these poems convey? Explain.

____

____

____

Suffixes

A suffix is a word part added to the end of a base word. Sometimes a suffix changes the meaning of the word. Sometimes a suffix changes the word's part of speech. The suffix *-ism* means "the state of being like something or someone, or having a particular quality" or "a political belief or religion based on a particular principle or the ideas and beliefs of a particular person." This suffix is used to form nouns.

Examples

Base Word	Resulting Noun	Meaning
hero + -ism	heroism	the state of being like a hero or showing the qualities of a hero
capital + -ism	capitalism	an economic and political system in which businesses belong mostly to private owners, not to the government

Now You Do It

Add the suffix *-ism* to the following words. Then, use each noun in a sentence. Consult a dictionary if necessary.

magnet	
Buddha	

TALK ABOUT IT **A Show of Heroism** Tell a partner about a time when you behaved with heroism or when you witnessed heroism.

WRITE ABOUT IT **Create an *Ism*** Think about ideas or beliefs that are important to you. Use one word to identify an idea or belief, and add the suffix *-ism* to the end of the word. Then, write a definition explaining the idea or belief. For example, you may enjoy playing soccer, so you would add the suffix *-ism* to this word to create *soccerism:* a belief that soccer is the most exciting sport.

Vocabulary

Listen to each word. Say it. Then, read the definition and the example sentence.

lulled (LUHLD) *v.* When you have **lulled** someone, you have made that person feel calm or sleepy.

The mother lulled the newborn baby back to sleep.

dusky (DUHS kee) *adj.* Something that is **dusky** is dark or not very bright in color.

The dusky room was depressing.

liberty (LIB er tee) *n.* **Liberty** is the freedom and the right to do whatever you want without permission or being afraid.

The U. S. Constitution grants liberty and justice to all citizens.

Vocabulary Practice

Read the first sentence in each group of three. Then, complete Sentence *a* by substituting another word or phrase that means the same as the underlined vocabulary word. Complete Sentence *b* with your own ideas and words.

1. The soft music <u>lulled</u> the girl to sleep.

   a. The soft music _________________ the girl to sleep.

   b. ____ lulled the girl to sleep.

2. The <u>dusky</u> evening signaled the end of the day.

   a. The _______________ evening signaled the end of the day.

   b. The dusky evening ____.

3. The citizens fought for <u>liberty</u> against the tyrant.

   a. The citizens fought for _______________ against the tyrant.

   b. The citizens fought for liberty _________________________________.

Getting Ready to Read

The Harlem Renaissance was a flowering of African American arts centered in Harlem, an area of New York City, in the 1920s. Langston Hughes was one of the most popular poets of this period. With a partner, discuss what you know about African American writers or musicians today.

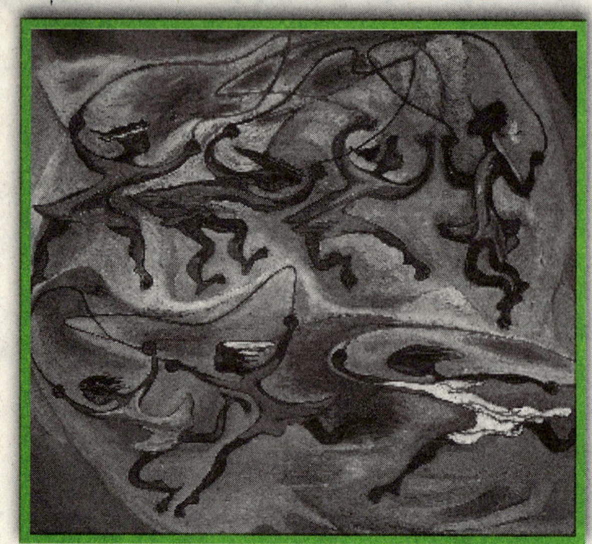

The Negro Speaks of Rivers • I, Too • Dream Variations • Refugee in America

Langston Hughes

Summaries In **"The Negro Speaks of Rivers,"** the speaker recalls the experience of his people along ancient rivers of the world. **"I, Too"** is Langston Hughes's response to a poem by Walt Whitman. Whitman's poem describes the variety that exists in America. The speaker in **"Dream Variations"** imagines a world in which he can play and rest freely and in which the blackness of his skin is accepted. **"Refugee in America"** challenges the reader to think more carefully about words such as *freedom* and *liberty*.

Note-taking Guide

As you read each poem, enter an example of what each speaker says and then explain what he means in the chart.

	What Does the Speaker Say?	What Does the Speaker Mean?
The Negro Speaks of Rivers		
I, Too		
Dream Variatons		
Refugee in America		

Thinking About the Selections

1. One purpose of the works from the Harlem Renaissance was to share aspects of African American culture with audiences. Complete the chart below with information from the poems.

Poem	What It Tells Readers About African American Culture or People
The Negro Speaks of Rivers	African American culture is old. It has existed since the beginning of time.
I, Too	
Dream Variatons	
Refugee in America	

2. Although Hughes's poetry recognizes injustice and oppression, the tone or mood of the works is hopeful because ________________________

____.

TALK ABOUT IT **Being America** In "I, Too," the speaker suggests that many voices, including his own, make up the song that is America. The speaker ends by stating, "I, too, am America." How are you part of the United States? How does your voice contribute to the song that is America? Discuss your ideas with a partner.

Writing About the Essential Question

What makes American literature American? In what ways do these poems capture some of the complexities of the African American experience?

____

____

____

____

Y as a Consonant or Vowel

When the letter *y* appears at the end of a word or syllable, or when there is no other vowel in the word, *y* performs as a vowel. At the end of single-syllable words, the letter *y* generally signifies the long *-i* sound as *fly*. At the end of multi-syllable words, the letters *y* or *ey* generally signify the long *-e* sound as in *happy*.

Examples

y as a vowel	fly, happy, monkey
y as a consonant	year, young

Now You Do It

Read the words below, and determine whether the *y* in each word acts as a consonant or a vowel. Write your answer on the line.

1. yeast _____________
2. sky _____________
3. rainy _____________
4. your _____________
5. yarn _____________

6. early _____________
7. youth _____________
8. myth _____________
9. lonely _____________
10. hymn _____________

TALK ABOUT IT **Play the Game** With a partner, practice determining whether *y* is a consonant or a vowel. Take a few minutes to list six words that contain the letter *y*, but do not share your list with your partner. Then say a word aloud, and ask your partner to determine whether the *y* is a consonant or a vowel in the word. Alternate roles with your partner, keeping track of the number of times each of you correctly determines whether *y* is a consonant or a vowel.

WRITE ABOUT IT **Family Write** Use words from the lesson and from the game you played with your partner to write a note to a family member. For example, you might write, "Dear Aunt Sue, I want you to know that I think you are a really great chef." Include at least three words that use the letter *y* as a consonant, and three that use the letter *y* as a vowel.

Vocabulary

Listen to each word. Say it. Then, read the definition and the example sentence.

benediction (ben uh DIK shuhn) *n.* A **benediction** is a type of prayer in the Christian religion that asks God to protect and help someone.

He asked the priest to give a special <u>benediction</u> for his ailing father.

countenance (KOWN tuh nuhnts) *v.* If you **countenance** something, you accept or approve of it.

The babysitter would not <u>countenance</u> the boy's tantrums.

beguile (bi GYL) *v.* When you **beguile** someone, you persuade or trick him into doing something, especially by saying nice things.

The children had planned to <u>beguile</u> their parents so they could stay out longer.

Vocabulary Practice

Read the first sentence in each group of three. Then, complete Sentence *a* by substituting another word or phrase that means the same as the underlined vocabulary word. Complete Sentence *b* with your own ideas and words.

1. The minister said a <u>benediction</u> for the sick woman.

   a. The minister said a ______________ for the sick woman.

   b. The minister said a benediction for ________________________.

2. I will not <u>countenance</u> tardiness or bad behavior.

   a. I will not ______________ tardiness or bad behavior.

   b. I will not countenance ________________________.

3. The politician tried to <u>beguile</u> voters with false promises.

   a. The politician tried to ______________ voters with false promises.

   b. The politician tried to beguile ________________________.

Getting Ready to Read

Some writers of the Harlem Renaissance express negative aspects of the African American experience. Tell a partner about a situation in your life that may be viewed both positively and negatively.

The Tropics in New York •
From the Dark Tower •
A Black Man Talks
of Reaping

Summaries In **"The Tropics in New York,"** a window fruit display in New York takes the speaker back home to the tropics. In **"From the Dark Tower,"** the speaker seems to say that better times are coming for those who plant "while others reap." He says the night is no less lovely because it is dark. He closes by referring to waiting in the dark, tending "our agonizing seeds." In **"A Black Man Talks of Reaping,"** the speaker describes his careful planting of a large crop from which he reaped only a small harvest. While his brother's sons gather the crops, his own children eat bitter fruit gathered from fields they have not sown.

Note-taking Guide

Use this diagram to record details from the three poems and the shared message the details suggest.

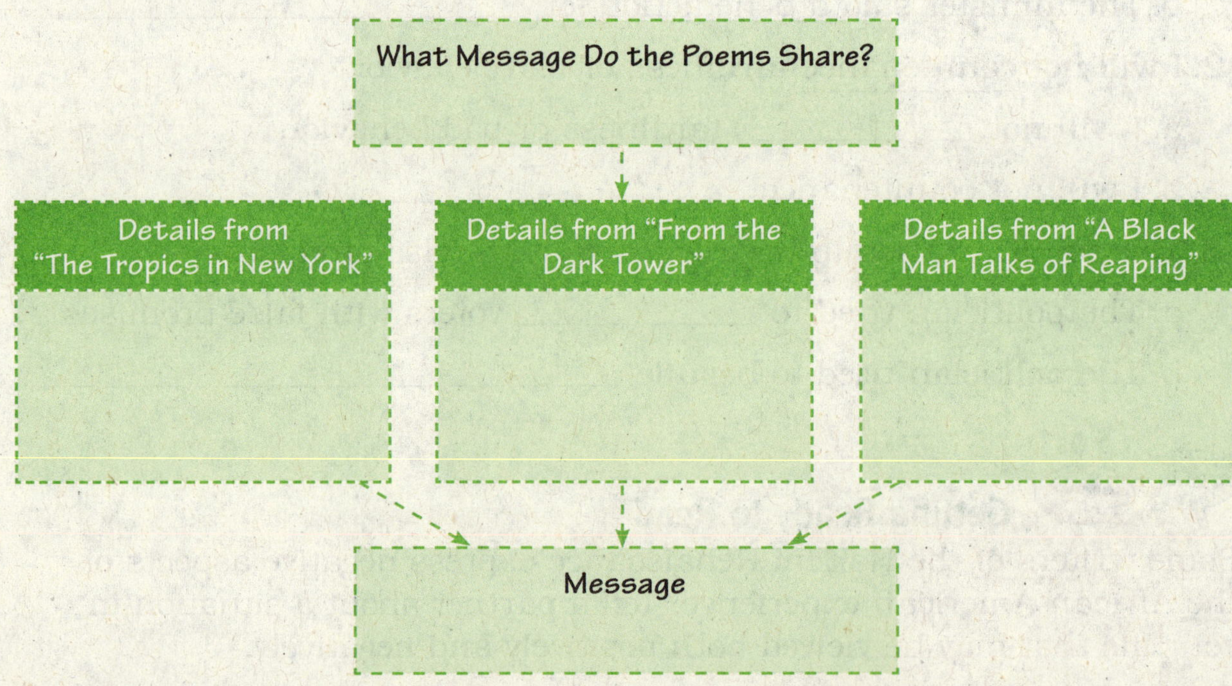

Thinking About the Selections

1. The three speakers use nature or farming to tell readers about their feelings and experiences regarding social issues, including racism. Complete the chart below by identifying additional images from the poems that deal with nature and farming.

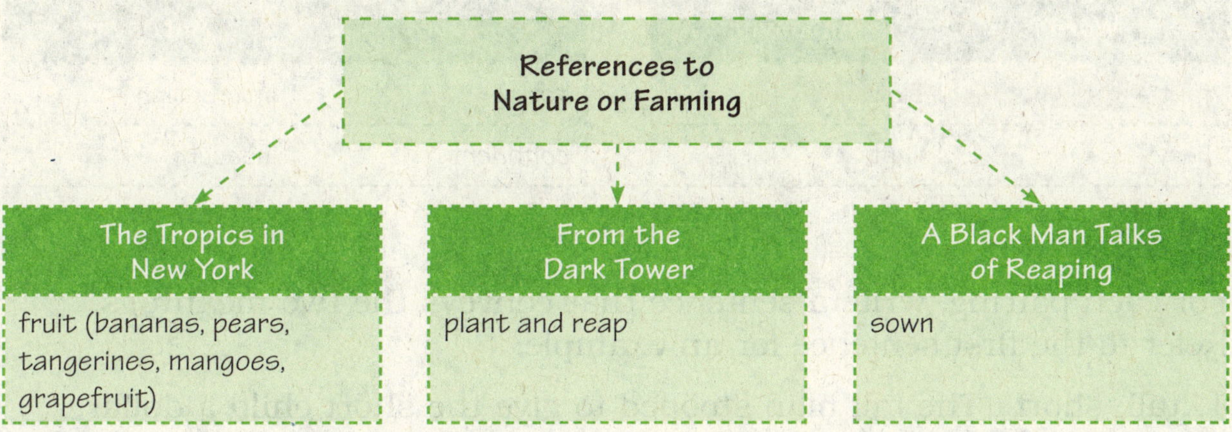

2. The three poems express feelings of longing for ________________________

____.

TALK **ABOUT IT** **Nature Comparison** In these poems, the writers compare nature to human situations through word choice. With a partner, create a nature simile or a comparison for a contemporary social situation. For example, you might say, *Poverty is like the autumn leaves falling from the trees, leaving the people stark and lonely.*

Writing About the Essential Question

What is the relationship between place and literature? Are these poets hopeful or pessimistic about the future for African Americans? Explain.

____

____

____

____

Antonyms

An antonym is a word that means the opposite of another word. For example, *tall* is an antonym of the word *short*. Sometimes, writers provide an antonym as a context clue to help readers understand the meaning of an unfamiliar term.

Examples

Word	Antonym
fast	slow
heavy	light

Word	Antonym
boring	interesting
confident	insecure

Now You Do It

For each pairing, write a sentence that conveys the two meanings. Refer to the first sentence for an example.

1. tall; short   The tall man stooped to give the short child a dollar.

2. fast; slow   _______________________________

3. heavy; light   _______________________________

4. boring; interesting   _______________________________

5. confident; insecure   _______________________________

TALK ABOUT IT **Reverse It** With a partner, practice using the antonyms in this lesson. Begin by saying a sentence that contains one of the words from the chart above. Have your partner reverse the meaning of the sentence by using an antonym for the word you choose. Switch roles, and continue the exercise.

WRITE ABOUT IT **Antonym Game** Create an antonym word game by writing note cards that give players two lists of words. For example, one list might include heavy items such as lead, a car, and so on. The second list might include light items such as a feather, a pencil, and so on. Write instructions so that players can use the lists to determine the antonyms.

Vocabulary

Listen to each word. Say it. Then, read the definition and the example sentence.

caper (KAY per) *n.* **Caper** is behavior or activity that is amusing or silly and not serious.

Selena's <u>caper</u> was inappropriate for the sad ceremony.

brazenness (BRAYZ uhn nuhs) *n.* When a person demonstrates **brazenness,** he or she is not embarrassed or ashamed to do something or to behave in a way that most people consider wrong or immoral.

Lloyd's <u>brazenness</u> regarding the theft concerned his friends.

duration (dŏŏ RAY shuhn) *n.* **Duration** is the length of time that something lasts.

Attendees remained standing for the <u>duration</u> of the ceremony.

Vocabulary Practice

Read the first sentence in each group of three. Then, complete Sentence *a* by substituting another word or phrase that means the same as the underlined vocabulary word. Complete Sentence *b* with your own ideas and words.

1. The boys' <u>caper</u> caused laughter during the ceremony.

   a. The boys' _______________ caused laughter during the ceremony.

   b. The boys' caper ____.

2. Myra showed <u>brazenness</u> when she refused to shake hands.

   a. Myra showed _______________ when she refused to shake hands.

   b. Myra showed brazenness when ___________________________________.

3. The test lasted for the <u>duration</u> of the afternoon.

   a. The test lasted for the _______________ of the afternoon.

   b. _______________ lasted for the duration of the afternoon.

Getting Ready to Read

As a child, Zora Neale Hurston loved to read Greek myths about the gods who ruled Mount Olympus and their interactions with human beings. Tell a partner about your favorite childhood stories. Give plot summaries and tell why you liked these stories.

from Dust Tracks on a Road

Zora Neale Hurston

Summary This is a section from a longer work. The author describes events from her childhood in a small Florida town. She used to wait at the side of the road for white travelers to pass by. She would ask to go with them for a short distance. Hurston also talks about an experience that changed her life. Her school had visitors one day. They were two white women. Hurston read aloud, and the women were impressed. They invited Hurston to visit them at their hotel. They gave her gifts. The gifts of books pleased Hurston more than the candy or pennies.

Note-taking Guide

As you read this selection, write down details about the characters in the chart below.

Character	What the Character Wants	What the Character Does
Zora		
Grandmother		
Mrs. Calhoun		
Mrs. Johnstone and Miss Hurd		

Thinking About the Selection

1. Hurston tells readers about an experience that changes her life. Complete the chart below with details from the story.

Why do the visitors choose to focus attention on Hurston rather than on one of the other children?	Hurston demonstrates the ability to read well, and other students struggle to read.
How do the visitors become involved in Hurston's life?	
Why does this attention change Hurston's life?	

2. Hurston is the kind of reader who ____.

TALK ABOUT IT **Life-Changing Events** Tell a partner about an event that changed your life in some way. Perhaps you moved. Perhaps you met an important person. Perhaps you enrolled in an unusual class. Use this sentence frame:

_______________________ changed my life because _______________________.

Writing About the Essential Question

How does literature shape or reflect society? Write about the details that reveal Hurston's self-confidence.

____

____

____

____

Parts of Speech

A noun is a word that represents a person, a place, a thing, an activity, a quality, or an idea. A verb is a word that describes an action, an experience, or a state of being. Some words can function as both nouns and verbs. Use context clues to determine the part of speech.

Examples

Word	Noun	Verb
block	piece of hard material with straight sides	prevent movement
deal	agreement or arrangement	give playing cards to players in a game
need	what someone has to have in order to live a healthy, comfortable life	require something or someone

Now You Do It

For each word, write two sentences. One sentence should contain the word used as a noun. The other sentence should contain the word used as a verb.

1. block ____

____

2. deal ____

____

3. need ____

____

TALK **ABOUT IT** **Share a Story** Share with a partner a brief story or anecdote, real or fictional, and include several of the words used as both nouns and verbs. Listen respectfully as your partner tells a story in which these words are used.

WRITE ABOUT IT **Describe a Game** Use the words in the chart to describe a game. Be sure to use the words as both nouns and verbs. Explain how the game is played and the purpose of the game.

Digital Tools

About Digital Tools

A **digital tool** is an electronic device or program that helps people perform tasks, such as research or writing. For example, students may consult Web sites to research information. They also use computers to write reports. Teachers expect students to cite, or give credit to, the sources that they use to write their reports. These sources may include books, articles, interviews, or Web sites from which the students gathered information. With a computer and Internet access, students can even find digital tools to help them cite their sources correctly.

Reading Skill

An essential step in the research process is to **locate appropriate information** about the topic. First, develop a research plan by listing questions you have about the topic. Next, choose which questions to use as the focus of your research, and develop a central idea for your report. Then, use the Internet and library sources to locate information that answers the questions. Finally, analyze the information to determine whether it is appropriate. Ask these questions:

- Does the information support the report's central idea?
- Is the author or source of the information objective?
- Does the material contain any bias?

Use the graphic organizer below to guide you as you read "Citation Machine."

Digital Resource			
Author or Creator			
Facts to Be Verified	Sources	Discrepancies	Result
1.			
2.			
3.			

Citation Machine™

CITATION MACHINE
Serving Students & Teachers
K-12, College, & University

Citation Machine™ is an interactive web tool designed to assist high school, college, and university students, their teachers, and independent researchers in their effort to respect other people's intellectual properties. To use Citation Machine™, simply …

Numbered items show how to use the organizer.

1. Click the citation format you need and then the type of resource you wish to cite.
2. Complete the Web form that appears with information from your source.
3. Click **Make Citations** to generate standard bibliographic and in-text citations.

The primary goal of this tool is to make it so easy for **high school**, **college**, and **university students** and other researchers to credit information sources that there is virtually no reason not to—because **SOMEDAY THE INFORMATION SOMEONE WANTS TO USE WILL BE YOURS.**

Warning: There are many nuances to how citations are formed, and this software may not pick up all of the circumstances that influence a citation's proper format. The Citation Machine™ cannot fully guarantee the accuracy of citations generated by this tool.

If you have questions about the proper citation of these or other source types, consult your local copy of:

Bullets beneath each format or style of citation list additional resources.

- MLA Handbook for Writers of Research Papers: 6th Edition or
- Publication Manual of the American Psychological Association: 5th Edition.

There will be copies in your school or public libraries.

Sidebar navigation

▼ **MLA**

Print
- Book: One or More Authors
- Encyclopedia or other reference work
- Journal Article: One or More Authors
- Magazine Article: One or More Authors

Non-Print
- Internet Journal or Magazine Article: One or More Authors
- Web Page
- Online Encyclopedia
- Encyclopedia (CD-ROM)

▼ **APA**

▼ **CHICAGO**

▼ **TURABIAN**

This input form is generated by clicking on the link for a book with two authors.

Input Screen

Results screen

The organizer generates a citation based on the input information.

Thinking About the Digital Tool

1. What does the Citation Machine help students do?

____

2. Which citation format was used to make the citation for *The Freedom Writers Diary?*

____

Reading Skill

3. Which link would you click if the teacher told you to use the Chicago format for citing sources?

____

4. Which link would you activate if you wanted to check the MLA format of a specific citation?

____

____

Timed Writing: Evaluation (25 minutes)

Write a brief essay in which you evaluate how you could best use the Online Citation Organizer and the Online Encyclopedia in your research. Consider both the benefits and drawbacks of each digital reference tool. Draw information from the documents you just studied and include methods for verifying information from both sources. Allow approximately five minutes to plan, fifteen minutes to draft, and five minutes to review, revise, and edit your paper.

Word Bank

depression	interpretation	transition
disillusion	metropolis	unresolved
exile	ordinary	wasteland

A. **Definition Matching** Next to each word listed in the column on the left, write the letter that corresponds to the word's definition.

Words	Definitions
depression _______	A. the process or period in which something changes from one form or state to another
interpretation _______	B. an unattractive area, often containing deserted buildings or factories
transition _______	C. unanswered or unsolved
disillusion _______	D. to force someone to leave his or her country, especially for political reasons
metropolis _______	E. to make someone realize that something which he or she thought was true or good is not really true or good
unresolved _______	F. a feeling of sadness that makes one think that there is no hope for the future
exile _______	G. a very large city that is the most important city in a country or an area
ordinary _______	H. the way in which someone explains or understands an event, information, or another's actions
wasteland _______	I. average, common, or usual, not different or special

B. Complete the chart by circling the part of speech of each word.

Word	Parts of Speech	
depression	adjective	noun
disillusion	verb	adverb
exile	adjective	verb
interpretation	noun	adjective
metropolis	noun	adverb
ordinary	adverb	adjective
transition	noun	adverb
unresolved	adjective	verb
wasteland	verb	noun

Discuss Disappointment The government of the United States is based on the principles of democracy and equality. The American Dream promises that financial security, civil liberties, and the pursuit of happiness are possible for ordinary citizens. However, at times in American history, citizens have been denied these goals. In these instances, Americans may be disillusioned. With a partner, discuss a time when you felt disappointed or disillusioned. Use the vocabulary words in your discussion.

Write About Disappointment Now, write about one experience of disillusionment or disappointment that you discussed. Begin by describing your hopes, dreams, or expectations in the situation. Then, explain why these hopes or dreams where not realized or fulfilled. Discuss the effects of your disappointment. Did you give up your hopes or dreams? Did you revise your hopes or dreams? Did you try again? Use the vocabulary words in your narrative.

Vocabulary

Listen to each word. Say it. Then, read the definition and the example sentence.

evacuated (i vak yoo AYT id) *v.* When a place is **evacuated,** it is made empty, such as when people leave it.

The police <u>evacuated</u> the city due to the hurricane warning.

volition (vuh LI shuhn) *n.* When you do something of your own **volition,** you do it as an act of using your will.

The athlete's desire and <u>volition</u> enabled her to win the medal.

rendezvous (RAHN day voo) *n.* A **rendezvous** is a meeting place that people have agreed upon.

That restaurant is the club's <u>rendezvous</u> point.

Vocabulary Practice

Read the first sentence in each group of three. Then, complete Sentence *a* by substituting another word or phrase that means the same as the underlined vocabulary word. Complete Sentence *b* with your own ideas and words.

1. The fire department <u>evacuated</u> the building.

   a. The fire department _______________ the building.

   b. _______________________________ evacuated the building.

2. The witness came to the police station of her own <u>volition</u>.

   a. The witness came to the police station of her own _____________.

   b. The witness _____________________ of her own volition.

3. We arranged a <u>rendezvous</u> for the committee.

   a. We arranged a _____________ for the committee.

   b. We arranged a rendezvous _________________________.

Getting Ready to Read

By August 1945, World War II had lasted six years. President Truman believed that the newly-developed atomic bomb would end the war quickly. The atomic bombing of Japan ended the war, but its effects were long lasting. How do you think the use of an atomic bomb changed the world? Discuss your thoughts with a partner.

from Hiroshima
John Hersey

Summary On August 6, 1945, at 8:15 in the morning, the United States dropped an atomic bomb on Hiroshima, Japan. More than 100,000 people died as a result of the bombing. Mr. Kiyoshi Tanimoto, Mrs. Hatsuyo Nakamura, Dr. Masakazu Fujii, and Miss Toshiko Sasaki survived. This excerpt tells part of their story.

Note-taking Guide

Use this chart to record what each person was doing when the bomb exploded.

	What were they doing?	How did they experience the blast?
Mr. Kiyoshi Tanimoto		
Mrs. Hatsuyo Nakamura		
Dr. Masakazu Fujii		
Miss Toshiko Sasaki		

Vocabulary

Listen to each word. Say it. Then, read the definition and the example sentence.

plexiglass (PLEKS i glas) *n.* **Plexiglass** is a strong, clear type of plastic that can be used instead of glass.

> *The glass windows shattered, so we replaced them with plexiglass.*

hunched (HUNCHT) *v.* If a person **hunched,** he or she bent down and forward, curving the back.

> *During the game of hide-and-seek, the child hunched under the table.*

loosed (LOOST) *v.* When something is **loosed,** it is set free.

> *The rescuer loosed the dogs when they smelled the missing hikers.*

Vocabulary Practice

Read the first sentence in each group of three. Then, complete Sentence *a* by substituting another word or phrase that means the same as the underlined vocabulary word. Complete Sentence *b* with your own ideas and words.

1. The plexiglass dome on the roof let in natural light.

   a. The _______________ dome on the roof let in natural light.

   b. The plexiglass dome on the roof _______________________________.

2. The tall woman hunched to fit through the doorway.

   a. The tall woman _______________ to fit through the doorway.

   b. The tall woman hunched _______________________________.

3. I loosed the bird after its wing had healed.

   a. I _______________ the bird after its wing had healed.

   b. I loosed the bird _______________________________.

Getting Ready to Read

Randall Jarrell joined the Army Air Force in 1942. He often wrote about young soldiers and their fears. How would it feel to be a gunner squeezed into a tiny space under a bomber high above Earth? Talk about your ideas in a small group.

The Death of the Ball Turret Gunner
Randall Jarrell

Summary In "The Death of the Ball Turret Gunner," the speaker uses images to show how deadly war is. The powerful final line shows the violence and finality of death in war.

Note-taking Guide

As you read, use this chart to list striking words and phrases from the poem.

Poem	Striking words	Striking phrases
"The Death of the Ball Turret Gunner"		

Thinking About the Selections

1. Both Hersey and Jarrell describe the destruction of war. Use the diagram below to list similarities and differences between their descriptions.

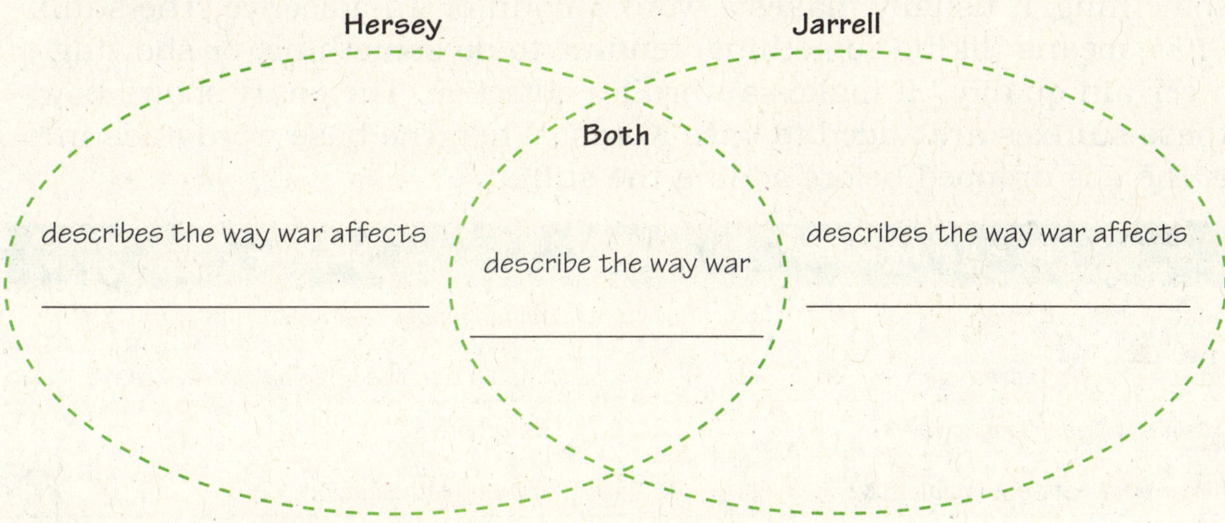

2. Hersey's purpose in writing *Hiroshima* is to show ________________

____ .

TALK ABOUT IT   **What Do You Think?** President Truman faced an extraordinarily difficult decision when considering whether to drop the atomic bomb on Hiroshima. What factors do you think he considered? Why do you think this decision was so difficult? Share your ideas with a partner.

Writing About the Essential Question

How does literature shape or reflect society? How do both the essay by Hersey and the poem by Jarrell create a societal memory of World War II? How important is that societal memory? Explain.

____

____

____

Suffixes

A suffix is a word part added to the end of a base word. Sometimes a suffix changes the word's meaning or part of speech.

Examples

The suffix *-ive* indicates that someone or something does or can do something. It usually makes a word a noun or an adjective. The suffix *-ative* means "liking something, tending to do something, or showing a certain quality." It makes a word an adjective. The chart shows how these suffixes are added to base words. When the base word ends in *e*, the *e* is dropped before adding the suffix.

Base word + suffix	Meaning
act + -ive = active	*adj.* doing things, taking actions
create + -ive = creative	*adj.* able to use the imagination to create
talk + -ative = talkative	*adj.* liking to talk
imagine + -ative = imaginative	*adj.* showing imagination

Now You Do It

Write a sentence that contains each word listed in the chart above.

1. active _______________________________________

2. creative _____________________________________

3. talkative ____________________________________

4. imaginative __________________________________

TALK ABOUT IT   **How Talkative Are You?** Discuss a topic in a small group. Use words you have learned with the suffixes *-ive* and *-ative*. Keep track of how often each person in the group adds to the discussion.

WRITE ABOUT IT   **Write a Dialogue** Write a dialogue, or conversation, between a teacher and a student that includes each word above.

____

____

Vocabulary

Listen to each word. Say it. Then, read the definition and the example sentence.

listed (LIST uhd) *v.* Something that has **listed** has tilted, or inclined, so it is no longer level.

The floor of the old house <u>listed</u> toward the door.

ravenous (RAV uh nuhs) *adj.* Someone who is **ravenous** is extremely eager, especially for food.

The <u>ravenous</u> birds quickly emptied the bird feeder.

morose (muh ROHS) *adj.* A person who is **morose** is feeling gloomy or sullen.

Gil was <u>morose</u> for days after his dog ran away.

Vocabulary Practice

Read the first sentence in each group of three. Then, complete Sentence *a* by substituting another word or phrase that means the same as the underlined vocabulary word. Complete Sentence *b* with your own ideas and words.

1. The ship <u>listed</u> to one side as the wind filled its sail.

   a. The ship _______________ to one side as the wind filled its sail.

   b. The ship listed to one side _________________________________.

2. The <u>ravenous</u> puppies ran to their food bowls.

   a. The _______________ puppies ran to their food bowls.

   b. The ravenous puppies _________________________________.

3. Her <u>morose</u> expression suggested that she had bad news.

   a. Her _______________ expression suggested that she had bad news.

   b. Her morose expression _________________________________.

Getting Ready to Read

During the Great Depression in the 1930s, many people were out of work. Some men became drifters, wandering from place to place looking for work. What would you have done if a drifter had come to your home looking for work? Would you try to help him or turn him away? Share

The Life You Save May Be Your Own
Flannery O'Connor

Summary A one-armed man, Mr. Shiftlet, approaches a woman and her mentally challenged daughter, Lucynell. He agrees to fix up the old woman's property in exchange for food and a place to sleep. The woman wants him to marry her daughter. Eventually, he agrees. The woman gives him money to take a wedding trip. When Mr. Shiftlet and his new wife stop for food, he leaves her at the counter. He heads toward Mobile in the car. On the way, he picks up a hitchhiker. They argue and the boy jumps out of the car. Mr. Shiflet drives toward Mobile alone.

Note-taking Guide

Use the chart to record what each character does in the story.

Character	Actions
Lucynell (daughter)	Learned the word *bird* Fell asleep in the restaurant
Mrs. Crater	
Mr. Shiftlet	

Thinking About the Selection

1. Mr. Shiftlet seems harmless to Mrs. Crater at first, and Mrs. Crater seems harmless to Mr. Shiftlet. Each wants something from the other, and both get it. Fill in the chart below to show each character's goal and the actions that he or she takes to reach it.

Character	Goal	Actions
Mr. Shiftlet		
Mrs. Crater		

2. Mrs. Crater wants Mr. Shiftlet to marry her daughter so that

____

____

____.

TALK ABOUT IT **A Good Decision?** Is Mrs. Crater's decision to marry her daughter to Mr. Shiftlet a good decision? Use one of the sentence starters below to help you frame your answer. Support your ideas with details from the story.

I think that she makes a good decision because _______________.

I think that she makes a bad decision because _______________.

Writing About the Essential Question

What makes American literature American? Based on this story, a good example of regionalism, do you think there is a single, unified body of American literature? Explain.

____

____

____

____

Word Families

Groups of words that share the same base word are called word families. A base word can stand alone or serve as the base of new words. Often, new words are formed by adding prefixes, suffixes, verb endings, and other words to the base word.

Example

Base Word	Words That Share the Base Word
heart	**disheartened:** *adj.* disappointed; having lost hope and the determination to continue doing something **heartfelt:** *adj.* very strongly felt and sincere **heartless:** *adj.* cruel and not feeling any pity **hearty:** *adj.* happy and friendly and usually loud

Now You Do It

Use your knowledge of the words from the table above to complete each sentence in a way that makes sense.

1. The builders were disheartened ____.

2. His heartfelt apology ____.

3. The heartless king ____.

4. Her hearty laughter ____.

TALK ABOUT IT **A Hearty Talk** Tell a partner about a personal experience. Use as many words as possible from the *heart* word family.

WRITE ABOUT IT **Write a Character Sketch** Write a description of a real or imaginary person. Use at least three of the words listed above in your character sketch.

Vocabulary

These words are underlined in the story. Listen to each word. Say it. Then, read the definition and the example sentence.

discerned (dI SERND) *v.* If you have **discerned** something, you have seen it and determined what it is.

> *He discerned the city's skyline through the haze.*

disappointment (dis uh POYNT muhnt) *n.* **Disappointment** is a feeling of unhappiness because something is not as good as you expected, or has not happened in the way you hoped.

> *Having studied hard, she could not hide her disappointment at her grade.*

lapsed (LAPST) *v.* When someone has **lapsed** into silence, he or she has become quiet.

> *Ed lapsed into silence after the teacher caught him lying.*

Vocabulary Practice

Read the first sentence in each group of three. Then, complete Sentence *a* by substituting another word or phrase that means the same as the underlined vocabulary word. Complete Sentence *b* with your own ideas and words.

1. Ari discerned the deer standing quietly beyond the bushes.

   a. Ari _____________ the deer standing quietly beyond the bushes.

   b. Ari discerned ____.

2. Despite her disappointment at losing, she acted graciously.

   a. Despite her _____________ at losing, she acted graciously.

   b. Despite her disappointment at losing, she _____________________.

3. Emily lapsed into silence when no one supported her idea.

   a. Emily _____________ into silence when no one supported her idea.

   b. Emily lapsed into silence when ________________________________.

Getting Ready to Read

Like many parents, the father in the story works hard so that his daughter might have a better, easier life. He even makes a plan for her life. Should parents plan their children's lives?

The First Seven Years

Bernard Malamud

Summary This story is about a shoemaker named Feld who runs a shop. He has an assistant named Sobel. He also has a daughter named Miriam. Feld wants his daughter to have a better life than he and his wife have had. He asks a college student named Max to call on her. He hopes the two will get married. Sobel hears the conversation Feld has with Max and runs out of the shop. He does not come back. Feld struggles to manage the shop and find a new assistant. When Feld meets Sobel again, Feld learns something about love and happiness.

Note-taking Guide

This story is about differences between people in what they value or desire. As you read, write down details that show the things each character finds important (values) and the things each character wants (desires).

Character	Values	Desires
Feld		
Miriam		
Max		
Sobel		

The First Seven Years

Bernard Malamud

Feld is a shoemaker who came to America from Poland. He has a helper named Sobel. Feld wishes that his daughter, Miriam, would go to college. Miriam enjoys reading books that Sobel lends her, but she would rather work than go to school. Feld admires a college student named Max because he has worked hard to get an education.

◆ ◆ ◆

A figure **emerged** from the snow and the door opened. At the counter the man **withdrew** from a wet paper bag a pair of battered shoes for repair. Who he was the shoemaker for a moment had no idea, then his heart trembled as he realized, before he had thoroughly <u>discerned</u> the face, that Max himself was standing there, embarrassedly explaining what he wanted done to his old shoes. Though Feld listened eagerly, he couldn't hear a word, for the opportunity that had burst upon him was **deafening.**

◆ ◆ ◆

Feld would like Max to date his daughter. He is afraid to suggest the idea. He does not know whether Max would agree or whether Miriam would be angry with him. Feld decides that there is no harm in bringing the idea up. If his daughter will not think about going to college herself, Feld wants her to marry an educated man. He wants her to have a better life.

Everyday Words

emerged (i MERJD) *v.* appeared or came out from somewhere

withdrew (with DROO) *v.* took an object out from inside something else

deafening (DEF uhn ing) *adj.* significant, or very important

---

Cultural Understanding

This story takes place in the 1950s in the United States. It was a time of peace and prosperity. Many parents had worked hard so that their children would have better lives.

Vocabulary Builder 

Suffixes The suffix *-ly* means "in a particular way." It is often added to an adjective to form an adverb. Circle three adverbs in the bracketed paragraph formed by adding the suffix *-ly*. What does each adverb mean?

____

____

____

Vocabulary Builder 

Idioms The idiom *bring something up* means "mention or start to talk about something." Complete this sentence:

While talking to Max, Feld decides

to bring up ______________

______________________.

Vocabulary Builder

Compound Adjectives Writers sometimes use a hyphen (-) to combine two words and create a compound adjective. *Dimly-lit* combines the adverb *dimly* and the adjective *lit* to form a new compound adjective. Normally, an adverb that ends in *-ly* when combined with an adjective does not need to be hyphenated. *Dimly-lit* means "not well lit" or "fairly dark." What noun does *dimly-lit* modify, or describe?

Vocabulary Builder

Parts of Speech Both *alert* and *battered* may be verbs or adjectives. The adjective *alert* means "always watching and ready to notice things," and the verb *alert* means "make someone aware of something important or dangerous." The adjective *battered* means "old and in bad condition," and the verb *battered* means "hit someone or something repeatedly." Are *alert* and *battered* adjectives or verbs in the bracketed paragraph?

Comprehension Builder 

Feld suggests that Max might be interested in and want to meet Miriam. Predict what Max will do.

Max describes to Feld what he wants done to his shoes. Then he asks about the price. Before answering, Feld asks Max to step into the hall for a conversation.

◆ ◆ ◆

"Ever since you went to high school," he said, in the dimly-lit hallway, "I watched you in the morning go to the subway[1] to school, and I said always to myself, this is a fine boy that he wants so much an education."

"Thanks," Max said, nervously alert. He was tall and **grotesquely** thin, with sharply cut features, particularly a beak-like nose. He was wearing a loose, long **slushy** overcoat that hung down to his ankles, looking like a rug draped over his bony shoulders, and a soggy, old brown hat, as battered as the shoes he had brought in.

"I am a business man," the shoemaker abruptly said to **conceal** his embarrassment, "so I will explain you right away why I talk to you. I have a girl, my daughter Miriam—she is nineteen—a very nice girl and also so pretty that everybody looks on her when she passes by in the street. She is smart, always with a book, and I thought to myself that a boy like you, an educated boy—I thought maybe you will be interested sometime to meet a girl like this." He laughed a bit when he had finished and was **tempted** to say more but had the good sense not to.

Everyday Words

grotesquely (groh TESK lee) *adv.* absurdly; strikingly
slushy (SLUHSH ee) *adj.* covered with partly melted snow or ice
conceal (kuhn SEEL) *v.* hide your real feelings or the truth about something
tempted (TEMPT id) *adj.* wanting to have or do something, especially something you know that you should not

1. **subway** (SUHB way) *n.* a railway system, or train, that runs under the ground beneath a city

Max stared down like a hawk. For an uncomfortable second he was silent, then he asked, "Did you say nineteen?"

"Yes."

"Would it be all right to inquire if you have a picture of her?"

"Just a minute." The shoemaker went into the store and hastily returned with a snapshot that Max held up to the light.

"She's all right," he said.

Feld waited.

"And is she sensible—not the flighty[2] kind?"

"She is very sensible."

After another short pause, Max said it was okay with him if he met her.

◆　◆　◆

Feld gives Max his telephone number. Max puts it away and asks again about the price of the shoes. Feld gives him a price of "a dollar fifty," which is less than he usually charges. Then Feld goes back into the store.

◆　◆　◆

Later, as he entered the store, he was startled by a violent clanging and looked up to see Sobel pounding with all his might upon the naked last.[3] It broke, the iron striking the floor and jumping with a thump against the wall, but before the enraged shoemaker could cry out, the assistant had torn his hat and coat from the hook and rushed out into the snow.

◆　◆　◆

Feld is upset that Sobel has left. He depends on Sobel because he has a heart condition. Sobel, a thirty-year-old Polish refugee, had come looking for work five years before. Now Feld trusts Sobel to run his business but feels guilty because he pays him so poorly. While Sobel does not seem to care about money, he is interested in books.

---

2. **flighty** (FLY tee) *adj.* changing one's ideas and opinions often; staying interested in something for only a short while

3. **last** *n.* a block shaped like a person's foot, on which shoes are made or repaired

Fluency Builder 

Lines of dialogue—or the characters' spoken words—appear between quotation marks. Underline the lines of dialogue in the bracketed passage. With a partner, take turns reading aloud the conversation between Feld and Max. One person should read Feld's lines, and the other should read Max's lines. Read with expression, as the characters would say the words.

Comprehension Builder 

How does Feld's assistant, Sobel, seem to feel when Feld returns to the store?

____

____

Circle two clues that tell you how Sobel feels.

Vocabulary Builder

Multiple-Meaning Words The verb *run* may mean "move very quickly by moving your legs more quickly than when you walk." It may also mean "organize or be in charge of a business, a group, or an activity." What does *run* mean in the underlined sentence?

____

____

Vocabulary Builder

Conjunctions The conjunctions *neither* and *nor* are often used together in a sentence when mentioning two things that are not true or possible. In the underlined sentence, what two things are not possible?

____

____

Vocabulary Builder

Multiple-Meaning Words The verb *received* may mean "got." It may also mean "welcomed." What does *received* mean in the bracketed paragraph?

____

____

Vocabulary Builder

Compound Nouns A compound noun combines two or more words to form a new noun. *Bathrobe* is a compound noun that refers to a robe, or piece of clothing similar to a coat, often worn before or after one takes a bath. Circle another compound noun in the same paragraph. What does it mean?

____

____

He has loaned books to Miriam and shared his written comments about them with her.

After working alone for a week, Feld goes to Sobel's rooming house to ask him to return. Sobel's landlady tells him that Sobel is not there. Feld is forced to hire a new assistant who is neither as trustworthy nor as skilled as Sobel is. Feld keeps his mind off his problems by thinking about Max and Miriam's first date. He hopes that they will like each other.

◆ ◆ ◆

At last Friday came. Feld was not feeling particularly well so he stayed in bed, and Mrs. Feld thought it better to remain in the bedroom with him when Max called. Miriam received the boy, and her parents could hear their voices, his throaty one, as they talked. Just before leaving, Miriam brought Max to the bedroom door and he stood there a minute, a tall, slightly **hunched** figure wearing a thick, droopy suit, and apparently at ease as he greeted the shoemaker and his wife, which was surely a good sign. And Miriam, although she had worked all day, looked fresh and pretty. She was a large-framed girl with a well-shaped body, and she had a fine open face and soft hair. They made, Feld thought, a first-class couple.

Miriam returned after 11:30. Her mother was already asleep, but the shoemaker got out of bed and after locating his bathrobe went into the kitchen, where Miriam, to his surprise, sat at the table, reading.

"So where did you go?" Feld asked pleasantly.

"For a walk," she said, not looking up.

"I advised him," Feld said, clearing his throat, "he shouldn't spend so much money."

"I didn't care."

Everyday Words

hunched (HUNCHT) *adj.* bent down so the back forms a curve

The shoemaker boiled up some water for tea and sat down at the table with a cupful and a thick slice of lemon.

"So how," he sighed after a sip, "did you enjoy?"

"It was all right."

He was silent. She must have sensed his <u>disappointment</u>, for she added, "You can't really tell much the first time."

"You will see him again?"

Turning a page, she said that Max had asked for another date.

"For when?"

"Saturday."

"So what did you say?"

"What did I say?" she asked, delaying for a moment—"I said yes."

◆　◆　◆

Miriam asks her father about Sobel. Feld tells her Sobel has another job. Throughout the week, Feld asks Miriam about Max. He is disappointed when he finds out that Max is taking business classes to become an accountant. Max and Miriam have a second date on Saturday. When Miriam comes home, she tells her father that Max bores her because he is only interested in things. Miriam says Max did not ask her on another date, but she has no interest in going out with him anyway. Feld still hopes that Max will call his daughter again. Instead, Max avoids the shoemaker's shop on his way to school.

One afternoon Max comes to the shop. He pays for his shoes and leaves without saying a word about Miriam. Later that night, Feld has a heart attack after finding out that his new assistant has been stealing from him. Feld stays in bed for three weeks. When Miriam offers to get Sobel, Feld reacts angrily. Once he returns to work, he feels tired. He

Vocabulary Builder 

Multiple-Meaning Expressions
The expression *all right* may mean that everything is good. It is often used to say that someone is not ill, hurt, or upset. The expression *all right* may also mean that something is okay or satisfactory but not great or excellent. What does *all right* mean when Miriam uses the expression to describe her date?

____

____

Vocabulary Builder 

Idioms The idiom *going out* with someone means "dating or having a romantic relationship with someone." Use the idiom to complete this sentence:

Miriam is not interested in

______________________.

Comprehension Builder

A heart attack is a sudden, serious medical condition in which someone's heart stops working properly. When does Feld have a heart attack?

____

____

Vocabulary Builder 

Idioms The idiom *burst out* means "suddenly said something in a forceful way." What did Sobel burst out in response to Feld's question?

____

Vocabulary Builder 

Contractions A contraction is a shortened form of one or more words. An apostrophe replaces one or more letters in a contraction. *Don't* is a contraction for *do not*. Underline another contraction on the page. What two words does the contraction represent?

____

Fluency Builder 

The letter *g* often has a hard pronunciation, as in *goat* or *grape.* Sometimes, it has a soft pronunciation, like that of a *j*. In *stingy,* the *g* is pronounced /j/. Practice saying *stingy* aloud, pronouncing the *g* like a *j*. Then, circle three more words on the page that have a soft *g* sound. With a partner, practice saying those words aloud.

realizes he needs Sobel's help. Feld visits Sobel at his rooming house. He notices stacks of books and wonders why Sobel reads so much.

◆　◆　◆

"So when you will come back to work?" Feld asked him.

To his surprise, Sobel burst out, "Never."

Jumping up, he strode over to the window that looked out upon the miserable street.
"Why should I come back?" he cried.

"I will raise your wages."

"Who cares for your wages!"

The shoemaker, knowing he didn't care, was at a loss what else to say.

"What do you want from me, Sobel?"

"Nothing."

"I always treated you like you was my son."

Sobel **vehemently** denied it. "So why you look for strange boys in the street they should go out with Miriam? Why you don't think of me?"

The shoemaker's hands and feet turned freezing cold. His voice became so **hoarse** he couldn't speak. At last he cleared his throat and croaked, "So what has my daughter got to do with a shoemaker thirty-five years old who works for me?"

"Why do you think I worked so long for you?" Sobel cried out. "For the stingy wages I sacrificed five years of my life so you could have to eat and drink and where to sleep?"

"Then for what?" shouted the shoemaker.

"For Miriam," he blurted—"for her."

The shoemaker, after a time, managed to say, "I pay wages in cash, Sobel," and lapsed into silence. Though he was **seething** with

Everyday Words

vehemently (VEE huh ment lee) *adv.* forcefully; intensely

hoarse (HOHRS) *adj.* having a rough sound to the voice, often due to a sore throat

seething (SEE<u>TH</u> ing) *adj.* boiling

excitement, his mind was coldly clear, and he had to admit to himself he had sensed all along that Sobel felt this way. He had never so much as thought it consciously, but he had felt it and was afraid.

"Miriam knows?" he muttered hoarsely.

"She knows."

"You told her?"

"No."

"Then how does she know?"

"How does she know?" Sobel said, "because she knows. She knows who I am and what is in my heart."

Feld had a sudden insight. In some devious way, with his books and commentary, Sobel had given Miriam to understand that he loved her. The shoemaker felt a terrible anger at him for his **deceit.**

"Sobel, you are crazy," he said bitterly.

"She will never marry a man so old and ugly like you."

◆ ◆ ◆

Sobel becomes very angry and then begins to cry. Feld feels sorry for Sobel. He realizes that Sobel barely escaped being killed by the Nazis during World War II and has patiently waited for five years for the girl he loves to grow up. Feld apologizes for calling Sobel ugly. He feels sad when he thinks about the kind of life his daughter will have if she marries Sobel. Feld believes his dreams for a better life for Miriam are dead.

◆ ◆ ◆

"She is only nineteen," Feld said **brokenly.** "This is too young yet to get married. Don't ask her for two years more, till she is twenty-one, then you can talk to her."

Everyday Words

deceit (duh SEET) *n.* deception; misrepresentation
brokenly (BROH kuhn lee) *adv.* as if crushed by grief

Fluency Builder 

A question mark (?) signals that someone is asking a question. When asking a question, English-speakers often raise the pitch—or sound—of their voice at the end of the question. With a partner, read aloud the bracketed dialogue. Pay attention to punctuation marks, and raise the pitch of your voice when asking a question.

Comprehension Builder 

What does Feld realize about Sobel?

____

____

Vocabulary Builder

Idioms The idiom *feels sorry for* means "pities or feels sympathy for someone because something bad has happened to him or her or because that person is in a difficult situation." Who feels sorry for whom on this page?

____

____

Vocabulary Builder

Multiple-Meaning Words The adverb *once* may mean "on one occasion only." It may also mean "as soon as." What does *once* mean in the bracketed paragraph?

Sobel didn't answer. Feld rose and left. He went slowly down the stairs but once outside, though it was an icy night and the crisp falling snow whitened the street, he walked with a stronger **stride.**

But the next morning, when the shoemaker arrived, **heavy-hearted,** to open the store, he saw he needn't have come, for his assistant was already seated at the last, pounding leather for his love.

© Pearson Education

Everyday Words
stride (STRYD) *n.* the way that a person walks
heavy-hearted (HEV ee HART id) *adj.* very sad

Thinking About the Selection

1. Feld has plans for his daughter, Miriam, but has to change them. Use the chart below to explain what Feld's plans are and why and how they change.

Feld's Original Plan	Why Feld's Plan Changes	Feld's New Plan
Feld wants Miriam to ________________ because ________________ .	Feld learns that ________________ ________________ .	Feld wants Sobel to ________________ ________________ .

2. Sobel is angry at Feld because ____ ____ .

A Better Life? Which is a better life for Miriam—the life her father planned for her, or the life she might have with Sobel? Why?

The life her father planned is a better life because ________________ ____

The life she could have with Sobel is a better life because ________ ____

Writing About the Essential Question

What makes American literature American? In your view, is Feld's definition of a successful and meaningful life one many Americans share? Explain.

____

____

____

Idioms

An idiom is a phrase with a special meaning that is different than the ordinary meaning of the words.

Examples

Idiom	Special Meaning	Sample Sentence
break cover	leave a hiding place	The soldiers decided to *break cover*.
break the ice	make people feel comfortable and willing to talk to each other	She suggested a game to *break the ice*.
break new ground	introduce new and exciting ideas	Their research was certain to *break new ground* in medicine.
break ranks	behave in a way that is different from other members of a group	He chose to *break ranks* with his political party on the issue.

Now You Do It

For each idiom listed below, write a sentence that uses the idiom in a way that makes sense.

1. break cover ______________________________________

____

2. break the ice ______________________________________

3. break new ground ______________________________________

____

4. break ranks ______________________________________

____

TALK ABOUT IT **Discuss Current Events** Use the four idioms above in a discussion of current events with a partner.

WRITE ABOUT IT **Write a Newspaper Article** Write a short newspaper article about a real or imagined event. In your article, use at least three idioms from the chart above.

Vocabulary

Listen to each word. Say it. Then, read the definition and the example sentence.

absurdity (uhb SERD uh tee) *n.* An **absurdity** is something that consists of nonsense or ridiculousness.

The comedian joked about the <u>absurdity</u> of driving to the North Pole.

realist (REE uh list) *n.* A **realist** is a person concerned with things as they are, rather than as they could or should be.

Nadia is a <u>realist</u> who knows that problems cannot be solved overnight.

taut (TAWT) *adj.* Something that is **taut** has been tightly stretched.

The fishing line was <u>taut</u> as I reeled in the fish.

Vocabulary Practice

Read the first sentence in each group of three. Then, complete Sentence *a* by substituting another word or phrase that means the same as the underlined vocabulary word. Complete Sentence *b* with your own ideas and words.

1. The children giggled at the <u>absurdity</u> of the clown's actions.

   a. The children giggled at the _______________ of the clown's actions.

   b. The children giggled at the absurdity _______________________.

2. As a <u>realist</u>, Manuel rarely daydreamed.

   a. As a _______________, Manuel rarely daydreamed.

   b. As a realist, Manuel _______________________________.

3. The <u>taut</u> plastic wrap covered the bowl.

   a. The _______________ plastic wrap covered the bowl.

   b. The taut _______________________________.

Getting Ready to Read

Some poems use free verse, which does not have a regular rhythm. "Constantly Risking Absurdity" is a free-verse poem. Think of a favorite poem. What characteristics does it share with other poems? What characteristics would you include in a poem you might write? Share your ideas with a small group.

Constantly Risking Absurdity

Lawrence Ferlinghetti

Summary In "Constantly Risking Absurdity," Lawrence Ferlinghetti explores what it means to be a poet. The speaker uses an extended metaphor to compare a poet to an acrobat who dares both danger and humiliation to entertain his or her audience. An extended metaphor describes one thing as something else throughout a piece of writing. In the end, the speaker states that the poet may or may not be successful in his or her performance, but the poem suggests that the result of the performance does not matter as much as the act of performing.

Note-taking Guide

Use the web to record details about what the poet—or acrobat—does, according to the speaker.

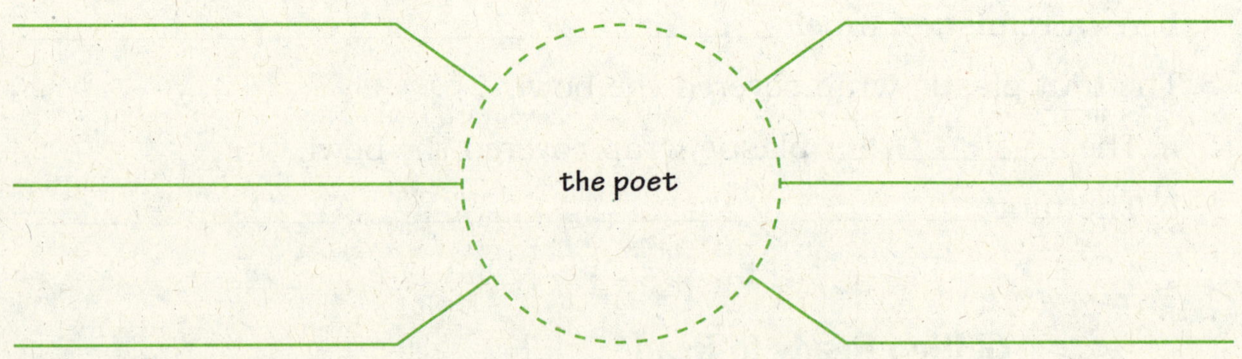

Thinking About the Selection

1. To describe what it is like to write poetry, Ferlinghetti compares a poet to an acrobat. How is a poet like an acrobat? Write your ideas in the web.

2. When Beauty leaps off her high perch, the poet _________________

____.

TALK ABOUT IT **Can You Picture It?** What images does the simile in this poem create for you? Share your ideas with others in a small group.

The comparison with an acrobat makes me imagine the poet

____.

? Writing About the Essential Question

How does literature shape or reflect society? What does this poem suggest about the reasons poetry is important to a society? Explain.

____

____

____

____

The Irregular Verb *To Have*

A conjugation is a complete list of the singular and plural forms of a verb in a particular tense. The chart below shows the conjugation of the irregular verb *to have* in the present and past tenses.

	Present Singular	Present Plural
First Person	I have	we have
Second Person	you have	you have
Third Person	he, she, it has	they have
	Past Singular	**Past Plural**
First Person	I had	we had
Second Person	you had	you had
Third Person	he, she, it had	they had

Now You Do It

Complete the sentences with the correct forms of the tenses of *to have*.

1. He _______ three sisters, and I _______ two brothers.

2. We now _______ a new name for our club.

3. They _______ a great time camping last weekend.

4. Before he spent $5 in the lunchroom, he _______ $30.

5. He says that he never _______ enough time to finish the assignment.

TALK **ABOUT IT** **Your Favorite Thing** Tell a partner about something you own that you like very much. Explain how you got it, how long you have owned it, and what you can do with it. Use at least four forms of the verb *to have*, two in the present tense and two in the past tense.

WRITE ABOUT IT **What Did You Learn?** Write a paragraph about your partner's favorite possession. Use singular and plural present and past-tense forms of the verb *to have* in your paragraph.

Vocabulary

Listen to each word. Say it. Then, read the definition and the example sentence.

preconceptions (pree kuhn SEP shuhns) *n.* **Preconceptions** are ideas that someone forms about something before knowing what it is really like.

Chen had <u>preconceptions</u> about the city before he moved there.

endured (in DOOD) *v.* Someone who **endured** a difficult situation was able to bear, or tolerate, it.

The sailors <u>endured</u> the frigid water until they were rescued.

transfusion (tranz FYOO zhuhn) *n.* When you get a **transfusion,** you receive a life-giving substance from someone or something else.

The patient received a blood <u>transfusion</u> during surgery.

Vocabulary Practice

Read the first sentence in each group of three. Then, complete Sentence *a* by substituting another word or phrase that means the same as the underlined vocabulary word. Complete Sentence *b* with your own ideas and words.

1. The group aimed to educate people about harmful <u>preconceptions</u>.

   a. The group aimed to educate people about harmful ______________.

   b. ______________________________ harmful preconceptions.

2. Sasha <u>endured</u> her parents' divorce when she was a child.

   a. Sasha ______________ her parents' divorce when she was a child.

   b. Sasha endured ______________________________.

3. The old dog received a <u>transfusion</u> of energy from the puppy.

   a. The old dog received a ______________ of energy from the puppy.

   b. The old dog received a transfusion of energy ______________.

Getting Ready to Read

Both "Mirror" and "Courage" include personification. "Mirror" gives human qualities to a mirror. "Courage" makes sorrow seem human. Why do poets use personification? What is its effect on readers? Share your thoughts with others in a small group.

Mirror • Courage
Sylvia Plath, Anne Sexton

Summaries In **"Mirror,"** Sylvia Plath describes a woman's feelings about growing older. The speaker is a mirror that shows life as it appears. A woman comes to the mirror again and again, watching her youth fade and old age approach. In **"Courage,"** Anne Sexton examines the nature of human courage. The speaker provides many examples of what it means to be courageous. The story reveals that the courage to face large and small challenges is what carries people through life.

Note-taking Guide

Both "Mirror" and "Courage" use a great deal of figurative language to describe what a mirror does and what courage is like. Think about the descriptions and metaphors in the chart below. Write what you think each one means.

Poem	Figurative Language	Meaning
"Mirror"	Whatever I see I swallow immediately/ Just as it is . . .	
	Most of the time I meditate on the opposite wall. / . . . Faces and darkness separate us over and over.	
	Then she turns to those liars, the candles or the moon.	
	In me she has drowned a young girl, and in me an old woman/Rises toward her . . .	
"Courage"	. . . you drank their acid/and concealed it.	
	. . . if you faced the death of bombs and bullets/you did not do it with a banner . . .	
	. . . each spring will be a sword you'll sharpen . . .	
	. . . when death opens the back door/you'll put on your carpet slippers/and stride out.	

Thinking About the Selections

1. The theme of a poem is its central idea or message. Note the theme of each poem in the center column. In the column to the right, identify words and images from the poem that support the theme.

Poem	Theme	Words and Images
"Mirror"		
"Courage"		

2. In "Courage," the speaker says that courage was not courage but love when ______________________________________

______________________________________.

TALK ABOUT IT **Make Connections** Which poem do you relate to more strongly? Tell a partner which poem connects to your life and why.

I connect with ________________ because ________________

______________________________________.

? Writing About the Essential Question

How does literature shape or reflect society? What do the private concerns expressed in these poems suggest about larger issues in society? Explain.

____

____

____

____

The Prefix *dis-*

A prefix is a word part added to the beginning of a base word. A prefix changes the meaning of the base word. The prefix *dis-* means "opposite of" or "not." It also shows the stopping or removing of a condition. The chart shows examples of these meanings.

Examples

dis- + Base Word	Meaning
dis- + order = disorder	the opposite of order
dis- + respect = disrespect	the opposite of respect
dis- + agree = disagree	not agree
dis- + obey = disobey	not obey
dis- + connect = disconnect	stop a connection
dis- + illusion = disillusion	remove illusion from

Now You Do It

For each word listed below, write a sentence that uses the word.

1. disorder _______________________________________

2. disrespect _____________________________________

3. disagree _______________________________________

4. disillusion _____________________________________

TALK ABOUT IT **Forms of Disrespect** With a partner, discuss how people show disrespect. Use the other words from this lesson.

WRITE ABOUT IT **Write an Editorial** In a one-page editorial, express your point of view on an issue about which you feel strongly, using words from this lesson.

____

____

Vocabulary

Listen to each word. Say it. Then, read the definition and the example sentence.

intricate (IN tri kuht) *adj.* Something that is **intricate** is very complex because it has many small, interrelated parts.

The threads in a piece of lace form an <u>intricate</u> pattern.

seeping (SEEP ing) *v.* A **seeping** substance is flowing slowly, usually through small cracks or holes.

Honey is <u>seeping</u> through the cracks in the jar.

quail (KWAYL) *v.* If you **quail,** you lose courage or step back in fear.

The bear's approach caused the hunter to <u>quail</u>.

Vocabulary Practice

Read the first sentence in each group of three. Then, complete Sentence *a* by substituting another word or phrase that means the same as the underlined vocabulary word. Complete Sentence *b* with your own ideas and words.

1. The <u>intricate</u> design demonstrated the weaver's skill.

   a. The _________________ design demonstrated the weaver's skill.

   b. The intricate design ____.

2. The water was <u>seeping</u> from the lawn into the basement.

   a. The water was _________________ from the lawn into the basement.

   b. The water was seeping ____.

3. The frightening movie poster caused the child to <u>quail</u>.

   a. The frightening movie poster caused the child to _________________.

   b. ____ caused the child to quail.

TALK ABOUT IT — ## Getting Ready to Read

A cutting is a plant part that is used to grow a new plant. A cutting can be a root, stem, or leaf. To grow roots, a stem cutting is usually placed in water or wet sand. What would be the rewards of using cuttings to grow new plants? Discuss your ideas with a partner.

Cuttings • Cuttings *(later)*
Theodore Roethke

Summaries Cuttings are pieces of plants that have been cut from the main body of the plant, usually to grow new plants. In **"Cuttings,"** Theodore Roethke describes the efforts of cuttings to keep living even after they have been cut. In **"Cuttings *(later),*"** Roethke examines the continuing struggle of the cuttings as they grow.

Note-taking Guide

These two poems tell how the cuttings struggle to grow. Use the graphic organizer below to show how Roethke describes their growth.

The small cells ______________.

One ______________ nudges a sandcrumb loose.

The tight ______________ part at last.

Cuttings

Cut stems struggle to ______________.

Sprouts ______________ slippery as fish.

Thinking About the Selections

1. Roethke creates vivid images of new plants growing from cuttings in two poems. How do the poems differ? Write your ideas in the diagram below.

<table>
<tr><td>Cuttings</td><td></td><td>Cuttings (later)</td></tr>
<tr><td>The speaker ______________________

______________________ .</td><td>+</td><td>The speaker ______________________

______________________ .</td></tr>
<tr><td>The process of growth is ____________

______________________ .</td><td></td><td>The process of growth is ____________

______________________ .</td></tr>
</table>

2. In the last three lines of "Cuttings (*later*)" the speaker describes how

____

____ .

TALK ABOUT IT   **A Natural Relationship?** What do the images in the poems suggest about the speaker's relationship with nature? Discuss your ideas in a small group.

The images in the poems suggest that the speaker ______________

____ .

Writing About the Essential Question

What is the relationship between place and literature? Do you think these poems document observed reality? Explain.

____

____

____

Multiple-Meaning Words

Many words have several meanings, depending on the way a word is used in a sentence. Often, the only way to determine the particular meaning of a word is to understand a word's context.

Examples

Word	Meanings
find: *verb*	• discover something by chance • have a particular feeling about someone or something
matter: *noun*	• a subject or situation • the material that everything in the universe is made of
hot: *adjective*	• having a high temperature • very popular or fashionable

Now You Do It

Complete the sentences with words from the chart. Then, write the meaning of the word on the lines provided.

He called a meeting to discuss a

very serious ____________.

____

She was surprised to ____________ a wallet lying on the sidewalk.

____

The pot of water on the stove was

____________ and bubbling.

____

Solids, liquids, and gases are

forms of ____________.

____

TALK ABOUT IT **First to Speak** Select one of the words from this page. Think of and say a sentence that uses one of its meanings. Then, have a partner use the other meaning in a sentence.

WRITE ABOUT IT **Flash Test** On flashcards, write sentences that use the multiple-meaning words from this page. Show a partner the cards. Ask your partner to define each multiple-meaning word.

Vocabulary

Listen to each word. Say it. Then, read the definition and the example sentence.

frayed (FRAYD) *adj.* When a rope or cloth is **frayed,** it is weakened or strained because its threads are loose.

The torn edges of the blanket were frayed.

wily (WY lee) *adj.* Someone who is **wily** is clever and good at using tricks to achieve a goal.

The wily thief convinced me that I was giving to charity.

gaudy (GAWD ee) *adj.* **Gaudy** items are brightly colored, and they look cheap and tasteless.

All of his ties were too gaudy to wear to a funeral.

Vocabulary Practice

Read the first sentence in each group of three. Then, complete Sentence *a* by substituting another word or phrase that means the same as the underlined vocabulary word. Complete Sentence *b* with your own ideas and words.

1. Jenna's nerves were <u>frayed</u> after the long, tense wait.

   a. Jenna's nerves were ______________ after the long, tense wait.

   b. Jenna's nerves were frayed ________________________________.

2. The <u>wily</u> criminal escaped from prison again.

   a. The ______________ criminal escaped from prison again.

   b. The wily criminal ________________________________.

3. Her <u>gaudy</u> clothing matched her obnoxious behavior.

   a. Her ______________ clothing matched her obnoxious behavior.

   b. Her gaudy clothing ________________________________.

Getting Ready to Read

Frederick Douglass worked to end slavery in the United States. He had been a slave in the South and fled to the North to find freedom. Douglass did not take freedom for granted. What would your life be like without freedom? What would you be willing to do so that others might be free? Share your thoughts in a small group.

The Explorer • Frederick Douglass

Gwendolyn Brooks, Robert Hayden

Summaries The speaker in **"The Explorer"** searches for peace in a noisy apartment building. In **"Frederick Douglass,"** the speaker longs for true freedom that will honor Douglass, one of the leading voices opposing slavery.

Note-taking Guide

Sometimes rewriting a line of poetry will help you understand its meaning. Use this chart to rewrite one line from each poem in your own words.

Poem	Line	Rewritten Line
The Explorer		
Frederick Douglass		

Thinking About the Selections

1. "The Explorer" includes many details that appeal to the senses. Use the chart below to explain what the person in the poem is seeking and what he finds. List the sensory details that describe each.

"The Explorer"	Sensory Details
He is seeking _______________.	
He finds _______________.	

2. The speaker in "Frederick Douglass" says freedom does not yet belong to all because ____

____.

TALK ABOUT IT   **What Does It Mean to You?** What does freedom mean to you? With a partner, discuss what freedom is.

Freedom is ____

____.

Writing About the Essential Question

How does literature shape or reflect society? What type of world do the speakers in these poems hope to see realized? Explain.

____

____

____

____

Short Vowels and Long Vowels

Some general rules guide the pronunciation of vowels. As always, vowels in some words do not follow the rules.

	General Pronunciation Rule	Examples
Short vowel	When a syllable ends in a consonant and has only one vowel, the vowel is short.	happy, tell, fit, hot, sum (The boldface vowel in each word is short.)
Long vowel	When a syllable ends in a vowel and it is the only vowel in the syllable, the vowel is usually long.	later, she, minor, over, uniform (The boldface vowel in each word is long.)

Now You Do It

Look at the underlined vowels in the words below. Then, use the rules above to decide whether the vowel is short or long. In the space provided, write *short* if a vowel is short and *long* if a vowel is long.

paper	__________	remedy	__________
obey	__________	bed	__________
govern	__________	operator	__________
exhaust	__________	gracious	__________

TALK ABOUT IT **Say and Check It** With a partner, check your pronunciation of the words above. Say each word and explain why you pronounced the underlined vowel with a long sound or a short sound.

WRITE ABOUT IT **Write a Poem** Write a humorous ten-line poem that includes as many of the words above as possible. Practice reading your poem aloud, and be sure to pronounce each word correctly. Then read your poem aloud in a small group.

Vocabulary

Listen to each word. Say it. Then, read the definition and the example sentence.

intent (in TENT) *n.* A person's **intent** is his or her purpose or aim.
His intent was to organize his baseball card collection.

permeated (PER mee ay tuhd) *adj.* When something is **permeated,** it is soaked through with a substance.
Her skirt was permeated with the spilled milk.

extraneous (ek STRAY nee uhs) *adj.* Something that is **extraneous** is not related or connected to the main item or topic.
The confusing article contained extraneous information.

Vocabulary Practice

Read the first sentence in each group of three. Then, complete Sentence *a* by substituting another word or phrase that means the same as the underlined vocabulary word. Complete Sentence *b* with your own ideas and words.

1. The intent of her speech was to encourage the students.

   a. The ______________ of her speech was to encourage the students.

   b. The intent of her speech ____.

2. The slip of paper was permeated with red ink.

   a. The slip of paper was ______________ with red ink.

   b. ________________________________ was permeated with red ink.

3. Extraneous details made the directions difficult to follow.

   a. ______________ details made the directions difficult to follow.

   b. Extraneous details ____.

Getting Ready to Read

"One Art" is an example of a villanelle, a poem with 19 lines, two repeating rhymes, and two refrains, or repeated phrases. With a partner, take turns reading "One Art" aloud. What is the effect of the repeated rhymes and refrains? Share your ideas with your partner.

One Art • Filling Station
Elizabeth Bishop

Summaries In **"One Art,"** Elizabeth Bishop comments on what it is like to lose things, including people whom we love. She points out that people lose things all the time. Losing things is easy, even though it often feels horrible. **"Filling Station"** describes the scene at a family-owned filling station, including some unusual details that demonstrate someone's love for the little business.

Note-taking Guide

In each poem, the speaker provides details to support the main idea. Use the chart below to list those details.

Poem	Main Idea	Details
"One Art"	The act of losing something is easy to do, even when it feels terrible.	
"Filling Station"	Something may seem unworthy of love, but it may still be very important to someone.	

Thinking About the Selections

1. "One Art" describes a variety of losses. Which losses are disasters? Which are not? Classify the losses in the chart below.

Disaster	Not a Disaster

2. In "Filling Station," small details of the filling station suggest that

____

____.

TALK ABOUT IT **How Does It Sound to You?** "One Art" has repeated rhymes and refrains. "Filling Station" has repeated *d* and *s* sounds. Which poem sounds better to you? Share your views in a small group.

I like the sound of _________________ because _________________

____.

Writing About the Essential Question

What is the relationship between place and literature? Are the places the speaker loses and finds in these poems parts of the actual, physical world, or parts of an emotional world? Explain.

____

____

____

____

____

Parts of Speech

Many words have more than one meaning, depending on their part of speech.

Examples

Word	Part of Speech	Meanings
delay	*noun*	a period in which someone or something has to wait
	verb	wait until a later time to do something
fire	*noun*	uncontrolled flames, light, and heat that destroy or damage things
	verb	force someone to leave his or her job
place	*noun*	a space or area
	verb	put something somewhere

Now You Do It

Complete the sentences with words from the chart, and write its part of speech on the line.

The _____________ broke out last night and burned until morning. _________

She needs to _____________ the amount of sugar in the recipe. _________

They finally arrived after a long _____________. _________

TALK ABOUT IT **Pick Parts of Speech** Have a conversation with a partner in which you use the words above as either nouns or verbs in sentences, and your partner uses the words in the other part of speech.

WRITE ABOUT IT **Write a Poem** Write a poem that uses both parts of speech and both meanings for the words above.

Vocabulary

These words are underlined in the story. Listen to each word. Say it. Then, read the definition and the example sentence.

hysterically (hi STER ik uh lee) *adv.* Someone who is behaving **hysterically** cannot control his or her behavior or emotions.

> *Janita cried <u>hysterically</u> when she learned that her dog had died.*

jubilant (JYOO bi luhnt) *adj.* Someone or something that is **jubilant** expresses great happiness and joy.

> *The crowd greeted the winning runner with <u>jubilant</u> shouts.*

perdition (per DI shuhn) *n.* **Perdition** is a complete loss that cannot be recovered.

> *Firefighters carried out most of his furniture, saving him from <u>perdition</u>.*

Vocabulary Practice

Read the first sentence in each group of three. Then, complete Sentence *a* by substituting another word or phrase that means the same as the underlined vocabulary word. Complete Sentence *b* with your own ideas and words.

1. The girls laughed <u>hysterically</u> as they watched the cartoon.

   a. The girls laughed _______________ as they watched the cartoon.

   b. The girls laughed hysterically _________________________________.

2. The winning team's <u>jubilant</u> cries filled the locker room.

   a. The winning team's _______________ cries filled the locker room.

   b. The winning team's jubilant cries _________________________________.

3. The loan may save his business from <u>perdition</u>.

   a. The loan may save his business from _______________.

   b. _________________________________ save his business from perdition.

Getting Ready to Read

The Great Depression was a period of great hardship and poverty. In Harlem, a section of New York City, many children did not have safe places to play outdoors. How important is it for children to have safe places to play? Discuss your ideas with a partner.

The Rockpile
James Baldwin

Summary This story is about a boy who disobeys his mother. When he is hurt, his father, a pastor, blames his older stepbrother for not watching him. His mother does not blame the older boy. The conflict between the parents shows that each parent has different expectations for each of the boys.

Note-taking Guide

Use this chart to record the reasons why the neighborhood is dangerous.

The danger	Why it is dangerous
There is a rockplie in the neighborhood.	

The Rockpile

James Baldwin

The setting of "The Rockpile" is Harlem, the New York City neighborhood where the author spent his childhood years. Dealing with family issues and relationships, this short story captures a scene from a day in the life of a struggling family.

This story takes place in the neighborhood of New York City called Harlem where a large pile of rock sits between two houses. Since it is such an unusual feature, it attracts many of the neighborhood boys to play and climb upon it. Roy, one such boy, believed that playing on the rockpile went along with living on in the area.

◆ ◆ ◆

Other boys were to be seen there each afternoon after school and all day Saturday and Sunday. They fought on the rockpile. Sure footed, dangerous, and reckless, they rushed each other and **grappled** on the heights, sometimes disappearing down the other side in a confusion of dust and screams and upended, flying feet.

◆ ◆ ◆

One parent in the neighborhood, Elizabeth, warned her children against going to the rockpile. Even though she addressed both of her sons, she only looked at Roy when she spoke. He was the one who enjoyed meeting his friends there. John feared the danger of playing in a rockpile. He also feared the boys who played there.

grappled (GRAP uhld) *v.* fought or struggled with someone, holding him or her tightly

---

Vocabulary Builder

Multiple-Meaning Words The verb *captures* may mean "gets control of a place or object that once belonged to an enemy." It may also mean "describes a situation or feeling, using words or pictures." Which meaning does *captures* have in the first paragraph?

Fluency Builder

With a partner, take turns reading aloud the bracketed paragraph with expression. Pause briefly after each comma, and pause slightly longer after each period. Break up difficult or long words into syllables, and practice saying them aloud individually.

Vocabulary Builder

Verb Tenses Regular verbs form the past tense by adding *-ed* or *-d* to the present form of the verb. For example, *warned* is the past tense of the regular verb *warn*. Underline four other regular past-tense verbs in the last paragraph. Irregular verbs do not follow this pattern. Circle the past-tense form of the irregular verb *speak* in the last paragraph.

Vocabulary Builder 

Multiple-Meaning Words The verb *tending* may mean that something happens often and is likely to happen again. It may also mean "taking care of someone by giving that person what he or she needs or by keeping him or her safe." What does *tending* mean in this paragraph?

____

____

Vocabulary Builder 

Proper Nouns A proper noun names a specific person, place, or thing. Proper nouns always begin with a capital letter. In the bracketed paragraph, circle the proper noun that names a specific thing. Underline three other proper nouns in the same paragraph.

Comprehension Builder

Why does Roy want to go downstairs?

____

____

____

____

One day the two brothers sat on the fire escape, watching people pass on the street below. Their mother was tending to the two younger children inside, and they expected that their father would soon be coming home.

From their view, Roy and John could see the Harlem River. During summers, boys swam and played in it. One time, a boy had drowned there. His mother knocked on people's doors looking for him all day. Later that evening, people throughout the neighborhood could hear the mother hysterically crying, as her husband carried the boy's drowned body back to their apartment. That incident put great fear into Elizabeth.

◆   ◆   ◆

Some friends of Roy passed beneath the fire escape and called him. Roy began to **fidget,** yelling down to them through the bars. Then a silence fell. John looked up. Roy stood looking at him.

"I'm going downstairs," he said.

◆   ◆   ◆

John argued with his younger brother. He reminded him that their father would be home soon, and that their mother was only a few feet away in the kitchen talking with her friend. Roy explained that he would only be gone for five minutes. Without giving John an **option**, Roy quickly went down and joined

© Pearson Education

Everyday Words

fidget (FIJ it) *v.* keep moving your hands or feet, especially because you are bored or nervous

option (AHP shun) *n.* a choice that a person can make in a particular situation

his friends. John refocused his attention on his schoolwork.

◆ ◆ ◆

When he looked up again he did not know how much time had passed, but now there was a gang fight on the rockpile. Dozens of boys fought each other in the harsh sun: **clambering** up the rocks and battling hand to hand, scuffed shoes sliding on the slippery rock; filling the bright air with curses and jubilant cries. They filled the air, too, with flying weapons: stones, sticks, tin cans, garbage, whatever could be picked up and thrown.

◆ ◆ ◆

John began to worry about Roy's absence. He realized his brother was also playing roughly with the others, although it was too bright to pinpoint which figure was Roy. When he finally saw Roy, Roy was standing at the top of the rockpile. Just then a tin can hit Roy directly on the head. He fell down on the rockpile, face first.

◆ ◆ ◆

Then for a moment there was no movement at all, no sound, the sun, arrested, lay on the street and the sidewalk and the arrested boys. Then someone screamed or shouted; boys began to run away, down the street, toward the bridge. The figure on the ground, having caught its breath and felt its own blood, began to shout. John cried, "Mama! Mama!" and ran inside.

◆ ◆ ◆

Everyday Words

clambering (KLAM ber ing) *v.* climbing something that is difficult to climb, using hands and feet

---

Vocabulary Builder

Idioms *Battling hand to hand* means fighting close to one's opponent. Use the idiom to complete this sentence:

Gangs of boys fought __________

______________________ on

the rockpile.

Vocabulary Builder 

Compound Words The compound verb *pinpoint* combines two words to form a new word. It means "find or show the exact position of something." Circle another compound word in the bracketed paragraph. What does it mean?

____

Vocabulary Builder 

Multiple-Meaning Words The verb *arrested* has different meanings. It can mean "taken away by the police because the person has done something illegal." It can also mean "stopped something that was happening." Which meaning does *arrested* have in the last paragraph? Underline the words that tell you.

____

____

Vocabulary Builder 

Idioms The idiom *paid attention to* can mean "carefully listened or watched someone or something." Complete this sentence:

John wanted to see whether their father was on his way home, so he

____

the street corner.

Comprehension Builder 

Predict what will happen when Roy's father returns home.

____

____

____

Vocabulary Builder

Parts of Speech *Delay* has different meanings, depending on how it is used in a sentence. It may be a noun meaning "a situation in which someone or something has to wait." It may also be a verb meaning "wait until a later time to do something." Is *delay* a noun or a verb in the bracketed paragraph?

____

By the time Elizabeth and her friend were halfway to the rockpile, a stranger was carrying the injured boy toward them. He explained that he thought the cut on Roy's head looked a lot worse than it actually was. Elizabeth was shaking with fear because she was so worried about the **potential** damage. Not looking at his brother, John paid more attention to the street corner to see if their father was on his way home already.

Back at the apartment, the women cleaned Roy's wound and remarked that it could have been so much worse. They questioned John about the incident. Elizabeth's friend blamed him for allowing Roy to leave, or at least for not telling his mother Roy's whereabouts. Nervously, Elizabeth looked to the door, wondering when her husband would be home. Her friend excused herself for the evening, after commenting that she knew that Roy's father, Reverend Gabriel Grimes, would be very upset upon his return from work for the day.

◆　　◆　　◆

Elizabeth turned slowly back into the room. Roy did not open his eyes, or move; but she knew that he was not sleeping; he wished to delay until the last possible moment any contact with his father. John put his newspaper and his notebook on the table and stood, leaning on the table, staring at her.

◆　　◆　　◆

Everyday Words

potential (puh TEN shuhl) *adj.* likely to develop into a particular type of person or thing in the future

Although Elizabeth tried to assure John that he should not worry about Gabriel's reaction, as long as he told the truth, they both continued to be concerned about it. Right before Gabriel came in, Delilah began to cry so Elizabeth went into her room to check on her. Delilah was one of Gabriel and Elizabeth's children. John, the oldest, had a different father.

Gabriel began angrily questioning John about what had happened. John stood paralyzed with fear. Elizabeth interrupted, telling her husband that Roy had brought this trouble on himself by not listening to her constant warnings. Gabriel addressed his hurt son with tenderness as Roy continued crying and acting worse than he had since the injury occurred. When Gabriel asked John directly about the situation again, Elizabeth blamed Roy and tried to dismiss everything saying that he would heal fine. Roy continued crying in the background as Gabriel's anger grew. He yelled at his wife, telling her to let the boy speak for himself. Then he asked where John had been during the whole **ordeal.** Terrified, John sat in silence, watching his mother, who was still holding Delilah. Gabriel threatened to whip John, but Elizabeth came to his defense. She also handed the baby to John, which provided a needed distraction. Wanting to take the focus off of John, Elizabeth challenged her husband, causing his anger to turn to rage.

◆　◆　◆

Everyday Words

ordeal (ahr DEEL) *n.* a very bad experience that continues for a long time

Vocabulary Builder 

Idioms The idiom *check on* means "make sure that someone or something is all right." Complete this sentence:

When Delilah began to cry,

Elizabeth _______________________

_______________________.

Vocabulary Builder

Common Expressions The expression *brought this trouble on himself* means "caused something bad to happen to himself." People use this expression to show that someone cannot blame someone else for something that has happened as a result of their own actions. How does Roy's mother say that Roy *brought this trouble on himself?*

____

____

Vocabulary Builder 

Adverbs An adverb is a word that adds to the meaning of a verb, an adjective, or another adverb. Most adverbs end in *-ly*. In the second paragraph, the adverb *angrily* means "in an angry manner." Circle another adverb that ends in *-ly* in the same paragraph. What does it mean?

____

____

TAKE NOTES

Comprehension Builder 

Was your prediction correct? Explain.

____

____

____

Fluency Builder 

With a partner, take turns reading aloud the bracketed paragraph until you can read it smoothly and with expression. Be sure to pause for punctuation marks.

His eyes were struck alive, unmoving, blind with malevolence[1]—she felt, like the pull of the earth at her feet, his longing to witness her perdition. Again, as though it might be propitiation,[2] she moved the child in her arms. And at this his eyes changed, he looked at Elizabeth, the mother of his children, the helpmeet[3] given by the Lord.

◆　◆　◆

Knowing her husband was beginning to calm down, Elizabeth took the baby out of the room. Before she left, she asked John to put away his father's lunchbox, in hopes of normalcy returning to their home.

◆　◆　◆

---

1. **malevolence** (muh LEV uh luhnts) *n.* a desire to harm other people
2. **propitiation** (proh PI shee ay shuhn) *n.* the act of making someone less angry or of stopping someone from attacking by giving him or her what he or she wants
3. **helpmeet** (HELP meet) *n.* helpmate, or a helpful companion, usually a wife

Thinking About the Selection

1. What happens in "The Rockpile"? Use the chart below to list events in the story in the order in which they occur.

Story Events
Elizabeth forbids ____.
Roy disobeys and ____.
Roy is injured when ____.
Gabriel returns home and ____.
Elizabeth challenges Gabriel and ____.

2. When Roy tells John that he is going downstairs, John ___________
____.

TALK ABOUT IT **Who Is to Blame?** Who do you think is to blame for what happens to Roy? Discuss your ideas in a small group.

I think ________________ is to blame because ________________

____.

Writing About the Essential Question

How does literature shape or reflect society? In which aspects of their lives are the characters in this story insiders or outsiders? Explain.

Idioms

Recall that an idiom is a word or phrase with a special meaning that is different than the literal meaning of the words.

Examples

Idiom	Special Meaning
live in the fast lane	have an exciting way of life that involves dangerous and expensive activities
live in the past	think only about the past
live it up	do things you enjoy and spend a great deal of money
live off the land	grow or catch all the food you need to live

Now You Do It

Write a sentence for each idiom that appears in the chart above.

1. a live in the fast lane _______________________________

____

2. live in the past _______________________________

____

3. live it up _______________________________

____

4. live off the land _______________________________

____

TALK ABOUT IT **Tell a Story** Make up a story to tell a partner, and use at least three idioms from the chart above. Be sure to use the idiom in a way that makes sense.

WRITE ABOUT IT **Write a Song** Write a song that uses one of the idioms from the chart as a title and features it as a refrain, or repeated phrase.

Vocabulary

These words are underlined in the selection. Listen to each word. Say it. Then, read the definition and the example sentence.

accessible (ak SES uh buhl) *adj.* Something that is **accessible** is easy to obtain, use, or understand.

> *Students found the novel accessible and interesting.*

contagious (kuhn TAY juhs) *adj.* If a feeling, attitude, or action is **contagious,** other people are quickly affected by it and begin to have it or do it.

> *The girls' laughter was contagious, and soon everyone was chuckling.*

calamity (kuh LAM uh tee) *n.* A **calamity** is a terrible and unexpected event that causes a great deal of damage or suffering.

> *The destructive train wreck was a huge calamity for the town.*

Vocabulary Practice

Read the first sentence in each group of three. Then, complete Sentence *a* by substituting another word or phrase that means the same as the underlined vocabulary word. Complete Sentence *b* with your own ideas and words.

1. Ana rephrased the words in more accessible language.

   a. Ana rephrased the words in more ______________ language.

   b. ______________________________ in more accessible language.

2. Charlie's contagious optimism encouraged the team.

   a. Charlie's ______________ optimism encouraged the team.

   b. Charlie's contagious optimism ______________________________.

3. The flood was the worst calamity people had endured.

   a. The flood was the worst ______________ people had endured.

   b. The flood was the worst calamity ______________________________.

Getting Ready to Read

Toni Morrison wrote this remembrance of James Baldwin a role model to her, at the time of his death. A role model is a person whose life people admire and try to copy. Whom do you consider a role model? Why? Share your thoughts with a partner.

from On James Baldwin
Toni Morrison

Summary In this excerpt from *On James Baldwin,* Toni Morrison honors and thanks an author who inspired her. Morrison wrote this tribute to Baldwin shortly after he died in 1987. In it, she identifies three gifts that Baldwin gave to her and to other writers.

Note-taking Guide

Use this graphic organizer to record the gifts that Morrison says Baldwin gave to her and to other writers.

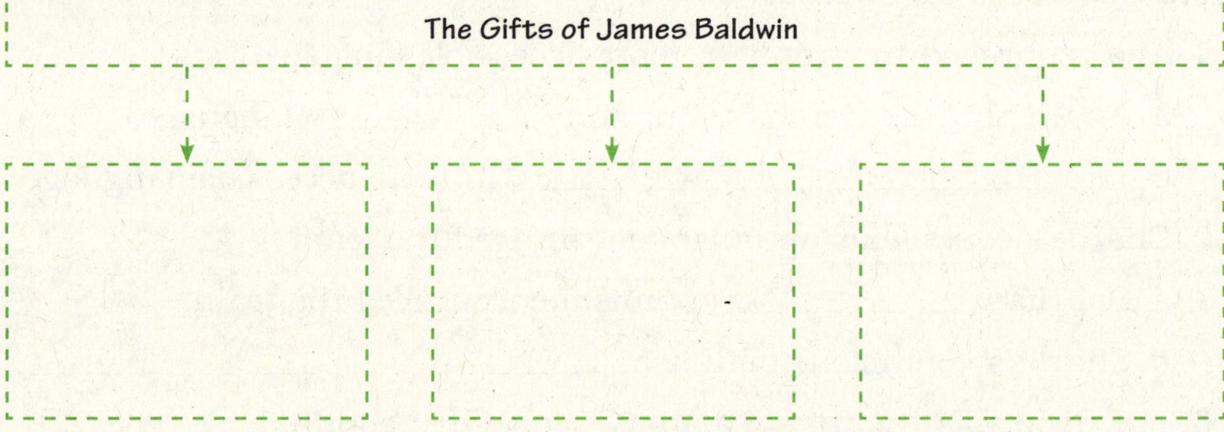

from On James Baldwin

Toni Morrison

Morrison opened her remembrance of James Baldwin by addressing him as Jimmy, showing the degree of closeness and **affection** that they shared. She thanked him for the many gifts he gave her and the lessons he taught her.

◆ ◆ ◆

I never heard a single command from you, yet the demands you made on me, the challenges you issued to me, were **nevertheless** unmistakable, even if unenforced: that I work and think at the top of my form, that I stand on **moral** ground but know that ground must be shored up by **mercy,** that "the world is before [me] and [I] need not take it or leave it as it was when [I] came in."

◆ ◆ ◆

The first gift that Morrison spoke of is Baldwin's use of the English language. She claimed he made it more accessible to all authors, but particularly black writers. She gave Baldwin credit for breaking down the more formal aspects of language

---

Everyday Words

affection (uh FEK shuhn) *n.* a feeling of liking, loving, or caring for someone

nevertheless (nev er thuh LES) *adv.* in spite of a fact that you have just mentioned

moral (MOHR uhl) *adj.* relating to the principles of what is right and wrong behavior

mercy (MER see) *n.* kindness, pity, and a willingness to forgive

---

Vocabulary Builder 

Multiple-Meaning Words
The verb *opened* may mean "removed the lid or top of a container." It may also mean "started an activity or event." What does *opened* mean in the first paragraph?

____

____

Vocabulary Builder 

Idioms The idiom *shored up* means "supported." Use the idiom to complete this sentence:

Toni Morrison learned from James Baldwin that moral ground must

be ______________ by mercy.

Vocabulary Builder 

Common Expressions The expression *breaking down* may mean "changing or removing something that prevents people from accomplishing a task or understanding something." What does Morrison give Baldwin credit for breaking down?

____

____

Vocabulary Builder

Multiple-Meaning Words The noun *fluff* may mean "soft, light hair or feathers." It may also mean "writing, news, or music that is not serious or important." What does *fluff* mean in underlined text?

____

____

Comprehension Builder 

Morrison uses figurative language to describe Baldwin's gift of courage. She says that he carved a path for other writers. This means that he opened the way for other writers to do something by first doing it himself. What did Baldwin's carving a path allow other writers to do?

____

____

Vocabulary Builder 

Suffixes The suffix *-ness* means "the state of being." When *-ness* is added to an adjective, the adjective changes to a noun. The adjective *tender* means "gentle in a way that shows love." What does the noun *tenderness* mean?

____

____

and stripping away the fluff so that words **genuinely** reflected valuable meaning. Morrison explained that Baldwin used language to create beauty and inspire others, including herself. He made writing desirable and alive.

Baldwin's second gift, according to Morrison, was his courage. Through writing, Baldwin gave others hope and strength to write about their passions, even if the majority resisted it. He carved a path for writers to explore previously **forbidden** topics. His **confidence** was both powerful and contagious.

Finally, the third gift Morrison described was Baldwin's tenderness. Morrison remembered how Baldwin's tenderness caused her to be a better person. His tenderness demanded a lot of a person, but also provided the means to meet those demands.

◆　◆　◆

Everyday Words

genuinely (JEN yoo uhn lee) *adv.* in a way that is truly or honestly felt and meant

forbidden (fohr BID uhn) *adj.* not allowed

confidence (KAHN fuh duhns) *n.* the belief that you have the power or ability to do things well or deal with situations successfully

You knew, didn't you, how I needed your language and the mind that formed it? How I relied on your fierce courage to **tame** wilderness for me? How strengthened I was by the certainty that came from knowing you would never hurt me? You knew, didn't you, how I loved your love? You knew. This then is no <u>calamity</u>. No. This is **jubilee.** "Our crown," you said, "has already been bought and paid for. All we have to do," you said, "is wear it."

And we do, Jimmy. You crowned us.

◆　◆　◆

Everyday Words

tame (TAYM) *v.* reduce the strength of something to prevent it from causing harm or trouble

jubilee (JOO buh lee) *n.* a celebration, or great rejoicing

Fluency Builder 

With a partner, take turns reading aloud the bracketed paragraph. Think about the love and respect that Morrison feels for Baldwin, and read the lines with appropriate emotion. Remember to pause appropriately at punctuation marks.

Thinking About the Selection

1. Morrison names three gifts that James Baldwin shared with her and others. In the chart below, explain why each gift was special.

Baldwin's Gifts

Baldwin's use of the English language was a gift because ___________ ___________	+ Baldwin's courage was a gift because ___________ ___________.	+ Baldwin's tenderness was a gift because ___________ ___________.

2. Morrison is confident that Baldwin knew ____________________________________ ____ ____.

TALK ABOUT IT **A Fitting Tribute?** What do you think of Toni Morrison's tribute to James Baldwin? Discuss your thoughts with a partner.

Morrison's tribute to Baldwin is ____________________________ because ____.

Writing About the Essential Question

How do the writer and society influence each other? Writers often influence other writers. How can these chains of influence affect society at a large?

____

____

____

____

____

The Irregular Verb *To Make*

The chart below shows the conjugation of the irregular verb *to make* in the present and past tenses.

	Present Singular	Present Plural
First Person	I make	we make
Second Person	you make	you make
Third Person	he, she, it makes	they make
	Past Singular	**Past Plural**
First Person	I made	we made
Second Person	you made	you made
Third Person	he, she, it made	they made

Now You Do It

Complete the sentences with the correct forms of the present and past tenses of the verb *to make*.

1. He ___________________ plenty of money at his new job.

2. She ___________________ the three cakes that won the competition.

3. I usually ___________________ soup on Saturday afternoon.

4. Last night, he ___________________ dinner and cleaned up afterward.

5. At each meeting, we ___________________ soft toys for children in hospitals.

TALK ABOUT IT **What Did You Make?** Tell a partner about something you made. Use singular and plural forms of the present and past tenses of the verb *to make* in your description.

WRITE ABOUT IT **Write an Ad** Write an advertisement for a product or service. In your ad, use singular and plural forms of the present and past tenses of the verb *to make*.

Vocabulary

Listen to each word. Say it. Then, read the definition and the example sentence.

alliance (uh LY uhns) *n.* An **alliance** is a group of nations that unite for a specific purpose.

Nations may form an <u>alliance</u> as protection in case of war.

invective (in VEK tiv) *n.* When people use **invective,** they make a verbal attack or a strong criticism.

Everyone involved in the vicious argument used <u>invective</u>.

eradicate (i RAD uh kayt) *v.* When you **eradicate** something, you eliminate it completely.

Scientists worked hard to <u>eradicate</u> smallpox.

Vocabulary Practice

Read the first sentence in each group of three. Then, complete Sentence *a* by substituting another word or phrase that means the same as the underlined vocabulary word. Complete Sentence *b* with your own ideas and words.

1. The groups formed an <u>alliance</u> and shared their resources.

   a. The groups formed an _______________ and shared their resources.

   b. The groups formed an alliance _______________________________.

2. His description of the enemy's strategy was full of <u>invective</u>.

   a. His description of the enemy's strategy was full of _______________.

   b. _______________________________ was full of invective.

3. The farmers tried to <u>eradicate</u> the harmful insects.

   a. The farmers tried to _______________ the harmful insects.

   b. The farmers tried to eradicate _______________________________.

Getting Ready to Read

John F. Kennedy delivered this address, or speech, at his inauguration as President of the United States in 1961. What goals for the nation would you set and describe in an inaugural address if you were elected President? Brainstorm goals in a small group.

Inaugural Address
John F. Kennedy

Summary An inaugural address is the speech a president gives when he takes office. John F. Kennedy delivered his inaugural address in 1961. Tensions were high between the United States and the Soviet Union. The possibility of a nuclear war was real. In his speech, Kennedy spoke to the fears of both the nation and the world. He reminded Americans that they had inherited a responsibility to defend freedom. The new President urged Americans to serve their country with the famous words, "Ask not what your country can do for you— ask what you can do for your country." Then, he called on the citizens of the world to work together for the freedom of people everywhere.

Note-taking Guide

In his speech, Kennedy calls on many groups of people to take action. In the chart, write what he asks each group to do.

	Actions that Kennedy Requests
Enemies of the U.S.	
American Citizens	
People of Other Nations	

Vocabulary

Listen to each word. Say it. Then, read the definition and the example sentence.

flagrant (FLAY gruhnt) *adj.* A **flagrant** action is one that is done in a noticeable and disrespectful way.

Jake's flagrant cheating resulted in a failing grade.

profundity (pruh FUN duh tee) *n.* Someone with **profundity** shows great knowledge and understanding.

The politician's colleagues respected her for her profundity.

disinherited (dis in HAYR uh tuhd) *adj.* When someone is **disinherited,** the person has had his or her natural or legal rights taken away.

The disinherited political group rebelled against the government.

Vocabulary Practice

Read the first sentence in each group of three. Then, complete Sentence *a* by substituting another word or phrase that means the same as the underlined vocabulary word. Complete Sentence *b* with your own ideas and words.

1. The student's <u>flagrant</u> disobedience resulted in detention.

    a. The student's _______________ disobedience resulted in detention.

    b. The student's flagrant disobedience _________________________.

2. Her simple words did not lessen the <u>profundity</u> of her ideas.

    a. Her simple words did not lessen the _______________ of her ideas.

    b. _________________________ the profundity of her ideas.

3. The <u>disinherited</u> people fought for their land rights.

    a. The _______________ people fought for their land rights.

    b. The disinherited people _________________________.

Getting Ready to Read

Civil rights are the basic privileges and liberties that every person should have, whatever the person's sex, race, or religion. What can citizens do to make sure that everyone has full equality, justice, and economic opportunity? Discuss your ideas with a partner.

Letter from Birmingham City Jail

Martin Luther King, Jr.

Summary Martin Luther King, Jr., was a civil rights leader. In April 1963, he was arrested for protesting segregation in Birmingham, Alabama. While in jail, King read a newspaper article that was critical of the civil rights movement. He responded to the article in this letter. In it, King criticized the police for their actions against protestors. He celebrated the real heroes who had the courage to take a stand against segregation. He also expressed confidence that the struggle for freedom would have a positive outcome.

Note-taking Guide

Answer the questions in the chart to keep track of the ideas that King expresses in his letter.

Question	Answer from King's Letter
Why will African Americans win freedom?	
Why doesn't King agree that the police deserve praise?	
How does King feel about the "sit-inners" and demonstrators?	

Thinking About the Selections

1. In his inaugural address, Kennedy makes pledges, or promises, to nations and people around the world. What does he say the United States pledges to the different groups? Write your answers in the chart below.

Pledges of the United States				
Old Allies	New Free States	Struggling People Around the World	Republics South of the Border	The United Nations

2. Dr. King believes that it is wrong to _______________________________

____.

What Can You Do? Kennedy urges Americans to ask what they can do for their country. What could you do to serve your country? Exchange ideas with a partner.

I could serve my country by _______________________________________.

Writing About the Essential Question

How does literature shape or reflect society? What do both of these documents suggest are the privileges and obligations of freedom?

____

____

____

____

Silent Letters

Letters such as *w* are sometimes silent. Generally, such silences are due to word origins or changes in pronunciation that have occurred over time.

Letter	Silent In	Examples
w	words that begin with *who-*	*who, whole, whose*
	words or syllables in which *w* comes before *r*	*wrap, write, wrong*

Now You Do It

Say each word aloud. Circle the words in which the w is silent.

worship	wreck
wrist	white
whoever	whom
wrinkle	whistle
world	wring

TALK ABOUT IT **Just in Time** Have a partner time you for sixty seconds as you write as many words as you can that contain a silent w. Then time your partner as he or she does the same. After you have both written your lists, read them aloud to each other. Note the words that your partner did not list, and discuss with your partner any additional words you think of.

WRITE ABOUT IT **Create a Word Search** Use graph paper to create a word search that includes ten words from this lesson or from the words you generated in your list. Rather than listing the words that are hidden in the word search, write the definitions of the words on a separate sheet of paper. You may consult a dictionary if necessary. Exchange word searches and definitions with a partner, and find the hidden words.

Vocabulary

Listen to each word. Say it. Then, read the definition and the example sentence.

predilection (pre di LEK shuhn) *n.* A **predilection** is a tendency to like a particular kind of person or thing.
   Felipe had a predilection for mystery novels.

ingratiating (in GRAY shee ayt ing) *n.* An **ingratiating** person tries to get others' approval by doing things to please them or by flattering them.
   The ingratiating tour guide charmed everyone on the tour bus.

inculcation (in kul KAY shuhn) *v.* When someone uses **inculcation,** he or she teaches by repetition and urging.
   The kindergarten teacher used inculcation to teach students the rules.

Vocabulary Practice

Read the first sentence in each group of three. Then, complete Sentence *a* by substituting another word or phrase that means the same as the underlined vocabulary word. Complete Sentence *b* with your own ideas and words.

 1. Malcolm had a <u>predilection</u> for caramel popcorn.

   a. Malcolm had a ____________ for caramel popcorn.

   b. Malcolm had a predilection for ________________________________.

 2. The <u>ingratiating</u> salesperson was successful at his work.

   a. The ____________ salesperson was successful at his work.

   b. The ingratiating salesperson ________________________________.

 3. Through <u>inculcation</u>, the teacher convinced students to study.

   a. Through ____________, the teacher convinced students to study.

   b. Through inculcation, the teacher convinced students ____________.

Getting Ready to Read

The Puritans believed in following the laws in the Bible in every area of their lives—church, home, and business. How do you think life as a Puritan teenager might have been similar to and different from your experience? Share your thoughts in a small group.

The Crucible, Act I

Arthur Miller

Summary It is 1692 in Salem, Massachusetts. The Reverend Parris is praying for his daughter Betty, who is ill. He says he saw his niece Abigail and Betty dancing in the woods. He asks Abigail why no one will hire her as a mother's helper since Mrs. Proctor fired her. Mary Warren comes in and says the village is accusing the girls of witchcraft. John Proctor comes for Mary and sends her back to his farm, where she works. Parris and all the girls but Abigail leave. Betty begins to wail. Others rush in, including kindly Rebecca Nurse, who calms Betty. Reverend Hale, an expert in witchcraft, enters. He questions Abigail, and she shifts the blame to Tituba, Reverend Parris's slave. Frightened, Tituba says that she saw Sarah Good and Goody Osburn with the Devil. Abby cries out other names, and soon all the girls are crying out names.

Note-taking Guide

Use this chart to record information about the setting, characters, and social or historical background of the play.

Setting	Characters	Background

Thinking About the Selection

1. What are characters' motives, or reasons, for behaving in a certain way? Consider the words and actions of the characters, and in the chart below, explain their motives.

Character	Words and Actions	Motive
Reverend Paris	demands that Abigail tell him everything that happened in the woods	
Abigail	insults John Proctor's wife	
Tituba	admits to witchcraft and seeing others with the Devil	

2. At the end of Act I, Abigail confesses that she and others danced with the Devil because she wants ___________________________

___________________________________.

TALK ABOUT IT **Make Judgments** What do you think of Abigail's actions at the end of Act I? What will be their outcome? Share your thoughts in a small group.

I think that Abigail ___________________________________.

Prefixes

A prefix is a word part added to the beginning of a base word. A prefix changes the meaning of the base word. The prefix *micro-* means "small."

Examples

| micro- + phone = microphone | The word *microphone* means "small piece of equipment that records the voice or makes it louder." |
| micro- + scope = microscope | the word *microscope* means "scientific equipment that makes small things appear larger." |

Now You Do It

Make new words by adding the prefix *micro-* to each word below. Consult a dictionary if necessary, and write a definition for each new word.

__________ wave __________________________________

__________ film __________________________________

__________ meter __________________________________

__________ manage __________________________________

TALK ABOUT IT **Coin Words** With a partner, use the prefix *micro-* to coin or invent your own words. For example, you might create the word *micronuisance* to describe something that is only a small annoyance.

WRITE ABOUT IT **Write Dictionary Entries** Select five invented words from your discussion, and write a dictionary entry for each word. In each entry, list the word, its pronunciation, its part of speech, and its definition. Consult a dictionary if necessary to develop a format for your entries.

____

____

____

____

Vocabulary

Listen to each word. Say it. Then, read the definition and the example sentence.

ameliorate (uh MI lyuh rayt) *v.* When you **ameliorate** something, you make it better.

> *Volunteers worked to <u>ameliorate</u> the home's shabby appearance.*

base (BAYS) *adj.* A **base** person exhibits little decency or honor.

> *The <u>base</u> dictator was the villain in the movie.*

deference (DEF uh ruhns) *n.* Behaving with **deference** shows that you respect someone and will accept his or her opinions.

> *The students treated the famous professor with <u>deference</u>.*

Vocabulary Practice

Read the first sentence in each group of three. Then, complete Sentence *a* by substituting another word or phrase that means the same as the underlined vocabulary word. Complete Sentence *b* with your own ideas and words.

1. The aid workers tried to <u>ameliorate</u> the situation at the camp.

   a. The aid workers tried to _____________ the situation at the camp.

   b. The aid workers tried to ameliorate ___________________________.

2. The <u>base</u> criminal did not seem to have a conscience.

   a. The _____________ criminal did not seem to have a conscience.

   b. The base criminal ____.

3. The townspeople treated the elderly gentleman with <u>deference</u>.

   a. The townspeople treated the elderly gentleman with _____________.

   b. ____ with deference.

Getting Ready to Read

Witchcraft is the use of magic powers to make things happen. Thousands of people in Europe were accused and convicted of witchcraft from the 1500s through the 1700s. This trend spread to colonial America. What do you think led people to accuse others of witchcraft in this period? Discuss your thoughts with a partner.

The Crucible, Act II
Arthur Miller

Summary Act II opens in the Proctor home, eight days later. Elizabeth Proctor says fourteen people have been arrested for witchcraft, based on what Abigail and the other girls have said. She urges John to testify that the girls are frauds. They quarrel over his previous affair with Abigail. Mary, back from court, gives Elizabeth a small doll. Mary says that those who confess will not be hanged. She says that Elizabeth's name has been mentioned. Elizabeth says she is sure that Abigail wants her dead. Hale appears at the door. To test John, Hale asks him to list the Ten Commandments. Ironically, John forgets the one about adultery. Then, two men burst in. They say their wives have been arrested. The marshal arrives and arrests Elizabeth. Over John's protests, she is taken away in chains.

Note-taking Guide

Use this chart to record information that you learn about characters in Act II based on the stage directions.

Character	Stage Direction	What it Says About the Character

Thinking About the Selection

1. Elizabeth Proctor is arrested on charges of witchcraft in Act II. Complete the sentences in the chart below to show the chain of events that lead to her arrest.

Mary ________________________________
____
________________________________.

Abigail ________________________________
____
________________________________.

Cheever ________________________________
____
________________________________.

Elizabeth is arrested for witchcraft and taken to jail.

2. John Proctor reacts to Elizabeth's arrest by ________________________________
____.

TALK **ABOUT IT** **A Fair Trial?** Hale says that the court will treat Elizabeth and the other accused women fairly. Do you think the women will get a fair trial? Why or why not?

I [think/do not think] the women will get a fair trial because ________
____.

Parts of Speech

A noun is a word that represents a person, a place, a thing, an activity, a quality, or an idea. A verb is a word that describes an action, an experience, or a state of being. Some words can function as both nouns and verbs. Use the position in the sentence and the context to determine the correct part of speech of a word.

Examples

Word	Noun	Verb
address	details of a place where one lives or works	solve a problem or speak formally to someone
give	ability of a material to bend or stretch under pressure	let someone have something or provide something for someone
pose	position in which something stands or sits	exist in a way that may cause danger or a problem

Now You Do It

Use each word as a noun in one sentence and as a verb in another sentence.

1. address ____

   ____

2. give ____

   ____

3. pose ____

   ____

TALK ABOUT IT **School Talk** With a partner, discuss school, using the words *address, give,* and *pose* as both nouns and verbs.

WRITE ABOUT IT **Describe Your Day** Use the words in the chart to describe a typical day in your life. Be sure to use the words as both nouns and verbs.

Vocabulary

Listen to each word. Say it. Then, read the definition and the example sentence.

contentious (kuhn TEN shuhs) *adj.* When someone or something is **contentious,** it is likely to cause an argument.

> *The contentious club members disagreed frequently.*

imperceptible (im per SEPT uh buhl) *adj.* Something **imperceptible** is impossible to notice.

> *The distant sound was almost imperceptible.*

effrontery (i FRUNT uh ree) *n.* **Effrontery** is behavior that is very bold and without shame.

> *The grandmother was stunned by the children's effrontery.*

Vocabulary Practice

Read the first sentence in each group of three. Then, complete Sentence *a* by substituting another word or phrase that means the same as the underlined vocabulary word. Complete Sentence *b* with your own ideas and words.

1. My contentious aunt quarreled with everyone in the family.

    a. My _______________ aunt quarreled with everyone in the family.

    b. My contentious aunt ____.

2. The change in the height of the grass was imperceptible.

    a. The change in the height of the grass was _______________.

    b. The change _______________ was imperceptible.

3. The effrontery of the new student shocked the teacher.

    a. The _______________ of the new student shocked the teacher.

    b. The effrontery of the new student _______________________________.

Getting Ready to Read

A crucible is a container in which substances can be heated to high temperatures. In this act, Danforth compares the court to a hot fire that melts down anything hidden. Which characters do you think will endure the crucible of the court by not giving up their beliefs or the principles that guide them? Discuss your ideas with a partner.

The Crucible, Act III
Arthur Miller

Summary Act III opens with Giles Corey pleading for his wife's life. Then, Francis Nurse says the girls are lying. Proctor leads in a terrified Mary. Mary admits that she never saw any spirits. Danforth tells John that Elizabeth is pregnant. He says that she will not be executed until after the baby is born. Abigail swears that Mary is lying. To stop Abigail, John admits his infidelity. Elizabeth is brought in to back up John's claim. To protect John, she lies, so John is not believed. Abigail begins pretending that Mary's spirit is bewitching her. Mary hysterically takes back her confession. John is arrested. Hale condemns the court and leaves.

Note-taking Guide
As you read, use this diagram to track the events in Act III.

Beginning Event	Event	Event	Event	Event	Final Outcome
Mary Warren confesses to lying.					

Thinking About the Selection

1. In the court, which characters tell the truth and which characters lie? What is the effect of each confession or lie?

Truth or Lie	Effect
Mary confesses that ________________ ________________________________.	________________________________ ________________________________.
Abigail lies and says that Mary __________ ________________________________.	________________________________ ________________________________.
Proctor confesses that ____________ ________________________________.	________________________________ ________________________________.
Elizabeth lies and says that ____________ ________________________________.	________________________________ ________________________________.

2. When Abigail and the other girls turn against her, Mary ____________ ____.

TALK ABOUT IT **Shared Responsibility?** What do you think of how the judges handle the trial? Do they share responsibility with the girls for the execution of innocent people? Explain.

____

____

____

____

____

Word Families

Word family is a group of words that share the same base word. A base word can stand alone or serve as the basis of new words. Generally, new words are formed by adding prefixes, suffixes, verb endings, or other words to the base word.

Example

Base Word	Words That Share the Base Word
able: *adj.* to have the skill, strength, or knowledge needed to do something	• ability: *n.* the state of being able to do something • doable: *adj.* able to be done • enable: *v.* make someone or something able to do something • inability: *n.* lack of the ability to do something

Now You Do It

For each word below, identify whether a prefix, a suffix, a word, or a combination of these elements has been added to the base word. Then write a sentence that includes the word.

1. ability _______ ______________________________

2. doable _______ ______________________________

3. enable _______ ______________________________

4. inability _______ ______________________________

TALK ABOUT IT **Talk About Ability** Tell a partner about your abilities. What are you capable of doing? What do you enable others to do? What inabilities bother you?

WRITE ABOUT IT **Able to Write** Use ideas from your discussion to write a short essay about your abilities. Use each word from the lesson at least once.

Vocabulary

Listen to each word. Say it. Then, read the definition and the example sentence.

retaliation (ri tal ee AY shuhn) *n.* **Retaliation** is the act of doing an injury or wrong to someone who has done the same to you.

The long-time enemies practiced continual retaliation.

adamant (A duh muhnt) *adj.* Someone who is **adamant** is determined not to change his or her opinion or decision.

She is adamant about buying the house on the corner.

cleave (CLEEV) *v.* When you **cleave** to an idea or position, you stick firmly or cling to it.

Followers cleave to the group's guiding principles.

Vocabulary Practice

Read the first sentence in each group of three. Then, complete Sentence *a* by substituting another word or phrase that means the same as the underlined vocabulary word. Complete Sentence *b* with your own ideas and words.

1. The treaty forbade the opponents to seek <u>retaliation</u>.

   a. The treaty forbade the opponents to seek ______________.

   b. ______________________________________ to seek retaliation.

2. The parents were <u>adamant</u> about their children's bedtime.

   a. The parents were ______________ about their children's bedtime.

   b. The parents were adamant about ______________________________.

3. Supporters <u>cleave</u> to the ideals of their political party.

   a. Supporters ______________ to the ideals of their political party.

   b. Supporters cleave to the ideals ______________________________.

Getting Ready to Read

After 19 people were hanged as witches, people began to oppose the Salem witch trials. This opposition led the governor of Massachusetts to close the special court. How do you think the victims' families felt after the governor's decision? Did they have a right to feel that way? Share your thoughts in a small group.

The Crucible, Act IV

Arthur Miller

Summary Act IV opens in the Salem jail. Danforth and Hathorne enter. Parris enters and tells the judges that Abigail and Mercy Lewis have stolen his money and run away. Parris, hoping that John or Rebecca will confess, asks for a postponement of their hangings. Danforth refuses. Hale enters to ask Danforth to pardon the condemned. Elizabeth is brought in. Hale asks her to urge John to confess. John is brought in and the couple is left alone. They express their love, but Elizabeth refuses to advise John about whether he should confess. John decides to confess but refuses to name others. He signs the confession but will not give it to Danforth. In a fury, he rips the paper, crying that he will not destroy his good name. He is taken away to be hanged.

Note-taking Guide

Use this diagram to record themes, or central ideas, of *The Crucible.*

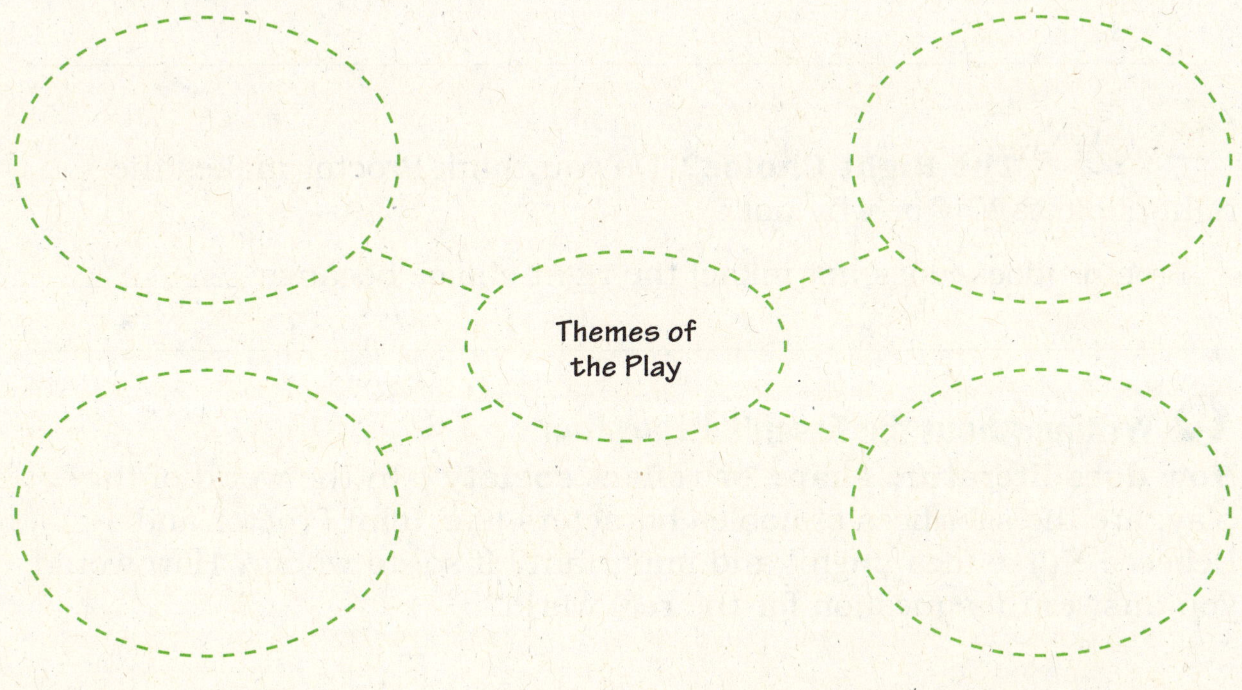

Thinking About the Selection

1. In the final act of the play, John Proctor has a chance to confess and avoid being hanged. He is not sure what to do. How do Proctor's actions show his conflict, or struggle? Complete the sentences in the chart below.

At first, Proctor ________________________ ____________________________________ __________________________________ .

Proctor changes his mind and __________ ____________________________________ __________________________________ .

However, he does not want ____________ ____________________________________ __________________________________ .

When Danforth tries to take the

confession, Proctor ________________ ____________________________________ .

2. John Proctor chooses to go to his death because ________________________ ____ ____ .

The Right Choice? Do you think Proctor makes the right choice? Why or why not?

Proctor [does/does not mkae] the right choice because ______________

____ .

Writing About the Essential Question

How does literature shape or reflect society? In the world of the play, are the sacrifices of noble characters like John Proctor and Rebecca Nurse meaningful and important? If so, to whom? How would you answer this question for the real world?

Suffixes

A suffix is a word part added to the end of a base word. A suffix changes the meaning of the base word. Sometimes it changes the word's part of speech. The suffix *-ee* refers to someone who receives or is the object of a particular action. This suffix is used to form nouns.

Examples

Base Word	Resulting Noun	Meaning
employ + -ee	employee	someone who is paid to work for someone else
pay + -ee	payee	person or organization receiving payment

Now You Do It

Add the suffix *-ee* to the following words. Then, use each noun in a sentence. Consult a dictionary if necessary.

address	
interview	
train	

1. ____

2. ____

3. ____

TALK ABOUT IT **Choose a Role** Choose one of the words from the charts above and tell a partner about a time when you were an employee, a payee, an addressee, interviewee, or a trainee. Perhaps you can combine some of these roles in the discussion. For example, as an employee, you may also be a trainee and a payee.

WRITE ABOUT IT **Describe Your Role** Now, use these ideas to write about the role you described. In your description, explain how you received an action or were the object of an action each time you use one of the words from the charts above.

Feature Articles

About Feature Articles

Feature articles provide information about topics of general interest. Although they are not news articles, feature articles answer the questions *who, what, when, where,* and *why.* They may also include direct quotations from people interviewed. However, the purpose of feature articles is both to inform and to entertain. Feature writers often describe their personal experience with a topic, and they may also share their opinions. Feature articles appear in newspapers and magazines and on Web sites.

Reading Skill

Before you accept information in a feature article, you should **evaluate the author's purpose and credibility.** When you evaluate the author's purpose, you judge his or her main reason for writing the article. Authors of feature articles write to entertain as well as inform. Look for details that support that purpose. When you evaluate the author's credibility, you judge whether he or she is knowledgeable and fair. Articles should contain accurate and balanced information. An author exhibits bias when only one side of an issue is presented. Credible authors avoid bias and present a balanced view, even when expressing their own opinions.

Use the graphic organizer below to guide you as you read "A Rock of the Modern Age, Arthur Miller is Everywhere."

Facts	Opinions
Summaries:	Evaluative Language:
Date/Events/People:	Emotional Language:

The New York Times

A Rock of the Modern Age, Arthur Miller is Everywhere

By Mel Gussow

When Arthur Miller was in Alaska to receive an award this year, he and a local environmental official went fishing for salmon in Prince William Sound. As they passed an iceberg, Mr. Miller's companion leaned over the side of the boat, chopped off pieces of blue glacial ice and threw them into the bucket with the fish. "That ice is probably millennia old," the playwright said in a recent interview. "Eight-million-year-old ice! It doesn't melt."

If ice can last that long, perhaps that says something about the survival of civilization—and art. Mr. Miller, who has never been known to sidestep a metaphor, smiled and said, "You hang around long enough . . . you don't melt."

In his 60-year career, Mr. Miller has been impervious to winds of fashion and periods of critical neglect. Even when receptivity for his work waned on Broadway, he found an audience in other countries, particularly in England, where he has been honored for his plays and also for his political consciousness.

Just turned 81, he finds himself in the middle of one of his busiest seasons. Nicholas Hytner's passionate film version of *The Crucible,* starring Daniel Day-Lewis and Winona Ryder, opened this week to generally favorable reviews. In *The New York Times,* Janet Maslin called it a "vibrant" and "beautifully acted" adaptation of Mr. Miller's 1953 play about witch hunts and marital betrayal in 17th-century Salem, Mass. Davis Thacker's television film of *Broken Glass* was shown last month on Masterpiece Theater, and his revival of *Death of a Salesman* recently opened at the Royal National Theater in London.

With both the film of *The Crucible* and the television production of *Broken Glass,* there is a trans-Atlantic creative alliance. Each is directed by an Englishman and has a British and American cast. Although Mr. Miller's work has been closely identified with American actors (from Lee J. Cobb to Dustin Hoffman in *Death of a Salesman*), certain English actors have also expressed a natural affinity for his work, including Mr. Day-Lewis and Paul Scofield in *The Crucible* and Michael Gambon, who gave a galvanizing performance in *A View From the Bridge* several years ago at the Royal National Theater.

Analyzing his English connection, Mr. Miller said, "Maybe because of the large amounts of work they do on classical plays, there's an assumption there that fundamentally a play is a metaphor, not simply a series of actions by characters."

From his perspective, his work is not basically naturalistic. With his assent, foreign productions often emphasize the symbolic aspects, as

The title clearly shows the reader this profile is about Arthur Miller.

The writer draws connections between various facts of Miller's life.

in a Swedish version of *The Last Yankee,* which had a six-foot rose as a life-enhancing emblem at the center of the production. There is no such flower in the text.

In the National Theater production of *Death of a Salesman,* Mr. Thacker has unmoored the play from its realistic roots. On an open turntable stage are aligned artifacts of Willy Loman's life: his old car and refrigerator and beds from Brooklyn to Boston. In a surprising, perhaps temporary turnabout for the playwright, the play and production received mixed reviews from London critics.

With the film of *The Crucible,* Mr. Hytner has made the drama more tangible and believable. The film was shot on rugged Hog Island, near Salem, where witch trials took place in the 17th century. Mr. Miller said the location was an asset, counteracting the "tendency to make it a static, photographed stage play." On Hog Island, "the environment kept moving in on you." . . .

Over the years, *The Crucible* has become his most produced play, seemingly transferrable to any country. No matter where it has been done—and he remembered one fanciful production in Georgia in the Soviet Union in which John Proctor was chased by a mob wearing balloon trousers and carrying scimitars—the most important thing is that Proctor is not meant to be heroic. He is "a damaged man" who rises against injustice.

In a recent speech, Robert Brustein said, "I defy you to name a single work of art that has ever changed anything." In response, Mr. Miller said, "I think works of art change the consciousness of people and their estimate of who they are and what they stand for." He pointed to John Steinbeck's *Grapes of Wrath* and to Mark Twain, "who gave America an image of itself, the idea of the innocent American, with his simple-minded appreciation of reality as against the complications of life." . . .

Speaking about his body of work, he said, "I have a feeling my plays are my character, and your character is your fate." Asked if he regretted any of his plays, he said, "That would be like regretting you lost your hair. They're part of my life. Each was terribly important to me at that moment."

As always, he works every day. He is writing a new play and he is revising *The Ride Down Mount Morgan* for its first New York production. And next season there will be a cycle of his plays in New York when he is playwright in residence Off Broadway with the Signature Theater Company.

Suddenly, he repeated his old refrain: "I never had a critic in my corner in this country." When it was pointed out that few playwrights have ever had critical champions, he readily agreed, adding, "As I look back, I honestly feel I have nothing to complain about." But still he keeps complaining.

"Well, yeah," he admitted, with a shrug. "You've got to keep the ball in the air."

Thinking About the Feature Article

1. What is the topic of the feature article?

____

2. What events may have prompted the author to write about this topic?

____

Reading Skill

3. What is the author's purpose? How do you know?

____

____

____

4. Does the author present a balanced view of his topic? How do you know?

____

____

____

WRITE ABOUT IT **Timed Writing: Position Statement** (25 minutes)

In 1953, theater critics like Brooks Atkinson had the power to make or break a Broadway production. Today, with the rise of the Internet and numerous forms of publishing, can any one critic still be as important or powerful? Write a position statement in which you address this question and express your opinion. Explain your views and use the theater reviews and feature article that appear as sources of supporting evidence. Spend approximately five minutes planning your response, ten minutes drafting, and another ten minutes reviewing, revising, and editing. Pay particular attention to the legibility of your handwriting so that readers will fully understand your thinking.

Word Bank

affluence	consumer	equality
anxiety	destruction	rebellion
conformity	dysfunctional	suburbia

A. Matching Draw an arrow from each word to its definition in the chart below.

Words	Definition
affluence	*n.* behavior that follows the accepted rules of a group
anxiety	*n.* suburbs in general, and the behavior, opinions, and ways of living that are typical of people who live there
conformity	*n.* feelling of being very worried about something
consumer	*n.* act or process of ruining something
destruction	*n.* great plenty or abundance
dysfunctional	*adj.* not working properly or normally
equality	*n.* someone who buys and uses products and services
rebellion	*n.* organized attempt to change the government or existing conditions
suburbia	*n.* situation in which people have the same rights and advantages

B. Complete the chart by writing the answer to each question.

Question	Response
Does a person with affluence have money or debt?	
Does a person with anxiety figet or relax?	
Does a person who is an example of conformity dress like everyone else or wear something unusual?	
Does a consumer use things up or produce new things?	
Does destruction usually cause sorrow or joy?	
Does a dysfunctional stove cook effectively or ineffectively?	
Does equality come from protecting civil rights or rejecting them?	
Does rebellion support or challenge existing conditions?	
Does a person in suburbia usually reside in a house or in a skyscraper?	

TALK ABOUT IT **Find Word Relationships** With a partner, discuss relationships among the vocabulary words. For example, people who live in *suburbia* may be accused of *conformity*. *Conformity* may breed *rebellion* as nonconformists seek freedom of expression. Talk about the similarities and differences between *conformity* and *equality*.

WRITE ABOUT IT **Write About Conformity and Rebellion** Write an article for your school newspaper about conformity and rebellion at your school. Consider the following questions as you draft your article:

- What are some examples of conformity?

- How does a consumer culture impact conformity?

- Is your school located in suburbia? How does living or not living in suburbia impact conformity?

- How do some students rebel against conformity? Do students at your school enjoy equality?

Vocabulary

Listen to each word. Say it. Then, read the definition and the example sentence.

dissuade (di SWAYD) *v.* When you **dissuade** a person, you convince him or her not to do something.

I could not dissuade him from getting a pet snake.

appease (uh PEEZ) *v.* When you **appease** someone, you satisfy him or her, or you make him or her less angry.

The clerk tried to appease the frustrated customer.

docile (DAH suhl) *adj.* A **docile** person or animal is obedient and easy to control.

A docile horse is the best choice for beginning riders.

Vocabulary Practice

Read the first sentence in each group of three. Then, complete Sentence *a* by substituting another word or phrase that means the same as the underlined vocabulary word. Complete Sentence *b* with your own ideas and words.

1. My mother tried to <u>dissuade</u> me from buying the camera.

   a. My mother tried to _______________ me from buying the camera.

   b. My mother tried to dissuade me from _______________________.

2. Kylie hoped to <u>appease</u> the crying baby with a bottle.

   a. Kylie hoped to _______________ the crying baby with a bottle.

   b. Kylie hoped to appease _____________________________________.

3. With training, the dog became <u>docile</u> and friendly.

   a. With training, the dog became _______________ and friendly.

   b. _________________________________ the dog became docile and friendly.

Getting Ready to Read

This story begins in Santo Domingo, the capital of the Dominican Republic. This city is the oldest European settlement in North America. What else do you know about the Dominican Republic? What do you know about early European settlements in North America? Share your knowledge with a small group of classmates.

Antojos
Julia Alvarez

Summary Yolanda's aunts warn her not to take a trip north by herself. She goes anyway. Yolanda stops to ask some boys to help her pick guavas. Yolanda finishes picking. By this time all the boys except Jose have left. She and Jose find that she has a flat tire. Jose goes for help. Yolanda stays alone with the car. Suddenly two men with machetes appear. Yolanda is frightened, but the men change her tire. They refuse any payment. Yolanda finds Jose walking on the road. He says that no one would help him because they did not believe his story.

Note-taking Guide

Use this chart to record key story events in the order in which they occur.

Beginning Event	Event	Event	Event
Yolanda cannot find guavas in the capital where her aunts live.			

Thinking About the Selection

1. In this story, one event leads to another in a cause and effect relationship. In the column on the right, write the effect of the event listed on the left.

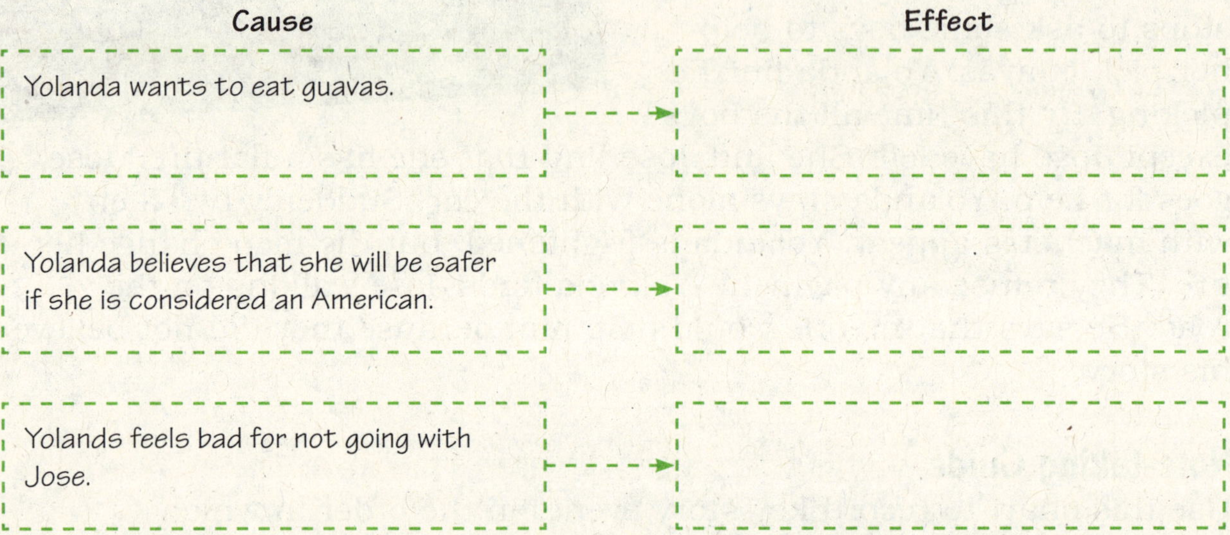

2. When Yolanda first sees the *campesinos,* she thinks that they

____, but they actually

____.

Yolanda's Dual Identity Yolanda misses parts of her homeland, but pretends not to understand Spanish when the *campesinos* arrive. How are the Dominican and American aspects of Yolanda's identity revealed in the story? Discuss your ideas with a partner. Be sure to identify details from the story that support your ideas.

Writing About the Essential Question

What is the relationship between place and literature? What details suggest that Yolanda longs for a deeper connection to her homeland?

Word Families

Word families are groups of words that share a common base word.
A base word is the word to which prefixes, suffixes, or other words
are added.

Example

Base Word	Words in the Word Family	Definition
resist *v.* stop yourself from having or doing something that you like or want	resistable	*adj.* able to be resisted
	irresistible	*adj.* too strong or powerful to be stopped
	resistance	*n.* refusal to accept new ideas or changes
	resistant	*adj.* not easily harmed or damaged by something

Now You Do It

Use each of the words from the "resist" word family in a sentence.

1. resist ____

2. resistible ____

3. irresistible ____

4. resistance ____

5. resistant ____

TALK ABOUT IT **That Was Hard!** With a partner, talk about a time when
you needed to resist a temptation or a desire. Did the situation seem
irresistible? How did you prove resistant in the end? Use words from
the *resist* word family in your conversation.

WRITE ABOUT IT **Resisting Temptation** Write four tips or "rules" for
resisting temptation that include words in the *resist* word family. Share
your work with a small group when you are done.

Vocabulary

These words are underlined in the story. Listen to each word. Say it. Then, read the definition and the example sentence.

sidle (SY duhl) *v.* When you **sidle,** you move sideways in a shy way.
The clown bent down when she saw the little boy sidle up to her.

oppress (uh PRES) *v.* To **oppress** a person means to treat him or her in an unfair and cruel way.
Many people believe that it is immoral to oppress others.

reserved (ree ZERVD) *v.* If someone **reserved** something, he or she kept it back or set it apart for later use.
I reserved the extra portion to have for lunch the next day.

Vocabulary Practice

Read the first sentence in each group of three. Then, complete Sentence *a* by substituting another word or phrase that means the same as the underlined vocabulary word. Complete Sentence *b* with your own ideas and words.

1. Fans often sidle up to celebrities to get autographs.

    a. Fans often _______________ up to celebrities to get autographs.

    b. Fans sidle up to ____.

2. Most dictators oppress people in countries under their control.

    a. Most dictators _______________ people in countries under their control.

    b. Most dictators oppress ____.

3. Taro reserved the scraps of paper to use in an art project.

    a. Taro _______________ the scraps of paper to use in an art project.

    b. Taro reserved the scraps of paper _________________________________.

Getting Ready to Read

People make quilts to provide warmth and to decorate their homes. Many people also pass down quilts to their descendants. What items or traditions have been passed down in your family? What would you like to pass down to your descendants? Discuss your ideas with a small group of classmates.

Everyday Use
Alice Walker

Summary The narrator and her daughter Maggie wait in the yard for the narrator's other daughter, Dee. The narrator is a hard-working woman from the Georgia countryside. Maggie is a shy young woman who was badly scarred during a house fire. Dee is an educated, confident woman. As a teenager, Dee abandoned her childhood home and culture. When Dee returns, she tries to take pieces of her heritage. Dee's visit helps Maggie and her mother discover their own pride.

Note-taking Guide
Use this plot diagram to keep track of the events in the story.

Climax:

Event ______________________________

Event ______________________________

Event ______________________________

Rising Action

Falling Action

Event ______________________________

Exposition

Resolution

Comprehension Builder 

What kind of mother does the narrator think that Dee would like to have? Underline the sentence that tells you. What kind of woman is the narrator? Circle the sentence that tells you.

Vocabulary Builder

Common Expressions The question *How do I look?* means "How do I look to you?" or "How do I appear?" People ask *How do I look?* when they want to know if they look nice, appropriate, or pretty or handsome. Complete this sentence:

Maggie wants to know how she

looks because ___________________

___________________________.

Vocabulary Builder 

Multiple-Meaning Words The noun *shuffle* may mean "a slow walk in which you do not lift your feet off the ground." It may also mean "the act of mixing playing cards into a different order." What does *shuffle* mean in the bracketed paragraph?

____

____

Discuss with a partner how you know the answer.

Everyday Use

Alice Walker

The narrator, or storyteller, waits anxiously for her daughter, Dee, to arrive. She knows that her other daughter, Maggie, will be nervous during Dee's visit. Maggie is embarrassed about the burn scars she has on her arms and legs. As she waits, the narrator dreams what it would be like if she and Dee were brought together for a surprise reunion on television. She imagines that Dee hugs her tearfully and pins a beautiful flower on her dress. In this dream, the narrator sees herself as **elegant** and **witty**. In reality, she is big, heavy, and strong with rough hands from hard work. She believes Dee would rather have a mother who is thin and has nice skin and hair.

◆ ◆ ◆

"How do I look, Mama?" Maggie says, showing just enough of her thin body **enveloped** in pink skirt and red blouse for me to know she's there, almost hidden by the door.

"Come out into the yard," I say.

Have you ever seen a **lame** animal, perhaps a dog run over by some careless person rich enough to own a car, sidle up to someone who is ignorant enough to be kind to him? That is the way my Maggie walks. She has been like this, chin on chest, eyes on ground, feet in shuffle, ever since the fire that burned the other house to the ground.

Everyday Words

elegant (EL uh guhnt) *adj.* beautiful, attractive, or graceful
witty (WIT ee) *adj.* using words in a clever and amusing way
enveloped (en VEL ohpt) *v.* surrounded
lame (LAYM) *adj.* unable to walk properly because your leg or foot is injured or weak

Dee is lighter than Maggie, with nicer hair and a fuller figure. She's a woman now, though sometimes I forget. How long ago was it that the other house burned? Ten, twelve years?

♦ ♦ ♦

The narrator can still remember the horror of the fire. Maggie was burned terribly.

♦ ♦ ♦

And Dee. I see her standing off under the sweet gum tree she used to dig gum out of; a look of **concentration** on her face as she watched the last dingy gray board of the house fall in toward the red-hot brick chimney.

♦ ♦ ♦

The narrator knows that Dee had hated the house. She wonders why Dee doesn't celebrate as the house burns down.

The narrator remembers how the church helped her raise enough money to send Dee to school in Augusta. The narrator says that Dee always got what she wanted. For example, she got a nice graduation dress and a pair of black shoes to match a suit. In the narrator's opinion, Dee was a stubborn teenager with a mind of her own.

The narrator was not educated. Her school was closed after second grade, but she doesn't know why. Maggie reads to her, although she struggles because she can't see well.

♦ ♦ ♦

She knows she is not bright. Like good looks and money, quickness passed her by. She will marry John Thomas (who has mossy teeth in an earnest face) and then I'll be free to sit here and I guess just sing church songs to myself.

♦ ♦ ♦

Fluency Builder 

Read aloud the first paragraph with expression. The paragraph tells what the narrator is thinking, so read the words as the narrator might say them. Pay attention to punctuation as you read.

Vocabulary Builder 

Idioms The idiom *to have a mind of one's own* means "to have strong opinions about things and to make your own decisions without being influenced by other people." Use the idiom to complete this sentence:

The narrator thinks that Dee

_________________________________.

Vocabulary Builder 

Multiple-Meaning Words
The adjective *bright* may mean "shining." It may also mean "intelligent." Which meaning of *bright* is used in the bracketed paragraph?

Everyday Words

concentration (kahn sen TRAY shun) *n.* close, undivided attention

Vocabulary Builder 

Regular and Irregular Verbs
In English, form the past tense of regular verbs by adding *-d* or *-ed* to the end of the base verb. Irregular verbs do not follow this rule. *Brought* is the past-tense form of the irregular verb *bring*. Circle the past-tense form of a regular verb in the first paragraph.

Vocabulary Builder 

Multiple-Meaning Words The verb *snaps* may mean "breaks with a sudden sharp noise." It may also mean "takes a photograph." What does *snaps* mean in the bracketed paragraph?

____

____

Comprehension Builder 

Why has Dee changed her name?

____

____

____

The narrator describes her house. It has three rooms, a tin roof, and holes for windows. The narrator believes Dee will hate this house. She says Dee never brought friends to visit. Maggie asks her mother if Dee ever had friends. The narrator remembers a few boys and girls who liked Dee because she was smart.

◆　◆　◆

When she comes I will meet—but there they are!

◆　◆　◆

Dee and a male friend arrive. Dee wears a flowing yellow and orange dress, long gold earrings, and bracelets. Her friend is short with long hair and a beard. Dee's friend tries to hug Maggie, but she **nervously** falls back against her mother's chair. While Dee snaps photographs, her mother sits with Maggie behind her. Finally, Dee puts the camera away and kisses her mother on the forehead. Dee's friend tries to shake Maggie's hand, but she doesn't want to.

Dee explains to her mother that her name is now Wangero Leewanika Kemanjo. Her mother wonders what happened to her real name, Dee.

◆　◆　◆

"She's dead," Wangero said. "I couldn't bear it any longer, being named after the people who oppress me."

"You know as well as me you was named after your aunt Dicie," I said. Dicie is my sister. She named Dee. We called her "Big Dee" after Dee was born.

"But who was *she* named after?" asked Wangero.

Everyday Words
nervously (NER vuhs lee) *adv.* in a way that shows that you are worried or frightened about something

"I guess after Grandma Dee," I said.

"And who was she named after?" asked Wangero.

"Her mother," I said, and saw Wangero was getting tired.

◆ ◆ ◆

To prevent further discussion, the narrator tells Dee (Wangero) that she doesn't know any more history. She actually does.

The narrator talks more about her daughter's new name. Dee (Wangero) tells her mother that she does not have to use this name, but the narrator tries to learn how to say it. The narrator also tries to say the name of Dee's friend. She has trouble, so he tells her to call him Hakim-a-barber.

◆ ◆ ◆

We sat down to eat and right away he said he didn't eat collards[1] and pork was unclean. Wangero, though, went on through the chitlins[2] and corn bread, the greens and everything else.

◆ ◆ ◆

Dee (Wangero) loves everything on the table. She even loves the handmade benches they are sitting on. Her daddy had made them because they didn't have money to buy chairs.

Dee (Wangero) tells Hakim-a-barber that she hadn't appreciated the benches until now. She carefully feels the wood.

◆ ◆ ◆

Then she gave a sigh and her hand closed over Grandma Dee's butter dish. "That's it!" she said. "I knew there was something I wanted to ask you if I could have."

◆ ◆ ◆

---

1   **collards** (KAHL erdz) *n.* leaves of the collard plant, often referred to as "collard greens"

2   **chitlins** (CHIT linz) *n.* chitterlings, a pork dish popular among southern African Americans

---

Vocabulary Builder

Possessive Pronouns Pronouns, such as *I, he, we, she,* and *you,* are used in place of nouns. Possessive pronouns, such as *my, his, her, your,* and *our,* show possession, or ownership. Circle two possessive pronouns in the bracketed paragraph. To whom does the first possessive pronoun refer?

____

To whom does the second one refer?

____

Vocabulary Builder 

Idioms The idiom *right away* means "immediately." What does Hakim-a-barber do right away?

____

____

Vocabulary Builder 

Contractions A contraction is a shortened form of one or more words. Often, an apostrophe replaces letters that have been dropped to shorten the word or words. *That's* is a contraction for "That is." Underline three more contractions on the page. Write out the complete words.

____

____

____

Cultural Understanding

Quilts are warm, thick blankets made by sewing two layers of cloth together with feathers or thick fabric between them. Throughout American history, people have sewed quilts from scraps, old clothes, and other fabrics. Some people use quilts as blankets on their beds; others hang them on their walls as art. Over time, quilters have developed specific patterns that have special names, such as Lone Star and Walk Around the Mountain. The Lone Star pattern consists of a series of squares sewn together. Each square has a star made of different types of fabric in the center.

Fluency Builder 

Underline the lines of dialogue on the page. With a partner, take turns reading aloud the dialogue between Wangero and her mother. One person should read Wangero's lines. The other should read the narrator's lines. Read with expression, as the characters would speak the words.

Comprehension Builder 

Dee wants to take her grandmother's quilts, but the narrator has promised them to Maggie. Predict what will happen to the quilts.

____

____

____

Dee (Wangero) asks her mother if she can have the top and handle to an old butter churn.[3] She wants to use the top as a centerpiece.[4] Dee (Wangero) asks who made it. Maggie says that their aunt's first husband, Stash, made it. Dee (Wangero) wraps up the pieces to the churn. After dinner, Maggie washes the dishes. Dee (Wangero) looks through a trunk[5] in her mother's room and finds two quilts. Dee's grandmother, mother, and aunt made the quilts from scraps of old dresses and shirts. One quilt pattern is Lone Star. The other is Walk Around the Mountain.

◆ ◆ ◆

"Mama," Wangero said sweet as a bird. "Can I have these old quilts?"

I heard something fall in the kitchen, and a minute later the kitchen door slammed.

◆ ◆ ◆

The narrator offers some other quilts instead. She explains that she made them but that Grandma had started them.

◆ ◆ ◆

"No," said Wangero. "I don't want those. They are stitched around the borders by machine."

"That'll make them last better," I said.

"That's not the point," said Wangero. "These are all pieces of dresses Grandma used to wear. She did all this stitching by hand. Imagine!" She held the quilts securely in her arms, stroking them.

◆ ◆ ◆

Dee (Wangero) is still admiring the quilts, but the narrator explains that she has promised them to Maggie as a wedding present.

◆ ◆ ◆

---

3. **butter churn** (BU ter CHERN) *n.* a large container used for shaking and stirring milk in order to make it into butter

4. **centerpiece** (SEN ter pees) *n.* a decoration placed in the middle of a table

5. **trunk** (TRUNK) *n.* a very large box made of wood or metal in which clothing or other items are stored

She gasped like a bee had stung her. "Maggie can't **appreciate** these quilts!" she said. "She'd probably be backward enough to put them to everyday use."

◆ ◆ ◆

The narrator exclaims that she hopes Maggie will use the quilts. No one has used them all this time that she has saved them. She also remembers that Dee (Wangero) had once told her that the quilts were old-fashioned and that she didn't want to take one to college with her.

◆ ◆ ◆

"But they're **priceless!**" she was saying now, **furiously;** for she has a temper. "Maggie would put them on the bed and in five years they'd be in rags. Less than that!"

◆ ◆ ◆

Dee (Wangero) becomes angry at the thought of Maggie having the quilts. The narrator asks Dee (Wangero) what she would do with them. Dee (Wangero) replies that she would hang them on the wall. Maggie listens nearby.

◆ ◆ ◆

"She can have them, Mama," she said, like somebody used to never winning anything, or having anything reserved for her. "I can 'member Grandma Dee without the quilts."

◆ ◆ ◆

The narrator looks at Maggie. She remembers that Maggie learned how to quilt from her grandmother and aunt. She sees that Maggie is slightly afraid of Dee (Wangero) but is not angry.

◆ ◆ ◆

Everyday Words

appreciate (uh PREE shee ayt) *v.* understand how good or useful something is
priceless (PRYS luhs) *adj.* extremely valuable
furiously (FYOOR ee uhs lee) *adv.* in a very angry way

Vocabulary Builder 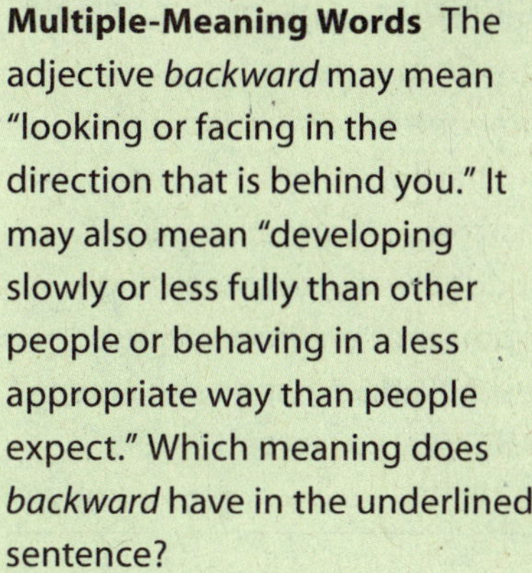

Multiple-Meaning Words The adjective *backward* may mean "looking or facing in the direction that is behind you." It may also mean "developing slowly or less fully than other people or behaving in a less appropriate way than people expect." Which meaning does *backward* have in the underlined sentence?

____

____

Vocabulary Builder 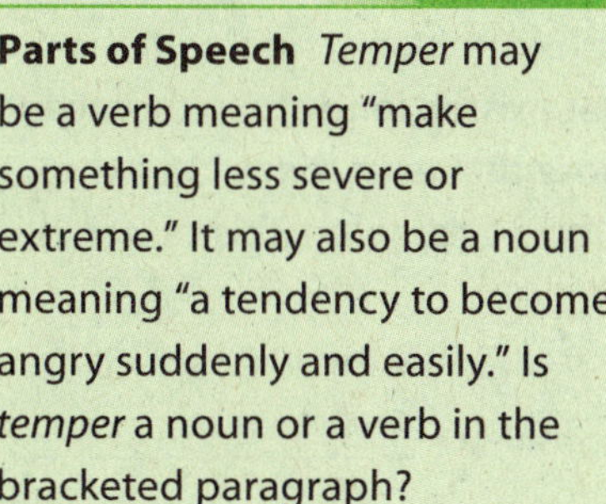

Parts of Speech *Temper* may be a verb meaning "make something less severe or extreme." It may also be a noun meaning "a tendency to become angry suddenly and easily." Is *temper* a noun or a verb in the bracketed paragraph?

____

Vocabulary Builder

Idioms The idiom *used to something* means "having experienced something so often or for such a long time that it no longer seems surprising, difficult, or strange." Complete this sentence:

According to the narrator,

Maggie is used to _____________

_______________________.

Vocabulary Builder

Multiple-Meaning Words The verb *hit* may mean "touch someone or something quickly and hard with your hand or an object." It may also mean "suddenly realize something's importance and feel surprised or shocked." What does *hit* mean in the first paragraph?

____

____

Vocabulary Builder

Idioms The idiom *living in the past* means "acting in accordance with conditions and traditions that existed long ago rather than those that exist today." Use the idiom to complete this sentence:

Dee says that Maggie and their

mother are _________________

______________________________.

Comprehension Builder

Was your prediction about the quilts correct? Explain.

____

____

____

When I looked at her like that something hit me in the top of my head and ran down to the soles of my feet. Just like when I'm in church and the spirit of God touches me and I get happy and shout. I did something I never had done before: hugged Maggie to me, then dragged her on into the room, snatched the quilts out of Miss Wangero's hands and dumped them into Maggie's lap. Maggie just sat there on my bed with her mouth open.

◆ ◆ ◆

The narrator tells Dee (Wangero) to choose other quilts, but Dee (Wangero) leaves and joins her friend, who is waiting in the car. Dee (Wangero) tells the narrator and Maggie that they do not understand their **heritage**. She also says they are living in the past. She puts on large, **modern** sunglasses.

◆ ◆ ◆

She put on some sunglasses that hid everything above the tip of her nose and her chin.

Maggie smiled; maybe at the sunglasses. But a real smile, not scared. After we watched the car dust settle I asked Maggie to bring me a dip of snuff.[6] And then the two of us sat there just enjoying, until it was time to go in the house and go to bed.

Everyday Words

heritage (HER uh tidj) *n.* the traditional beliefs, values, and customs of a group of people

modern (MAHD ern) *adj.* made or done by using the most recent designs and methods

6. **snuff** (SNUF) *n.* powdered tobacco

Thinking About the Selection

1. In the chart below, note how each of the narrator's daughters feels about the quilts.

<table>
<tr><td>Dee</td><td>Maggie</td></tr>
<tr><td>The quilts are</td><td>The quilts are</td></tr>
</table>

2. Dee changed her name to Wangero because ___________________________

____.

TALK ABOUT IT **Who Deserves Them?** Dee wants some of the quilts her grandmother had made, but the narrator refuses to give them to her because she has promised them to Maggie. Which daughter do you think deserves to have the quilts? Share your opinions with a partner.

I think that ___________________________ deserves the quilts because

____.

Writing About the Essential Question

How does literature shape or reflect society? Does this story suggest that there is a personal price for social change—even change for the better? Explain.

____

____

____

____

____

Prefixes

A prefix is a word part added to the beginning of a base word. A prefix changes the meaning of the base word. The prefix *inter-* means "between" or "among."

Examples

Prefix + Base Word	Definition
inter- + act = interact	The verb *interact* means "talk and work together with other people."
inter- + national = international	The adjective *international* means "between nations."
inter- + section = intersection	The noun *intersection* is the place where two roads or lines meet and cross each other.

Now You Do It

Make new words by adding the prefix *inter-* to each word below. Write a definition for each new word. You may consult a dictionary.

state ________________

Definition: ____

dependent _______________

Definition: ____

personal ________________

Definition: ____

TALK ABOUT IT **Interact!** In a small group take turns making up sentences that correctly use the *inter-* words above. One group member should say one of the words, and then another group member should respond by saying a sentence that uses the word. Continue until all group members have said a sentence.

WRITE ABOUT IT **An International Interaction** Write a short sketch about a boy and a girl from different nations who meet for the first time. How do they interact? Use as many words with the prefix *inter-* as you can.

Vocabulary

Listen to each word. Say it. Then, read the definition and the example sentence.

coincide (koh in SYD) *v.* Two or more events **coincide** when they happen at the same time.

Tamira's birthday party will <u>coincide</u> with the parade.

ambitions (am BI shuhnz) *n.* A person's **ambitions** are his or her strongly desired goals.

Arturo has <u>ambitions</u> to sing and play in a band.

fitfully (fit FUHL ee) *adv.* Something that is done **fitfully** is not regular and is always starting and stopping.

Chris moved <u>fitfully</u> around the room while waiting.

Vocabulary Practice

Read the first sentence in each group of three. Then, complete Sentence *a* by substituting another word or phrase that means the same as the underlined vocabulary word. Complete Sentence *b* with your own ideas and words.

1. Our trip to the city will <u>coincide</u> with the festival.

   a. Our trip to the city will ______________ the festival.

   b. Our trip to the city will coincide with ____________________.

2. One of Ana's <u>ambitions</u> is to study chemistry.

   a. One of Ana's ______________ is to study chemistry.

   b. One of Ana's ambitions is to ____________________.

3. The feverish child slept <u>fitfully</u> through the night.

   a. The feverish child slept ______________ through the night.

   b. ____________________ fitfully though the night.

Getting Ready to Read

In this story, a young adult must make a choice about how to fulfill his responsibilities. How have your responsibilities changed as you have aged? Talk about your thoughts with a group of classmates.

Everything Stuck to Him
Raymond Carver

Summary In "Everything Stuck to Him" the speaker tells his adult daughter a story about something that happened when she was still a baby. He had planned to go on a hunting trip, but the baby had cried most of the night. Her mother tells him to choose either hunting or his family. He leaves but hesitates and then returns.

Note-taking Guide

Complete the sentences in the chart to describe the main events in the story in the order in which they happened.

1. The father begins his story by describing

2. During a telephone call with an old hunting friend, the boy

3. That evening the couple goes to bed, but

4. The next morning after the boy dresses for his hunting trip, the girl

5. The boy leaves, but he returns, and they both say

Thinking About the Selection

1. The young man in this story has many responsibilities. Complete the graphic organizer below by listing some of those responsibilities.

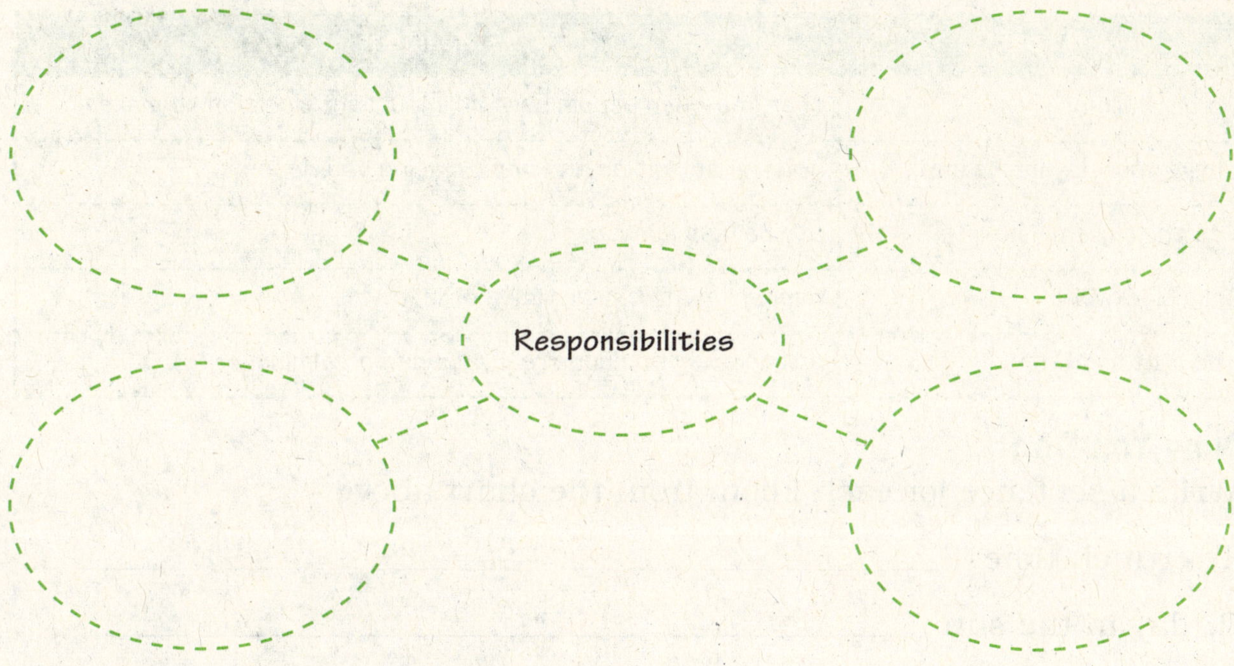

2. The title of this story refers to ________________________________ ____.

Making Choices In this story, the boy is forced to choose between his family and a hunting trip. What choice do you think he should have made? Talk about your opinions with a partner.

I think that the boy should have ________________________________.

Writing About the Essential Question

What makes American literature American? Although the frame story is set in Italy, the characters are from the United States. What aspects of their speech strike you as distinctly American? Explain.

____

____

Idioms

Recall that an idiom is an expression that has a special meaning different from the ordinary meaning of its words.

Examples

The following idioms all contain references to time.

Idiom	Meaning
crunch time	the time when people have an important decision to make
have your day in the sun	get the attention and appreciation you deserve
at the eleventh hour	at the last minute
like clockwork	happening at regular times or intervals
hour of need	a time when someone really needs something

Now You Do It

Write a sentence for each idiom from the chart above.

1. crunch time ______________________________________

2. day in the sun ______________________________________

3. at the eleventh hour ______________________________________

4. like clockwork ______________________________________

5. hour of need ______________________________________

TALK ABOUT IT **Deadlines** Tell a partner about a time when you had to meet a tight due date or accomplish something difficult in a short amount of time. Use at least three idioms from the chart above in your explanation.

WRITE ABOUT IT **Cartoon Time** Create a comic strip in which two characters have a dialogue. Use at least four of the idioms from this lesson in the dialogue or in captions below the comic strip.

Vocabulary

Listen to each word. Say it. Then, read the definition and the example sentence.

swerve (SWERV) *v.* When you **swerve,** you turn aside sharply and suddenly.

> *I had to swerve to avoid hitting the dog in the road.*

exhaust (eg ZAWST) *n.* **Exhaust** is the used steam or gas that an engine sends out.

> *A cloud of gray exhaust is coming from that truck.*

shard (SHARD) *n.* A **shard** is a sharp fragment of glass or metal from a broken object.

> *A metal shard punctured my bicycle tire.*

Vocabulary Practice

Read the first sentence in each group of three. Then, complete Sentence *a* by substituting another word or phrase that means the same as the underlined vocabulary word. Complete Sentence *b* with your own ideas and words.

1. Skilled bicyclists can <u>swerve</u> quickly around obstacles.

   a. Skilled bicyclists can _______________ quickly around obstacles.

   b. _____________________________ swerve quickly around obstacles.

2. The service station smelled of <u>exhaust</u> fumes and gasoline.

   a. The service station smelled of _______________ fumes and gasoline.

   b. _____________________________ smelled of exhaust fumes and gasoline.

3. Marcus picked up a <u>shard</u> of broken glass from the floor.

   a. Marcus picked up a _______________ of broken glass from the floor.

   b. Marcus picked up a shard of broken glass _____________________.

Getting Ready to Read

Each of the poems in this collection tells a story. This kind of poetry, called narrative poetry, is one of the oldest forms of poetry. Many early stories were told as narrative poems. Why do you think early people may have told stories in the form of poems? Do you think poetry or prose is a better way to tell a story? Talk about your opinions with a small group of classmates.

Traveling Through the Dark • The Secret • The Gift

William Stafford,
Denise Levertov, Li-Young Lee

Summaries In **"Traveling Through the Dark,"** the speaker finds a dead doe on the edge of the road. The speaker hesitates before pushing the animal into a river. In **"The Secret,"** two girls discover the secret of life in a line of poetry. In **"The Gift,"** the speaker removes a splinter from his wife's hand and recalls how his father once pulled a splinter from the speaker's hand.

Note-taking Guide

In each of these poems, the speaker responds to a situation or an event. Use the chart to provide details about the event in each poem. One poem has been done for you.

Poem	Event	Response
"Traveling Through the Dark"		
"The Secret"	Two girls tell the speaker that they have found the secret of life in one of her poems, but they cannot recall which poem or which line.	The speaker feels grateful that the girls found such meaning in one of her poems and loves them for it. She is also glad that they forgot so that they can find it again.
"The Gift"		

Thinking About the Selections

1. The speakers in "The Gift" and "The Secret" are each grateful for something. Complete the chart below by noting what each speaker is grateful for.

"The Gift"	"The Secret"

2. In "Traveling Through the Dark," the speaker must move the body of a deer because ____ ____ .

TALK ABOUT IT **Trading Positions** In "Traveling Through the Dark," the speaker must push the body of a deer into a canyon even though the deer is pregnant, and its unborn fawn is still alive. How do you think the speaker feels about doing this? Share your ideas with a partner, and use details from the poem and from your own experience to support your response.

Writing About the Essential Question

How does literature shape or reflect society? What do each of these poems suggest about the connections between small events and larger meanings?

____

____

____

Parts of Speech

A noun is a word that represents a person, a place, a thing, an activity, a quality, or an idea. A verb is a word or phrase that describes an action, an experience, or a state of being. Some words can function as both nouns and verbs. Use context and a word's position in a sentence to determine whether it is used as a noun or a verb.

Examples

Word	Noun	Verb
light	the energy from the sun or a lamp that allows you to see things	to make something start to burn
wave	an area of raised water that moves across the surface of the ocean	to move your hand as a signal or a greeting
glow	the pink color you have in your face when you are happy or excited	to shine with a gentle, steady light

Now You Do It

In each sentence below, determine whether the underlined word is a noun or a verb, and write the part of speech on the line.

1. a) _________ The <u>light</u> of the sun filled the room.

   b) _________ Dad will <u>light</u> the fire and we can toast marshmallows.

2. a) _________ The <u>wave</u> toppled my sandcastle.

   b) _________ <u>Wave</u> goodbye when we leave.

3. a) _________ Thousands of stars <u>glow</u> in the night sky.

   b) _________ The <u>glow</u> in her cheeks told me that she was thrilled.

TALK ABOUT IT **Have a Conversation** Have a partner identify a word from the chart and a part of speech. Then, you say a sentence that uses the word as that part of speech. Continue the exercise, taking turns.

WRITE ABOUT IT **Double Duty** Write a sentence for each word from this lesson. Use it as both a noun and a verb in the same sentence.

Vocabulary

These words are underlined in the selection. Listen to each word. Say it. Then, read the definition and the example sentence.

manufactured (man yuh FAK cherd) *v.* Someone who **manufactured** something made that thing using machines.

> *The electronics company manufactured record numbers of televisions.*

exact (ig ZAKT) *adj.* **Exact** describes something that is completely correct in all its details.

> *The candidate's speech contained the exact message I hoped to hear.*

crevices (KREV is iz) *n.* **Crevices** are narrow cracks or splits that may occur in rock or ice.

> *Crevices in glaciers may be hidden by snow.*

Vocabulary Practice

Read the first sentence in each group of three. Then, complete Sentence *a* by substituting another word or phrase that means the same as the underlined vocabulary word. Complete Sentence *b* with your own ideas and words.

1. Many factories in the city manufactured automobile parts.

    a. Many factories in the city ______________ automobile parts.

    b. Many factories in the city manufactured ______________________.

2. The measurements must be exact for the door to fit.

    a. The measurements must be ______________ for the door to fit.

    b. The measurements must be exact ______________________________.

3. The explorer examined all the crevices of the cave.

    a. The explorer examined all the ______________ of the cave.

    b. ______________________________ all the crevices of the cave.

Getting Ready to Read

A legal pad is a writing tablet that measures 8½ by 14 inches. In this poem, the speaker describes making legal pads at an after-school job. With a partner, discuss the after-school jobs you have had.

Who Burns for the Perfection of Paper
Martín Espada

Summary In "Who Burns for the Perfection of Paper," the speaker recalls working at a printing plant as a teenager. Now older and attending law school, the speaker acknowledges the pain and work that went into the pads of paper that students use.

Note-taking Guide

In this poem, the speaker describes what it was like to work in a printing plant. Use the web to record details about his experiences.

working in the
printing plant

Who Burns for the Perfection of Paper

Martín Espada

At sixteen, I worked after high school hours
at a printing plant
that manufactured legal pads;
Yellow paper
5   stacked seven feet high
and leaning
as I slipped cardboard
between the pages,
then brushed red glue
10 up and down the stack.
No gloves: fingertips required
for the perfection of paper,
smoothing the exact rectangle.
Sluggish by 9 pm, the hands
15 would slide along suddenly sharp paper,
and gather slits thinner than the crevices
of the skin, hidden.
Then the flue would sting,
hands oozing
20 till both palms burned
at the punchclock.

Ten years later, in law school,
I knew that every legal pad
was glued with the sting of hidden cuts,
25 that every open lawbook
was a pair of hands
upturned and burning.

Vocabulary Builder 

Multiple-Meaning Words The noun *plant* can mean "a living thing, smaller than a tree, that has roots and leaves and usually grows in the ground." It can also mean "a factory and all its equipment." What does *plant* mean in line 2?

____

____

Comprehension Builder

For what two reasons do workers get paper cuts?

____

____

____

Cultural Understanding

Punchclock is another word for a time clock. A time clock is a special clock that records the exact time at which an employee arrives at or leaves work. A worker inserts a card in the clock to record the time.

Vocabulary

Listen to each word. Say it. Then, read the definition and the example sentence.

terrain (tuh RAYN) *n.* **Terrain** is an area of ground and its features, such as mountains and forests.

The rocky, uneven terrain was difficult for hiking.

refuge (REF yooj) *n.* A **refuge** is a place where people or animals find shelter or protection from danger.

Carla manages a refuge for stray cats and dogs.

tirelessly (TYR les lee) *adv.* Someone who does something **tirelessly** does so in a determined way without stopping.

Sheldon campaigned tirelessly for the protection of the rain forest.

Vocabulary Practice

Read the first sentence in each group of three. Then, complete Sentence *a* by substituting another word or phrase that means the same as the underlined vocabulary word. Complete Sentence *b* with your own ideas and words.

1. The engineer studied the terrain to plan for the new road.

   a. The engineer studied the _______________ to plan for the new road.

   b. The engineer studied the terrain _________________________________.

2. In the barn they found refuge from the storm.

   a. In the barn they found _______________ from the storm.

   b. In the barn they found refuge _________________________________.

3. Ando studied tirelessly through the night.

   a. Ando studied _______________ through the night.

   b. Ando studied tirelessly _________________________________.

Getting Ready to Read

Between 1954 and 1975, Vietnam experienced a period of warfare. During that time, the country was divided into North Vietnam and South Vietnam. Many movies and books deal with with U.S. involvement in the conflict. In 1975, North Vietnam and South Vietnam reunified. What do you know about the Vietnam War? Share you knowledge with a partner.

Camouflaging the Chimera • Streets

Yusef Komunyakaa, Naomi Shihab Nye

Summaries In **"Camouflaging the Chimera,"** the speaker describes his experiences during the Vietnam War. He tells how soldiers used branches, mud, and grass to camouflage themselves. He relates his memories of being in combat. In **"Streets,"** the speaker describes what happens when someone dies. The speaker then explores the different ways that people live their lives.

Note-taking Guide

Use this chart to paraphase important details or events from each poem.

Poem	Important Details and Events
"Camouflaging the Chimera"	
"Streets"	

Thinking About the Selections

1. What images from "Camouflaging the Chimera" suggest that the soldier's are becoming part of the jungle? Write your answers in the graphic organizer below.

> Images That Suggest the Soldiers Are Becoming Part of the Jungle

2. According to the speaker in "Streets," the people who live in two worlds sleep once for _________________________________ and once for _________________________________.

TALK ABOUT IT **Two Different Experiences** The speaker of "Who Burns for the Perfection of Paper" describes two experiences with legal pads. How does the speaker's first experience affect the second? In your opinion, how does the speaker feel about legal pads? Discuss your ideas with a partner. Be sure to cite details from the poem to support your ideas.

Writing About the Essential Question

How does literature shape or reflect society? What do these poems suggest about the power of poetry to convey experience that is both private and public? Explain.

____

____

Irregular Verbs

To form the past tense and past participle of a regular verb, add the suffix *-d* or *-ed* to the base *(call, called)*. Irregular verbs, however, do not follow this pattern. The past tense and past participle forms of irregular verbs are formed in other ways. You must memorize the forms of common irregular verbs.

Examples

Present	Past	Past Participle
see	saw	seen
wear	wore	worn
go	went	gone
take	took	taken

Now You Do It

In the left column, complete the sentences with the past tense form of the verb in parentheses. In the right column, complete the sentences with the past participle of the verb in parentheses.

I ___________ my favorite plaid shirt. (wear)

James had ___________ to the store before the party. (go)

We ___________ turns playing the new video game. (take)

We have ___________ several good movies this year. (see)

TALK ABOUT IT **Talking Tenses** With a partner, take turns creating sentences that use the past and past participle forms of each verb listed in the chart above. Correct each other's use of the verbs if necessary.

WRITE ABOUT IT **Shopping Story** Write a short story about a trip to a store to buy clothes. Use as many of the verbs and tenses from the chart as possible.

Vocabulary

These words are underlined in the selection. Listen to each word. Say it. Then, read the definition and the example sentence.

proclaiming (proh KLAYM ing) *v.* When someone is **proclaiming** something, he or she is announcing it.

> *The principal was proclaiming the winner of the science fair.*

repent (ri PENT) *v.* If you **repent,** you feel sorry for what you did and you promise to behave differently.

> *The boy was mean to the dog, and he will not repent.*

steal (STEEL) *v.* To **steal** means to move carefully and quietly so that no one will notice you.

> *She plans to steal through the yard to pick her neighbor's flowers.*

Vocabulary Practice

Read the first sentence in each group of three. Then, complete Sentence *a* by substituting another word or phrase that means the same as the underlined vocabulary word. Complete Sentence *b* with your own ideas and words.

1. The coach was proclaiming the team's victory.

   a. The coach was _______________ the team's victory.

   b. The coach was proclaiming _______________________________.

2. The criminal refused to repent before his execution.

   a. The criminal refused to _______________ before his execution.

   b. The criminal refused to repent _______________________________.

3. Sometimes, he would steal into the kitchen for a snack.

   a. Sometimes, he would _______________ into the kitchen for a snack.

   b. Sometimes, he would steal _______________________________.

Getting Ready to Read

Halley's Comet is named for English astronomer Edmond Halley. A comet is an object in the sky that looks like a very bright ball with a tail. Comets orbit, or move around, the sun. In this poem, the speaker believes that the appearance of the comet might signal the end of the world. Why might the appearance of a comet cause people to think that the world might be ending? Discuss your ideas with a partner.

Halley's Comet
Stanley Kunitz

Summary In **"Halley's Comet,"** the speaker remembers learning about Halley's comet as a young boy. His teacher warns that if the comet strays off course, the world might be destroyed. The speaker remembers feeling afraid but also excited. After his family goes to sleep that night, he crawls up to the roof to watch the sky and wait.

Note-taking Guide

The speaker and several other characters contribute to the story told in this poem. Use the chart to paraphrase what each person thinks, feels, does, or says.

Person	What He or She Thinks or Says
Miss Murphy	
a red-bearded preacher	
the speaker, at dinner	
the speaker's mother	
the speaker, on the roof	

Thinking About the Selection

1. What does the speaker learn about Halley's Comet from Miss Murphy? Complete the sentences in the graphic organizer.

Miss Murphy tells the speaker's class that . . .

2. At dinner, the speaker is sad because _______________________________________ ____.

TALK ABOUT IT **What Is the Effect?** How do Miss Murphy and the preacher affect the speaker's view of the world? How does the speaker feel about the possible effects of the comet? Discuss your ideas with a small group.

Miss Murphy and the preacher affect the speaker by _______________ ____.

 **Writing About the Essential Question**

What is the relationship between place and literature? How does the "place" described in the last seven lines differ from the places mentioned in lines 1–29? Why might the poet have wanted to revisit this particular spot in the landscape of his memories?

____

____

____

Consonant Digraphs

A consonant digraph is a group of letters that represents a single sound. For example, the letters *ph* have an /f/ sound. The letters *gn* have an /n/ sound in words of one syllable.

Example

Digraph	Example	Pronunciation
gn	sign	SYN
	gnat	NAT
	align	uh LYN
	gnaw	NAW
ph	paragraph	PAR uh graf
	physical	FIZ i kuhl
	philosophy	fi LAHS uh fee
	elephant	EL uh fuhnt

Now You Do It

Use the words from the chart to answer the questions below.

1. Which word has the same beginning sound as *gnaw?* ___________

2. Which word has the same ending sound as *align?* ___________

3. Which word ends with an /f/ sound? ___________

4. Which words have the same beginning sound as *photo?* ___________

TALK ABOUT IT **Ping Pong** Make up a question to ask a partner, the answer to which is a word from the chart. Take turns asking and answering questions and pronouncing each answer word.

WRITE ABOUT IT **Write a Poem** Write a short poem that includes at least three words from the chart. Your poem may contain nonsense lines, such as: *In my philosophy/an elephant/outranks a gnawing gnat.* Read your poem aloud to a small group.

Vocabulary

Listen to each word. Say it. Then, read the definition and the example sentence.

heady (HED ee) *adj.* Something **heady** is intense and has a strong effect on one's senses.

> *The heady aroma of roses surrounded us in the garden.*

ample (AMP uhl) *adj.* An **ample** item is very large or plentiful.

> *The ample armchair can hold both children.*

divine (duh VYN) *v.* When you **divine,** you make a guess based on your intuition.

> *Kim tried to divine Tavon's reason for leaving.*

Vocabulary Practice

Read the first sentence in each group of three. Then, complete Sentence *a* by substituting another word or phrase that means the same as the underlined vocabulary word. Complete Sentence *b* with your own ideas and words.

1. The <u>heady</u> smell of ripe fruit filled the rain forest.

   a. The _______________ smell of ripe fruit filled the rain forest.

   b. The heady smell of ripe fruit _________________________________.

2. She denied no one her <u>ample</u> generosity.

   a. She denied no one her _______________ generosity.

   b. ____ her ample generosity.

3. We tried to <u>divine</u> the meaning of the coded letter.

   a. We tried to _______________ the meaning of the coded letter.

   b. We tried to divine the meaning of _________________________________.

Getting Ready to Read

People who move to a different country may miss the familiar goods of their native lands. Specialized stores in the United States sell imported products from many parts of the world. Have you ever visited a specialized store? What kinds of things did you see there? Talk about your experiences with a small group of classmates.

The Latin Deli: An Ars Poetica

Judith Ortiz Cofer

Summary In **"The Latin Deli: An Ars Poetica,"** the speaker describes a deli, or delicatessen store, in America. There, Latin American immigrants come to shop for foods from their homelands and talk to one another in their native language, Spanish.

Note-taking Guide

Use the chart to describe the owner of the deli.

The speaker describes the owner of the deli as . . .
• the Patroness of Exiles.
• _________________________
• _________________________
• _________________________
• _________________________
• _________________________
• _________________________
• _________________________
• _________________________

Thinking About the Selection

1. Complete the graphic organizer by identifying the goods sold at the Latin deli.

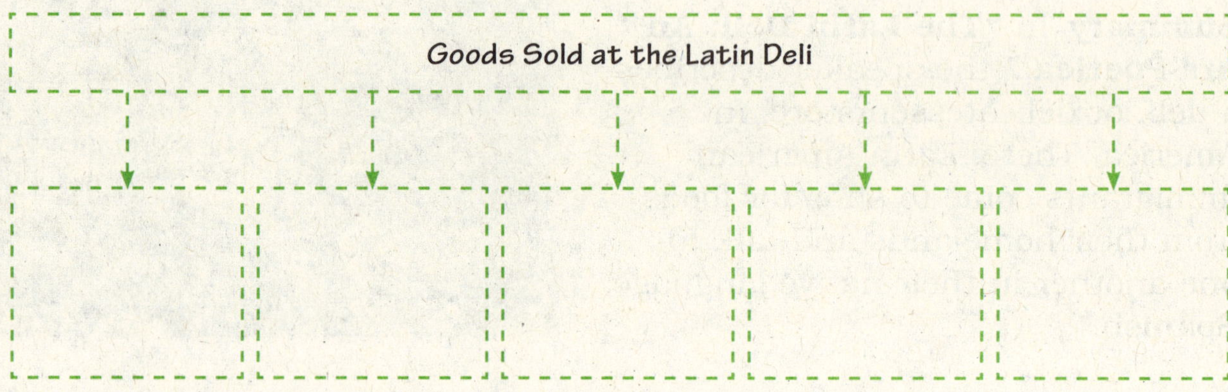

2. People shop at the Latin deli mainly because _________________________

____.

TALK ABOUT IT **Ars Poetica** The subtitle of this poem, "An Ars Poetica," means "the art of poetry." Usually, the phrase describes a poem about poetry. Why do you think the poet included the subtitle in this piece? What meaning do you think it has? Discuss your ideas with a partner.

In this poem, the phrase *ars poetica* means ____________________

____.

Writing About the Essential Question

What is the relationship between place and literature? What geographical, cultural, and emotional boundaries does the poet explore or even merge in this poem?

____

____

____

____

Suffixes

Recall that a suffix is word part added to the end of a base word. The suffix *-ment* often forms nouns when it is added to verbs. The suffix *-ment* means "result or product of doing something," or "the state of being something."

Examples

Base Word + Suffix	Definition
entertain + ment = entertainment	the result or product of entertaining
agree + ment = agreement	the result or product of agreeing
amaze + ment = amazement	the state of being amazed
commit + ment = commitment	the state of being committed

Now You Do It

Make new words by adding the suffix *-ment* to each word below. Write a definition for each new word. You may consult a dictionary.

achieve _______________________ ____

content _______________________ ____

measure _______________________ ____

excite _______________________ ____

TALK ABOUT IT **Your Assignment** In a small group take turns saying sentences that correctly use the *-ment* words from this lesson.

WRITE ABOUT IT **Showing the Result** Write a description of the way a person would look when feeling or experiencing each of the *-ment* words from this lesson. Do not use the *-ment* word in the description. With a partner, take turns reading your descriptions aloud. Ask your partner to guess the *-ment* word to which each description refers.

Vocabulary

These words are underlined in the selection. Listen to each word. Say it. Then, read the definition and the example sentence.

synonymous (si NAHN uh muhs) *adj.* Something that is **synonymous** has the same, or almost the same, meaning.

His name is synonymous with generosity.

derive (di RYV) *v.* When you **derive** something, you get it from someone or something else.

We derive satisfaction from working cooperatively.

speculation (spek yuh LAY shuhn) *n.* **Speculation** is a guess that a person makes without knowing all the facts.

His prediction about the election is just speculation.

Vocabulary Practice

Read the first sentence in each group of three. Then, complete Sentence *a* by substituting another word or phrase that means the same as the underlined vocabulary word. Complete Sentence *b* with your own ideas and words.

1. The team's name is synonymous with perfection.

    a. The team's name is ______________ with perfection.

    b. The team's name is synonymous with ____________________.

2. I derive my name from my aunt.

    a. I ______________ my name from my aunt.

    b. I derive my name __________________________________.

3. Her speculation about the weather today was correct.

    a. Her ______________ about the weather today was correct.

    b. Her speculation about the weather __________________________.

Getting Ready to Read

Onomatopoeia is figure of speech in which a word sounds like what it means. Some examples of onomatopoeia include *buzz* and *hiss*. With a partner, list different types of literary works that might use onomatopoeia. What would the use of onomatopoeia add to each work? Discuss your ideas with your partner.

Onomatopoeia
William Safire

Summary "Onomatopoeia" is a humorous essay. In it, William Safire explains the meaning and history of the term *onomatopoeia*. Onomatopoeia refers to words that sound like the action they describe, such as *buzz* or *hiss*. He then talks about the word *zap*, which takes the concept one step further. It imitates an imaginary noise—the sound of a paralyzing ray gun.

Note-taking Guide
Use this word map to explore the meaning of *onomatopoeia*.

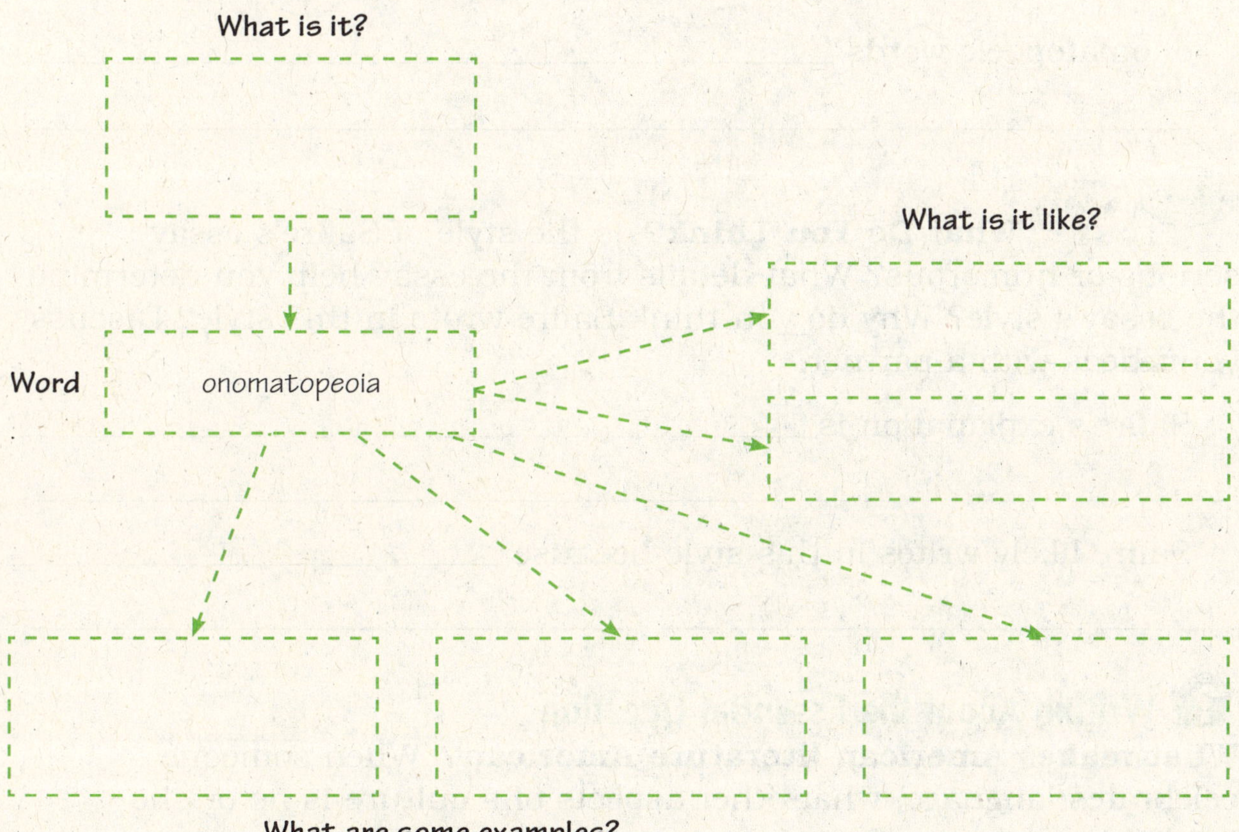

Thinking About the Selection

1. According to Safire, two theories explain how language began. Use the chart below to describe the *bow-wow theory* and the *pooh-pooh theory*.

Bow-wow Theory	Pooh-pooh Theory

2. At the end of the essay, Safire makes the point that many

   onomatopoeic words _______________________________

   ____ .

What Do You Think? Is the style of Safire's essay serious or humorous? What details from the essay help you determine the essay's style? Why do you think Safire wrote in this style? Discuss your ideas with a partner.

Safire's explanation is _______________________________

____ .

Safire likely writes in this style because _______________

____ .

Writing About the Essential Question

What makes American literature American? When someone celebrates language, what other aspects of a culture is he or she implicitly celebrating?

____

____

____

Multiple-Meaning Words

Recall that many words can have different meanings depending on their use in a sentence. Context clues help determine the meaning of a word. Context includes surrounding words, phrases, and sentences.

Examples

The verb *miss* can mean
A) not arrive in time for something
B) feel sad because you are no longer with a particular person

The verb *start* can mean
A) begin doing something
B) move one's body suddenly, especially when surprised or afraid

Now You Do It

Beside each sentence below, write whether the A or B definition applies to the underlined word.

_____ 1. We will <u>miss</u> the president's speech if we do not hurry.

_____ 2. I will <u>start</u> writing the final draft of my essay tomorrow.

_____ 3. I <u>miss</u> my sister when she is away at college.

_____ 4. They <u>miss</u> each other when she leaves for her business trip.

_____ 5. The sudden clap of thunder caused me to <u>start</u>.

_____ 6. Do not <u>start</u> something you cannot finish.

TALK ABOUT IT **Identify the Meaning** Say aloud a sentence that uses one of the meanings of *miss.* Ask a partner to identify which meaning of the word you used in your sentence. Switch roles with your partner and identify the meaning of the word *start.*

WRITE ABOUT IT **A Near Miss** Write a humorous story about missing an opportunity, a deadline, or an event. Use both meanings of the word *miss* and both meanings of the word *start* in your story.

Vocabulary

Listen to each word. Say it. Then, read the definition and the example sentence.

contiguous (kuhn TIG yoo uhs) *adj.* Things that are **contiguous** are next to each other or share a border.

> *We toured California and its contiguous states.*

vigorously (VI guhr uhs lee) *adj.* Something that is done **vigorously** is done forcefully or powerfully.

> *Deondra complained vigorously about the new rule.*

systemic (sis TEM ik) *adj.* Something that is **systemic** affects the entire body.

> *Drinking plenty of water has beneficial systemic effects.*

Vocabulary Practice

Read the first sentence in each group of three. Then, complete Sentence *a* by substituting another word or phrase that means the same as the underlined vocabulary word. Complete Sentence *b* with your own ideas and words.

1. Our geography class studied the contiguous 48 states.

   a. Our geography class studied the _______________ 48 states.

   b. Our geography class studied the contiguous _______________.

2. Kwame exercised vigorously to prepare for the track meet.

   a. Kwame exercised _______________ to prepare for the track meet.

   b. Kwame exercised vigorously _______________.

3. Dr. Vargas noted the systemic effects of the poison.

   a. Dr. Vargas noted the _______________ effects of the poison.

   b. Dr. Vargas noted the systemic effects _______________.

Getting Ready to Read

Wile E. Coyote is a well-known cartoon character. Wile E. Coyote always chases the Road Runner but never succeeds in catching it. Wile E. Coyote often suffers comical physical injury from products built by the fictional Acme Corporation. Have you ever seen a Wile E. Coyote cartoon? Describe what you saw to a partner.

Coyote v. Acme

Ian Frazier

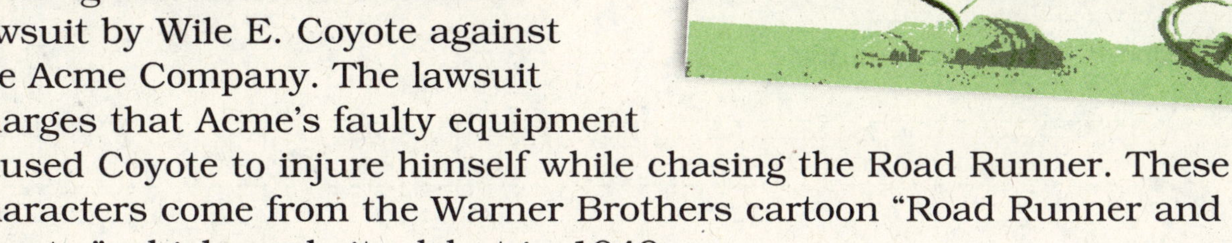

Summary "Coyote v. Acme" is the opening statement of a fictional lawsuit by Wile E. Coyote against the Acme Company. The lawsuit charges that Acme's faulty equipment caused Coyote to injure himself while chasing the Road Runner. These characters come from the Warner Brothers cartoon "Road Runner and Coyote," which made its debut in 1949.

Note-taking Guide

Use this diagram to draw conclusions about "Coyote v. Acme."

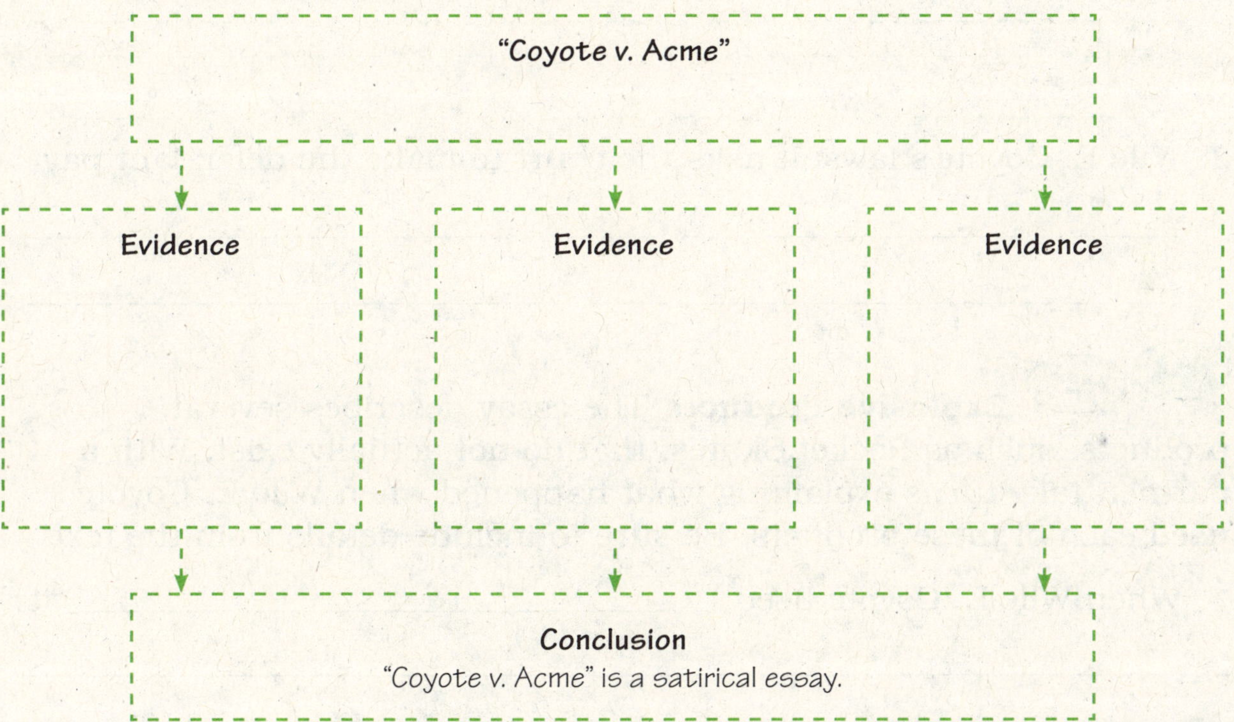

Thinking About the Selection

1. What five things happened as a result of the Acme Bomb (Catalogue #78-832)? Complete the graphic organizer below with details from the selection.

> Explosion of the Acme Bomb

2. Wile E. Coyote's lawsuit asks the court to make the defendant pay

____

____.

TALK ABOUT IT **Explosive Products** The essay describes several products, such as Rocket Skates, that do not actually exist. With a partner, take turns explaining what happened when Wile E. Coyote used each of these products. Be sure to include details from the text.

When Wile E. Coyote used ________________________________, it

____.

? Writing About the Essential Question

How does literature shape or reflect society? Based on this essay, do you think humorous exaggeration is an effective way to make a serious point? Why or why not?

Word Families

Recall that a group of words that share the same base word is called a word family. New words are formed by adding suffixes, prefixes, verb endings, and other words to the base word.

Example

Base Word	Words in the Word Family	Definition
agree: v. to have the same opinion about something	agreeable	*adj.* nice, acceptable, or enjoyable
	disagree	*v.* to have or express a different opinion from someone else
	disagreeable	*adj.* not enjoyable or pleasant
	agreement	*n.* an arrangement or promise to do something
	disagreement	*n.* a situation in which people express different opinions about something

Now You Do It

Complete each sentence below by writing the appropriate word from the word family.

1. Their ________________ caused their friendship to end.

2. The boys reached an ________________ about sharing the game.

3. The conflict at work became a ________________ situation.

4. Ali has many friends because she is so ________________.

5. People often ________________ about politics.

TALK ABOUT IT **How Did It Start?** Tell a partner about a disagreement you have had recently. What was it about? With whom did you disagree and why? Use words that belong to the *agree* word family.

WRITE ABOUT IT **Becoming Agreeable** Write a set of tips or "rules" for avoiding disagreements. Use words that belong to the *agree* word family in your tips or rules. Share your work with a small group when you are done. See whether they agree with advice.

Vocabulary

These words are underlined in the selection. Listen to each word. Say it. Then, read the definition and the example sentence.

mundane (mun DAYN) *adj.* Something **mundane** is ordinary and not very interesting or exciting.

> *His boring job consisted of mundane daily tasks.*

induce (in DOOS) *v.* To **induce** means to cause a particular condition or feeling.

> *Some medications induce drowsiness.*

prosperity (prah SPAYR uh tee) *n.* **Prosperity** is the condition of having money and being successful.

> *The booming economy created years of prosperity.*

Vocabulary Practice

Read the first sentence in each group of three. Then, complete Sentence *a* by substituting another word or phrase that means the same as the underlined vocabulary word. Complete Sentence *b* with your own ideas and words.

1. Jana did some mundane chores before going to bed.

   a. Jana did some _____________ chores before going to bed.

   b. Jana did some mundane chores _________________________.

2. Yukio played soft music to induce calm feelings.

   a. Yukio played soft music to _____________ calm feelings.

   b. Yukio played soft music to induce _____________________.

3. Elisa enjoyed the prosperity that came with her new job.

   a. Elisa enjoyed the _____________ that came with her new job.

   b. Elisa enjoyed the prosperity _______________________.

TALK ABOUT IT ## Getting Ready to Read

On the morning of September 11, 2001, terrorists killed almost three thousand people when they flew airplanes into three buildings in the United States. A fourth hijacked airplane crashed into a Pennsylvania field, killing everyone on board. Where were you on September 11, 2001? What do you remember about that day? How has that day affected you? With a partner, discuss your answers.

One Day, Now Broken in Two
Anna Quindlen

Summary In this essay, Anna Quindlen looks at the impact of the events of 9-11 on Americans. She thinks that Americans have become better people as a result of having to face this tragedy.

Note-taking Guide
Use this chart to analyze the effects of 9-11.

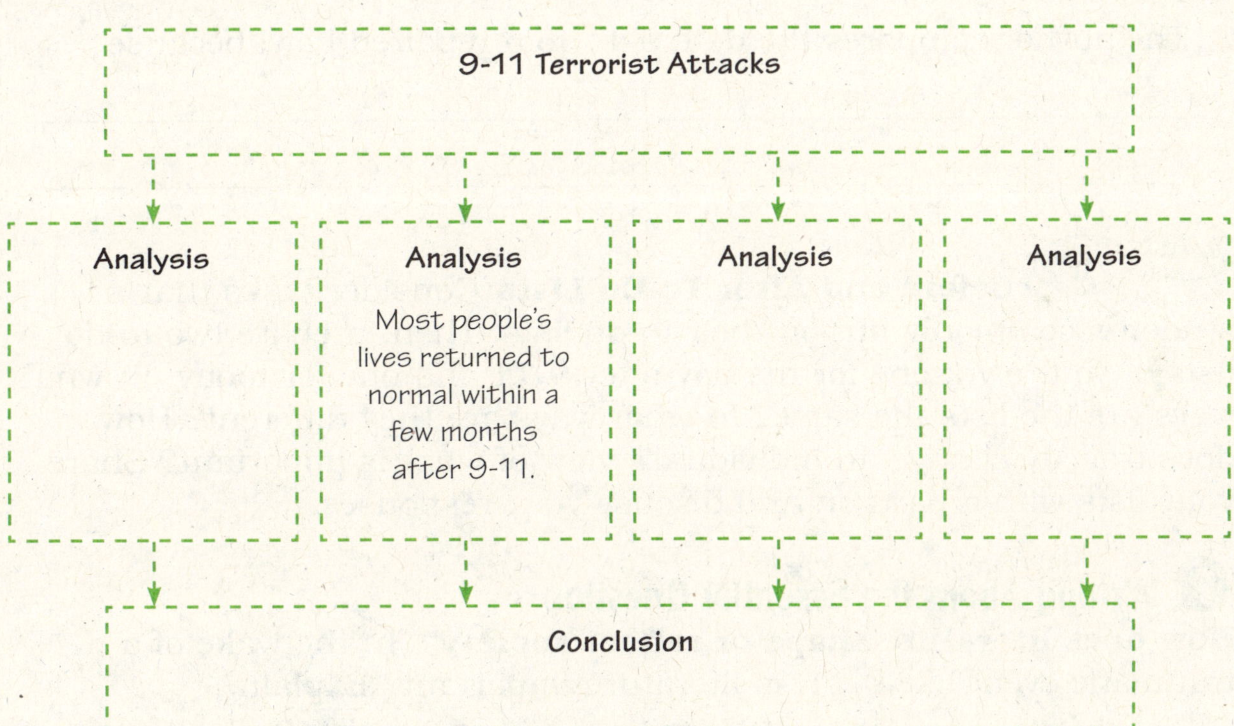

Thinking About the Selection

1. The author of the selection gives different meanings to the same date, depending on the way in which it is named: September 11 or 9-11. List these different meanings in the chart below.

September 11	9-11

2. The author compares the date 9-11 to a repaired bowl because

____

____.

TALK **ABOUT IT** **Before and After To-Do Lists** Consider tasks that students commonly put on their to-do lists. Then, prepare two to-do lists of your own: one for the day after 9-11 and one for today. In what ways are the lists the same? In what ways are they different? How does tragedy change an individual's view of what is important? Share your lists with a partner, and discuss your responses.

Writing About the Essential Question

How does literature shape or reflect society? In the wake of a traumatic event like 9-11, is literature important? Explain.

____

____

____

____

____

Idioms

Recall that an idiom is a word or phrase that has a special meaning different from the ordinary meaning of the words. The following idioms contain references to light and dark.

Examples

Idiom	Meaning
see the light	finally realize or understand something
light a fire under	motivate or cause someone or something to do something
make light of	joke about something or treat it as unimportant
in the dark	knowing nothing about something other people know about

Now You Do It

Beside each idiom, write a sentence that uses the idiom in a way that makes sense.

1. see the light ____

2. light a fire under ____

3. make light of ____

4. in the dark ____

TALK ABOUT IT   **Out of the Darkness . . .** Have you ever been "in the dark" about something and then later "seen the light"? Discuss your experience with a partner. Use any of the other idioms in your conversation if you can.

WRITE ABOUT IT   **. . . Into the Light** Write the story of the experience you described in the previous activity. Include all of the idioms of light and dark that you used in your conversation. Try to use at least three of the idioms from this lesson.

Vocabulary

These words are underlined in the selection. Listen to each word. Say it. Then, read the definition and the example sentence.

evoke (i VOHK) *v.* When you **evoke** something, such as an emotion or a memory, you call it forth or draw it out.

> *A national anthem can evoke feelings of patriotism.*

wince (WINS) *v.* To **wince** is to cringe or draw back slightly as if in pain.

> *Whenever I eat ice cream, I wince when the cold hits my teeth.*

ashamed (uh SHAYMD) *adj.* When someone feels **ashamed,** he or she feels embarrassed or guilty about something.

> *Ami was ashamed to be seen driving an old, rusty car to school.*

Vocabulary Practice

Read the first sentence in each group of three. Then, complete Sentence *a* by substituting another word or phrase that means the same as the underlined vocabulary word. Complete Sentence *b* with your own ideas and words.

1. Dirk knows that lying will evoke his father's anger.

   a. Dirk knows that lying will _______________ his father's anger.

   b. Dirk knows that lying will evoke _______________________________.

2. Students often wince when teachers announce weekend homework.

   a. Students often _______________ when teachers announce homework.

   b. Students often wince when teachers announce _______________.

3. Diara felt ashamed for hurting her best friend's feelings.

   a. Diara felt _______________ for hurting her best friend's feelings.

   b. Diara felt ashamed for _________________________________.

Getting Ready to Read

The term *mother tongue* is the first language that an individual learns as a child. Think about the two words in this term. Why would the words *mother* and *tongue* be used to describe a child's first language? Discuss your ideas with a partner.

Mother Tongue
Amy Tan

Summary In "Mother Tongue," Amy Tan describes her mother as an intelligent and perceptive woman. However, her mother is regularly confronted by problems because of her non-standard English. Tan writes about the differences between the lessons she has learned from her mother with the English-speaking world's view of her mother. Tan explains that when she began to think of her mother as her reader, she found her voice as a writer.

Note-taking Guide

Use the following cluster diagram to take notes about Amy Tan's mother.

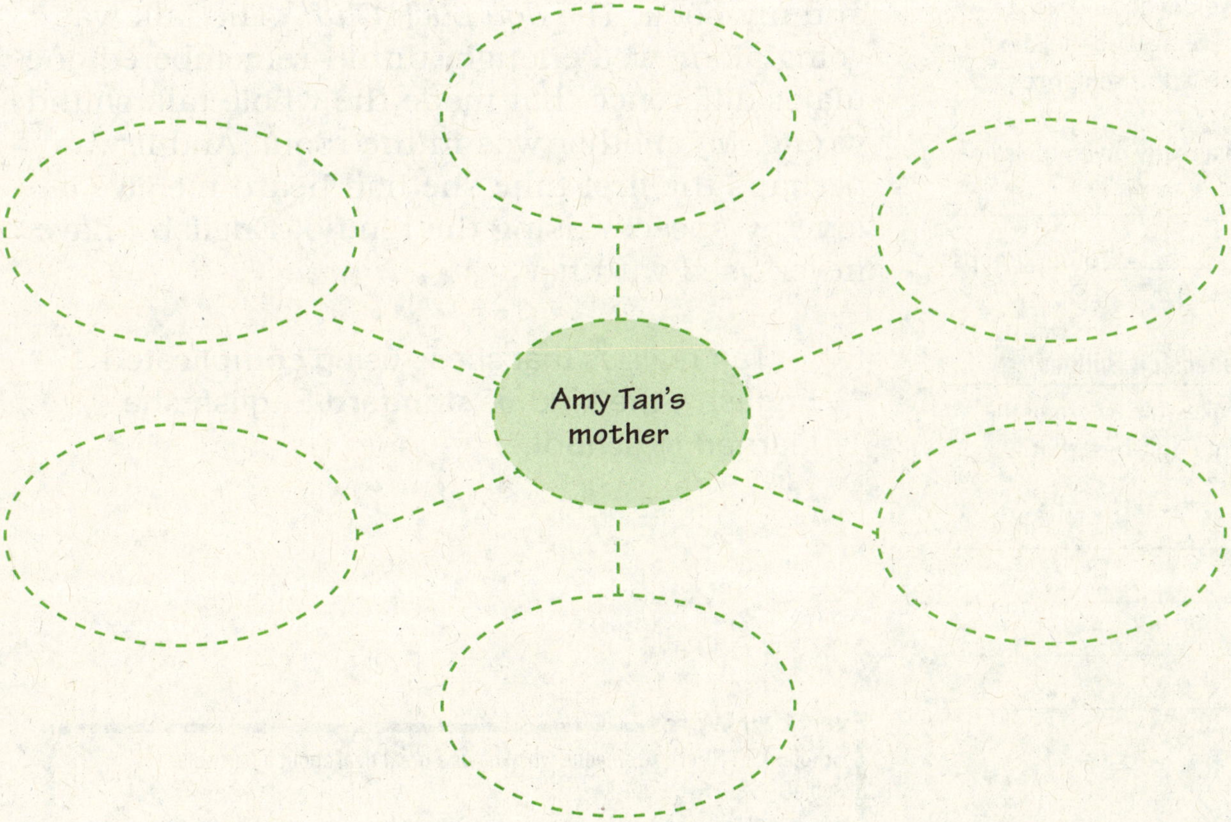

Amy Tan's mother

Vocabulary Builder 

Multiple-Meaning Words The noun *trade* may mean "the act of buying, selling, or exchanging goods." It may also mean "a particular job, especially one that requires a special skill." What does *trade* mean in the bracketed paragraph?

____

____

Vocabulary Builder 

Idioms A *dozen* means "twelve of something." *Half* means "one of two equal parts of something." So, half of a dozen would equal six, but people more commonly use the idiom *half a dozen* to mean "several." Use the idiom to complete this sentence:

Tan had already given the same

speech to ___________________

___________________ other groups.

Comprehension Builder 

What makes Tan aware of the "different Englishes" that she uses?

____

____

____

____

Mother Tongue

Amy Tan

I am not a **scholar** of English or literature. I cannot give you much more than personal opinions on the English language and its variations in this country or others.

I am a writer. And by that definition, I am someone who has always loved language. I am fascinated by language in daily life. I spend a great deal of my time thinking about the power of language—the way it can evoke an emotion, a visual image, a complex idea, or a simple truth. Language is the tool of my trade. And I use them all—all the Englishes I grew up with.

Recently, I was made **keenly** aware of the different Englishes I do use. I was giving a talk to a large group of people, the same talk I had already given to half a dozen other groups. The nature of the talk was about my writing, my life, and my book, *The Joy Luck Club*.[1] The talk was going along well enough, until I remembered one major difference that made the whole talk sound wrong. My mother was in the room. And it was perhaps the first time she had heard me give a lengthy speech, using the kind of English I have never used with her.

♦ ♦ ♦

Tan realizes that she is using complicated English—the kind of **standard** English she learned in school.

♦ ♦ ♦

Everyday Words

scholar (SKAHL er) *n.* someone who knows a great deal about a particular subject

keenly (KEEN lee) *adv.* strongly

standard (STAN derd) *adj.* considered correct and used by most people

1. *The Joy Luck Club* Amy Tan's highly praised 1989 novel about four Chinese American women and their mothers

Just last week, I was walking down the street with my mother, and I again found myself **conscious** of the English I was using, the English I do use with her. We were talking about the price of new and used furniture and I heard myself saying this: "Not waste money that way." My husband was with us as well, and he didn't notice any switch in my English. And then I realized why. It's because over the twenty years we've been together I've often used the same kind of English with him, and sometimes he even uses it with me. It has become our language of **intimacy,** a different sort of English that relates to family talk, the language I grew up with.

◆　◆　◆

Tan shares a conversation she had with her mother, demonstrating what her "family talk" sounds like. When Tan's mother speaks, she does not use standard English. However, Tan's mother understands more than her limited use of English suggests. For example, Tan's mother follows complicated business and finance news. While Tan's friends do not always completely understand her mother, Tan understands her mother's English because it is what she grew up with. Tan explains that the way her mother speaks English influences the way she views the world.

◆　◆　◆

Lately, I've been giving more thought to the kind of English my mother speaks. Like others, I have described it to people as "broken," or "fractured" English. But I wince when I say that. It has always bothered me that I can think of no way to describe

---

Everyday Words

conscious (KAHN shuhs) *adj.* noticing or realizing something

intimacy (IN tuh muh see) *n.* a state of having a close personal relationship with someone

Fluency Builder 

With a partner, take turns reading aloud the underlined sentence as it is written. This is an example of dialect, or nonstandard English spoken by a particular group of people. Rewrite the sentence in standard English.

____

____

Read the rewritten sentence aloud.

Vocabulary Builder

Multiple-Meaning Words The verb *follows* may mean "goes, walks, or drives behind or after someone else." It may also mean "is interested in and likes to learn about something." What does *follows* mean in the bracketed paragraph?

____

____

Vocabulary Builder 

Synonyms The adjective *fractured* means "cracked or split apart." Circle the synonym for *fractured* that appears in the last paragraph. Both words describe the way that Tan's mother speaks English.

Vocabulary Builder

Suffixes The suffix -*ness* is added to adjectives to form nouns. It means "the state or quality of being a particular thing." The adjective *whole* means "all of something, or complete." The adjective *sound* means "in good condition, not damaged." What do the nouns *wholeness* and *soundness* mean?

____

____

Comprehension Builder

How does Tan say that she used to feel about her mother's English? Underline the sentence that tells you.

Vocabulary Builder

Parts of Speech *Check* may be a noun meaning "a printed piece of paper that you write an amount of money on, sign, and use instead of money to pay for things." It may also be a verb meaning "do something in order to find out whether something really is correct, true, or in good condition." Is *check* a noun or a verb in the bracketed paragraph?

____

it other than "broken," as if it were damaged and needed to be fixed, as if it lacked a certain wholeness and soundness. I've heard other terms used, "limited English," for example. But they seem just as bad, as if everything is limited, including people's **perceptions** of the limited English speaker.

I know this for a fact, because when I was growing up, my mother's "limited" English limited my perception of her. I was ashamed of her English. I believed that her English reflected the quality of what she had to say. That is, because she expressed them imperfectly her thoughts were imperfect. And I had plenty of **empirical** evidence to support me: the fact that people in department stores, at banks, and at restaurants did not take her seriously, did not give her good service, pretended not to understand her, or even acted as if they did not hear her.

◆　◆　◆

Tan explains that her mother herself also realized how her limited use of English created problems. When Tan was fifteen, she was asked to call people to get information for her mother. For example, Tan once called a stockbroker to find out about a missing check. More recently, Tan's mother went to the hospital to learn the results of a brain scan.[2] After the hospital claimed to have lost the scan, Mrs. Tan refused to leave until the doctor called her daughter. Tan arranged to get the information her mother wanted. She also received an apology for the hospital's mistake.

◆　◆　◆

2. **brain scan** (BRAYN SKAN) *n.* a process in which detailed photographs of a person's brain are taken and examined by a doctor

I think my mother's English almost had an effect on limiting my possibilities in life as well. Sociologists[3] and linguists[4] probably will tell you that a person's developing language skills are more influenced by **peers.** But I do think that the language spoken in the family, especially in immigrant families which are more **insular,** plays a large role in shaping the language of the child. And I believe that it affected my results on achievement tests, IQ tests, and the SAT.[5] While my English skills were never judged as poor, compared to math, English could not be considered my strong suit.

◆　◆　◆

Tan did fairly well in English in school. However, she always had higher scores in math and science achievement tests. Tan believes she did well on math tests because there was only one right answer. On the other hand, she had problems with English tests because she felt that the answers depended on personal experience and opinions. Tan could not sort through all the vivid images that came to mind when she tried to answer fill-in-the-blank sentence completions or word analogies.

◆　◆　◆

I have been thinking about all this lately, about my mother's English, about achievement tests. Because lately I've been asked, as a writer, why

Cultural Understanding

In the United States, students must take a series of achievement tests at different grade levels. An achievement test measures a particular skill, such as writing, or a person's knowledge of a particular subject, such as science. An IQ test is a special test that measures someone's intelligence, or ability to learn, understand, and think about things.

Vocabulary Builder 

Idioms The idiom *on the other hand* refers to the second thing to consider when you are talking about or describing two different facts or two opposite ways of thinking about something. Use the idiom to complete this sentence:

Tan had some difficulties with

English tests. _________________

_________________, she did

well on _________________

_________________.

Comprehension Builder 

What has Tan been thinking about lately?

____

____

Vocabulary Builder

Multiple-Meaning Words The adjective *broad* may mean "wide." It may also mean "concerning the main ideas or parts of something rather than the details." What does *broad* mean in the underlined sentence?

____

____

Vocabulary Builder

Compound Words Many compound words have meanings that reflect the meanings of their individual words. Others have different meanings. The compound noun *stereotypes* means "beliefs or ideas about what particular people or groups of people are like." The compound adjective *freelance* means "working independently for different companies rather than working for one particular company."

Vocabulary Builder

Idioms The idiom *with something in mind* means "considering someone or something when doing something and taking an appropriate action." Use the idiom to complete this sentence:

Tan began writing stories with

___________________.

there are not more Asian Americans represented in American literature. Why are there few Asian Americans enrolled in creative writing programs? Why do so many Chinese students go into engineering? Well, these are broad sociological questions I can't begin to answer. But I have noticed in surveys—in fact, just last week—that Asian students, as a whole, always do significantly better on math achievement tests than in English. And this makes me think that there are other Asian-American students whose English spoken in the home might also be described as "broken" or "limited." And perhaps they also have teachers who are **steering** them away from writing and into math and science, which is what happened to me.

◆ ◆ ◆

Tan describes how she **rebelled** against Asian-American stereotypes to become a writer. First, she chose to study English rather than science in college. Then, she became a freelance writer after an employer told her that she could not write. In 1985, Tan started writing fiction. At first, she wrote difficult sentences to prove she could use English well.

◆ ◆ ◆

Fortunately, for reasons I won't get into today, I later decided I should **envision** a reader for the stories I would write. And the reader I decided upon was my mother, because these were stories about mothers. So with this reader in mind—and in fact she did read my early drafts—I began to write stories using all the Englishes I grew up with: the English I spoke to my mother, which for lack of a better term might be described as

Everyday Words

steering (STEER ing) *v.* guiding; directing
rebelled (ri BELD) *v.* opposed or fought against someone in authority or against an idea or situation
envision (en VIZH uhn) *v.* picture in the mind; imagine

"simple"; the English she used with me, which for lack of a better term might be described as "broken"; my translation of her Chinese, which could certainly be described as "watered down";[6] and what I imagined to be her translation of her Chinese if she could speak in perfect English, her internal language, and for that I sought to **preserve** the **essence,** but neither an English nor a Chinese **structure.** I wanted to capture what language ability tests can never reveal: her **intent,** her **passion,** her imagery, the rhythms of her speech and the **nature** of her thoughts.

Apart from what any critic had to say about my writing, I knew I had succeeded where it counted when my mother finished reading my book and gave me her **verdict:** "So easy to read."

Everyday Words

preserve (pri ZERV) *v.* make something continue without changing

essence (ES uhns) *n.* the most basic and important quality of something

structure (STRUK cher) *n.* the way in which the parts of something are connected with one another and form a whole, or the thing that these parts make up

intent (in TENT) *n.* what someone intends, or plans, to do

passion (PASH uhn) *n.* a very strong belief or feeling about something

nature (NAY chur) *n.* the qualities or features that something has

verdict (VER dikt) *n.* someone's conclusion or decision about something

6. **"watered down"** usually written "watered-down"; having been changed so that it is less extreme or forceful than when first written or said

Comprehension Builder 

What four Englishes does Tan use in her writings?

____

____

____

____

Vocabulary Builder 

Multiple-Meaning Words

The verb *counted* may mean "calculated the total number of things in a group." It may also mean that something "was important or valuable." What does *counted* mean in the last paragraph?

____

____

Vocabulary

These words are underlined in the selection. Listen to each word. Say it. Then, read the definition and the example sentence.

ecstasy (EK stuh see) *n.* **Ecstasy** is a feeling of extreme happiness or overpowering joy.

> *Downhill skiing gave Maya a feeling of ecstasy.*

daunting (DAHN Ting) *adj.* Something that is **daunting** is frightening and makes a person feel less confident.

> *Climbing Mount Everest is a daunting challenge.*

aspirations (as puh RAY shuhnz) *n.* When you have **aspirations,** you have strong desires or ambitions.

> *Raul has aspirations to become a famous athlete.*

Vocabulary Practice

Read the first sentence in each group of three. Then, complete Sentence *a* by substituting another word or phrase that means the same as the underlined vocabulary word. Complete Sentence *b* with your own ideas and words.

1. The dancer had feelings of ecstasy after the performance.

   a. The dancer had feelings of ______________ after the performance.

   b. The dancer had feelings of ecstasy ______________________________.

2. Kita faced the daunting task of giving her speech first.

   a. Kita faced the ______________ task of giving her speech first.

   b. Kita faced the daunting task of ______________________________.

3. Pablo has aspirations to be a painter because he loves color.

   a. Pablo has ______________ to be an artist because he loves color.

   b. Pablo has aspirations to be a painter because ______________________.

Getting Ready to Read

The author of the selection names *A Thousand and One Nights* as her favorite fairy tale. It is the story of Scheherezade, a woman who tricks her new husband—an evil king—into letting her live by telling him a collection of stories, none of which can be finished in one night. What is your favorite fairy tale? Discuss your answer with a partner.

For the Love of Books
Rita Dove

Summary In "For the Love of Books," Rita Dove says her career as a writer came from her love of books. Since childhood, Dove loved to read books. She not only loved to read them, she loved holding them, smelling them, and turning their pages. She read everything from Shakespeare to science fiction. When her eleventh-grade English teacher took her to a book-signing, she realized writers were real people.

Note-taking Guide
Use the chart below to list experiences that influenced Rita Dove's life and career.

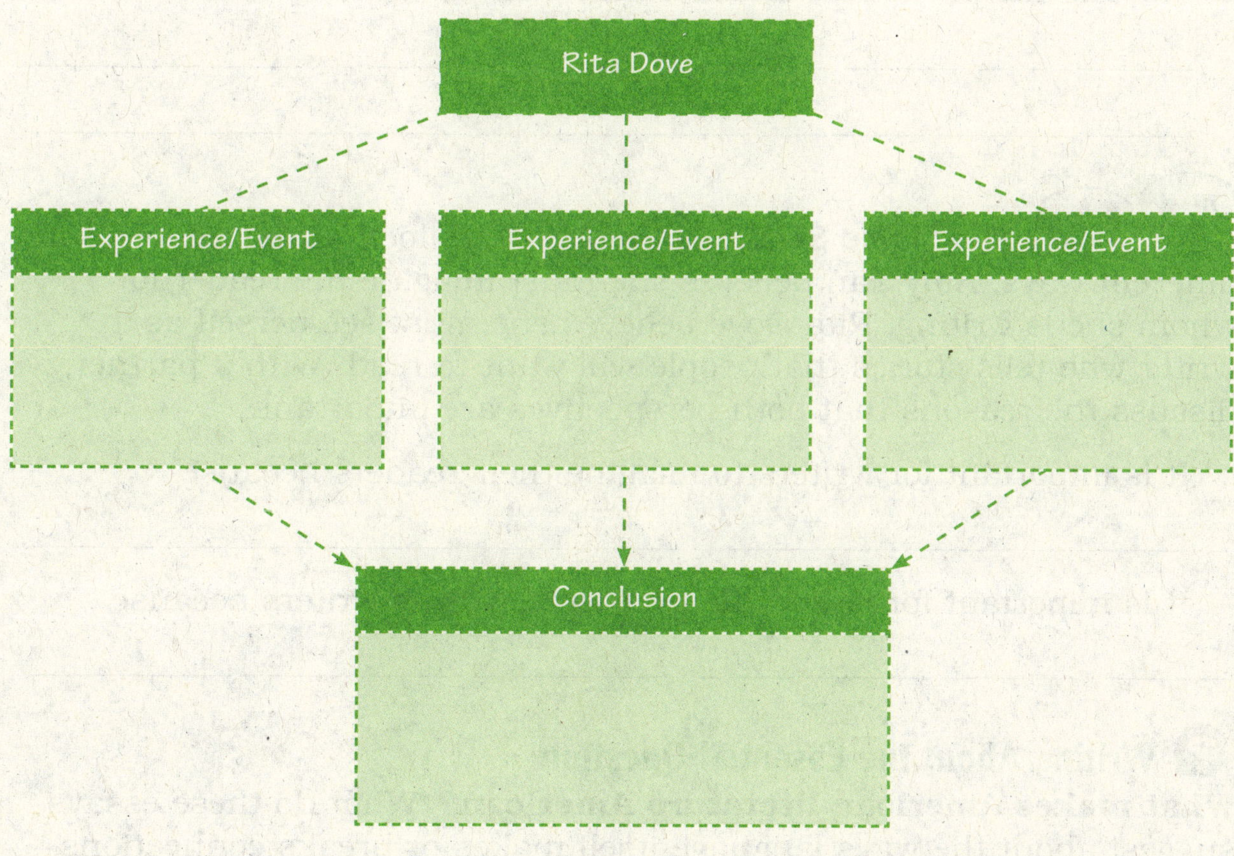

Thinking About the Selections

1. Use the graphic organizer below to list and explain the different "Englishes" that Amy Tan identifies in "Mother Tongue."

Amy Tan's "Englishes"

2. Meeting the poet John Ciardi helped Rita Dove understand that

____

____.

TALK ABOUT IT **The Write Stuff** Different writers look at their careers in different ways. Amy Tan believes she must imagine the reader for whom she is writing. Rita Dove believes she must see herself as a writer who tells stories that people will want to read. With a partner, discuss the reasons that both perspectives are important.

It is important for writers to imagine their readers because

____.

It is important for writers to see themselves as writers because

____.

 **Writing About the Essential Question**

What makes American literature American? What do these essays suggest about the ways language itself makes or breaks connections among people, both within families and communities?

Multiple-Meaning Words

Recall that many words can have different meanings depending on their use in a sentence. Look for clues in the words and sentences around the word—its context—to help you determine its meaning.

Example

The noun *point* can mean

- a single fact or opinion in a discussion or argument
- a unit used for showing the score in a game or contest

The noun *chair* can mean

- a piece of furniture for one person to sit on, which has a back, a seat, and four legs
- the position of being in charge of a meeting or committee, or the person who is in charge of it

Now You Do It

Use each of the meanings of *point* and *chair* in a sentence.

1. *point* ____

____

2. *chair* ____

____

TALK ABOUT IT **List It** With a partner, discuss different situations in which people might make points, score points, sit in chairs, and listen to chairs. Work together to write lists of the different situations you think of in your discussion.

WRITE ABOUT IT **Write Them All** Using your lists as an aid, write a short story that includes both meanings of the words *point* and *chair*. Be sure that your story makes logical sense.

Vocabulary

These words are underlined in the selection. Listen to each word. Say it. Then, read the definition and the example sentence.

inaudibly (in AW duh blee) *adv.* When something is done **inaudibly,** it is done in a way that it cannot be heard.

> *Jake walked inaudibly down the carpeted hallway.*

gravity (GRA vuh tee) *n.* **Gravity** is the seriousness or importance of an event or situation.

> *Their somber expressions revealed the gravity of the conflict.*

oblivious (uh BLI vee uhs) *adj.* When you are **oblivious,** you are unaware of objects or events around you.

> *The worried driver was oblivious to the roadside flowers.*

Vocabulary Practice

Read the first sentence in each group of three. Then, complete Sentence *a* by substituting another word or phrase that means the same as the underlined vocabulary word. Complete Sentence *b* with your own ideas and words.

1. The lawyer whispered inaudibly to her client during the trial.

   a. The lawyer whispered ______________ to her client during the trial.

   b. The lawyer whispered inaudibly to her client ____________________.

2. The child did not understand the gravity of telling a lie.

   a. The child did not understand the ______________ of telling a lie.

   b. The child did not understand the gravity of ____________________.

3. The couple kissed passionately, oblivious to the crowd.

   a. The couple kissed passionately, ______________ the crowd.

   b. ____________________________________, oblivious to the crowd.

Getting Ready to Read

In this selection, a 68-year-old woman sits in an airport for many hours waiting anxiously for her sister to arrive. Think of a time when you have waited anxiously for someone or something. With a partner, take turns discussing your experiences.

The Woman Warrior
Maxine Hong Kingston

Summary Brave Orchid goes to the San Francisco airport. She waits for her sister to arrive from Hong Kong. The sisters have not seen each other in thirty years. Brave Orchid has brought her niece and two of her children. They wait at the airport for more than nine hours. Finally, the plane lands. Then, they must wait another four hours. Finally, the sisters greet each other. Neither can believe how old the other looks.

Note-taking Guide

Use this chart to find details in the memoir that show what Brave Orchid is like.

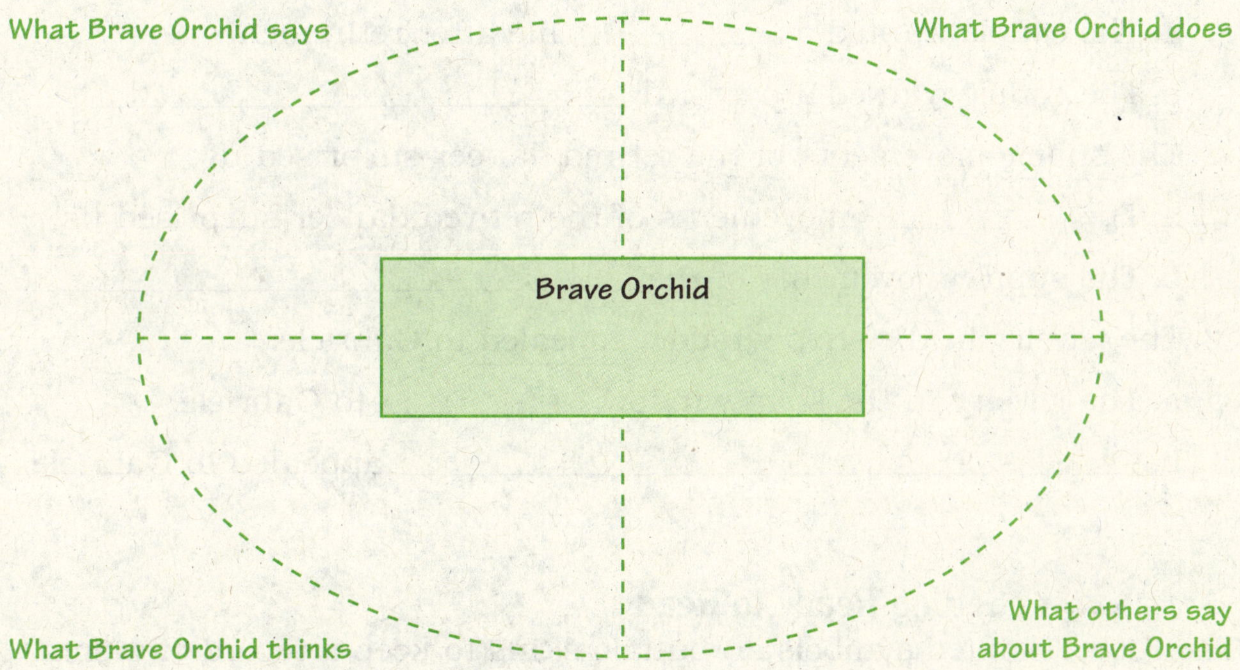

Vocabulary

These words are underlined in the selection. Listen to each word. Say it. Then, read the definition and the example sentence.

pastoral (PAS tuh ruhl) *adj.* Something that is **pastoral** has the quality of rural life, usually imagined as peaceful, simple, and natural.

>   *She usually paints pastoral scenes of rural America.*

supple (SU puhl) *adj.* Something that is **supple** is able to bend and move easily.

>   *The champion gymnast was very supple.*

appealed (uh PEELD) *v.* Something that has **appealed** to someone has seemed attractive and desirable.

>   *The thought of taking a vacation appealed to the overworked doctor.*

Vocabulary Practice

Read the first sentence in each group of three. Then, complete Sentence *a* by substituting another word or phrase that means the same as the underlined vocabulary word. Complete Sentence *b* with your own ideas and words.

1. The couple wanted a pastoral life after retirement.

    a. The couple wanted a ______________ life after retirement.

    b. The couple wanted a pastoral ________________________________.

2. The supple movements of the retired dancer surprised us.

    a. The ______________ movements of the retired dancer surprised us.

    b. The supple movements of the ________________________________.

3. The jewelry in the shop window appealed to Gabriele.

    a. The jewelry in the shop window ______________ to Gabriele.

    b. ________________________________ appealed to Gabriele.

Getting Ready to Read

The Kiowa painted symbols on buffalo skins to keep a record of events. In this selection, N. Scott Momaday, a Kiowa, records events from his life as a young teen. What events from your life do you think you should record? With a partner, take turns discussing your answers.

from The Names
N. Scott Momaday

Summary *The Names* is from a longer work. In this section, the author tells about the horse that his parents gave him as a child. The horse's name was Pecos. The author still thinks about Pecos.

Note-taking Guide
Use the chart below to record important details about the subjects of the essay.

Essay	Subject	Details
from *The Names*		

Thinking About the Selections

1. In what order did events take place in the selection from *The Names*? Complete the graphic organizer below by writing the numbers that show the order in which the events happened.

Order of Events	Events
	The writer loses most races when he tries to mount his horse during the race.
	The writer falls from his horse and badly hurts his thumb.
	The writer receives a horse from his parents.
	The writer learns to mount his horse while his horse runs.
	The writer decides to take a journey on his horse.

2. In the selection from *The Woman Warrior*, the phrase "two old women with faces like mirrors" means that _________________________

____.

TALK ABOUT IT **It Takes Two** With a partner, compare and contrast two relationships: the one between Brave Orchid and Moon Orchid and the one between N. Scott Momaday and his horse, Pecos. In what ways are the two relationships similar? In what ways are they different?

These relationships are similar because _____________________.

These relationships are different because _____________________.

Writing About the Essential Question

What is the relationship between place and literature? Based on these two memoirs, what does the idea of homeland mean?

____

____

____

Vowel Combinations

A vowel combination is a grouping of two vowels that produce a single sound. The vowel combination may be pronounced differently in different words. For example, the vowel combination *ou* can be pronounced in several ways.

Example

OU vowel combination		
pronounced as a long /u/ sound	you soup coupon	YOO SOOP KOO pahn
pronounced as a long /o/ sound	soul poultry	SOHL POHL tree
pronounced as an /ow/ sound	out round bounce	OWT ROWND BOWNS

Now You Do It

Use the words in the chart to answer the questions below.

1. Which words in the chart have the same sound as "roll"?

   ____

2. Which word has an /ow/ sound, *dough* or *found*? _______________

3. To which sound group does the word *shoulder* belong? _____________

4. Which word rhymes with *ounce*? _______________

TALK ABOUT IT **Ping Pong** Make up a question to ask a partner, the answer to which is a word from the chart. For example, you might ask, "What could you eat for lunch?" (*soup*) Be sure that the answer word is pronounced correctly. Take turns asking and answering questions and pronouncing each answer word.

WRITE ABOUT IT **Write a Short Poem** Write a nonsense rhyme that uses at least three words from the chart above. Read your poem aloud to a small group.

Public Documents

About Public Documents

You may already have a job, or you may be planning for your career. Either way, you are likely to read **public documents** that describe guidelines or policies that you should follow in the workplace. Sometimes, government agencies write guidelines to help businesses obey laws about workplace issues, such as health and safety. Sometimes, private organizations develop policy statements to encourage businesses to provide products and services that will benefit all people. Before guidelines and policies become public documents, agencies and organizations review them as internal reports.

Reading Skill

Public documents can cover a broad range of information. To find the information that you need, it helps to **preview the text** by skimming and scanning. To **skim the text,** glance through the document quickly to get a general idea about the topic it covers. Skim the title and the first sentence of each paragraph. Stop and read headings and other text that is set off, such as underlined text. To **scan the text,** run your eyes over the document and look for specific words related to your needs. Stop and read the paragraphs that contain these words.

Use the graphic organizer below to guide you as you read "How People with Disabilities Use the Web."

Strategy	Unfamiliar	Familiar	Clarification
Reread	GRDDL is a mechanism for getting RDF data out of XML documents.	Mechanism; data; documents	The software gets data from formatted documents.
Use context clues	Data formats like XML and XHTML are used in the Web.	Data formats	XML and XHTML are data formats used for Web sites.

This report was issued by the Worldwide Web Consortium (W3C), an international governing body for the development of Web standards and specifications.

Gleaning Resource Descriptions from Dialects of Languages (GRDDL)

W3C *Team Submission 16 May 2005*

Abstract

This document presents GRDDL, a mechanism for Gleaning Resource Descriptions from Dialects of Languages; that is, for getting RDF data out of XML and XHTML documents using explicitly associated transformation algorithms, typically represented in XSLT.

Contents

1. Introduction
2. The GRDDL profile for XHTML
3. The GRDDL transformation attribute in XML
4. GRDDL for XML Namespace and HTML Profile Documents
5. GRDDL Transformations
6. Security Considerations
7. References & Appendices

The list of contents (which is also hyperlinked for use on the Internet) shows the organization of the information contained in the entire report.

1. Introduction: Data and Documents

Data formats like XML and XHTML are used in the Web for a large spectrum of purposes, from poetry and drama to spreadsheets and databases. The information in a poem may be rich and subtle; we might use a computer to pick out the author's name, but themes and opposing forces are not readily computable. When extracting data from documents, preserving meaning is important: if a document says "It is highly unlikely that the king was more than twenty years old" and a computation returns "the king was more than twenty years old," that computation does not preserve meaning.

The Resource Description Framework[RDFC04] codifies certain forms of data—simple logical statements like age (king, 20)—and specifies basic rules for preserving meaning. The framework includes a constrained XML concrete syntax, but it also includes an abstract

syntax. GRDDL is a mechanism for Gleaning Resource Descriptions from Dialects of Languages; that is, for getting RDF data out of XML and XHTML documents.

For example, Dublin Core meta-data can be written in HTML dialect[RFC2731] that has a clear correspondence to an encoding in RDF/XML[DCRDF]. The correspondence can be expressed in an XSLT transformation, dc-extract.xsl:

Transforming HTML meta-data to a RDF/XML (svg)

The transformation preserves the author's meaning, provided the author understood the conventions of this dialect. But an author may have accidentally conformed to the syntactic conventions without any knowledge of Dublin Core at all. In that case, the mapping most likely does not preserve the author's meaning. In GRDDL, documents contain explicit references to the conventions that the author used to encode data.

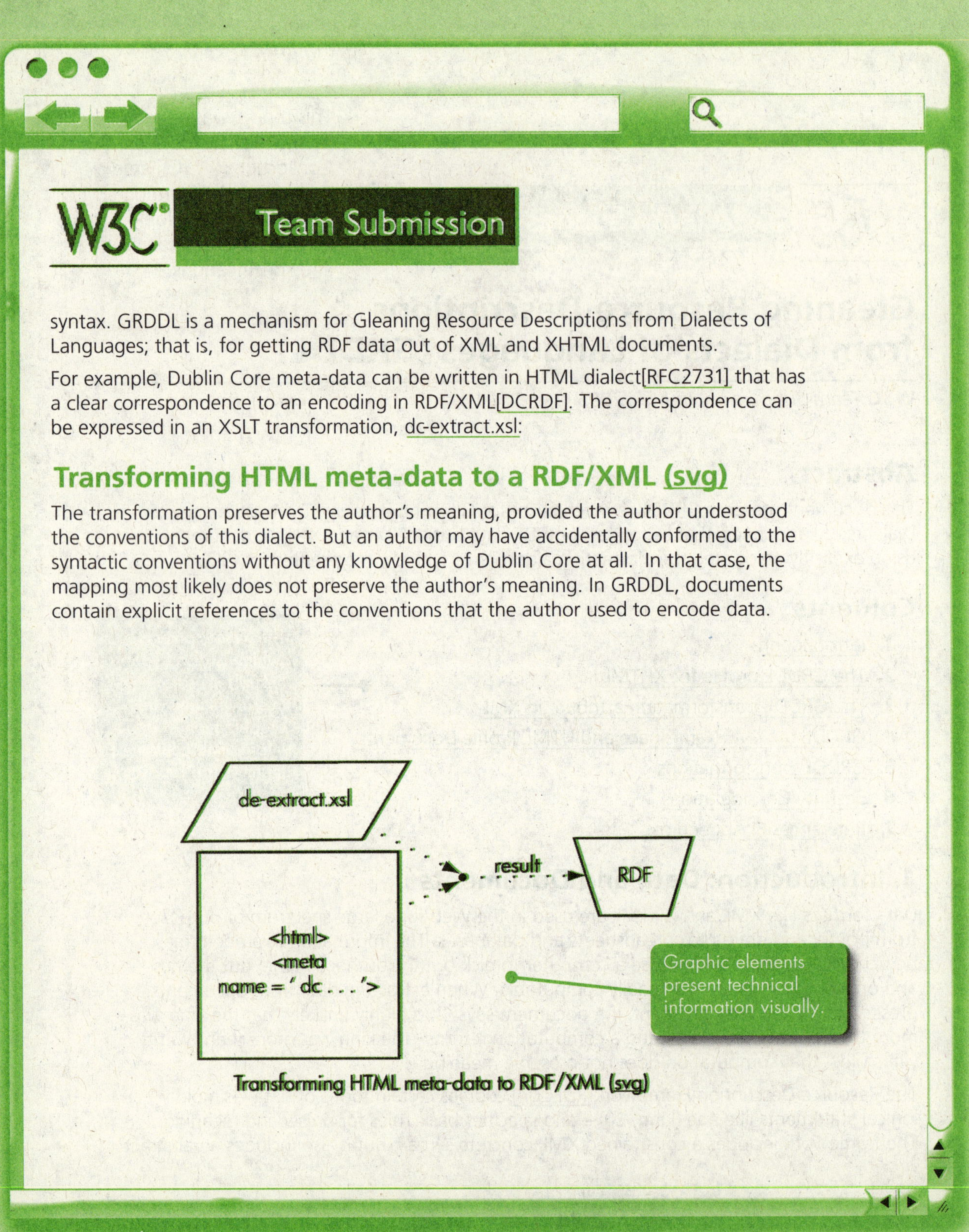

Transforming HTML meta-data to RDF/XML (svg)

Thinking About Public Documents

1. What is the Web Accessibility Initiative?

   ____

2. Why is it important for people with disabilities to have access to the Web?

   ____

TALK ABOUT IT Reading Skill

3. How many Web scenarios, or possible Web situations, does the document describe? Use skimming skills to answer the question.

   ____

4. Why are style sheets important to online shoppers with color blindness? To answer this question, scan the text for the term *style sheets*; then, read the paragraph that contains this term.

   ____

   ____

WRITE ABOUT IT Timed Writing: Public Documents (25 minutes)

Use the public document "How People with Disabilities Use the Web" to verify and clarify the following statement:

Technology makes it possible for people of all abilities to use the World Wide Web with ease.

Answer the questions below to help you organize your writing.

- What disabilities keep individuals from using the Web with ease?

   ____

- How can access to the Web be improved for people with disabilities?

   ____

- What role do public documents play in the development of the Web and its use?

   ____

Word Bank

commercial	cyberspace	information
communication	digital	innovation
crossover	diversity	transform

A. Matching Draw an arrow from each word to its definition in the chart below.

Words	Definition
diversity	facts and details that tell you about something
innovation	using a system in which information is recorded or sent out electronically in the form of numbers
crossover	the inclusion of many different types of people or things
cyberspace	relating to business; buying and selling
transform	the introduction of new ideas or methods
communication	the fact of liking, using, or supporting different types of things or groups
information	to change the appearance of something completely
commercial	all the connections between computers in different places
digital	expressing thoughts and feelings to other people

B. **Syllables** A syllable is part of a word that contains a vowel sound. Vowel sounds are usually represented by the letters *a, e, i, o u,* and sometimes *y.* Say each word in the word bank on the previous page and emphasize the breaks between syllables. If the word has two syllables, write it in the column on the left. If it has three syllables, write it in the middle column. If it has four or more syllables, write the word in the column on the right.

Two syllables	Three syllables	Four or more syllables

TALK ABOUT IT **Crossing Over** With a partner, discuss the equation "*Communication* plus *diversity* equals *innovation.*" Do you think that this equation is logical? Can you think of examples that demonstrate this outcome from American history or from your own experiences?

WRITE ABOUT IT **Tomorrow Land** Use ideas from your discussion to write a short essay on innovations that you believe society will see in the future. What causes or needs will lead to these innovations? What changes to today's world will the innovations produce? Try to use as many of the word bank's terms in your essay as you can.

Selection Summaries in Eight Languages

Part 2 contains summaries of all selections in Prentice Hall Literature. Summaries are in:

- English
- Spanish
- Haitian Creole
- Filipino
- Hmong
- Chinese
- Vietnamese
- Korean

Use the summaries in Part 2 to preview or review the seletions.

The Earth on Turtle's Back

from the Onondaga

Summary The Onondaga are one of the Iroquois tribes of the Northeast woodlands. They tell about a time before Earth was above water. A brave muskrat brings a tiny piece of earth out of the water to help a woman who falls from the sky. A turtle's back then becomes the base for Earth. Then, life on Earth begins. Such a story about the beginning of life gives an understanding to the beliefs and thinking of the Onondaga people.

La Tierra desde el caparazón de una tortuga

de los Indios Onondaga

Resumen Los Onondagas conforman una de las tribus iroquesas de los bosques del Noreste. Describen una época en que la Tierra estaba sobre el agua. Una valiente rata almizclera extrae un diminuto pedazo de Tierra que estaba en el agua para ayudar a una mujer que cae del cielo. El caparazón de una tortuga se convierte en la base de la Tierra. Y luego comienza la vida en la Tierra. Esta historia sobre el comienzo de la vida nos ayuda a comprender las creencias e ideas del pueblo onondaga.

Latè sou do yon tòti

se yon mit tribi endyen Onondaga

Rezime Onondaga a se youn nan tribi iwokwa yo ki abite nan forè nòdès la. Yo rakonte yon epòk anvan latè te anlè sifas dlo a. Yon rat miske ki brav pote yon ti moso latè sot nan dlo a pou ede yon dam ki tonbe sot nan syèl la. Ansuit se do yon tòti ki vin sèvi kòm baz pou latè. Ansuit, lavi sou latè kòmanse. Yon istwa konsa konsènan kòmansman lavi bay yon limyè sou kwayans ak panse pèp Onondaga a.

Ang Daigdig sa Likod ng Pagóng

mula sa Ang Onondaga

Buod Ang Onondaga ay isa sa mga tribo ng Iroquois sa mga kagubatan ng Hilagang-Silangan. Ito'y tungkol sa panahon bago umahon ang Mundo sa ibabaw ng tubig. Isang matapang na "muskrat" ang nagdalá ng maliit na piraso ng lupa mula sa tubig upang tulungan ang isang babae na nahulog mula sa langit. Ang likod ng isang pagóng ang siyang naging patungán ng Mundo. Pagkatapos ay nagsimula na ang buhay sa Mundo. Ang isang kuwento tulad nito ay nakakatulong sa mambabasá na maunawaan ang mga paniniwala at pag-iisip ng mga taong Onondaga.

Lub Ntiaj Teb nyob saum Vaub Kib Nrob Qaum

los ntawm Haiv Neeg Onondaga

Lub Ntsiab Cov Onondaga yog ib pab neeg Iroquois uas nyob hauv cov hav zoov qaum teb sab hnub tuaj. Lawv qhia txog ib lub sijhawm ua ntej lub Ntiaj Teb no nyob sab saum cov dej. Ib tug nas loj uas muaj peev xwm heev mus nqa tau ib thooj av me me tawm hauv cov dej los kom pab tau ib tug pojniam uas poob saum ntuj los. Ib tug vaub kib lub nrob qaum thiaj li los ua lub chaw pib rau lub Ntiaj Teb. Ces kev ua neej hauv ntiaj teb thiaj li pib. Ib zaj dabneeg zoo li zaj no pab tau kom tus nyeem to taub txog cov kev ntseeg thiab kev xav ntawm cov neeg Onondaga.

《烏龜背上的地球》(The Earth on Turtle's Back)

來自 歐諾達卡人 (Onondaga)

摘要 歐諾達卡族是東北林地印第安部族的其中一枝。他們描述一段陸地浮在水面上之前發生的故事。一隻勇敢的麝鼠從水裡帶來一小搓的泥土，想幫助一名從天上掉下來的女子。一隻烏龜的背脊隨後成為地球的底座。接下來，地球上開始繁衍生命。類似這樣的故事幫助讀者瞭解了歐諾達卡族人的信仰及思想。

Trái Đất Trên Lưng Rùa

huyền thoại của Bộ Lạc Onondaga

Tóm Tắt Onondaga là một trong những bộ lạc người Iroquois thuộc vùng rừng Đông Bắc. Họ kể lại thời kỳ khi Trái Đất chưa trồi lên khỏi nước. Một con chuột xạ dũng cảm mang một nhúm đất ra khỏi nước để giúp một người phụ nữ từ trên trời rơi xuống. Lưng một con rùa trở thành cơ sở để tạo dựng Trái Đất. Sau đó, sự sống trên Trái Đất bắt đầu. Một câu truyện như vậy giúp độc giả hiểu được tín ngưỡng và cách tư duy của người Onondaga.

플리머스 농장 중에서 (The Earth on Turtle's Back)

오논다가 부족의 신화 중에서 (Onondaga)

요약 오노다가는 미국 북동부 숲 속에 살았던 이로쿼이 인디언의 한 부족이다. 이야기는 육지가 아직 물 위로 올라오기 전부터 시작된다. 하늘에서 한 여인이 떨어지고 그 여인을 구하기 위해 용감한 사향쥐 한 마리가 작은 땅 조각을 물에서 꺼낸다. 그러자 한 거북이가 자신의 등으로 그 작은 땅 조각이 머물 수 있는 토대를 만들어 준다. 그때부터 육지 위에 생명이 싹트기 시작한다. 이런 전설을 통해 독자는 오노다가 사람들의 생각과 신념을 이해할 수 있게 된다.

When Grizzlies Walked Upright

from the Modoc

Summary The Modoc lived in areas that became part of the western United States. They tell a story that explains the arrival of the first Native Americans. A daughter of the Chief of the Sky Spirits comes to Earth and marries a grizzly bear. Their children become the first Native Americans.

Cuando los osos pardos caminaban erguidos

de los Indios Modoc

Resumen Los Modocs vivían en áreas que luego se convirtieron en parte de la zona oeste de los Estados Unidos. Cuentan una historia que describe la llegada de los primeros nativos norteamericanos. Una de las hijas del jefe de los espíritus del cielo viene a la Tierra y se casa con un oso pardo. Sus hijos se convierten en los primeros nativos norteamericanos.

Lè grizli yo mache sou pye yo

se yon mit tribi endyen Modoc

Rezime Pèp Modoc la te abite nan rejyon ki te vin fè pati zòn lwès Etazini. Yo rakonte yon istwa ki eksplike arive premye endyen ameriken yo. Yon pitit fi chèf lespri nan syèl vin sou latè epi li marye ak yon lous grizli. Se pitit yo ki te vin premye endyen ameriken yo.

Noong ang mga "Grizzly" ay Lumalakad nang Patayó

mula sa Ang Modoc

Buod Ang mga Modoc ay nakatirá sa mga pook na naging bahagi ng gawing-kanluran ng Estados Unidos. Sila ay may kuwento na nagpapaliwanag kung saan nanggaling ang mga unang Katutubong Amerikano. Isang anak ng Hepe ng mga Kaluluwang-Langit ang bumabá sa lupa at nagpakasál sa isang osong "grizzly." Ang kanilang mga anak ay ang mga naging unang Katutubong Amerikano.

Thaum Cov Dais Grizzlies Taug Kev Sawv Ntsug

los ntawm Haiv Neeg Modoc

Lub Ntsiab Cov Modoc nyob rau thaj chaw uas tamsim no yog thaj chaw sab hnub poob ntawm Tebchaws Meskas. Lawv piav ib zaj dabneeg uas qhia tias thawj pab neeg Khab los qhov twg los. Ib tug ntxhais ntawm tus huab tais qaum ntuj Chief of the Sky Spirits los rau hauv ntiaj teb thiab los yuav ib tug dais. Nkawd cov menyuam tshwm sim los ua thawj cov neeg Khab.

《當灰熊站立行走時》(When Grizzlies Walked Upright)

來自 摩達克人 (Modoc)

摘要 摩達克人住在屬於美國西部的區域。他們講述一個可說明第一批美洲原住民起源的故事。一名天空之魂酋長的女兒來到地球，並嫁給一隻灰熊。他們的孩子成為第一位北美原住民。

Khi Những Con Gấu Xám Biết Đi Thẳng Đứng

huyền thoại của Bộ Lạc Modoc

Tóm Tắt Bộ lạc Modoc từng sinh sống ở những khu vực sau này đã trở thành một phần của phía Tây Hợp Chủng Quốc Hoa Kỳ. Họ kể một câu chuyện giải thích nguồn gốc của Thổ Dân Mỹ. Con gái của Thủ Lĩnh Các Linh Hồn Trên Trời xuống Trái Đất và lấy một con gấu xám Bắc Mỹ. Những đứa con ra đời chính là những Thổ Dân Mỹ đầu tiên.

플리머스 농장 중에서 (When Grizzlies Walked Upright)

모도크 부족의 신화 중에서 (Modoc)

요약 모도크 부족은 미국 서부 지역에 살았던 인디언 부족이다. 이 글은 아메리칸 인디언의 유래에 관한 이야기이다. 모도크 부족의 전해져 내려오는 이야기에 의하면 하늘의 신령들 중 우두머리 신의 딸이 이 땅에 내려와 회색 곰과 결혼한다. 거기서 태어난 아이들이 최초의 아메리칸 인디언이 된다.

from The Navajo Origin Legend

Summary This part of the Navajo legend tells how the wind breathes life into corn to create the First Man and First Woman. This creation myth shows the importance of nature, corn, animal skins, feathers, and the wind.

de La leyenda de origen navajo

Resumen Esta parte de la leyenda de los navajos cuenta cómo el viento exhala vida dentro del maíz para crear al primer hombre y a la primera mujer. Este mito de la creación muestra la importancia de la naturaleza, el maíz, las pieles de los animales, las plumas y el viento.

yon ekstrè nan Lejann sou orijin Navajo a

Rezime Pati sa a nan lejann Navajo a rakonte fason van an ensifle lavi nan mayi pou l kreye premye gason an ak premye fi a. Mit kreyasyon sa a montre enpòtans lanati, mayi, po bèt, plim ak van genyen.

mula sa Ang Alamat ng Pinanggalingan ng mga Navajo

Buod Ikinukuwento ng bahaging ito ng alamat ng mga Navajo kung paano nagbugá ng buhay ang hangin sa maís para ilikhá ang Unang Lalaki at ang Unang Babae. Ipinapakita ng alamat ng unang paglikhá na ito kung gaano kahalaga para sa mga Navajo ang kalikasan, ang maís, ang mga balát ng hayop, ang mga balahibo, at ang hangin.

los ntawm Dabneeg Navajo Qhia Txog Kev Pib Ua Neeg Los Mus

Lub Ntsiab Zaj no ntawm cov dabneeg Navajo qhia txog cov cua uas tshuab tau txoj sia rau cov pob kws uas tsim tau Thawj Tug Txiv Neej thiab Thawj Tug PojniamZaj dabneeg txog kev pib muaj ub no qhia tau hais tias tej yam hauv ntiaj teb tseem ceeb npaum li cas rau cov neeg Navajo xws li pob kws, tsiaj cov tawv, plaub noog, thiab cov cua.

取材自《納瓦荷族起源傳奇》 (The Navajo Origin Legend)

摘要 這則納瓦荷族傳奇講述的是風如何將生命吹入玉米田，從而創造出第一個男人以及第一個女人。這則創造神話證明了大自然、玉米、動物毛皮、羽毛、以及風對納瓦荷人來說有多重要。

trích từ Truyền Thuyết Về Nguồn Gốc Của Bộ Lạc Navajo

Tóm Tắt Phần này của truyền thuyết Navajo kể lại làm thế nào gió truyền sự sống vào cây bắp để tạo ra Người Đàn Ông và Người Đàn Bà đầu tiên. Huyền thoại sáng thế này cho thấy tầm quan trọng của thiên nhiên, cây bắp, da thú, lông vũ, và gió đối với bộ lạc Navajo.

플리머스 농장 중에서 (The Navajo Origin Legend)

요약 이 글은 어떻게 바람이 옥수수에 생명을 불어넣고 그 옥수수에서 최초의 남자와 여자가 탄생하는지를 설명하고 있다. 이 창조 신화를 통하여 자연, 옥수수, 동물 가죽, 깃털, 바람이 나바호 인디언에게는 얼마나 소중한 것들인지 알 수 있다.

from The Iroquois Constitution

Translated by Arthur C. Parker

Summary This selection is an excerpt, or a section, from The Iroquois Constitution. Dekanawidah, who is an Iroquois prophet, speaks here of the Tree of Great Peace that gives shelter and protection to the Iroquois nations. He explains why and how the Five Nations, a group of five Iroquois tribes, should come together to form a union or confederacy for their common good.

de La Constitución iroquesa

Traducido por Arthur C. Parker

Resumen Esta selección es un extracto o sección de "La constitución iroquesa". Dekanawidah, un profeta iroqués, habla aquí acerca del Árbol de la gran paz que brinda refugio y protección a las naciones iroquesas. Él explica cómo y por qué las Cinco naciones, un grupo de cinco tribus iroquesas, deben unirse para formar una unión o confederación a fin de lograr el bien común.

yon ekstrè nan Konstitisyon iwokwa a

Tradui pa Arthur C. Parker

Rezime Seleksyon sa a se yon ekstrè, oswa yon seksyon, nan Konstitisyon iwokwa a. Dekanawidah, ki se yon pwofèt iwokwa, pale la a konsènan Pyebwa kokennchenn lapè a ki bay abri ak pwoteksyon pou nasyon iwokwa a. Li eksplike rezon ak fason senk nasyon yo, yon gwoup senk tribi iwokwa, dwe reyini ansanm pou fòme yon sendika oswa yon alyans pou enterè tout moun.

mula sa Ang Konstitusyon ng mga Iroquois

Isinalin ni Arthur C. Parker

Buod Ang seleksiyón na ito ay isang nakuhang bahagi, o isang seksiyon, mula sa Ang Konstitusyon ng mga Iroquois. Si Dekanawidah, isang propetong Iroquois, ay nagsasalitá tungkol sa Puno ng Dakilang Kapayapaan na nagbibigay ng silong at proteksiyón sa mga lahi ng Iroquois. Kanyang pinaliliwanag kung bakit at paano dapat magkaisa ang Limang Lahi o Nasyon, isang grupo ng limang tribo ng mga Iroquois, upang magtatag ng unyón para sa kabutihan nilang lahat.

los ntawm Daim Ntawv Tuav Cai Ntawm Pawg Khab Iroquois

Txhais los ntawm Arthur C. Parker

Lub Ntsiab Zaj no yog ib feem ntawm ib zag xwb, lossis ib nqe me me xwb, uas yog los ntawm zaj Daim Ntawv Tuav Cai Ntawm Pawg Khab Iroquois. Dekanawidah, uas yog ib tug saub ntawm hom neeg Iroquois, tham ntawm no txog Tsob Ntoo Muaj Kev Ywj Pheej uas muab tau kev pab thiab tiv thaiv cov neeg Iroquois. Nws piav hais tias yog vim licas thiab ua licas uas cov tsib pab pawg khab hu ua Five Nations yuav tsum los uake kom sib koom tau ua ib pawg lossis ua ib tsoom neeg sib pab rau qhov zoo.

選自《北美印第安部族憲法》(The Iroquois Constitution)

翻譯者：Arthur C. Parker

摘要 這篇文選是《北美印第安部族憲法》的其中一部分摘錄（或一項條款）。達卡納威達是一位印第安部族的先知，他在此談到給印第安人提供避護所及保護的偉大和平之樹。他說明了由五個印第安部族所組成之五國應該團結在一起為了共同利益成立一個聯邦或聯盟的原因及方法。

trích từ Hiến Pháp Iroquois

Được Dịch Bởi Arthur C. Parker

Tóm Tắt Đây chỉ là một đoạn trích, một phần trong Hiến Pháp Iroquois. Dekanawidah, một nhà tiên tri Iroquois, nhắc đến Cây Hòa Bình (Tree of Great Peace) luôn che chở và bảo vệ các bộ lạc Iroquois. Ông giải thích tại sao và làm thế nào Năm Bộ Lạc, một nhóm gồm năm tộc người Iroquois, nên sát cánh bên nhau để thành lập nên một liên minh hay khối thống nhất vì lợi ích chung.

플리머스 농장 중에서 (The Iroquois Constitution)

Arthur C. Parker 번역

요약 이 글은 이로쿼이 헌장 중에서 발췌한 것이다. 이로쿼이 부족의 예언가인 데카나위다는 자신의 종족에게 보호와 피난처를 제공해 주는 위대한 평화의 나무에 대해 이야기한다. 그리고 이로쿼이 다섯 부족이 공동 번영을 위해 하나가 되어 연맹을 결성해야 하는 이유와 방법을 설명하고 있다.

A Journey Through Texas

Alvar Núñez Cabeza de Vaca

Summary In this narrative, the author describes his journey into what is now the state of Texas. There, he meets many Native Americans who help him on his journey. The Native Americans share food with him and help him find his way. The author learns to appreciate the different ways people have found to live.

Un viaje por Texas

Alvar Núñez Cabeza de Vaca

Resumen En esta narración el autor describe su viaje por el territorio que actualmente constituye el estado de Texas. Allí conoce a muchos nativos norteamericanos que lo ayudan en el viaje. Los nativos norteamericanos comparten su comida con él y lo ayudan a encontrar su camino. El autor aprende a valorar las diferentes maneras de vivir que las personas han descubierto.

Yon vwayaj atravè Teksas

Pa Alvar Núñez Cabeza de Vaca

Rezime Nan resi sa a, otè a dekri vwayaj li atravè eta ki rele Teksas jounen jodi a. Se la li rankontre anpil endyen ameriken ki ede l nan vwayaj li a. Endyen ameriken yo pataje manje avèk li epi ede l jwenn wout li. Otè a aprann pou l apresye diferan fason moun te jwenn pou yo ka viv.

Isang Paglalakbay sa Texas

Alvar Núñez Cabeza de Vaca

Buod Sa salaysay na ito, inilalarawan ng manunulát ang lugar na ngayon ay tinatawag na estado ng Texas. Dito'y marami siyang nakilalang mga Katutubong Amerikanong tumulong sa kanyang pagbiyahe. Siya'y binigyan ng pagkain ng mga Katutubong Amerikano, at tinulungan nila siya upang 'di siya maligáw. Natutunan ng awtor na pahalagahan ang mga naiibang uri ng pamumuhay ng iba't-ibang tao.

Ua Si Ncig Texas

Alvar Núñez Cabeza de Vaca

Lub Ntsiab Hauv zaj sau no, tus sau piav txog nws txoj kev mus ncig ua si thoob thaj chaw uas niaj hnub no peb hu ua Texas. Nyob rau ntawd, nws tau ntsib coob leej neeg Khab uas pab nws rau nws txoj kev ncig tebchaws. Cov Khab pub zaub mov rau nws tau nrog lawv noj thiab pab nws nrhiav nws txoj kev mus. Tus sau zaj no kawm tau kev qhuas txog lwm haiv neeg txoj kev ua noj ua haus.

《穿越德州的一趟旅程》 (A Journey Through Texas)

Alvar Núñez Cabeza de Vaca

摘要 作者在故事中描述自己進入現今德州地區的旅程。他在那裡遇到許多美洲原住民，而他們也協助他完成旅程。這些美洲原住民與他分享食物，並幫他找到正確的道路。作者學會欣賞不同的求生方式。

Một Cuộc Hành Trình Qua Texas

Alvar Núñez Cabeza de Vaca

Tóm Tắt Trong câu truyện tường thuật này, tác giả miêu tả chuyến đi của mình ở nơi ngày nay là tiểu bang Texas. Ở đó, ông gặp nhiều Thổ Dân Mỹ và họ giúp ông trong cuộc hành trình này. Họ chia lương thực cho ông và giúp ông tìm đường. Tác giả học được cách hiểu rõ giá trị các phương thức khác nhau mà con người khám phá ra để sinh tồn.

플리머스 농장 중에서 (A Journey Through Texas)

Alvar Núñez Cabeza de Vaca

요약 이 글은 현재 텍사스 주로 불리는 지역에 저자가 여행 갔던 일을 쓰고 있다. 거기서 그는 아메리칸 인디언들을 만나게 되고 그들은 저자의 여정을 도와 준다. 인디언들은 가지고 있던 식량을 나누어 주며 저자가 길을 찾을 수 있도록 도와 준다. 저자는 사람들이 가지고 있는 저마다의 다른 생활 방식에 감사해 한다.

Boulders Taller Than the Great Tower of Seville

García Lôpez de Cárdenas

Summary This narrative tells about the first time that Europeans come to the Grand Canyon. The author describes the canyon's vast size, difficult landscape, and cold weather. He explains what happens when his group tries to explore the canyon.

Rocas más grandes que la gran torre de Sevilla

García López de Cárdenas

Resumen Esta narración trata sobre la primera vez que los europeos llegaron al Gran Cañón. El autor describe el enorme tamaño del cañón, el duro paisaje y el clima frío. Y explica lo que sucede cuando su grupo intenta explorar el cañón.

Wòch ki pi wo pase gran tou Sevil la

García Lôpez de Cárdenas

Rezime Resi sa a pale konsènan premye fwa ewopeyen yo te vin nan Grand Canyon. Otè a dekri kokennchenn gwosè canyon an, peyizaj difisil sa a ak tanperati frèt canyon an. Li eksplike ki sa ki rive lè gwoup li a eseye eksplore canyon an.

Mga Batong Mas Mataas Kaysa sa Malaking Tore ng Sevilla

García Lôpez de Cárdenas

Buod Ikinukuwento ng salaysay na ito ang unang beses ng pagdating ng mga European sa Grand Canyon. Inilalarawan ng awtor ang kalawakan nito, ang malalim at magaspang na mukha ng lupain, at ang kalamigan ng panahon rito. Kanyang ipinaliwanag ang mga pangyayari nang subukan ng kanyang grupong galugarin ang kanyon.

Cov Pob Zeb Loj Siab Tshaj Lub Tsev Siab Siab Seville

García López de Cárdenas

Lub Ntsiab Zaj lus no qhia txog thawj zaug uas hom neeg Europeans tuaj txog rau thaj chaw muaj pob zeb pob tsuas hu ua Grand Canyon. Tus sau zaj no qhia txog cov pob tsuas tias loj npaum li cas, qhia txog cov chaw uas nyuaj nce, thiab huab cua txias heev. Nws piav tias muaj dabtsi tshwm sim thaum nws pawg neeg sim mus saib lub roob loj ntawd.

《比塞爾維亞高塔還高的大圓石》 (Boulders Taller Than the Great Tower of Seville)

García López de Cárdenas

摘要 這則故事描述歐洲人第一次到達大峽谷的情形。作者描述了大峽谷廣闊的面積、險峻的景觀、以及寒冷的天氣。他描述當自己這一群人嘗試要探索大峽谷時所發生的事。

Những Tảng Đá Cao Lớn Hơn Tháp Seville

García López de Cárdenas

Tóm Tắt Câu truyện tường thuật này kể lại lần đầu tiên người Châu Âu đến đại vực Grand Canyon. Tác giả miêu tả sự hùng vĩ,cảnh đẹp khắc nghiệt và thời tiết giá lạnh của vực sâu này. Tác giả miêu tả điều gì xảy ra khi nhóm của mình cố gắng khám phá đại vực.

플리머스 농장 중에서 (Boulders Taller Than the Great Tower of Seville)

García López de Cárdenas

요약 이 글은 유럽인들이 처음으로 그랜드 캐년을 방문했을 당시를 묘사하고 있다. 추운 날씨 속에 펼쳐지는 광활한 계곡과 험준한 바위들의 경치를 그리고 있다. 또한 계곡을 탐험하면서 벌어지는 일에 대해서도 쓰고 있다.

from Of Plymouth Plantation

William Bradford

Summary This narrative account tells of the Puritans' first journey to the New World. The first part of the narrative describes their voyage. The second section describes the hardships of their first winter in Massachusetts. The third part tells how the Puritans received help from Native Americans and made a peace treaty with them.

de De la plantación de Plymouth

William Bradford

Resumen Este relato trata sobre el primer viaje de los puritanos hacia el Nuevo Mundo. La primera parte de la narración describe el viaje. La segunda sección describe las dificultades que debieron atravesar en su primer invierno en Massachussetts. La tercera parte cuenta cómo los puritanos recibieron ayuda de los nativos de Estados Unidos e hicieron un tratado de paz con ellos.

yon ekstrè nan Plantasyon Plimout

William Bradford

Rezime Resi sa a rakonte premye vwayaj piriten yo nan Nouvo Monn lan. Premye pati nan resi a dekri vwayaj yo a. Dezyèm seksyon an dekri difikilte yo te rankontre nan premye ivè yo te pase nan Massachusetts. Twazyèm pati a pale konsènan fason piriten yo te resevwa èd nan men endyen ameriken yo epi yo te fè yon trete de pè avèk yo.

mula sa Sa Pataníman ng Plymouth

William Bradford

Buod Ikinikuwento ng salaysay na ito ang unang biyahe ng mga Puritan sa "Bagong Mundo," o "New World." Inilalarawan ng unang bahagi ng salaysay ang kanilang biyahe. Inilalarawan ng ikalawang bahagi ang kanilang mga paghihirap noong unang winter nila sa Massachusetts. Isinasalaysay ng ikatlong bahagi kung paano tinulungan ang mga Puritan ng mga Katutubong Amerikano, at ang paggawá nila ng isang kasunduan ng kapayapaan sa mga ito.

los ntawm zaj **Hais Txog Thaj Teb Plymouth Plantation**

William Bradford

Lub Ntsiab Zaj lus no qhia txog pawg neeg Puritan thawj zaug tuaj txog rau lub tebchaws no uas hu ua New World. Qhov ua ntej qhia txog lawv txoj kev uas tuaj txog. Qhov thib ob qhia txog tej kev nyuaj siab uas lawv tau ntsib rau thawj lub caij ntuj no nyob rau hauv lub xeev MassachusettsQhov thib peb qhia txog tias cov neeg Puritan tau kev pab los ntawm haiv neeg Khab thiab tau sau ntaub ntawv cog lus cia txog kev thaj yeeb.

改編自《普利茅斯殖民地》(Of Plymouth Plantation)

William Bradford

摘要 這則故事講述的是清教徒第一次的新世界之旅。故事的第一部分描述他們航行的過程。第二部分則描述他們在麻薩諸塞州第一個冬天的艱苦情形。第三部分則敍述這些新教徒如何獲得當地美洲原住民的援助，並與其訂立了一個和平協定。

trích từ **Nhật Ký Về Đồn Điền Plymouth**

William Bradford

Tóm Tắt Câu truyện tường thuật này kể về hành trình đầu tiên đến Tân Thế Giới của những người theo Thanh Giáo. Phần đầu mô tả chuyến đi biển của họ. Phần hai nói về những gian khổ của họ trong mùa đông đầu tiên ở Massachusetts. Phần ba kể về việc làm thế nào những người theo Thanh Giáo nhận được sự giúp đỡ của Thổ Dân Mỹ và đạt được hiệp ước hòa bình với họ.

플리머스 농장 중에서 (Of Plymouth Plantation)

William Bradford

요약 이 글은 신세계를 향한 청교도들의 첫 번째 여정을 그리고 있다. 제 1부는 신세계까지의 항해를 묘사하고 있고 제 2부는 메사추세츠에서 처음으로 맞게 된 혹독한 겨울을 그리고 있다. 제 3부는 청교도들이 아메리칸 인디언들로부터 어떻게 도움을 받았고 평화 협정을 맺게 되는지를 설명하고 있다.

Huswifery • To My Dear and Loving Husband

Summary Taylor's poem is addressed to God. The speaker in the poem compares himself to a spinning wheel that turns yarn into cloth. The speaker wants to be changed by God into a person who is worthy of being saved. In Bradstreet's poem, the speaker addresses her husband. She expresses her deep love for him, which will last even after their lives on earth are over.

Huswifery • A mi querido y amado esposo

Resumen El poema de Taylor está dirigido a Dios. El narrador del poema se compara con una rueca que convierte el hilo en tela. El narrador quiere que Dios lo convierta en una persona que merezca la salvación. En el poema de Bradstreet, la narradora le habla a su esposo. Ella expresa su profundo amor hacia él, que durará incluso después de que sus vidas en la Tierra terminen.

Metrès kay • Pou chè mari m ki afektye

Rezime Se a Bondye Taylor adrese powèm li a. Oratè a nan powèm lan konpare tèt li a yon wou ki fè fil tounen twal. Oratè a vle pou Bondye fè l tounen yon moun ki diy pou l sove. Nan powèm Bradstreet la, oratè a adrese mari l. Li eksprime lanmou pwofon li gen pou li, ki pral dire menm aprè lavi yo sou latè fini.

Huswifery • Para sa Aking Minamahal at Nagmamahal na Asawa

Buod Ang tulá ni Taylor ay naka-ukol sa Diyos. Sa tulá na ito, inihahambing ng nagsasalita ang kanyang sarili sa isang "spinning wheel," isang makina na humahabi ng tela mula sa sinulid. Nais ng nagsasalita na baguhin siya ng Diyos para siya'y maging isang taong karapat-dapat na mailigtas nito. Sa tulá ni Bradstreet, kinakausap ng nagsasalita ang kanyang asawa. Kanyang ipinahahayag ang kalaliman ng pag-ibig niya para dito, na siyang mananatili kahit nagwakas na ang kanilang mga buhay sa mundo.

Huswifery • Rau Kuv Tus Txiv Uas Hlub thiab Tshua

Lub Ntsiab Taylor zaj pajhuam yog sau mus rau Vajtswv. Tus neeg hais lus hauv zaj pajhuam muab nws tus kheej piv rau ib lub tshuab ua xov uas muab xov fiab tau los ua ntaub. Tus neeg hais lus xav kom Vajtswv muab nws hloov mus ua ib tug neeg uas tsim nyog yuav cawm txoj sia. Hauv Bradstreet zaj pajhuam, tus neeg hais lus tham rau nws tus txiv. Nws nthuav txog nws txoj kev hlub uas tob heev rau tus txiv, uas yuav tseem nyob mus txawm tias nkawd lub neej nyob hauv ntiaj teb no tau xaus lawm.

《丈夫妻室》(Huswifery) 《給我最親愛及摯愛的丈夫》(To My Dear and Loving Husband)

摘要 泰勒寫這首詩獻給上帝。詩裡的敘述者將自己比作一個將紗線紡成布的紡輪。他希望上帝能將他改變成一個值得被救贖的人。布瑞德史崔特的詩作中的敘述者則對自己的丈夫傾訴。她向他表達自己的愛意，這份愛即便在他們的生命結束後都將持續下去。

Việc Nội Trợ • Dành Tặng Cho Người Chồng Yêu Thương Của Tôi

Tóm Tắt Bài thơ của Taylor viết cho Chúa Trời. Nhân vật trong bài thơ so sánh chính mình với một chiếc guồng quay tơ có thể biến những sợi tơ thành vải vóc. Anh ta muốn được Chúa Trời biến mình thành một người đáng được cứu vớt. Nhân vật trong bài thơ của Bradstreet làm thơ cho chồng mình. Cô diễn tả tình yêu sâu đậm của mình dành cho chồng và tình yêu đó sẽ mãi vĩnh cửu kể cả khi hai người không còn trên cõi đời này.

플리머스 농장 중에서 (Huswifery) • 플리머스 농장 중에서 (To My Dear and Loving Husband)

요약 테일러의 시는 신에게 말을 하는 형식을 빌어 표현하고 있다. 이 시에서 화자는 그 자신을 실로 옷감을 짜는 물레에 비유한다. 그리고 신이 자신을 마땅히 구원 받을 만한 인간으로 바꿔 주기를 바란다. 브래드스트리트의 시는 자신의 남편에 대해 이야기한다. 남편에 대한 깊은 사랑을 표현하며 그 사랑은 이 세상에서 죽어 없어진 후에도 계속될 것이라고 이야기한다.

from Sinners in the Hands of an Angry God

Jonathan Edwards

Summary Edwards's sermon tells about God's anger toward the sinners in his audience. He compares God's anger to floods and to a bow bent ready to shoot an arrow. The only thing that keeps God from dropping sinners into the fire is his mercy, according to Edwards. He tells the people that they can be reborn and save themselves from the anger.

de Pecadores en las manos de un Dios airado

Jonathan Edwards

Resumen El sermón de Edwards trata sobre la ira de Dios hacia los pecadores que se encuentran en la audiencia. Compara la ira de Dios con las inundaciones y un arco doblado listo para disparar una flecha. Según Edwards, el único motivo que impide que Dios envíe a todos los pecadores al fuego es su misericordia. Les advierte a las personas que pueden volver a nacer y salvarse de su ira.

yon ekstrè nan Pechè nan men yon Bondye ki an kòlè

Jonathan Edwards

Rezime Sèmon Edward la pale konsènan kòlè Bondye genyen kont pechè ki nan oditwa li a. Li konpare kòlè Bondye ak delij epi ak yon ak koube ki prè pou l tire yon flèch. Selon Edwards, sèl bagay ki anpeche Bondye jete pechè yo nan dife se mizerikòd li. Li di moun yo konsa yo ka ne ankò epi sove tèt yo de kòlè a.

mula sa Mga Makakasalanan sa Kamay ng Galít na Diyos

Jonathan Edwards

Buod Sinasabi ng sermon ni Edwards ang poot ng Diyos para sa mga makasalanan sa mga nakikiníg. Kanyang inihahambing ang poot ng May-Kapal sa mga bahá at sa isang panang nakabaluktot at handa nang humagis ng palasa. Ang tanging bagay na nagpipigil sa May-Kapal na itapon ang mga makasalanan sa apoy ay ang kanyang habag, ayon kay Edwards. Sinasabi niya sa mga tao na maaari silang muling isilang, at maisasalbá nila ang kanilang sarili mula sa poot na ito.

los ntawm **Cov Neeg Ua Txhaum uas nyob rau hauv Xib Teg ntawm ib tug Vajtswv Chim Heev**

Jonathan Edwards

Lub Ntsiab Edwards zaj lus no qhia txog Vajtswv txoj kev chim rau ib txhia neeg uas tab tom mloog nws uas yog neeg tau ua txhaum lawm. Nws muab Vajtswv txoj kev chim siab coj los piv rau tej dej uas nyab ntiaj teb thiab piv rau rab hneev uas tab tom npaj yuav tua ib xib xub. Tib yam uas tseem cheem Vajtswv ntawm kev muab cov neeg ua txhaum ntawd pov rau hauv hluav taws ces yog nws txoj kev siab zoo zam txim xwb, raws li Edwards hais. Nws qhia rau cov neeg tias lawv muaj kev yuav rov yug dua tshiab thiab pab lawv tus kheej ntawm txoj kev chim siab ntawd.

改編自《憤怒之神手中的罪人》 (Sinners in the Hands of an Angry God)

Jonathan Edwards

摘要 作者的這則佈道講述上帝對他的聽眾席中的罪人的憤怒。他將上帝的憤怒比喻成洪水以及一把彎曲著準備射出箭的弓。根據作者的說法，唯一能阻止上帝將罪人丟入火堆的關鍵是他的仁慈。他告訴眾人，他們可以重生並拯救自己免於遭受這種憤怒的後果。

trích từ **Những Tội Đồ trong Tay Chúa Trời Giận Dữ**

Jonathan Edwards

Tóm Tắt Bài thuyết giáo của Edwards kể về sự giận dữ của Chúa Trời với những người có tội lỗi trong đám thính giả. Ông so sánh cơn giận của Chúa Trời với các cơn lũ lụt và với một cây cung đã giương lên sẵn sàng để bắn đi một mũi tên. Theo Edwards, điều duy nhất giữ không để Chúa Trời quẳng những người có tội lỗi vào lửa chính là sự nhân từ của Ngài. Ngài nói với những người đó rằng họ có thể được tái sinh và cứu họ thoát khỏi cơn giận dữ.

플리머스 농장 중에서 (Sinners in the Hands of an Angry God)

Jonathan Edwards

요약 에드워드는 죄인들을 향한 신의 분노에 대해 설교한다. 그는 신의 분노를 홍수와 화살을 장전해 이제 당기기만 하면 되는 활에 비유한다. 신이 죄인들을 불구덩이 속으로 떨어뜨리는 것을 막을 수 있는 유일한 길은 신이 자비를 베푸는 것뿐이다. 저자는 죄인들도 다시 태어나 신의 분노에서 자신들을 구할 수 있다고 말한다.

Speech in the Virginia Convention

Patrick Henry

Summary In this speech, Patrick Henry says that he must respectfully disagree with the previous speeches. He believes that the actions of the British mean that they are preparing for war. The colonists have tried to discuss the problem, but they are being ignored. Henry claims that the war has already begun. The colonists' only choices are to fight or to become slaves.

Discurso en la convención de Virginia

Patrick Henry

Resumen En este discurso Patrick Henry dice que, respetuosamente, debe disentir de sus discursos anteriores. Cree que las acciones de los británicos significan que se están preparando para la guerra. Los colonos han intentado hablar acerca del problema, pero han sido ignorados. Henry sostiene que la guerra ya ha comenzado. Las únicas alternativas de los colonos son luchar o convertirse en esclavos.

Diskou nan Konvansyon Vijini a

Patrick Henry

Rezime Nan diskou sa a, Patrick Henry di respektyezman li pa dakò ak diskou ki sot fèt yo. Li kwè aksyon anglè yo siyifi y ap prepare yo pou lagè. Kolon yo te eseye diskite sou pwoblèm lan, men yo iyore yo. Henry fè konnen lagè a deja kòmanse. Sèl chwa kolon yo genyen se swa yo konbat swa yo vin tounen esklav.

Talumpati sa Pagtitipon sa Virginia

Patrick Henry

Buod Sinimulan ni Patrick Henry ang talumpati sa pamamagitan ng pagsabi na, mawalang-galang lamang, 'di raw siya sumasang-ayon sa mga naunang diskurso. Makikita sa mga pagkilos nila, 'ika niya, na ang mga Englatera ay naghahanda para sa digmáan. Sinubukan na nating pag-usapan ang problema. Tayo'y binabale-walá; wala nang urungán kundi patungo sa pagkabuhay-alipin. Ang panahon ng matiwasay na pakikisama ay tapós na. Nagsimula na ang digmáan. "Bigyan mo ako ng kalayaan o kaya'y bigyan mo ako ng kamatayan" ay ang makapangyarihan at tanyag na pagtatapós ni Henry.

Zaj Lus Hauv Rooj Sib Tham Nyob Virginia

Patrick Henry

Lub Ntsiab Nyob rau zaj lus no, Patrick Henry pib tham txog tias, nws tsis xav saib tsis taus leej twg, tiam sis nws tsis pom zoo raws li cov lus uas tau hais los lawm. Nws hais tias raws li nws saib pom lawv txoj kev coj mas, cov neeg British tab tom npaj yuav ua tsov rog. Peb twb tau tham txog cov teeb meem tas lawm. Lawv tsis mloog peb hais li; tsis muaj kev dim tsuas yog muaj kev hais tias yuav raug mus ua qhev xwb. Lub sijhawm uas tseem yuav sib haum ua ke ces twb dhau mus lawm. Tsov rog twb pib lawm. "Muab kev thaj yeeb rau kuv los yog muab kev tuag." Nqe no yog nqe lus uas Henry hais muaj fwjchim heev thiab coob leej paub txog tshaj.

《維吉尼亞州會議中的演說》 (Speech in the Virginia Convention)

Patrick Henry

摘要 作者在這篇演說中一開頭就說,他沒有任何不尊重的意思,只是不得不對之前的演說表示不同的意見。他說,依其舉止來判斷,英國人正準備要開戰。我們已經試圖要討論這個問題。我們一直都受到輕視;除了變成奴隸之外,沒有其他退路。和平共處的時代已經結束。戰爭已經開始。「不自由,毋寧死」是作者強烈而廣為人知的結語。

Bài Diễn Văn Tại Hội Nghị Virginia

Patrick Henry

Tóm Tắt Patrick Henry bắt đầu bài diễn văn này bằng cách nói một cách cung kính rằng ông không tán thành các bài phát biểu trước. Ông cho rằng cách hành xử của nước Anh cho thấy họ đang chuẩn bị cho một cuộc chiến. Chúng ta đã thử thảo luận vấn đề nhưng chúng ta không được người ta đếm xỉa đến; không còn cách lùi bước trừ phi chúng ta chịu làm nô lệ. Thời điểm để có thể chung sống hòa bình đã qua rồi. Cuộc chiến đã thực sự bắt đầu. "Hãy cho tôi tự do hoặc hãy giết tôi đi" là câu kết hùng hồn và nổi tiếng của Henry.

플리머스 농장 중에서 (Speech in the Virginia Convention)

Patrick Henry

요약 이 연설은 "무례를 무릅쓰고 말하건대 이전 연설에 나는 동의하지 않는다" 라는 말로 시작한다. 패트릭 헨리는 계속해서 다음과 같이 말한다. 그들의 행동을 보고 판단컨대 영국은 전쟁을 준비하고 있다. 우리는 이 문제를 해결하고자 많은 애를 썼다. 그러나 우리는 무시 당하고 있으며 노예 제도로의 후퇴만 있을 뿐이다. 평화롭게 공존하던 시간은 이제 끝났다. 전쟁은 이미 시작됐다. "내게 자유가 아니면 죽음을 달라" 라는 유명한 말로 이 연설을 끝맺고 있다.

Speech in the Convention

Benjamin Franklin

Summary Benjamin Franklin expresses his doubts about the Constitution. However, he still approves of the document. He supports his opinions with several reasons. Franklin feels that this Constitution is the best document that imperfect men can offer. He also thinks that it is important to show complete support for the Constitution.

Discurso en la convención

Benjamin Franklin

Resumen Benjamin Franklin expresa sus dudas con respecto a la Constitución. Sin embargo, aprueba el documento. Argumenta sus opiniones a través de varias razones. Franklin siente que esta Constitución es el mejor documento que los hombres imperfectos pueden escribir. También piensa que es importante demostrar apoyo total hacia la Constitución.

Diskou nan Konvansyon an

Benjamin Franklin

Rezime Benjamin Franklin eksprime dout li genyen konsènan Konstitisyon an. Sepandan, li toujou apwouve dokiman an. Li sipòte opinyon li avèk plizyè rezon. Franklin santi Konstitisyon sa a se meyè dokiman moun ki enpafè ka ofri. Epitou li panse li enpòtan pou montre sipò total pou Konstitisyon an.

Talumpati sa Pagtitipon

Benjamin Franklin

Buod Ipinahahayag ni Benjamin Franklin ang kanyang mga duda ukol sa Konstitusyon. Gayunman, ipinagtibay pa rin niya ang dokumento. Sinuportahan niya ang kanyang mga opinyon sa pamamagitan ng maraming dahilan. Nararamdaman ni Franklin na ang Konstitusyon na ito ay ang pinakamahusay na dokumento na maaaring ihandog ng mga hindi perpektong nilaláng. Kanya ring iniisip na mahalaga ang magpakita ng buong suporta para sa Konstitusyon.

Zaj Lus Ntawm Rooj Sib Tham

Benjamin Franklin

Lub Ntsiab Benjamin Franklin tham txog nws cov kev txhawj txog daim ntawv tswj cai hu ua Constitution. Txawm li ntawd los, nws yeej pom zoo txog daim ntawv ntawd. Nws siv ob peb nqe lus coj los txhawb nws txoj kev xav. Franklin xav tias daim Constitution no yog daim zoo tshaj uas ib pawg txiv neej zoo tsis tag yuav sau tau. Nws ho xav tias tseem ceeb heev rau kev yuav tsum txhawb nqa daim Constitution kom tas siab nrho.

《會議中的演說》 (Speech in the Convention)

Benjamin Franklin

摘要 作者班傑明　富蘭克林表達了自己對憲法的疑慮。即便如此，他還是批准了這份文件。他提出幾個理由來支持他的論點。富蘭克林覺得這套憲法是不完美的人類所能提出的最佳文件。他也認為對憲法給予完全的支持極為重要。

Bài Diễn Văn Tại Đại Hội Hiến Pháp

Benjamin Franklin

Tóm Tắt Benjamin Franklin bày tỏ những băn khoăn của mình đối với Bản Hiến Pháp. Tuy nhiên, ông vẫn tán thành văn kiện này. Ông bảo vệ các ý kiến của mình với rất nhiều lý do. Franklin cảm thấy rằng Bản Hiến Pháp là văn kiện tốt nhất mà những người không hoàn hảo có thể đưa ra. Ông cũng cho rằng một điều quan trọng là phải thể hiện sự ủng hộ hết mình đối với Bản Hiến Pháp.

플리머스 농장 중에서 (Speech in the Convention)

Benjamin Franklin

요약 벤자민 프랭클린은 헌법에 대해 아직 미덥지 못한 점은 있으나 이 문서에 찬성한다. 여러 가지 이유를 들어 자신의 찬성 의견을 설명한다. 그리고 이 헌법이야말로 불완전한 인간이 만들어 낼 수 있는 최상의 문서라고 하며 헌법에 전적인 지지를 보내는 것이 중요하다고 주장한다.

The Declaration of Independence

Thomas Jefferson

Summary Thomas Jefferson explains that it is important to state why America is separating from Britain. He claims certain basic rights for the colonists. He says that the English king abuses those rights. Based on these abuses, the colonies are independent of Britain and the colonists pledge their support of this declaration.

La declaración de la independencia

Thomas Jefferson

Resumen Thomas Jefferson explica la importancia de declarar por qué Norteamérica se independiza de Gran Bretaña. Y reclama ciertos derechos básicos para los colonizadores. Dice que el rey de Inglaterra se abusa de esos derechos. Debido a estos abusos, las colonias son independientes de Gran Bretaña y los colonizadores prometen brindar su apoyo a esta declaración.

Deklarasyon Endepandans la

Thomas Jefferson

Rezime Thomas Jefferson eksplike li enpòtan pou deklare rezon ki fè Amerik ap separe ak Angletè. Li reklame kèk dwa fondamantal pou kolon yo. Li di konsa wa anglè a abize dwa sa yo. Akoz de abi sa yo, koloni yo endepandan de peyi Angletè epi kolon yo pwomèt pou yo sipòte deklarasyon sa a.

Talumpati sa Pagtitipon sa Virginia

Patrick Henry

Buod Sinimulan ni Patrick Henry ang talumpati sa pamamagitan ng pagsabi na, mawalang-galang lamang, 'di raw siya sumasang-ayon sa mga naunang diskurso. Makikita sa mga pagkilos nila, 'ika niya, na ang mga Englatera ay naghahanda para sa digmáan. Sinubukan na nating pag-usapan ang problema. Tayo'y binabale-walá; wala nang urungán kundi patungo sa pagkabuhay-alipin. Ang panahon ng matiwasay na pakikisama ay tapós na. Nagsimula na ang digmáan. "Bigyan mo ako ng kalayaan o kaya'y bigyan mo ako ng kamatayan" ay ang makapangyarihan at tanyag na pagtatapós ni Henry.

Daim Ntawv Hais Txog Kev Ywj Pheej Declaration of Independence

Thomas Jefferson

Lub Ntsiab Thomas Jefferson piav tias tseem ceeb heev uas yuav tsum hais txog tias vim li cas Tebchaws Meskas thiaj li faib tawm ntawm Britain lawm. Nws hais tias muaj tej yam cai uas cov neeg nyob tebchaws no yuav tsum muaj. Nws hais tias tus Huab Tais Askiv coj tsis ncaj ncees rau cov cai ntawd lawm. Vim cov kev coj tsis ncaj ncees no, cov neeg tebchaws tshiab yuav tsum nyob ywj pheej nrug Britain thiab cov neeg tshiab yuav tsum cog lus pab lub tswv yim no.

《獨立宣言》(The Declaration of Independence)

Thomas Jefferson

摘要 作者解釋表明美國應該離開英國而獨立的決心極為重要。他為殖民地人民爭取某些基本權利。他說英國國王濫用了這些權利。由於這種濫權的情況，殖民地必須脫離英國獨立，而殖民地人民也誓言要支持這項宣言。

Bản Tuyên Ngôn Độc Lập

Thomas Jefferson

Tóm Tắt Thomas Jefferson cho rằng điều quan trọng là tuyên bố tại sao nước Mỹ tách ra khỏi nước Anh. Ông khẳng định một số quyền cơ bản đối với những người dân thuộc địa. Ông cho rằng vua Anh lạm dụng các quyền này và do vậy các thuộc địa tuyên bố độc lập và những người dân thuộc địa cam kết ủng hộ bản tuyên bố này.

플리머스 농장 중에서 (The Declaration of Independence)

Thomas Jefferson

요약 토마스 제퍼슨은 왜 미국이 영국으로부터 분리되어야 하는지 그 중요성을 설명한다. 그리고 미국 개척자들이 누려야 할 기본적 권리를 주장한다. 그러나 영국의 왕은 그런 권리들을 악용했으며 그로 인해 이 식민지는 영국으로부터 독립해야만 하며 미국인들은 독립 선언 지지를 맹세한다.

from The Crisis, Number 1

Thomas Paine

Summary Thomas Paine writes his essay to the American colonists. He wants to encourage them to fight against the British. Paine writes that God supports the American cause. He also argues that a good father will fight. If the fathers fight, their children may live in peace. Paine then asks Americans in every state to unite.

de La crisis, número 1

Thomas Paine

Resumen Thomas Paine escribe un ensayo dirigido a los colonizadores norteamericanos. Quiere alentarlos para que peleen contra los británicos. Paine afirma que Dios apoya la causa norteamericana. También sostiene que un buen padre peleará. Si los padres pelean, sus hijos vivirán en paz. Luego, Paine les pide a los norteamericanos de todos los estados que se unan.

yon ekstrè nan Kriz la, Nimewo 1

Thomas Paine

Rezime Thomas Paine ekri disètasyon l lan pou kolon ameriken yo. Li vle ankouraje yo pou yo konbat kont anglè yo. Paine ekri Bondye ap sipòte kòz ameriken an. Epitou li fè konnen yon bon papa pral goumen. Si papa yo goumen, pitit yo ka viv an pè. Ansuit Paine mande ameriken yo nan chak eta pou yo fè tèt ansanm.

mula sa Ang Krisis, Bilang 1

Thomas Paine

Buod Sinulat ni Thomas Paine ang kanyang sanaysay para sa mga kolonistang Amerikano. Nais niya silang hikayatin na lumaban sa mga taga-Britanya. Sinulat ni Paine na sinusuportahan ng Diyos ang panig ng mga Amerikano. Kanya ring ipinahayag na ang mabuting ama ay lalaban. Kung ang mga ama ay lumaban, ang kanilang mga anak ay maaaring mabuhay ng mapayapa. Pagkatapos ay hiniling ni Paine na magkaisa ang mga Amerikano sa bawat estado.

los ntawm Qhov Teeb Meem, Lej 1

Thomas Paine

Lub Ntsiab Thomas Paine sau nws zaj lus txog cov neeg Meskas uas xub tuaj ua neej nyob rau tebchaws Meskas. Nws xav txhawb kom lawv tawm tsam cov British. Paine sau tias Vajtswv txhawb cov neeg Meskas lub hom phiaj. Nws ho hais ntxiv mus tias ib leej txiv zoo ces yeej yuav nrog lawv tawm tsam. Yog tias cov leej txiv mus tua rog lawm, lawv cov menyuam thiaj yuav muaj kev thaj yeeb. Ces Paine nug cov neeg Meskas hauv txhua lub xeev kom lawv sawv los uake.

改編自《危機，1號》(The Crisis, Number 1)

Thomas Paine

摘要 作者寫這篇文章獻給美國殖民地居民。他希望鼓勵他們對抗英國政府。作者描述上帝也支持美國人的行動。他也主張一位好的父親會起而抗爭。假如父親願意抗爭，他們的子女即可望生活在和平當中。作者接著要求各州的美國人應該團結起來。

trích từ Cuộc Khủng Hoảng, Số 1

Thomas Paine

Tóm Tắt Thomas Paine viết một bài tiểu luận cho những người dân thuộc địa Mỹ. Ông muốn khuyến khích họ đấu tranh chống lại người Anh. Paine viết rằng Chúa ủng hộ cuộc đại nghĩa của người Mỹ. Ông lập luận rằng một người cha tốt sẽ đấu tranh. Nếu những người cha đấu tranh, con của họ có thể được sống trong hòa bình. Rồi Paine kêu gọi người Mỹ ở các tiểu bang cùng đoàn kết.

위기, 제 1번 중에서 (The Crisis, Number 1)

Thomas Paine

요약 저자는 미국 개척자들에게 이 글을 쓰고 있다. 그는 영국과 맞서 싸우기를 권하며 신도 미국의 대의명분을 지지한다고 이야기한다. 또한 훌륭한 아버지라면 맞서 싸워야 하며, 아버지들이 싸워 자유를 얻는다면 그 아이들은 평화 속에 살게 될 것이라고 주장한다. 그리고 미국 모든 주의 사람들에게 서로 단결할 것도 당부한다.

UNIT 1

To His Excellency, General Washington

Phillis Wheatley

Summary "To His Excellency, General Washington" praises the revolutionary cause. The poem personifies America as the goddess Columbia. It also praises George Washington for his bravery and leadership.

A su excelencia, general Washington

Phillis Wheatley

Resumen "A su excelencia, general Washington" elogia la causa revolucionaria. El poema personifica a Norteamérica como la diosa Columbia. También elogia a George Washington por su valentía y liderazgo.

Pou Son Ekselans, jeneral Washington

Phillis Wheatley

Rezime Powèm "Pou Son Ekselans, jeneral Washington" lan fè lwanj pou kòz revolisyonè a. Powèm lan pèsonifye Amerik kòm deyès Kolonbi. Epitou li fè lwanj pou George Washington pou bravou li ak lidèchip li.

Para kay Excellency, Henerál Washington

Phillis Wheatley

Buod Pinupuri ng "Sa Kanyang Excellency, Henerál Washington" ang panig ng mga naghihimagsik. Ang tulá ay nagbibigay sa Amerika ng parang-taong-anyó ng diyosang si Columbia. Pinupuri rin nito si George Washington para sa kanyang katapangan at pamumuno.

Hawm Txog, General Washington

Phillis Wheatley

Lub Ntsiab "Hawm Txog, General Washington" sau qhuas txog kev tawm tsam tsoom fwv Askiv Teb. Lub Ntsiab "Rau Tus Neeg Txawj Thiab Zoo Heev, General Washington" yog hais lus zoo txog txoj kev tawm tsam no. Zaj pajhuam no muab Tebchaws Meskas saib piv rau tus ntxhais qaum ntuj Columbia. Thiab nws hais lus zoo siab txog George Washington rau nws txoj kev siab tawv thiab txoj kev txawj coj.

《致華盛頓將軍》(To His Excellency, General Washington)

Phillis Wheatley

摘要 此篇文章稱頌革命的理想。這首詩將美國擬人化為哥倫比亞女神。詩中也對喬治　華盛頓的英勇與領導大表讚揚。

Gửi Tặng Đại Tướng Washington

Phillis Wheatley

Tóm Tắt "Gửi Tặng Đại Tướng Washington" là lời ca ngợi sự nghiệp cách mạng. Bài thơ coi nước Mỹ là hiện thân của nữ thần Columbia. Bài thơ cũng ngợi ca George Washington vì sự dũng cảm và khả năng lãnh đạo của ông.

위대하신 워싱턴 장군에게 (To His Excellency, General Washington)

Phillis Wheatley

요약 이 시는 독립 혁명의 정당한 이유를 칭송하며 미국을 컬럼비아라는 여신으로 형상화하고 있다. 또한 조지 워싱턴 장군의 리더십과 용맹을 칭송하고 있다.

from The Autobiography

Benjamin Franklin

Summary Franklin is working on a plan to reach moral perfection. He will work on thirteen virtues, or qualities. Franklin writes the virtues in a notebook to see how well he is doing. He makes a black mark beside a virtue every time he forgets to follow it. He works on a different virtue each week. Franklin thinks his plan is helpful but not completely successful.

de La autobiografía

Benjamin Franklin

Resumen Franklin trabaja en un plan destinado a alcanzar la perfección moral. Trabajará sobre trece virtudes o cualidades. Franklin escribe sus virtudes en un cuaderno para ver cómo progresa. Cada vez que se olvida de seguir una virtud, coloca una marca negra al lado. Trabaja sobre una virtud diferente cada semana. Franklin cree que su plan es útil, pero no del todo perfecto.

yon ekstrè nan Otobyografi a

Benjamin Franklin

Rezime Franklin ap travay sou yon plan pou rive jwenn pèfeksyon moral. Li pral travay sou trèz vèti oswa kalite. Franklin ekri vèti yo nan yon kaye pou l wè ki jan li travay sou yo. Li mete yon mak nwa akote yon vèti chak fwa li bliye pou l suiv vèti a. Li travay sou yon diferan vèti chak semèn. Franklin panse plan l lan itil men li pa konplètman reyisi.

mula sa Ang Sariling Talambuhay

Benjamin Franklin

Buod Si Franklin ay gumagawá ng plano upang maabot ang ganáp na kabanalan. Susubukan niyang gawin ang labing-tatlong kalinisang-budhi, o mga mabuting katangian. Sinusulat ni Franklin ang mga uri ng kalinisang-budhi sa isang aklat-sulatán upang makita niya ang kanyang progreso. Gumuguhit siya ng markang itim sa tabí ng bawat isang katangian tuwing nalilimutan niyang sundin ito. Bawat linggo ay ibang katangian ang binibigyang-diin niya. Sa wari ni Franklin, ang kanyang plano ay nakatutulong, ngunit 'di lubos na matagumpay.

los ntawm Zaj Sau Txog Tus Kheej

Benjamin Franklin

Lub Ntsiab Franklin tab tom npaj ib lub tswv yim tias yuav ua li cas thiaj li yog tau ib tug neeg zoo tshaj plaws. Nws yuav saib txog kaum peb txoj kev zoo, lossis yam zoo. Franklin sau cov kev zoo rau hauv ib phau ntawv kom paub tau tias nws ua li cas lawm xwb. Nws kos ib kab dub loj loj rau ntawm ib sab txhua txoj kev coj zoo thaum twg uas nws tsis nco qab ua raws li ntawd lawm. Txhua lub lim piam nws xyaum ib qho kev zoo. Franklin xav tias nws lub tswv yim no pab tau thiab tiamsis tsis tau zoo tas.

改編自《自傳》(The Autobiography)

Benjamin Franklin

摘要 作者正在努力達到一項道德完美的計劃。他將致力於十三種美德或特質。作者在一本筆記本上寫出這些美德，想瞭解自己做得有多好。每當他忘了實行某項美德時，他就在這項美德旁做一個黑色的標示。他每星期都致力不同的美德。作者認為自己的計劃很有幫助，但並沒有完全成功。

trích từ Tự Truyện

Benjamin Franklin

Tóm Tắt Franklin đang thực hiện một kế hoạch để đạt được sự hoàn hảo về đạo đức. Ông sẽ thực hiện kế hoạch này lấy tiêu chí là 13 đức tính tốt. Franklin ghi các đức tính tốt đó vào một quyển sổ để theo dõi xem mình làm tốt đến đâu. Ông đánh dấu đen bên cạnh từng đức tính mỗi lần ông quên không thực hiện theo. Mỗi tuần ông tập một đức tính khác nhau. Franklin cho rằng kế hoạch của ông hữu ích nhưng không thành công trọn vẹn.

플리머스 농장 중에서 (The Autobiography)

Benjamin Franklin

요약 프랭클린은 도덕적 완벽을 지향하기 위해 계획을 세운다. 그 계획에는 열세 개의 지켜야 할 덕목도 있다. 그 덕목을 공책에 적고는 자신이 그것을 잘 지키고 있는지 체크한다. 지키지 못한 덕목이 있을 때마다 그 옆에 검은 점으로 표시해 둔다. 매주마다 지켜야 할 덕목이 다르다. 프랭클린은 이 계획이 완벽하게 성공적이지는 않아도 유익할 것이라고 생각한다.

from Poor Richard's Almanack

Benjamin Franklin

Summary Franklin gives advice about how people should behave. He presents his thoughts in aphorisms, or short sayings with a message. Many of his aphorisms come from traditional folk sayings. Sayings such as "Well done is better than well said" tell something about Franklin and what he values.

de El almanaque del pobre Ricardo

Benjamin Franklin

Resumen Franklin da consejos a las personas sobre cómo deben comportarse. Presenta sus pensamientos en aforismos, o dichos cortos que contienen un mensaje. Varios de sus aforismos provienen de refranes populares tradicionales. Refranes como "Bien hecho es mejor que bien dicho" hablan sobre Franklin y las cosas que valora.

yon ekstrè nan Almanak pòv Richard la

Benjamin Franklin

Rezime Franklin bay konsèy konsènan fason moun dwe konpòte yo. Li prezante panse l yo an aforis, oswa pwovèb kout ki gen yon mesaj ladan l. Anpil nan aforis li yo soti nan pwovèb popilè tradisyonèl. Kèk pwovèb tankou "Byen fè miyò pase byen di" di kichòy sou pèsonalite Franklin ak sa li bay valè.

mula sa "Poor Richard's Almanack"

Benjamin Franklin

Buod Si Franklin ay nagbibigay ng payô tungkol sa karapat-dapat na pagkilos ng mga tao. Kanyang ipinahahayag ang kanyang mga kuru-kuro sa "aphorisms," o mga maiikling kasabihan na may mensahe. Marami sa kanyang mga maiikling kasabihan ay galing sa mga tradisyunál na sabi-sabi. Ang mga kasabihan tulad ng "Ang mahusay na paggawá ay mas mainam kaysa sa mabuting pagsasalitá" ay nagpapakita ng pagkatao ni Franklin at ng kanyang binibigyang-halaga.

los ntawm Richard Phau Almanack

Benjamin Franklin

Lub Ntsiab Franklin muab kev pab rau cov neeg uas yuav tsum txawj coj kom zoo tshaj qub. Nws qhia txog nws cov kev xav nyob rau hauv aphorisms, lossis yog ib co lus sau uas luv thiab muaj ib lub ntsiab lus nyob rau hauv. Nws muaj ntau qhov aphorism uas los ntawm cov paj lug uas neeg ib txwm siv los. Tej nqe lus hais xws li "Ua tau zoo ces zoo tshaj qhov hais tau zoo" qhia tau tias Franklin yog tus neeg zoo li cas thiab nws thwm txoj kev coj zoo li cas.

改編自《窮理查的曆書》(Poor Richard's Almanack)

Benjamin Franklin

摘要 作者針對人類行為提出他的意見。他以格言或是內含某種訊息的簡短諺語的方式提出自己的想法。他的格言有許多都來自傳統的民間諺語。譬如「做得好更勝說得好」之類的諺語就道出了作者本人的想法及他重視的觀念。

trích từ Niên Lịch Về Chàng Richard Nghèo Khổ

Benjamin Franklin

Tóm Tắt Franklin khuyên mọi người cách cư xử. Ông thể hiện suy nghĩ của mình dưới dạng cách ngôn, tức là những câu nói ngắn gọn nhưng có ý nghĩa. Nhiều câu cách ngôn của ông xuất phát từ những câu tục ngữ dân gian truyền thống. Ví như câu "Làm nhiều tốt hơn nói nhiều" cho chúng ta biết đôi điều về Franklin và những giá trị của ông.

플리머스 농장 중에서 (Poor Richard's Almanack)

Benjamin Franklin

요약 이 책에서 프랭클린은 사람이 어떻게 행동해야 하는지에 관해 조언한다. 자신의 생각을 격언의 형식을 빌어 표현한다. 여기 나오는 많은 격언들은 속담에서 유래되었다. "훌륭한 행동이 훌륭한 말보다 낫다" 라는 격언은 프랭클린과 그의 가치관을 잘 표현한 말이다.

from The Interesting Narrative of the Life of Olaudah Equiano

Olaudah Equiano

Summary Olaudah Equiano tells what happened to him aboard a slave ship. He describes the crowded conditions and sickening smells. He also tells of the slaves' despair. He explains that the ship's crew chained, starved, and beat the slaves. Many people died during the terrible journey. Those who lived were examined and sold when they reached Barbados.

de La Interesante narrativa de la vida de Olaudah Equiano

Olaudah Equiano

Resumen Olaudah Equiano cuenta lo que le sucede a bordo de un barco de esclavos. Describe el hacinamiento y los olores repugnantes. También habla de la desesperación de los esclavos. Y cuenta que la tripulación del barco encadenaba, golpeaba y privaba de alimentos a los esclavos. Muchas personas murieron en ese terrible viaje. Aquéllos que sobrevivieron fueron revisados y vendidos cuando llegaron a Barbados.

yon ekstrè nan Resi enteresan sou lavi Olaudah Equiano

Olaudah Equiano

Rezime Olaudah Equiano rakonte sa k te rive l abò yon bato ki t ap transpòte esklav. Li dekri kondisyon moun ki antase nan bato a ak sant ki ta fè w malad. Epitou li rakonte dezespwa esklav yo te santi. Li eksplike manm ekipaj bato a te anchene, pa bay esklav yo manje epi bat yo. Anpil moun te mouri pandan vwayaj tèrib sa a. Yo te egzamine rès ki te siviv yo epi yo te vann yo lè yo te rive nan peyi Babad.

mula sa Ang Interesanteng Salaysay ng Buhay ni Olaudah Equiano

Olaudah Equiano

Buod Kinukuwento ni Olaudah Equiano kung ano ang nangyari sa kanya sa isang barkong nagdadalá ng mga taong-inalipin. Inilalarawan niya ang masikip na kalagayan at ang mga amoy na kasuká-suká. Sinabi rin niya ang kawaláng-pag-asa ng mga inalipin. Sinabi niya na ang mga inalipin ay tinikalá, ginutom, at ginulpí ng mga tauhan ng barko. Maraming taong namatáy sa marahas na biyahe. Ang mga naiwang buháy ay ineksamen at ipinagbilí nang sila'y umabot sa Barbados.

los ntawm Zaj Sau Zoo Mloog Heev txog Lub Neej ntawm Olaudah Equiano

Olaudah Equiano

Lub Ntsiab Olaudah Equiano qhia txog yam uas tshwm sim rau nws thaum nws nyob rau saum lub nkoj thauj cov neeg tuaj ua qhev. Nws piav txog tias lub nkoj mas ti heev li thiab tsw phem heevNws ho qhia txog cov neeg qhev ntawd txoj kev tu siab thiab. Nws piav tias cov neeg ua haujlwm hauv lub nkoj ntawd muab cov qhev xauv tes taw, tsis pub mov rau noj, thiab muab lawv ntaus. Coob leej tau tag sim neej rau txoj kev phem no lawm. Cov uas tseem ciaj sia ces raug kuaj zoo zoo tas thiab raug muag thaum uas lub nkoj mus txog Barbados.

改編自《歐拉達　伊奎諾一生的有趣故事》(The Interesting Narrative of the Life of Olaudah Equiano)

Olaudah Equiano

摘要 作者歐拉達　伊奎諾描述自己搭乘一艘奴隸船時發生的事。他描寫那種擁擠不堪的環境以及令人作嘔的味道。他也描述了這些奴隸的絕望。船員會將奴隸用鐵鍊銬起來，讓他們挨餓，並毆打他們。許多人在這趟惡劣的旅程期間死亡。當他們抵達巴爾巴度斯時，存活的人會受到檢查並被賣掉。

trích từ Câu Truyện Tường Thuật Đáng Chú Ý về Cuộc Đời của Olaudah Equiano

Olaudah Equiano

Tóm Tắt Olaudah Equiano kể về những điều đã xảy ra với ông trên một con tàu chở nô lệ. Ông mô tả điều kiện sống chật chội và những cái mùi ghê tởm, đồng thời cũng nhắc đến nỗi tuyệt vọng của các nô lệ. Ông kể rằng thủy thủ đoàn xiềng xích, bỏ đói, và đánh dập các nô lệ. Nhiều người đã bỏ mạng trong chuyến đi kinh hoàng đó. Những người còn sống sót được kiểm tra và bán khi họ đến được Barbados.

플리머스 농장 중에서 (The Interesting Narrative of the Life of Olaudah Equiano)

Olaudah Equiano

요약 저자는 자신이 노예선에 타게 되었을 때 벌어진 일들을 이야기한다. 사람으로 가득 차고 지독한 냄새가 코를 찌르는 노예선의 모습을 그리고 있을 뿐만 아니라 노예들의 절망에 대해서도 이야기한다. 선원들은 노예에 쇠사슬을 채우고 굶기며 때리기도 한다. 이 끔찍한 항해를 하는 동안 많은 사람이 죽어간다. 살아남은 노예들은 바베이도스에 도착하자 건강 진단을 받고 팔려간다.

The Devil and Tom Walker

Washington Irving

Summary Tom Walker meets the Devil ("Old Scratch") in a swamp. The Devil offers the pirate Captain Kidd's treasure to Tom on certain conditions. Tom's wife encourages him to accept, but Tom refuses. She leaves to find the Devil and make her own bargain. After her second try, she doesn't come back. Later, Tom finds her apron with a heart and liver in it. He assumes that the Devil has killed her. Almost grateful, Tom looks for the Devil again. This time, he makes a deal. Tom will get Captain Kidd's treasure if he becomes a moneylender. Later, Tom regrets his deal and starts going to church often. But the Devil returns and sends Tom off on horseback into a storm. Tom never comes back, though his troubled spirit appears on stormy nights.

El diablo y Tom Walker

Washington Irving

Resumen Tom Walker conoce al diablo (el "Maligno") en un pantano. El diablo le ofrece a Tom el tesoro del pirata capitán Kidd a cambio de ciertas condiciones. La esposa de Tom lo incita a aceptarlo, pero Tom se niega. Entonces ella parte en busca del diablo para hacer su propio negocio. Luego del segundo intento, ella no regresa. Luego Tom encuentra su delantal con un corazón y un hígado adentro. Supone que el diablo la ha matado. Casi agradecido, Tom va en busca del diablo otra vez. Y esta vez hace un trato. Tom se quedará con el tesoro del capitán Kidd si se convierte en prestamista. Pero luego Tom se arrepiente del trato y comienza a ir frecuentemente a la iglesia. Pero el diablo regresa y obliga a Tom a enfrentarse a una tormenta montado en un caballo. Tom nunca regresa, pero su perturbado espíritu aparece en las noches tormentosas.

Dyab la ak Tom Walker

Washington Irving

Rezime Tom Walker rankontre Dyab la ("Old Scratch") nan yon marekaj. Dyab la ofri Tom trezò pirat kaptenn Kidd la men a kondisyon. Madanm Tom ankouraje l pou l aksepte, men Tom refize. Li pati al chèche Dyab la pou l fè pwòp negosyasyon l. Aprè dezyèm esè li, li pa retounen. Pita, Tom jwenn tabliye li ki gen yon kè ak yon fwa ladan l. Li sipoze Dyab la te touye madanm li. Prèske rekonesan, Tom al chèche Dyab la ankò. Fwa sa a, li fè yon akò avèk li. Tom pral genyen trezò kaptenn Kidd la si l vin yon pretè lajan. Pita, Tom regrèt akò li te fè epi li kòmanse retounen al legliz souvan. Men Dyab la retounen epi li ranvwaye Tom sou do yon chwal nan yon tanpèt. Tom pa janm retounen, byenke lespri twouble li a parèt nan nuit ki gen tanpèt.

Ang Demonyo at si Tom Walker

Washington Irving

Buod Nasalubong ni Tom Walker ang Demonyo (si "Tandáng Kalmot") sa isang latian. Inalok ng Demonyo kay Tom ang kayamanan ng pirate o tulisáng-dagat na si Kapitan Kidd, ngunit may ilang kondisyon. Sinusulsulan ng asawa ni Tom na tanggapin niya ito, ngunit si Tom ay tumanggi. Siya ay umalis para hanapin ang Demonyo upang siya naman ang makipagtawarán dito. Pagkatapos ng kanyang ikalawang pagsubok, siya ay 'di bumalik. Makaraan ang panahon ay nahanap ni Tom ang kanyang apron na naglalamán ng isang puso at atay. Inakala ni Tom na pinatáy siya ng Demonyo. Si Tom ay halos magpasalamat, at kanya na namang hinanap ang Demonyo. Ngayon, siya ay nakipagkasundo. Makukuha ni Tom ang kayamanan ni Kapitan Kidd kung siya ay naging isang tagapag-pautang ng pera. Makaraan ang panahon, pinagsisihan ni Tom ang kanyang pakikipagkasundo, at siya'y nagsimba nang malimit. Pero bumalik ang Demonyo at kanyang pinasakay si Tom sa isang kabayo at pinasulong ito sa bagyó. Si Tom ay 'di na nagbalik, pero ang kanyang ligalig na kaluluwa ay lumilitaw sa mga gabíng bumabagyo.

Tus Dab thiab Tom Walker

Washington Irving

Lub Ntsiab Tom Walker ntsib tus Dab ("Old Scratch") hauv ib lub pas hav iav. Tus Dab hais tias nws mam li muab Captain Kidd cov nyiaj kub los rau Tom yog tias nws kam ua ib yam. Tom tus pojniam hais kom nws txais, tiamsis Tom tsis kam. Tus pojniam tawm mus nrhiav tus Dab thiab mus hais ib yam rau nws tus kheej. Tom qab nws rov sim dua zaum ob, nws cia li tsis rov los lawm. Tom qab ntawd, Tom nrhiav tau nws tus pojniam daim ntaub npua xub ntiag nrog ib lub plawv thiab lub siab nyob rau hauv. Nws xav kiag hais tias tus Dab yog tus tua nws pojniam. Zoo siab me ntsis, Tom mus nrhiav tus Dab dua. Zaum no, nws nrog tus dab sib cog lus. Tom yuav tau Captain Kidd cov nyiaj yog tias Tom kam ua ib tug neeg txais nyiaj rau lwm tus. Tom qab, Tom tsis xav ua raws nws cov lus cog tseg thiab pib mus tom tsev teev ntuj heev. Tiamsis tus Dab rov qab los thiab xa Tom caij nees tawm rau sab nraum zoov thaum ntuj nag los hlob heev. Tom tsis rov los li lawm, tiamsis thaum twg los nag hlob heev tseem pom nws tus ntsuj plig nyuaj siab.

《惡魔與湯姆・華克》(The Devil and Tom Walker)

Washington Irving

摘要 湯姆・華克在一處沼澤遇到惡魔。惡魔提議可在某種條件下將海盜基德船長的寶藏送給湯姆。湯姆的妻子鼓勵他接受，但湯姆拒絕了。她於是前去找惡魔，並提出她自己的交易條件。在她第二次嘗試後，她並沒有回來。之後，湯姆發現她的圍裙，裡面有一顆心及肺。他認定惡魔已經殺死她了。湯姆有慶幸的感覺，他於是再次去找惡魔。這次，他達成了一項交易。湯姆假如能成為一位放債人，即可取得基德船長的寶藏。湯姆在之後又很後悔自己的交易，並開始經常上教堂。但惡魔回來了，並且將湯姆送上一匹馬，奔馳入暴風雨中。湯姆從未回來，不過他惶惑不安的靈魂在暴風雨的夜裡會出現。

Quỷ Xa Tăng và Tom Walker

Washington Irving

Tóm Tắt Tom Walker gặp Quỷ Xa Tăng ("Lão Scratch") ở một đầm lầy. Quỷ Xa Tăng hứa sẽ cho Tom kho báu của Tàu Trưởng Kidd, một trùm băng hải tặc, với một số điều kiện nhất định. Vợ Tom khuyến khích anh ta chấp nhận nhưng Tom từ chối. Chị ta bỏ đi tìm Quỷ Xa Tăng để tự thỏa thuận. Sau nỗ lực thỏa thuận lần thứ hai, chị ta không trở về. Sau đó, Tom tìm thấy chiếc tạp dề của vợ trong đó có một quả tim và gan. Cho rằng Quỷ Xa Tăng đã giết vợ mình, Tom thấy thật dễ chịu nên tìm gặp lại Quỷ Xa Tăng. Lần này, anh đồng ý thỏa thuận. Tom sẽ nhận được kho báu của Tàu Trưởng Kidd nếu anh ta trở thành một kẻ cho vay lãi. Sau đó, Tom lại thấy hối tiếc vì thỏa thuận của mình và bắt đầu đi lễ nhà thờ thường xuyên. Nhưng Quỷ Xa Tăng quay lại và đẩy anh ta vào một cơn bão trên lưng ngựa. Tom không bao giờ quay trở về mặc dù linh hồn đau khổ của anh ta vẫn xuất hiện trong các đêm có bão.

악마와 탐 워커 (The Devil and Tom Walker)

Washington Irving

요약 어느 날 탐 워커는 늪에서 "올드 스크래치" 라는 악마를 만나게 된다. 악마는 어떤 조건 하에 해적 선장 키드의 보물을 주겠다고 제안한다. 탐의 아내는 그가 그 제안을 수락할 것을 종용하나 그는 거절한다. 그러자 아내는 자신이 직접 악마와 거래하기 위해 악마를 찾아 나선다. 그런데 두 번째로 악마를 찾아 떠난 날 아내는 돌아오지 않는다. 나중에 탐은 아내의 앞치마를 발견하게 되나 그 앞치마에는 심장과 간이 놓여져 있다. 악마가 아내를 죽였다고 생각한 탐은 악마를 찾아가게 되고 이번에는 자신이 고리대금업자가 된다는 조건 하에 키드의 보물을 얻는다. 나중에 탐은 악마와의 거래를 후회하며 교회에 자주 나가게 된다. 이에 악마가 찾아와 탐을 말에 태워 폭풍 속으로 떠나 보낸다. 그 이후 탐을 본 사람은 아무도 없으나 폭풍이 몰아치는 밤이면 고통스런 탐의 영혼이 나타난다.

"The Tide Rises, The Tide Falls" and *from* The Song of Hiawatha
Henry Wadsworth Longfellow

"Thanatopsis"
William Cullen Bryant

"Old Ironsides"
Oliver Wendell Holmes

Summaries The subjects of these poems connect to life in New England. In "The Tide Rises, The Tide Falls," Bryant compares the cycle of tides in the ocean to the cycle of life and death. Longfellow paints a picture of the wild country in the opening verses from The Song of Hiawatha. In "Thanatopsis," Bryant also explores the theme of death through images from nature, such as the earth and the ocean. Holmes celebrates a ship's history at sea in "Old Ironsides."

"La marea sube, la marea baja" y *de* La canción de Hiawatha
Henry Wadsworth Longfellow

"Thanatopsis"
William Cullen Bryant

"Viejos valientes"
Oliver Wendell Holmes

Resúmenes Los temas de estos poemas están relacionados con la vida en Nueva Inglaterra. En "La marea sube, la marea baja", Bryant compara el ciclo de las mareas en el océano con el ciclo de la vida y la muerte. Longfellow pinta un cuadro del país salvaje en los primeros versos de La canción de Hiawatha. En "Thanatopsis" Bryant también investiga el tema de la muerte a través de imágenes de la naturaleza, como la tierra y el océano. Holmes celebra la historia de un barco en el océano en "Viejos valientes".

"Mare a monte, mare a desann" epi *yon ekstrè nan* Chanson Hiawatha a
Henry Wadsworth Longfellow

"Thanatopsis"
William Cullen Bryant

"Old Ironsides"
Oliver Wendell Holmes

Rezime Sijè powèm sa yo konekte lavi nan Nouvèl Angletè. Nan "Mare a monte, mare a desann" Bryant konpare sik mare yo nan lanmè a ak sik lavi ak lanmò. Longfellow pentire yon imaj peyi sovaj la nan estwòf ouvèti nan Chanson Hiawatha a. Nan "Thanatopsis," Bryant eksplore tou tèm lanmò atravè imaj lanati, tankou latè ak lanmè a. Holmes selebre istwa yon bato nan lanmè nan "Old Ironsides."

"Tumataas ang Tide, Bumababa ang Tide" at *mula sa* Ang Awit ni Hiawatha
Henry Wadsworth Longfellow

"Thanatopsis"
William Cullen Bryant

"Ang Lumang Ironsides"
Oliver Wendell Holmes

Mga Buod Ang mga paksâ ng mga tuláng ito ay may ugnay sa buhay sa New England. Sa "Tumaatas ang Tide, Bumababa ang Tide," inihahambing ni Longfellow ang siklo ng mga tide sa karagatan sa siklo ng buhay at kamatayan. Nagpinta si Longfellow ng larawan ng mailap na kagubatan sa mga unang taludtod ng Ang Awit ni Hiawatha. Sa "Thanatopsis," tinatalakay rin ni Bryant ang tema ng kamatayan sa pamamagitan ng mga anyó mula sa kalikasan, tulad ng lupa at ng karagatan. Ipinagdiriwang ni Holmes ang kasaysayan ng isang barko sa dagat sa "Lumang Ironsides."

"Nthwv Dej Siab, Nthwv Dej Qis" thiab *los ntawm* Hiawatha Zaj Nkauj

Henry Wadsworth Longfellow

"Thanatopsis"

William Cullen Bryant

"Old Ironsides"

Oliver Wendell Holmes

Cov ntsiab Tej yam hauv cov pajhaum no yog txog lub neej nyob hauv New England. Hauv "Nthwv Dej Siab, Nthwv Dej Qis," Bryant muab cov dej hiav txwv uas ntws mus ntws los coj los piv rau kev ua neej thiab kev tuag uas ntws ib yam. Longfellow tham txog lub tebchaws uas tseem tshiab tshiab nyob rau hauv cov nqe lus qhib ntawm Hiawatha Zaj Nkauj. Hauv "Thanatopsis," Bryant rov qab tham txog kev ploj tuag uas siv tej yam hauv ntiaj teb los qhia txog, uas yog xws li lub ntiaj teb thiab hiav txwv. Holmes muaj kev zoo siab txog keeb kwm ntawm ib lub nkoj hauv zaj hu ua "Old Ironsides."

《潮起潮落》(The Tide Rises, The Tide Falls) 以及取材自希阿哇薩歌曲 (The Song of Hiawatha)

Henry Wadsworth Longfellow

《對死的觀感》(Thanatopsis)

William Cullen Bryant

《老鐵殼》(Old Ironsides)

Oliver Wendell Holmes

摘要 這些詩作的主題皆與新英格蘭地區的生活有關。隆費羅在《潮起潮落》中將大海的潮汐週期比喻成生命及死亡的循環。隆費羅在取材自《希阿哇薩之歌》的開頭詩句中描繪出荒野國度的景象。拜倫在《對死的觀感》中也透過各種大自然的畫面，例如地球及大海等，探討死亡的主題。荷姆斯則在《老鐵殼》中稱頌一艘船的海上歷史。

"Thủy Triều Lên, Thủy Triều Xuống" và *trích từ* Bài Ca Về Hiawatha

Henry Wadsworth Longfellow

"Thanatopsis"

William Cullen Bryant

"Chiến Hạm Thành Sắt Cổ"

Oliver Wendell Holmes

Tóm Tắt Chủ đề của những bài thơ này có liên quan đến cuộc sống ở vùng New England. Trong bài "Thủy Triều Lên, Thủy Triều Xuống", Longfellow so sánh chu kỳ thủy triều trên biển với chu kỳ sống chết. Longfellow vẽ lên bức tranh một xứ sở hoang vu ngay từ những vần thơ đầu tiên trong Bài Ca Về Hiawatha. Trong bài "Thanatopsis", Bryant cũng khai thác chủ đề cái chết qua những hình ảnh thiên nhiên như trái đất và đại dương. Holmes ngợi ca lịch sử một con tàu trên biển trong bài "Chiến Hạm Thành Sắt Cổ."

"밀물이 들어오고 썰물이 나간다" 와 하이어와서의 노래 중에서 ("The Tide Rises, The Tide Falls" and from The Song of Hiawatha)

Henry Wadsworth Longfellow

"타나탑시스" ("Thanatopsis")

William Cullen Bryant

"늙은 철기병" ("Old Ironsides")

Oliver Wendell Holmes

요약 이 시들의 주제는 모두 뉴 잉글랜드의 생활과 관련 있다. "밀물이 들어오고 썰물이 나간다" 에서 시인 롱펠로는 되풀이되는 밀물과 썰물을 삶과 죽음의 순환에 비유하고 있으며 "하이어워서의 노래" 의 처음 구절은 황량한 시골 경치를 그리고 있다. "타나탑시스" 에서 시인 브라이언트는 육지와 바다라는 자연의 이미지를 통해 죽음이라는 주제를 이야기하며 "늙은 철기병" 에서 홈스는 배 한 척의 역사를 칭송하고 있다.

The Minister's Black Veil

Nathaniel Hawthorne

Summary The parson, Mr. Hooper, arrives at church wearing a black veil over his face. He wears the veil without explanation through his sermon, through the following sermon, and then through a funeral and a wedding. The congregation whispers among themselves. They fear the veil. Only Mr. Hooper's fiancée has the courage to ask him why he wears the veil. She does not understand the answer and leaves him. Mr. Hooper wears the veil for the rest of his life. In fact, he offers no other explanation for it until his death.

El velo negro del ministro

Nathaniel Hawthorne

Resumen El reverendo Hooper llega a la iglesia con un velo negro sobre la cara. Usa el velo sin ninguna explicación durante todo su sermón, y en el próximo, y luego en un funeral y en una boda. Los miembros de la congregación cuchichean entre ellos. Le temen al velo. Solamente la prometida del Sr. Hooper tiene el valor de preguntarle por qué usa ese velo. Ella no comprende la respuesta y lo abandona. El Sr. Hooper usa el velo por el resto de su vida. Y sólo explicará cuál es motivo el día de su muerte.

Vwal nwa minis la

Nathaniel Hawthorne

Rezime Minis la, mesye Hooper, rive nan legliz la avèk yon vwal nwa sou figi l. Li mete vwal la pandan tout sèmon li an, pandan pwochen sèmon an, epi pandan yon fineray ak yon maryaj, san l pa bay ankenn eksplikasyon. Kongregasyon an ap chichote pami yo menm. Yo pè vwal la. Se sèl fiyanse mesye Hooper ki gen kouraj pou l mande l poukisa li mete vwal la. Li pa konprann repons li bay la epi li kite misye. Mesye Hooper kite vwal la sou figi l pandan tout rès vi l. Anfèt, li pa bay ankenn eksplikasyon pou vwal la jiskaske l mouri.

Ang Itim na Belo ng Minístro

Nathaniel Hawthorne

Buod Ang pastor na si Gg. Hooper ay dumating sa simbahan nang may suót na itim na belong nagtatakip sa kanyang mukha. Suot niya ang belo sa kanyang buong sermon, sa sumunod na sermon, at pagkatapos noon, sa isang libing at isang kasalan, nang walang pagpapaliwanag. Ang mga nasa simbahan ay nagbulungan. Kinatakutan nila ang belo. Ang nobya lamang ni Gg. Hooper ang may lakas-loob na magtanong sa kanya kung bakit niya suót ang belo. Hindi niya naintindihan ang sagot, at kanyang iniwanan ito. Buong buhay na suót ni Gg. Hooper ang belo. Sa katunayan, hindi niya ipinaliwanag ito hanggang sa kanyang kamatayan.

Tus Txiv Plig Daim Ntaub Dub

Nathaniel Hawthorne

Lub Ntsiab Tus txiv plig, Mr. Hooper, hnav ib daim ntaub dub npog nws ntsej muag tuaj txog tom lub tsev teev ntuj. Thoob nws qhov sermon los nws yeej tsis qhia tias vim li cas nws thiaj hnav daim ntaub dub no, thiab nws hnav li no rau ib lub ntees thiab rau ib rooj tshoob tib si. Cov neeg hais lus ntxhi cuag tsi uake. Lawv/ ntshai daim ntaub. Tsuas yog Mr. Hooper's tus hluas nkauj qhaib tib leeg thiaj li tsis ntshai los nug nws tias vim li cas nws hnav daim ntaub dub. Tus hluas nkauj qhaib ntawd tsis to taub nqe lus teb thiab txiav txim tsis sib qhaib lawm. Mr. Hooper hnav daim ntaub ntawd mus tas nws lub neej. Qhov tseeb, nws tsuas qhia tias yog vim li cas thaum uas nws tag sim neej kiag lawm xwb.

《牧師的黑色面紗》 (The Minister's Black Veil)

Nathaniel Hawthorne

摘要 教區牧師胡伯先生來到教堂時臉上戴了層黑色面紗。他戴著面紗進行講道、下一場講道、以及之後的喪禮及婚禮，並且對於戴面紗的原因未做任何解釋。教堂裡的人群彼此間竊竊私語。他們很害怕這層面紗。只有胡伯先生的未婚妻敢鼓起勇氣問他戴面紗的原因。她不能理解牧師的回答，於是離開了他。結果胡伯先生終其一生都戴著這個面紗。事實上，他直到死前都未曾再對此提出過任何解釋。

Chiếc Mạng Che Mặt Màu Đen Của Vị Mục Sư

Nathaniel Hawthorne

Tóm Tắt Ông Hooper, một vị mục sư, đến nhà thờ và đội một chiếc mạng che mặt màu đen. Ông đeo chiếc mạng đó hết bài thuyết giáo của mình, hết bài thuyết giáo tiếp theo, rồi hết một đám ma và một đám cưới mà không hề giải thích gì. Giáo đoàn thì thầm với nhau. Họ sợ chiếc mạng. Chỉ có vị hôn thê của Ông Hooper đủ can đảm để hỏi ông tại sao ông lại đeo chiếc mạng đó. Cô không hiểu câu trả lời và bỏ đi. Ông Hooper đeo chiếc mạng suốt phần đời còn lại của mình và không hề đưa ra lời giải thích nào khác cho mãi đến khi ông qua đời.

검은 베일을 쓴 목사 (The Minister's Black Veil)

Nathaniel Hawthorne

요약 후퍼 목사는 얼굴에 검은 베일을 쓰고 교회에 나타난다. 목사는 베일에 대한 아무런 설명 없이, 설교를 하는 동안에도 내내 베일을 벗지 않았으며 다음 설교 때도 결혼식과 장례식 때도 내내 베일을 쓰고 있다. 신도들은 수근대기 시작하며 무서워한다. 오직 목사의 약혼녀가 용기를 내어 그 이유를 물어 보지만 목사의 답변을 이해하지 못한 그녀는 그를 떠난다. 후퍼 목사는 이후 남은 일생을 베일을 쓴 채 살아가며 죽는 날까지도 베일을 쓴 이유를 설명하지 않는다.

The Fall of the House of Usher

Edgar Allan Poe

Summary Roderick Usher has asked the narrator to stay with him while he is ill. The narrator answers his old friend's request and travels to Usher's gloomy mansion. There, he learns that Usher is not well physically or mentally. The narrator also finds out that Usher's twin sister, Madeline, is ill. One evening, Usher tells the narrator that his sister has died. Usher and the narrator take her coffin to a vault within the mansion. After they seal her inside, strange things begin to happen.

La caída de la casa Usher

Edgar Allan Poe

Resumen Roderick Usher le ha pedido al narrador que se quede con él mientras está enfermo. El narrador acepta acompañar a su viejo amigo y viaja hacia la triste mansión Usher. Allí se da cuenta de que Usher no está física ni mentalmente sano. El narrador también descubre que Madeline, la hermana melliza de Usher, está enferma. Una tarde, Usher le cuenta al narrador que su hermana ha muerto. Usher y el narrador llevan el ataúd hasta una bóveda dentro de la mansión. Después de que sellan la bóveda, comienzan a suceder cosas extrañas.

Chit kay Usher a

Edgar Allan Poe

Rezime Roderick Usher te mande naratè a pou l rete avèk li pandan l malad la. Naratè a reponn a demann zanmi long dat li a epi li vwayaje al nan chato sonb Usher a. Pandan l la, li aprann Usher pa byen ni fizikman ni mantalman. Epitou naratè a aprann sè jimèl Usher a, Madeline, malad. Yon jou swa, Ushwe di naratè a konsa sè l la te mouri. Usher ak naratè a pran sèkèy sè a epi yo mete l nan yon kòf nan chato a. Aprè yo fin fèmen l andedan kòf la, kèk bagay etranj kòmanse rive.

Ang Pagbagsák ng Tahanan ng Usher

Edgar Allan Poe

Buod Nakiusap si Roderick Usher sa nagsasalaysay na samahan siya habang siya ay may sakít. Pumayag ang nagsasalaysay sa hiling ng kanyang matagal nang kaibigan, at siya'y nagpunta sa malamlam na mansiyón ni Usher. Doon ay nalaman niya na 'di mahusay ang kalagayan ng katawan at isipan ni Usher. Nalaman din ng nagsasalaysay na ang kambal na kapatid na babae ni Usher na si Madeline ay may sakít din. Isang gabí, sinabi ni Usher sa nagsasalaysay na ang kanyang kapatid ay namatáy. Dinalá ni Usher at ng nagsasalaysay ang kanyang kabaong sa isang silid na libingan sa loob ng mansiyón. Pagkatapos nilang ilibing siya doon at sarhán ang libingan, nagsimulang maganáp ang mga kataká-takáng pangyayari.

Kev Xaus Ntawm Lub Ts Usher

Edgar Allan Poe

Lub Ntsiab Roderick Usher tau hais kom tus neeg hauv zaj no nyob nrog nws lub sijhawm uas nws mob. Tus neeg hauv zaj no teb nws tus phooj ywg qhov lus thiab mus rau Usher lub tsev uas tsaus ntuj nti. Nyob rau hauv, nws mam paub tau tias Usher tsis yog puas cev xwb, nws tseem puas hlwb lawm thiab. Tus neeg hauv zaj no ho paub tau ntxiv tias Usher tus muam ntxaib, Madeline, tab tom muaj mob. Muaj ib hmo, Usher qhia tus neeg hauv zaj no tias nws tus muam ntxaib tau tag sim neej lawm. Usher thiab tus neeg hauv zaj no nqa tus muam lub hleb mus rau hauv ib lub chav hauv lub tsev vaj loog loj. Tom qab nkawd kaw nws rau hauv lawm, muaj ntau yam txawv txawv pib tshwm sim.

《厄榭府的崩塌》(The Fall of the House of Usher)

Edgar Allan Poe

摘要 羅德瑞克・厄榭要求敘事者在他生病時陪在他身邊。敘事者於是應他老朋友的要求啟程前往厄榭的宅第。他到那裡時才瞭解厄榭在身體或心理方面都有問題。敘事者還發現，厄榭的雙胞胎姊姊 麥德琳也生病了。一天晚上，厄榭告訴敘事者，他的姊姊已經死亡。厄榭和敘事者於是將她的棺木放入宅第內的一處地窖。在他們將她封閉在裡面之後，離奇的事情開始發生。

Sự Sụp Đổ Của Gia Đình Usher

Edgar Allan Poe

Tóm Tắt Roderick Usher yêu cầu người thuật truyện ở với mình khi ông ta ốm. Người thuật truyện đáp lại lời thỉnh cầu của người bạn cũ và đến lâu đài u ám của gia đình Usher. Khi ở đó, ông phát hiện ra rằng Usher không khỏe và tinh thần cũng không được bình thường. Người thuật truyện cũng phát hiện ra rằng người em gái song sinh của Usher là Madeline đang ốm. Một tối nọ, Usher nói với ông rằng em gái mình đã chết. Usher và ông ta mang quan tài của cô ấy xuống hầm ngầm trong tòa lâu đài. Sau khi họ đóng kín hầm lại, những sự việc lạ kỳ bắt đầu xảy ra.

어셔 가의 몰락 (The Fall of the House of Usher)

Edgar Allan Poe

요약 로데릭 어셔는 화자에게 자신의 병이 나을 때까지 같이 있어 주기를 부탁한다. 화자는 옛 친구의 부탁을 들어 주기로 하고 음산한 어셔 가의 집으로 들어가게 된다. 거기서 그는 어셔가 신체적으로뿐만 아니라 정신적으로도 병들어 있음을 알게 된다. 또 어셔에게는 매들린이라는 쌍둥이 여동생이 있으며 그녀 또한 아프다는 것을 알게 된다. 어느 날 저녁 어셔는 화자에게 여동생이 죽었다고 이야기한다. 둘은 여동생의 관을 지하실로 옮기고 그 관을 봉한다. 그런데 그때부터 이상한 일이 벌어지기 시작한다.

The Raven

Edgar Allan Poe

Summary The speaker in this poem sits alone reading at night. A mysterious raven comes knocking at his door. The speaker has been grieving for his lost love, Lenore. He begins to ask the raven questions, but the raven only has one response. Through the man's conversation with the raven, Poe explores a mind falling into madness.

El cuervo

Edgar Allan Poe

Resumen El narrador de este poema se sienta solo a leer a la noche. Un misterioso cuervo comienza a tocar la puerta. El narrador ha estado llorando por la pérdida de su amor, Lenore. Comienza a hacerle preguntas al cuervo, pero el cuervo sólo tiene una respuesta. A través de la conversación del hombre con el cuervo, Poe explora una mente que cae en la locura.

Kòbo a

Edgar Allan Poe

Rezime Oratè a nan powèm sa a chita poukont li pou l li lèswa. Yon kòbo misterye vin frape nan pòt li a. Oratè a te an dèy akoz li pèdi lanmou li, Lenore. Li kòmanse poze kòbo a kèk kesyon, men kòbo a gen sèlman yon repons. Atravè konvèsasyon mesye a genyen avèk kòbo a, Poe eskplore yon sèvo k ap tonbe nan foli.

Ang Uwak

Edgar Allan Poe

Buod Ang nagsasalita sa tulá na ito ay mag-isang nakaupo na nagbabasá sa gabí. Isang mahiwagang uwak ang kumatok sa kanyang pintuan. Tinatangis ng nagsasalita ang pagkawalá ng kanyang pag-ibig na si Lenore. Nagsimula siyang magbigkas ng mga katanungan sa uwak, ngunit iisa lamang ang kasagutan nito. Sa pamamagitan ng pag-uusap ng lalaki at ng uwak, tinatalakay rin ni Poe ang isang isipan na nagiging baliw.

Noog Dub

Edgar Allan Poe

Lub Ntsiab Tus neeg hais lus hauv zaj pajhuam no zaum ib leeg nyeem ntawv thaum tsaus ntuj. Ib tug noog dub cia li los khob nws lub qhov rooj. Tus neeg hais lus no tseem tab tom muaj kev tu siab nco txog nws tus hlub uas ploj mus lawm hu ua Lenore. Nws pib nug ib co lus rau tus noog dub, tiamsis tus noog dub tsuas teb tib lo lus xwb. Thaum saib txog tus txiv neej cov lus tham nrog tus noog dub, Poe xyuas txog txoj kev uas ib tug neeg pib vwm.

《渡鴉》 (The Raven)

Edgar Allan Poe

摘要 這首詩的敘述者在夜裡獨自坐著看書。一隻神秘的渡鴉來敲他的門。敘述者一直以來都在為他失去的愛人 — 莉濃爾哀傷。他開始詢問這隻渡鴉問題，但渡鴉只有一種答案。作者透過這個男人與渡鴉間的對話探討一個陷入瘋狂的心靈。

Con Quạ

Edgar Allan Poe

Tóm Tắt Nhân vật trong bài thơ này ngồi đọc sách một mình trong đêm. Một con quạ bí hiểm đến gõ cửa. Anh ta đang đau lòng trước cái chết của người yêu mình là Lenore. Anh ta bắt đầu hỏi con quạ, nhưng con quạ chỉ có độc một câu trả lời. Qua cuộc đối thoại giữa người đàn ông và con quạ, Poe tìm hiểu một tâm trí đang dần điên loạn.

까마귀 (The Raven)

Edgar Allan Poe

요약 이 시에서 화자는 밤에 독서를 하며 혼자 앉아 있다. 그때 이상한 까마귀 한 마리가 날아와 문을 두드린다. 화자는 사랑하는 여인 리노어가 죽어 슬퍼하고 있었다. 화자는 그 까마귀에게 여러 질문을 던지나 까마귀의 대답은 오직 하나이다. 화자와 까마귀와의 대화를 통해 시인은 서서히 미쳐 가는 정신세계를 그리고 있다.

from Moby-Dick

Herman Melville

Summary Captain Ahab has led the crew of the Pequot on a whale hunt. In the first excerpt from Moby-Dick, Ahab explains that they are not hunting for business. Instead, Ahab is looking for revenge. He wants to hunt and kill the great white whale called Moby-Dick. He blames the whale for the loss of his leg. The second excerpt is the final chapter. Here, the narrator tells what happens when Ahab and his crew finally catch up with the whale.

de Moby-Dick

Herman Melville

Resumen El capitán Ahab guía a la tripulación del barco ballenero Pequod en una caza de ballenas. En el primer extracto de Moby-Dick, Ahab explica que no cazan para hacer negocios. En lugar de eso, Ahab busca venganza. Quiere cazar y matar a la gran ballena blanca llamada Moby-Dick. Culpa a la ballena por la pérdida de su pierna. El segundo extracto presenta el capítulo final. Allí el narrador cuenta lo que sucede cuando Ahab y su tripulación finalmente atrapan a la ballena.

yon ekstrè nan Moby-Dick

Herman Melville

Rezime Kaptenn Ahab te alatèt manm ekipaj Pequot la nan yon lachas dèyè balèn. Nan premye ekstrè Moby-Dick la, Ahab eksplike se pa pou biznis y ap fè lachas la. Okontrè, se revanj Ahab ap chèche. Li vle chase epi touye gwo balèn blan an ki rele Moby-Dick. Li blame balèn la paske l te pèdi janm li. Dezyèm ekstrè a se chapit final la. Nan ekstrè sa a naratè a rakonte sa k rive lè Ahab ak manm ekipaj li a finalman ratrape balèn lan.

mula sa Moby-Dick

Herman Melville

Buod Dinalá ni Kapitan Ahab ang mga manggagawa ng barkong Pequot para manghuli ng balyena. Sa unang bahagi na kinuha mula sa Moby-Dick, ipinaliwanag ni Ahab na hindi sila nanghuhuli para magbenta. Imbes na ito, ang hinahanap ni Ahab ay ang paghihigantí. Ibig niyang hulihin at patayín ang malaking putíng balyena na tinatawag na Moby-Dick. Ibinibintang niya sa balyena ang pagkawalá ng kanyang binti. Ang ikalawang bahagi ay ang hulíng kabanata. Dito'y isinasalaysay ng manunulát kung ano ang nangyari noong maabutan ni Ahab at ng kanyang mga kasamahán ang balyena.

los ntawm zaj Moby-Dick

Herman Melville

Lub Ntsiab Captain Ahab tau coj ib pab neeg Pequot nrog nws mus tua cov ntses nyav. Hauv thawj nqe uas los ntawm zaj Moby-Dick, Ahab piav tias lawv tsis yog nrhiav haujlwm ua. Tiamsis, Ahab tab tom nrhiav kev pauj kua zaub ntsuab. Nws xav mus nrhiav thiab tua tus ntse nyav hu ua Moby-Dick. Nws hais tias yog tim tus ntse nyav es nws thiaj li tu ib sab taw lawm. Nqe thib ob yog nqe kawg. Ntawm zaj no, tus sau qhia txog tias ua li cas rau Ahab thiab nws cov neeg lawm thaum uas lawv mus caum tau tus ntse nyav ntawd.

改編自《莫比迪克》(Moby-Dick)

Herman Melville

摘要 阿哈貝船長帶領印第安皮科特族人進行一場獵鯨的航程。在《莫比迪克》的第一篇節錄中，阿哈貝說明他們並非為了商業利益而進行獵鯨。阿哈貝反而是為了復仇。他希望獵到偉大的白鯨莫比迪克，並殺了它。他歸咎這頭鯨魚使他喪失了一條腿。第二篇節錄則是最後一章。此時敘事者描述阿哈貝及他的船員最後捕捉到這頭鯨魚時所發生的事。

trích từ Moby-Dick

Herman Melville

Tóm Tắt Thuyền trưởng Ahab dẫn đầu thủy thủ đoàn của tàu Pequot đi săn cá voi. Trong đoạn trích đầu tiên từ truyện Moby-Dick, Ahab giải thích rằng họ không đi săn cá voi để kiếm tiền mà là đi trả thù. Anh ta muốn săn và giết con cá voi trắng lớn tên là Moby-Dick. Anh ta cho rằng nó chính là thủ phạm làm mất chân của anh ta. Đoạn trích thứ hai là chương cuối. Trong chương này, người thuật truyện kể lại điều gì xảy ra khi Ahab và các thủy thủ cuối cùng cũng bắt được con cá voi đó.

모비딕 중에서 (Moby-Dick)

Herman Melville

요약 에이하브 선장은 피쿼트 호의 선원을 데리고 고래 사냥을 간다. 모비딕에서 발췌한 첫 부분은 에이하브 선장이 돈을 벌기 위해 고래를 잡으러 가는 것이 아니라 자신의 복수를 위해 고래를 잡으러 간다고 설명하는 내용이다. 그는 자신의 한쪽 다리를 잃게 한 장본인인 모비딕이라 불리는 거대한 흰 고래를 쫓고 있다. 두 번째 부분은 모비딕의 마지막 장으로, 에이하브 선장과 선원이 마침내 모비딕을 따라잡았을 때 벌어진 일을 이야기하고 있다.

from Nature

Ralph Waldo Emerson

Summary In this selection, Emerson writes about the harmony between himself and nature. He believes all living things are connected and reflect each other. Emerson descries how beauty, peace, and spirituality can be found in the natural world.

de Naturaleza

Ralph Waldo Emerson

Resumen En esta selección Emerson escribe sobre la armonía que existe entre él y la naturaleza. Piensa que todas las cosas vivientes están conectadas y se reflejan unas en otras. Emerson describe cómo se puede encontrar la belleza, la paz y la espiritualidad en el mundo natural.

yon ekstrè nan Lanati

Ralph Waldo Emerson

Rezime Nan seleksyon sa a, Emerson ekri konsènan amoni ki egziste ant li menm ak lanati. Li kwè tout bagay vivan konekte epi yo reflete youn lòt. Emerson wè ki jan ou ka jwenn bote, lapè ak espirityalite nan monn natirèl la.

mula sa Kalikasan

Ralph Waldo Emerson

Buod Sa sanaysay na ito, si Emerson ay nagsusulat tungkol sa mabuting pagsasama niya at ng kalikasan. Naniniwala siya na ang lahat ng mga bagay na may buhay ay konektado at nagsasalamin sa isa't-isa. Ipinakikita ni Emerson kung paano ang kagandahan, ang katiwasayan, at ang espiritwal ay maaaring mahanap sa likás na mundo.

los ntawm Ntiaj Teb Sab Nraud

Ralph Waldo Emerson

Lub Ntsiab Hauv zaj no, Emerson sau txog kev thaj yeeb uas muaj ntawm nws tus kheej thiab ntiaj teb sab nraud. Nws ntseeg tau tias txhua yam uas muaj sia nyob hauv ntiaj teb yeej sib txuas thiab sib txheeb. Emerson sau txog txoj kev zoo nkauj, kev thaj yeeb, thiab kev ntseeg fab ntsuj plig uas yuav nrhiav tau nyob rau hauv lub ntiaj teb.

改編自《大自然》(Nature)

Ralph Waldo Emerson

摘要 作者在這篇文選中描述自己與自然間的和諧。他相信所有的生物都相互關聯，並且彼此影響。作者描述如何發現大自然世界中的美麗、和平、與靈性。

trích từ Thiên Nhiên

Ralph Waldo Emerson

Tóm Tắt Trong đoạn trích này, Emerson viết về sự hài hòa giữa bản thân mình và thiên nhiên. Ông tin rằng tất cả các sự vật sống đều gắn kết và phản ảnh lẫn nhau. Emerson mô tả bằng cách nào vẻ đẹp, hòa bình, và sự duy linh có thể được tìm thấy trong thế giới tự nhiên.

자연 중에서 (Nature)

Ralph Waldo Emerson

요약 이 글에서 저자는 자신과 자연의 조화에 대해 쓰고 있다. 그는 모든 살아 있는 것들은 연관성이 있어 서로를 거울처럼 비추어 준다고 믿는다. 그리고 자연 세계에서 발견할 수 있는 아름다움과 평화와 깨끗한 정신을 묘사하고 있다.

from Self-Reliance

Ralph Waldo Emerson

Summary In this excerpt, Emerson speaks to the individual. He urges readers to avoid conforming to the standards of society. Instead, Emerson urges readers to think and act independently.

de Confía en ti mismo

Ralph Waldo Emerson

Resumen En este extracto Emerson le habla al ser individual. Insta a los lectores a que eviten someterse a las normas de la sociedad. En cambio, les aconseja que piensen y actúen de manera independiente.

yon ekstrè nan Endepandans

Ralph Waldo Emerson

Rezime Nan ekstrè sa a', Emerson pale ak endividi a. Li ankouraje lektè yo pou yo evite konfòme yo ak nòm lasosyete. Olye de sa, Emerson ankouraje lektè yo pou yo panse epi aji de fason endepandan.

mula sa Pagtiwala sa Sarili

Ralph Waldo Emerson

Buod Dito sa kapirasong sanaysay na ito, kinakausap ni Emerson ang indibidwál. Hinihimok niya ang mga mambabasá na iwasan ang pagsang-ayon sa mga pamantayan ng lipunan. Sa halip nito, hinihimok ni Emerson ang mga mambabasá na mag-isip at kumilos nang malaya.

from Ntseeg-Tus Kheej

Ralph Waldo Emerson

Lub Ntsiab Hauv nqe ntawm no, Emerson tham rau tus kheej. Nws txhawb kom cov neeg nyeem ntawv no tsis txhob ua raws nkaus li txoj kev uas neeg sawvdaws pheej yuav kom ua xwb. Emerson txhawb kom cov neeg nyeem no txawj xav thiab txawj coj rau nyias tus kheej.

改編自《自力更生》(Self-Reliance)

Ralph Waldo Emerson

摘要 在這篇摘錄的文章中，作者向每個人提出意見，他鼓勵讀者避免遵從社會的成規。作者鼓勵讀者應該獨立地思考與行動。

trích từ Tự Lực

Ralph Waldo Emerson

Tóm Tắt Trong đoạn trích này, Emerson nói về tính cá nhân. Ông kêu gọi độc giả tránh tuân theo những chuẩn mực của xã hội. Thay vì đó, Emerson mong muốn mọi người hãy suy nghĩ và hành động độc lập.

자기신뢰 중에서 (Self-Reliance)

Ralph Waldo Emerson

요약 이 글에서 저자는 개개인에게 이야기한다. 독자들에게 사회적 기준에 순응하지 말고 독자적으로 사고하고 행동하기를 주문한다.

Concord Hymn

Ralph Waldo Emerson

Summary "Concord Hymn" honors the minutemen who fought at Lexington and Concord during the American Revolution. The poem suggests that those who make great sacrifices for others should not be forgotten.

Himno a Concord

Ralph Waldo Emerson

Resumen "Himno a Concord" homenajea a los milicianos conocidos como "minutemen" u "hombres minuto" (hombres siempre listos para actuar de inmediato), que pelearon en Lexington y Concord durante la revolución norteamericana. El poema sugiere que no se debe olvidar a aquéllos que hacen grandes sacrificios por los demás.

Im Konkòd

Ralph Waldo Emerson

Rezime "Im Konkòd" onore sòlda yo ki te konbat nan Leksingtonn ak Konkòd pandan revolisyon ameriken an. Powèm sa a sijere yo pa dwe bliye moun ki fè gwo sakrifis pou lòt moun.

Ang Kantá ng Concord

Ralph Waldo Emerson

Buod Binibigyan-dangál ng "Kantá ng Concord" ang mga "minutemen" na siyang lumaban sa Lexington at Concord noong himagsikan sa Amerika. Iminumungkahi ng tulá na ang mga gumawa ng mga dakilang pagpapapakasakit para sa iba ay dapat 'di makalimutan.

Zaj Nkauj Hawm Txog Concord

Ralph Waldo Emerson

Lub Ntsiab "Zaj Nkauj Hawm Txog Concord" hawm txog cov tub rog minutemen uas tau tua rog rau tom Lexington thiab Concord thaum muaj tsov rog American Revolution. Zaj pajhuam hais tias kom yuav tsum tsis txhob nov qab txog cov neeg uas tau muab lawv txoj sia pauv ntau yam rau neeg sawvdaws.

《康科德之歌》(Concord Hymn)

Ralph Waldo Emerson

摘要 本書表揚在美國革命期間於列辛頓及康科德地區奮戰的民兵。這首詩認為這些為其他人做出極大犧牲的人不應被遺忘。

Bài Thánh Ca Concord

Ralph Waldo Emerson

Tóm Tắt "Bài Thánh Ca Concord" thể hiện sự kính trọng đối với những dân quân đã chiến đấu tại Lexington và Concord trong Cuộc Cách Mạng Mỹ. Bài thơ nhắc nhở rằng những ai đã hy sinh vì người khác không nên bị lãng quên.

콩코드 찬가 (Concord Hymn)

Ralph Waldo Emerson

요약 이 글은 미국 독립 혁명 전쟁 당시 렉싱턴과 콩코드에서 전투를 벌였던 미니어트 맨이라는 민병들을 기리기 위해 쓰여졌다. 다른 이들을 위해 자신을 희생한 자들을 절대 잊어서는 안 된다고 저자는 말한다.

from Walden

Henry David Thoreau

Summary For two years, Henry David Thoreau lived alone in a small cabin. He had built the cabin above Walden Pond. Seven years after he left the cabin, he used his journal to write Walden. In these selections, Thoreau shares his Transcendentalist vision. He believes human society has become too complex. He encourages people to simplify their lives, to slow down and do less, and to enjoy more.

de Walden

Henry David Thoreau

Resumen Durante dos años Henry David Thoreau vivió solo en una pequeña cabaña. Había construido la cabaña en lo alto del lago Walden. Siete años después de dejar la cabaña, utilizó su diario para escribir Walden. En estas selecciones Thoreau comparte su visión trascendental. Cree que la sociedad humana se ha vuelto demasiado compleja. Insta a las personas a que simplifiquen sus vidas, se relajen, hagan menos cosas y disfruten más la vida.

yon ekstrè nan Walden

Henry David Thoreau

Rezime Pandan dezan, Henry David Thoreau te abite poukont li nan yon ti kabin. Li te konstwi kabin nan sou tèt etan Walden lan. Sèt ane aprè l fin kite kabin nan, li te itilize jounal li a pou l ekri Walden. Nan seleksyon sa yo, Thoreau pataje vizyon transandansalis li a. Li kwè lasosyete imèn te vin twò konplèks. Li ankouraje moun yo pou yo senplifye lavi yo, pou yo ralanti epi fè mwens aktivite, epi pou yo anmize yo plis.

mula sa Walden

Henry David Thoreau

Buod Dalawang taóng tumirá si Henry David Thoreau nang mag-isa sa isang kubo o maliit na bahay. Kanyang itinayo ang kubo sa may Lawa ng Walden. Makalipas ang pitong taón pagkatapos niyang iniwanan ang kubo, ginamit niya ang kanyang talaarawan upang isulat ang Walden. Sa mga seleksiyón na ito, ipinamahagi ni Thoreau ang kanyang Transendentál na pananaw. Naniniwala siya na ang kapisanan ng mga tao ay naging masyado nang komplikado. Inaanyayahan niya ang mga tao na gawing mas simple ang kanilang buhay, na maghinay-hinay, at bawasan ang kanilang mga ginagawa, at dagdagan ang kanilang kasiyahan.

Los ntawm Walden

Henry David Thoreau

Lub Ntsiab Rau ob xyoos, Henry David Thoreau tau nyob ib leeg rau hauv ib lub tsev ntoo me me.. Nws tau mus txua lub tsev ntoo no nyob ntawm ntug pas dej Walden Pond. Xya xyoo tom qab uas nws tau ncaim lus tsev ntoo no lawm, nws siv nws phau ntawv khaws tseg coj los sau tau phau hu ua Walden. Hauv cov zaj lus no, Thoreau qhia txog nws txoj kev pom tshiab hu ua Transcendentalist vision. Nws ntseeg tau tias tib neeg tau rais los ua lub neej uas muaj ntau yam kev nyuaj dhau lawm. Nws txhawb kom neeg sawvdaws ua lawv lub neej kom yooj yim mentsis, kom tsis txhob maj maj thiab txhob ua ntau ntau, thiab kom sawvdaws yuav tsum muaj kev zoo siab rau lawv lub neej tshaj qub.

改編自 《湖濱散記》 (Walden)

Henry David Thoreau

摘要 作者獨自住在一間小屋中長達兩年的時間。他將這座小屋蓋在華爾登湖畔。在他離開這間小屋七年之後，他利用他當時的日記寫下這本《湖濱散記》。在這些文選中，作者透露自己的先驗論者的觀點。他相信人類社會已經變得過於複雜。他鼓勵人們簡化自己的生活，放慢速度並減少工作，而且多享受大自然。

trích từ Walden

Henry David Thoreau

Tóm Tắt Henry David Thoreau sống một mình trong một nhà gỗ nhỏ trong hai năm. Ông xây căn nhà này phía trên Ao Walden. Bảy năm sau khi dời căn nhà đó, ông sử dụng nhật ký của mình để viết Walden. Trong các đoạn trích này, Thoreau chia sẻ quan điểm của mình theo Thuyết Tiên Nghiệm. Ông tin rằng xã hội loài người đã trở nên quá phức tạp. Ông khuyến khích mọi người đơn giản hóa cuộc sống, sống bớt gấp gáp, làm ít hơn và tận hưởng cuộc sống nhiều hơn.

월든 중에서 (Walden)

Henry David Thoreau

요약 저자는 월든 호숫가에 작은 오두막을 짓고 거기서 이년 동안 홀로 생활했다. 그리고 오두막을 떠난 지 칠년 만에 거기서 쓴 일기를 토대로 이 책을 쓰게 된다. 이 글에서 저자는 그의 초월주의적 사상을 이야기한다. 저자는 사람들이 살고 있는 이 사회가 너무 복잡해지고 있다고 여긴다. 사람들은 생활을 좀 단순화하여 서두르지 말고 덜 일하며 삶을 즐겨야 한다고 촉구한다.

from Civil Disobedience

Henry David Thoreau

Summary In 1846, Henry David Thoreau spent a night in jail. He had refused to pay his taxes because he believed the tax money would support the war against Mexico. He opposed the war. After he was released, he wrote "Civil Disobedience." In this essay. Thoreau argues that people should oppose laws that violate their principles. In this excerpt, he explains his views on government.

de Desobediencia civil

Henry David Thoreau

Resumen En 1846 Henry David Thoreau pasó una noche en prisión. Se negó a pagar sus impuestos porque creía que el dinero de los impuestos se destinaba a apoyar la guerra contra México. Y él estaba en contra de esa guerra. Después de ser liberado, escribió "Desobediencia civil". En este ensayo Thoreau sostiene que las personas deben oponerse a las leyes que violan sus principios. En este extracto presenta sus opiniones acerca del gobierno.

yon ekstrè nan Rezistans pasiv

Henry David Thoreau

Rezime Nan ane 1846, Henry David Thoreau te pase yon nuit nan prizon. Li te refize peye taks paske l te kwè lajan taks la ta va sipòte lagè kont Meksik. Li te kont lagè a. Aprè li te fin libere, li te ekri "Rezistans pasiv." Nan disètasyon sa a, Thoreau fè konnen moun dwe opoze kèk lwa ki vyole prensip yo genyen. Nan ekstrè sa a, li eksplike pwennvi l sou gouvènman.

mula sa Pagsusuwáy na Sibíl

Henry David Thoreau

Buod Noong 1846, si Henry David Thoreau ay nagpalipas ng isang gabí sa loob ng bilangguan. Ayaw niyang magbayad ng buwis sapagkat naniniwala siya na ang perang buwis ay gagamitin sa pagsuporta ng digmáan laban sa Mexico. Siya ay tutol sa digmáang ito. Pagkatapos siyang pakawalán, isinulat niya ang "Pagsusuwáy na Sibíl." Sa sanaysay na ito, ipinagtibay ni Thoreau na dapat lang suwayín ng mga tao ang mga batás na labag sa kanilang mga prinsipyo. Dito sa bahaging ito, kanyang ipinaliwanag ang kanyang pagtingin sa pamahalaan.

Los ntawm zaj Neeg Kev Ua Tsis Raws Tej Cai

Henry David Thoreau

Lub Ntsiab Thaum cov xyoo 1846, Henry David Thoreau tau siv ib hmos nyob hauv nkuaj kaw neeg. Nws tsis kam them nws cov se vim nws ntseeg tau hais tias cov nyiaj them se ntawd yuav yog ib feem mus pab rau kev ua tsov rog nyob Mexico. Nws tsis nyiam txoj kev ua tsov rog. Tom qab nws tau raug tso tawm lawm, nws sau tau zaj hu ua "Neeg Kev Ua Tsis Raws Tej Cai." Hauv zaj sau no, Thoreau hais tias neeg yuav tsum tawm tsam txog tej cai uas ua tsis raws li cov neeg tej kev ntseeg. Hauv nqe no, nws piav nws txoj kev xav txog tsoom fwv.

改編自《不合作主義》(Civil Disobedience)

Henry David Thoreau

摘要 作者梭羅在 1846 年時在牢裡待了一晚。他拒絕繳稅，原因是他認為這些稅金將被用來支持對抗墨西哥的戰爭。他反對這場戰爭。在他被釋放後，他寫下本書。在這篇文章裡，作者主張人民應該反對違反他們的原則的法律。在這篇節錄的內容中，他描述了自己對政府的觀點。

trích từ Bất Phục Tùng Dân Sự

Henry David Thoreau

Tóm Tắt Vào năm 1846, Henry David Thoreau ở tù một đêm. Ông từ chối đóng thuế vì cho rằng tiền thu được từ thuế sẽ được dùng để phục vụ cho cuộc chiến tranh chống lại Mehicô. Ông phản đối chiến tranh. Sau khi được thả, ông đã viết bài "Bất Phục Tùng Dân Sự". Trong tiểu luận này, Thoreau lập luận rằng mọi người nên phản đối các luật vi phạm những nguyên tắc của họ. Trong đoạn trích này, ông giải thích cách nhìn của mình về việc cai trị đất nước.

시민의 불복종 중에서 (Civil Disobedience)

Henry David Thoreau

요약 1846년 저자는 감옥에서 하룻밤을 보내게 된다. 이유는 세금이 멕시코와 벌이는 전쟁에 쓰여지고 있다고 판단하여 세금을 내는 것을 거부했기 때문이다. 그는 전쟁을 반대하고 있다. 그가 감옥에서 풀려난 후 "시민의 불복종"을 썼는데, 이 글에서 저자는 자신의 신조에 어긋나는 법에는 반대해야 한다고 주장한다. 또 정부에 관한 자신의 의견도 피력한다.

Emily Dickinson's Poetry

Summary In "Because I could not stop for Death," the poet imagines that a carriage takes her to her grave after she dies. The poet also writes about her own death in "I heard a fly buzz—when I died." "There's a certain Slant of light" tells about the sad afternoon light of winter. In "My life closed twice before its close," the poet thinks about enduring a terrible event. The poet speaks of the soul's tendency to prefer one person over all others in "The Soul selects her own Society." "The Brain—is wider than the sky—" is a poem that claims that all of nature and even God can be contained in the mind. In "There is a solitude of space," the soul offers more solitude than any earthly place. The poet suggests that things can only be known through their opposites in "Water, is taught by thirst."

La poesía de Emily Dickinson

Resumen En "Porque yo no podía detener la muerte", la poetisa imagina que un carruaje la lleva hasta su tumba después de morir. También escribe acerca de su propia muerte en "Al morir, sentí el zumbido de una mosca". "Hay una cierta luz sesgada" describe la triste luz de las tardes de invierno. En "Dos veces terminó mi vida antes del fin", la poetisa piensa en una terrible situación que deberá soportar. La poetisa habla de la tendencia del alma a preferir a una persona en lugar de otras en "El alma elige su propia compañía". "El cerebro es más grande que el cielo" es un poema que afirma que toda la naturaleza, incluido Dios, puede contenerse en la mente. En "Hay una soledad en el espacio" el alma ofrece más soledad que cualquier lugar terrenal. La poetisa sugiere que las cosas sólo se pueden conocer a través de sus opuestos en "El agua se conoce por la sed".

Pwezi Emily Dickinson

Rezime Nan "Paske m pa t ka kanpe pou lanmò," powèt la imajine se yon kawòs ki mennen l nan tonm li aprè l fin mouri. Powèt la ekri tou konsènan pwòp lanmò li nan "Mwen te tande yon mouch boudonnen—lè m te mouri." "Gen yon sèten liyè limyè" pale konsènan limyè ivè nan yon aprèmidi ki tris. Nan "Lavi m te fèmen de fwa anvan fèmti l," powèt la panse sou fason pou l andire yon evenman tèrib. Powèt la pale konsènan tandans nanm nan genyen pou l prefere yon moun pami tout lòt moun nan "Nanm nan chwazi pwòp sosyete l." "Sèvo a—pi laj pase syèl la—" se yon powèm ki fè konnen sèvo a ka kontni tout lanati e menm Bondye. Nan "Genyen yon solitid espas," nanm nan ofri plis solitid pase nenpòt kote sou latè. Powèt la sijere gen kèk bagay se sèlman atravè sa ki lenvès yo nou ka rive konnen yo nan "Se swaf ki aprann nou dlo."

Ang Panunulá ni Emily Dickinson

Buod Sa "Dahil Hindi Ako Makahintô para sa Kamatayan," ginuguni-guni ng manunulá na siya'y hinatid ng isang karwahe patungo sa kanyang libingan pagkatapos niyang mamatáy. Nagsulat din ang manunulá tungkol sa kanyang kamatayan sa "May narinig akong langaw na humaging—nang ako'y namatáy." Pinag-uusapan ng "May Isang Hilis ng Ilaw" ang malamlam na ilaw ng hapon kapag winter. Sa "Ang Aking Buhay ay Dalawang Beses Nagsará Bago Ito Magsará," nag-isip ang manunulá tungkol sa pagtiis sa isang malubhang pangyayari. Sinasabi ng manunulá ang gawí o ugali ng kaluluwa na magkagustó sa isang tao sa ibabaw ng lahat ng iba sa "Ang Kaluluwa ay Namimili ng Kanyang Sariling Kasamahán." Ang "Ang Utak—ay higit na malawak sa Langit—" ay isang tuláng naghahayag na ang buong kalikasan at pati na rin ang Diyos ay maaaring mailaman sa isipan. Sa "May Pag-iisa sa Kalawakan," ang kaluluwa ay nagdudulot ng higit na pag-iisa kaysa pa sa kahit na anong pook sa daigdig. Iminumungkahi ng manunulá na ang mga bagay ay maaari lamang makilala sa pamamagitan ng kanilang kataló sa "Ang Tubig, ay itinuturo ng Kauhawan."

Emily Dickinson Cov Pajhuam

Lub Ntsiab Hauv "Vim kuv nres tsis tau tos Death," tus sau pajhuam no xav txog lub laub caij uas yuav cab nws mus rau nws lub ntxa tom qab thaum nws tag sim neej lawm. Tus sau pajhuam no ho sau txog nws tus kheej txoj kev tag sim neej nyob rau hauv zaj "kuv ib lub suab buzz—thaum kuv tuag lawm." "Muaj ib lub Teb Ci Ntsa Tom Ib Sab Tuaj" qhia txog ib tav su pom kev nruab hnub nrig tau tu siab heev nyob rau lub caij ntuj no. Hauv "Kuv lub neej xaus ob zaug ua ntej nws xaus lawm tiag," tus sau pajhuam xav txog kev uv ib yam uas tshwm sim phem heev. Tus sau pajhuam tham txog tus ntsuj plig txoj kev nyiam ib tug neeg heev tshaj lwm cov tagnrho lawm nyob rau hauv zaj "Tus Ntsuj Plig Xaiv Cov Neeg Nws Nyiam." "Lub Paj Hlwb – dav tshaj lub ntuj –" yog ib zaj pajhuam uas hais tias tagnrho txhua yam hauv ntiaj teb nrog rau Vajtswv tib si muaj peev xwm coj los khaws cia tau rau hauv yus lub hlwb . Hauv zaj "Muaj Ib Qho Chaw Zoo Rau Yus Nyob Ib Leeg," tus ntsuj plig muaj chaw rau yus nyob xav ib leeg zoo tshaj txhua qhov chaw hauv ntiaj teb li. Tus sau pajhuam hais tias txhua yam yog paub los ntawm yam uas rov uas nyob rau hauv zaj, "Dej, paub vim nqis dej."

《愛蜜莉　狄更生的詩》(Emily Dickinson's Poetry)

摘要 詩人在《因為我無法停下來等死》中想像一輛四輪馬車在她死後將她載運至墓地。詩人也在《我聽到一隻蒼蠅嗡嗡叫 — 當我死去時》中描寫自己的死亡。《光線的某種角度》則描寫冬日裡黯淡午後的光線。詩人在《我的人生在結束之前會關閉兩次》中思考如何忍受一件討厭的事情。《靈魂選擇她自己的社團》中詩人描寫靈魂在一群人中偏好某個人的傾向。《頭腦 — 比天空還寬 —》這首詩主張我們的心靈能包含大自然的萬物、甚至上帝。《空間的隱密》描寫靈魂比任何世俗的地方可提供更多的隱密。《水受到口渴的啟發》這首詩認為萬事萬物只有透過與其相反的事物才能被瞭解。

Thơ của Emily Dickinson

Tóm Tắt Trong bài thơ "Bởi vì tôi không thể dừng chờ Thần Chết", nhà thơ tưởng tượng cảnh một chiếc xe ngựa đưa cô ra mồ sau khi cô chết. Nhà thơ cũng viết về cái chết của chính mình trong bài "Tôi nghe thấy tiếng ruồi vo ve—khi tôi chết." Bài "Có một tia sáng xuyên chéo qua" kể về ánh sáng chiều mùa đông buồn bã. Trong bài "Cuộc đời tôi đã chết hai lần trước khi kết thúc nhà thơ nghĩ đến việc phải chịu đựng một sự kiện khủng khiếp. Trong bài "Tâm hồn chọn cho riêng mình một Người Bạn", nhà thơ nói về bản chất của tâm hồn, thường thích một người hơn tất cả những người khác". "Não—lớn hơn cả bầu trời—" là một bài thơ với ý chủ đạo rằng tất cả tự nhiên và thậm chí cả Chúa Trời đều có thể được chứa đựng trong tâm trí. Trong bài thơ "Góc bình yên", tâm hồn cho ta sự yên bình hơn bất cứ nơi nào trên trái đất. Trong bài thơ "Nước, được biết đến nhờ cơn khát" tác giả cho rằng chúng ta chỉ có thể thực sự hiểu biết một vật khi đã hiểu biết về vật đối lập của nó.

에밀리 디킨슨의 시 (Emily Dickinson's Poetry)

요약 "내가 죽음을 향해 멈출 수 없어서"에서 시인은 자신의 운구를 실은 마차가 무덤으로 가는 것을 상상하고 있으며 "내가 죽었을 때 파리 한 마리가 윙윙대는 소리를 들었다" 에서도 자신의 죽음에 대해 쓰고 있다. "비스듬히 비치는 불빛이 있다" 는 어느 겨울 오후에 본 슬픈 불빛을 묘사하고 있고 "내 인생은 종말을 고하기도 전에 두 번 끝났다" 에서는 끔찍한 일을 견뎌내는 과정을 그리고 있다. "영혼은 자신만의 사회가 있다" 에서는 영혼도 자기가 좋아하는 사람을 고르는 경향이 있다고 이야기한다. "뇌는 하늘보다 넓다" 에서는 자연의 모든 것과 심지어 신도 마음에 담을 수 있다고 말한다. "공간의 고독" 에서는 그 어떤 세속적인 장소보다 영혼이 고독을 더 많이 느끼게 한다고 주장하며 "물, 목마름으로 가르침을 받다" 에서는 사물은 오직 그 반대가 되는 것을 통하여 알 수 있다고 주장한다.

Walt Whitman's Poetry

Summary In the Preface to the 1855 Edition of Leaves of Grass, the speaker says the United States is a great poem. In "Song of Myself," he describes himself. Then, he considers the grass as a symbol of immortality. The speaker leaves a lecture on the stars to view the heavens in "perfect silence" in "When I Heard the Learn'd Astronomer." "By the Bivouac's Fitful Flame" is a poem that considers the army, life, and death. The speaker tells about carpenters, masons, and other workers in "I Hear America Singing." In "A Noiseless Patient Spider," the speaker compares a spider's work to that of a soul trying to become attached to something.

La poesía de Walt Whitman

Resumen En el prólogo de la edición de 1855 de Hojas de hierba, el narrador describe a los Estados Unidos como un gran poema. En "Canción de mí mismo" el poeta se describe. Luego considera a la hierba como un símbolo de la inmortalidad. El narrador presenta un discurso sobre las estrellas para aprender a observar el cielo en un "silencio absoluto" en "Cuando escuché al sabio astrónomo". "Al lado de las llamas intermitentes del campamento" es un poema que habla del ejército, la vida y la muerte. El narrador habla acerca de los carpinteros, albañiles y otros trabajadores en "Oigo cantar a América". En "Una araña paciente y silenciosa", el narrador compara el trabajo de una araña con el de un alma que intenta aferrarse a algo.

Pwezi Walt Whitman lan

Rezime Nan prefas edisyon 1855 Fèy Gazon an, oratè a fè konnen Etazini se yon gran powèm. Nan "Chan tèt mwen," li dekri tèt li. Ansuit, li konsidere gazon kòm yon senbòl imòtalite. Oratè a kite yon lekti sou zetwal yo l al pou wè syèl la nan yon "silans pafè" nan powèm "Lè mwen te tande astwonòm savan an." "Akote flam entèmitan bivwak la" se yon powèm ki konsidere lame, lavi ak lanmò. Oratè a pale konsènan chapant, mason ak lòt travayè nan powèm "Mwen tande Amerik k ap chante." Nan "Yon arenyen pasyan ki pa fè bwi," oratè a konpare travay yon arenyen avèk yon nanm k ap eseye vin atache ak yon bagay.

Ang Tulá ni Walt Whitman

Buod Sa paunang-salitá ng edisyóng 1855 ng Mga Dahon ng Damó, sinabi ng nagsasalita na ang Estados Unidos ay isang dakilang tulá. Sa "Awit Tungkol sa Akin," kanyang inilalarawan ang kanyang sarili. Pagkatapos ay inaayunan niya ang damó bilang isang simbolo ng walang-kamatayan. Nag-iwan ang tagapagsalitá ng isang panayam ukol sa mga bituin upang tanawin ang langit sa "sakdal na katahimikan" sa "Noong Aking Narinig ang Dalubhasang Astronomo." Ang "Sa Tabi ng Sumpunging Ningas ng Bivouac" ay isang tulá na nagsasaalang-alang sa hukbo, buhay, at kamatayan. Pinag-usapan ng nagsasalita ang mga karpintero, mga mason at iba pang mga manggagawa sa "Naririnig Kong Umaawit ang Amerika." Sa "Isang Tahimik at Matiyagang Gagamba," inihahambing ng nagsasalita ang gawain ng isang gagamba sa gawain ng isang kaluluwa na nagsisikap ikabit ang kanyang sarili sa isang bagay.

Walt Whitman Cov Pajhuam

Lub Ntsiab Hauv nqe Lus Pib ntwm phau Leaves of Grass xyoo 1855, tus neeg hais lus ntawd hais tias Tebchaws Meskas yog ib zag pajhuam. Hauv "Zaj Nkauj Txog Kuv Tus Kheej," nws piav txog nws tus kheej. Ces, nws xam hais tias cov nyom zoo tam li kev ua neeg nyob tsis txawj ploj tuag. Tus neeg hais lus tham txog cov hnub qub kom ntsia saum lub ntuj "ntsiag to" hauv zaj "Thaum Kuv Hnov Tus Kws Kawm Txog Hnub Qub." "By the Bivouac's Fitful Flame" yob ib zaj pajhuam uas tham txog cov tub rog, lub neej, thiab kev ploj tuag. Tus neeg hais lus qhia txog cov neeg txua ntoo, tus neeg muab pob zeb los ua tsev nyob, thiab lwm cov neeg ua haujlwm hauv zaj "Kuv Hnov Tebchaws Meskas Hu Nkaj Uake." Hauv "Tus Kab Laug Sab Tos Ntsiag To," tus neeg hais lus muab ib tug poj kab laug sab txoj haujlwm los piv rau ib tug neeg uas xav nyiam ib yam khoom twg.

《沃爾特・惠特曼的詩》 (Walt Whitman's Poetry)

摘要 《草葉集》(Leaves of Grass) 1855 年版的敘述者在前言中說美國是一首偉大的詩。在《我自己的歌》中，他則描述自己。接著他認為草是一種不朽的象徵。為了看到《當我聽到那博學的天文學家》中的《完美的靜默》的天堂，敘述者留下一篇有關星星的訓誡。《比沃艾克的不規則火燄》則是一首思考軍隊、生命、及死亡的詩。《我聽到美國唱歌》的敘述者描述木匠、泥水匠、以及其他工人。《一隻無聲而有耐心的蜘蛛》的敘述者將一隻蜘蛛的工作比喻成一個試圖依附在某種東西上的靈魂。

Thơ của Walt Whitman

Tóm Tắt Trong Lời Tựa cho Ấn Bản Lá Cỏ in năm 1855, nhân vật trong bài nói rằng Hoa Kỳ là một áng thơ tuyệt vời. Trong bài thơ "Hát Về Chính Mình", ông miêu tả chính bản thân. Rồi ông coi cỏ là biểu tượng của sự bất tử. Nhân vật trong bài "Khi Tôi Nghe Tiếng Nhà Thiên Văn Thông Thái" bỏ không nghe một bài giảng về các vì sao để ngắm nhìn bầu trời ban đêm trong "sự tĩnh lặng khôn cùng". "Bên Ngọn Lửa Bập Bùng Ở Trại Quân" là một bài thơ nói về quân đội, cuộc sống và cái chết. Nhân vật trong bài thơ "Tôi Nghe Nước Mỹ Hát" kể về những người thợ mộc, thợ nề và các công nhân khác. Nhân vật trong bài "Một Con Nhện Kiên Nhẫn, Im Lặng" so sánh công việc của một con nhện với công việc của một tâm hồn đang cố gắng gắn kết với cái gì đó.

월트 휘트먼의 시 (Walt Whitman's Poetry)

요약 1855년판 시집 풀잎의서문에서 시인은 미국 그 자체가 위대한 시 한 편이라고 이야기한다. "나 자신의 노래" 에서는 자기 자신에 대해 그리고 있으며 풀잎을 불멸의 상징이라 간주한다. "내가 그 박식한 천문학자의 말을 들었을 때" 에서는 별에 대한 강의를 듣다가 도중에 나와 "아무 말 없이" 하늘을 올려다본다. "야영지 캠프 파이어 옆에서" 는 군대와 죽음과 삶을 생각해 보고 있고 "나는 미국이 노래하는 것을 듣는다" 에서는 목수와 벽돌공 또 그 외 직업에 종사하는 사람들을 이야기하고 있다. "참을성 있는 거미" 에서는 거미줄을 만드는 거미의 작업을 무언가를 탐구하려 하는 영혼의 작업에 비유하고 있다.

An Occurrence at Owl Creek Bridge

Ambrose Bierce

Summary A southern plantation owner is about to be hanged. He stands at the edge of the Owl Creek Bridge. Union soldiers prepare to put him to death for trying to burn down the bridge. A sergeant releases the plank that supports the plantation owner, and the author describes what happens as the man falls.

El puente sobre el Río búho

Ambrose Bierce

Resumen El dueño de una plantación sureña está a punto de ser colgado. Y se coloca en el borde del puente sobre el Río búho. Los soldados de la Unión se preparan para matarlo por haber intentado quemar el puente. Un sargento suelta el tablón donde está parado el dueño de la plantación; el autor describe lo que sucede a medida que el hombre cae.

Yon evenman sou pon Owl Creek la

Ambrose Bierce

Rezime Yo ta pral pandye yon pwopriyetè plantasyon nan lesid. Li kanpe arebò pon Owl Creek la. Sòlda inyon yo ap prepare pou touye misye paske l t ap eseye boule pon an. Yon sèjan lache moso planch ki sipòte pwopriyetè plantasyon an, epi otè a dekri ki sa ki rive pandan misye ap grinngole desann.

Isang Pangyayari sa Tulay ng Owl Creek

Ambrose Bierce

Buod Ang may-ari ng isang hasyenda sa South ay malapit ng bitayin. Tumayo siya sa dulo ng Tulay ng Owl Creek. Inihahanda siyang patayin ng mga sundalo ng Unyón dahil sinubukan niyang sunugin ang tulay. Pinakawalán ng sarhento ang tabla na tinatayuan ng hasendero, at inilarawan ng awtor kung ano ang nangyari nang nahuhulog ang lalaki.

Ib Yam Tshwm Sim Tom Owl Creek Bridge

Ambrose Bierce

Lub Ntsiab Ib tug tswv teb nyob rau sab qab teb tab tom yuav raug dai caj dab. Nws sawv ntawm ntug choj Owl Creek Bridge. Cov tub rog nyob pab pawg Union npaj muab nws tua vim nws sim yuav hlawv tus choj ntawd. Ib tug tub rog tshem daim txiag ntoo uas txheem tus tswv teb ntawd, thiab tus sau piav txog muaj dabtsi tshwm sim thaum tus txiv neej ntawd poob.

《貓頭鷹溪水橋上發生的事》(An Occurrence at Owl Creek Bridge)

Ambrose Bierce

摘要 一位南方農場的主人即將被吊死。他站在貓頭鷹溪水橋的邊緣。聯邦的士兵準備以燒毀橋的方式將他處死。一名士兵將支撐著這名農場主人的木板放開，而作者描述了當這個男人掉下去時所發生的事。

Một Sự Cố Trên Cầu Owl Creek

Ambrose Bierce

Tóm Tắt Một chủ đồn điền ở miền nam nước Mỹ sắp bị treo cổ. Ông ta đứng bên rìa Cầu Owl Creek. Quân Liên Bang Miền Bắc chuẩn bị xử tử ông vì tội định đốt cầu. Một viên trung sĩ rút chiếc ván đỡ ông ta, và tác giả mô tả điều gì xảy ra khi người đàn ông đó ngã.

아울 크리크 다리에서 생긴 일 (An Occurrence at Owl Creek Bridge)

Ambrose Bierce

요약 한 남부 농장 주인이 막 교수형에 처해지려고 한다. 그는 아울 크리크 다리 난간에 서 있다. 그는 이 다리를 불태워 없애려 했다는 이유로 연합군들이 그를 교수형에 처하려 하고 있다. 한 하사관이 그를 지탱해 주던 판자를 내려 놓는다. 저자는 그가 떨어지는 순간 벌어지는 일을 묘사하고 있다.

An Episode of War

Stephen Crane

Summary A soldier fighting in the Civil War prepares the day's portions of coffee for his squad. As he measures the coffee, a bullet strikes him in the arm and changes his life. This story follows the soldier as he confronts the tragedy of war.

Un episodio de guerra

Stephen Crane

Resumen Un soldado de la guerra civil prepara el café del día para su escuadra. Mientras prepara el café, una bala se incrusta en su brazo y le cambia la vida. Esta historia sigue al soldado mientras enfrenta la tragedia de la guerra.

Yon epizòd lagè

Stephen Crane

Rezime Yon sòlda k ap batay nan lagè sivil la prepare pòsyon kafe pou jounen an pou ploton l lan. Pandan l ap mezire kafe a, yon bal frape misye nan bra l epi sa chanje lavi l. Istwa sa a suiv sòlda pandan l ap afwonte trajedi lagè a.

Isang Kabanata ng Digmáan

Stephen Crane

Buod Isang sundalong lumalaban sa Digmáang Sibíl ang naghahanda ng kapé na gagamitin ng kanyang pangkat sa araw na iyon. Habang kanyang sinusukat ang kapé, ang kanyang braso ay natamaan ng isang bala at ito ay nakapagbago ng kanyang buhay. Sinusundan ng kuwentong ito ang sundalo habang kanyang hinaharap ang trahedya ng digmáan.

Ib Zaj Hais Txog Kev Ua Tsov Rog

Stephen Crane

Lub Ntsiab Ib tug tub rog uas mus ua rog rau hauv Tsov Rog Pejxeem tab tom npaj cov khas-fes hnub ntawd rau nws pawg tub rog. Thaum nws tseem tab tom ntsuas cov khas-fes, ib lub mos txwv ya los raug nws sab caj npab thaib ua rau nws lub neej hloov kiag lawm. Zaj dabneeg sau raws tus tub rog lub neej uas muaj kev nyuaj siab los ntawm kev uas tsov rog los.

《戰爭的一件插曲》(An Episode of War)

Stephen Crane

摘要 一名在南北戰爭中作戰的士兵為自己的小隊準備了一天所需的咖啡。當他在量咖啡時，一顆子彈擊中了他的手臂，並改變了他的人生。故事的情節隨著士兵面對戰爭的悲劇展開。

Một Câu Truyện Về Chiến Tranh

Stephen Crane

Tóm Tắt Một người lính đang chiến đấu trong Cuộc Nội Chiến chuẩn bị phần cà phê trong ngày cho đội mình. Trong khi đang đo khẩu phần cà phê, một viên đạn bắn trúng vào tay anh và thay đổi cuộc đời anh. Câu truyện này kể về những gì xảy ra khi người lính đó đối mặt với bi kịch chiến tranh.

전쟁에서 생긴 일 (An Episode of War)

Stephen Crane

요약 남북전쟁 당시 한 군인이 자신의 부대원이 마실 커피를 준비하고 있었다. 커피를 재고 있을 때 총알이 날아와 그의 팔을 관통하고 이 일은 그의 인생을 바꾸어 놓는다. 이 이야기는 전쟁이라는 비극과 만나게 된 한 군인에 대해 쓰고 있다.

Swing Low, Sweet Chariot • Go Down, Moses

Summary In the spiritual "Swing Low, Sweet Chariot," the chorus describes a chariot coming to take the singer home to heaven. The singer also describes crossing the river Jordan with a band of angels. If listeners get to heaven first, they are encouraged to tell everyone that the singer is on the way. In "Go Down, Moses," the singer tells the story of Moses following God's command to free the Israelites from Egypt. Moses tells the Pharaoh to "let my people go!" or God will punish the Egyptians.

Muévete suavemente, dulce carroza • Desciende, Moisés

Resumen En la canción religiosa "Muévete suavemente, dulce carroza", el coro describe una carroza que viene para llevarse al cantante hasta el cielo. El cantante también describe el cruce del río Jordán con un grupo de ángeles. Si los oyentes llegan primero al cielo, se los alienta para que les digan a todos que el cantante está en camino. En "Desciende, Moisés", el cantante cuenta la historia de Moisés, que sigue las órdenes de Dios para liberar a los israelitas de Egipto. Moisés le dice al faraón: "¡libere a mi pueblo!", o Dios castigará a los egipcios.

Balanse ba, charyo dou • Desann, Moyiz

Rezime Nan chan espirityèl "Balanse ba, charyo dou," kè a dekri yon charyo k ap vin pou pran chantè a pou mennen l nan syèl. Chantè a dekri tou lè l travèse larivyè Jouden an avèk yon bann zanj. Si oditè yo rive nan syèl la anvan, yo ankouraje yo pou yo fè tout moun konnen chantè a nan wout. Nan "Desann, Moyiz," chantè a rakonte istwa Moyiz ki te suiv lòd Bondye pou l libere izrayelit yo ann Ejip. Moyiz di Farawon pou l "kite pèp mwen an ale !" oswa Bondye pral pini ejipsyen yo.

Swing Low, Sweet Chariot • Bumabá ka, Moses

Buod Sa espirituwál na awit na "Swing Low, Sweet Chariot," inilalarawan ng koro ang isang karong paratíng para iuwí sa langit ang umaawit. Inilalarawan rin ng umaawit ang pagtawid sa Ilog Jordan kasama ng isang banda ng mga anghel. Kung ang mga nakikiníg ay maunang makarating sa langit, hinihikayat silang sabihin sa lahat na ang umaawit ay paratíng na. Ang "Bumabá ka, Moses" ay kuwento ng kumakanta tungkol sa pagsunód ni Moses sa utos ng Diyos na palayain ang mga taga-Israel mula sa Egypt. Sinabi ni Moses sa "Pharoah" na "palayain mo ang mga tao ko!" o kaya'y parurusahan ng Diyos ang mga taga-Egypt.

Mus Kom Qis, Lub Laub Thauj Neeg • Nqis Mus Sab Hauv, Moses

Lub Ntsiab Hauv zaj "Swing Low, Sweet Chariot," zaj nkauj hais txog ib lub laub caij uas yuav los tos tus kws hu nkauj rov mus tsev rau saum qaum ntuj. Tus hu nkauj ho hais txog kev hla tus dej Jordan nrog ib co ntsuj plig thiab. Yog cov mloog ho mus txog saum ntuj ua ntej lawm, lawv yuav tau qhia rau sawvdaws saud tias tus hu nkauj tab tom los lawm. Hauv "Nqis Mus Sab Hauv, Moses," tus hu nkauj qhia zaj dabneeg txog Moses txoj kev ua raws Vajtswv cov lus kom pab tso tau cov neeg Israelites tawm ntawm Egypt. Moses hais rau tus Pharaoh tias "cia kuv cov neeg mus!" lossis Vajtswv yuav rau txim rau cov Egyptians.

《歡樂的馬車》(Swing Low, Sweet Chariot) •《走下去，摩西》(Go Down, Moses)

摘要 聖歌《歡樂的馬車》的合唱曲描述一輛即將來帶歌手返回天堂的家的馬車。歌手也描述了與一群天使跨過喬丹河的歷程。假如聽眾先一步到達天堂，他們應該告訴每個人這位歌手已經在路上了。歌手在《走下去，摩西》中講述摩西追隨上帝的命令將以色列人從埃及手中解救出來的故事。摩西告訴法老王「讓我的人民離開！」，否則上帝將懲罰埃及人。

Xe Ngựa Yêu, Hãy Bay Thấp Nhé • Hãy Xuống Đi Moses

Tóm Tắt Bài dân ca tôn giáo "Xe Ngựa Yêu, Hãy Bay Thấp Nhé" miêu tả một xe ngựa đến để đưa người hát từ nhà lên thiên đường. Người hát cũng miêu tả cảnh vượt sông Jordan cùng một đoàn thiên thần. Nếu những người nghe đến được thiên đường trước, người hát nhờ họ nói với mọi người rằng mình cũng đang trên đường tới. Bài hát "Hãy Xuống Đi Moses" kể câu chuyện về Moses vâng lệnh Chúa Trời đưa những người Do Thái ra khỏi Ai Cập đến tự do. Moses yêu cầu vị Pharaông Cổ "hãy để người của tôi đi!", nếu không Chúa Trời sẽ trừng phạt những người Ai Cập.

낮게 날아라, 행복의 마차여 (Swing Low, Sweet Chariot) • 모세가 내려오신다 (Go Down, Moses)

요약 흑인 영가인 "낮게 날아라, 행복의 마차여" 에서는 노래하는 이를 천국으로 데려가 줄 마차가 오고 있다. 그 마차를 타고 천사들의 음악대와 함께 요르단 강을 건넌다. 만약 노래를 듣는 이들 가운데 누군가가 먼저 천국에 간다면 노래하는 이도 곧 천국에 도착할 것임을 말해 달라고 한다. "모세가 내려오신다" 는 하나님의 명령을 받들어 이집트의 속박에서 이스라엘 백성을 구하려는 모세를 그리고 있다. 모세는 파라오에게 "내 민족을 가게 해 달라!" 그렇지 않으면 하나님이 이집트를 벌하실 것이라고 이야기한다.

The Gettysburg Address

Abraham Lincoln

Letter to His Son

Robert E. Lee

Summary Lincoln delivers a brief speech to honor those who died at the battle of Gettysburg, Pennsylvania. In "The Gettysburg Address," he calls on people to continue fighting to preserve the Union.

Robert E. Lee writes this "Letter to His Son" shortly before the Civil War starts. Lee discusses the conflict he feels over his belief in the Union and his commitment to his state of Virginia.

El discurso de Gettysburg

Abraham Lincoln

Carta a su hijo

Robert E. Lee

Resumen Lincoln pronuncia un breve discurso en homenaje a los que murieron en la batalla de Gettysburg, en Pensilvania. En "El discurso de Gettysburg", Lincoln pide a sus oyentes que continúen peleando para mantener la Unión.

Robert E. Lee escribe esta "Carta a su hijo" justo antes de que comience la guerra civil. Lee habla sobre la disyuntiva que se le presenta entre su creencia en la Unión y su compromiso con el estado de Virginia.

Diskou Gettysburg la

Abraham Lincoln

Lèt pou pitit gason l

Robert E. Lee

Rezime Lincoln fè yon diskou brèf pou l onore moun ki te mouri nan batay Gettysburg la, nan eta Pennsilvani. Nan "Diskou Gettysburg la," li mande moun yo pou yo kontinye goumen pou yo ka prezève Inyon an.

Robert E. Lee ekri "Lèt pou pitit gason l " sa a toujis anvan lagè sivil la kòmanse. Lee diskite konfli li santi ki genyen sou kwayans li nan Inyon an ak angajman li genyen pou Vijini, eta kote l rete a.

Ang Talumpati sa Gettysburg

Abraham Lincoln

Liham sa Kanyang Anak na Lalaki

Robert E. Lee

Buod Nagbigay si Lincoln ng maikling talumpati upang bigyang-dangál ang mga namatáy sa labanán ng Gettysburg, Pennsylvania. Sa "Ang Talumpati sa Gettysburg," hinihikayat niya ang mga tao na ipagpatuloy ang labanán para panatilihin ang Unyón.

Isinulat ni Robert E. Lee ang "Liham sa Kanyang Anak na Lalaki" na ito bago lamang nagsimula ang Digmáang Sibíl. Tinatalakay ni Lee ang paglalaban-ng-loob na naramdaman niya hinggil sa kanyang paniniwala sa Unyón at sa kanyang pangako sa kanyang home state ng Virginia.

Hais Txog Kev Sib Tua Nyob Gettysburg

Abraham Lincoln

Tsab Ntawv Rau Nws Tus Tub

Robert E. Lee

Lub Ntsiab Lincoln hais mentsis lus los hawm txog cov uas tau tag sim neej rau kev sib tua tom Gettysburg, Pennsylvania. Hauv zaj "Hais Txog Kev Sib Tua Nyob Gettysburg," nws hais kom neeg sawvdaws kav tsij ntau ntxiv los tiv thaiv pawg Union.

Robert E. Lee sau zaj "Tsab Ntawv Rau Nws Tus Tub" tsis ntev ua ntej Tsov Rog Pejxeem tau pib. Lee tham txog txoj kev nyuaj siab uas nws muaj txog pawg Union thiab nws txoj kev cog siab tau rau lub xeev Virginia.

《蓋茨堡演說》(The Gettysburg Address)

Abraham Lincoln

《寫給兒子的一封信》(Letter to His Son)

Robert E. Lee

摘要 林肯發表了一篇簡短的演說表揚那些在賓州蓋茨堡戰役中喪生的人。他在《蓋茨堡演說》中呼籲人民繼續戰鬥，以維護聯邦政府。

《寫給兒子的一封信》的作者則在南北戰爭開打不久寫了這封信。他論述自己對聯邦政府的信念以及保衛自己的家鄉維吉尼亞州的承諾。

Diễn Văn Gettysburg

Abraham Lincoln

Lá Thơ Cho Con Trai

Robert E. Lee

Tóm Tắt Lincoln đọc một bài diễn văn ngắn gọn để vinh danh những người đã hy sinh trong trận đánh ở Gettysburg, Pennsylvania. Trong bài "Diễn Văn Gettysburg", ông kêu gọi mọi người tiếp tục tranh đấu để gìn giữ Liên Bang Hoa Kỳ.

Robert E. Lee viết "Lá Thơ Cho Con Trai" ngay trước khi Cuộc Nội Chiến bùng nổ. Lee nói về những cảm nghĩ của mình về sự mâu thuẫn giữa niềm tin của ông vào Liên Bang Hoa Kỳ và cam kết của ông với quê hương của mình là tiểu bang Virginia.

게티즈버그 연설 (The Gettysburg Address)

Abraham Lincoln

아들에게 보내는 편지 (Letter to His Son)

Robert E. Lee

요약 링컨은 펜실베이니아 주 게티즈버그 전투의 전사자들을 기리기 위해 짤막한 연설을 한다. "게티즈버그 연설"에서 그는 사람들에게 미 합중국을 지키기 위해 계속 싸워줄 것을 당부한다.

로버트 E 리는 남북 전쟁이 발발하기 직전에 "아들에게 보내는 편지"를 쓴다. 미 합중국에 대한 신념과 자신의 고향인 버지니아 주에 대한 의무 사이에 겪는 갈등을 이야기하고 있다.

An Account of an Experience With Discrimination

Sojourner Truth

Summaries In "An Account of an Experience With Discrimination," Sojourner Truth tells about the discrimination she experiences six months after the end of the Civil War.

Informe de una experiencia discriminadora

Sojourner Truth

Resumen En "Informe de una experiencia discriminadora" Sojourner Truth cuenta acerca de la discriminación que sufre seis meses después de que termine la guerra civil.

Resi yon eksperyans avèk diskriminasyon

Sojourner Truth

Rezime Nan "Resi yon eksperyans avèk diskriminasyon," Sojourner Truth pale konsènan diskriminasyon li te sibi sis (6) mwa anvan lafen lagè sivil la.

Kuwento Ukol sa Isang Karanasan ng Diskriminasyón

Sojourner Truth

Buod Sa "Kuwento Ukol sa Isang Karanasan ng Diskriminasyón," kinukuwento ni Sojourner Truth ang diskriminasyon na naranasan niya anim na buwan matapos ang Digmáang Sibíl.

Nco Qab Txog Ib Zaug Uas Tau Raug Luag Coj Tsis Ncaj Ncees Rau

Sojourner Truth

Lub Ntsiab Hauv zaj "Nco Qab Txog Ib Zaug Uas Tau Raug Luag Coj Tsis Ncaj Ncees Rau," Sojourner Truth qhia txog ib zaug uas nws rau luag coj tsis ncaj ncees rau thaum uas yog rau lub hlis tom qab tsov rog Civil War tau xaus lawm.

《一次歧視的經驗》(An Account of an Experience With Discrimination)

Sojourner Truth

摘要 作者在《一次歧視的經驗》中描述她在南北戰爭結束後六個月所經歷到的歧視。

Bản Miêu Tả Một Lần Bị Phân Biệt Đối Xử

Sojourner Truth

Tóm Tắt Trong "Bản Miêu Tả Một Lần Bị Phân Biệt Đối Xử" Sojourner Truth kể lại sự phân biệt đối xử mà chính cô trải nghiệm 6 tháng sau khi cuộc Nội Chiến kết thúc.

인종차별 경험에 대한 생각 (An Account of an Experience With Discrimination)

Sojourner Truth

요약 "인종차별 경험에 대한 생각"은 남북전쟁이 끝나고 반년 후 저자가 경험했던 인종차별에 대해 이야기하고 있다.

The Boys' Ambition *from* Life on the Mississippi • The Notorious Jumping Frog of Calaveras County

Mark Twain

Summary In "The Boys' Ambition," a boy dreams of becoming a steamboat captain. This selection comes from the book Life on the Mississippi. In that book Mark Twain shares the thoughts and hopes of a young boy who grows up along the Mississippi River. "The Notorious Jumping Frog of Calaveras County," is a humorous tale about a betting man and his frog.

La ambición de los niños *de* Vida en el Mississippi • La célebre rana saltarina del Condado de Calaveras

Mark Twain

Resumen En "La ambición de los niños", un niño sueña con convertirse en capitán de un barco de vapor. Esta selección ha sido extraída del libro Vida en el Mississippi. En ese libro Mark Twain comparte los pensamientos y expectativas de un joven que crece junto al río Mississippi. "La célebre rana saltarina del Condado de Calaveras" es una divertida leyenda sobre un hombre a quien le gusta apostar y su rana.

Anbisyon tigason yo ki se *yon ekstrè nan* Lavi sou Misisipi a • Krapo notwa k ap sote a nan konte Calaveras

Mark Twain

Rezime Nan "Anbisyon ti gason yo," yon ti gason reve pou l vin kaptenn yon bato a vapè. Seleksyon sa a soti nan liv Lavi sou Misisipi a. Nan liv sa a Mark Twain pataje panse ak espwa yon jèn ti gason ki te grandi bò larivyè Misisipi a. "Krapo notwa k ap sote nan konte Calaveras," se yon istwa komik konsènan yon mesye ki konn fè paryaj ak krapo l la.

Ang Ambisyón ng mga Batang Lalaki *mula sa* Buhay sa Mississippi • Ang Bantog na Lumulundag na Palaká ng Nayong Calaveras

Mark Twain

Buod Sa "Ang Ambisyón ng mga Batang Lalaki," nangangarap ang isang batang lalaki na maging kapitan ng isang "steamboat". Ang sanaysay na ito ay mula sa aklat na Buhay sa Mississippi. Sa aklat na iyon, ipinamamahagi ni Mark Twain ang mga iniisip at inaasahan ng isang batang lalaking lumaki sa may Ilog ng Mississippi. Ang "Ang Bantog na Lumulundag na Palaká ng Nayong Calaveras," ay isang katawá-tawáng kuwento tungkol sa isang lalaking mahilig pumusta at ang kanyang palaká.

Cov Menyuam Tub Txoj Kev Mob Siab *los ntawm* Lub Neej Nyob Ntawm Tus Dej Mississippi • Tus Qav Uas Txawj Dhia Ntawm Thaj Chaw Calaveras County

Mark Twain

Lub Ntsiab Hauv "Cov Menyuam Tub Txoj Kev Mob Siab," ib tug menyuam tub xav kom muaj ib hnub nws tau mus ua tus coj nyob saum ib lub nkoj. Cov nqe lus no yog muab los ntawm phau ntawv Lub Neej Nyob Ntawm Tus Dej Mississippi. Hauv phau ntawv no Mark Twain sau txog nws cov kev xav thiab kev npau suav rau ib tug menyuam tub uas loj hlob ntawm ntug dej Mississippi River. "Tus Qav Uas Txawj Dhia Ntawm Thaj Chaw Calaveras County," yog ib zaj dabneeg txaus luag heev txog ib tug txiv neej thiab nws tus qav.

《男孩的野心》(The Boys' Ambition)，*改編自*《密西西比河上的生活》(Life on the Mississippi) • 《克拉皮拉斯郡惡名昭彰的飛蛙》(The Notorious Jumping Frog of Calaveras County)

Mark Twain

摘要《男孩的野心》描寫一位夢想成為一個汽船船長的男孩。這則文選改編自《密西西比河上的生活》這本書。作者馬克·吐溫在書中分享一個在密西西比河畔成長的小男孩的想法及希望。《克拉皮拉斯郡惡名昭彰的飛蛙》則是一則妙趣橫生的傳說，描述一個乞丐和他的青蛙的故事。

Hoài Bão Của Cậu Bé *trích từ* Cuộc Sống Trên Dòng Sông Mississippi • Con Ếch Nổi Tiếng Nhảy Thi Của Quận Calaveras

Mark Twain

Tóm Tắt Trong truyện "Hoài Bão Của Cậu Bé", một cậu bé mơ trở thành thuyền trưởng một tàu thủy chạy bằng hơi nước. Câu truyện này nằm trong cuốn sách Cuộc Sống Trên Dòng Sông Mississippi. Trong cuốn sách đó, Mark Twain kể về những suy nghĩ và hy vọng của một cậu bé lớn lên bên Dòng Sông Mississippi. "Con Ếch Nổi Tiếng Nhảy Thi Của Quận Calaveras" là một câu truyện hài ước về một người đàn ông chuyên cá cược và con ếch của anh ta.

소년의 야망, 미시시피에서의 생활 중에서 (The Boys' Ambition *from* Life on the Mississippi) • 캘라버라스 카운티의 악명 높은 뜀뛰는 개구리 (The Notorious Jumping Frog of Calaveras County)

Mark Twain

요약 "소년의 야망"에서는 한 소년이 증기선 선장이 되는 것을 꿈꾼다. 이 글은 "미시시피에서의 생활"이란 책에서 발췌하였다. 이 책에서 저자는 미시시피강과 함께 자란 소년의 희망과 생각을 이야기한다. "캘라버라스 카운티의 악명 높은 뜀뛰는 개구리"는 한 도박사와 그의 개구리에 관한 재미있는 이야기이다.

To Build a Fire

Jack London

Summary This story focuses on a man who has been searching for gold in the Yukon, a frozen wilderness in Alaska. The man and his dog are walking toward a camp. The man does not recognize the danger of his journey. He does not realize that the temperature is far too cold for him to be traveling alone. Then he builds his fire in the wrong place. The man's terrible mistakes turn out to be deadly.

Encender una hoguera

Jack London

Resumen Esta historia se centra en un hombre que ha estado buscando oro en Yukon, una región helada de Alaska. El hombre y su perro caminan hacia un campamento. El hombre no reconoce los peligros de este viaje. No comprende que el clima es demasiado frío para viajar solo. Luego enciende una fogata en el lugar equivocado. Los terribles errores del hombre se convierten en una trampa mortal.

Fè yon dife

Jack London

Rezime Istwa sa a fokalize sou yon mesye ki te alarechèch lò nan Yukon lan, yon dezè jele nan Alaska. Mesye a ak chyen li ap mache nan direksyon yon kan. Mesye a pa rekonèt danje ki genyen nan vwayaj li a. Li pa reyalize tanperati a twò frèt pou l vwayaje poukont li. Ansuit li fè yon dife nan move kote a. Erè tèrib mesye a te vin yon erè mòtèl.

Gumawa ng Apoy

Jack London

Buod Ang kuwentong ito ay naka-sentro sa isang lalaking naghahanap ng ginto sa Yukon, isang nagyelong liblib na lugar sa Alaska. Ang lalaki at ang kanyang aso ay naglalakad patungo sa isang kampo. Hindi naisip ng lalaki ang peligro ng kanyang biyahe. Hindi niya naisip na ang temperatura ay labis na malamig para magbiyahe siya nang mag-isa. Gumawa siya ng apoy sa malíng lugar. Ang mga malubhang pagkakamali ng lalaki ay naging nakamamatay.

Rauv Taws

Jack London

Lub Ntsiab Zaj dabneeg no saib txog ib tug txiv neej uas tau xawb nrhiav kub rau hauv Yukon, uas yog ib thaj chaw hav fab hav tsuag nyob rau hauv Alaska. Tus txiv neej thiab nws tus aub tab tom taug kev los rau ib lub chaw so. Tus txiv neej tsis pom tias nws txoj kev mus ntawd phom sij npaum li casNws tsis pom tau tias cov huab cua txias heev dhau lawm rau ib tug neeg mus ncig ib leeg xwb. Ces nws taws tau hluav taws rau ib qho chaw tsis zoo. Tus txiv neej txoj kev ua tsis yog ntawd tshwm sim los ua ib yam tsis zoo kiag li.

《生火》(To Build a Fire)

Jack London

摘要 這則故事主要敘寫一個男人在阿拉斯加結冰的荒野大地 — 幽肯尋找黃金。這個男人和他的狗正走向一處營地。男人並未體認到自己旅程的危險。他不瞭解氣溫實在太低，他不應該單獨外出。接著他又在錯誤的地點生火。這個男人糟糕的錯誤結果造成致命的下場。

Nhóm Lửa

Jack London

Tóm Tắt Câu truyện này tập trung kể về một người đàn ông đi tìm vàng ở Yukon, một vùng hoang sơ giá lạnh ở Alaska. Anh ta và con chó của mình đang đi về phía một cái trại. Người đàn ông này không nhận thấy mối hiểm nguy của chuyến đi này. Anh ta không nhận ra răng nhiệt độ quá lạnh và anh ta không thể đi một mình. Sau đó, anh ta nhóm lửa ở một nơi không thích hợp. Sai lầm đó hóa ra là một sai lầm chết người.

불 지피기 (To Build a Fire)

Jack London

요약 한 남자가 알래스카의 얼어붙은 황무지 유콘에서 금을 찾아 헤매고 있었다. 그와 그의 개는 야영지를 찾아 걷고 있었다. 그러나 그는 이 여정이 위험하며 혼자서 여행을 지속하기엔 날씨가 너무 춥다는 사실조차 깨닫지 못한다. 그리고 잘못된 장소에서 불을 지피게 되고 이 끔찍한 실수가 치명적인 결과를 불러온다.

The Story of an Hour

Kate Chopin

Summary Mrs. Mallard has just learned that her husband has died in a train accident. She goes to her room, sits in a comfortable armchair, and looks out her window. She feels something she does not understand. She cries for her lost husband but she feels something else she has never felt before—freedom.

La historia de una hora

Kate Chopin

Resumen La Sra. Mallard se acaba de enterar que su marido ha fallecido en un accidente de tren. Se dirige a su dormitorio, se sienta en un cómodo sillón y mira por la ventana. Y siente algo que no comprende de qué se trata. Llora por su marido perdido, pero siente algo más que nunca antes había sentido: libertad.

Istwa yon èdtan

Kate Chopin

Rezime Madan Mallard fèk aprann mari l sot mouri nan yon aksidan tren. Li al nan chanm li, kote li chita nan yon chèz konfòtab, epi l ap gade nan fenèt la. Li santi yon bagay li pa konprann. Li kriye pou mari l li pèdi a men li santi yon lòt bagay li pa t janm te konn santi anvan sa—libète.

Ang Kuwento ng Isang Oras

Kate Chopin

Buod Nalaman ni Gng. Mallard na ang kanyang asawa ay namatáy sa isang aksidente sa tren. Siya ay nagpunta sa kanyang silid, umupo sa isang komportableng silya, at dumungaw sa kanyang bintana. Mayroon siyang naramdaman na 'di niya maintindihan. Iniyakan niya ang kanyang nawaláng asawa ngunit mayroon siyang nadarama na 'di pa niya nadarama kahit kailan—ang kalayaan.

Zaj Dabneeg Txog Ib Teev

Kate Chopin

Lub Ntsiab Mrs. Mallard nyuam qhuav paub tau tias nws tus txiv tau tag sim neej hauv kev tsheb nqaj hlau sib nraus lawmNws mus rau tom nws chav, zaum hauv ib lub rooj zoo zaum, thiab ntsia tawm nws lub qhov rai. Nws hnov ib yam hauv siab uas nws tsis to taub. Nws qhuaj rau nws tus txiv tiamsis nws ho hnov ib yam uas nws yeej tsis tau mloog tau ib zauj kiag li—kev ywj pheej.

《一小時的故事》(The Story of an Hour)

Kate Chopin

摘要 馬勒太太才剛得知她的丈夫在一場火車意外事故中喪失。她走到自己的房間，坐在一個舒適的扶椅上，並望向窗外。她感到某種自己無法理解的感覺。她為自己死去的丈夫哭泣，但她覺得自己感到了其他某種過去不曾感覺到的事物 — 自由。

Câu Truyện Một Giờ

Kate Chopin

Tóm Tắt Bà Mallard vừa nhận được tin chồng mình chết trong một vụ tai nạn tàu hỏa. Bà đi vào phòng mình, ngồi vào chiếc ghế bành thoải mái, và nhìn ra ngoài cửa sổ. Bà có một cảm giác không hiểu nổi. Bà khóc thương cho người chồng đã mất của mình nhưng lại có một cảm giác chưa từng thấy bao giờ—đó chính là cảm giác được tự do.

한 시간의 이야기 (The Story of an Hour)

Kate Chopin

요약 맬라드 부인은 남편이 기차 사고로 죽었다는 소식을 막 접한다. 그리고 자신의 방으로 가서 안락의자에 앉아 창밖을 바라본다. 그런데 무언가 이해할 수 없는 감정을 느끼게 된다. 남편이 죽어 슬피 우는 가운데 그녀는 전에 느껴 보지 못했던 그 어떤 것을 느낀다. 그것은 자유였다.

Douglass • We Wear the Mask

Paul Laurence Dunbar

Summary In "Douglass," Dunbar appeals to Frederick Douglass. Douglass was a nineteenth-century abolitionist known for his strong speeches and writing. He worked to gain equal rights for African Americans. In his sonnet to Douglass, Dunbar writes that the fight for equality is not over.

In "We Wear the Mask," Dunbar describes the daily struggles of African Americans. He suggests that African Americans may appear content, but they are not. Dunbar describes how African Americans hid their despair from the eyes of white America.

Douglass • Usamos la máscara

Paul Laurence Dunbar

Resumen En "Douglass" Dunbar apela a Frederick Douglass. Douglass era un abolicionista del siglo diecinueve, conocido por sus poderosos discursos y artículos. Trabajó para lograr que los afroamericanos alcancen la igualdad de derechos. En su soneto para Douglass, Dunbar escribe que la pelea por la igualdad no ha terminado.

En "Usamos la máscara", Dunbar describe la lucha diaria de los afroamericanos. Insinúa que los afroamericanos pueden parecer estar contentos, pero no lo están. Dunbar describe cómo los afroamericanos esconden su desesperación ante los ojos de la sociedad blanca.

Douglass • Nou mete mask la

Paul Laurence Dunbar

Rezime Nan "Douglass," Dunbar fè apèl a Frederick Douglass. Douglass se te yon abolisyonis nan diznevyèm syèk la ki koni pou diskou ak ekri l yo ki pisan. Li te travay pou l jwenn egalite dwa pou afriken amériken yo. Nan sonè li te fè pou Douglass la, Dunbar ekri batay pou egalite a poko fini.

Nan "Nou mete mask la," Dunbar dekri lit afriken ameriken yo mennen chak jou. Li sijere afriken ameriken yo ka parèt satisfè, men se pa vre. Dunbar dekri fason afriken ameriken yo te kache dezespwa yo pou je blan Amerik la pa wè.

Douglass • Suót Namin ang Maskara

Paul Laurence Dunbar

Buod Sa "Douglass," si Dunbar ay nakikiusap kay Frederick Douglass. Si Douglass ay isang "abolitionist," o isang tutol sa pang-aalipin, noong ika-labíngsiyam na siglo, na kilalá sa kanyang mga makapangyarihang mga talumpati at kasulatán. Nagsikap siya para makamit ang pantay na mga karapatan para sa mga Aprikano-Amerikano. Sa kanyang "sonnet" o tulá kay Douglass, isinulat ni Dunbar na ang laban para sa pagkakapantay-pantay ay 'di pa tapós.

Sa "Suót Namin ang Maskara," inilalarawan ni Dunbar ang mga pang-araw-araw na paghihirap ng mga Aprikano-Amerikano. Kanyang iminumungkahi na maaaring mukhang kontento ang mga Aprikano-Amerikano, ngunit hindi ito tunay. Inilalarawan ni Dunbar kung paano ikinukublí ng mga Aprikano-Amerikano ang kanilang pagkawaláng-pagasa mula sa mga mata ng mga putíng Amerikano.

Douglass • Peb Looj Ntsej Muag

Paul Laurence Dunbar

Lub Ntsiab Hauv "Douglass," Dunbar tham rau Frederick Douglass. Douglass yog ib tug neeg uas tsis nyiam kev quab yuam lwm tus ua qhev uas sawvdaws paub vim nws cov ntaub ntawv thiab cov lus hais tau muaj zog heev. Nws ua haujlwm kom muaj kev vaj huam sib luag rau cov Meskas Dub. Hauv nws zaj sonnet mus rau Douglass, Dunbar sau tias txoj kev xub kom tau vaj huam sib luag mas yeej tseem tsis tau tiav.

Hauv "Peb Looj Ntsej Muag," Dunbar piav txog Meskas Dub cov kev nyuaj siab uas muaj txhua hnub liNws xav hais tias cov Meskas Dub zoo li lawv yeej zoo siab lawm, tiamsis lawv yeej tsis tau zoo siab li. Dunbar piav txog tias cov Meskas Dub muab lawv txoj kev tag kev cia siab nkaum ntawm cov dawb nyob Tebchaws Meskas lawm xwb.

《道格拉斯》(Douglass)《我們戴著面具》(We Wear the Mask)

Paul Laurence Dunbar

摘要 作者在《道格拉斯》中向佛瑞德瑞克・道格拉斯求助。道格拉斯是一位十九世紀的廢奴主義者，他以具影響力的演說及寫作著稱。他致力於為非洲裔美國人爭取平等的權利。作者在寫給道格拉斯的這首十四行詩中寫道，爭取平等的奮鬥尚未結束。

而在《我們戴著面具》中，作者則描寫非洲裔美國人每天的內心掙扎。他暗示非洲裔美國人可能表面上看來甘於現狀，實則不然。作者描述非洲裔美國人如何隱藏自己的絕望，使得白種美國人看不出來。

Douglass • Chúng Tôi Đeo Mặt Nạ

Paul Laurence Dunbar

Tóm Tắt Trong "Douglass," Dunbar thỉnh cầu Frederick Douglass. Douglass là một người theo chủ nghĩa bãi nô ở thế kỷ 19, nổi tiếng với những bài diễn văn và bài viết hùng hồn. Ông hoạt động để dành quyền bình đẳng cho người Mỹ gốc Phi. Trong bản xônê gửi cho Douglass, Dunbar viết rằng cuộc đấu tranh vì sự bình đẳng chưa kết thúc.

Trong "Chúng Ta Đeo Mặt Nạ", Dunbar mô tả cuộc tranh đấu diễn ra hằng ngày của người Mỹ gốc Phi. Ông cho rằng có thể người Mỹ gốc Phi tỏ ra hài lòng nhưng thực chất không phải vậy. Dunbar miêu tả làm thế nào họ giấu được nỗi tuyệt vọng của mình khỏi ánh mắt của người Mỹ da trắng.

더글라스 (Douglass) • 우리는 가면을 쓴다 (We Wear the Mask)

Paul Laurence Dunbar

요약 "더글라스" 에서 저자는 프레드릭 더글라스에게 호소한다. 더글라스는 19 세기 노예제도 폐지론자로서 강렬한 연설과 작품으로 유명하다. 그는 미국 흑인의 평등권 쟁취를 위해서도 애썼다. 저자는 더글라스에게 바치는 소네트를 통해 평등권 쟁취를 위한 싸움은 아직 끝나지 않았다고 이야기한다.

"우리는 가면을 쓴다" 에서는 흑인들이 일상 생활에서 겪는 좌절을 그리고 있다. 저자는 흑인들이 만족한 것처럼 보이나 실은 그렇지 않다고 말한다. 이 글에서는 흑인들이 백인들이 볼 수 없도록 자신들의 절망을 어떻게 숨기고 있는지 묘사하고 있다.

Luke Havergal • Richard Cory • Lucinda Matlock • Richard Bone

Edgar Lee Masters
Edwin Arlington Robinson

Summaries The two poems by Robinson focus on the pain of loss. In "Luke Havergal," the speaker describes how Luke Havergal is grieving for his beloved. Havergal questions whether he can go on living. In contrast, "Richard Cory" describes a whole town in shock and grief over the suicide of wealthy man.

The two poems by Masters describe characters who have the ability to face life in a changing world. From the grave, both characters speak about their lives. "Lucinda Matlock" died when she was ninety-six after a hard but fulfilling life. She does not listen to the complaints of young people who she thinks do not embrace life. "Richard Bone" tells the story of the man who carves messages on tombstones.

Luke Havergal • Richard Cory • Lucinda Matlock • Richard Bone

Edgar Lee Masters
Edwin Arlington Robinson

Resúmenes Los dos poemas de Robinson se concentran en el dolor que ocasiona una pérdida. En "Luke Havergal" el narrador describe cómo Luke Havergal llora la pérdida de su amada. Havergal se pregunta si podrá continuar viviendo sin ella. Por el contrario, "Richard Cory" describe un pueblo completo conmocionado y dolorido por el suicidio de un hombre rico.

Los dos poemas de Masters describen a personajes que tienen la capacidad de enfrentarse a la vida en un mundo en constante cambio. Desde el sepulcro, ambos personajes hablan sobre sus vidas. "Lucinda Matlock" murió a los noventa y cinco años después de una vida dura pero satisfactoria. No escucha las quejas de los jóvenes, que en su opinión no aprecian la vida. "Richard Bone" cuenta la historia de un hombre que esculpe mensajes en las lápidas.

Luke Havergal • Richard Cory • Lucinda Matlock • Richard Bone

Edgar Lee Masters
Edwin Arlington Robinson

Rezime De powèm Robinson ekri yo fokalize sou doulè lè w pèdi yon moun. Nan "Luke Havergal," oratè a dekri ki jan Luke Havergal an dèy pou yon moun li renmen. Havergal kesyone si wi ou non li ka kontinye viv. An kontras, "Richard Cory" dekri ki jan tout yon vil an chòk epi ki tris akoz yon mesye rich ki touye tèt li.

De powèm sa yo Masters te ekri dekri pèsonaj ki te gen kapasite pou yo fè fas ak lavi nan yon monn an chanjman. Nan tonb yo, toulède pèsonaj yo pale konsènan lavi yo. "Lucinda Matlock" te mouri lè l te gen katreven sis an aprè yon vi ki te difisil men satisfezan. Li pa koute plent jèn moun yo paske l panse yo pa anbrase lavi a. "Richard Bone" rakonte istwa yon mesye ki konn taye kèk mesaj sou tonb yo.

Luke Havergal • Richard Cory • Lucinda Matlock • Richard Bone

Edgar Lee Masters
Edwin Arlington Robinson

Mga Buod Ang dalawang tulá ni Robinson ay nakasentro sa hapdí ng kawalán. Sa "Luke Havergal," inilalarawan ng nagsasalita kung paano nagdadalamhati si Luke Havergal para sa kanyang minamahal. Tinatanong ni Havergal kung kaya pa niyang mabuhay. Kaiba rito ang "Richard Cory" na naglalarawan ng pagkabiglá at dalamhati ng isang buong nayon nang ang isang mayamang lalaki ay nagpakamatáy.

Inilalarawan ng dalawang tulá ni Masters ang mga taong mayroong kakayahang humarap sa buhay sa pabagu-bagong mundo. Mula sa libingan, pinag-uusapan ng mga taong ito ang kanilang mga buhay. Namatáy si "Lucinda Matlock" noong siya ay siyamnapu't-anim na taóng gulang, pagkatapos ng isang mahirap ngunit ganáp na buhay. Siya ay 'di nakikinig sa mga reklamo ng mga kabataang sa wari niya ay hindi yumayakap sa buhay. Ang "Richard Bone" ay nagsasalaysay tungkol sa isang lalaking nag-uukit ng mga mensahe sa mga lápida.

Luke Havergal • Richard Cory • Lucinda Matlock • Richard Bone

Edgar Lee Masters
Edwin Arlington Robinson

Cov ntsiab Ob zaj pajhuam los ntawm Robinson yog saib txog kev mob siab thaum tus kheej tau ploj ib yam lawm. Hauv "Luke Havergal," tus neeg hais lus piav txog tias Luke Havergal tab tom muaj kev tu siab txog nws tus hlub uas tau ploj mus lawm. Havergal nug nws tus kheej tias nws puas yuav ua tau neej nyob ntxiv mus li lawm. Ho zaj txawv hu ua, "Richard Cory" piav txog ib lub zos uas ceeb tag li thaum uas ib tug txiv neej nplua nuj heev tau txov nws tus kheej txoj sia.

Ob zaj pajhuam los ntawm Masters no piav txog cov neeg uas muaj rab peev xwm ua neej tauj ntxiv mus rau ib lub neej uas tau hloov lawm. Ob tug uas tau tag sim neej hauv ob zaj no piav txog nkawd lub neej. "Lucinda Matlock" tau tag sim neej thaum nws muaj cuaj caum rau xyoo tom qab ib lub neej nyuaj tiamsis ho muaj kev sov siab heev. Nws tsis mloog cov hluas tej lus nroo uas nws xav tias tsis muaj kev zoo siab rau lub neej. "Richard Bone" qhia zaj dabneeg txog tus txiv neej uas carve lus rau saum tej daim phiaj pob zeb.

《路克·哈沃葛》(Luke Havergal) 《李查·科瑞》(Richard Cory) 《露辛姐·麥特洛克》(Lucinda Matlock) 《李查·波恩》(Richard Bone)

Edgar Lee Masters
Edwin Arlington Robinson

摘要 這兩首由羅賓森寫的詩主要描述失去的痛苦。《路克·哈沃葛》的敘述者描述路克·哈沃葛如何為自己摯愛的人哀傷。哈沃葛對於自己是否能繼續活下去都心存懷疑。相反地，《李查·科瑞》則描述一個極為震驚的小鎮，鎮上的居民全都為一個有錢人的自殺哀悼。

馬斯特斯寫的兩首詩則描述有能力面對處於變動世界的生活的人物。這兩個人在墳墓中談論自己的人生。《露辛姐·麥特洛克》在渡過一個艱辛但充實的人生後於九十六歲過逝。她不想聽她認為並沒有勇敢面對人生的年輕人的抱怨。《李查·波恩》則講述在墓碑上雕刻文字的人的故事。

Luke Havergal • Richard Cory • Lucinda Matlock • Richard Bone

Edgar Lee Masters
Edwin Arlington Robinson

Tóm Tắt Hai bài thơ của Robinson tập trung nói về nỗi đau của sự mất mát. Nhân vật trong bài "Luke Havergal" miêu tả Luke Havergal đau buồn như thế nào khi mất người yêu. Havergal tự hỏi không biết liệu mình có thể tiếp tục sống hay không. Như một sự tương phản với bài thơ đó, bài "Richard Cory" miêu tả cả một thị trấn bị choáng váng và đau buồn trước vụ tự sát của một người đàn ông giàu có.

Hai bài thơ của Masters kể về các nhân vật có khả năng đối mặt với cuộc sống trong một thế giới đang đổi thay. Từ dưới mồ, cả hai nhân vật nói về cuộc sống của mình. "Lucinda Matlock" chết khi bà 96 tuổi. Bà đã sống một cuộc sống tuy cực nhọc nhưng trọn vẹn. Bà không nghe những lời than phiền của thanh niên. Theo bà, họ không nắm bắt được cuộc sống. "Richard Bone" kể câu chuyện một người đàn ông chuyên khắc bia mộ.

루크 하버갤 (Luke Havergal) • 리차드 코리 (Richard Cory) • 루신다 매트록 (Lucinda Matlock) • 리차드 본 (Richard Bone)

Edgar Lee Masters
Edwin Arlington Robinson

요약 로빈슨의 두 시는 상실감을 노래한다. "루크 하버갤" 에서 루크는 사랑하는 사람을 애도하며 자신이 계속해서 살아야만 하는지 의문을 갖는다. "리차드 코리" 는 한 부자의 자살로 인해 충격과 슬픔에 빠진 마을을 그리고 있다.

매스터스가 쓴 두 시는 변화하는 세상에서 삶과 맞서 싸웠던 인물을 그리고 있다. 이 두 인물은 모두 무덤 속에서 자신들의 삶을 이야기하고 있다. "루신다 매트록" 은 고달프지만 만족스런 삶을 산 후 아흔여섯의 나이에 죽는다. 그녀는 아직 제대로 인생을 살아 보지도 않은 젊은이들의 불평을 듣지 않는다. 리차드 본" 은 묘비에 글을 새겨 넣는 한 남자의 이야기를 하고 있다.

A Wagner Matinée

Willa Cather

Summary Aunt Georgiana was a music teacher who lived in Boston. She met her husband and moved to the Nebraska Territory. She returns to Boston many years later. The narrator meets her at the train station. He remembers his early years with her in Nebraska. He wants to share something special with her, so he takes her to hear a performance of an opera by Wagner. The narrator is surprised by the effect the music has on his aunt.

Una matiné de Wagner

Willa Cather

Resumen La tía Georgiana era una profesora de música que vivía en Boston. Conoció a quien sería su esposo y se mudó al territorio de Nebraska. Y regresa a Boston varios años después. El narrador se encuentra con ella en la estación de trenes. Recuerda su infancia con ella en Nebraska. Desea compartir algo especial con ella, entonces la lleva a escuchar una ópera de Wagner. El narrador está sorprendido por el efecto que causa la música en su tía.

Yon matine avèk Wagner

Willa Cather

Rezime Matant Georgiana se te yon pwofesè mizik ki te abite nan Boston. Se la li te rankontre mari li epi yo te demenaje al nan teritwa Nebraska. Li retounen Boston plizyè ane aprè sa. Naratè a rankontre l nan estasyon tren an. Li sonje ane li te pase ansanm avèk li lontan nan Nebraska. Li vle pataje yon bagay espesyal avèk li, kidonk li mennen l nan yon pèfòmans yon opera Wagner t ap fè. Naratè a sipri akoz efè li wè mizik la genyen sou matant li.

Isang Wagner Matinée

Willa Cather

Buod Si Tiya Georgiana ay isang tagapagturo ng musika na naninirahan sa Boston. Kanyang nakilala ang kanyang naging asawa, at lumipat siya sa Teritoryo ng Nebraska. Bumalik siya sa Boston matapos ang ilang taón. Sinalubong siya ng nagsasalita sa istasyon ng tren. Naalala niya ang kanyang kabataan noong sila ay magkasama sa Nebraska. Nais niyang magkaroon ng magandang panahon kasama ng kanyang tiya, kaya ito'y dinalá niya para makinig sa isang opera ni Wagner. Ang nagsasalita ay nagulat sa naging epekto ng musika sa kanyang tiya.

Ib Zag Yeeb Yam Los Ntawm Wagner

Willa Cather

Lub Ntsiab Phauj Georgiana yog ib tug xib fwb qhia suab nkauj uas nyob hauv Boston. Nws ntsib nws tus txiv thiab tsiv mus nyob rau hauv Nebraska Territory lawm. Ntau xyoo tom qab ces nws rov los nyob hauv Boston. Tus sau tau mus ntsib nws tom chaw tos tsheb nqaj hlau. Nws nco qab txog cov xyoo uas tau nrog tus phauj nyob hauv Nebraska. Nws xav ua ib yam tshwj xeeb nrog nws phauj, yog li no nws thiaj li coj nws tus phauj mus mloog ib zaj yeeb yam hu suab nkauj opera los ntawm Wagner. Tus sau zaj no ceeb tias cov suab nkauj no ua rau nws tus phauj xav ntau yam.

《一場華格納音樂會》(A Wagner Matinée)

Willa Cather

摘要 喬吉安娜嬸嬸是一位住在波士頓的音樂老師。她嫁給她的丈夫後就搬到內布拉斯加地區。她在多年後返回波士頓。敘事者在火車站遇到她。他想起自己小時候在內布拉斯加和她相處的時光。他希望與她共享一些特別的事物,於是帶她去聆聽一場華格納的歌劇表演。敘事者對於這些音樂對他的嬸嬸造成的影響深感訝異。

Buổi Biểu Diễn Nhạc Wagner Ban Chiều

Willa Cather

Tóm Tắt Dì Georgiana là một giáo viên dạy nhạc sống ở Boston. Dì gặp chồng mình và chuyển đến Hạt Nebraska sinh sống. Dì trở về Boston nhiều năm sau đó. Người thuật truyện gặp dì tại nhà ga tàu hỏa. Ông nhớ đến những năm hồi còn bé chơi cùng dì ở Nebraska. Ông muốn chia sẻ điều gì đó đặc biệt với dì, vì vậy ông đưa dì tới nghe một buổi hát opêra của Wagner. Người thuật truyện ngạc nhiên trước tác động của buổi nhạc đó đối với dì.

바그너 음악 공연 (A Wagner Matinée)

Willa Cather

요약 조지아나 아주머니는 음악선생님으로 보스턴에 사시다가 남편을 따라 네브라스카로 이사를 가셨다. 수년이 흐른 뒤 아주머니는 보스턴으로 돌아오시고 화자는 그녀를 기차역에서 만나게 된다. 화자는 당시 네브라스카에 살았던 아주머니 댁에서 유년 시절을 보낸 적이 있다. 아주머니와 함께 그 때의 추억을 이야기할 겸 바그너 오페라 공연장으로 같이 간다. 그런데 화자는 바그너의 음악이 아주머니에게 끼친 영향을 알고는 놀라게 된다.

The Love Song of J. Alfred Prufrock

T. S. Eliot

Summary J. Alfred Prufrock invites someone to go for a walk in a city at evening. The city he describes is gloomy and sad. Then, Prufrock asks some questions about himself: Could he have done more with his life? Can he express love for a woman? Is he able to do anything important? Do the answers to his questions even matter? Prufrock sees himself and others as drowning in a sea of troubles.

La canción de amor de J. Alfred Prufrock

T. S. Eliot

Resumen J. Alfred Prufrock invita a alguien a pasear por una ciudad a la tarde. La ciudad que describe es melancólica y triste. Luego Prufrock se hace algunas preguntas: ¿Podría haber hecho más cosas en su vida? ¿Puede expresarle amor a una mujer? ¿Puede hacer algo importante? ¿Acaso las respuestas a sus preguntas tienen alguna importancia? Prufrock se ve a sí mismo y a los demás como si se ahogaran en un mar de problemas.

Chan lanmou J. Alfred Prufrock la

T. S. Eliot

Rezime J. Alfred Prufrock envite yon moun pou al pwomennen avèk li nan yon vil nan sware. Vil li dekri a se yon vil ki sonb epi ki tris. Ansuit, Prufrock poze kèk kesyon konsènan tèt li : Èske l ta ka fè plis avèk lavi li ? Èske l ka eksprime lanmou pou yon fanm ? Èske l ka fè anyen ki enpòtan ? Èske repons kesyon l yo gen enpòtans ? Prufrock wè ni li menm ni lòt moun ap nwaye nan yon lanmè pwoblèm.

Ang Awit ng Pag-Ibig ni J. Alfred Prufrock

T. S. Eliot

Buod Kinumbida ni J. Alfred Prufrock ang isang tao na maglakád sa siyudad sa gabí. Ang siyudad na inilarawan niya ay madilim at malungkot. Pagkatapos ay tinanong siya ni Prufrock tungkol sa kanyang sarili: Maaari kayang mas marami siyang nagawá sa kanyang buhay? Kaya ba niyang magtapat ng pag-ibig sa isang babae? Kaya ba niyang gumawá ng anumang bagay na mahalaga? May kabuluhan ba ang mga sagot sa mga katanungan niya? Nakita ni Prufrock ang kanyang sarili at ang ibang taong nalulunod sa isang dagat ng kaguluhan.

Zaj Nkauj Sib Hlub Ntawm J. Alfred Prufrock

T. S. Eliot

Lub Ntsiab J. Alfred Prufrock caw ib tug neeg mus nrog nws taug kev ua si ib hmos. Lub nroog uas nws piav txog mas tsaus thiab muaj kev tu siab heev. Ces, Prufrock nug ib co lus txog nws tus kheej: Puas muaj lwm yam uas nws twb yuav tsum ua nrog nws lub neej lawm? Nws puas qhia tau txog nws txoj kev hlub rau ib tug pojniam? Nws puas muaj rab peev xwm ua tau ib yam dabtsi tseem ceeb li? Cov lus teb rau nws cov lus nug puas tseem ceeb li? Prufrock pom zoo tias nws tus kheej thiab lwm cov neeg muaj teeb meem ntau heev.

《艾爾佛瑞德 • 普魯佛洛克的愛之歌》(The Love Song of J. Alfred Prufrock)

T. S. Eliot

摘要 艾爾佛瑞德 • 普魯佛洛克一天晚上邀請某個人在一座城市裡散步。他將這座城市描述成陰沉而悲哀。普魯佛洛克接著問了有關自己的一些問題。他對自己的人生可能多努力些甚麼嗎？他能表達出對某位女性的愛意嗎？他能夠做任何重要的事情嗎？他這些問題的答案重要嗎？普魯佛洛克認為自己和其他人正陷入困境中。

Bản Tình Ca của J. Alfred Prufrock

T. S. Eliot

Tóm Tắt J. Alfred Prufrock mời ai đó đi dạo tối trong một thành phố. Thành phố này dưới ngòi bút của ông thật buồn và ảm đạm. Sau đó, Prufrock tự hỏi mình: Liệu mình đã có thể thực hiện nhiều việc hơn trong cuộc đời này hay không? Mình có thể thể hiện tình yêu với một người phụ nữ? Hoặc làm một việc quan trọng nào đó? Liệu đáp án cho những câu hỏi này có thực sự quan trọng? Prufrock thấy mình và những người khác như đang bị ngập chìm bởi hàng núi vấn đề.

J. 알프레드 프루프록의 사랑 노래 (The Love Song of J. Alfred Prufrock)

T. S. Eliot

요약 J. 알프레드 프루프록은 어느 저녁에 누군가를 초대해 도시 산책을 나간다. 그가 묘사하는 도시는 음산하고 슬프다. 프루프록은 스스로에 관한 몇 가지 질문을 던진다. 이제까지 살아오면서 더 많은 일을 할 수 있지는 않았는가? 한 여인에게 사랑을 말할 수 있는가? 무언가 중요한 일을 할 수 있는가? 이런 질문의 답이 그리 중요한가? 프루프록은 자신과 다른 사람들이 근심의 바다 속에 빠져 허우적거리고 있다고 생각한다.

The Imagist Poets

Summaries In the essay "A Few Don'ts by an Imagiste," Ezra Pound talk about the rules for writing Imagist poetry. He says it is important to use few words and to make sure they are strong and specific.

In "In a Station of the Metro," the speaker compares faces in crowded subway station to flower petals on a tree branch.

In "The Red Wheelbarrow," the speaker describes a wheelbarrow and some chickens.

In "The Great Figure," the speaker describes a moving fire truck.

"This Is Just to Say" is in the style of a personal note. The speaker is sorry for eating plums someone left in the refrigerator.

In "Pear Tree," the speaker describes a tree in bloom.

In "Heat," the speaker talks to the wind. The speaker asks the wind to attack and break up the extreme heat.

Los poetas imaginistas

Resúmenes En el ensayo "Lo que no se debe hacer según un imaginista", Ezra Pound habla acerca de las reglas para escribir poesía imaginista. Dice que es importante utilizar pocas palabras y asegurarse de que sean poderosas y específicas.

En "En una estación del metro", el narrador compara los rostros de las personas en la concurrida estación de metro con los pétalos de las flores en la rama de un árbol.

En "La carretilla roja" el narrador describe una carretilla y unas gallinas.

En "La gran figura" el narrador describe un camión de bomberos en movimiento.

El poema "Esto es sólo para decir" está escrito como si fuese una carta personal. El narrador se arrepiente de haberse comido las ciruelas que alguien dejó en el refrigerador.

En "El peral" el narrador describe un árbol en flor.

En "El calor" el narrador habla acerca del viento. El narrador le pide al viento que ataque y destroce el calor extremo.

Powèt imajis yo

Rezime Nan disètasyon "Kèk bagay yon imajis entèdi," Ezra Pound pale konsènan kèk règ pou ekri pwezi imajis. Li fè konnen li enpòtan pou itilize mwens mo epi pou asire mo yo fò epi yo presi.

Nan "Nan yon estasyon metwo," oratè a konpare figi moun nan yon estasyon tren ki ankonbre ak petal flè sou yon branch pyebwa.

Nan "Bourèt wouj la," oratè a dekri yon bourèt ak kèk poul.

Nan "Gran senbòl la," oratè a dekri yon kamyon ponpye k ap deplase.

"Se senpleman pou m di" se nan estil yon nòt pèsonèl. Oratè a dezole paske l te manje kèk prin yon moun te kite nan frijidè a.

Nan "Pye pwar," oratè a dekri yon pyebwa ki an flè.

Nan "Chalè," oratè a ap pale ak van an. Oratè a mande van an pou l atake epi pou l entèwonp chalè ekstrèm lan.

Ang mga Manunuláng "Imagist"

Mga Buod Sa sanaysay na "Kaunting mga Huwag ng isang Imagiste," tinatalakay ni Ezra Pound ang mga alituntunin para sa pagsusulat ng mga tuláng "imagist" o tagapaglarawan. Sinasabi niya na mahalagang gumamit ng kaunting salitá at siguraduhing ito ay malakas at tiyak.

Sa "Sa Istasyon ng Metro," ang mga mukha sa isang masikíp na istasyon ng subway ay inihahambing ng nagsasalita sa mga talulot ng bulaklak sa sanga ng isang puno.

Sa "Ang Pulang Karetilya," inilalarawan ng nagsasalita ang isang "wheelbarrow" o karetilya, at ang ilang mga manok.

Sa "Ang Malaking Pigura," inilalarawan ng nagsasalita ang isang tumatakbong trak ng bombero.

Ang "Ito Ay Para Sabihin Lamang" ay nasa istilo ng isang liham na personál. Ang tagapagsalitá ay nagsisisi na kinain niya ang mga "plum" na iniwanan ng iba sa refrigerator.

 Sa "Puno ng Peras," inilalarawan ng nagsasalita ang isang punong namumulaklak.

Sa "Init," ang nagsasalitá ay nakikipag-usap sa hangin. Hinihiling ng nagsasalitá sa hangin na salakayin at sirain nito ang labis na init.

Cov Neeg Sau Pajhuam Imagist

Cov ntsiab Hauv zaj sau "A Few Don'ts by an Imagiste," Ezra Pound tham txog cov cai rau kev sau hom pajhuam Imagist. Nws hais tias tseem ceeb heev uas yus yuav tsum siv tsawg los lus xwb thiab xaiv cov lus kom muaj zog thiab raug lub ntsiab.

Hauv "In a Station of the Metro," tus neeg hais lus muab cov ntsej muag uas pom ntawm ib pab neeg coob coob hauv lub chaw tos npav nqaj hlau coj los piv rau cov nplaim paj uas nyob rau ib ceg ntoo.

Hauv zaj "The Red Wheelbarrow," tus neeg hais lus qhia txog ib lub laub thiab ib co qaib.

Hauv "The Great Figure," tus neeg hais lus piav txog ib lub tsheb loj tua hluav taws uas tab tom khiav hauv kev luv.

This Is Just to Say" yog ib zaj uas sau raws li ib daim ntawv. Tus neeg hais lus thov txim vim tau noj ib co txiv ntoo uas ib tug neeg tau tseg rau hauv lub taub txias.

Hauv "Pear Tree," tus neeg hais lus piav txog ib tsob ntoo uas tab tom tawg paj.

Hauv "Heat," tus neeg hais lus tham nrog cov cua. Tus neeg hais lus nug cov cua kom los ntau thiab rhuav cov huab cua uas kub dhau heev lawm.

《意象派詩人》 (The Imagist Poets)

摘要 《一個意象派詩人不能做的幾件事》的作者談論有關寫作意象派詩的規則。他說，重要的是必須使用少數幾個字並確保這些字夠震撼及具體。

《在一個大都會車站中》的敘述者將擁擠的地下鐵車站中的面容比喻成樹枝上的花瓣。

《紅色的手推車》的敘述者描述一輛手推車及幾隻雞。

《偉大的人物》中的敘述者則描述一輛移動中的消防車。

《只是要說》的風格像是一篇私人記事。敘述者對於吃了別人留在冰箱中的梅子感到後悔。

《桃子樹》的敘述者描述一棵花朵盛開的樹。

《熱氣》中的敘述者與風對談。敘述者要求風攻擊及瓦解高溫的熱氣。

Các Nhà Thơ Theo Chủ Nghĩa Hình Tượng

Tóm Tắt Trong tiểu luận "Một Số Điều Cấm Ky Đối Với Các Nhà Thơ Theo Chủ Nghĩa Hình Tượng," Ezra Pound đề cập đến những niêm luật đối với việc sáng tác thơ theo chủ nghĩa hình tượng. Theo ông, quan trọng là sử dụng ít ngôn từ nhưng đảm bảo rằng đó là những ngôn từ cụ thể và gây ấn tượng.

Nhân vật trong bài "Trong Một Nhà Ga Xe Điện Ngầm" ví những gương mặt trong nhà ga xe điện ngầm như những cánh hoa trên cành.

Nhân vật trong bài "Xe Cút Kít Đỏ" miêu tả một chiếc xe cút kít và vài con gà.

Nhân vật trong bài "Vật To Lớn" miêu tả một chiếc xe cứu hỏa đang chạy.

"Chỉ Biết Nói Vậy" được viết dưới dạng ghi chép cá nhân. Nhân vật trong đó thấy có lỗi vì đã ăn những quả mận ai đó để trong tủ lạnh.

Nhân vật trong bài "Cây Lê" miêu tả một cái cây nở hoa.

Nhân vật trong bài "Cái Nóng" nói chuyện với gió. Nhân vật đó yêu cầu gió tấn công và xóa tan cái nóng như thiêu như đốt.

사상주의 시인들 (The Imagist Poets)

요약 "사상주의자가 해서는 안될 것들" 에서 에즈라 파운드는 사상주의 시를 쓰는 데 필요한 규칙을 이야기한다. 단어는 최소한으로 하되 강렬하고 구체적인 단어로 선정해야 한다.

"지하철 역에서" 에서 화자는 붐비는 지하철 역 안에 있는 사람들의 얼굴을 나뭇가지 위의 꽃잎에 비유하고 있다.

"빨간 손수레" 에서 화자는 손수레와 몇 마리의 닭들을 묘사하고 있다.

"커다란 형상" 에서 화자는 움직이는 소방차를 그리고 있다.

"이것은 그냥 말하는 것이다" 는 개인적인 메모의 형식을 취하고 있다. 화자는 누군가가 냉장고에 남긴 자두를 먹어 버린 것이 미안하다.

"배나무" 에서 화자는 꽃이 활짝 핀 배나무를 묘사하고 있다.

"열기" 에서 화자는 바람에게 이야기를 한다. 화자는 바람에게 이 더운 열기를 공격하여 없애주기를 부탁한다.

Winter Dreams

F. Scott Fitzgerald

Summary Dexter Green is the son of a grocer in a small Minnesota town. He loves Judy Jones, the daughter of a wealthy local family. Dexter and Judy meet at a country club when he is fourteen and she is eleven. He is attracted to her and quits his caddying job to avoid the humiliation of carrying her clubs. After college they meet again and begin a serious romance for one summer. Judy, however, does not want a commitment and dates other men. Dexter decides to marry the more sensible Irene Scheerer. On the eve of the engagement, Judy returns. She renews the relationship with Dexter, which causes Dexter to lose Irene. Judy then leaves Dexter once more. Years later, Dexter learns that Judy is now trapped in an unhappy marriage and has lost her beauty.

Sueños de invierno

F. Scott Fitzgerald

Resumen Dexter Green es el hijo de un almacenero que vive en un pequeño pueblo de Minnesota. Está enamorado de Judy Jones, la hija de una adinerada familia del lugar. Dexter y Judy se conocen en un club de campo cuando él tiene catorce años y ella, once. Se siente atraído por ella y renuncia a su trabajo como caddie en el club para no sentirse humillado al tener que llevar sus palos de golf. Después de la universidad, se encuentran otra vez y comienzan formalmente un romance durante un verano. Sin embargo, Judy no quiere compromisos y sale con otros hombres. Dexter decide casarse con Irene Scheerer, una mujer más sensata. Pero justo en la víspera del compromiso, Judy regresa. Y renueva su relación con Dexter, lo que hace que Dexter pierda a Irene. Judy vuelve a abandonar a Dexter. Años más tarde Dexter se entera de que Judy está atrapada en un infeliz matrimonio y que ya no es tan bella como lo era antes.

Rèv ivè

F. Scott Fitzgerald

Rezime Dexter Green se pitit gason yon episye nan yon ti vil nan Minesota. Li renmen Judy Jones, pitit fi yon fanmi rich nan zòn nan. Dexter ak Judy rankontre nan yon klib lwazi lè Dexter te gen katòz an epi Judy te gen onz an. Judy te atire misye epi li kite djòb li te genyen kòm transpòtè klib gòlf pou l ka evite imilyasyon li ta ka santi pou l pote klib gòlf Judy. Aprè yo te vin fè klas inivèsite yo, yo te vin rankontre ankò epi yo te kòmanse yon womans serye pandan yon ete. Sepandan, Judy pa vle yon angajman epi li kòmanse sòti ak lòt gason. Dexter deside marye avèk Irene Scheerer, yon fi ki te pi rezonab. Nan lavèy angajman an, Judy retounen. Li renouvle relasyon l avèk Dexter, sa ki vin lakoz Dexter pèdi Irene. Aprè sa Judy kite Dexter ankò. Dèzane aprè, Dexter aprann Judy pyeje nan yon maryaj malere epi li te pèdi bote l.

Mga Panaginip ng Winter

F. Scott Fitzgerald

Buod Si Dexter Green ay anak ng isang may-ari ng groseri sa isang maliit na bayan sa Minnesota. Umiibig siya kay Judy Jones, ang anak ng isang mayamang pamilya sa bayan. Sila ay nagkakilala noong si Dexter ay labing-apat na taóng gulang at si Judy ay labing-isa, sa isang "country club". Siya'y naakit sa dalagita, at binitiwan niya ang kanyang trabaho bilang tagakargá ng mga club na gamit sa "golf," dahil ibig niyang iwasan ang kahihiyan ng pagdadalá ng mga club ng dalagita. Pagkatapos ng kolehiyo, sila'y nagkita muli at nagsimula ng isang seryosong pagmamahalan na nagtagal ng isang summer. Gayunman, ayaw ni Judy na mangakong maging tapat, at siya ay lumabas pa rin kasama ng mga ibang lalaki. Nagpasiya si Dexter na pakasalán ang masmatino na si Irene Scheerer. Sa gabí ng kanilang pagkakasunduang magpakasál, si Judy ay bumalik. Kanyang muling binuhay ang relasyon nila ni Dexter, at dahil dito ay nawalá ni Dexter si Irene. Tapos, iniwanan muli ni Judy si Dexter. Makalipas ang mga taón, nalaman ni Dexter na si Judy ay 'di makawalá sa isang hindi maligayang kasal, at lumipas na ang kanyang kagandahan.

Kev Npau Suav Lub Caij Ntuj No

F. Scott Fitzgerald

Lub Ntsiab Dexter Green yog tus tub ntawm ib tug tswv khw nyob rau ib lub zos me hauv Minnesota. Nws hlub Judy Jones, uas yog tus ntxhais ntawm ib tsev neeg muaj nyiaj. Dexter thiab Judy sib ntsib hauv ib lub chaw ua si thaum nws muaj kaum plaub xyoos thiab tus ntxhais muaj kaum ib xyoos. Nws cia li nyiam tus ntxhais thiab thiaj li tawm nws txoj haujlwm nqa pas ntaus pob rau neeg kom tsis txhob txaj muag vim yuav tau nqa tus ntxhais cov pas ntaus pob. Tom qab kawm ntawv qib siab tag ces nkawd rov sib ntsib dua thiab pib muaj kev sib hlub thaum lub caij ntuj so. Tiamsis Judy tsis xav sib hlub tiag nws thiaj li tham lwm cov txiv neej thiab. Dexter txiav txim siab yuav tus ntxhais uas txawj xav mentsis hu ua Irene Scheerer. Nyob rau hmo uas nkawd tab tom yuav sib qhaib, Judy rov qab los. Nws rov los muaj kev hlub nrog Dexter, uas ua rau Dexter plam Irene lawm. Judy rov qab tso Dexter dua ib zaug ntxivNtau xyoo tom qab, Dexter paub tau tias Judy tau poob mus rau ib lub neej nrog luag uas tsis muaj kev zoo siab li thiab nws txoj kev zoo nkauj tau ploj lawm.

《冬天的夢境》 (Winter Dreams)

F. Scott Fitzgerald

摘要 德斯特·葛林是一個明尼蘇達小鎮的食品雜貨商之子。他愛上了茱蒂·瓊斯，她是當地有錢人家的女兒。德斯特和茱蒂在一個鄉村俱樂部中相識，當時他十四歲，而她才十一歲。他被她深深吸引，並辭去自己當球僮的工作，以避免搬運她的球具的羞辱。他們在大學中再度相遇，並開始了一段維持了一個夏天的熱戀。然而，茱蒂卻不希望承諾任何事，而且還與其他男子約會。德斯特於是決定娶更門當戶對的艾琳·席瑞爾。在訂婚前一晚，茱蒂卻回來了。她與德斯特再續前緣，但此舉卻使德斯特失去了艾琳。茱蒂之後又再度離開德斯特。多年後，德斯特得知茱蒂的婚姻並不美滿，而且她也已經失去了自己的美貌。

Những Giấc Mơ Mùa Đông

F. Scott Fitzgerald

Tóm Tắt Dexter Green là con trai một người bán tạp phẩm ở thị trấn nhỏ bé thuộc Minnesota. Cậu yêu Judy Jones, con gái một gia đình giàu có trong thị trấn. Dexter và Judy gặp nhau tại một câu lạc bộ trong thi trấn khi cậu 14 và cô nàng 11 tuổi. Cậu bị cô nàng hút hồn và bỏ ngay việc vác gậy và nhặt bóng ở sân gôn để tránh bị xấu hổ khi phải vác gậy cho cô. Sau khi tốt nghiệp đại học, họ gặp lại nhau và bắt đầu một cuộc tình lãng mạn nghiêm túc trong một mùa hè. Tuy nhiên, Judy không muốn cam kết điều gì và hẹn hò với những người đàn ông khác. Dexter quyết định kết hôn với Irene Scheerer, một cô gái khôn ngoan hơn. Vào đêm đính hôn, Judy quay trở lại. Cô ta nối lại mối quan hệ với Dexter, khiến cho anh ta mất Irene. Sau đó, Judy lại bỏ rơi Dexter một lần nữa. Nhiều năm sau, Dexter biết được rằng Judy không còn xinh đẹp nữa và đang mắc kẹt trong một cuộc hôn nhân không hạnh phúc.

겨울의 꿈 (Winter Dreams)

F. Scott Fitzgerald

요약 덱스터 그린은 미네소타에 있는 한 작은 마을의 상점 주인 아들이다. 그는 그 마을 유지의 딸 주디 존스를 사랑한다. 그들은 덱스터가 열네 살, 주디가 열한 살이었을 때 골프장에서 처음 만난다. 덱스터는 그녀에게 호감을 느끼고 그녀의 골프 클럽 가방을 매고 다니는 것이 창피해 캐디 일을 그만둔다. 대학 졸업 후 그들은 다시 만나게 되고 어느 해 여름 동안 열렬한 로맨스에 빠진다. 그러나 주디는 사랑의 언약은 원하지도 않았고 다른 남자와 데이트를 시작한다. 덱스터는 현명한 아이린 쉬어러와 결혼하기로 결심한다. 약혼식 전날 밤 주디는 다시 돌아오고 덱스터와 관계를 지속하고 싶어한다. 이로 인해 덱스터는 아이린을 잃게 된다. 그러나 주디는 다시 덱스터를 떠난다. 수년 후 덱스터는 주디가 불행한 결혼의 덫에 걸려 있고 미모도 잃었음을 알게 된다.

The Turtle *from* The Grapes of Wrath

John Steinbeck

Summary A turtle crawls over some grass toward a highway. As he moves, some wild oat seeds become attached to the turtle's legs. With great effort, the turtle gets onto the highway. One car nearly hits the turtle. Another vehicle does hit the turtle, and it rolls off the highway onto its shell. After some time, the turtle rolls itself over. As it rolls, the wild oat seeds fall onto the ground. As the turtle moves, it drags dirt over the seeds.

La tortuga *de* Las uvas de la ira

John Steinbeck

Resumen Una tortuga camina sobre el césped en dirección a una carretera. A medida que avanza, algunas semillas de avena silvestre se adhieren a sus patas. Con gran sacrificio, la tortuga logra llegar hasta la carretera. Un automóvil casi la atropella. Luego aparece otro vehículo que sí le pega y la tortuga rueda por la carretera sobre su caparazón. Después de un rato, la tortuga se da vuelta. Mientras voltea, las semillas de avena silvestre caen al suelo. A medida que avanza, arrastra mugre sobre las semillas.

Tòti *ki sot nan* Grap kòlè a

John Steinbeck

Rezime Yon tòti ap rale sou kèk gazon nan direksyon yon otowout. Pandan l ap avanse, kèk grenn avwàn sofaj vin kole nan pye tòti a. Avèk anpil efò, tòti a rive sou otowout la. Yon machin manke frape tòti a. Yon lòt machin frape tòti a epi li woule sot sou bò otowout la sou karapas li. Aprè kèk tan, tòti a woule tèt li pou l kanpe sou pye li. Pandan l ap woule, grenn avwàn sovaj yo tonbe atè a. Pandan tòti a ap deplase, li trenne pousyè sou grenn yo.

Ang Pagóng *mula sa* Ang mga Ubas ng Poot

John Steinbeck

Buod Gumagapang ang isang pagóng sa damó patungo sa lansangan. Habang siya'y kumikilos, may mga butil ng ligáw na "oats" na dumidikit sa mga binti ng pagóng. Nakarating ang pagóng sa highway pagkatapos nito magsikap nang husto. Muntik na mabundól ang pagóng ng isang sasakyan. Ang pagóng ay tunay ngang nabundól ng isa pang sasakyan, at ito ay gumulong nang palayó sa highway, at lumapág ito sa kanyang balatan. Maya-maya pa, ginulong ng pagóng ang kanyang sarili nang pabaliktád. Habang ito ay gumugulong, ang mga ligáw na butil ng "oats" ay nahuhulog sa lupa. Habang kumikilos ang pagóng, kinakaladkad nito ang alikabok sa ibabaw ng mga butil.

Tus Vaub Kib *los ntawm zaj* The Grapes of Wrath

John Steinbeck

Lub Ntsiab Ib tug vaub kib nkag saum cov nyom mus rau ib txoj kev loj. Thaum nws mus, ib co noob qus khuam tau rau ntawm nws ob sab ceg. Vim rau siab heev, tus vaub kib tau mus txog tom kev loj. Ib lub tsheb yuav luag luam tus vaub kib. Lwm lub tsheb ho cia li tsoo tus vaub kib, thiab ua rau nws kiv lees los nres ntxeev tiaj rau nws lub plhaub tawv tawv lawm. Tom qab sijhawm dhau mentsis, tus vaub kib dov tau nws tus kheej rov qab los. Thaum nws dov tau rov los, cov noob qus poob rau hauv av. Thaum tus vaub kib txav, nws ua rau ib co av npog cov noob.

《烏龜》(The Turtle)，改編自 《憤怒的葡萄》(The Grapes of Wrath)

John Steinbeck

摘要 一隻烏龜爬行過某處通往一座高速公路的草地。當他移動時，一些野生燕麥的種子附著在烏龜的腿上。烏龜費盡力氣，終於抵達高速公路。一輛汽車幾乎撞上烏龜。另一輛車則真的撞到了烏龜，而它因此滾出了高速公路，並縮進自己的殼裡。一段時間後，這隻烏龜自己翻身。當它翻身時，野生燕麥的種子就掉在地面上。當烏龜移動時，它耙了一些地上的泥土在種子上。

Con Rùa *trích từ* Chùm Nho Uất Hận

John Steinbeck

Tóm Tắt Một con rùa bò qua một đám cỏ để ra đường quốc lộ. Khi nó di chuyển, vài hạt yến mạch dại mắc vào chân nó. Nó cố gắng hết sức để lên được đường. Một chiếc ô tô suýt đâm vào nó. Một chiếc xe khác đâm vào nó và nó lăn lông lốc xuống lề đường. Khi ngừng lại, nó nằm ngược trên tấm mai của mình. Sau một hồi, con rùa mới lật mình được. Khi nó bị lăn, những hạt yến mạch dại rơi xuống đất. Khi con rùa lại đi được, chân của nó kéo đất lấp đầy các hạt yến mạch.

거북이, 분노의 포도 중에서 (The Turtle *from* The Grapes of Wrath)

John Steinbeck

요약 거북이 한 마리가 풀밭을 지나 고속도로를 향해 기어가고 있다. 움직일 때마다 야생 오트밀 씨앗들이 거북이의 다리에 엉겨 붙는다. 온갖 고난을 무릅쓰고 고속도로에 도달한다. 지나가던 차 한대가 거북이를 칠 뻔 한다. 뒤이어 달려오던 또 다른 차에 치여 고속도로 밖으로 나뒹군다. 한참이 지난 후 거북이는 뒹굴기 시작하며 그럴 때마다 몸에 붙어 있던 오트밀 씨앗들이 땅에 떨어진다. 거북이는 움직이기 시작하고 땅에 떨어진 씨앗들 위로 먼지가 날린다.

The Unknown Citizen

W. H. Auden

Summary "The Unknown Citizen" honors a model citizen of his society. The speaker calls this man a saint because he served the Greater Community. However, no one knows anything about his true life experiences.

El ciudadano desconocido

W. H. Auden

Resumen "El ciudadano desconocido" elogia a un ciudadano modelo de su sociedad. El narrador describe a este hombre como un santo porque prestó sus servicios a la Gran Comunidad. Sin embargo, nadie sabe nada acerca de sus verdaderas experiencias de vida.

Sitwayen enkoni an

W. H. Auden

Rezime "Sitwayen enkoni an" onore yon sitwayen modèl nan sosyete l la. Oratè a rele mesye sa a yon sen paske l te sèvi tout kominote a. Sepandan, pèsòn pa konnen anyen konsènan vrè eksperyans li nan lavi.

Ang Di-Kilalang Mamamayan

W. H. Auden

Buod "Ang Di-Kilalang Mamamayan" ay nagbibigay-dangál sa isang modelong mamamayan ng kanyang lipunan. Ang taong ito ay tinatawag ng nagsasalita na isang santo sapagkat kanyang pinagsilbihan ang Malawak na Komunidad. Gayunman, walang nakaaalam ng kahit anuman tungkol sa kanyang mga tunay-na-buhay na karanasan.

Tus Pejxeem Uas Tsis Muaj Leej Twg Paub

W. H. Auden

Cov ntsiab "Tus Pejxeem Uas Tsis Muaj Leej Twg Paub" hawm txog ib tug neeg zoo heev nyob rau hauv zos. Tus neeg hais lus hu tus txiv neej ntawd ua ib tug neeg uas sawvdaws hawm vim nws tau pab lub Zej Zog. Txawm li ntawd los, yeej tsis muaj leej twg paub txog nws lub neej tiag li.

《默默無聞的市民》(The Unknown Citizen)

W. H. Auden

摘要 《默默無聞的市民》表揚一位社會中的模範市民。敘述者稱這個人為聖人，因為他為「更偉大的社區」提供服務。但卻沒有人知道任何有關他的真實人生的經歷。

Công Dân Không Được Ai Biết Đến

W. H. Auden

Tóm Tắt Bài thơ "Công Dân Không Được Ai Biết Đến" vinh danh một công dân kiểu mẫu của cộng đồng. Nhân vật trong bài gọi người đàn ông này là một thánh nhân bởi vì anh ta đã phục vụ cho Cộng Đồng Mở Rộng. Tuy nhiên, không ai biết gì về những điều diễn ra trong cuộc sống thực của anh.

알려지지 않은 시민 (The Unknown Citizen)

W. H. Auden

요약 "알려지지 않은 시민" 은 그 사회의 모범이 되는 한 시민을 기리고 있다. 화자는 그 사람이 사회를 위해 봉사하기 때문에 그를 성자라고도 부른다. 그러나 아무도 그의 진짜 생활을 알지 못한다.

old age sticks • anyone lived in a pretty how town

E. E. Cummings

Summaries In "old age sticks," the speaker says that the young ignore the warnings of the elderly. He suggests that although the young tear down warning "signs," one day they will be posting such "signs" themselves. In "anyone lived in a pretty how town," the speaker tells about an anonymous town in which people live routine and ordinary lives. The main characters, "anyone" and "noone," do nothing special and are basically unnoticed by other people in the town.

De madera vieja • Alguien vivió en un bonito pueblo

E. E. Cummings

Resúmenes En "De madera vieja", el narrador afirma que los jóvenes ignoran las advertencias de los mayores. Y sugiere que aunque los jóvenes destruyan las "señales" de advertencia, algún día serán ellos mismos los que den esas "señales". En "Alguien vivió en un bonito pueblo", el narrador habla sobre un pueblo anónimo en donde las personas viven una vida rutinaria y normal. Los personajes principales, "alguien" y "nadie" no hacen nada en especial y son básicamente inadvertidos por los demás habitantes del pueblo.

baton vyeyès • nenpòt moun te abite nan yon bèl vil

E. E. Cummings

Rezime Nan "baton vyeyès," oratè a fè konnen jèn yo iyore avètisman granmoun yo ba yo. Li sijere byenke jèn yo chire "siy" avètisè sa yo, gen yon jou se yo menm ki pral poste "siy" sa yo poukont yo. Nan "nenpòt moun te abite nan yon bèl vil," oratè a pale konsènan yon vil ki pa gen non kote moun viv vi nòmal epi òdinè. Pèsonaj prensipal yo, "nenpòt moun" ak "noone," pa fè anyen ki espesyal epi esansyèlman lòt moun pa menm remake yo nan vil la.

ang katandaan ay dumidikit • kahit sinuman ay tumirá sa isang marikit na paanong bayan

E. E. Cummings

Mga Buod Sa "ang katandaan ay dumidikit," sinabi ng nagsasalitá na binabale-walá ng mga kabataan ang mga babalâ ng mga may-edad. Kanyang iminumungkahi na kahit sinisira ng mga kabataan ang mga "karatula" ng babalâ, isang araw ay sila mismo ay magtatayo ng mga "karatulang" ito. Sa "kahit sinuman ay tumirá sa isang marikit na paanong bayan," kinukuwento ng nagsasalita ang isang di-kilalang bayan kung saan ang mga tauhan ay may mga kinagawian at karaniwang mga buhay. Ang mga pangunahing tauhan, si "sinuman" at "wala-ni-sinuman," ay walang katangi-tanging ginagawá, at sila'y talagang hindi napapansin ng mga ibang tao sa bayan.

cov pas laus laus• anyone lived in a pretty how town

E. E. Cummings

Cov ntsiab Hauv "cov pas laus laus," tus neeg hais lus hais tias cov neeg hluas tsis mloog tej lus ceeb toom ntawm cov laus li. Nws xav hais tias txawm cov hluas yuav pov tseg tej lus ceeb toom lawm los muaj ib hnub lawv/ yuav tau hais cov lus ceeb toom no lawv tus kheej thiab. Hauv "anyone lived in a pretty how town," tus neeg hais lus qhia txog ib lub zos tsis paub npe uas muaj neeg nyob ua neej xws li luag thiab. Cov neeg tseem uas yog, "anyone" thiab "noone," tsis ua dabtsi tshwj xeeb li thiab lwm cov neeg hauv zos yeej tsis xav dabtsi ntau txog nkawd li.

《老傢伙》(old age sticks)《住在美麗何如鎮的任何人》(anyone lived in a pretty how town)

E. E. Cummings

摘要《老傢伙》的敘述者描述年輕人不理會年長者的警告。他認為雖然年輕人撕毀警告「標誌」，有一天他們自己就會張貼這類「標誌」。《住在美麗何如鎮的任何人》的敘述者描述一個不知名的小鎮，人們在此過著日復一日的平凡生活。其中的兩個主人翁「任何人」以及「弩恩」平凡地過日子，而且基本上小鎮上的其他人也不會注意到他們 。

lão niên • có ai đó sống ở thị trấn nhỏ xinh

E. E. Cummings

Tóm Tắt Nhân vật trong bài "lão niên," nói rằng thanh niên phớt lờ những lời cảnh báo của người già. Ông cho rằng mặc dù thanh niên hay xé bỏ những "biển" cảnh báo, một ngày nào đó chính họ sẽ dán lên những "biển" của chính mình. Nhân vật trong bài "có ai đó sống ở thị trấn nhỏ xinh" kể về một thị trấn không tên. Ở đó, mọi người sống một cuộc sống bình thường, đều đều. Các nhân vật chính "ai đó" và "không ai" không làm gì đặc biệt và về cơ bản những người khác trong thị trấn cũng không để ý đến họ.

늙은이의 지팡이 (old age sticks) • 귀여운 하우 타운에 살았던 그 누구 (anyone lived in a pretty how town)

E. E. Cummings

요약 "늙은이의 지팡이" 에서 화자는 젊은이들이 나이든 사람이 해 주는 경고를 무시한다고 한다. 젊은이들이 지금은 경고의 "표지판" 을 찢어 버리지만은 언젠가는 자신들이 직접 그런 "표지판" 을 세우는 날이 올 것이라고 저자는 말한다. "귀여운 하우 타운에 살았던 그 누구" 는 사람들이 평범한 일상을 살아가는 익명의 한 마을에 대해 이야기한다. 두 주인공 "애니원" 과 "노원" 은 평범한 일을 하며 마을의 그 누구도 주목하지 않는 인물들이다.

Of Modern Poetry

Wallace Stevens

Ars Poetica

Archibald MacLeish

Poetry

Marianne Moore

Summaries All of these poems are about poems. Each poet says what he or she thinks a poem is or should be. They say what they like or do not like about poems. Sometimes, they say these things directly. Sometimes, they use images to give you a feeling about what they mean. In "Of Modern Poetry," the speaker says that a poem must use the language of its own time. In "Ars Poetica," the speaker compares a poem to several other things. He says that the image is the most important part of a poem. The meaning of the poem does not matter as much. In "Poetry," the speaker feels sad for those who do not like poems. She thinks poems should be written so that readers can understand them.

De la poesía moderna

Wallace Stevens

Ars Poética

Archibald MacLeish

Poesía

Marianne Moore

Resúmenes Todos estos poemas hablan acerca de poemas. Cada poeta dice lo que él o ella considera que es un poema o debería serlo. Mencionan lo que les gusta o disgusta de los poemas. Algunas veces los poetas dicen las cosas de manera directa. Otras veces utilizan imágenes para que el lector se imagine lo que el poeta quiere significar. En "De la poesía moderna", el narrador dice que un poema debe usar el lenguaje de su tiempo. En "Ars Poética" el narrador compara un poema con varias otras cosas. Dice que la imagen es la parte más importante de un poema. El significado del poema no importa tanto. En "Poesía" la narradora siente tristeza por aquéllos a quienes no les gusta la poesía. Piensa que los poemas deben estar escritos de manera que los lectores puedan comprenderlos.

Pwezi modèn

Wallace Stevens

Atizay powetik

Archibald MacLeish

Pwezi

Marianne Moore

Rezime Tout powèm sa yo se konsènan powèm. Chak powèt di ki sa li panse yon powèm ye oswa ta dwe ye. Yo di sa yo renmen oswa sa yo pa renmen konsènan powèm yo. Pafwa, yo di bagay sa yo dirèkteman. Pafwa, yo itilize imaj ki ba w yon santiman sou sa yo vle di. Nan "Pwezi modèn," oratè a di yon powèm dwe itilize langaj epòk li. Nan "Atizay powetik," oratè a konpare yon powèm ak plizyè lòt bagay. Li di konsa imaj se pati ki pi enpòtan nan yon powèm. Siyifikasyon powèm nan pa gen menm valè enpòtans. Nan "Pwezi," oratè a santi l tris pou moun ki pa renmen powèm. Li panse powèm yo dwe ekri yon fason pou lektè yo ka konprann yo.

Sa Panunuláng Moderno

Wallace Stevens

Ars Poetika (Ang Sining ng Panunulá)

Archibald MacLeish

Mga Panunulá

Marianne Moore

Mga Buod Ang lahat ng mga tuláng ito ay tungkol sa mga tulá. Sinasabi ng bawat manunulá kung ano sa isip niya ang isang tulá, o kung ano dapat ito. Sinasabi nila ang kanilang gustó at 'di-gustó tungkol sa mga tulá. Minsan, tuwiran silang magsalitá. Minsan, gumagamit sila ng mga larawang-isip para iparamdam sa inyo ang kanilang nais ipakahulugan. Sa "Sa Panunuláng Moderno," sinasabi ng nagsasalita na ang isang tulá ay dapat gumamit ng wika ng sarili nitong panahon. Sa "Ars Poetika" (Ang Sining ng Panunulá), inihahambing ng nagsasalita ang isang tulá sa marami pang ibang bagay. Sinasabi niya na ang larawang-isip ay ang pinaka-mahalagang bahagi ng isang tulá. Ang kahulugan ng tulá ay 'di kasing-halagá nito. Sa "Panunulá," ang nagsasalita ay nalulungkot para sa mga hindi mahilig sa mga tulá. Iniisip niya na ang mga tulá ay dapat isulat para maunawaan ito ng mga mambabasá.

Cov Pajhuam Nim No

Wallace Stevens

Ars Poetica

Archibald MacLeish

Pajhuam

Marianne Moore

Cov ntsiab Tagnrho cov pajhuam no yog hais txog pajhaum. Txhua tus sau pajhuam hais txog nws txoj kev xav tias ib zaj pajhuam yuav tsum zoo li cas. Lawv hais txog tej yam uas lawv nyiam lossis tsis nyiam txog cov pajhuam. Tej thaum, lawv yeej hais kiag raws li qhov lawv xav. Tej thaum, lawv siv lus coj los hais kom tawm ib daim duab txog tias lawv txhais tau li cas̗ tiag. Hauv "Cov Pajhuam Nim No," tus neeg hais lus hais tias ib zaj pajhuam cov lus uas los ntawm lub sijhawm ntawd los. Hauv "Ars Poetica," tus neeg hais lus piv ib zaj pajhuam rau ntau yam. Nws hais tias tus duab uas pom tau ces yog yam tseem ceeb tshaj ntawm zaj pajhuam. Lub ntsiab ntawm zaj pajhuam tsis tseem ceeb tshaj. Hauv "Pajhuam," tus neeg hais lus muaj kev tu siab rau cov uas tsis nyiam pajhuam. Nws xav tias pajhuam sau kom cov neeg nyeem to taub tau.

《現代詩》(Of Modern Poetry)

Wallace Stevens

《詩藝》(Ars Poetica)

Archibald MacLeish

《詩歌藝術》(Poetry)

Marianne Moore

摘要 這些詩作全都與詩有關。每一位詩人說出自己對一首詩的看法或這首詩應該表達的方式。他們說出自己對詩喜歡或不喜歡的地方。有時他們會直接說出這些事情。有時他們則用一些形象化的描述，讓讀者瞭解他們的意思。《現代詩》的敘述者說一首詩必須使用詩詞本身時代的語言。《詩藝》的敘述者則將一首詩比喻成幾種其他的事物。他說，形象化的描述是一首詩最重要的部分。詩的意義則沒那麼重要。《詩歌》的敘述者為那些不喜歡詩的人感到難過。她認為詩的寫作方式應該有助於讀者瞭解詩的內容。

Về Thi Ca Hiện Đại

Wallace Stevens

Ars Poetica

Archibald MacLeish

Thi Ca

Marianne Moore

Tóm Tắt Tất cả các bài thơ này đều nói về thơ. Mỗi nhà thơ bộc lộ suy nghĩ của mình về thế nào là một bài thơ hoặc một bài thơ thì nên như thế nào. Họ nói lên những điều họ thích hoặc không thích về thơ. Đôi chỗ, họ bày tỏ những điều này một cách trực tiếp. Đôi chỗ, họ sử dụng các hình ảnh để giúp cho bạn cảm nhận được điều họ muốn nói. Nhân vật trong bài "Thi Ca Hiện Đại" nói rằng một bài thơ phải sử dụng ngôn ngữ hợp thời. Nhân vật trong bài "Ars Poetica" so sánh một bài thơ với rất nhiều thứ khác. Ông cho rằng hình ảnh là phần quan trọng nhất của một bài thơ, còn quan trọng hơn ý nghĩa của bài thơ. Nhân vật trong bài "Thi Ca" cảm thấy tiếc cho những ai không thích thơ. Bà nghĩ rằng thơ cần được sáng tác sao để các độc giả có thể hiểu được.

현대시 중에서 (Of Modern Poetry)

Wallace Stevens

시론 (Ars Poetica)

Archibald MacLeish

시 (Poetry)

Marianne Moore

요약 이 시들은 모두 시에 관해 쓰고 있다. 각각의 시인은 시란 어떤 것인지 혹은 어때야 하는지를 나름대로 이야기한다. 시에 대해 좋은 점과 싫은 점도 이야기한다. 그들은 직접적으로 말하기도 하며 때로는 이미지를 사용하여 자신이 말하고자 하는 것을 독자가 느끼게 하기도 한다. "현대시 중에서" 에서 화자는 시란 그 시대의 언어를 사용해서 써야 한다고 주장한다. "시론" 에서는 시를 여러 가지 것에 비유한다. 그리고 시에서 중요한 것은 이미지이며 시의 의미는 그다지 중요하지 않다고 이야기한다. "시" 에서 화자는 시를 좋아하지 않는 사람들이 있다는 것에 슬퍼하며 시란 독자들이 이해할 수 있도록 쓰여져야 한다고 말한다.

In Another Country

Ernest Hemingway

Summary In "In Another Country," an American officer recovering from a war injury meets three young Italian officers and an older major. All of the men are wounded. The major helps the American with his Italian grammar, advises him not to marry, and mourns the death of his own wife.

En otro país

Ernest Hemingway

Resumen En la historia "En otro país", un oficial estadounidense que se recupera de una herida de guerra conoce a tres oficiales italianos y a un viejo comandante. Todos ellos están heridos. El comandante ayuda al estadounidense con la gramática italiana, le aconseja no casarse y llora la muerte de su propia esposa.

Nan yon lòt peyi

Ernest Hemingway

Rezime Nan "Nan yon lòt peyi," yon ofisye ameriken k ap rekipere akoz li te blese nan yon gè rankontre twa jèn ofisye italyen ak yon kòmandan ki pi aje. Tout mesye yo te blese. Kòmandan an ede ameriken an avèk gramè italyen li an, li konseye l pou l pa marye, epi li an dèy pou lanmò pwòp madanm li.

Sa Ibang Bansa

Ernest Hemingway

Buod Sa "Sa Ibang Bansa," ang isang Amerikanong opisyal na nagpapagaling ng pinsala mula sa digmáan ay nakasalubong ng tatlong batang Italyanong opisyal at isang nakatatandang komandante. Lahat sila ay sugatán. Tinulungan ng komandante ang Amerikano sa kanyang balarilang Italyano, pinayuhan siyang huwag mag-asawa, at nagdalamhati siya sa pagkawalá ng sarili niyang asawa.

Hauv Lwm Lub tebchaws

Ernest Hemingway

Lub Ntsiab Hauv zaj "Hauv Lwm Lub tebchaws," ib tug tub rog Meskas uas tseem tsis tau zoo tus mob los ntawm kev ua tsov rog tau ntsib peb tug tub rog tseem hluas uas yog haiv neeg Italian thiab ib tug major uas muaj hnub nyoog lawm. Tagnrho cov txiv neej ntawd rau mob lawm tibsi. Tus major pab tau tus Meskas ntawd nrog nws cov lus Italian, pab qhia rau nws tias kom tsis txhob yuav pojniam, thiab tseem niaj hnub nco txog nws tus pojniam.

《在另一個國度》(In Another Country)

Ernest Hemingway

摘要 《在另一個國度》描寫一位在戰場上受了傷、正在康復中的美國軍官遇到了三個年輕的義大利軍官以及一位較年長的少校。這幾個人全都受了傷。少校幫助這個美國人學義大利文文法，建議他不要結婚，並為他自己的妻子的過逝服喪。

Ở Một Đất Nước Xa Lạ

Ernest Hemingway

Tóm Tắt Trong truyện "Ở Một Đất Nước Xa Lạ" một sĩ quan Mỹ đang dưỡng thương gặp ba sĩ quan trẻ người Ý và một vị thiếu tá nhiều tuổi hơn. Tất cả bọn họ đều bị thương. Vị thiếu tá giúp viên sĩ quan Mỹ học ngữ pháp tiếng Ý và khuyên anh ta không nên kết hôn, rồi than khóc trước cái chết của chính vợ ông.

다른 나라에서 (In Another Country)

Ernest Hemingway

요약 전쟁에서 입은 부상에서 회복 중인 한 미국 장교가 세 명의 젊은 이탈리아 장교들과 나이든 소령을 만나게 된다. 그들도 모두 부상을 당하였다. 소령은 미국 장교에게 이탈리아어 문법을 가르쳐 주며 결혼하지 말 것을 충고하나 자신은 아내의 죽음을 슬퍼한다.

A Rose for Emily

William Faulkner

Summary Emily Grierson is a woman in a small Southern town. She lives under the watchful eyes of the community. Because she is secretive and private, the townspeople believe that she may be crazy. When Emily shows interest in a man from another town, people wonder whether she will marry him. When the man disappears from town, Emily begins keeping to herself again. After her death, people find something shocking in her bedroom.

Una rosa para Emily

William Faulkner

Resumen Emily Grierson es una mujer que vive en un pequeño pueblo del Sur. Vive bajo la atenta mirada de toda la comunidad. Los habitantes del pueblo piensan que está loca porque se comporta de manera reservada y sigilosa. Cuando Emily se interesa por un hombre que vive en otro pueblo, las personas se preguntan si se casará con él. Cuando el hombre desaparece del pueblo, Emily comienza a encerrarse otra vez. Después de su muerte, la gente encuentra algo impactante en su habitación.

Yon woz pou Emily

William Faulkner

Rezime Emily Grierson se yon fanm nan yon ti vil nan Lesid. L ap viv sou je atantif kominote a. Paske l se yon moun ki diskrè epi prive, moun nan vil la kwè li ka fòl. Lè Emily montre li enterese ak yon mesye ki abite nan yon lòt vil, moun yo mande tèt yo si Emily pral marye ak mesye sa a. Lè mesye a disparèt nan vil la, Emily kòmanse vin diskrè ankò. Aprè Emily fin mouri, moun yo jwenn yon bagay chokan nan chanm li a.

Isang Rosas para kay Emily

William Faulkner

Buod Si Emily Grierson ay isang babaeng nakatirá sa isang maliit na bayan sa South. Siya ay palaging pinanunood ng mga mapagpunang mata ng komunidad. Dahil siya ay masekreto at mapag-isa, naniwala ang mga taong-bayan na maaaring siya ay balíw. Nang si Emily ay nagpakita ng pagkakagustó sa isang lalaking taga ibang bayan, pinag-isipan ng mga tao kung papakasalán niya ito. Nang mawalá ang lalaki sa bayan, si Emily ay nagsimula na namang magsarilí. Pagkatapos ng kanyang pagkamatáy, ang mga tao ay mayroong nahanap na nakabibiglá sa kanyang silid-tulugan.

Ib Lub Paj Ntshua Nplaim Rau Emily

William Faulkner

Lub Ntsiab Emily Grierson yog ib tug pojniam nyob hauv ib lub zos me nyob sab qab teb. Nws ua lub neej nyob hauv lub zej zog uas sawv daws nyiam saib raws nws nruj heev li. Vim nws yog ib tug neeg uas nyiam nyob twm zeej ib leeg heev, neeg hauv zos thiaj xav tias nws yog ib tug neeg vwm. Thaum Emily pib nyiam ib tug txiv neej nyob rau lwm lub zos, neeg xav tias nws puas yuav tus txiv neej ntawd. Thaum tus txiv neej ntawd cia li ploj lawm, Emily pib nyob ntsiag to dua. Tom qab nws tag sim neej lawm, cov neeg sawvdaws nrhiav tau ib yam hauv nws chav pw.

《獻給愛蜜莉的玫瑰》 (A Rose for Emily)

William Faulkner

摘要 愛蜜莉・葛瑞爾森是一位住在一座南方小鎮的婦女。她生活在社區居民的監視下。由於她都躲躲藏藏，生活又很隱密，鎮民因此認為她可能瘋了。當愛蜜莉對一位從另一個小鎮來的男子表現出興趣時，大家都很好奇她是否將嫁給他。當這個男人從小鎮上消失時，愛蜜莉開始再次不與其他人往來。在她死後，大家在她的臥室發現了驚人的東西。

Một Đóa Hồng Dành Cho Emily

William Faulkner

Tóm Tắt Emily Grierson là một phụ nữ sống ở một thị trấn nhỏ miền Nam. Cô sống dưới con mắt dò xét của cộng đồng. Bởi vì cô là người kín đáo, ít thổ lộ nên người trong thị trấn tin rằng có thể cô bị điên. Khi Emily để ý một người đàn ông đến từ thị trấn khác, mọi người băn khoăn không biết cô có lấy anh ta không. Khi người đàn ông biến mất khỏi thị trấn, Emily lại sống khép kín. Sau khi cô chết, mọi người khám phá ra một điều gây sốc trong phòng ngủ của cô.

에밀리에게 장미를 (A Rose for Emily)

William Faulkner

요약 에밀리 그리어슨은 남부의 한 조그만 마을에 살고 있는 여인이다. 그 마을 사람들은 그녀에게 경계의 눈초리를 보낸다. 그녀는 자기 생활을 밖으로 드러내지 않으며 무언가 비밀스러워 보이기 때문에 마을 사람들은 그녀가 미쳤을 지도 모른다고 생각한다. 에밀리가 다른 마을에서 온 남자에게 관심을 보이자 사람들은 그녀가 그와 결혼할 것인지 궁금해 한다. 그 남자가 마을에서 사라지자 에밀리도 원래의 모습으로 돌아간다. 그녀가 죽고 나서 마을 사람들은 그녀의 방에서 충격적인 것을 발견한다.

Nobel Prize Acceptance Speech

William Faulkner

Summary William Faulkner received the Nobel Prize for literature in 1950. In his acceptance speech, Faulkner presents his opinions about world affairs. He also talks about the role of literature in helping people make sense of the world. Faulkner tells young writers to set aside their fear of world destruction and address the basic problems of love, honor, and caring for others. He explains that it is the writer's duty to help people carry on. Writers can do this by reminding people of the glory of their past.

Discurso de aceptación del Premio Nobel

William Faulkner

Resumen William Faulkner recibió el Premio Nobel de literatura en 1950. En su discurso de aceptación, Faulkner presenta sus opiniones sobre diferentes asuntos mundiales. También habla acerca del rol de la literatura para ayudar a que las personas le encuentren sentido a la vida. Faulkner les dice a los jóvenes escritores que dejen a un lado su miedo a la destrucción del mundo e identifica los problemas básicos del amor, el honor y el cuidado al prójimo. Explica que es deber del escritor ayudar a la gente a no bajar los brazos. Los escritores pueden hacer esto, recordándoles a las personas acerca de la gloria que disfrutaban en el pasado.

Diskou akseptasyon pou pri Nobel

William Faulkner

Rezime William Faulkner te resevwa pri Nobel pou literati an 1950. Nan diskou akseptasyon l lan, Faulkner prezante opinyon l konsènan zafè lemonn. Epitou li pale konsènan wòl literati genyen pou l ede moun konprann monn lan. Faulkner di jèn ekriven yo pou yo mete laperèz yo genyen konsènan destriksyon monn lan epi pou yo abòde pwoblèm fondamantal lanmou, onè ak sousi pou lòt moun. Li eksplike se devwa ekriven an pou l ede moun yo kontinye viv. Ekriven yo ka fè sa lè yo raple moun laglwa nan pase yo.

Talumpati sa Pagtanggáp ng Nobel Prize

William Faulkner

Buod Natanggáp ni William Faulkner ang Nobel Prize para sa panitikan noong 1950. Sa kanyang talumpati sa pagtanggáp ng premyo, sinabi ni Faulkner ang kanyang mga kuru-kuro tungkol sa mga pangyayari sa mundo. Tinalakay din niya ang papel ng panitikan sa pagtulong sa mga taong maunawaan ang mundo. Sinabi ni Faulker sa mga batang manunulát na kalimutan na ang kanilang pangangamba sa pagkasira ng mundo, at talakayin ang mga saligang problema ng pag-ibig, karangalan, at pag-aalaga sa kapwa. Ipinaliwanag niya na tungkulin ng manunulát ang tumulong sa mga tao na magpursigí. Magagawá ito ng mga manunulát sa pamamagitan ng pagpapaalala sa mga tao ng kaluwalhatian ng kanilang nakaraan.

Zaj Lus Hais Thaum Tau Yeej Qhov Nobel Prize

William Faulkner

Lub Ntsiab William Faulkner tau txais qhov Nobel Prize rau kev sau ntawv thaum xyoo 1950. Nyob rau nws zaj lus hais thaum nws los txais qhov Nobel Prize, Faulkner tham txog nws txoj kev xav txog tej haujlwm khiav kom sib to taub ntawm cov tebchawsNws ho tham txog kev sau ntawv uas pab tau neeg to taub txog lub ntiaj teb. Faulkner qhia rau cov hluas uas tseem tab tom kawm sau ntawv kom lawv tsis txhob muab tej kev tsis zoo hauv ntiaj teb coj los xav es kom lawv sau txog cov teeb meem ntawm kev hlub, kev hwm, thiab kev sib tshua. Nws piav tias yog ib tug neeg sau ntawv lub luag haujlwm los pab neeg nrhiav kev ua neej ntxiv mus. Cov neeg sau ntawv yuav ua tau li no los ntawm kev sau kom sawvdaws nco qab ntsoov txog tej yam zoo ntawm lawv lub neej uas tau muaj los.

《諾貝爾獎領獎演說》 (Nobel Prize Acceptance Speech)

William Faulkner

摘要 作者在 1950 年被頒發諾貝爾文學獎。他在領獎演說中表達了自己對於世界局勢的看法。他也談論了文學在幫助世人理解世界局勢上的重要性。作者告訴年輕的作家不要去理會自己對世界毀滅的恐懼，而要探討愛、榮譽、及關懷其他人的基本問題。他認為幫助其他人繼續生存是作家的責任。作家可以藉著提醒人們自己過去的光榮事蹟辦到這點。

Bài Phát Biểu Nhân Dịp Nhận Giải Nobel

William Faulkner

Tóm Tắt William Faulkner nhận giải Nobel văn học năm 1950. Trong bài phát biểu nhận giải, Faulkner trình bày quan điểm của mình về các sự kiện thế giới. Ông cũng nói đến vai trò của văn học trong việc giúp mọi người hiểu được thế giới. Faulkner khuyên các nhà văn trẻ gạt bỏ nỗi sợ hãi thế giới bị huỷ diệt và tập trung vào những vấn đề cơ bản của tình yêu, danh dự, và việc quan tâm chăm sóc người khác. Ông giải thích rằng nhiệm vụ của nhà văn là giúp mọi người tiếp tục đứng lên. Các nhà văn có thể làm được điều này bằng cách gợi nhớ họ đến quá khứ vinh quang của họ.

노벨상 수락 연설 (Nobel Prize Acceptance Speech)

William Faulkner

요약 월리엄 포크너는 1950년 노벨 문학상을 수상한다. 수상 수락 연설에서 그는 세계 정세에 관해 자신의 의견을 피력한다. 또한 사람들이 세상을 현명하게 만들어 나가는 데 있어 문학의 역할에 대해서도 이야기한다. 포크너는 젊은 작가들에게 세상이 무너진다는 두려움은 뒤로하고 사랑이나 명예와 같은 좀더 근원적인 문제를 글로 다루어 보라고 말한다. 사람들에게 힘을 주는 것이 작가의 의무이며 과거의 영광을 되살려 보여줌으로써 사람들에게 힘을 불어넣을 수 있다고 주장한다.

The Jilting of Granny Weatherall

Katherine Anne Porter

Summary Ellen Weatherall is on her deathbed. Her thoughts drift between moments in the present and memories of the past. She receives visits from her daughter, her doctor, and her priest. She recalls the people and events that filled her life. Her thoughts wander freely among the good and the bad memories.

La muerte de Granny Weatherall

Katherine Anne Porter

Resumen Ellen Weatherall está en su lecho de muerte. Sus pensamientos se mueven entre momentos del presente y recuerdos del pasado. Su hija, su médico y un sacerdote llegan a visitarla. Y recuerda los momentos y a las personas que llenaron su vida. Sus pensamientos deambulan libremente entre los buenos y los malos recuerdos.

Refi granny Weatherall

Katherine Anne Porter

Rezime Ellen Weatherall sou kabann lanmò li. Panse l flote ant kèk moman nan leprezan ak kèk souvni nan lepase. Li resevwa vizit pitit fi l, doktè l ak prèt li. Li sonje kèk moun ak evenman ki te ranpli lavi l. Panse l pwomennen libè libè ant bon ak move souvni yo.

Kev Tso Granny Weatherall

Katherine Anne Porter

Lub Ntsiab Ellen Weatherall tab tom yuav tag sim neej. Nws txoj kev xav hloov mus los txog nws lub neej nim no thiab tej yam uas dhau los lawm. Nws tus ntxhais, nws tus kws kho mob, thiab nws tus txiv plig tuaj saib nws. Nws nco qab txog cov neeg thiab tej yam uas tau tshwm sim hauv nws lub neej. Nws cov kev xav dhia mus los txog tej yam zoo thiab tej yam uas tsis zoo.

Ang Pagtatakwíl kay Granny Weatherall

Katherine Anne Porter

Buod Si Ellen Weatherall ay naghihingaló. Ang kanyang isipan ay lumulutang-lutang mula sa mga sandali ng kasalukuyan at mga alaala ng nakaraan. Siya'y nakatanggap ng mga bisita mula sa kanyang anak na babae, kanyang doktor, at kanyang pastor. Naaalala niya ang mga tao at mga pangyayari na pumunó ng kanyang buhay. Ang kanyang isipan ay malayang lumilibot sa mga magaganda at mga masasamáng alaala.

《葛瑞妮・威德羅爾的負心》 (The Jilting of Granny Weatherall)

Katherine Anne Porter

摘要 艾倫・威德羅爾正在彌留狀態。她的思緒漂流在現在與過去的時光之間。她的女兒、醫生、及牧師都來探望她。她回想一生中發生的人與事。她的思緒自由地遊走於好與壞的時光之中。

Cuộc Phụ Tình Của Bà Weatherall

Katherine Anne Porter

Tóm Tắt Ellen Weatherall đang hấp hối. Suy nghĩ của bà cứ trôi từ những khoảnh khắc hiện tại về các ký ức trong quá khứ. Con gái, bác sĩ và linh mục đến thăm bà. Bà nhớ lại mọi người và các sự kiện trong suốt cuộc đời mình. Những suy nghĩ cứ miên man giữa những ký ức đẹp và những ký ức xấu.

웨더롤 할머니의 버리기 (The Jilting of Granny Weatherall)

Katherine Anne Porter

요약 엘렌 웨더롤은 임종이 가까워지고 있다. 할머니의 생각은 현재 순간들과 과거의 추억들 사이에서 떠다닌다. 딸과 의사와 신부님이 할머니를 찾아온다. 할머니는 자신의 인생을 채웠던 사건들과 사람들을 회상한다. 할머니는 좋은 기억과 나쁜 기억을 모두 생각해 본다.

A Worn Path

Eudora Welty

Summary In "A Worn Path," an old woman makes her way along a country path. Once in town, she goes to a doctor's office to get medicine for her grandson. She has been taking care of him since he swallowed lye some years before.

Un camino desgastado

Eudora Welty

Resumen En "Un camino desgastado", una anciana mujer atraviesa un camino por el campo. Una vez en el pueblo, acude al consultorio de un médico para conseguir un medicamento para su nieto. Lo ha cuidado incansablemente desde que tragó lejía hace algunos años.

Yon chemen ize

Eudora Welty

Rezime Nan "Yon chemen ize," yon ti granmoun fi fè wout li sou yon chemen lakanpay. Yon fwa li rive lavil, li al kay yon doktè pou l jwenn medikaman pou pitit pitit gason l. Li t ap pran swen pitit pitit gason l lan depi l te vale alkalin kèk ane oparavan.

Isang Upód na Daanan

Eudora Welty

Buod Sa "Isang Upód ng Daanan," ang isang matandang babae ay naglalakad sa isang daanan sa bukid. Pagdating niya sa bayan, pumunta siya sa opisina ng isang doktor para kumuha ng gamot para sa kanyang apóng lalaki. Kanyang inaalagaan ito mula nang ito ay nakalunok ng lihiya mga ilang taóng nakaraan.

Ib Txoj Kev Taug Ntau Zaus Lawm

Eudora Welty

Lub Ntsiab Hauv "Ib Txoj Kev Taug Ntau Zaus Lawm," ib tug pojniam laus laus taug kev raws ib txoj kev uas nyob sab nraum zos. Thaum txog hauv zos, nws mus nqa tshuaj hauv kws kho mob lub chav haujlwm los rau nws tus xeeb ntxwv. Nws tau zov tus menyuam txij li thaum tus menyuam tau nqos laib ib co tshuaj hu ua lye ob peb xyoos dhau los lawm.

《熟路》 (A Worn Path)

Eudora Welty

摘要 《熟路》描寫一位老婦人沿著一條鄉間小徑行走。到了鎮上後，她就前往一間醫生的診所，為她的孫子拿藥。自從他在幾年前吞下鹼液後，她就一直在照顧他。

Con Đường Mòn

Eudora Welty

Tóm Tắt Trong bài "Con Đường Mòn" một người phụ nữ già đi dọc con đường quê. Khi đã vào trong thị trấn, bà đến phòng mạch của một bác sĩ để lấy thuốc cho cháu trai. Bà đã chăm sóc cậu bé kể từ khi cậu nuốt phải dung dịch kiềm vài năm trước.

오래 다닌 길 (A Worn Path)

Eudora Welty

요약 한 늙은 여인이 시골 길을 따라 걸어가고 있다. 여인은 손자가 먹을 약을 가지러 마을에 하나밖에 없는 진료소에 가는 중이다. 손자가 몇 년 전 잿물을 삼켜서 아프게 되었을 때부터 여인은 계속 손자를 돌보고 있는 중이다.

The Night the Ghost Got In

James Thurber

Summary One night, the narrator hears footsteps. He wakes up his family. All of the confusion makes the narrator's crazy grandfather angry.

La noche en que entraron los fantasmas

James Thurber

Resumen Una noche el narrador escucha unos pasos. Y despierta a su familia. Toda la confusión hace enfurecer al loco abuelo del narrador.

Nuit fantòm lan te rantre

James Thurber

Rezime Yon nuit, naratè a tande kèk pa. Li reveye fanmi l. Tout konfizyon yo vin fè granpè fou naratè a fache.

Ang Gabí nang Nakapasok ang Multo

James Thurber

Buod Isang gabí, narinig ng tagapagsalitá ang tunóg ng paáng naglalakád. Ang balíw na lolo ng tagapagsalitá ay nagalit dahil sa lahat ng guló.

Hmo Tus Dab Nkag Los Tau

James Thurber

Lub Ntsiab Muaj ib hmos, tus piav zaj no hnov leej twg mus kev. Nws tsa nws tsev neeg. Cov kev tsis to taub txog yam tshwm sim ntawd ua rau tus piav zaj no yawg chim heev.

《鬼魂進來的夜晚》(The Night the Ghost Got In)

James Thurber

摘要 敘事者在一天晚上聽到腳步聲。他叫醒家人。所有發生的令人不解的情況都令敘事者瘋狂的爺爺憤怒不已。

Đêm Có Ma Xuất Hiện

James Thurber

Tóm Tắt Một đêm, người thuật chuyện nghe thấy tiếng bước chân. Anh ta đánh thức gia đình dậy. Cảnh rối loạn ồn ào khiến cho người ông điên dại của anh ta nổi giận.

유령이 찾아오던 날 밤(The Night the Ghost Got In)

James Thurber

요약 어느 날 밤 화자는 발소리를 듣는다. 그는 가족을 다 깨운다. 이런 일련의 소동이 제정신이 아닌 화자의 할아버지를 화나게 만든다.

Chicago • Grass

Carl Sandburg

Summaries In "Chicago," Sandburg uses simple words to express his love and admiration for the city of Chicago. He challenges the reader to find a city with more life. In "Grass," the grass explains that there is only grass where once important battles between great armies took place. The calmness of nature hides the horror and senselessness of war.

Chicago • Hierba

Carl Sandburg

Resúmenes En "Chicago" Sandburg usa palabras sencillas para expresar su amor y admiración por la ciudad de Chicago. Desafía al lector a que encuentre una ciudad con más vida. En "Hierba", la hierba explica que sólo hay hierbas en donde alguna vez se pelearon batallas importantes entre grandes ejércitos. La tranquilidad de la naturaleza esconde el horror y el sinsentido de la guerra.

Chikago • Gazon

Carl Sandburg

Rezime Nan "Chikago," Sandburg itilize kèk mo senp pou eksprime lanmou l ak admirasyon l pou vil Chikago. Li defye lektè a pou l jwenn yon vil ki gen plis vi. Nan "Gazon," gazon eksplike gen gazon sèlman kote te konn gen batay enpòtan ant gwo lame yo. Serenite lanati kache atwosite ak estipidite lagè.

Chicago • Damó

Carl Sandburg

Mga Buod Sa "Chicago," gumagamit si Sandburg ng mga simpleng salitá para ipahayag ang kanyang pag-ibig at paghanga sa siyudad ng Chicago. Hinahámon niya ang mambabasá na maghanap ng isang siyudad na mas-may-buhay kaysa rito. Sa "Damó," ipinaliliwanag ng damó na damó na lamang ang natirá kung saan noong naganáp ang mga malalakíng labanán ng mga dakilang hukbo. Kinukublí ng katiwasayan ng kalikasan ang sindak at pagkawaláng-katuturán ng digmáan.

Chicago • Nyom

Carl Sandburg

Cov ntsiab Hauv "Chicago," Sandburg siv tej lo lus yooj yim coj los qhia txog nws txoj kev nyiam thiab qhuas lub nroog Chicago. Nws hais kom cov nyeem mus nrhiav ib lub nroog nyob uas muaj sia mentsisHauv "Nyom," cov nyom piav tias tsuas tshuav nyom lawm xwb uas yog tej thaj chaw uas tau muaj kev ua tsov rog loj heev dhau los lawm. Ntiaj teb txoj kev nyob tus yees zais tau txoj kev phem thiab tsis zoo ntawm kev ua tsov rog.

《芝加哥》(Chicago) • 《草地》(Grass)

Carl Sandburg

摘要 作者在《芝加哥》中利用簡單的文字表達自己對芝加哥這座城市的熱愛與欣賞。他要求讀者找出一座更具生命力的城市。《草地》中的草地主張，只有草地上曾經發生過偉大軍隊間的重要戰役。大自然的安寧掩藏了戰爭的可怕及愚蠢。

Chicago • Đồng Cỏ

Carl Sandburg

Tóm Tắt Trong bài "Chicago", Sandburg sử dụng ngôn từ giản đơn để bày tỏ tình yêu và sự thán phục của mình đối với thành phố Chicago. Ông thách thức độc giả tìm được một thành phố sôi động hơn. Trong bài "Đồng Cỏ", chính đồng cỏ là nhân vật giải thích rằng bây giờ chỉ còn những đồng cỏ nơi đã từng diễn ra các trận chiến quan trọng giữa các đội quân hùng mạnh. Sự tĩnh lặng của thiên nhiên che giấu đi sự kinh hoàng và nhẫn tâm của chiến tranh.

시카고 (Chicago) • 풀 (Grass)

Carl Sandburg

요약 "시카고" 에서 저자는 단순한 단어를 사용하여 시카고에 대한 사랑과 숭배를 이야기한다. 독자들로 하여금 좀더 생기가 넘치는 도시를 찾아보도록 권하고 있다. "풀" 에서는 풀이 말하기를 큰 전투가 있었던 자리에 오직 풀만이 덮고 있다고 한다. 자연의 고요함 속에는 전쟁의 공포와 무자비함이 숨어 있다.

Robert Frost's Poetry

Summaries In "Birches," the speaker recalls the pleasure of swinging from birch trees as a child. "Stopping by Woods on a Snowy Evening" describes a man tempted to linger in the peaceful woods. In "Mending Wall," the speaker and his neighbor meet to repair breaks in the wall that separates their fields. The speaker wonders about the purpose of the wall and the forces of nature that continually pull it down. "Out, Out—" tells the harsh story of a young farm boy who loses control of his chain saw while cutting wood. "The Gift Outright" examines the colonial spirit that struggled to tame a new land and form a nation. In "Acquainted With the Night," the speaker admits to moments of loneliness in his life.

La poesía de Robert Frost

Resúmenes En "Los abedules" el narrador evoca el placer de treparse a los abedules cuando era niño. "Junto a los árboles en una noche nevada" describe a un hombre que siente deseos de quedarse entre la paz de los árboles. En "Reparando la cerca", el narrador y su vecino se juntan para reparar las roturas en la pared que separa sus terrenos. El narrador se pregunta acerca del propósito de la pared y las fuerzas de la naturaleza que continuamente la derriban. "Fuera, fuera" cuenta la dura historia de un joven granjero que pierde el control de su motosierra mientras corta leña. "El regalo indiscutible" explora el espíritu colonial que luchó por dominar una nueva tierra y formar una nación. En "Familiarizado con la noche", el narrador admite caer vencido ante los momentos de soledad de su vida.

Pwezi Robert Frost la

Rezime Nan "Boulo," oratè a sonje plezi li te genyen lè l te konn balanse nan pye boulo lè l te timoun. "Estope avèk bwa nan yon sware anneje" dekri yon mesye ki tante pou l rete pi lontan nan bwa pezib yo. Nan "Reparasyon mi," oratè a ak vwazen li rankontre pou yo repare yon ripti nan mi ki separe chan yo a. Oratè a ap mande tèt li ki bi mi an genyen ak fòs lanati ki kontinyèlman ap kraze l. "Deyò, Deyò—" rakonte istwa dezagrayab yon jèn fèmye ki pèdi kontwòl si li a pandan l ap koupe bwa. "Kado dirèk la" egzamine lespri kolonyal ki te konbat pou l donte yon tè nèf epi fòme yon nasyon. Nan "Familye avèk lannuit," oratè a admèt li pase kèk moman solitid nan lavi l.

Mga Tulá ni Robert Frost

Mga Buod Sa "Mga Birch," natatandaan ng nagsasalitá ang galak ng pagbabaging sa mga puno ng "birch" noong siya'y bata pa. Inilalarawan ng "Pagtitigil sa Gubat sa Isang May Snow na Gabí" ang isang lalaking nauudyok na magtagal sa tahimik na kagubatan. Sa "Pagtatagpí ng Pader," ang nagsasalitá at ang kanyang kapitbahay ay nagtagpo upang tagpian ang mga puwang sa pader na naghihiwalay ng kanilang mga bukid. Nagtataká ang nagsasalitá tungkol sa gamit ng pader, at sa mga puwersa ng kalikasan na paulit-ulit na gumigibá dito. Ang "Labas, Labas—" ay nagsasalaysay ng isang magaralgál na kuwento tungkol sa isang batang lalaki na nawalán ng kontrol sa kanyang "chain saw" habang siya'y naglalagari ng kahoy. Sa "Kilalá ang Gabí," inamin ng nagsasalita na may mga sandalí ng kalungkutan sa kanyang buhay.

Robert Frost Cov Pajhuam

Cov ntsiab Hauv "Birches," tus neeg hais lus nco qab txog txoj kev zoo siab thaum ua viav vias saum tsob ntoo birch thaum uas tseem yog ib tug menyuam yaus. "Stopping by Woods on a Snowy Evening" piav txog ib tug txiv neej uas xav nyob kom ib nyuag ntev mentsis hauv ib lub hav zoov uas muaj kev ywj pheej nyob ntsiag twb to heev. Hauv "Mending Wall," tus neeg hais lus thiab nws tus neeg nyob hauv zej zog sib ntsib vim ob leeg tab tom tuaj kho daim laj kab uas thaiv nkawd ciam teb. Tus neeg hais lus xav txog hais tias vim li cas thiaj li muaj daim laj kab ntawd thaiv thiab nws xav txog tej yam uas ua rau yus yuav tau tsa laj kab thaiv. Out, Out—" qhia zaj dabneeg ntawm ib tug menyuam tub nyob ib daim teb uas tau plam tes rau nws rab kaws ntoo thaum nws tab tom kaws ntoo. Hauv "Acquainted With the Night," tus neeg hais lus lees txog tej lub sijhawm uas nws nyob ib leeg kho siab khuav hauv nws lub neej.

《羅伯特・佛洛斯特的詩》(Robert Frost's Poetry)

摘要 「樺木」的敘述者回想小時候在白樺樹上擺盪的快樂回憶。「在一個下雪的夜晚在森林中逗留」則描述一個男人受到誘惑而在寧靜的森林中流連忘返。「修補圍牆」中的敘述者和他的鄰居一道修補分隔彼此農場的圍牆上的裂縫。敘述者對於這座圍牆的功能以及不斷拆毀圍牆的大自然力量感到疑惑。《飛出去、飛出去了》講述一個農場小男孩在砍木頭時無法控制自己的鏈鋸而發生的殘酷故事。《熟悉夜晚》中的敘述者坦承自己人生中感到孤寂的時刻。

Thơ của Robert Frost

Tóm Tắt Nhân vật trong bài thơ "Những Cây Bulô" hồi tưởng lại sự thoải mái khi đánh đu trên những cái cây bulô hồi còn nhỏ. Bài "'Dừng Chân Bên Rừng Giữa Chiều Tuyết Rơi" miêu tả một người đàn ông định lưu lại trong một khu rừng yên tĩnh. Nhân vật trong bài "Chữa Tường" gặp người hàng xóm để sửa những chỗ vỡ trên bức tường ngăn cách cánh đồng của hai nhà. Nhân vật này băn khoăn về mục đích của bức tường và các lực của thiên nhiên liên tục làm hỏng bức tường. Bài thơ "Tắt, Tắt—" kể một câu truyện nghiệt ngã về một cậu bé trên nông trang không kiểm soát được chiếc cưa xích của mình khi đang cưa gỗ. Nhân vật trong bài thơ "Làm Quen Với Bóng Đêm" thú nhận về những khoảnh khắc cô đơn trong cuộc đời mình.

로버트 프로스트의 시 (Robert Frost's Poetry)

요약 "자작나무" 에서 화자는 어린 시절 자작 나무에 매달린 그네를 타면서 놀았던 즐거움을 회상한다. "눈 내리는 저녁 숲가에 서서" 는 평화로운 숲을 거닐고 싶어하는 한 남자를 표사하고 있다. "담장 고치기" 에서 화자는 밭의 경계선이 되어 주는 담장의 부서진 곳을 고치기 위해 이웃과 만난다. 화자는 그 담장이 있어야 하는 목적과 그 담장을 계속 부수는 자연의 힘에 대해 생각해 본다. "아웃, 아웃—" 은 한 어린 농장 소년이 나무를 자르다 기계톱을 잘못 다루어 생기는 가혹한 이야기이다. "밤을 잘 알고 있다" 에서 화자는 삶의 고독의 순간들을 받아들이고 있다.

The Negro Speaks of Rivers • I, Too • Dream Variations • Refugee in America

Langston Hughes

Summaries In "The Negro Speaks of Rivers," the speaker recalls the experience of his people along ancient rivers of the world. "I, Too" is Langston Hughes's response to a poem by Walk Whitman. Whitman's poem describes the variety that exists in America. The speaker in "Dream Variations" imagines a world in which he can play and rest freely and in which the blackness of his skin is accepted. "Refugee in America" challenges the reader to think more carefully about words such as freedom and liberty.

El negro habla de los ríos • Yo también • Variaciones de sueños • Refugiado en los Estados Unidos

Langston Hughes

Resúmenes En "El negro habla de los ríos", el narrador recuerda la experiencia de la gente de su pueblo junto a antiguos ríos del mundo. "Yo también" es la respuesta de Langston Hughes a un poema de Walt Whitman. El poema de Whitman describe la diversidad que existe en los Estados Unidos. El narrador de "Variaciones de sueños" imagina un mundo donde puede jugar y descansar libremente, y en donde se acepta el color negro de su piel. "Refugee in America" desafía al lector a analizar más detenidamente conceptos como libertad y autonomía.

Nèg la ap pale konsènan kèk rivyè • Mwenmenm, tou • Varyasyon nan rèv • Refijye ann Amerik

Langston Hughes

Rezime Nan "Nèg la ap pale konsènan kèk rivyè," oratè a raple eksperyans pèp li a te fè bò rivyè antik monn lan. "Mwenmenm, tou" se repons Langston Hughes te bay pou yon powèm Walk Whitman te ekri. Powèm Whitman lan dekri varyete ki egziste ann Amerik. Oratè nan "Varyasyon nan rèv" imajine yon monn kote li ka jwe epi repoze libè libè epi nan yon monn kote yo aksepte nwasè po li. "Refijye ann Amerik" defye lektè a pou l panse avèk plis atansyon sou kèk mo tankou li afranchisman ak libète.

Ang Negro ay Nagsasalitá Tungkol sa mga Ilog • Ako Rin • Sari-Saring mga Panaginip • Refugee sa Amerika

Langston Hughes

Mga Buod Sa "Ang Negro ay Nagsasalitá Tungkol sa mga Ilog," iniisip ng tagapagsalitá ang karanasan ng kanyang mga ninuno sa tabi ng mga matatandang ilog ng mundo. Ang "Ako Rin" ay ang sagot ni Langston Hughes sa isang tulá ni Walt Whitman. Inilalarawan ng tulá ni Whitman ang pagkakaroon ng pagkakaiba-iba sa Amerika. Pinag-iisipan ng nagsasalita sa "Sari-saring mga Panaginip" ang isang mundo kung saan maaari siyang maglaró at mamahingá nang malaya, at kung saan tinatanggap ang kaitiman ng kanyang balát. Ang "Refugee sa Amerika" ay naghahámon sa mga mambabasá na mas maingat na pag-isipan ang mga salitá tulad ng kalayaan at kasarinlan.

Cov Khej Dub Tham Txog Cov Kwj Deg • Kuv Thiab • Ntau Zaj Npau Suav Sib Txawv • Neeg Thoj Nam Nyob Tebchaws Meskas

Langston Hughes

Cov ntsiab Hauv "Cov Khej Dub Tham Txog Cov Kwj Deg," tus neeg hais lus nco qab txog tej yam uas tshwm hauv nws lub neej ntawm nws cov neeg uas nyob raws ntug dej ntawm cov dej nyob thoob lub ntiaj teb. "Kuv Thiab" yog Langston Hughes cov lus teb rau ib zaj pajhuam los ntawm Walk Whitman los. Whitman zaj pajhuam piav txog ntau yam uas muaj nyob hauv Tebchaws Meskas. Tus neeg hais lus hauv "Ntau Zaj Npau Suav Sib Txawv" npau suav toog txog ib lub ntiaj teb us nws yuav ua si tau kaj siab lug thiab ib lub ntiaj teb uas nws xim tawv nqaij dub los yeej muaj kev saib taus thiab. "Neeg Thoj Nam Nyob Rau Tebchaws Meskas" ua rau cov nyeem xav zoo zoo txog ob nqe lus xws li kev ywj pheej thiab kev thaj yeeb.

《黑人描述河流》(The Negro Speaks of Rivers) • 《我也是》(I, Too) • 《夢境的變化》(Dream Variations) • 《美國境內的難民》(Refugee in America)

Langston Hughes

摘要 在《黑人描述河流》中，敘述者回憶自己的同胞在世界古老河流沿岸生活的經驗。作者在《我也是》中對一首沃特·惠特曼的詩提出回應。惠特曼的詩描述存在美國境內的多樣性。《夢境的變化》中的敘述者則想像一個他可以自由地玩耍及休息的世界，而且他的黝黑膚色在那裡也能被接受。《美國境內的難民》則要求讀者更謹慎地思考諸如獨立自主與自由這些字眼。

Người Da Đen Nói Về Các Con Sông • Tôi Cũng Là Người Mỹ • Biến Tấu Ước Mơ • Người Tị Nạn ở Mỹ

Langston Hughes

Tóm Tắt Nhân vật trong bài "Người Da Đen Nói Về Các Con Sông" hồi tưởng lại người dân của ông đọc các con sông cổ trên thế giới. "Tôi Cũng Là Người Mỹ" là sự phản hồi của Langston Hughes đối với một bài thơ của Walt Whitman. Bài thơ của Whitman miêu tả sự đa dạng tồn tại trên đất Mỹ. Nhân vật trong bài "Biến Tấu Ước Mơ" tưởng tưởng ra một thế giới mà ở đó ông có thể chơi và nghỉ ngơi thoải mái, là nơi màu da đen của ông được chấp nhận. "Người Tị Nạn ở Mỹ" thách đố các độc giả suy nghĩ cẩn trọng hơn về các từ như quyền tự do và sự tự do.

흑인이 강에 대해 말한다 (The Negro Speaks of Rivers) • 나 역시 (I, Too) • 꿈의 변주곡 (Dream Variations) • 미국에서의 피난민 (Refugee in America)

Langston Hughes

요약 "흑인이 강에 대해 말한다" 에서 화자는 예부터 존재하는 강을 따라오며 그 의 부족이 겪게 되는 경험을 회상하고 있으며, "나 역시" 는 휘트먼의 시에 대한 응답시이다. 휘트먼의 시는 미국에 존재하는 다양성을 묘사하고 있다. "꿈의 변주곡" 에서 시인은 자유롭게 뛰놀 수도 쉴 수도 있으며 검은 피부도 받아들여지는 세상을 상상해 본다. "미국에서의 피난민" 은 독자로 하여금 자유와 해방과 같은 말을 좀더 주의 깊게 생각해 보도록 한다.

The Tropics in New York • From The Dark Tower • A Black Man Talks of Reaping

Claude McKay
Countee Cullen
Arna Bontemps

Summaries In "The Tropics in New York," a window fruit display in New York takes the speaker back home to the tropics. In "From the Dark Tower," the speaker seems to say that better times are coming for those who plant "while others reap." He says the night is no less lovely because it is dark. He closes by referring to waiting in the dark, tending "our agonizing seeds." In "A Black Man Talks of Reaping," the speaker describes his careful planting of a large crop from which he reaped only a small harvest. While his brother's sons gather the crops, his own children eat bitter fruit gathered from fields they not sown.

Los trópicos en Nueva York • Desde la torre oscura • Un hombre negro habla de cosechar

Claude McKay
Countee Cullen
Arna Bontemps

Resúmenes En "Los trópicos en Nueva York", el narrador ve un arreglo frutal en Nueva York que lo lleva de vuelta a los trópicos. En "Desde la torre oscura", el narrador parece decir que se aproximan mejores épocas para aquellos que plantan "mientras otros cosechan". Dice que la noche no es menos bella porque todo esté oscuro. Y cierra el poema refiriéndose a la espera en la oscuridad, cuidando de "nuestras agonizantes semillas". En "Un hombre negro habla de cosechar", el narrador describe su cuidadoso procedimiento para realizar un gran cultivo del que tuvo una pequeña cosecha. Mientras los hijos de su hermano recogen la cosecha, sus propios hijos comen frutas amargas que juntan de los campos que no sembraron.

Twopik yo nan Nouyòk • Sot nan tou nwa a • Yon mesye nwa ap pale konsènan rekòt

Claude McKay
Countee Cullen
Arna Bontemps

Rezime Nan "Twopik yo nan Nouyòk," yon fenèt kote yo etale fwi nan Nouyòk transpòte oratè a lakay li nan twopik yo. Nan "Sot nan tou nwa a," oratè a sanble l ap di tan miyò ap vini pou moun ki plante "pandan lòt ap rekòlte." Li di konsa paske l fè nwa sa pa retire nan bote nuit la. Li klotire lè l refere a tann nan fènwa, ap siveye "grenn agonizan nou yo." Nan "Yon mesye nwa ap pale konsènan rekòt," oratè a dekri fason li plante yon gwo kilti avèk anpil prekosyon kote se sèlman yon ti rekòt li te fè. Pandan pitit gason frè l la t ap ranmase kilti yo, pwòp pitit pa l ap manje fwi anmè yo te ranmase nan chan yo pa t plante.

Ang Tropiko sa New York • Mula sa Madilim na Tore • Isang Itim na Lalaki'y Nagsasalitá Tungkol sa Pag-aani

Claude McKay
Countee Cullen
Arna Bontemps

Mga Buod Sa "Ang Tropiko sa New York," dinala ng mga prutas na nakalantad sa isang window display sa New York ang tagapagsalitá pabalik sa kanyang sariling bayan sa mga tropiko. Sa "Mula sa Madilim na Tore," tila sinasabi ng nagsasalitá na darating ang mga maginhawang panahon para sa mga nagtatanim "habang ang iba ay nag-aani." Sinabi niya na 'di nababawasan ang kagandahan ng gabí dahil ito ay madilim. Nagtapós siya sa pamamagitan ng pagtukoy sa paghihintay sa dilim, habang pinangangalagaan "ang ating mga naghihirap na binhi." Sa "Isang Itim na Lalaki'y Nagsasalitá Tungkol sa Pag-aani," inilalarawan ng nagsasalitá ang maingat niyang paghahasik ng maraming tanim kung saan kaunti lamang ang kanyang nagapas na ani. Habang iniipon ng mga anak ng kanyang kapatid ang ani, ang kanyang mga sariling anak ay kumakain ng mapapait na bungang galing sa mga bukid na 'di nila tinamnan.

Cov Chaw Sov Hauv New York • Los Ntawm Lub Tsev Dub Siab Siab • Ib Tug Txiv Neej Dub Tham Txog Kev Sau Qoob Loo

Claude McKay
Countee Cullen
Arna Bontemps

Cov ntsiab Hauv "Cov Chaw Sov Hauv New York," tus neeg hais lus pom ib co txiv ntoo nyob ntawm lub qhov rai ua rau nws nco qab txog nws tsev uas nyob rau thaj chaw uas tshav ntuj nrig sov so. Hauv "Los Ntawm Lub Tsev Dub Siab Siab," tus neeg hais lus hais tias yeej yuav muaj hnub zoo tshaj rau cov neeg uas siv sijhawm cog qoob loo uas lwm tus tsuas tos "sijhawm sau" xwb. Nws hais tias yav tsaus ntuj tsis yog tsis zoo nkauj vim lub ntuj tsausNws xaus nrog kev tham txog txoj kev uas yus tos tsaus ntuj nti, zov thiab saib rawv txog "yus cov noob nyuaj siab." Hauv "Ib Tug Txiv Neej Dub Tham Txog Kev Sau Qoob Loo," tus neeg hais lus piav txog nws txoj kev maj mam cog ib plag zaub loj heev uas tsuas tau me me los xwb. nws tus kwv tij tej tub tuaj sau cov qoob loo, nws cov menyuam ho noj cov txiv ntoo iab uas los ntawm lwm daim teb uas lawv tsis yog cov cog los.

《紐約的熱帶》 (The Tropics in New York) • 《來自黑暗的高塔》 (From The Dark Tower) • 《一個黑人談論收割》 (A Black Man Talks of Reaping)

Claude McKay
Countee Cullen
Arna Bontemps

摘要 《紐約的熱帶》中，紐約的一個水果展示窗使敘述者想起自己位於熱帶的家。《從黑暗的高塔》的敘述者似乎在說，「當其他人在收割時」，對於種植的人來說，更好的時光即將來臨。他說夜晚並不會因為是黑暗的而較不迷人。他的結論是我們必須在黑暗中等候，並照料「我們苦悶的種子」。「一個黑人談收割」的敘述者描述自己小心翼翼地栽種了一大片農作物，而卻只獲得其中的一小部分收成。當他的兄長的兒子在收取作物時，他自己的孩子卻在啃咬從他們不播種的田地裡取得的苦澀水果。

Vùng Nhiệt Đới ở NewYork • Từ Trong Tháp Tối • Một Người Đàn Ông Da Đen Kể Chuyện Về Thu Hoạch Vụ Mùa

Claude McKay
Countee Cullen
Arna Bontemps

Tóm Tắt Trong "Vùng Nhiệt Đới ở NewYork" một cuộc trưng bày hoa quả trên các ô kính ở New York đưa nhân vật trong bài thơ trở về nhà mình ở vùng nhiệt đới. Nhân vật trong bài "Từ Trong Tháp Tối" dường như muốn nói rằng những ai phải trồng cây "trong khi người khác đi thu hoạch" sắp sửa gặp thời kỳ tốt đẹp hơn. Theo ông, vẻ đẹp của đêm không vì đen tối mà giảm. Tác giả kết thúc bài thơ bằng việc nhắc đến việc chờ đợi trong đêm, chăm nom "những hạt giống đau đớn của chúng ta". Nhân vật trong bài "Một Người Đàn Ông Da Đen Kể Chuyện Về Thu Hoạch Vụ Mùa" miêu tả việc anh ta gieo trồng cẩn thận một vụ mùa lớn nhưng chỉ thu hoạch được ít. Trong khi con của những người khác thu hoạch, các con của anh ăn những trái cây đắng được thu lượm về từ những cánh đồng mà chúng không gieo hạt.

뉴욕에서 느낀 열대지방 (The Tropics in New York) • 어두운 탑에서 (From The Dark Tower) • 한 흑인이 수확을 말하다 (A Black Man Talks of Reaping)

Claude McKay
Countee Cullen
Arna Bontemps

요약 "뉴욕에서 느낀 열대지방" 은 쇼윈도에 전시된 과일을 보며 화자가 고향인 열대지방을 떠올린다. "어두운 탑에서" 에서 화자는 "다른 이들이 수확하는 동안" 씨를 뿌리는 자들에게 더 좋은 때가 오리라고 말해 주는 듯 하다. 밤은 어둡기 때문에 마찬가지로 멋지다. 어둠 속에서 "고통스러워 하는 씨" 를 보살피며 기다린다는 말로 이 시를 끝맺고 있다. "한 흑인이 수확을 말하다" 에서 화자는 거둬들일 것은 작지만 작물을 조심스럽게 심고 있는 과정을 표사하고 있다. 형의 아들들이 그 작물을 수확하는 동안 자신의 아이들은 그들이 씨 뿌리지 않은 밭에서 주어온 쓴 과일을 먹는다.

from Dust Tracks on a Road

Zora Neale Hurston

Summary This is a section from a longer work. The author describes events from her childhood in a small Florida town. She used to wait at the side of the road for white travelers to pass by. She would ask to go with them for a short distance. Hurston also talks about an experience that changed her life. Her school had visitors one day. These were two white women. Hurston read aloud and the women were impressed. They invited Hurston to visit them at their hotel. They gave her gifts. The gifts of books pleased Hurston more than the candy or pennies.

de Huellas de polvo en el camino

Zora Neale Hurston

Resumen Ésta es sólo una parte de un trabajo más extenso. La autora describe vivencias de su niñez en un pequeño pueblo de Florida. Solía aguardar a un lado del camino a los viajeros blancos que pasaban cerca. Les pedía si podía acompañarlos un corto trecho. Hurston también habla acerca de una experiencia que le cambió la vida. Un día llegaron visitantes a su escuela. Eran dos mujeres blancas. Hurston leyó en voz alta y las mujeres quedaron impresionadas. La invitaron a visitar su hotel. Y le dieron algunos obsequios. Hurston estaba más contenta con los libros que con los dulces y los centavos que las mujeres le obsequiaron.

yon ekstrè nan Anprent pousyè sou yon wout

Zora Neale Hurston

Rezime Sa se yon seksyon nan yon ouvraj ki pi long. Otè a dekri kèk evenman ki te pase nan anfans li nan yon ti vil nan Florid. Li te konn rete tann sou bò wout la pou lè vwayajè blan yo ap pase. Li konn mande yo pou l akonpaye yo sou wout la pandan yon ti distans. Hurston pale tou konsènan yon eksperyans ki te chanje lavi l. Lekòl li a te gen kèk vizitè yon jou. Se te de dam blanch. Hurston te li byen fò epi dam yo te enpresyone avèk lekti a. Yo te envite Hurston al vizite yo nan otèl yo a. Yo te ba l kèk kado. Kado liv yo te satisfè Hurston plis pase sirèt oswa kèk penich.

mula sa Mga Bakás ng Alikabok sa Kalye

Zora Neale Hurston

Buod Ito ay isang bahagi mula sa isang mas-mahabang likhá. Inilalarawan ng awtor ang mga pangyayari nang bata pa siya sa isang maliit na bayan sa Florida. Dati-rati ay naghihintay siya sa may tabí ng kalye para sa mga putíng mambibiyahe na magdaan. Hinihiling niya sa mga ito kung maaari siyang sumabay sa kanila nang kaunti. Pinag-usapan din ni Hurston ang isang karanasan na nakapagbago ng kanyang buhay. Isang araw, ang kanyang paaralan ay nagkaroon ng mga panauhin. Ito ay dalawang putíng babae. Nagbasá nang malakas si Hurston at humanga ang mga babae. Kinumbida nila si Hurston na bisitahin sila sa kanilang hotel. Binigyan nila siya ng mga regalo. Ang mga regalong aklat ay higit na nagustuhan ni Hurston kaysa sa mga kendi o mga mamera.

Los ntawm Hneev Taw Nyob Rau Txoj Kev Luv

Zora Neale Hurston

Lub Ntsiab Nqe no yog los ntawm lwm zaj uas ntev tshaj nov. Tus sau piav txog tej yam uas tshwm sim thaum nws tseem yog menyuam yaus hauv ib lub zos me nyob Florida. Nws nyiam nyob ntawm kev tos cov neeg dawb uas tuaj ncigNws mus nug seb lawv puas kam nws nrog lawv taug kev mentsis. Hurston ho tham txog ib yam tshwm sim uas tau hloov nws lub neej lawm thiab. Muaj ib hnub muaj ib tug neeg tuaj saib nws tom tsev kawm ntawv. Yog ob tug pojniam Meskas dawbHurston nyeem ntawv thiab ob tug pojniam ntawd qhuas heevNkawd caw Hurston mus saib nkawd tom nkawd lus chaw so. Nkawd muab khoom plig rau nws. Cov khoom plig uas yog tej phau ntawv nyeem ua rau Hurston zoo siab tshaj cov qhob noom lossis cov nyiaj npib.

改編自《道路上的塵跡》(Dust Tracks on a Road)

Zora Neale Hurston

摘要 此篇文選改編自一個較長的作品。作者描寫自己兒時在一個佛羅里達州小鎮上的事情。她習慣在路邊等待白人旅客經過。她會要求與他們同行一段短距離。作者也談到一段改變她的人生的經驗。她的學校一天來了幾位訪客。這是兩位白人女性。作者大聲朗讀，讓這兩名女士留下深刻印象。她們邀請作者到她們住的旅館作客。她們給了她一些禮物。這幾本書籍禮物帶給作者的快樂勝過糖果或是金錢。

trích từ Những Dấu Chân Cát Bụi trên một Con Đường

Zora Neale Hurston

Tóm Tắt Đây là phần trích đoạn của một tác phẩm dài. Tác giả miêu tả các sự kiện trong tuổi thơ của mình ở một thị trấn nhỏ bang Florida. Cô bé thường đợi bên lề đường để được gặp những du khách da trắng đi ngang qua. Cô bé sẽ nói với họ cho mình đi cùng một đoạn đường ngắn. Hurston cũng kể về một sự việc đã làm thay đổi cuộc đời mình. Một ngày nọ, trường học của cô bé có khách đến thăm. Họ là hai phụ nữ da trắng. Hurston đọc chuyện to cho họ nghe khiến cho hai người phụ nữ bị gây ấn tượng. Họ mời cô bé đến khách sạn và cho quà. Trong các quà tặng này, cô bé thích nhất những quyển sách còn hơn cả kẹo hay những đồng xu.

길 위의 먼지 자욱 중에서 (Dust Tracks on a Road)

Zora Neale Hurston

요약 이 글은 장편의 한 부분이다. 저자는 플로리다의 어느 한 마을에서 유년시절을 보내게 되는데, 그때 있었던 일들을 쓰고 있다. 그녀는 백인 여행자들이 지나가는 것을 길가에 앉아 기다리곤 했었다. 짧은 거리였다면 그들에게 같이 가자고 하곤 했었다. 저자는 자신의 인생을 바꾼 경험에 대해서도 이야기한다. 어느 날 그녀가 다니는 학교에 손님이 두 명 방문한다. 그들은 백인 여성이었다. 저자는 큰소리로 책을 읽고 그 백인 여자들은 깊은 인상을 받는다. 그들은 저자를 자신들이 머물고 있는 호텔로 초대하고 선물을 준다. 선물은 책 이였고 사탕이나 돈을 받는 것보다 더 좋았다.

from Hiroshima

John Hersey

Summary On August 6, 1945, at 8:15 in the morning, the United States dropped an atomic bomb on Hiroshima, Japan. More than 100,000 people died as a result of the bombing. Miss Toshiko Sasaki, Dr. Masakazu Fujii, Mrs. Hatsuyo Nakamura, and Mr. Kiyoshi Tanimoto survived. This excerpt tells part of their story.

de Hiroshima

John Hersey

Resumen El 6 de agosto de 1945, a las 8:15 de la mañana, los Estados Unidos arrojaron una bomba atómica en Hiroshima, Japón. Más de 100,000 personas murieron a causa de la explosión. La señorita Toshiko Sasaki, el Dr. Masakazu Fujii, la Sra.Hatsuyo Nakamura y el Sr. Kiyoshi Tanimoto sobrevivieron. Este extracto cuenta partes de su historia.

yon ekstrè nan Iwochima

John Hersey

Rezime Le 6 out 1945, a 8 è 15 dimaten, Etazini te lage yon bonm atomik sou vil Iwochima, Japon. Plis pase 100 000 moun te mouri akoz bonbadman an. Mis Toshiko Sasaki, doktè Masakazu Fujii, madan Hatsuyo Nakamura ak mesye Kiyoshi Tanimoto te siviv. Ekstrè sa a rakonte yon pati nan istwa yo.

mula sa Hiroshima

John Hersey

Buod Noong ika-6 ng Agosto 1945, 8:15 ng umaga, ang Estados Unidos ay naghulog ng isang bombang atomiko sa Hiroshima, Japan. Higit sa 100,000 na tao ang namatáy bilang resulta nitong pagbobomba. Si Bb. Toshiko Sasaki, Doktor Masakazu Fujii, Gng. Hatsuyo Nakamura, at Gg. Kiyoshi Tanimoto ay nakaligtás. Ikinukuwento ng sanaysay na ito ang bahagi ng kanilang kasaysayan.

Los ntawm zaj Hiroshima

John Hersey

Lub Ntsiab Thaum lub yim hli ntuj hnub tim 6, 1945, thaum 8:15 sawv ntxov, Tebchaws Meskas tau tso ib lub foob pob loj heev poob los rau Hiroshima, Tebchaws Yivpoon. Tshaj 100,000 leej neeg tau tuag vim txoj kev tso foob pob loj no. Miss Toshiko Sasaki, Dr. Masakazu Fujii, Mrs. Hatsuyo Nakamura, thiab Mr. Kiyoshi Tanimoto tsis tuag. Nqe lus sau no yog qhia txog lawv cov zaj lus piav.

改編自《廣島》(Hiroshima)

John Hersey

摘要 1945年8月6日上午8:15，美國在日本廣島投下了一顆原子彈。超過 100,000 的人由於這場轟炸而死亡。佐佐木俊子小姐、藤井正一醫師、中村津裕夫人、以及谷本清詞先生則是生還者。這篇摘錄描寫了他們的部分故事。

trích từ Hiroshima

John Hersey

Tóm Tắt Vào lúc 8:15 sáng ngày mùng 6, Tháng Tám, năm 1945, Mỹ ném bom nguyên tử xuống thành phố Hiroshima, Nhật Bản. Hơn 100,000 người đã chết trong vụ ném bom. Cô Toshiko Sasaki, Bác Sĩ Masakazu Fujii, Bà Hatsuyo Nakamura và Ông Kiyoshi Tanimoto đã thoát chết. Đoạn trích này kể lại một phần câu truyện của họ.

히로시마 중에서 (Hiroshima)

John Hersey

요약 1945년 8월 6일 아침 8시 15분 미국은 원자 폭탄을 일본 히로시마에 투하한다. 그 결과 십만 명 이상의 희생자를 낸다. 이 발췌문은 생존자 사사키 토시히코 씨, 후지 마사카즈 박사, 나카무라 하쯔오 씨, 타니모토 키요시 씨가 그 날의 경험을 이야기하는 것이다.

The Death of the Ball Turret Gunner

Randall Jarrell

Summary In "The Death of the Ball Turret Gunner," the speaker uses images to show how deadly war is. The powerful final line shows the violence and finality of death in war.

La muerte del artillero de la cúpula blindada

Randall Jarrell

Resumen En "La muerte del artillero de la cúpula blindada", el narrador utiliza imágenes para mostrar la fatalidad de la guerra. La poderosa línea final muestra la violencia y la finalidad de la muerte en la guerra.

Lanmò bonbadye a

Randall Jarrell

Rezime Nan "Lanmò bonbadye a," oratè a itilize kèk imaj pou montre ki jan lagè se yon bagay ki mòtèl. Liy final pisan an montre vyolans ak finalite lanmò nan lagè.

Ang Pagkamatáy ng Mammaríl sa "Ball Turret"

Randall Jarrell

Buod Sa "Ang Pagkamatáy ng Mamamaríl sa Ball Turret," gumagamit ang nagsasalita ng mga larawang-isip para ipakita kung paano nakamamatay ang digmáan. Ipinapakita ng makapangyarihang hulíng linya ang dahás at ganáp-na-katapusan ng kamatayan sa digmáan.

Thaum Tus Neeg Tua Phom Hauv Qab Dav Hlau Tuag

Randall Jarrell

Lub Ntsiab Hauv zaj "Thaum Tus Neeg Tua Phom Hauv Qab Dav Hlau Tuag," tus neeg hais lus siv duab coj los qhia txog tias kev ua tsov rog phem npaum li cas. Kab lus muaj zog uas kawg qhia tau tias muaj kev sib ntaus sib tua thiab kev tuag ntau npaum li cas los ntawm kev ua tsov rog.

《旋轉炮塔炮手之死》(The Death of the Ball Turret Gunner)

Randall Jarrell

摘要 《旋轉炮塔炮手之死》一詩的敘述者利用一些畫面來描述致命的戰爭。令人震撼的最後一行文字顯示出戰爭中的暴力與死亡的終結。

Cái Chết Của Người Lính Pháo Binh Tháp Tròn

Randall Jarrell

Tóm Tắt Nhân vật trong "Cái Chết Của Người Lính Pháo Binh Tháp Tròn" sử dụng các hình ảnh để chỉ ra sự chết chóc của chiến tranh. Câu thơ mạnh mẽ cuối bài cho thấy chiến tranh chỉ gây ra bạo lực và cuối cùng là cái chết.

폭격기 조종사의 죽음 (The Death of the Ball Turret Gunner)

Randall Jarrell

요약 "폭격기 조종사의 죽음" 에서 화자는 이미지를 사용하여 전쟁이 얼마나 끔찍한가를 보여 준다. 특히 마지막 문장은 가장 강렬한 이미지로 전쟁의 폭력성과 죽음의 결말을 보여 준다.

The Life You Save May Be Your Own

Flannery O'Connor

Summary A one-armed man, Mr. Shiftlet, approaches a woman and her mentally challenged daughter, Lucynell. He agrees to fix up the old woman's property in exchange for food and a place to sleep. The woman wants him to marry her daughter. Eventually, he agrees. The woman gives him money to take a wedding trip. When Mr. Shiftlet and his new wife stop for food, he leaves her at the counter. He heads toward Mobile in the car. On the way, he picks up a hitchhiker. They argue and the boy jumps out of the car. Mr. Shiftlet drives toward Mobile alone.

La vida que usted salva puede ser la suya

Flannery O'Connor

Resumen El Sr. Shiftlet, un hombre manco, se acerca a una mujer y a su hija Lucynell, que tiene algunos problemas mentales. Acepta reparar la casa de la mujer a cambio de comida y un lugar para dormir. La mujer quiere que el hombre se case con su hija. Y finalmente, él acepta. La mujer les regala dinero para que hagan un viaje de recién casados. Cuando el Sr. Shiftlet y su nueva esposa se detienen a comer, él la abandona en el mostrador. Y se dirige a Mobile en el automóvil. En el camino recoge a un autoestopista. Luego discuten y el muchacho sale del automóvil. El Sr. Shiftlet conduce solo hasta Mobile.

Lavi ou sove a ka lavi pa w

Flannery O'Connor

Rezime Yon mesye ki gen yon sèl bra, mesye Shiftlet, apwoche yon dam ansanm ak pitit fi l la, Lucynell, ki gen yon andikap mantal. Mesye a dakò pou l fikse pwopriyete dam lan anretou dam lan ap ba l manje ak yon kote pou l dòmi. Dam lan vle pou misye marye ak pitit fi l la. Evantyèlman li dakò. Dam lan ba l lajan pou l ka al nan lin de myèl. Lè mesye Shiftlet ak nouvo madam li fè yon estòp pou manje, li kite madanm li sou kontwa a. Li dirije nan direksyon Mobil nan machin nan. Sou wout la, li ranmase yon moun k ap fè otostòp. Yo fè yon diskisyon epi ti gason an sote sot nan machin nan. Mesye Shiftlet kontinye kondui nan direksyon Mobil poukont li.

Ang Buhay na Iyong Iligtás ay Maaaring sa Iyo

Flannery O'Connor

Buod Si Gg. Shiftlet, isang lalaking iisa lamang ang braso, ay lumapit sa isang babae at sa kanyang anak na babaeng may kapansanan sa kaisipan na nagngangalang Lucynell. Pumayag siyang ayusin ang bahay ng babae kapalit ang pagkain at isang lugar na tutulugan. Nais ng babae na pakasalán nito ang kanyang anak. Maya-maya pa ay pumayag ito. Binigyan siya ng pera ng babae para sa isang biyaheng pagpapapakasal. Nang si Gg. Shiftlet at ang kanyang bagong asawa ay tumigil para kumain, iniwanan niya ang babae sa may lamesa. Siya'y tumungo sa Mobile, nang nakasakay sa kotse. Sa kanyang biyahe, pinasakay niya ang isang hitchhiker. Sila ay nagkasagutan, at ang batang lalaking nakisakáy ay tumalón palabás sa kotse. Mag-isang nagmaneho si Gg. Shiftlet patungong Mobile.

Ntshe Tej Zaum Txoj Sia Koj Cawm Tau Yuav Yog Koj Txoj

Flannery O'Connor

Lub Ntsiab Ib tug txiv neej uas muaj ib sab tes lawm xwb hu ua Mr. Shiftlet, los ntsib ib tug pojniam thiab nws tus ntxhais uas xiam oob khab hu ua Lucynell. Nws txaus siab yuav pab kho tus pojniam ntawd lub tsev thiab chaw nyob yog los pauv zaub mov thiab ib qho chaw pw. Tus pojniam xav kom tus txiv neej ntawd yuav nws tus ntxhais. Tsis ntev, tus txiv neej txaus siab ua li hais. Tus pojniam muab nyiaj rau nws coj tus ntxhais mus ncig ua si rau nkawd txoj kev sib yuav tag. Thaum Mr. Shiftlet thiab nws tus pojniam tau nres so noj mov, tus txiv neej tseg tus pojniam nyob rau ntawm chaw ua ntaub ntawvNws tsav tsheb mus rau tom lub chaw sam roj Mobile. Thaum tseem mus, nws pab thauj ib tug neeg taug kev. Nkawd sib cav thiab tus menyuam tub ntawd nrhia tawm ntawm lub tsheb. Mr. Shiflet tsav tsheb mus rau tom Mobile ib leeg.

《你拯救的也許是你自己的生命》 (The Life You Save May Be Your Own)

Flannery O'Connor

摘要 一位獨臂男人希佛特烈先生向一位女士及她的智障女兒露西奈爾搭訕。他同意修理這位老婦人的房子，以交換食物及睡覺的地方。這位婦人則希望他能娶自己的女兒。最後他也同意了。這位婦人給了他錢，讓他們去蜜月旅行。當希佛特烈先生及他的新婚妻子中途停下來用餐時，他將她留在櫃台。他朝汽車走去。在途中他載了一名搭便車的旅行者。他們吵了起來，而這名男孩跳出了車子。希佛特烈先生於是獨自開著車子。

Cuộc Sống Bạn Dang Tay Cứu Vớt Có Thể Mang Lại Cuộc Sống Cho Chính Bạn

Flannery O'Connor

Tóm Tắt Một người đàn ông bị cắt cụt một cánh tay tên là Shiftlet đến nói chuyện với một người phụ nữ và cô con gái thiểu năng trí tuệ của bà là Lucynell. Anh ta đồng ý sửa nhà cho bà để đổi lấy thức ăn và một nơi để ngủ. Người phụ nữ muốn anh ta cưới con gái mình. Rốt cuộc anh ta cũng đồng ý. Bà đưa tiền cho anh ta để họ đi hưởng tuần trăng mật. Khi Shiftlet và người vợ mới cưới của mình dừng lại để mua thức ăn, anh ta bỏ cô ấy lại quầy hàng. Anh ta đi về phía Mobile trên chiếc xe ô tô. Trên đường đi, anh ta cho một người đi nhờ. Họ cãi nhau và cậu trai đi nhờ nhảy ra khỏi xe. Shiftlet một mình lái xe về hướng Mobile.

당신이 구한 그 생명은 당신의 것일지도 모른다 (The Life You Save May Be Your Own)

Flannery O'Connor

요약 외팔이 남자 쉬프틀렛은 한 늙은 여인과 정신이 약간 이상한 딸 루시넬에게 다가간다. 먹을 것과 잠잘 곳을 제공 받는다는 조건에 쉬프틀렛은 그 늙은 여인의 집을 고쳐 주기로 한다. 그 여인은 그가 자신의 딸과 결혼해 주기를 바란다. 결국 그는 동의한다. 여인은 그에게 돈을 주며 신혼여행을 다녀 오라고 한다. 그와 루시넬은 여행을 떠나게 되고 식사를 위해 잠시 멈춘다 그는 루시넬을 식당 카운터에 남겨 놓고 주유소로 향한다. 도중에 히치하이커를 만나 차에 태워주나 곧 말다툼을 벌여 소년은 차에서 뛰어나간다. 쉬프틀렛은 혼자서 주유소를 향한다.

The First Seven Years

Bernard Malamud

Summary This story is about a shoemaker named Feld who runs a shop. He has an assistant named Sobel. He also has a daughter named Miriam. Feld wants his daughter to have a better life than he and his wife have had. He asks a college student named Max to call on her. He hopes the two will get married. Sobel hears the conversation Feld has with Max and runs out of the shop. He does not come back. Feld struggles to manage the shop and find a new assistant. When Feld meets Sobel again, Feld learns something above love and happiness.

Los primeros siete años

Bernard Malamud

Resumen Esta historia trata sobre un zapatero llamado Feld que posee una tienda. Y tiene un asistente llamado Sobel. También tiene una hija llamada Miriam. Feld desea que su hija tenga una mejor vida que la que han tenido él y su esposa. Le pide a un estudiante de la universidad llamado Max que la invite a salir. Espera que ambos se casen. Sobel escucha la conversación entre Feld y Max y sale corriendo de la tienda. Y no regresa. Feld se esfuerza por atender la tienda y encontrar a un nuevo asistente. Cuando Feld se vuelve a encontrar con Sobel, Feld aprende algo acerca del amor y la felicidad.

Sèt premye ane yo

Bernard Malamud

Rezime Istwa sa a pale konsènan yon kòdonye ki rele Feld k ap jere yon magazen. Li gen yon asistan ki rele Sobel. Epitou li gen yon pitit fi ki rele Miriam. Feld vle pou pitit fi l genyen yon lavi ki miyò pase lavi limenm ak madanm li te genyen. Li mande yon etidyan inivèsite ki rele Max rann pitit fi l la yon vizit. Li espere yo de a pral marye. Sobel tande konvèsasyon Feld genyen avèk Max epi li kouri sot nan magazen an. Li pa retounen. Feld ap lite pou l jere magazen an epi pou l jwenn yon nouvo asistan. Lè Feld rankonte Sobel ankò, Feld aprann yon bagay ki pi wo pase lanmou ak lakontantman.

Ang mga Unang Pitóng Taón

Bernard Malamud

Buod Ang kuwentong ito ay tungkol sa isang sapaterong nagngangalang Feld, na siyang nagpapatakbo ng isang tindahan. Mayroon siyang katulong na nagngangalang Sobel. Mayroon din siyang anak na babae na nagngangalang Miriam. Nais ni Feld na magkaroon ang kanyang anak ng mas-maginhawang kabuhayan kaysa sa kabuhayan nila ng kanyang asawa. Hiniling niya sa isang estudyante sa kolehiyo na nagngangalang Max na dalawin ang kanyang anak. Umaasa siya na ang dalawa ay magpapakasál. Narinig ni Sobel nang kausap ni Feld si Max, at siya'y tumakbo palabás sa tindahan. Hindi na siya bumalik. Nahirapan si Feld magpatakbó ng tindahan at maghanáp ng bagong katulong. Nang nakita muli ni Feld si Sobel, may natutunan si Feld na higit sa pag-ibig at kaligayahan.

Thawj Xya Xyoo

Bernard Malamud

Lub Ntsiab Zaj dabneeg no yog hais txog ib tug kws xaws khau hu ua Feld uas muaj ib lub khwNws muaj ib tug neeg pab ua haujlwm hu ua Sobel. Nws ho muaj ib tug ntxhais hu ua Miriam. Feld xav kom nws tus ntxhais muaj lub neej zoo tshaj nws thiab nws pojniam nkawd muaj. Nws hais kom ib tug tub kawm ntawv hu ua Max tuaj nrog tus ntxhais tham. Nws cia siab tias ob tug yuav sib yuav. Sobel hnov cov lus uas Feld tau muaj nrog Max ces nws txawm khiav tawm hauv lub khw lawm. Nws tsis rov qab los lawm. Feld khiav tsis taus haujlwm ib leeg hauv lub khw thiab mus nrhiav ib tug neeg pab tshiab. Thaum Feld tau ntsib Sobel dua, Feld kawm tau ib yam txog kev hlub thiab kev zoo siab.

《剛開始的七年》 (The First Seven Years)

Bernard Malamud

摘要 這則故事描寫一位名叫菲爾德的鞋匠，他經營一間商店。他的助理叫梭貝爾。他還有一位名叫梅莉恩的女兒。菲爾德希望女兒能過一種比他和妻子更好的生活。他要求一位大學生麥斯來找她。他希望這兩人能結婚。梭貝爾聽到菲爾德與麥斯的對話，就從店裡跑了出去。他沒有回來。菲爾德辛苦地經營這間店，並找了一位新助理。當菲爾德再度遇見梭貝爾時，菲爾德瞭解了某種超出愛與幸福的事物。

Bảy Năm Đầu

Bernard Malamud

Tóm Tắt Câu truyện này kể về một thợ làm giày tên là Feld. Ông ta có một cửa hàng và thuê một nhân viên phụ giúp tên là Sobel. Ông có một cô con gái tên là Miriam. Feld muốn con gái mình có một cuộc sống tốt hơn cuộc sống của vợ chồng ông. Ông yêu cầu một sinh viên đại học tên là Max ghé thăm cô bé. Ông hy vọng hai người sẽ kết hôn. Sobel nghe được cuộc nói chuyện giữa Feld với Max và chạy ra khỏi cửa hàng. Cậu ta không quay trở lại. Feld phải vất vả để quản lý cửa hàng và tìm một người phụ giúp mới. Khi Feld gặp lại Sobel, Feld nhận ra một số điều về tình yêu và sự hạnh phúc.

처음 칠 년 (The First Seven Years)

Bernard Malamud

요약 이 글은 펠드라는 이름의 구두 만드는 사람의 이야기이다. 펠드는 구두 가게를 운영하고 있으며 소벨이라는 조수를 데리고 일한다. 미리엄이라는 딸도 한 명 있었는데 그는 딸이 자신과 아내보다 더 좋은 삶을 살기를 원한다. 그는 맥스라는 한 대학생에게 딸을 찾아와 줄 것을 부탁하며 둘이 나중에 결혼하기를 바란다. 소벨은 맥스와 펠드의 대화를 듣고는 그 가게를 떠나서 돌아오지 않는다. 펠드는 가게를 운영하는 데 애를 먹고 새 조수를 구한다. 펠드가 소벨을 다시 만나게 되었을 때 그는 사랑과 행복 이상의 그 어떤 것을 깨닫게 된다.

Constantly Risking Absurdity…

Lawrence Ferlinghetti

Summary The narrator of "Constantly Risking Absurdity…" compares poets to acrobats. The comparison explains that both poets and acrobats perform for crowds, and both are judged by the success of their acts.

Constantemente al borde del absurdo…

Lawrence Ferlinghetti

Resumen El narrador de "Constantemente al borde del absurdo…" compara a los poetas con acróbatas. La comparación explica que los poetas y los acróbatas trabajan para complacer al público y ambos son juzgados según el éxito de sus trabajos.

Konstamman ap riske absidite…

Lawrence Ferlinghetti

Rezime Naratè a nan "Konstammman ap riske absidite…" konpare powèt yo ak akwobat. Konparezon an eksplike ni powèt ni akwobat pèfome pou foul moun, epi yo jije toulède selon siksè ak pèfòmans yo.

Palagiang Nanganganib sa Pagka-Waláng-Katuturán…

Lawrence Ferlinghetti

Buod Inihahambing ng nagsasalitá sa "Palagiang Nanganganib sa Pagka-Waláng-Katuturán…" ang mga manunulá sa mga acrobat. Ipinaliliwanag ng paghahambing na kapwa ang mga manunulá at mga acrobat ay gumaganáp para sa madla, at kapwa silang hinuhusgahán ayon sa tagumpáy ng kanilang mga pagganáp.

Constantly Risking Absurdity…

Lawrence Ferlinghetti

Lub Ntsiab Tus piav zaj "Constantly Risking Absurdity…" muab cov neeg sau pajhuam piv rau cov neeg txawj qoj tes taw nrhia. Qhov sib piv no piav tias cov neeg txawj pajhuam thiab cov txawj qoj tes taw dhia tib si ua yeeb yam rau neeg saib, thiab neeg txiav txim tias puas nyiam los tsis nyiam raws li lawv rab peev xwm ua tau zoo los tsis zoo.

《不斷遭受怪誕事物的危險…》 (Constantly Risking Absurdity…)

Lawrence Ferlinghetti

摘要 本書的敘事者將詩人比喻成特技演員。這種比較說明了詩人和特技演員都是為群眾表演，而兩者也都以其行動的成功受到評斷。

Luôn Có Nguy Cơ Bị Chê Là Vô Lý…

Lawrence Ferlinghetti

Tóm Tắt Người thuật truyện trong "Luôn Có Nguy Cơ Bị Chê Là Vô Lý…" so sánh các nhà thơ với các diễn viên nhào lộn. Sự ví von đó muốn nói lên một điều là cả nhà thơ và diễn viên nhào lộn đều phục vụ công chúng, và cả hai đều được đánh giá bởi sự thành công trong nghề của họ.

부조리를 끊임없이 감수하며… (Constantly Risking Absurdity…)

Lawrence Ferlinghetti

요약 "부조리를 끊임없이 감수하며…"에서 화자는 시인을 곡예사에 비유한다. 왜냐하면 둘 다 군중을 위해 행위를 보여 주며 그 행위의 성공 여부에 따라 판단되기 때문이다.

Mirror

Sylvia Plath

Courage

Anne Sexton

Summary "Mirror" shows a woman's feelings about growing older, as reflected in a mirror. "Courage" tells of the situations throughout life that require courage.

El espejo

Sylvia Plath

Coraje

Anne Sexton

Resumen "El espejo" muestra los sentimientos de una mujer sobre el envejecimiento, mientras se mira al espejo. "Coraje" describe las situaciones de la vida donde es necesario tener coraje.

Miwa

Sylvia Plath

Kouraj

Anne Sexton

Rezime "Miwa" montre santiman yon fanm genyen konsènan vyeyisman, jan yon miwa reflete sa. "Kouraj" rakonte kèk sitiyasyon atravè lavi ki mande pou gen kouraj.

Salamin

Sylvia Plath

Katapangan

Anne Sexton

Buod Ipinapakita ng "Salamin" ang damdamin ng isang babae tungkol sa pagtandá, bilang isang repleksiyón sa isang salamin. Tinatalakay ng "Katapangan" ang mga sitwasyon sa buhay na nangangailangan ng katapangan.

Daim Iav

Sylvia Plath

Ua Siab Tawv

Anne Sexton

Lub Ntsiab "Daim Iav" yog txog ib tug pojniam txoj kev xav thaum nws laus zuj zus lawm, xws li qhov pom nyob rau hauv daim iav "Ua Siab Tawv" qhia tej yam uas tshwm sim hauv kev ua neeg uas yuav tsum muaj lub siab tawv qhawv.

《鏡子》(Mirror)

Sylvia Plath

《勇氣》(Courage)

Anne Sexton

摘要 《鏡子》描寫一位女子對變老時在鏡中反映出的影像的感覺。《勇氣》則講述人生中需要勇氣的時機。

Chiếc Gương

Sylvia Plath

Sự Dũng Cảm

Anne Sexton

Tóm Tắt Bài "Chiếc Gương" lột tả những xúc cảm của một người phụ nữ về việc thấy mình già đi khi soi trong gương. Bài "Sự Dũng Cảm" kể về các tình huống trong cuộc đời đòi hỏi sự dũng cảm.

거울 (Mirror)

Sylvia Plath

용기 (Courage)

Anne Sexton

요약 "거울" 은 한 여인이 거울에 비친 자신의 나이든 모습을 보고 느끼는 감정을 그리고 있고 "용기" 는 인생을 살아가며 용기가 필요한 상황에 대해 쓰고 있다.

CUTTINGS and CUTTINGS (later)

Theodore Roethke

Summaries These two related poems describe how plants grow from small cuttings. In "CUTTINGS," Roethke illustrates the slow beginning, leaving the reader with a sense that there is more to come. In "CUTTING (later)," the poet continues the story, and reveals his amazement at the struggle.

RECORTES y RECORTES (más tarde)

Theodore Roethke

Resúmenes Estos dos poemas relacionados entre sí describen cómo crecen las plantas después de hacerles pequeños recortes. En "RECORTES" Roethke ilustra un comienzo lento y le deja al lector la idea de que muchas cosas más están por suceder. En "RECORTES (más tarde)", el poeta continúa la historia y revela su asombro ante la lucha.

BOUTI ak BOUTI (pita)

Theodore Roethke

Rezime De powèm sa yo ki asosye dekri fason plant yo grandi apati de bouti. Nan "BOUTI," Roethke ilistre debi lant lan, epi li kite lektè a avèk yon sans kote gen plis bagay k ap vini toujou. Nan "BOUTI (pita)," powèt la kontinye istwa a, epi li revele etonman li konsènan lit la.

MGA PINUTOL at MGA PINUTOL (mayá-mayá)

Theodore Roethke

Mga Buod Inilalarawan ng dalawang magkaugnay na tulá na ito kung paano tumutubo ang mga halaman mula sa maliliit na mga pinutol na sanga. Sa "MGA PINUTOL," ipinaliliwanag ni Roethke ang mabagal na pagsimulá, na nagpapadama sa mambabasá na mayroon pang higit na darating. Sa "MGA PINUTOL (mayá-mayá)," tinutuloy ng manunulá ang kuwento, at ibinubunyag niya ang kanyang pagtataká sa pagpupunyagi nito.

CUTTINGS thiab CUTTINGS (later)

Theodore Roethke

Cov ntsiab Ob zaj pajhuam uas sib txheeb no piav txog tias tej nplooj ntoos loj hlob ntawm tej tsob uas me me xwb. Hauv "CUTTINGS," Roethke hais txog txoj kev uas maj mam pib, uas ua tus nyeem mloog tau tias tseem muaj lwm yam yuav los ntxiv thiab. Hauv "CUTTING (later)," tus sau pajhuam tauj zaj dabneeg, thiab qhia txog nws tus kheej txoj kev ceeb thaum pom tias nyuaj npaum li cas.

《插條》(CUTTINGS) 以及《插條後續》(CUTTINGS (later))

Theodore Roethke

摘要 這兩首相關的詩作描述植物如何從小插條開始生長。作者在《插條》中描寫了緩慢的開端，讓讀者感覺即將有進一步的發展。而在《插條 — 後續》中，詩人繼續這個故事，並透露自己對於過程中的艱辛感到驚奇。

CÀNH GIÂM và CÀNH GIÂM (bài tiếp theo)

Theodore Roethke

Tóm Tắt Hai bài thơ liên quan đến nhau, cùng miêu tả cây cối mọc lên như thế nào từ những cành giâm nhỏ bé. Trong bài "CÀNH GIÂM" Roethke vẽ lên một sự khởi đầu chậm chạp để cho độc giả cảm nhận được rằng còn nhiều điều hơn nữa sắp diễn ra. Thi sĩ trong bài thơ "CÀNH GIÂM (bài tiếp theo)" tiếp tục câu chuyện và hé lộ sự ngạc nhiên của mình trước quá trình sinh trưởng của cây.

자른 가지 (CUTTINGS), 자른 가지 (후) (CUTTINGS (later))

Theodore Roethke

요약 서로 관련된 이 두 시는 작은 자른 가지에서 식물이 생겨나는 과정을 묘사하고 있다. "자른 가지"는 더딘 시작을 그리며 독자로 하여금 뭔가 더 올 것이라는 여운을 남긴다. "자른 가지 (후)"에서 시인은 첫 번째 시의 내용을 계속해서 이어나가고 식물이 안간힘을 쓰며 나오는 것에 경이로움을 느낀다.

UNIT
5

The Explorer • Frederick Douglass

Gwendolyn Brooks
Robert Hayden

Summaries The speaker in "The Explorer" searches for peace in a noisy apartment building. In "Frederick Douglass," the speaker longs for true freedom that will honor Douglass, one of the leading voices opposing slavery.

El explorador • Frederick Douglass

Gwendolyn Brooks
Robert Hayden

Resúmenes El narrador de "El explorador" busca paz en un ruidoso apartamento. En "Frederick Douglass" el narrador desea alcanzar la verdadera libertad que hará honor a Douglass, una de las voces principales que se oponen la esclavitud.

Eksploratè a • Frederick Douglass

Gwendolyn Brooks
Robert Hayden

Rezime Oratè a nan "Eksploratè a" ap chèche lapè nan yon imèb ki gen apatman kote gen anpil bwi. Nan "Frederick Douglass," oratè a ap tann avèk enpasyans vrè libète ki pral onore Douglass, youn nan vwa prensipal yo ki te opoze esklavaj.

Ang Nagsisiyasat • Frederick Douglass

Gwendolyn Brooks
Robert Hayden

Mga Buod Hinahanap ng nagsasalita sa "Ang Nagsisiyasat" ang katiwasayan sa isang maingay na apartment building. Sa "Frederick Douglass," ang nagsasalita ay nangangarap ng tunay na kalayaan na magbibigay-karangalan kay Douglass, isa sa mga pangunahing boses na tutol sa pang-aalipin.

Tus Neeg Nyiam Ncig Saib Tebchaws • Frederick Douglass

Gwendolyn Brooks
Robert Hayden

Cov ntsiab Tus neeg hais lus hauv zaj "Tus Neeg Nyiam Ncig Saib Tebchaws" nrhiav kev nyob ntsiag to hauv ib lub tsev uas muaj ntau yim nyob thiab taug ntsej heevHauv "Frederick Douglass," tus neeg hais lus xav tau kev ywj pheej kom hawm tau txog Douglass, uas yog ib tug neeg nquag tawm suab txog kev tawm tsam quab yuam lwm tus ua qhev.

《探險者》 (The Explorer) • 《佛瑞德瑞克·道格拉斯》 (Frederick Douglass)

Gwendolyn Brooks
Robert Hayden

摘要 《探險者》的敘述者想在一棟吵雜的公寓大樓中尋找平靜。《佛瑞德瑞克·道格拉斯》的敘述者渴求能讓道格拉斯感到光榮的真正自由，道格拉斯是反對奴隸制度的領導人。

Kẻ Đi Kiếm Tìm • Frederick Douglass

Gwendolyn Brooks
Robert Hayden

Tóm Tắt Nhân vật trong bài "Kẻ Đi Kiếm Tìm" kiếm tìm sự yên tĩnh trong một tòa chung cư ồn ào. Nhân vật trong bài "Frederick Douglass" ngóng trông sự tự do thực sự tương xứng công lao của Douglass, một trong những nhân vật có tiếng nói trọng lượng trong cuộc đấu tranh chống chế độ nô lệ.

탐험자 (The Explorer) • 프레드릭 더글라스 (Frederick Douglass)

Gwendolyn Brooks
Robert Hayden

요약 "탐험자" 에서 화자는 시끄러운 한 아파트 건물에서 평화를 찾아다닙니다. "프레드릭 더글라스" 는 진정한 자유를 열망하는 글로서 노예 제도 반대에 목소리를 높였던 더글라스를 기리고 있다.

"The Filling Station" and "One Art"

Elizabeth Bishop

Summaries In "The Filling Station," the speaker describes the sight of a gas station and everything around it. In "One Art," the speaker discusses how to deal with loss.

"La gasolinera" y "Un arte"

Elizabeth Bishop

Resúmenes En "La gasolinera", la narradora describe una estación de servicio y todo lo que la rodea. En "Un arte" la narradora habla sobre cómo afrontar una pérdida.

"Estasyon desans lan" ak "Yon atizay"

Elizabeth Bishop

Rezime Nan "Estasyon desans lan," oratè a dekri vizyon yon estasyon gazolin ak tout bagay ki antoure l. Nan "Yon atizay," oratè a diskite fason pou fè fas ak yon pèt.

"Ang Gasolinahan" at "Isang Sining"

Elizabeth Bishop

Mga Buod Sa "Ang Gasolinahan," inilalarawan ng nagsasalitá ang itsura ng gasolinahan at ang lahat ng nasa paligid nito. Sa "Isang Sining," tinatalakay ng nagsasalitá kung paano pasanín ang pagkakawalán.

"Lub Khw Sam Roj" thiab "One Art"

Elizabeth Bishop

Cov ntsiab Hauv "Lub Khw Sam Roj," tus neeg hais lus piav txog ib lub khw sam roj thiab txhua yam uas nyob ib ncig ntawd. Hauv "One Art," tus neeg hais lus tham txog txoj kev ua yuav ua neeg mus li cas thaum uas tau ploj ib yam lossis ib tug lawm.

《加油站》 (The Filling Station) 以及 《一種藝術》 (One Art)

Elizabeth Bishop

摘要 敘述者在《加油站》中描述一座加油站的景象以及有關此地的一切事物。《一種藝術》的敘述者則論述如何處理損失。

"Trạm Bán Xăng" và "Một Loại Nghệ Thuật"

Elizabeth Bishop

Tóm Tắt Nhân vật trong bài thơ "Trạm Bán Xăng" mô tả cảnh một trạm xăng và mọi thứ xung quanh đó. Nhân vật trong bài "Một Loại Nghệ Thuật" nói về việc làm thế nào để đối mặt với sự mất mát.

"주유소" 와 "예술 하나" ("The Filling Station" and "One Art")

Elizabeth Bishop

요약 "주유소" 에서 화자는 주유소와 그 주변을 묘사하고 있고, "예술 하나" 는 손실에 어떻게 대처해야 하는지를 이야기하고 있다.

The Rockpile

James Baldwin

Summary This story is about a boy who disobeys his mother. When he is hurt, his father, a pastor, blames his older stepbrother for not watching him. His mother does not blame the older boy. The conflict between the parents shows that each parent has different expectations for each of the boys.

Rockpile

James Baldwin

Resumen Esta historia trata sobre un niño que desobedece a su madre. Cuando el niño se lastima, su padre, un pastor, le echa la culpa a su hermanastro mayor por no cuidarlo. Pero la madre no culpa al hijo mayor. El conflicto entre los padres muestra que cada uno de ellos tiene diferentes expectativas con respecto a cada uno de sus hijos.

Rockpile la

James Baldwin

Rezime Istwa sa a pale konsènan yon ti gason ki dezobeyi manman l. Lè l frape, papa l, ki se yon pastè, blame demi-frè l la ki pi gran pase l paske l pa t siveye l. Manman l pa blame ti gason ki pi gran an. Konfli ki gen ant paran yo montre chak paran genyen diferan atant pou chak ti gason yo.

Ang Tumpok ng Bato

James Baldwin

Buod Itong kuwento ay tungkol sa isang batang lalaki na hindi sumunod sa kanyang ina. Nang siya ay masaktan, sinisi ng kanyang ama, isang pastor, ang kanyang nakatatandang stepbrother dahil 'di siya binantayan nito. Hindi sinisi ng ina ang nakatatandang bata. Ipinakita ng pagkakasalungat ng mga magulang na ang bawat magulang ay may mga ibang inaasahan para sa bawat bata.

Pawg Pobzeb

James Baldwin

Lub Ntsiab Zaj dabneeg no yog hais txog ib tug menyuam tub uas tsis mloog nws niam. Thaum nws raug mob, nws txiv, uas yog ib tug xib fwb teev ntuj cem nws tus tij laug hlob uas muaj niam txawv, tias tsis saib tus yau. Nws niam tsis cem tus menyuam tub hlob. Qhov kev tsis sib haum ntawm leej niam thiab txiv qhia tau tias leej niam leej txiv nyias muaj nyias kev xav tias ob tug tub yuav tsum coj li cas.

《石堆》 (The Rockpile)

James Baldwin

摘要 這則故事描寫一個不聽母親話的小男孩。當他受傷時，他的父親（一位牧師）責怪他同父異母的哥哥沒有看好他。他的母親則不怪這個哥哥。父母親間的衝突顯示出每位身為父母者對於每個男孩都抱有不同的期望。

Đống Đá

James Baldwin

Tóm Tắt Câu truyện này kể về một cậu bé không nghe lời mẹ. Khi cậu bị thương, bố cậu bé, một mục sư, đổ lỗi cho người anh trai cùng mẹ khác cha của cậu bé đã không trông em. Mẹ thì không trách người anh. Mâu thuẫn giữa cha và mẹ cho thấy mỗi người có kỳ vọng của riêng mình với từng đứa con.

바위 더미 (The Rockpile)

James Baldwin

요약 이 이야기는 어머니의 말을 듣지 않는 한 소년에 관한 것이다. 소년이 다치자 아버지와 목사님이 동생을 잘 돌보지 않았다며 이복 형을 나무라신다. 하지만 어머니는 형의 잘못이 아니라고 말한다. 이로 인해 부모님 사이에 일어나는 갈등은 부모님이 두 소년에게 기대하는 것이 각각 다르다는 것을 보여 준다.

from On James Baldwin

Toni Morrison

Summary In this excerpt, Toni Morrison remembers her colleague and friend James Baldwin, a distinguished African-American novelist and essayist. She talks about how he impacted her life both as a person and as a writer. Morrison claims that through his craft and interactions with others, Baldwin left three gifts to future generations of writers: language, courage, and tenderness.

extraído de On James Baldwin

Toni Morrison

Resumen En este extracto, Toni Morrison rememora a su colega y amigo James Baldwin, distinguido novelista y ensayista afroamericano. Cuenta la influencia que Baldwin tuvo sobre su vida, tanto a nivel personal como en su profesión de escritora. Morrison expresa que, a través de su arte e interacciones con los demás, Baldwin dejó tres legados a las futuras generaciones de escritores: el idioma, el coraje y la ternura.

yon ekstrè nan Sou James Baldwin

Toni Morrison

Rezime Nan ekstrè sa a, Toni Morrison sonje kòlèg li ki se zanmi li James Baldwin, yon womansye ak eseyis afriken ameriken. Li pale konsènan fason li te enfliyanse lavi l ni antank yon moun ni antank yon ekriven. Morrison pretann atravè abilite l epi entèaksyon l avèk lòt moun, Baldwin te kite twa kado pou jenerasyon fiti ekriven : langaj, kouraj ak tandrès.

Mula sa Tungkol kay James Baldwin [On James Baldwin]

Toni Morrison

Buod Sa maikling bahagi na ito, natatandaan ni Toni Morrison ang kanyang kasamahan at kaibigang si James Baldwin, isang tanyag na Aprikano-Amerikanong nobelista at mananalaysay. Pinag-uusapan ni Morrison kung paano nito naapektohan ang kanyang buhay bilang isang tao at isang manunulat. Ayon kay Morrison, sa pamamagitan ng husay ni Baldwin sa pagsusulat at sa kanyang pakikihalubilo sa iba, nag-iwan siya ng tatlong regalo sa mga darating na henerasyon ng manunulat: wika, katapangan, at pagiging malambing.

los ntawm zaj Hais Txog James Baldwin

Toni Morrison

Lub Ntsiab Nyob rau nqe no, Toni Morrison xav txog nws tus phoojywg James Baldwin, uas yog ib tug neeg Meskas Dub txawj sau ntawv heev. Nws tham txog tias tus phoojywg no tau txhawb tau nws npaum li cas hais txog tus kheej thiab kev sau ntawv tib si. Morrison hais tias tus phoojywg no txoj kev sau ntawv thiab kev ua phoojywg nrog tibneeg tsim tau muaj peb yam khoom plig zoo rau cov tub ntxhais yav tom ntej: cov lus siv, lub siab tawv, thiab kev ua zoo.

《論關詹姆士·鮑德溫》(On James Baldwin) 作者

Toni Morrison

摘要 在這篇節錄文章中，作者回憶她的同事兼好友、也是傑出的非洲裔美國小說家與散文家 — 詹姆士·鮑德溫。她談到他本人及以作家的身份對她的生命造成的影響。 作者表示，透過他的作品及與其他人的互動，鮑德溫對未來世代的作家留下了三件禮物：語言、勇氣、以及溫柔。

trích từ Về James Baldwin (On James Baldwin)

Toni Morrison

Tóm Tắt Trong đoạn trích này, Toni Morrison tưởng nhớ một người vừa là đồng nghiệp vừa là người bạn là James Baldwin, nhà văn Mỹ viết tiểu thuyết và tiểu luận xuất sắc. Bà giải thích ông ta đã tác động đến đời sống của bà, đến tác phẩm và chính con người của bà, như thế nào. Morrison cho rằng thông qua văn phong tinh xảo và giao tiếp với nhiều người, Baldwin và đã gửi gắm cho thế hệ viết văn trẻ ba món quà quý: đó là ngôn từ, sự can đảm, và tính nhẹ nhàng.

제임스 볼드윈에 관하여에서 (from On James Baldwin)

Toni Morrison

요약 이 발췌문에서 Toni Morrison 은 자신의 동료이자 친구로서 특출한 아프리카계 미국인 소설가 겸 수필가인 제임스 볼드윈에 대하여 회상한다. 그녀는 볼드윈이 그녀의 인생에 있어서 한 인간으로서 그리고 또 한 작가로서 얼마나 지대한 영향을 주었는가에 대해 말한다. 볼드윈은 자신의 작품과 다른 사람들과의 관계를 통하여 다음 세대의 작가들에게 언어와 용기와 정감이라는 세 가지 선물을 남겼다고 모리슨은 주장한다.

Inaugural Address

John F. Kennedy

Summary An inaugural address is the speech a president gives when he takes office. John F. Kennedy delivered his inaugural address in 1961. Tensions were high between the United States and the Soviet Union. The possibility of a nuclear war was real. In his speech, Kennedy spoke to the fears of both the nation and the world. He reminded Americans that they had inherited a responsibility to defend freedom. The new President urged Americans to serve their country with the famous words. "Ask not what your country can do for you—ask what you can do for your country." Then, he called on the citizens of the world to work together for the freedom of people everywhere.

Discurso inaugural

John F. Kennedy

Resumen Un discurso inaugural es el discurso que pronuncia un presidente cuando asume su cargo. John F. Kennedy pronunció su discurso inaugural en 1961. Había mucha tensión entre los Estados Unidos y la Unión Soviética. Existía la posibilidad de una guerra nuclear. En su discurso Kennedy habló de los miedos de la nación y el mundo. Les recordó a los estadounidenses que han heredado la responsabilidad de defender la libertad. Con sus famosas palabras, el nuevo presidente impulsó a los estadounidenses a que sirvieran al país. "No se pregunten qué puede hacer el país por ustedes; pregúntense qué pueden hacer ustedes por el país". Luego les habló a los ciudadanos del mundo para que trabajen juntos por la libertad de todas las personas.

Diskou inogirasyon

John F. Kennedy

Rezime Yon diskou inogirasyon se diskou yon prezidan fè lè l pral kòmanse dirije. John F. Kennedy te fè diskou inogirasyon l lan nan ane 1961. Tansyon yo te wo ant Etazini ak Inyon Sovyetik. Posiblite yon lagè nikleyè te yon bagay ki reyèl. Nan diskou l la, Kennedy te pale konsènan laperèz toulède nasyon yo ak lemonn genyen. Li te fè ameriken yo sonje yo te eritye yon responsablite pou yo defann libète. Nouvo prezidan an te ankouraje ameriken yo pou yo sèvi peyi yo avèk mo selèb sa yo. "Piga mande ki sa peyi w ka fè pou ou—mande pito ki sa ou ka fè pou peyi w." Ansuit, li te mande pou tout sitwayen nan lemonn travay ansanm pou libète moun tout kote.

Pang-Umpisáng Talumpati

John F. Kennedy

Buod Ang pang-umpisáng talumpati ay ang diskurso na ibinibigay ng isang pangulo kapag siya ay nagsimula sa kanyang katungkulan. Inihatid ni John F. Kennedy ang kanyang pang-umpisáng talumpati noong 1961. Mataas ang tensiyón noon sa pagitan ng Estados Unidos at ng Unyóng Sobyet. Mayroon noong tunay na posibilidád ng digmáang nukliyár. Sa kanyang talumpati, sinabi ni Kennedy ang mga takot ng kapwa bansa at ng mundo. Pinaalala niya sa mga Amerikano na sila ay nakamana ng tungkuling ipagtanggol ang kalayaan. Inanyayahan ng bagong Pangulo ang mga Amerikano na pagsilbihan nila ang kanilang bansa sa pamamagitan ng mga tanyag na pagbibigkas. "Huwag itanong kung ano ang magagawa ng inyong bansa para sa inyo—itanong kung ano ang magagawa ninyo para sa inyong bansa." Pagkatapos nito, tinawagan niya ang mga mamamayan ng mundo na magtulong-tulong para sa kalayaan ng mga tao sa lahat ng dako ng mundo.

Zaj Lus Tos Txais Lub Luag Haujlwm

John F. Kennedy

Lub Ntsiab Zaj lus tos txais lub luag haujlwm yog ib zaj lus uas tus thawj tswj tebchaws hais thaum uas nws sawv kev los ua haujlwm tshiab. John F. Kennedy hais nws zaj lus tos txais lub luag haujlwm thaum xyoo 1961. Tab tom yog sijhawm uas muaj kev tsis sib haum ntawm Tebchaws Meskas thiab Soviet UnionThaum ntawd muaj kev yuav ua tsov rog sib tua. Hauv nws zaj lus, Kennedy hais txog txoj kev ntshai ntawm ob lub tebchaws thiab lub ntiaj teb tib si. Nws hais kom cov neeg Meskas nco txog tias lawv ib txwm muaj lub luag haujlwm los tiv thaiv kev ywj pheej. Tus Thawj Tswj Tebchaws siv nqe lus uas nrov npe heev no los hais kom cov neeg Meskas ua haujlwm txhawb lawv lub tebchaws. Nws hais tias, "Tsis txhob nug seb koj lub tebchaws yuav ua tau dabtsi rau koj—nug seb koj ua tau dabtsi rau koj lub tebchaws." Ces nws hais txog cov pej xeem nyob thoob lub ntiaj teb kom sib sau uake los txhawb txoj kev ywj pheej ntawm tib neeg txhua txhia qhov chaw.

《就職演說》 (Inaugural Address)

John F. Kennedy

摘要 就職演說是總統上任時發表的演說。作者約翰・甘迺迪於 1961 年發表他的就職演說。當時美國與蘇聯間的緊張情勢高漲。核子戰爭一觸即發。甘迺迪在他的演說中提及全國與全世界的恐懼。他提醒美國人民，他們承接先人捍衛自由的責任。這位新上任的總統用以下這段著名的話敦促美國人民為國服務。「不要問國家能為你做甚麼 — 問自己能為國家貢獻甚麼。」他接著請求全世界的人民為了世界自由而團結在一起。

Diễn Văn Nhậm Chức

John F. Kennedy

Tóm Tắt Một bài diễn văn nhậm chức là bài diễn văn một tổng thống sẽ đọc khi nhậm chức. John F. Kennedy đọc diễn văn nhậm chức năm 1961. Vào thời điểm đó sự căng thẳng giữa Mỹ và Liên Bang Xô Viết đang rất cao. Khả năng xảy ra một cuộc chiến tranh hạt nhân là có thực. Trong bài diễn văn của mình, Kennedy nói về nỗi sợ hãi của hai quốc gia và của thế giới. Ông nhắc nhở người dân Mỹ rằng họ phải gánh trách nhiệm bảo vệ nền tự do. Vị Tổng Thống mới của nước Mỹ đã yêu cầu dân chúng hãy phục vụ đất nước mình bằng một câu đã trở thành nổi tiếng. "Đừng hỏi Tổ Quốc có thể làm gì cho mình—mà hãy hỏi mình có thể làm gì cho Tổ Quốc". Rồi sau đó, ông kêu gọi người dân trên thế giới cùng hợp tác vì tự do của mọi người khắp nơi.

대통령 취임 연설 (Inaugural Address)

John F. Kennedy

요약 1961년 존 에프 케네디가 대통령 취임 시에 한 연설이다. 당시는 미국과 소련 사이에 긴장이 고조된 시기였으며 핵 전쟁의 가능성도 점쳐지던 때였다. 이 연설에서 대통령은 우선 미국과 세계가 느끼는 두려움을 이야기한다. 그리고 미 국민에게 자유를 지켜야 하는 책임을 물려받았음을 상기시키며 다음의 유명한 구절로 나라를 위해 헌신할 것을 촉구한다. "국가가 당신을 위해 무엇을 해 줄지 묻지 말고 당신이 국가를 위해 무엇을 할 수 있는지 물어 보아라". 그리고 전 세계 사람들을 향해 어디에 있든지 간에 자유를 위해 같이 싸워 나가자고 호소한다.

Letter from Birmingham City Jail

Martin Luther King, Jr.

Summary Martin Luther King, Jr., was a civil rights leader. In April 1963, he was arrested for protesting segregation in Birmingham, Alabama. While in jail, King read a newspaper article that was critical of the civil rights movement. He responded to the article in this letter. In it, King criticized the police for their actions against protestors. He celebrated the real heroes who had the courage to take a stand against segregation. He also expressed confidence that the struggle for freedom would have a positive outcome.

Carta desde la cárcel de la ciudad de Birmingham

Martin Luther King, Jr.

Resumen Martin Luther King, Jr. fue un líder de los derechos civiles. En abril de 1963, fue arrestado por protestar por la segregación en Birmingham, Alabama. Mientras estaba en prisión, King leía un artículo del periódico que criticaba el movimiento por los derechos civiles. Y respondió al artículo a través de una carta. En su carta King critica a la policía por tomar medidas contra los protestantes. Y conmemora a los héroes reales que tuvieron el coraje de ponerse firmes ante la segregación. También se muestra confiado en que el conflicto por la libertad tendrá un resultado positivo.

Yon lèt ki sot nan prizon Birmingham City

Martin Luther King, Jr.

Rezime Martin Luther King, Jr., se te yon lidè nan zafè dwa sivil. Ann avril 1963, yo te arete l paske l t ap pwoteste segregasyon nan vil Birmingham, Alabama. Pandan l te nan prizon, King te li yon atik nan jounal ki t ap kritike mouvman dwa sivil la. Li te reponn a atik la nan lèt sa a. Nan lèt la, King te kritike lapolis pou aksyon yo te pran kont pwotestatè yo. Li te selebre vrè ewo yo ki te gen kouraj pou yo pran pozisyon kont segregasyon. Epitou li te eksprime konfyans li genyen kote lit pou libète ta va gen yon rezilta pozitif.

Liham mula sa Bilangguan ng Siyudad ng Birmingham

Martin Luther King, Jr.

Buod Si Martin Luther King, Jr. ay isang lider ng kilusan para sa mga karapatang sibíl. Noong Abril 1963, siya'y dinakip dahil sa kanyang pagpoprotesta laban sa segregasyón sa Birmingham, Alabama. Habang siya'y nasa bilangguan, nakabasa si King ng isang artikulo sa pahayagan na pumipintas sa kilusan para sa mga karapatang sibíl. Sinagot niya ang artikulo sa liham na ito. Dito, pinuna ni King ang mga pulis dahil sa mga pagkilos nila laban sa mga nagpoprotesta. Kanyang ipinagdiwang ang mga tunay na bayani na may katapangan na manindigan laban sa segregasyón. Kanya ring ipinahayag ang kanyang kompiyansa na ang paglaban para sa kalayaan ay magkakaroon ng mabuting resulta.

Tsab Ntawv Los Ntawm Lub Tsev Kaw Neeg Birmingham City Jail

Martin Luther King, Jr.

Lub Ntsiab Plaub Hlis xyoo 1963, nws tau raug ntes vim nws tawm suab hauv Birmingham, Alabama txog kev tsis nyiam txoj kev muab cai faib tsis sib luag rau txhua hom neeg. Thaum nws tseem tab tom raug kaw, King nyeem ib tsab ntawv xov xwm uas tseem ceeb heev rau kev tawm suab kom muaj vaj huam sib luagNws teb tsab ntawv ntawd nyob nrog tsab ntawv no. Hauv tsab no, King hais lus cem txog cov tub ceev xwm vim lawv txoj kev coj rau cov neeg uas tsis txaus siab rau lawv txoj kev ua haujlwm. Nws muaj lus zoo siab thiab qhuas txog cov neeg uas tau ua siab tawv qhawv los sawv cev tawm tsam kev coj tsis ncaj ncees rau hom neeg txawv. Nws ho hais txog nws txoj kev ntseeg tias yam nyuaj ntawm kev txhawb kom muaj kev ywj pheej tsuas yuav rov los txhawb tau rau sawvdaws xwb.

《來自伯明罕市監獄的信》 (Letter from Birmingham City Jail)

Martin Luther King, Jr.

摘要 作者馬丁・路德・金是一位民權領袖。他於1963年4月因為在阿拉巴馬州的伯明罕市抗議種族隔離政策而被捕。金在獄中讀到一篇批判民權運動的報紙文章。他在這封信中回應這篇文章。金在裡面批評警方壓制抗議者的行動。他讚揚有勇氣挺身而出對抗種族隔離政策的真正英雄。他還對這場自由的奮戰將有一個正面結果表達了信心。

Lá Thơ Từ Nhà Tù Thành Phố Birmingham

Martin Luther King, Jr.

Tóm Tắt Martin Luther King, Jr. là nhà lãnh đạo phong trào đòi quyền công dân. Vào Tháng Tư, năm 1963, ông bị bắt giữ ở Birmingham, Alabama vì phản đối chính sách phân biệt chủng tộc. Trong tù, King đọc một bài báo đả kích phong trào đòi quyền công dân. Ông đã phản hồi bài báo trong lá thơ này. King chỉ trích cảnh sát vì những hành động chống lại những người phản đối. Ông ngợi ca những người hùng thực sự, có đủ can đảm để bày tỏ quan điểm chống lại chính sách phân biệt chủng tộc. Ông cũng bày tỏ niềm tin rằng cuộc đấu tranh vì tự do sẽ có kết quả tích cực.

버밍엄 시 감옥에서 온 편지 (Letter from Birmingham City Jail)

Martin Luther King, Jr.

요약 저자는 인권 운동가이다. 1963 년 4월 앨라배마 주 버밍엄 시에서 인종 차별에 반대하는 데모를 벌이다 체포된다. 감옥에서 저자는 인권 보호 운동에 비판적인 한 신문 기사를 읽고 이 편지를 써서 응답한다. 편지에서 저자는 데모자들을 체포하는 경찰의 행동을 비판하며 인종 차별에 항거할 수 있는 용기를 가진 사람들을 찬양한다. 그리고 자유를 쟁취하기 위한 이 씨움이 긍정적인 결과를 가져올 것이라고 자신한다.

The Crucible, Act I

Arthur Miller

Summary It is 1692 in Salem, Massachusetts. The Reverend Parris is praying for his daughter Betty, who is ill. He says he saw his niece Abigail and Betty dancing in the woods. He asks Abigail why no one will hire her as a mother's helper since Mrs. Proctor fired her. Mary Warren comes in and says the village is accusing the girls of witchcraft. John Proctor comes for Mary and sends her back to his farm, where she works. Parris and all the girls but Abigail leave. Betty begins to wail. Others rush in, including kindly Rebecca Nurse, who calms Betty. Reverend Hale, an expert in witchcraft, enters. He questions Abigail, and she shifts the blame to Tituba, reverend Parris's slave. Frightened, Tituba says that she saw Sarah Good and Goody Osborn with the Devil. Abby cries out other names, and soon all the girls are crying out names.

El crisol, Acto I

Arthur Miller

Resumen Corre el año 1692 en Salem, Massachussets. El reverendo Parris reza por su hija Betty, que está enferma. Dice que vio a su sobrina Abigail y a Betty, bailando en el bosque. Y le pregunta a Abigail por qué nadie la ha contratado como niñera desde que la Sra. Proctor la despidió. Mary Warren entra y les dice que el pueblo acusa a las muchachas de hacer brujerías. John Proctor busca a Mary y la envía de regreso a la granja, donde ella trabaja. Parris y las demás muchachas parten, salvo Abigail. Betty comienza a lamentarse. Otras muchachas entran corriendo, incluida la amable enfermera Rebecca, que intenta calmar a Betty. Ingresa el reverendo Hale, un experto en brujerías. El reverendo interroga a Abigail, y ella le echa culpa a Tituba, la esclava del reverendo Parris. Aterrada, Tituba explica que ella vio a Sarah Good y a Goody Osborn con el demonio. Abby da otros nombres y pronto todas las muchachas comienzan a dar ciertos nombres.

Krezè a, Ak I

Arthur Miller

Rezime Nou nan ane 1692 nan vil Salem, Massachusetts. Reveran Parris ap priye pou pitit fi l Betty, ki malad. Li di konsa li te wè nyès li a Abigail ak Betty ki t ap danse nan bwa yo. Li mande Abigail poukisa pèsòn moun pa vle anboche l kòm yon èd manman piske madan Proctor te revoke l. Mary Warren rantre epi l di konsa vilaj la akize ti fi yo kòm moun k ap fè sòsèlri. John Proctor vini pou Mary epi li voye l retounen nan fèm li an, kote Mary travay. Parris ansanm ak tout ti fi yo pati eksepte Abigail. Betty kòmanse ap jemi. Lòt moun kouri rantre, ikonpri Rebecca Nurse ki emab, epi li kalme Betty. Reveran Hale, yon ekspè nan sòsèlri rantre. Li kesyone Abigail, epi Abigail voye responsablite a sou Tituba, esklav reveran Parris la. Tou efreye, Tituba di konsa li te wè Sarah Good ak Goody Osborn avèk Dyab la. Abby rele kèk lòt non, epi anvan lontan tout ti fi yo ap rele non moun.

Ang "Crucible", Ika-I Akto

Arthur Miller

Buod 1692 sa Salem, Massachusetts. Si Reverend Parris ay nagdarasal para sa kanyang anak na babaeng si Betty, na siyang may sakít. Sabi niya na nakita niya ang kanyang pamangking babaeng si Abigail at si Betty na nagsasayaw sa gubat. Tinanong niya si Abigail kung bakit walang kumukuha sa kanya para magtrabaho bilang isang katulong ng ina mula nang nasisante siya ni Gng. Proctor. Pumasok si Mary Warren at sinabi niya na sabi raw ng mga taong-bayan na ang mga babae ay mga mangkukulam. Sinundo ni John Proctor si Mary at pinabalik ito sa kanyang bukid, kung saan siya nagtatrabaho. Si Parris at ang lahat ng mga babae ay umalis maliban kay Abigail. Nagsimulang umungol si Betty. May mga ibang nagmadalíng pumasok, kabilang na rin ang mabait na si Rebecca Nurse, na siyang nagpahinahon kay Betty. Pumasok si Reverend Hale, isang eksperto sa pangkukulam, ay pumasok. Nag-usisa siya kay Abigail, at pinasa naman niya ang bintang kay Tituba, ang alipin ni reverend Parris. Sa kanyang takot, sinabi ni Tituba na nakita niya si Sarah Good at Goody Osborn na kasama ng Demonyo. Isinigaw ni Abby ang iba pang mga pangalan, at maya-maya, lahat na ng mga babae ang nagsisigawan ng mga pangalan.

The Crucible, Tshooj Ib

Arthur Miller

Lub Ntsiab Yog xyoo 1692 hauv Salem, Massachusetts. Reverend Parris tab tom thov tswv ntuj rau nws tus ntxhais Betty, uas muaj mob lawm. Nws hais tias nws pom nws tus ntxhais xeeb ntxwv Abigail thiab Betty seev cev hauv hav zoov. Nws nug Abigail tias vim li cas tsis muaj ib tug niam tsev uas yuav kam ntiav nws mus ua lawv tus neeg pab hauv tsev tom qab uas Mrs. Proctor tau muab nws rho tawm haujlwm lawm. Mary Warren tuaj txog thiab hais tias cov neeg hauv zos liam tias cov ntxhais yog poj dab. John Proctor tuaj ntsib Mary thiab hais kom nws rov qab mus rau nws daim teb, uas nws tau ua haujlwm. Parris thiab tagnrho cov ntxhais mus lawm thiab tsuas tshuav Abigail lawm xwb. Betty pib quaj. Lwm cov neeg khiav rov los hauv, nrog rau Rebecca Nurse, uas pab Betty. Reverend Hale, ib tug kws paub ntau yam txog poj dab cov kev ua khwv koob, nkag los thiab. Nws nug Abigail, thiab nws hloov cov lus iab liam mus rau Tituba, uas yog Reverand Parris tus qhev. Tituba ntshai heev ces nws thiaj hais tias nws tau pom Sarah Good thiab Goody Osborn nrog tus Dab thiab. Abby hu ob peb lub npe tawm, thiab tsis ntev txhua tus ntxhais iab liam ntau lub npe tawm.

《激情年代，第一幕》(The Crucible, Act I)

Arthur Miller

摘要 故事背景是1692年麻州的薩勒姆郡。派瑞斯牧師為生病的女兒貝蒂祈禱。他說他看到自己的姪女艾比蓋兒及貝蒂在樹林中舞蹈。他詢問艾比蓋兒，自從波洛克特夫人解雇她之後為何無人願意雇用她當母親幫手。瑪莉・華倫進入屋內，她說村裡正指控這些女孩玩巫術。約翰・波洛克特前來找瑪莉，並送她回到他的農場裡，她在此工作。除了艾比蓋兒外，派瑞斯以及所有的女孩都離開了。貝蒂開始嚎啕大哭。其他人趕忙進來，其中包括仁慈的瑞貝卡護士，她安撫著貝蒂。專精於巫術的海爾牧師進來了。他質問艾比蓋兒，而她卻轉而將過錯推卸給派瑞斯的奴隸堤杜巴。堤杜巴在極度害怕下說，她看到莎拉・古德以及古迪・歐斯朋和魔鬼在一起。艾比喊出了其他幾個名字，很快地，所有的女孩也都喊出一些名字。

Cuộc Thử Thách, Hồi I

Arthur Miller

Tóm Tắt Bối cảnh truyện là năm 1692 tại Salem, Massachusetts. Mục Sư Parris đang cầu nguyện cho cô con gái đang ốm của mình là Betty. Ông nói mình đã nhìn thấy cháu gái của mình là Abigail và Betty đang nhảy múa trong rừng. Ông hỏi Abigail tại sao không ai mướn cô ta làm người giúp việc kể từ khi bị Chị Proctor sa thải. Mary Warren đi vào và nói rằng ngôi làng buộc tội các cô gái có phép thuật ma quái. John Proctor đến tìm Mary và bảo cô quay trở về trang trại của anh ta, nơi cô làm việc. Ngoại trừ Abigail, còn Parris và tất cả cô gái bỏ đi. Betty bắt đầu khóc thét lên. Mọi người chạy xô vào, cả Rebecca Nurse tốt bụng cũng vào để trấn tĩnh cô bé. Mục Sư Hale, một người chuyên nghiên cứu về phép thuật bước vào. Ông ta hỏi Abigail, và cô ta đổ lỗi cho Tituba, một nô lệ của Mục Sư Parris. Hoảng sợ, Tituba nói mình nhìn đã thấy Sarah Good và Goody Osborn đi cùng Quỷ Xa Tăng. Abby gào lên những cái tên khác, và chẳng mấy chốc tất cả các cô gái cùng gào lên tố cáo người này người kia.

시련, 제 1막 (The Crucible, Act I)

Arthur Miller

요약 때는 1692년, 장소는 메사추세츠 주의 세일럼이다. 패리스 목사는 아픈 딸 베티를 위해 기도를 올린다. 그는 조카딸 아비게일과 베티가 숲 속에서 춤추는 것을 보았노라고 말하며, 아비게일에게 프록터 부인에게 해고 당한 후 왜 아무도 그녀를 고용하려 하지 않는지 그 이유를 묻는다. 이때 메리 워렌이 등장하고 마을 사람들이 소녀들을 마녀라고 비난하고 있음을 알려 준다. 따라 들어온 존 프록터는 메리를 그녀가 일하는 농장으로 돌려보낸다. 아비게일을 뺀 모든 소녀와 패리스 목사가 퇴장한다. 베티가 아파서 울부짖는다. 그러자 베티를 돌봐 주는 친절한 간호사 레베카와 마녀 사냥 전문가인 할리 목사를 비롯한 여러 사람이 등장한다. 할리 목사는 아비게일을 심문한다. 아비게일은 모든 것을 패리스 목사의 노예 티투바의 탓으로 돌린다. 겁에 질린 나머지 티투바는 사라 굿과 구디 오스번이 악마들과 같이 있는 걸 보았다고 말한다. 아비게일은 다른 사람의 이름을 소리치고 곧 거기 있던 소녀들도 제각각 다른 사람의 이름을 부른다.

The Crucible, Act II

Arthur Miller

Summary Act II opens in the Proctor home, eight days later. Elizabeth Proctor says fourteen people have been arrested for witchcraft, based on what Abigail and the other girls said. She urges John to testify that the girls are frauds. They quarrel over his previous affair with Abigail. Mary, back from court, gives Elizabeth a small doll. Mary says those who confess will not be hanged. She says that Elizabeth's name has been mentioned. Elizabeth says she is sure that Abigail wants her dead. Hale appears at the door. To test John, Hale asks him to list the ten Commandments. Ironically, John forgets the one about adultery. Then two men burst in. They say their wives have been arrested. The marshal arrives and arrests Elizabeth. Over John's protests, she is taken away in chains.

El crisol, Acto II

Arthur Miller

Resumen El Acto II comienza en la casa de Proctor, ocho días más tarde. Elizabeth Proctor dice que catorce personas fueron arrestadas por hacer brujerías, según lo que dijeron Abigail y otras muchachas. Y le pide a John que declare que las muchachas son unas farsantes. Discuten con Abigail sobre otros temas anteriores. Cuando Mary vuelve del tribunal, le regala a Elizabeth una pequeña muñeca. Mary dice que aquéllos que confiesen no serán colgados. Ella dice que se ha mencionado el nombre de Elizabeth. Elizabeth dice que está segura de que Abigail la quiere matar. Hale aparece en la puerta. Para poner a prueba a John, Hale le pide que recite los Diez mandamientos. Irónicamente, John olvida el que habla sobre adulterio. Luego, dos hombres entran precipitadamente. Dicen que sus esposas han sido arrestadas. El alguacil llega y arresta a Elizabeth. Sin importar las protestas de John, se la llevan encadenada.

Krezè a, Ak II

Arthur Miller

Rezime Ak II ouvri sou kay Proctor, uit jou aprè. Elizabeth Proctor fè konnen yo te arete katòz moun pou sòsèlri, selon deklarasyon Abigail ak lòt ti fi yo. Li ankouraje John pou l temwaye pou l fè konnen se manti ti fi yo ap bay. Yo fè diskisyon sou yon lyezon li te genyen avèk Abigail. Mary, ki sot nan tribinal, bay Elizabeth yon ti poupe. Mary di konsa yo pa pral pann moun ki konfese yo. Li di konsa yo te mansyone non Elizabeth. Elizabeth di konsa li sèten Abigail vle pou l mouri. Hale parèt nan pòt la. Pou l ka teste John, Hale mande misye pou l site di kòmandman yo. Iwonikman, John bliye kòmandman sou adiltè a. Ansuit de mesye parèt tou cho tou bouke. Yo di konsa yo sot arete madanm yo. Marechal la vini epi li arete Elizabeth. Malgre John pwoteste, yo anchene Elizabeth epi yo ale avèk li.

Ang "Crucible", Ika-II Akto

Arthur Miller

Buod Ang ika-II Akto ay nagbukás sa tahanan ng mga Proctor, pagkalipas ng walong araw. Sinabi ni Elizabeth Proctor na labing-apat na tao ang inaresto dahil sa pagiging mangkukulam, ayon sa mga pinagsasabi ni Abigail at ng ibang mga babae. Pinipilit niya si John na tumestigo at sabihing ang mga babaeng iyon ay mga manloloko. Sila ay nag-away tungkol sa nakaraan niyang relasyon kay Abigail. Si Elizabeth ay binigyan ni Mary, na kababalik lamang galing sa hukuman, ng isang maliit na manyika. Sinabi ni Mary na ang mga magkukumpisal ay hindi bibitayin. Sinabi niya na ang pangalan ni Elizabeth ay nabanggit. Sinabi ni Elizabeth na sigurado siyang nais ni Abigail siyang mamatáy. Lumitaw si Hale sa may pintuan. Para subukan si John, hiniling niyang ilista nito ang sampung "Commandments" o mga "Utos." Parang panunuyá, nalimutan ni John ang isang Utos tungkol sa pangangaliwá. Pagkatapos nito, may dalawang lalaking biglang pumasok. Sinabi nila na ang kanilang mga asawa ay inaresto. Dumating ang marsyal at inaresto nito si Elizabeth. Sa ibabaw ng mga pagpoprotesta ni John, siya ay dinaláng naka-kadena.

The Crucible, Tshooj Ob

Arthur Miller

Lub Ntsiab Tshooj Ob pib hauv Proctor lub tsev, yim hnub tom qab. Elizabeth Proctor hais tias muaj kaum plaub tus neeg tau raug txhom vim kev ua khawv koob dab, raws li Abigail thiab lwm cov ntxhais tau liam. Nws hais rau John tias kom qhia qhov tseeb tias cov ntxhais tsuas yog hais lus dag xwb. Nkawd sib ceg txog thaum nws tau tham Abigail dhau los. Mary rov los nram tsev hais plaub los thiab muab tau ib tug roj hmab me me rau Elizabeth. Mary hais tias cov neeg uas lees lub txim yuav tsis raug dai caj dab. Nws hais tias Elizabeth lub npe tau traug iab liam lawm thiab. Elizabeth hais tias nws yeej paub lawm tias Abigail xav kom nws tuag xwb. Hale tuaj txog ntawm qhov rooj. Hale sim John siab thiab nug nws txog kaum txoj cai kev ua neeg ncaj ncees hu ua Ten Commandments. Txawv kawg li uas John tsis nco qab txog nqe uas hais kom tsis txhob tham luag tus pojniam lossis tus txiv. Ces ob tug txiv neej nkag hlo los txog. Nkawd hais tias nkawv ob tug pojniam raug txhom lawm. Tus tub ceev xwm nkag los thiab txhom Elizabeth. Txawm John txwv npaum cas los lawv muab nws xauv tes coj mus lawm.

《激情年代，第二幕》(The Crucible, Act II)

Arthur Miller

摘要 第二幕一開始的場景是八天後的波洛克特家。依莉莎白・波洛克特說，由於艾比蓋兒及其他女孩的說詞，已經有十四個人因為巫術而被逮捕。她敦促約翰作證這些女孩是騙子。兩人為了約翰之前與艾比蓋兒有染的事而發生口角。瑪莉從法庭回來，給了依莉莎白一個小玩偶。瑪莉說，主動自白的人將不會受到絞刑。她說依莉莎白的名字已經被提起。依莉莎白說她很肯定艾比蓋兒希望她死。海爾出現在門口。為了試探約翰，海爾要求他列出十誡。諷刺的是，約翰竟然忘了其中一項有關通姦的戒律。接著兩個男人闖入。他們說自己的妻子已經被逮捕。警長也來了，他逮捕了依莉莎白。在約翰的抗議聲中，她被銬上鐵鍊帶走。

Cuộc Thử Thách, Hồi II

Arthur Miller

Tóm Tắt Hồi II mở ra với cảnh nhà Proctor tám ngày sau. Elizabeth Proctor cho biết, dựa vào lời nói của Abigail và các cô bé khác, 14 người đã bị bắt vì bị coi là có phép thuật. Chị yêu cầu John ra làm chứng rằng các cô bé đã khai gian. Họ cãi nhau về vụ ngoại tình trước đây của anh ta với Abigail. Mary trở về từ phiên tòa và đưa cho Elizabeth một con búp bê nhỏ. Mary nói rằng người nào chịu thú tội sẽ không bị treo cổ. Cô ta nói rằng tên của Elizabeth cũng bị nhắc đến. Elizabeth cho biết cô chắc rằng Abigail muốn cô chết. Mục Sư Hale xuất hiện ở cửa. Để kiểm tra John, Mục Sư yêu cầu anh ta đọc Mười Điều Răn. Nực cười thay, John quên mất một điều răn về tội ngoại tình. Sau đó, hai người đàn ông mở tung cửa bước vào. Họ cho biết vợ họ đã bị bắt. Viên cảnh sát trưởng đến bắt Elizabeth. Cho dù John chống đối, chị vợ vẫn bị xích tay đưa đi.

시련, 제 2막 (The Crucible, Act II)

Arthur Miller

요약 제 2막은 그 후 여드레가 지난 프록터의 집에서 시작된다. 아비게일과 다른 소녀들의 증언을 토대로 열네 명의 사람이 체포되었다는 것을 프록터 부인은 전한다. 부인은 프록터에게 소녀들이 거짓말을 하고 있음을 법정에 나가 증언하라고 촉구한다. 그러다가 둘은 프록터가 전에 아비게일과 가졌던 부적절한 관계에 대해 논쟁을 벌이게 된다. 법정에서 돌아온 메리가 부인에게 작은 인형을 주면서 자백하는 사람들은 교수형에 처해지지 않을 거라고 말하며 부인의 이름도 거론되었음을 말한다. 이에 부인이 아비게일은 자신의 죽음을 원한다는 것을 확신한다고 말한다. 할리 목사가 법정 문 앞에 모습을 드러낸다. 그는 프록터를 심문하기 전에 십계명을 외워 보라고 한다. 아이러니하게도 프록터는 간음에 관한 덕목을 잊어 버린다. 그때 두 명의 남자가 법정 안으로 뛰어 들어오고 자신들의 아내가 붙잡혀 있다고 말한다. 경찰이 프록터의 집에 들이닥치고 프록터 부인이 체포된다. 프록터의 저항에도 불구하고 그녀는 쇠사슬에 묶인 채 끌려간다.

The Crucible, Act III

Arthur Miller

Summary Act III opens with Giles Corey pleading for his wife's life. Then, Francis Nurse says the girls are lying. Proctor leads in a terrified Mary. Mary admits that she never saw any spirits. Danforth tells John that Elizabeth is pregnant. He says that she will not be executed until after the baby is born. Abigail swears that Mary is lying. To stop Abigail, John admits his infidelity. Elizabeth is brought in to back up John's claim. To protect John, she lies, so John is not believed. Abigail begins pretending that Mary's spirit is bewitching her. Mary hysterically takes back her confession. John is arrested. Hale condemns the court and leaves.

El crisol, Acto III

Arthur Miller

Resumen El Acto III abre con Giles Corey, que suplica le perdonen la vida a su esposa. Luego, Francis Nurse dice que las muchachas mienten. Proctor presenta a una Marry aterrada. Mary confiesa que jamás vio un espíritu. Danforth le dice a John que Elizabeth está embarazada. Él dice que Elizabeth no será ejecutada hasta que nazca el bebé. Abigail jura que Mary miente. Para detener a Abigail, John confiesa su adulterio. Elizabeth tiene que dar su declaración para respaldar las afirmaciones de John. Para proteger a John, Elizabeth miente, entonces nadie le cree a John. Abigail comienza a simular que el espíritu de Mary ha empezado a embrujarla. Histéricamente, Mary retira su confesión. John es arrestado. Hale declara culpable al tribunal y abandona el lugar.

Krezè a, Ak III

Arthur Miller

Rezime Ak III ouvri avèk Giles Corey k ap enplore pou yo pa touye madanm li. Ansuit, Francis Nurse di konsa ti fi yo ap bay manti. Proctor dirije l sou Mary ki tèrifye. Mary admèt li pa t janm wè ankenn espri. Danforth di John konsa Elizabeth ansent. Li di konsa yo pa pral touye Mary pazavan li akouche tibebe a. Abigail sèmante Mary ap bay manti. Pou l estope Abigail, John admèt li te gen yon lyezon avèk Abigail. Yo fè Elizabeth vini pou l ka kore sa John ap di a. Pou l ka pwoteje John, li bay manti, pou yo ka pa kwè John. Abigail kòmanse pretann espri Mary a ap ansòsele l. Nan yon fason isterik Mary repran konfesyon l lan. Yo arete John. Hale kondane tribinal la epi li pati.

Ang "Crucible", Ika-III Akto

Arthur Miller

Buod Ang ika-III Akto ay nagbukás nang si Giles Corey ay nagmamakaawa para sa buhay ng kanyang asawa. Tapos, sinabi ni Francis Nurse na ang mga babae ay nagsisinungaling. Inakay ni Proctor ang takot-na-takot na si Mary. Inamin ni Mary na 'di kailanman siya nakakita ng mga espirito. Sinabi ni Danforth kay John na si Elizabeth ay nagdadaláng-tao. Sinabi niya na ito ay hindi bibitayin hanggang pagkatapos ipanganak ang sanggol. Sinumpa ni Abigail na si Mary ay nagsisinungaling. Para pigilan si Abigail, inamin ni John ang kanyang pangangaliwá. Ipinasok si Elizabeth para pagtibayin ang pahayag ni John. Para protektahan si John, siya ay nagsinungaling, kaya si John ay hindi pinaniwalaan. Nagsimula si Abigail na magkunwaríng kinukulam siya ng kaluluwa ni Mary. Magulóng binawi ni Mary ang kanyang kinumpisal. Si John ay inaresto. Hinatulan ni Hale ang hukuman at ito'y umalis.

The Crucible, Tshooj Peb

Arthur Miller

Lub Ntsiab Tshooj peb pib thaum Giles Corey thov thov rau nws pojniam txoj siaCes Francis Nurse hais tias cov ntxhais dag xwb. Proctor coj Mary los thiab Mary ntshai heev li. Mary lees tias nws yeej tsis tau pom dab li. Danforth qhia John tias Elizabeth lub cev tab tom xeeb tub lawm. Nws hais tias nws yuav tsis raug tua kom txog tom qab yug tas tus menyuam tso. Abigail cog lus tias Mary tsuas yog dab xwb. Yuav kom nres tau Abigail, John lees txog nws txoj kev tham AbigailElizabeth raug coj rov qab los hais txog John txoj kev dag. Nws tsis lees vim nws tiv thaiv John, uas ua rau lawv tsis ntseeg John cov lus. Abigail pib dag tias Mary tus ntsuj plig los ua dab rau nws lawm thiab. Mary ntshai heev thiab rov nws cov lus tas. John raug txhom. Hale foom hmoov phem rau lub tsev hais plaub thiab tawm mus lawm.

《激情年代，第三幕》(The Crucible, Act III)

Arthur Miller

摘要 第三幕一開場則是吉爾斯・科瑞為自己妻子的性命求情。法蘭希斯護士接著表示，這些女孩在說謊。波洛克特將嚇壞的瑪莉帶了進來。瑪莉承認自己從未看過任何幽靈。丹恩佛斯告訴約翰，依莉莎白懷有身孕。他說她在嬰兒出生後才會被處決。艾比蓋兒發誓瑪莉在說謊。為了阻止艾比蓋兒，約翰承認了自己的不貞。依莉莎白被帶來證明約翰的聲明。為了保護約翰，她說了謊，因此約翰的話未被採信。艾比蓋兒開始假裝瑪莉的靈魂正在對她施法。瑪莉在歇斯底里下收回自己的自白。約翰被逮捕了。海爾譴責法庭的做法，接著就離開了。

Cuộc Thử Thách, Hồi III

Arthur Miller

Tóm Tắt Hồi III mở ra với cảnh Giles Corey nài xin tha mạng cho vợ mình. Sau đó, Francis Nurse cho biết các cô gái nói dối. Proctor đưa Mary vào. Mary hoảng sợ nhưng thú nhận rằng cô chưa bao giờ nhìn thấy bất kỳ một linh hồn nào. Danforth nói với John rằng Elizabeth đang mang thai. Ông cho biết chị ta sẽ không bị xử tử cho đến khi đứa bé ra đời. Abigail thề rằng Mary đang nói dối. Để ngăn Abigail lại, John thừa nhận vụ ngoại tình của mình. Elizabeth được đưa đến để chứng thực lời khai của John. Để bảo vệ John, chị nói dối, vì vậy không ai tin John. Abigail bắt đầu giả vờ rằng linh hồn của Mary đang bỏ bùa cô ta. Sợ quá, Mary rút lại lời khai của mình. John bị bắt. Mục Sư Hale lên án phiên toà và bỏ đi.

시련, 제 3막 (The Crucible, Act III)

Arthur Miller

요약 제 3막은 질레스 코레이가 자신의 아내를 변호하는 것으로 시작된다. 그리고 프랜시스 너스도 소녀들이 거짓말을 하고 있다고 전한다. 프록터는 겁에 질린 메리를 데리고 온다. 메리는 한번도 어떤 영을 본 적이 없다고 자백한다. 댄포스는 프록터에게 그의 부인이 임신했다는 것을 알려주며 아기가 태어날 때까지는 교수형에 처하지 않을 것임을 말한다. 아비게일은 메리가 거짓말을 하고 있다고 주장한다. 아비게일을 막기 위해 프록터는 과거 그녀와 있었던 일을 말하게 되고 프록터 부인이 이를 증명하기 위해 무대로 끌려 나온다. 그러나 프록터를 보호하고자 부인은 거짓말을 하고 아무도 존의 말을 믿지 않는다. 아비게일은 메리의 영이 자신에게 마술을 걸고 있는 척 하기 시작한다. 메리는 신경질을 부리며 자신의 고백을 취소한다. 존 프록터는 체포된다. 할리 목사는 재판을 비난하고 떠난다.

The Crucible, Act IV

Arthur Miller

Summary Act IV opens in the Salem jail. Danforth and Hathorne enter. Parris enters and tells the judges that Abigail and Mercy Lewis have stolen his money and run away. Parris, hoping that John or Rebecca will confess, asks for a postponement of their hangings. Danforth refuses. Hale enters to ask Danforth to pardon the condemned. Elizabeth is brought in. Hale asks her to urge John to confess. John is brought in and the couple is left alone. They express their love, but Elizabeth refuses to advise John about whether he should confess. John decides to confess but refuses to name others. He signs the confession but will not give it to Danforth. In a fury, he rips the paper, crying that he will not destroy his good name. He is taken away to be hanged.

El crisol, Acto IV

Arthur Miller

Resumen El Acto IV comienza en la cárcel de Salem. Entran Danforth y Hathorne. Entra Parris y les dice a los jueces que Abigail y Mercy Lewis le han robado su dinero y han escapado. Esperando que John o Rebecca confiesen, Parris pide que se postergue la ejecución. Danforth se niega. Entra Hale para pedirle a Danforth que perdone a los condenados. Elizabeth tiene que ingresar al tribunal. Hale le pide que convenza a John para que confiese. Traen a John, y la pareja queda sola. Se expresan su amor, pero Elizabeth se niega a aconsejarle a John que confiese. John decide confesar, pero se niega a dar nombres. Firma la confesión, pero no se la dará a Danforth. Furioso, rompe el papel mientras grita que no destruirá su buena reputación. Y se lo llevan para ejecutarlo.

Krezè a, Ak IV

Arthur Miller

Rezime Ak IV ouvri nan prizon Salem lan. Danforth ak Hathorne rantre. Parris rantre epi li di jij yo konsa Abigail ak Mercy Lewis te vòlè lajan l epi yo te sove. Parris, ki espere John oswa Rebecca pral konfese, mande pou yo ranvwaye pandezon yo a. Danforth refize. Hale rantre pou l mande Danforth pou l padone moun yo kondane yo. Yo mennen Elizabeth. Hale mande l pou ankouraje John pou l konfese. Yo mennen John epi yo kite koup la poukont yo. Yo eksprime lanmou yo, men Elizabeth refize konseye John si wi ou non li dwe konfese. John deside pou l konfese men li refize site non lòt moun. Li siyen konfesyon an men li pa vle bay Danforth li. An kolè, li chire papye a, l ap kriye epi li di konsa li pa pral detwi bon repitasyon l. Yo pran l al avèk li pou yo pann li.

Ang "Crucible", Ika-IV na Akto

Arthur Miller

Buod Ang ika-IV na Akto ay nagbukás sa bilangguan ng Salem. Pumasok si Danforth at Hathorne. Pumasok si Parris at kanyang sinabi sa mga huwes na ninakaw ni Abigail at Mercy Lewis ang kanyang pera, at sila ay lumayas. Umasa si Parris na magtatapat si John o si Rebecca kaya't humingi siya ng pagpapaliban ng kanilang pagbibitay. Tumanggi si Danforth. Pumasok si Hale at hiniling kay Danforth na patawarin ang mga hinatulan. Ipinasok si Elizabeth. Hiniling ni Hale sa kanya na kumbinsihing magtapat si John. Ipinasok si John at ang mag-asawa ay naiwang mag-isa. Ipinahayag nila ang kanilang pag-ibig, ngunit ayaw payuhan ni Elizabeth si John tungkol sa kung siya'y dapat magkumpisal. Nagpasiya si John na magtapat ngunit ayaw niyang magbanggit ng ibang pangalan. Pinirmahan niya ang kumpisyon pero ayaw niyang ibigay ito kay Danforth. Sa galit niya, kanyang pinunit ang papel, at sumigaw na 'di raw niya sisirain ang kanyang mabuting pangalan. Siya ay dinalá para bitayin.

The Crucible, Tshooj Plaub

Arthur Miller

Lub Ntsiab Tshooj plaub pib hauv lub tsev kaw neeg nyob hauv Salem. Danforth thiab Hathorne nkag los. Parris nkag los thiab qhia kws txiav txim hais tias Abigail thiab Mercy Lewis tau nyiag nws cov nyiaj thiab khiav lawmParris xav kom John lossis Rebecca lees thiab hais kom tsis txhob rawm muab leej twg dai li. Danforth tsis kam. Hale nkag los nug Danforth kom zam lub txim. Lawv coj Elizabeth los rau hauv. hais kom nws hais kom John lees tximJohn raug coj los thiab lawv tseg ob niam txiv nyob uake. Nkawd tham txog nkawd txoj kev hlub, tiamsis Elizabeth tsis kam hais rau John hais tias seb txiav txim siab yuav lam lees los tsis lees. John txiav txim siab lam lees tiamsis tsis kam iab liam txog lwm tus npe. Nws tis npe rau daim ntawv lees txim tiamsis tsis kam muab rau Danforth. Nws chim siab heev thiab cia li muab daim ntawv dua pov tseg lawm. Nws quaj hais tias nws yuav tsis rhuav nws lub npe zoo. Lawv coj nws mus dai tuag.

《激情年代，第四幕》(The Crucible, Act IV)

Arthur Miller

摘要 第四幕的開場是在薩勒姆監獄。丹恩佛斯和哈梭恩進來。派瑞斯也走了進來並告訴法官，艾比蓋兒和莫西‧路易斯偷了他的錢，然後逃跑了。派瑞斯希望約翰或是瑞貝卡可以自白，因此要求延後他們的絞刑。丹恩佛斯拒絕了。海爾進來要求丹恩佛斯赦免這些被判有罪的人。依莉莎白被帶了進來。海爾要求她鼓勵約翰自白。約翰也被帶進來，然後這對夫妻被單獨留下。他們表達對彼此的愛意，但依莉莎白拒絕對約翰是否應該自白的事提供意見。約翰決定自白，但拒絕指名其他人。他簽下自白書，但不將其交給丹恩佛斯。在狂怒之下，他撕了自白書，並嘶吼他將不會毀了自己清白的名聲。他最後被帶走吊死。

Cuộc Thử Thách, Hồi IV

Arthur Miller

Tóm Tắt Hồi IV mở ra với cảnh trong nhà tù Salem. Danforth và Hathorne bước vào. Mục Sư Parris cũng vào và nói với các thẩm phán rằng Abigail và Mercy Lewis đã ăn cắp tiền của ông và bỏ trốn. Với hy vọng rằng John và Rebecca sẽ thú tội, Parris yêu cầu được hoãn việc treo cổ. Danforth từ chối. Mục Sư Hale bước vào yêu cầu Danforth tha cho những người bị kết tội. Elizabeth được đưa vào. Hale bảo cô thuyết phục John thú tội. John được đưa vào và mọi người để hai người họ lại một mình. Họ bày tỏ tình yêu của mình dành cho nhau nhưng Elizabeth từ chối khuyên John về việc anh ta có nên thú tội hay không. John quyết định thú tội nhưng từ chối khai tên người khác. Anh ta ký vào giấy thú tội nhưng không đưa cho Danforth. Trong lúc tức giận, anh ta xé nát tờ giấy, kêu gào lên rằng anh ta sẽ không hủy hoại thanh danh của mình. Người ta đưa anh ta đi treo cổ.

시련, 제 4막 (The Crucible, Act IV)

Arthur Miller

요약 제 4막은 세일럼의 감옥에서 시작된다. 댄포스와 호오손 판사가 등장한다. 패리스 목사가 등장하여 존 프록터와 레베카가 자백하기를 바라며 그들의 교수형을 연기해 줄 것을 판사들에게 부탁한다. 그리고 아비게일과 머시 루이스가 자신의 돈을 훔치고 달아났다는 말도 전한다. 그러나 댄포스는 거절한다. 할리 목사가 등장하고, 선고 받은 사람들을 사면해 줄 것을 댄포스에게 요청한다. 프록터 부인이 등장하고 할리 목사는 그녀에게 존이 자백하도록 설득시키라고 종용한다. 이어 존 프록터가 등장하고 무대에는 이 부부만 남게 된다. 그들은 자신의 사랑을 확인하지만, 부인은 프록터에게 자백할 것을 권하지 않는다. 프록터는 자백하기로 결심하나 다른 사람들의 이름을 말하는 것은 거부한다. 자백서에 서명은 하지만 그 종이를 댄포스 판사에게 넘겨 주지 않을 것이다. 성난 그는 자신의 명예를 더럽히지 않을 거라 절규하며 자백서를 찢는다. 그리고는 교수형장으로 끌려간다.

Antojos

Julia Alvarez

Summary Yolanda's aunts warn her not to take a trip north by herself. She goes anyway. Yolanda stops to ask some boys to help her pick guavas. Yolanda finishes picking. By this time, all the boys except Jose have left. She and Jose find that she has a flat tire. Jose goes for help. Yolanda stays alone with the car. Suddenly two men with machetes appear. Yolanda is frightened, but the men change her tire. They refuse any payment. Yolanda finds Jose walking on the road. He says that no one would help him because they did not believe his story.

Antojos

Julia Alvarez

Resumen Una tía le advierte a Yolanda que no viaje sola al norte. Pero ella se va de todas formas. Yolanda se detiene y les pide a unos muchachos que la ayuden a recoger algunas guayabas. Yolanda termina de recogerlas. En ese momento se da cuenta de que todos los muchachos se han ido, salvo Jose. Yolanda y Jose descubren que ella tiene un neumático desinflado. Jose sale a buscar ayuda. Yolanda se queda sola junto al automóvil. De pronto aparecen dos hombres con machetes. Yolanda tiene miedo, pero los hombres le cambian el neumático. Y se niegan a recibir dinero a cambio. Yolanda encuentra a Jose caminando por la carretera. Él le dice que nadie lo ayudaba porque no le creían esa historia.

Antojos

Julia Alvarez

Rezime Matant Yolanda avèti l pou l pa vwayaje al nan lenò poukont li. Li pati kanmenm. Yolanda kanpe pou l mande kèk ti gason pou ede l ranmase kèk gwayav. Yolanda fin ranmase gwayav yo. Nan lè sa a, tout tigason yo te pati eksepte Jose. Limenm ak Jose reyalize yon kawotyou l plat. Jose al chèche èd. Yolanda rete poukont li nan machin nan. Toudenkou de mesye parèt avèk manchèt nan men yo. Yolanda pè, men mesye yo chanje kawotyou a pou li. Yo refize pou Yolanda peye yo. Yolanda jwenn Jose k ap mache sou wout la. Li di konsa pèsòn pa vle ede l paske yo pa t kwè istwa li a.

Antojos

Julia Alvarez

Buod Binabalaán si Yolanda ng kanyang mga tiya na huwag magbiyahe sa hilaga nang nag-iisa. Umalis din siya. Nakiusap si Yolanda sa ilang mga batang lalaki na tulungan siyang mamitás ng mga bayabas. Natapos na si Yolanda sa pamimitás. Nang natapos siya, nakaalis na ang lahat ng mga batang lalaki maliban kay Jose. Natuklasan niya at ni Jose na walang hangin ang isa niyang gulóng. Umalis si Jose para maghanap ng tulong. Naiwang mag-isa si Yolanda sa kotse. Biglang may dumating na dalawang lalaking may mga daláng bolo. Natakot si Yolanda, ngunit pinalitán ng mga lalaki ang kanyang gulóng. Sila'y tumanggi sa bayad. Nahanap ni Yolanda si Jose na naglalakad sa kalye. Sabi niya na walang nais tumulong sa kanya dahil hindi sila naniwala sa kanyang kuwento.

Antojos

Julia Alvarez

Lub Ntsiab Yolanda tus phauj ceeb toom nws kom tsis txhob mus sab qaum teb ib leeg. Nws tsis mloog thiab mus lawm. Yolanda mus nug kom ib co menyuam tub pab nws de txiv cuab thoj. Yolanda de tag. Txog thaum no, tagnrho cov menyuam tub twb mus tsev tas lawm thiab tshuav nws lawm xwb. Nws thiab Jose pom tau tias nkawd lub log tsheb tawm pa tas lawm. Jose mus nrhiav kev pab. Yolanda nyob ib leeg nrog lub tsheb. Ib pliag cia li muaj ob tug txiv neej tawm los uas nqa rab txuas. Yolanda ntshai heev, tiamsis cov txiv neej pab nws hloov log tsheb. Nkawd tsis kam txais nyiaj. Yolanda pom Jose taug kev los. Nws hais tias tsis muaj neeg kam pab nws vim lawv tsis ntseeg nws zaj dabneeg.

《安東荷斯》 (Antojos)

Julia Alvarez

摘要 尤蘭達的姑姑警告她不可獨自朝北旅行。她還是去了。尤蘭達中途停下來要求幾個男孩幫她摘番石榴。尤蘭達終於摘完了。此時，除了荷西外，其他所有的男孩都離開了。她和荷西發現，她的一個輪胎爆胎了。荷西於是去找人幫忙。尤蘭達單獨留在車子旁。有兩個帶著大砍刀的男人卻忽然出現了。尤蘭達極為害怕，但這兩個男人幫她換了輪胎。他們也拒絕任何報酬。尤蘭達看見走在路上的荷西。他說沒人願意幫他，因為他們全都不相信他的說詞。

Antojos

Julia Alvarez

Tóm Tắt Các dì của Yolanda cảnh báo cô ta không nên ra miền Bắc một mình. Dẫu vậy, cô vẫn đi. Yolanda dừng lại để nhờ vài cậu bé giúp mình hái ổi. Yolanda hoàn thành xong việc đó. Lúc này, tất cả các cậu bé đều đã bỏ đi, chỉ còn lại mình Jose. Cô ta và Jose phát hiện xe của cô bị xịt lốp. Jose đi tìm người giúp đỡ. Yolanda ở lại một mình bên chiếc xe. Đột nhiên, có hai người đàn ông cầm dao rựa xuất hiện. Yolanda hoảng sợ nhưng họ thay bánh xe cho cô. Họ từ chối không nhận tiền. Yolanda thấy Jose đang đi trên đường. Cậu ta nói sẽ không có ai đến giúp vì họ không tin câu truyện của cậu.

안토조스 (Antojos)

Julia Alvarez

요약 욜란다의 아주머니들은 욜란다 혼자서 북쪽으로 여행가는 것을 만류하신다. 그래도 어쨌든 그녀는 여행을 떠난다. 욜란다는 소년들에게 구아바 따는 것을 도와 달라고 부탁한다. 구아바를 다 따서 보니 호세만 남고 나머지 소년들은 다 가버렸다. 욜란다와 호세는 욜란다의 차 타이어에 펑크가 난 것을 알게 되고 호세는 도움을 청하러 간다. 욜란다 혼자 차 안에서 기다리고 있는데, 갑자기 칼을 든 남자 두 명이 나타난다. 그녀는 무서워진다. 그러나 그 두 남자는 펑크 난 타이어를 갈아 주고 보답으로 돈을 주려 해도 안 받는다. 욜란다는 걸어오고 있는 호세를 발견한다. 호세는 아무도 자기 이야기를 믿지 않아 도와줄 사람을 찾지 못했다고 말한다.

Everyday Use

Alice Walker

Summary The narrator and her daughter Maggie wait in the yard for the narrator's other daughter, Dee. The narrator is a hard-working woman from the Georgia countryside. Maggie is a shy young woman who was badly scarred during a house fire. Dee is an educated, confident woman. As a teenager, Dee abandoned her childhood home and culture. When Dee returns, she tries to take pieces of her heritage. Dee's visit helps Maggie and her mother discover their own pride.

Uso diario

Alice Walker

Resumen La narradora y su hija Maggie aguardan en el jardín a la otra hija de la narradora, Dee. La narradora es una mujer que trabaja con gran dedicación en el campo de Georgia. Maggie es una tímida jovencita que está llena de cicatrices a causa de un incendio que hubo en su casa. Dee es una mujer educada y segura de sí misma. En su adolescencia Dee abandonó el hogar y la cultura de su niñez. Cuando Dee regresa intenta quedarse con algo de su herencia. La visita de Dee ayuda a Maggie y a su madre a descubrir su propio orgullo.

Izaj kotidyen

Alice Walker

Rezime Naratè a ansanm ak pitit fi l Maggie ret tann nan lakou a pou lòt pitit fi naratè a, Dee. Naratè a se yon fanm ki travay di ki sot nan yon zòn riral nan Jòji. Maggie se yon jèn dam ki timid epi ki te boule anpil nan yon dife ki te pase lakay li. Dee se yon dam ki enstwi, ki gen konfyans nan tèt li. Lè l te yon adolesan, Dee te abandone kay ak kilti danfans li. Lè Dee retounen, li eseye pran kèk moso nan eritaj li. Vizit Dee a ede Maggie ak manman l dekouvri pwòp fyète yo.

Pang-Araw-Araw na Gamit

Alice Walker

Buod Ang tagapagsalitá at ang kanyang anak na babaeng si Maggie ay naghihintay sa bakuran para sa isa pa niyang anak na babaeng si Dee. Ang tagapagsalitá ay isang masipag na babae na galing sa bukirin ng Georgia. Si Maggie ay isang mahiyaing dalaga na siyang nagkaroon ng mga malubhang peklat dahil sa isang sunog sa bahay. Si Dee ay isang edukadang babae, na may kompiyansa sa kanyang sarili. Noong siya ay isang tinedyer, itinakwíl ni Dee ang kanyang tahanan nang siya'y bata pa at ang kanyang kultura. Nang magbalik si Dee, kanyang sinubukang angkinín ang mga piraso ng kanyang minanang-lahi. Ang pagdalaw ni Dee ay nakatulong kay Maggie at sa kanyang ina na matuklasán ang kanilang sariling karangalan.

Siv Txhua Hnub

Alice Walker

Lub Ntsiab Tus piav zaj no thiab nws tus ntxhais Maggie nyob hauv lub vaj vim tseem tos nws lwm tus ntxhais, Dee. Tus piav zaj no yog ib tug pojniam uas nquag ua haujlwm heev nyob rau hauv lub zos sab nraum ciam teb Georgia. Maggie yog ib tug ntxhais hluas thiab txaj muag heev uas tau raug mob thaum tsev kub hnyiab dhau los. Dee yog ib tug ntxhais kawm ntaub ntawv thiab tsis muaj siab ntshai dabtsi li. Thaum tseem yog menyuam yaus, Dee tau tso tsev thiab tej kab lis kev cai ntawm nws cov neeg tseg. Thaum Dee rov los, nws xav rov qab los nqa tej yam ntawm nws haiv neeg. Dee txoj kev rov los ntawd pab tau Maggie thiab nws niam pom tau nkawd ob tug kheej txoj kev qhua txog nkawd.

《日常用法》(Everyday Use)

Alice Walker

摘要 故事主人翁和女兒麥姬在院子裡等候她的另一位女兒 — 迪。故事主人翁是一位來自喬治亞州鄉間、辛苦工作的婦女。麥姬是一位害羞的年輕女性，她在一場住宅火災中留下嚴重的疤痕。迪則是一位受過良好教育、極有自信的女性。迪在青少女時期就捨棄了自己兒時的家及文化。迪返家後試圖拾回自己的文化傳統。迪的到來幫助了麥姬及她的母親發現屬於自己的驕傲。

Sử Dụng Hàng Ngày

Alice Walker

Tóm Tắt Người thuật truyện và con gái Maggie của mình đợi ở sân để gặp một người con gái khác của bà là Dee. Bà là một phụ nữ làm lụng chịu khó đến từ vùng quê của tiểu bang Georgia. Maggie là một phụ nữ trẻ nhút nhát mang rất nhiều sẹo trên người do một vụ cháy nhà. Dee là một phụ nữ có học và tự tin. Khi còn là một thiếu niên, Dee từ bỏ nhà của mình ở quê hương và nền văn hóa của mình. Khi Dee quay lại, cô cố gắng tiếp nhận từng chút di sản của mình. Chuyến viếng thăm của Dee giúp Maggie và mẹ mình khám phá ra niềm tự hào của chính họ.

매일 사용한다 (Everyday Use)

Alice Walker

요약 화자와 딸 매기는 마당에서 딸 디를 기다린다. 화자는 조지아주 시골 출신으로 부지런한 여성이다. 딸 매기는 부끄러움을 많이 타며 집에서 난 화재로 심한 화상을 입었다. 디는 교육을 받은 자신만만한 여성이다. 디는 십대였을 때 자신의 집과 문화를 등진다. 디는 돌아오고 자신이 물려받은 유산을 조금씩 알려고 한다. 디의 방문은 어머니와 매기에게 자부심을 심어 준다.

Everything Stuck to Him

Raymond Carver

Summary A young couple's baby will not stop crying. The wife thinks the baby is sick. The husband disagrees. The husband must choose between taking a trip and staying home with his wife.

Todo le sucede a él

Raymond Carver

Resumen El bebé de una joven pareja no deja de llorar. La esposa piensa que el bebé está enfermo. Su marido no opina lo mismo. El marido debe elegir entre irse de viaje, o quedarse con su esposa en casa.

Tout bagay te kole sou li

Raymond Carver

Rezime Tibebe yon jèn koup pa vle sispann kriye. Madanm nan panse tibebe a malad. Mari a pa dakò. Mari a dwe chwazi ant fè yon vwayaj oswa rete nan kay la avèk madanm li.

Ang Lahat ay Nakadikít sa Kanya

Raymond Carver

Buod Ayaw tumigil sa pag-iyak ang sanggol ng isang batang mag-asawa. Inakala ng babae na ang sanggol ay may sakít. Hindi sumasang-ayon ang lalaki. Kinakailangang pagpasiyahan ng lalaki kung siya ay bibiyahe o kaya'y maiiwan sa bahay kasama ang kanyang asawa.

Txhua Yam Daig rau Nws

Raymond Carver

Lub Ntsiab Ob niam txiv hluas hluas tus menyuam pheej tsis ntsiag liTus pojniam xav tias tus menyuam muaj mob. Tus txiv tsis xav li ntawdTus txiv yuav tau xaiv seb yuav mus kev deb raù ib txoj haujlwm los yog yuav nyob tsev nrog nws pojniam.

《困住他的每件事》(Everything Stuck to Him)

Raymond Carver

摘要 一對年輕夫妻的嬰兒不斷地哭鬧。妻子認為嬰兒生病了。但丈夫不同意。丈夫必須在外出旅行以及留在家中陪妻子之間做出選擇。

Mọi Thứ Đeo Bám Anh Ta

Raymond Carver

Tóm Tắt Một em bé con một cặp vợ chồng trẻ cứ khóc mãi không thôi. Người vợ cho rằng con mình bị ốm nhưng người chồng lại không nghĩ vậy. Anh ta phải lựa chọn giữa việc đi săn một chuyến hoặc ở nhà với vợ.

모든 것이 그에게 달라붙었다 (Everything Stuck to Him)

Raymond Carver

요약 한 젊은 부부의 아기가 멈추지 않고 계속 울고 있다. 아내는 아기가 아프다고 생각하지만 남편은 그렇게 생각하지 않는다. 남편은 여행을 떠나든가 아니면 아내와 같이 집에 있든가 둘 중의 하나를 선택해야 한다.

Traveling Through the Dark
William Stafford

The Secret
Denise Levertov

The Gift
Li-Young Lee

Summaries In "Traveling Through the Dark," the speaker finds a dead doe on the edge of the road. He hesitates before he pushes the animal into a river. In "The Secret," the speaker talks about two girls who discover the secret of life from reading a poem. In "The Gift," the speaker recalls a time when his father pulled a metal splinter from his finger. The speaker uses the technique years later to remove a splinter from his wife's hand.

Viaje a través de la oscuridad
William Stafford

El secreto
Denise Levertov

El regalo
Li-Young Lee

Resúmenes En "Viaje a través de la oscuridad", el narrador encuentra una liebre muerta al costado de la carretera. Y duda antes de arrojar el animal al río. En "El secreto", el narrador habla sobre dos muchachas que descubren el secreto de la vida cuando leen un poema. En "El regalo", el narrador recuerda una vez en que su padre se quitó del dedo una astilla de metal. Años más tarde, el narrador utiliza la mismà técnica para quitarle a su esposa una astilla de la mano.

Vwayaj nan fè nwa
William Stafford

Sekrè a
Denise Levertov

Kado a
Li-Young Lee

Rezime Nan "Vwayaj nan fè nwa," oratè a jwenn yon bich ki mouri sou bò wout la. Li ezite anvan l pouse bèt la nan yon rivyè. Nan "Sekrè a," oratè a pale konsènan de ti fi ki dekouvri sekrè lavi lè yo fin li yon powèm. Nan "Kado a," oratè a sonje yon epòk lè papa l te rale yon klis an metal nan dwèt li. Oratè a itilize teknik la dèzane aprè pou l retire yon klis nan men madanm li.

Pagbibiyahe sa Dilim
William Stafford

Ang Lihim
Denise Levertov

Ang Regalo
Li-Young Lee

Mga Buod Sa "Pagbibiyahe sa Dilim," nakahanap ang nagsasalita ng isang patáy na usa sa tabi ng daanan. Siya'y nagdalawang-isip bago niya itulak ang hayop sa isang ilog. Sa "Ang Lihim," kinuwento ng nagsasalita ang dalawang batang babae na silang nakatuklás ng lihim ng buhay mula sa pagbabasá ng isang tulá. Sa "Ang Regalo," natandaan ng nagsasalita ang isang panahon nang hinila ng kanyang ama ang isang bakal na sipak mula sa kanyang daliri. Makalipas ang ilang taón, ginamit ng nagsasalita ang parehong paraan para tanggalín ang isang sipak mula sa kamay ng kanyang asawa.

Ncig Tebchaws Thaum Tsaus Ntuj
William Stafford

Yam Zais Cia
Denise Levertov

Qhov Khoom Plig
Li-Young Lee

Cov ntsiab Hauv zaj "Ncig Tebchaws Thaum Tsaus Ntuj," tus neeg hais lus pom ib tug menyuam kauv tuag rau ntawm ntug kev. Nws xav ua ntej nws mam li muab thawb rau huav tus kwj deg lawm. Hauv zaj "Yam Zais Cia," tus neeg hais lus tham txog ob tug ntxhais uas nrhiav tau lub ntsiab ntawm kev ua neeg uas nyob rau hauv ib zaj pajhuam. Hauv "Qhov Khoom Plig," tus neeg hais lus nco qab txog ib lub sijhawm thaum nws txiv rub tau ib tug pos hlau tawm ntawm nws tus ntiv tes los. Tus neeg hais zaj lus no siv tib txoj kev ntawd coj los rho tus menyuam pos uas chob nws tus pojniam txhais tes.

《穿過黑暗旅行》(Traveling Through the Dark)
William Stafford

《秘密》(The Secret)
Denise Levertov

《禮物》(The Gift)
Li-Young Lee

摘要 《穿越黑暗旅行》的敘述者在路邊發現一隻死去的雌鹿。他在將這隻動物推入河裡之前有些遲疑。《秘密》的敘述者描述兩個女孩從閱讀一首詩中發現了人生的秘密。而在《禮物》中的敘述者則想起自己的父親曾經從他的手指中挑出一塊金屬碎片。敘述者多年後也利用這種技巧從他的妻子的手上移出一塊碎片。

Xuyên Qua Bóng Tối
William Stafford

Bí Mật
Denise Levertov

Món Quà
Li-Young Lee

Tóm Tắt Nhân vật trong bài "Xuyên Qua Bóng Tối" tìm thấy một con hươu cái đã chết bên rìa đường. Ông do dự trước khi đẩy xác con vật xuống sông. Nhân vật trong bài "Bí Mật" nói chuyện về hai cô gái khám phá ra bí mật của cuộc sống sau khi đọc một bài thơ. Nhân vật trong bài "Món Quà" nhớ lại lúc cha mình rút một mảnh dăm bằng kim loại ra khỏi ngón tay của cậu. Nhiều năm sau đó, cậu sử dụng đúng cách này để lấy một mảnh dăm ra khỏi tay vợ.

어둠 속을 여행하기 (Traveling Through the Dark)
William Stafford

비밀 (The Secret)
Denise Levertov

재능 (The Gift)
Li-Young Lee

요약 "어둠 속을 여행하기" 에서 화자는 길가에서 죽어 있는 암사슴을 한 마리 발견한다. 화자는 망설이다 죽은 암사슴을 강물에 밀어 넣는다. "비밀" 은 시를 읽으며 인생의 비밀을 발견하게 된 두 소녀에 관해 쓰고 있다. "재능" 에서 화자는 아버지가 자기 손에 박힌 금속 조각을 뽑아내던 것을 기억한다. 세월이 흐른 지금 화자는 기술을 사용하여 아내 손에 박힌 조각을 제거한다.

Who Burns for the Perfection of Paper

Martín Espada

Summary In "Who Burns for the Perfection of Paper," the speaker describes the physical labor of an after-school job.

¿Quién se quema por la perfección del papel?

Martín Espada

Resumen En "¿Quién se quema por la perfección del papel?", el narrador describe la actividad física que debe realizar en un trabajo después de la escuela.

Kiyès ki boule pou pèfeksyon papye

Martín Espada

Rezime Nan "Kiyès ki boule pou pèfeksyon papye," oratè a dekri travay fizik yon djòb li genyen aprè lekòl.

Sino ang Nagsusunog Para sa Kaganapan ng Papel

Martín Espada

Buod Sa "Sino ang Nagsusunog Para sa Kaganapan ng Papel," inilalarawan ng nagsasalita ang pisikal ng pagtatrabaho pagkatapos ng klase.

Leej Twg Mob Siab Rau Cov Ntawv Zoo Heev

Martín Espada

Lub Ntsiab Hauv zaj "Leej Twg Mob Siab Rau Cov Ntawv Zoo Heev," tus neeg hais lus piav txog txoj haujlwm ua tom qab tsev kawm ntawv lawb lawm.

《有人為了報告完美而燒毀》(Who Burns for the Perfection of Paper)

Martín Espada

摘要 本書的敘述者描述一份課後工作的體能勞動。

Chịu Phỏng Để Làm Ra Những Tập Giấy Hoàn Hảo

Martín Espada

Tóm Tắt Nhân vật trong "Chịu Phỏng Để Làm Ra Những Tập Giấy Hoàn Hảo" miêu tả cảnh lao động cực nhọc khi đi làm việc sau giờ học.

누가 종이를 완벽히 태울 것인가 (Who Burns for the Perfection of Paper)

Martín Espada

요약 "누가 종이를 완벽히 태울 것인가"에서 화자는 방과 후 맡게 된 육체 노동을 묘사하고 있다.

Camouflaging the Chimera

Yusef Komunyakaa

Summary In "Camouflaging the Chimera," the poet describes his experiences during the Vietnam War. He tells how soldiers used branches, mud, and grass to camouflage themselves. He relates his memories of being in combat.

Cómo ocultar la quimera

Yusef Komunyakaa

Resumen En "Cómo ocultar la quimera", el poeta describe sus vivencias durante la guerra de Vietnam. Cuenta cómo los soldados utilizaban ramas, barro y hierbas para ocultarse. Relata sus recuerdos de cuando estaba en combate.

Kamoufle mons lejandè a

Yusef Komunyakaa

Rezime Nan "Kamoufle mons lejandè a," powèt la dekri eksperyans li te fè pandan lagè Vyetnàm lan. Li rakonte ki jan sòlda yo te itilize kèk branch, labou ak gazon pou yo kamoufle tèt yo. Li rakonte souvni li yo lè l t ap batay.

Pagbabalatkayo ng "Chimera"

Yusef Komunyakaa

Buod Sa "Pagbabalatkayo ng Chimera," inilalarawan ng manunulá ang kanyang mga karanasan noong Digmáan sa Vietman. Ikinukuwento niya kung paano gumagamit ang mga sundalo ng mga sanga, putik, at damó para pagbalatkayohin ang kanilang mga sarili. Ikinukuwento niya ang kanyang mga alaala ng pagigíng nasa loob ng labanán.

Camouflaging the Chimera

Yusef Komunyakaa

Lub Ntsiab Hauv "Camouflaging the Chimera," tus sau pajhuam piav txog nws lub sijhawm nyob tsov rog Vietnam War. Nws qhia tias cov tub rog siv ceg ntoo, av nkos, thiab siv nyom coj los looj thaiv lawv tus kheej. Nws qhia txog tej yam nws nco qab txog kev sib tua.

《偽裝怪獸》 (Camouflaging the Chimera)

Yusef Komunyakaa

摘要 詩人在《偽裝怪獸》中描述自己在越戰時的經歷。他描寫士兵利用樹枝、泥土、以及草來掩飾自己。他聯想到自己在作戰時的回憶。

Ngụy Trang

Yusef Komunyakaa

Tóm Tắt Trong bài "Ngụy Trang," nhà thơ miêu tả những trải nghiệm của mình trong Cuộc Chiến Tranh Việt Nam. Ông kể lại các binh sĩ đã sử dụng cành cây, bùn đất, và cỏ như thế nào để tự ngụy trang. Ông thuật lại các ký ức khi tham chiến.

키메라를 위장시키기 (Camouflaging the Chimera)

Yusef Komunyakaa

요약 이 시에서 시인은 베트남 전쟁에서 겪었던 일을 묘사한다. 군인들이 나뭇가지와 진흙과 풀을 사용하여 어떻게 위장하는지를 말해 준다. 전투에 임했던 기억들을 이야기하고 있다.

Halley's Comet

Stanley Kunitz

Summary In "Halley's Comet," a young boy reacts to news that a comet is headed toward earth. He is both excited and frightened by what might happen when the comet lands.

El cometa Halley

Stanley Kunitz

Resumen En "El cometa Halley", un niño se sorprende por la noticia de que un cometa se dirige hacia la Tierra. El niño está entusiasmado y a la vez temeroso de lo que pueda ocurrir cuando el cometa aterrice.

Komèt Halley a

Stanley Kunitz

Rezime Nan "Komèt Halley a," yon jèn tigason reyaji devan nouvèl ki fè konnen gen yon komèt k ap vin nan direksyon latè. Tigason an eksite epi li pè alafwa pou sa ki ka rive lè komèt la ateri.

Ang Kometa ni Halley

Stanley Kunitz

Buod Sa "Ang Kometa ni Halley," ang isang batang lalaki ay tumugon sa balita na may isang kometa na patungo sa mundo. Siya'y kapwa nananabik at natatakot sa maaaring maganáp pagdating ng kometa.

Halley Lub Hnub Qub

Stanley Kunitz

Lub Ntsiab Hauv "Halley Lub Hnub Qub," ib tug menyuam tub hnov xov xwm tias ib lub hnub qub poob tab tom ya ceev ceev los rau ntiaj tebNws xav paub ntxiv txog thiab ho ntshai thiab hais tias thaum poob los txog ntiaj teb ces yuav muaj dabtsi tshwm sim.

《哈雷慧星》 (Halley's Comet)

Stanley Kunitz

摘要 《哈雷慧星》描寫一個小男孩對即將有慧星朝地球飛來的新聞產生的反應。他對於慧星降落地面時可能發生的事既興奮又害怕。

Sao Chổi Halley

Stanley Kunitz

Tóm Tắt Trong bài "Sao Chổi Halley", một cậu bé phản ứng trước tin rằng một sao chổi đang dịch chuyển về phía trái đất. Cậu bé vừa thích vừa sợ trước những gì có thể xảy ra khi sao chổi xuống mặt đất.

핼리 혜성 (Halley's Comet)

Stanley Kunitz

요약 이 글은 혜성이 지구를 향하고 있다는 뉴스를 들었을 때 한 소년이 보이는 반응을 이야기하고 있다. 소년은 혜성이 지구와 충돌했을 때 벌어질지도 모르는 일로 인해 흥분되기도 하고 무섭기도 하다.

The Latin Deli: An Ars Poetica

Judith Ortiz Cofer

Summary This poem describes a Latin deli where people of many different Latin cultures gather together. They come there because everyone speaks Spanish, and the food reminds them of home. The memories that customers get from the old-fashioned deli are more important than the things they actually buy.

El Deli latino: El arte poético

Judith Ortiz Cofer

Resumen Este poema describe un deli latino (tienda donde venden comidas) en el que se reúnen personas de diferentes culturas latinas. Se juntan allí porque todos hablan español y la comida les recuerda a su hogar. Los recuerdos que tienen del viejo deli son realmente más importantes que las cosas que compran allí.

Deli laten an : Yon atizay powetik

Judith Ortiz Cofer

Rezime Powèm sa a dekri yon deli laten kote moun ki gen diferan kilti laten rasanble. Yo vin la paske tout moun pale panyòl, epi manje a fè yo sonje lakay yo. Souvni kliyan yo fè nan deli konsèvatè a pi enpòtan pase sa yo achte nan deli a.

Ang Latinong "Deli": Isang Ars Poetika (Isang Sining ng Panunulá)

Judith Ortiz Cofer

Buod Inilalarawan ng tuláng ito ang isang Latinong "deli" o bilihan ng pagkain, kung saan nagpupulong-pulong ang mga taong galing sa iba't-ibang mga kulturang Latino. Nagpupunta sila doon dahil lahat ay nagsasalitá ng Espanyol, at ang pagkain ay nagpapaalala sa kanila ng kanilang inang bayan. Ang mga alaala na nakakamit ng mga suki sa matandang-usong "deli" ay mas-mahalaga kaysa sa mga mismong bagay na kanilang binibilí.

The Latin Deli: An Ars Poetica

Judith Ortiz Cofer

Lub Ntsiab Zaj pajhuam piav txog ib lub khw muag khoom noj uas yog Mev uas ntau hom neeg tuaj sib sau ua ke. Lawv tuaj ntawd vim sawvdaws hais lus Mev, thiab cov zaub mov ua rau lawv nco txog tsev. Cov zaub mov uas ua tau rau cov neeg nco qab txog ntau yam ntawd tseem ceeb tshaj tej khoom uas lawv tuaj yuav.

《拉丁熟食店：一種詩藝》(The Latin Deli: An Ars Poetica)

Judith Ortiz Cofer

摘要 這首詩描寫一間聚集許多不同拉丁文化背景的人的拉丁熟食店。他們來此的原因是這裡的每個人都會說西班牙語，而且供應有他們家鄉味的食物。顧客從這間老式熟食店獲得的回憶比起他們真正購買的物品更彌足珍貴。

Cửa Hàng Latin Bán Đồ Ăn Ngon : Một Bài Ars Poetica

Judith Ortiz Cofer

Tóm Tắt Bài thơ này miêu tả một cửa hàng Latin bán thức ăn ngon. Đó là nơi mọi người thuộc các nền văn hóa Latin khác nhau tụ họp. Họ đến đó vì mọi người đều nói tiếng Tây Ban Nha, và vì thức ăn ở đây gợi nhớ về quê nhà. Những ký ức khách hàng có được từ cửa hàng truyền thống này quan trọng hơn nhiều so với những thứ họ mua ở cửa hàng.

라틴 음식점: 시론 (The Latin Deli: An Ars Poetica)

Judith Ortiz Cofer

요약 이 시는 많은 라틴계 사람들이 모이는 라틴 음식점을 묘사하고 있다. 그 사람들은 스페인 말도 잘 통하고 음식들이 고향을 생각나게 해 주기 때문에 그 음식점에 간다. 이 오래된 음식점에서 얻는 추억은 실제로 거기서 사는 음식보다 더 중요하다.

Onomatopoeia

William Safire

Summary "Onomatopoeia" is a humorous essay. In it, William Safire explains the meaning and history of the term *onomatopoeia*. Onomatopoeia refers to words that sound like the action they describe, such as *buzz* or *hiss*. He then talks about the word zap, which takes the concept one step further. It imitates an imaginary noise—the sound of a paralyzing ray gun.

Onomatopeya

William Safire

Resumen "Onomatopeya" es un ensayo humorístico. En este ensayo William Safire explica el significado y la historia del término onomatopeya. Onomatopeya se refiere a palabras que suenan como la acción que describen, tales como mu o guau. Luego habla sobre la palabra zap, que lleva el concepto un poco más allá. Imita un ruido imaginario (el sonido de una pistola de rayos paralizantes).

Onomatopoeia

William Safire

Rezime "Onomatopoeia" se yon disètasyon komik. Ladan l, William Safire eksplike siyifikasyon ak istwa mo onomatopoeia a. Onomatopoeia refere a mo ki gen menm son ak aksyon yo dekri a, tankou *buzz* oswa *hiss*. Ansuit li pale konsènan mo zap, ki fè konsèp la rive yon etap pi lwen. Li imite yon bwi imajinè—son yon zàm k ap bay reyon paralizan.

Onomatopoeia

William Safire

Buod Ang "Onomatopoeia" ay isang katawá-tawáng sanaysay. Dito, ipinaliwanag ni William Safire ang kahulugan at kasaysayan ng salitáng onomatopoeia. Ang Onomatopoeia ay tumutukoy sa mga salitáng kasing tunog ng mga aksiyón na kanilang inilalarawan, tulad ng *buzz* o *hiss*. Pagkatapos ay tinalakay naman niya ang salitáng zap, na siyang nagpapalawak pa sa konseptong ito. Ginagaya nito ang isang tunóg na sa guni-guni lamang—ang tunóg ng isang nakapanínigas na "ray gun".

Onomatopoeia

William Safire

Lub Ntsiab "Onomatopoeia" yog ib zaj sau tau txaus luag heev. Hauv zaj no, William Safire piav lub ntsiab thiab keeb kwm ntawm lo lus tias *onomatopoeia*. Onomatopoeia yog hais txog cov lus uas nrov tau ib yam li txoj kev ua ntawd, xws li lo tias *buzz* lossis *hiss*. Nws tham txog lo lus zap, thiab ntau yam tauj ntxiv. Lo lus no hias tau nrov raws ib lub suab uas yus tsim tawm los - uas yog lub suab ntawm ib rab phom tshauv fais fab rau neeg.

《擬聲法》 (Onomatopoeia)

William Safire

摘要 本文是一篇幽默小品。作者在其中說明擬聲法這個名詞的意義及由來。擬聲法指聽起來類似字面形容的動作的文字，譬如嗡嗡叫或是嘶嘶聲。他接著描述掃射 *(zap)* 這個字，這個字賦予了這個概念更深刻的意義。這個字模擬了一種想像的雜音 — 一支有癱瘓作用的雷射槍的聲音。

Từ Tượng Thanh

William Safire

Tóm Tắt "Từ Tượng Thanh" là một tiểu luận hài ước. Trong tiểu luận này, William Safire giải thích ý nghĩa và lịch sử của thuật ngữ *từ tượng thanh*. Từ tượng thanh dùng để chỉ những từ có âm thanh giống như chính hành động mà từ đó miêu tả, ví dụ như từ *buzz* hoặc *hiss*. Rồi ông nói về từ zap. Từ này đưa khái niệm tượng thanh đi thêm một bước nữa, vì nó bắt chước một âm thanh tưởng tưởng—thứ âm thanh của một khẩu súng tia điện gây liệt người.

의성어 (Onomatopoeia)

William Safire

요약 "의성어"는 재미있는 에세이이다. 이 글에서 저자는 의성어라는 용어의 의미와 유래를 설명한다. 의성어란 벌이 윙윙거리거나(buzz) 뱀이 쉿쉿 하는(hiss) 등 행동을 소리로 나타내는 단어이다. zap이란 의성어도 설명하고 있는데 한발 더 나간다는 개념을 가지고 있고 마치 방사선 총의 소리를 상상하여 만든 단어이다.

Coyote v. Acme

Ian Frazier

Summary "Coyote v. Acme" is the opening statement of a fictional lawsuit by Wile E. Coyote against the Acme Company. The lawsuit charges that Acme's faulty equipment caused Coyote to injure himself while chasing the Road Runner. These characters come from the Warner Brothers cartoon "Road Runner and Coyote," which made its debut in 1949.

Coyote contra Acme

Ian Frazier

Resumen "Coyote contra Acme" es la declaración de apertura de un juicio ficticio de Wile E. Coyote contra la empresa Acme. El veredicto del juicio establece que el equipo defectuoso de Acme le ocasionó heridas al Coyote mientras éste perseguía a un correcaminos. Estos personajes provienen de los dibujos animados de Warner Brothers "El coyote y el correcaminos", que debutaron en 1949.

Coyote kont Acme

Ian Frazier

Rezime "Coyote kont Acme" se diskou douvèti yon pwosè fiktif Wile E. Coyote fè kont konpayi Acme a. Pwosè a fè konnen ekipman defektye Acme a te lakoz Coyote blese pandan l t ap fè lachas dèyè Road Runner. Pèsonaj sa yo soti nan desen anime Warner Brothers yo ki rele "Road Runner ak Coyote," ki te debite nan ane 1949.

Coyote Laban sa Acme

Ian Frazier

Buod Ang "Coyote Laban sa Acme" ay ang panimuláng pahayag ng isang di-tunay na paghahablá ni Wile E. Coyote laban sa Kompaniyang Acme. Ayon sa paghahablá, nasaktan ni Coyote ang kanyang sarili dahil sa may-sirang gamit ng Acme habang kanyang hinahabol ang "Road Runner". Ang mga ito ay galing sa cartoon ng "Warner Brothers" na "Si Road Runner at si Coyote," na nagdibú noong 1949.

Coyote sib foob nrog Acme

Ian Frazier

Lub Ntsiab "Coyote sib foob nrog Acme" yog ib zaj lus qhib ntawm ib rooj plaub tsim los ntawm Wile E. Coyote foob txog lub chaw haujlwm Acme Company. Rooj plaub foob tias Acme cov khoom ua rau Coyote raug mob thaum tseem caum tus qaib Road Runner. Cov tas lauv nyob hauv Warner Brothers cov duab kos "Road Runner thiab Coyote," uas tawm thaum xyoo 1949.

《威利狼與阿克米的訴訟》
(Coyote v. Acme)

Ian Frazier

摘要 本文是威利狼控告阿克米公司的一場虛構訴訟的開場陳述。這場訴訟指控阿克米公司的錯誤設備導致威利狼在追必必鳥時受了傷。這些角色出自 1949 年推出的華納兄弟卡通「比比鳥與威利狼」。

Coyote chống Acme

Ian Frazier

Tóm Tắt "Coyote chống Acme" là câu mở màn vụ kiện hư cấu của Wile E. Coyote chống lại Công Ty Acme. Theo như vụ kiện thì các sản phẩm của Acme có lỗi khiến cho Coyote bị thương khi rượt theo Road Runner. Các nhân vật này xuất hiện trong bộ phim hoạt hình của Warner Brothers có tên là "Road Runner và Coyote" được công chiếu lần đầu năm 1949.

코요테 대 애키미 (Coyote v. Acme)

Ian Frazier

요약 월리 E. 코요테가 애키미 회사를 상대로 가상의 소송을 벌인다. 이 글은 그 소송에 나오는 첫 번째 진술이다. 코요테는 이 진술에서 애키미 회사가 만든 장비 결함으로 로드러너를 쫓다가 다치게 되었다고 주장한다. 1949년 처음 선보인 워너 브러더스의 만화 영화 "로드러너와 코요테" 의 캐릭터들이 이야기 속에 등장한다.

One Day, Now Broken in Two

Anna Quindlen

Summary In this essay, Anna Quindlen looks at the impact of the events of 9-11 on Americans. She thinks that Americans have become better people as a result of having to face this tragedy.

Un día partido en dos

Anna Quindlen

Resumen En este ensayo Anna Quindlen observa el impacto que produjo el 11 de septiembre en los estadounidenses. Piensa que los estadounidenses se han convertido en mejores personas después de haberse enfrentado a esta tragedia.

Yon jou, kounye a kase an de

Anna Quindlen

Rezime Nan disètasyon sa a, Anna Quindlen gade enpak evenman 9-11 yo genyen sou ameriken yo. Li panse ameriken yo te vin miyò akoz trajedi sa a yo te afwonte.

Isang Araw, Ngayo'y Baság na sa Dalawa

Anna Quindlen

Buod Sa sanaysay na ito, tinitingnan ni Anna Quindlen ang naging epekto ng mga pangyayari ng 9-11 sa mga Amerikano. Sa kanyang palagay, ang mga Amerikano ay naging mas-mabuting mga tao bilang resulta ng kanilang pangangailangang humaráp sa trahedyang ito.

Ib Hnub, Dam Ua Ob Hnub Lawm

Anna Quindlen

Lub Ntsiab Hauv zaj sau no, Anna Quindlen saib txog txoj kev uas tej yam tshwm sim nyob rau hnub 9-11 tau tsim kev kub ntxhov li cas rau cov neeg nyob Tebchaws Meskas. Nws xav tias cov neeg nyob Tebchaws Meskas tau hloov los ua ib co neeg zoo tshaj qub lawm vim tias tau muaj txoj kev txom nyem no raug rau sawvdaws.

《一天，現在破裂成兩個》(One Day, Now Broken in Two)

Anna Quindlen

摘要 作者在本文中描寫 9-11 事件對美國人造成的影響。她認為美國人已經因為必須面對這種悲劇而變得更好。

Rồi Có Một Ngày, Đời Sống Người Dân Bị Vỡ Đôi

Anna Quindlen

Tóm Tắt Trong tiểu luận này, Anna Quindlen kể về các ảnh hưởng của sự kiện 11 tháng 9 đối với người dân Mỹ. Bà nghĩ rằng người Mỹ đã trở thành những người tốt hơn sau khi phải đối mặt với thảm kịch này.

어느 하루, 지금은 둘로 부서진 (One Day, Now Broken in Two)

Anna Quindlen

요약 이 에세이에서 저자는 9.11 테러 사건이 미국인에게 남긴 충격과 영향을 살펴 본다. 그런 비극을 맞이한 결과 미국인들은 좀더 나은 사람들이 되었다고 저자는 생각한다.

SUMMARY TRANSLATIONS

Mother Tongue

Amy Tan

Summary In "Mother Tongue," Amy Tan describes her mother as an intelligent and perceptive woman. However, her mother is regularly confronted by problems because of her non-standard English. Tan writes about the differences between the lessons she has learned from her mother with the English-speaking world's view of her mother. Tan explains that when she began to think of her mother as her reader, she found her voice as a writer.

Lengua materna

Amy Tan

Resumen En "Lengua materna" Amy Tan describe a su madre como una mujer inteligente y perceptiva. Sin embargo, su madre a menudo enfrenta diversos problemas por su inglés poco convencional. Tan escribe sobre las diferencias entre las clases que su madre le ha dictado desde la perspectiva del mundo angloparlante de su madre. Tan explica que cuando empezó a pensar en su madre como su lectora, encontró su voz como escritora.

Lang matènèl

Amy Tan

Rezime Nan "Lang matènèl," Amy Tan dekri manman l kòm yon fanm ki entèlijan epi ki pèspikas. Sepandan, manman an regilyèman konfwonte ak pwoblèm akoz anglè l ki pa estanda. Tan ekri konsènan diferans yo ant leson li te aprann nan men manman l ak pwennvi manman l sou monn ki pale anglè a. Tan eksplike lè l te kòmanse panse de manman l kòm yon lektè li, li te jwenn vwa l kòm yon ekriven.

Inang Wika

Amy Tan

Buod Sa "Inang Wika," inilalarawan ni Amy Tan ang kanyang ina bilang isang matalino at mapagmasid na babae. Gayunman, ang kanyang ina ay karaniwang nababahala ng mga problema dahil sa kanyang Ingles na 'di-ayon sa pamantayan. Isinulát ni Tan ang mga pagkakaiba ng mga liksiyón na natutunan niya sa kanyang ina, at ang paningin ng mundong nagsasalitá ng Ingles sa kanyang ina. Ipinaliwanag ni Tan na nang nagsimula niyang isipin ang kanyang ina bilang kanyang mambabasá, noon niya nahanap ang kanyang boses bilang isang manunulát.

Hom Lus Niam Siv

Amy Tan

Lub Ntsiab Hauv "Hom Lus Niam Siv," Amy Tan piav txog nws niam hais tias txawj ntse thiab yog ib tug pojniam txawj xav heevTiamsis, nws niam pheej muaj teeb meem los ntawm kev tsis txawj lus Askiv kom meej meej. Tan sau txog tej yam uas nws kawm tau los ntawm nws niam coj los piv rau cov neeg uas txawj lus Askiv txoj kev xav txog nws niam. Tan piav tias thaum nws pib xav txog tias nws niam ua ib tug neeg nyeem nws cov ntawv sau thiab, ces thaum ntawd nws thiaj li nrhiav tau nws lub suab coj los ua ib tug neeg sau ntawv lawm.

《母語》 (Mother Tongue)

Amy Tan

摘要 作者在本書中將自己的母親描寫成一位有智慧又很敏銳的女性。然而，她的母親卻由於自己不標準的英語經常遭遇困難。作者於是描寫自己從母親身上領悟到的道理與母親對英語世界的觀點間的差異。作者描述當自己開始將母親視為自己的讀者時，她就能將自己的聲音視為一位作家。

Tiếng Mẹ Đẻ

Amy Tan

Tóm Tắt Trong bài "Tiếng Mẹ Đẻ" Amy Tan miêu tả mẹ mình là một người phụ nữ thông minh và sâu sắc. Tuy nhiên, bà thường xuyên gặp rắc rối do thứ tiếng Anh không chuẩn của mình. Tan viết về những khác biệt giữa những bài học cô học được từ mẹ mình với cái nhìn của những người nói tiếng Anh về mẹ cô. Tan giải thích rằng khi cô bắt đầu nghĩ đến mẹ với tư cách là một độc giả của mình, cô mới tìm thấy được giọng văn của mình.

모국어 (Mother Tongue)

Amy Tan

요약 저자는 자신의 어머니를 똑똑하고 지각 있는 여성으로 묘사한다. 그러나 어머니는 올바르지 못한 영어표현 때문에 언제나 문제에 직면하게 된다. 저자는 어머니에게서 배운 교훈과 영어를 말하는 사람들이 어머니를 바라보는 관점의 차이점을 기술한다. 그리고 어머니를 자신이 쓴 책을 읽는 독자로 간주하기 시작했고 자신의 목소리는 작가의 목소리로 간주한다.

For the Love of Books

Rita Dove

Summary In "For the Love of Books," Rita Dove says her career as a writer came from her love of books. Since childhood, Dove loved to read books. She not only loved to read them, she loved holding them, smelling them, and turning their pages. She read everything from Shakespeare to science fiction. When her eleventh-grade English teacher took her to a book-signing, she realized writers were real people.

Por amor a los libros

Rita Dove

Resumen En "Por amor a los libros", Rita Dove cuenta que su profesión como escritora vino de su amor por los libros. Desde pequeña, Dove amaba leer libros. Y no sólo amaba leerlos, también le encantaba tenerlos en sus manos, olerlos y dar vuelta sus páginas. Leía de todo, desde Shakespeare hasta ciencia ficción. Cuando su maestro de inglés del 11º grado la llevó a una reunión donde autografiaban libros, Rita se dio cuenta de que los escritores eran personas reales.

Pou lanmou liv yo

Rita Dove

Rezime Nan "Pou lanmou liv yo," Rita Dove di konsa karyè l antank yon ekriven te pran nesans nan lanmou li genyen pou liv yo. Depi l te piti, Dove te renmen li liv. Li pa t senpleman renmen li yo, li te renmen kenbe yo, santi yo, epi tounen paj yo. Li te li tout kalite liv sot nan Shakespeare pou rive nan syans fiksyon. Lè pwofesè anglè onzyèm klas li a te mennen l nan yon seyans dedikas, li te vin reyalize ekriven yo se moun reyèl yo ye.

Para sa Pagmamahal sa mga Aklat

Rita Dove

Buod Sa "Para sa Pagmamahal sa mga Aklat," sabi ni Rita Dove na ang kanyang karera bilang isang manunulát ay nanggaling sa kanyang pagmamahal sa mga aklat. Mula kabataan, si Dove ay mahilig na magbasá ng mga libro. Hindi lamang siya mahilig magbasá nito, hilig din niyang tanganan sila, amuyin sila, at buklatin ang kanilang mga pahina. Binasa niya lahat mula Shakespeare hanggang sa mga science fiction. Nang dalhin siya ng kanyang guro sa ika-labíng-isang baitang sa isang pagpirma-ng-libro, naunawaan niya na ang mga manunulát ay mga tunay na tao.

Vim Kev Nyiam Cov Phau Ntawv Nyeem

Rita Dove

Lub Ntsiab Hauv "Vim Kev Nyiam Cov Phau Ntawv Nyeem," Rita Dove pib nws txoj haujlwm ua ib tug neeg sau ntawv vim nws nyiam nyeem ntawv heev. Txij thaum yog ib tug menyuam yaus los, Dove yeej nyiam nyeem ntawv lawm. Nws tsis yog nyiam nyeem ntawv xwb, tiam sis nws nyiam tuav, hnia, thiab nthuav lawv cov nplooj ntawv. Nws nyeem txog Shakespeare mus rau tej yam xws li cov dabneeg txog lwm yam kev tsim tshiab. Thaum nws tus xib fwb qhia ntawv qib kaum tau coj nws mus koom rau ib qho kev sib sau uas muaj tus txawj sau ntawv tuaj kos npe rau sawvdaws, ua rau nws paub tias cov neeg sau ntawv yog ib co neeg siab zoo heev.

《愛之書》 (For the Love of Books)

Rita Dove

摘要 作者在本書中道出自己會以作家為業實則起因於對書籍的熱愛。作者從小就熱愛閱讀。她不只喜歡讀，還喜歡抱著書本，聞上面的味道及翻裡面的書頁。她讀每種書，莎士比亞到科幻小說都看。當她的十一年級英文教師帶她參加一場簽書會時，她才瞭解作家確有其人。

Bắt Nguồn Từ Tình Yêu Sách

Rita Dove

Tóm Tắt Trong bài "Bắt Nguồn Từ Tình Yêu Sách", Rita Dove cho biết sự nghiệp viết văn của bà xuất phát từ tình yêu sách. Từ thủa thơ ấu, Dove đã ham đọc sách. Bà không những chỉ thích đọc sách mà còn thích được ôm những quyển sách, ngửi mùi giấy, và lật giở những trang sách. Bà đọc tất cả mọi thứ, từ Shakespeare cho đến truyện khoa học viễn tưởng. Khi cô giáo tiếng Anh lớp 11 đưa Rita Dove đến một dịp tác giả ký tặng độc giả, cô bé nhận ra răng các nhà văn là những con người thật.

책에 대한 사랑 (For the Love of Books)

Rita Dove

요약 "책에 대한 사랑" 에서 저자는 책을 좋아한 나머지 작가가 된 자신을 이야기한다. 어렸을 때부터 저자는 책 읽기를 좋아하였다. 읽는 것뿐만 아니라 들고 다니고 냄새를 맡고 책장을 넘기는 것도 좋아했다. 셰익스피어에서 과학 공상 소설까지 모두 두루 읽었다. 고등학교 이학년 때 영어 선생님을 따라 책 사인회에 가게 되는데, 거기서 저자는 작가들도 현실 속에서 생활하는 보통 사람이라는 것을 알게 된다.

The Woman Warrior

Maxine Hong Kingston

Summary Brave Orchid goes to the San Francisco airport. She waits for her sister to arrive from Hong Kong. The sisters have not seen each other in thirty years. Brave Orchid has brought her niece and two of her children. They wait at the airport for more than nine hours. Finally, the plane lands. Then, they must wait another four hours. Finally, the sisters greet each other. Neither can believe how old the other looks.

La mujer guerrera

Maxine Hong Kingston

Resumen Brave Orchid se dirige al aeropuerto de San Francisco. Espera que su hermana llegue de Hong Kong. Las hermanas no se han visto en treinta años. Brave Orchid ha ido acompañada por su sobrina y dos de sus hijos. Y esperan en el aeropuerto más de nueve horas. Finalmente, el avión aterriza. Luego deben esperar cuatro horas más. Después de la larga espera, las hermanas se saludan. Ninguna de las dos puede creer lo vieja que se ve la otra hermana.

Fanm gèrye a

Maxine Hong Kingston

Rezime Brave Orchid al nan ayewopò San Francisco a. Li ret ap tann sè l la k ap soti nan peyi Hong Kong. Sè yo gen trant an depi yo pa wè youn lòt. Brave Orchid te mennen avèk li nyès li ak de pitit li yo. Yo ret tann nan ayewopò a pandan plis pase nevèdtan. Finalman, avyon an ateri. Ansuit, yo dwe ret tann yon lòt katrèdtan. Finalman, sè yo salye youn lòt. Yo pa ka kwè jan youn lòt parèt granmoun.

Ang Babaeng Mandirigma

Maxine Hong Kingston

Buod Si "Brave Orchid" ay pumunta sa airport ng San Francisco. Hinintay niya ang kanyang kapatid na babaeng dumating mula sa Hong Kong. Tatlumpung taón silang 'di nagkikita. Sinama ni Brave Orchid ang kanyang pamangking babae at dalawa sa kanyang mga anak. Mahigit na siyam na oras silang naghintay sa airport . Sa wakas ay dumating ang eroplano. Ngayon ay kailangan nilang maghintay ng apat pang oras. Sa wakas ay nagbatián ang magkapatid. Kapwa silang 'di makapaniwala sa katandaán ng itsura ng isa't-isa.

Tus Ntxhais Tub Rog

Maxine Hong Kingston

Lub Ntsiab Brave Orchid mus rau lub tshav dav hlau hauv San Francisco. Nws tos nws tus viv ncaus tuaj Hong Kong tuaj. Ob tug viv ncaus tsis tau sib ntsib tshaj peb caug xyoo lawm. Brave Orchid coj nws tus xeeb ntxwv thiab nws ob tug menyuam. Lawv tau muaj cuaj teev hauv lub tsev dav hlau. Thaum kawg, lub dav hlau los tsaws. Ces, lawv yuav tau tos plaub teev ntxiv. Thaum kawg, ob tug viv ncaus tau sib ntsib. Nkawd ob leeg yeej ntseeg tsis tau tias nyias zoo nyias li cas lawm.

《女戰士》 (The Woman Warrior)

Maxine Hong Kingston

摘要 勇敢的蘭花前往舊金山機場。她在等候姊姊從香港飛抵此地。這兩姊妹已經有三十年未曾謀面。勇敢的蘭花帶來了她的姪子以及兩個小孩。他們在機場等了九個鐘頭以上。飛機終於降落了。他們還必須再等另外四個小時。最後兩姊妹迎接彼此。兩個人都不相信對方竟然看來這麼蒼老。

Nữ Chiến Binh

Maxine Hong Kingston

Tóm Tắt Brave Orchid ra sân bay San Francisco. Bà đợi em gái từ Hồng Kông đến. Hai chị em đã không gặp nhau 30 năm rồi. Đi cùng với bà còn có cháu gái và hai người con của bà. Họ đợi ở sân bay hơn chín tiếng đồng hồ. Cuối cùng thì máy bay cũng hạ cánh. Sau đó, bà phải đợi thêm 4 tiếng nữa mới được chào đón em gái mình. Hai chị em ngạc nhiên vì không ngờ người kia trông lại già như vậy.

여전사 (The Woman Warrior)

Maxine Hong Kingston

요약 브레이브 오키드는 홍콩에서 오는 여동생을 맞이하러 샌프란시스코 공항으로 간다. 이 자매는 30년 동안이나 못 만났다. 브레이브 오키드는 조카딸과 자신의 두 아이를 데리고 공항에서 아홉 시간 이상을 기다린다. 그리고 비행기는 도착하지만 또 네 시간을 더 기다려야 했다. 마침내 자매는 서로를 만나 인사를 할 수 있었고 서로 늙어 버린 얼굴에 깜짝 놀란다.

from The Names

N. Scott Momaday

Summary *The Names* is from a longer work. In this section, the author tells about the horse his parents gave him as a child. The horse's name was Pecos. The author still thinks about Pecos.

de Los nombres

N. Scott Momaday

Resumen *Los nombres* es una parte de un trabajo más extenso. En esta sección el autor nos cuenta sobre el caballo que sus padres le regalaron cuando era pequeño. El nombre del caballo era Pecos. El autor todavía piensa en Pecos.

yon ekstrè nan Non yo

N. Scott Momaday

Rezime *Non yo* se yon ekstrè nan yon ouvraj ki pi long. Nan seksyon sa a, otè a pale konsènan chwal paran l te ba li lè l te timoun. Non chwal la se te Pecos. Otè a toujou panse sou Pecos.

mula sa Ang Mga Pangalan

N. Scott Momaday

Buod Ang *Ang mga* Pangalan ay galing sa isang mas-mahabang likhá. Sa bahaging ito, nagkukuwento ang awtor tungkol sa kabayo na ibinigay sa kanya ng kanyang mga magulang noong siya ay bata pa. Ang pangalan ng kabayo ay Pecos. Naiisip pa rin ng awtor si Pecos.

Los ntawm zaj Cov Npe

N. Scott Momaday

Lub Ntsiab *The Names* yog los ntawm lwm zaj uas ntev tshaj nov. Hauv zaj no, tus sau qhia txog tus nees uas nws niam thiab txiv tau muab rau nws thaum nws tseem yog ib tug menyuam yaus. Tus sau zaj no tseem nco qab ntsoov txog Pecos.

改編自《姓名》 (The Names)

N. Scott Momaday

摘要 此文取材自一本更長篇的作品。在這段文章中，作者描寫父母在他小時候送給他的一匹馬。這隻馬的名字是佩可斯。作者到現在依然會想起佩可斯。

trích từ Những Cái Tên

N. Scott Momaday

Tóm Tắt *Những Cái* Tên được trích từ một tác phẩm dài. Trong truyện, tác giả kể về con ngựa cha mẹ cho mình hồi nhỏ. Tên con ngựa là Pecos. Tác giả vẫn nghĩ về Pecos.

이름들 중에서 (The Names)

N. Scott Momaday

요약 이 작품은 장편으로서 여기 발췌한 이 부분에서 저자는 자신이 아이였을 때 부모님이 주신 말 한 마리에 관해 쓰고 있다. 그 말의 이름은 피코스였고 저자는 지금도 그 말을 생각하곤 한다.

The exercises and tools presented here are designed to help you increase your vocabulary. Review the instruction and complete the exercises to build your vocabulary knowledge. Throughout the year, you can apply these skills and strategies to improve your reading, writing, speaking, and listening vocabulary.

Prefixes V2

Word Roots V4

Suffixes V6

Learning About Etymologies V8

How to Use a Dictionary V12

Academic Words V14

Word Attack Skills: Phonics and Word Patterns V16

Vocabulary and the SAT® V18

Communication Guide: Diction and Etiquette V22

Words in Other Subjects V26

Vocabulary Flash Cards V27

Vocabulary Fold-a-List V33

Commonly Misspelled Words V39

Personal Thesaurus V41

The following list contains common prefixes with meanings and examples. On the blank lines, write other words you know that begin with the same prefixes. Write the meanings of the new words.

Prefixes	Meaning	Example and Meaning	Your Words	Meanings
Anglo-Saxon *fore-*	before	*foretell:* to tell beforehand; predict		
Greek *auto-*	self	*autobiography:* the story of one's own life written by oneself		
Greek *di-*	away; apart	*digress:* to move away from a subject		
Greek *dys-*	difficult; bad	*dystopia:* a place with dreadful conditions		
Greek *mono-*	alone; one; single	*monologue:* a long speech by one speaker		
Latin *con-*	with; together	*conference:* a meeting for discussion		
Latin *dis-*	apart; not	*dishonest:* not honest		
Latin *ex-*	out	*extort:* to squeeze out		

 English Learner's Notebook

Prefixes	Meaning	Example and Meaning	Your Words	Meanings
Latin *in-*	in; into; not; without	*inescapable:* that cannot be escaped		
Latin *mal-*	bad	*malice:* desire to harm another		
Latin *multi-*	many; much	*multiply:* to increase in number		
Latin *ob-*	against	*object:* showing disapproval		
Latin *omni-*	all; every	*omnipotent:* all-powerful		
Latin *pro-*	forward	*protruded:* thrust forward		
Latin *re-*	again; back	*evolve:* to move in a circle around a point		
Latin *trans-*	across; through	*transportation:* means of moving passengers or goods		

The following list contains common word roots with meanings and examples. On the blank lines, write other words you know that have the same roots. Write the meanings of the new words.

Root	Meaning	Example and Meaning	Your Words	Meanings
Greek -archy-	to rule	*anarchy*: without government; without rule		
Greek -psych-	soul; mind	*psychology*: the science that deals with the mind		
Latin -aud-	hearing, sound	*auditorium*: a room for gathering an audience to hear concerts or speeches		
Latin -bene-	good	*benefit*: to do good for		
Latin -equi-	equal	*equivalent*: equal in quantity, value, or meaning		
Latin -fid-	faith; trust	*confident*: full of certainty or trust		
Latin -grat-	pleasing	*grateful*: expressing thankfulness		
Latin -ject-	to throw	*eject*: to throw out		

Root	Meaning	Example and Meaning	Your Words	Meanings
Latin *-lib-*	free	*liberty:* freedom		
Latin *-mort-*	death	*mortuary:* a place where dead bodies are kept		
Latin *-patr-*	father	*paternal:* fatherly		
Latin *-press-*	push	*compress:* to squeeze or push together; make compact		
Latin *-scrib-*	write	*transcribe:* to write out or type out in full		
Latin *-sol-*	alone	*solitary:* being alone; without others		
Latin *-terr-*	earth; land	*terrarium:* a glass container holding small plants or small land animals		
Latin *-vid-*	to see	*video:* the process of recording and showing television programs, movies, and real events		

The following list contains common suffixes with meanings and examples. On the blank lines, write other words you know that have the same suffixes. Write the meanings of the new words.

Suffix	Meaning	Example and Meaning	Your Words	Meanings
Anglo-Saxon -fold	a specific number of times or ways	*tenfold:* ten times		
Anglo-Saxon -ful	full of	*joyful:* happy; full of joy		
Anglo-Saxon -hood	state or quality of	*parenthood:* the state of being a parent		
Anglo-Saxon -less	without	*helpless:* not able to help oneself		
Anglo-Saxon -ness	the state of being	*handedness:* the quality of using one hand more skillfully than the other		
Anglo-Saxon -some	tending toward being	*awesome:* impressive; inspiring awe		
Greek -ate	forms verbs	*evaporate:* to change into a vapor		
Greek -ic	forms adjectives	*hypnotic:* causing sleep		

Suffix	Meaning	Example and Meaning	Your Words	Meanings
Greek *-itis*	disease; inflammation	*bronchitis:* inflammation of the bronchial tubes		
Greek *-logy*	the science or study of	*biology:* the study of living organisms		
Latin *-able/-ible*	capable of being	*lovable:* able to be loved		
Latin *-al*	of, like, suitable for	*theatrical:* having to do with the theater		
Latin *-ance/-ence*	quality of; state of being	*permanence:* the state of being permanent; remaining		
Latin *-er*	one who	*geographer:* one whose profession deals with the study of geography		
Latin *-ity*	turns adjectives into nouns	*complexity:* the state of being complex or difficult		
Latin *-tion*	turns a noun into a verb	*deliberation:* the act of deliberating or thinking about very carefully		

Etymology is the history of a word. It shows where the word came from, or its **origin.** It also shows how it got its present meaning and spelling. Understanding word origins, or etymology, can help you understand and remember the meanings of words you add to your vocabulary.

A good dictionary will tell you the etymology of a word. The word's etymology usually appears in brackets, parentheses, or slashes near the beginning or the end of the dictionary entry. Part of the etymology is the language from which the word comes.

Abbreviations for Languages	
Abbreviation	Language
OE	Old English
ME	Middle English
F	French
Gr	Greek
L	Latin
ML	Medieval Latin
LL	Late Latin

You can find these abbreviations and more in a dictionary's key to abbreviations.

Words From Other Languages

The English that you speak today began in about the year 500. Tribes from Europe settled in Britain. These tribes, called the Angles, the Saxons, and the Jutes, spoke a Germanic language. Later, when the Vikings attacked Britain, their language added words from Danish and Norse. Then, when Christian missionaries came to Britain, they added words from Latin. The resulting language is called Old English, and it looks very different from modern English.

For example, to say "Listen!" in Old English, you would have said "Hwaet!"

The Normans conquered Britain in 1066. They spoke Old French, and the addition of this language changed Old English dramatically. The resulting language, called Middle English, looks much more like modern English, but the spellings of words are very different.

For example, the word *knight* in Middle English was spelled *knyght,* and the word *time* was spelled *tyme.*

During the Renaissance, interest in classical cultures added Greek and Latin words to English. At this time, English started to look more like the English you know. This language, called Modern English, is the language we still speak.

Modern English continues to add words from other languages. As immigrants have moved to the United States, they have added new words to the language.

For example, the word *boycott* comes from Ireland and the word *burrito* comes from Mexico.

Note-taking Using a dictionary, identify the language from which each of the following words came into English. Also identify the word's original and current meaning.

Word	Original Language	Original Meaning	Current Meaning
comb			
costume			
guess			
mile			
panther			

Words That Change Meaning Over Time

English is a living language. It grows by giving new meanings to existing words and by incorporating words that have changed their meaning over time and through usage.

For example, the word *dear* originally meant "expensive."

Note-taking Using a dictionary, identify the original meaning and the current meaning of each of the following words.

	original meaning	current meaning
1. havoc	_______________________	_______________________
2. magazine	_______________________	_______________________

Words That Have Been Invented, or *Coined,* to Serve New Purposes.

New products or discoveries need new words.

For example, the words *paperback* and *quiz* are coined words.

Note-taking Identify one word that has been coined in each of the following categories.

Category	Coined Word
sports	
technology	
transportation	
space travel	
medicine	

Words That Are Combinations of Words or Shortened Versions of Longer Words

New words can be added to the language by combining words or by shortening words.

For example, the word *greenback* is a combination of the words *green* and *back,* and the word *flu* is a shortened version of the word *influenza.*

Note-taking Generate a word to fill in the blanks in each of the following sentences correctly. Your word should be a combination of two words or a shortened version of a longer word.

Jerome served one of our favorite dinners, spaghetti and ____________________.

Many years ago, people might take an omnibus to work, but today they would call that vehicle a ____________________.

We took the most direct route to Aunt Anna's house, which meant driving forty miles on the ____________________.

We thought we could get to shelter before the storm started, but we did not quite make it. A few ____________________ dampened our jackets.

A dictionary lists words in alphabetical order. Look at this sample dictionary entry. Notice the types of information about a word it gives.

Example of a Dictionary Entry

dictionary (dik´ shə ner´ ē) **n.** pl. **–aries** [ML *dictionarium* < LL *dictio*] **1** a book of alphabetically listed words in a language, with definitions, etymologies, pronunciations, and other information **2** a book of alphabetically listed words in a language with their equivalents in another language [a Spanish-English *dictionary*)

Answer the questions based on the dictionary entry.

1. What is the correct spelling? _______________________________________

2. How do you form the plural? _______________________________________

3. What language does the word come from? _______________________________

4. How many definitions are there? _____________________________________

5 What example is given?____

Here are some abbreviations you will find in dictionary entries.

Pronunciation Symbols	Parts of Speech	Origins of Words
´ means emphasize this syllable as you say the word	adj. = adjective	Fr = French
¯ means pronounce vowel with a long sound, such as -ay- for a and -ee- for e	adv. = adverb	Ger = German
ə means a sound like -uh-	n. = noun	L = classical Latin
o͞o means the sound of *u* in cute	v. = verb	ME = Middle English OE = Old English

As you read, look up new words in a dictionary. Enter information about the words on this chart.

My Words

New Word	Pronunciation	Part of Speech	Origin	Meanings and Sample Sentence

Academic words are words you use often in your schoolwork. Knowing what these words mean and how to use them will help you think and write better.

The following chart provides definitions and pronunciations for academic words. When you come across one of these words in your reading, write the sentence in which it appears in the middle column. In the right column, use your own words to explain what these sentences mean.

Academic Word	Example You Find	Meaning of Example
analyze (AN uh LYZ) break down into parts and explain		
apply (uh PLY) tell how you use information in a specific situation		
categorize (KAT uh gaw ryz) group similar items together		
clarify (KLA ri FY) make something more understandable		
conclude (kuhn KLOOD) use reasoning to reach a decision or opinion		
deduce (dee DOOS) figure something out by applying a general idea		
define (dee FYN) tell the qualities that make something what it is		
demonstrate (DEM uhn STRAYT) use examples to prove a point		
differentiate (dif er EN shee AYT) explain what makes two things different		

Academic Word	Example You Find	Meaning of Example
evaluate (ee VAL yoo AYT) determine the value or importance of something		
identify (y DEN ti FY) name or show you recognize something		
illustrate (IL uhs TRAYT) give examples that show you know what something means		
interpret (in TER pret) explain the underlying meaning of something		
judge (JUHJ) assess or form an opinion about something		
label (LAY bel) attach the correct name to something		
predict (pree DIKT) tell what will happen based on details you know		
recall (ri KAWL) tell details that you remember		

When you are reading, you will find many unfamiliar words. Here are some tools that you can use to help you read unfamiliar words.

Phonics

Phonics is the science or study of sound. When you learn to read, you learn to associate certain sounds with certain letters or letter combinations. You know most of the sounds that letters can represent in English. When letters are combined, however, it is not always so easy to know what sound is represented. In English, there are some rules and patterns that will help you determine how to pronounce a word. This chart shows you some of the common **vowel digraphs,** which are combinations like ea and oa. Two vowels together are called vowel digraphs. Usually, vowel digraphs represent the long sound of the first vowel.

Vowel Digraphs	Examples of Unusual Sounds	Exceptions
ee and *ea*	steep, each, treat, sea	head, sweat, dread
ai and *ay*	plain, paid, may, betray	
oa, ow, and *oe*	soak, slow, doe	
ie and *igh*	lie, night, delight, my	myth

As you read, sometimes the only way to know how to pronounce a word with an *ea* spelling is to see if the word makes sense in the sentence. Look at this example:

The water pipes were made of *lead.*

First, try out the long sound "ee." Ask yourself if it sounds right. It does not. Then, try the short sound "e." You will find that the short sound is correct in that sentence.

Now, try this example:

Where you *lead,* I will follow.

Word Patterns

Recognizing different vowel-consonant patterns will help you read longer words. In the following section, the **V** stands for "vowel" and the **C** stands for "consonant."

Single-Syllable Words

CV–go: In two-letter words with a consonant followed by a vowel, the vowel is usually long. For example, the word *go* is pronounced with a long "o" sound.

In a single-syllable word, a vowel followed only by a single consonant is usually short.

CVC–got: If you add a consonant to the word *go,* such as the *t* in *got,* the vowel sound is a short *o.* Say the words *go* and *got* aloud and notice the difference in pronunciation.

Multi-Syllable Words

In words of more than one syllable, notice the letters that follow a vowel.

VCCV–robber: A single vowel followed by two consonants is usually short.

VCV–begin: A single vowel followed by a single consonant is usually long.

VCe–beside: An extension of the VCV pattern is vowel-consonant-silent *e.* In these words, the vowel is long and the *e* is not pronounced.

When you see a word with the VCV pattern, try the long vowel sound first. If the word does not make sense, try the short sound. Pronounce the words *model, camel,* and *closet.* First, try the long vowel sound. That does not sound correct, so try the short vowel sound. The short vowel sound is correct in those words.

Remember that patterns help you get started on figuring out a word. You will sometimes need to try a different sound or find the word in a dictionary.

As you read and find unfamiliar words, look up the pronunciations in a dictionary. Write the words in this chart in the correct column, to help you notice patterns and remember pronunciations.

Syllables	Example	New Words	Vowel
CV	go		long
CVC	got		short
VCC	robber		short
VCV	begin open		long long
VCe	beside		long

FAQs About the SAT®

What Is the SAT®?

- The SAT® is a national test intended to predict how well you will do with college-level material.

What Does the SAT® Test?

- The SAT® tests vocabulary, math, and reasoning skills in three sections:
  - Critical Reading: two 25-minute sections and one 20-minute section
  - Math: two 25-minute sections and one 20-minute section
  - Writing: one 35-minute multiple-choice section and one 25-minute essay

Why Should You Take the SAT®?

- Many colleges and universities require you to submit your SAT® scores when you apply. They use your scores, along with other information about your ability and your achievements, to evaluate you for admission.

How Can Studying Vocabulary Help Improve Your SAT® Scores?

- The Critical Reading section of the SAT® asks two types of questions that evaluate your vocabulary.
  - Sentence Completions ask you to fill in one or more blanks in a sentence with the correct word or words. To fill in the blanks correctly, you need to know the meaning of the words offered as answers.
  - Vocabulary in Context questions in Passage-based Reading ask you to determine what a word means based on its context in a reading passage.
- With a strong vocabulary and good strategies for using context clues, you will improve the likelihood that you will score well on the SAT®.

Using Context Clues on the SAT®

When you do not know the meaning of a word, nearby words or phrases can help you. These words or phrases are called context clues.

Guidelines for Using Context Clues

1. Read the sentence or paragraph, concentrating on the unfamiliar word.

2. Look for clues in the surrounding words.

3. Guess the possible meaning of the unfamiliar word.

4. Substitute your guess for the word.

5. When you are reviewing for a test, you can check the word's meaning in a dictionary.

Types of Context Clues

Here are the most common types of context clues:

- formal definitions that give the meaning of the unfamiliar word
- familiar words that you may know that give hints to the unfamiliar word's meaning
- comparisons or contrasts that present ideas or concepts either clearly similar or clearly opposite to the unfamiliar word
- synonyms, or words with the same meaning as the unfamiliar word
- antonyms, or words with a meaning opposite to that of the unfamiliar word
- key words used to clarify a word's meaning

Note-taking List several new words that you have learned recently by figuring out their meanings in context. Then, explain how you used context to decide what the word meant.

New Word	How You Used Context to Understand the Word

Sample SAT® Questions

Here are examples of the kinds of questions you will find on the SAT®. Read the samples carefully. Then, do the Practice exercises that follow.

Sample Sentence Completion Question:

Directions: The sentence that follows has one blank indicating that something has been omitted. Beneath the sentence are five words or sets of words labeled **A** through **E.** Choose the word or set of words that, when inserted in the sentence, best fits the meaning of the sentence as a whole.

1. Though he is ______________________________, his nephew still invites him to Thanksgiving dinner every year.

   A cheerful

   B entertaining

   C misanthropic

   D agile

   E healthy

The correct answer is C. The uncle is *misanthropic.* You can use the context clues "though" and "invites him" to infer that the uncle has some negative quality. Next, you can apply your knowledge of the prefix *mis-* to determine that *misanthropic,* like *mistake* and *misfortune,* is a word indicating something negative. Eliminate the other answer choices, which indicate positive or neutral qualities in this context.

Sample Vocabulary in Context Question:

Directions: Read the following sentence. Then, read the question that follows it. Decide which is the best answer to the question.

Martin Luther King, Jr., whose methods motivated many to demand equal rights in a peaceful manner, was an inspiration to all.

1. In this sentence, the word *inspiration* means—

   A politician

   B motivation to a high level of activity

   C the process of inhaling

   D figurehead

The correct answer is *B.* Both *B* and *C* are correct definitions of the word *inspiration,* but the only meaning that applies in the context of the sentence is "motivation to a high level of activity."

Practice for SAT® Questions

Practice Read the following passage. Then, read each question that follows the passage. Decide which is the best answer to each question.

Many people are becoming Internet savvy, exhibiting their skills at mastering the Web. The Internet is also becoming a more reliable source of factual information. A Web-surfer can find information provided by reputable sources, such as government organizations and universities.

1. In this passage, the word *savvy* means—

   A incompetent

   B competent

   C users

   D nonusers

2. The word *reliable* in this passage means—

   A existing

   B available

   C dependable

   D relevant

 English Learner's Notebook

3. In this passage, the term *Web-surfer* means—

   A someone who uses the Internet

   B a person who uses a surfboard

   C a person who know a great deal about technology

   D a student

4. The word *reputable* in this passage means—

   A an approved Internet provider

   B well-known and of good reputation

   C purely academic

   D costly

Practice Each sentence that follows has one or two blanks indicating that something has been omitted. Beneath the sentence are five words or sets of words labeled A through E. Choose the word or set of words that, when inserted in the sentence, best fits the meaning of the sentence as a whole.

1. "I wish I had a longer _________________ between performances," complained the pianist. "My fingers need a rest."

   A post-mortem   C prelude   E solo

   B circumlocution   D interval

2. Instead of revolving around the sun in a circle, this asteroid has a(n)

   _________________ orbit.

   A rapid   C interplanetary   E regular

   B eccentric   D circular

3. He was the first historian to translate the _________________ on the stone.

   A impulsion   C excavation   E inscription

   B aversion   D circumspection

4. To correct your spelling error, simply _________________ the i and the e.

   A translate   C transcent   E integrate

   B transpose   D interpolate

5. Spilling soda all over myself just when the movie got to the good part was

   a(n) _________________ event.

   A fortunate   C tenacious   E constructive

   B premature   D infelicitous

Diction

Diction is a writer's or a speaker's word choice. The vocabulary, the vividness of the language, and the appropriateness of the words all contribute to diction, which is part of a writing or speaking **style.**

- Hey, buddy! What's up?

- Hi, how're you doing?

- Hello, how are you?

- Good morning. How are you?

These four phrases all function as greetings. You would use each one, however, in very different situations. This word choice is called *diction,* and for different situations, you use different *levels of diction.*

Note-taking Here are some examples of levels of diction. Fill in the blanks with the opposite level of diction.

Level of Diction	Formal	Informal
Example	Good afternoon. Welcome to the meeting.	

Level of Diction	Ornate	Plain
Example		I need more coffee.

Level of Diction	Abstract	Concrete
Example		The mayor has asked for volunteers to pick up litter along the river next Saturday.

Level of Diction	Technical	Ordinary
Example	My brother is employed as a computer system design manager.	

Level of Diction	Sophisticated	Down-to-Earth
Example	Thank you very much. I appreciate your help.	

Level of Diction	Old-fashioned	Modern/Slangy
Example	Yes, it is I. Shall we sample the bill of fare?	

With close friends and family, most of your conversations will probably be informal, down-to-earth, even slangy. In school or in elegant surroundings, or among people you do not know well or people who are much older than you, you will probably choose language that is more formal. Sometimes the distinctions can be subtle, so try to take your cues from others and adjust your diction accordingly.

Note-taking Complete the following activities.

1. Make a list of words and phrases that would be appropriate for you to use as you escort a visiting school board member on a tour of your school.

____

____

____

____

2. Make a second list of words and phrases that you might use as you escort your teenage cousin on a tour of your school.

____

____

____

____

3. Study the following pairs of phrases. Then, identify one phrase in each pair as formal and the other as informal.

	Phrase	Formal / Informal	Phrase	Formal / Informal
1.	Hello, it's nice to meet you.		How do you do?	
2.	What is your opinion, Professor Hughes?		What do you think, Pat?	
3.	Please accept my deepest sympathy.		That's too bad.	
4.	Sorry. I didn't hear you.		I beg your pardon. Please repeat the question.	
5.	I don't get it.		I do not quite understand.	

4. List several common phrases. Then, identify whether each phrase is formal or informal, and give its formal or informal opposite.

	Phrase	Formal / Informal	Phrase	Formal / Informal
1.				
2.				
3.				
4.				
5.				

Etiquette: Using the Vocabulary of Politeness

No matter how many words you know, the way you use those words will impact how your friends, your family, your teachers, and all the people in your life react to you. For almost every interaction you have, choosing a vocabulary of politeness will help you avoid conflicts and communicate your ideas, thoughts, and feelings effectively to others.

When in doubt, always choose the polite word or phrase.

Formal or Informal?

Polite vocabulary does not have to be formal. In fact, the definition of the word *polite* is "behaving or speaking in a way that is correct for the social situation." People often think that *etiquette,* which consists of rules for polite behavior, applies only in formal situations. All interactions with other people, though, should follow the etiquette that is appropriate for the situation.

Etiquette for Classroom Discussions

Use the following sentences starters to help you express yourself clearly and politely in classroom discussions.

Use these sentence starters to help you express yourself clearly in different classroom situations.

To Express an Opinion

I think that ____.

I believe that ____.

It seems to me that ____.

In my opinion, ____.

To Agree

I agree with _________________ that _________________________.
I see what you mean.
That's an interesting idea.
My idea is similar to _________________'s idea.
I hadn't thought of that.

To Disagree

I don't completely agree with _______________ because _______________________.
My opinion is different from yours.
My idea is slightly different from yours.
I see it a different way.

To Report the Ideas of a Group

We agreed that ____.
We concluded that ____.
We had a similar idea.
We had a different approach.

To Predict or Infer

I predict that ____.
Based on _________________________, I infer that _______________________.
I hypothesize that ____.

To Paraphrase

So you are saying that ____.
In other words, you think ____.
What I hear you saying is ____.

To Offer a Suggestion

Maybe we could ____.
What if we ____.
Here's something we might try.

To Ask for Clarification

Could you explain that another way?
I have a question about that.
Can you give me another example of that?

To Ask for a Response

What do you think?
Do you agree?
What answer did you get?

Practice With a partner, discuss an issue about which you disagree. At the end
of five minutes, list five or more polite words or phrases that you used to
communicate your conflicting opinions.

____

____

Use this page to write down academic words you come across in other subjects, such as social studies or science. When you are reading your textbooks, you may find words that you need to learn. Following the example, write down the word, the part of speech, and an explanation of the word. You may want to write an example sentence to help you remember the word.

dissolve *verb* to make something solid become part of a liquid by putting it in a liquid and mixing it

The sugar *dissolved* in the hot tea.

____

____

____

____

____

____

____

____

____

____

____

____

____

Use these flash cards to study words you want to remember. The words on this page come from Unit 1. Cut along the dotted lines on pages V29 through V32 to create your own flash cards or use index cards. Write the word on the front of the card. On the back, write the word's part of speech and definition. Then, write a sentence that shows the meaning of the word.

confederate	entreated	subsisted
protruded	deliberation	mortality
ablutions	disposition	feigned

adjective united with others for a common purpose The *confederate* Iroquois nations worked well together.	*verb* jutted out A tuft of hair *protruded* from under her hat.	*noun* cleansing the body as part of a religious rite The people performed their *ablutions* before beginning the scared dance.
verb begged; pleaded The children *entreated* the parents not to be angry with them.	*noun* careful consideration After much *deliberation*, we decided to go to the Grand Canyon for our vacation.	*noun* an inclination or tendency Neither side shows a *disposition* to compromise in the conflict.
verb remained alive; were sustained The lost hunters *subsisted* on berries and tree bark.	*noun* death on a large scale The infant *mortality* rate has been on the increase in certain areas.	*verb* pretended; faked Joe *feigned* sleep so that his brother would not talk to him.

Use these flash cards to study words you want to remember. Cut along the dotted lines on pages V29 through V32 to create your own flash cards or use index cards. Write the word on the front of the card. On the back, write the word's part of speech and definition. Then, write a sentence that shows the meaning of the word.

Use these flash cards to study words you want to remember. Cut along the dotted lines on pages V29 through V32 to create your own flash cards or use index cards. Write the word on the front of the card. On the back, write the word's part of speech and definition. Then, write a sentence that shows the meaning of the word.

Use a fold-a-list to study the definitions of words. The words on this page come from Unit 1. Write the definition for each word on the lines. Fold the paper along the dotted line to check your definition. Create your own fold-a-lists on pages V35 through V38.

exquisite

affliction

indications

abundance

pilfer

palisades

conceits

mollified

peril

loath

Fold

Write the word that matches the definition on each line.
Fold the paper along the dotted line to check your work.

very beautiful; delicate;
carefully wrought

something causing
pain or suffering

signs; things that point
out or signify

a great supply;
more than enough

steal

large, pointed stakes set
in the ground to form a
fence used for defense

strange or fanciful ideas

soothed; calmed

danger

reluctant; unwilling

Fold →

Write the words you want to study on this side of the page. Write the definitions on the back. Then, test yourself. Fold the paper along the dotted line to check your answers.

Word: _______________________________________

____

Word: _______________________________________

____

Word: _______________________________________

____

Word: _______________________________________

____

Word: _______________________________________

____

Word: _______________________________________

____

Word: _______________________________________

____

Word: _______________________________________

____

Word: _______________________________________

____

Word: _______________________________________

____

Word: _______________________________________

____

Fold →

Write the word that matches the definition on each line.
Fold the paper along the dotted line to check your work.

Definition: _______________________________

____

Definition: _______________________________

____

Definition: _______________________________

____

Definition: _______________________________

____

Definition: _______________________________

____

Definition: _______________________________

____

Definition: _______________________________

____

Definition: _______________________________

____

Definition: _______________________________

____

Definition: _______________________________

____

Fold →

Write the words you want to study on this side of the page.
Write the definitions on the back. Then, test yourself. Fold
the paper along the dotted line to check your answers.

Word: ____

____

Word: ____

____

Word: ____

____

Word: ____

____

Word: ____

____

Word: ____

____

Word: ____

____

Word: ____

____

Word: ____

____

Word: ____

____

Fold →

Write the word that matches the definition on each line.
Fold the paper along the dotted line to check your work.

Definition: _______________________________

____

Definition: _______________________________

____

Definition: _______________________________

____

Definition: _______________________________

____

Definition: _______________________________

____

Definition: _______________________________

____

Definition: _______________________________

____

Definition: _______________________________

____

Definition: _______________________________

____

Fold →

The list on these pages presents words that cause problems for many people. Some of these words are spelled according to set rules, but others follow no specific rules. As you review this list, check to see how many of the words give you trouble in your own writing. Then, add your own commonly misspelled words on the lines that follow.

abbreviate	auxiliary	census	deficient
absence	awkward	certain	definitely
absolutely	bandage	changeable	delinquent
abundance	banquet	characteristic	dependent
accelerate	bargain	chauffeur	descendant
accidentally	barrel	chief	description
accumulate	battery	clothes	desert
accurate	beautiful	coincidence	desirable
ache	beggar	colonel	dessert
achievement	beginning	column	deteriorate
acquaintance	behavior	commercial	dining
adequate	believe	commission	disappointed
admittance	benefit	commitment	disastrous
advertisement	bicycle	committee	discipline
aerial	biscuit	competitor	dissatisfied
affect	bookkeeper	concede	distinguish
aggravate	bought	condemn	effect
aggressive	boulevard	congratulate	eighth
agreeable	brief	connoisseur	eligible
aisle	brilliant	conscience	embarrass
all right	bruise	conscientious	enthusiastic
allowance	bulletin	conscious	entrepreneur
aluminum	buoyant	contemporary	envelope
amateur	bureau	continuous	environment
analysis	bury	controversy	equipped
analyze	buses	convenience	equivalent
ancient	business	coolly	especially
anecdote	cafeteria	cooperate	exaggerate
anniversary	calendar	cordially	exceed
anonymous	campaign	correspondence	excellent
answer	canceled	counterfeit	exercise
anticipate	candidate	courageous	exhibition
anxiety	capacity	courteous	existence
apologize	capital	courtesy	experience
appall	capitol	criticism	explanation
appearance	captain	criticize	extension
appreciate	career	curiosity	extraordinary
appropriate	carriage	curious	familiar
architecture	cashier	cylinder	fascinating
argument	catastrophe	deceive	February
associate	category	decision	fiery
athletic	ceiling	deductible	financial
attendance	cemetery	defendant	fluorescent

foreign
fourth
fragile
gauge
generally
genius
genuine
government
grammar
grievance
guarantee
guard
guidance
handkerchief
harass
height
humorous
hygiene
ignorant
immediately
immigrant
independence
independent
indispensable
individual
inflammable
intelligence
interfere
irrelevant
irritable
jewelry
judgment
knowledge
lawyer
legible
legislature
leisure
liable
library
license
lieutenant
lightning
likable
liquefy
literature
loneliness
magnificent
maintenance
marriage
mathematics
maximum
meanness
mediocre
mileage
millionaire
minimum

minuscule
miscellaneous
mischievous
misspell
mortgage
naturally
necessary
neighbor
neutral
nickel
niece
ninety
noticeable
nuisance
obstacle
occasion
occasionally
occur
occurred
occurrence
omitted
opinion
opportunity
optimistic
outrageous
pamphlet
parallel
paralyze
parentheses
particularly
patience
permanent
permissible
perseverance
persistent
personally
perspiration
persuade
phenomenal
phenomenon
physician
pleasant
pneumonia
possess
possession
possibility
prairie
precede
preferable
prejudice
preparation
previous
primitive
privilege
probably
procedure

proceed
prominent
pronunciation
psychology
publicly
pursue
questionnaire
realize
really
recede
receipt
receive
recognize
recommend
reference
referred
rehearse
relevant
reminiscence
renowned
repetition
restaurant
rhythm
ridiculous
sandwich
satellite
schedule
scissors
secretary
siege
solely
sponsor
subtle
subtlety
superintendent
supersede
surveillance
susceptible
tariff
temperamental
theater
threshold
truly
unmanageable
unwieldy
usage
usually
valuable
various
vegetable
voluntary
weight
weird
whale
wield
yield

Using the Personal Thesaurus

The Personal Thesaurus provides students with the opportunity to make connections between words academic words, familiar words, and even slang words. Students can use the Personal Thesaurus to help them understand the importance of using words in the proper context and also avoid overusing words in their writing.

Use the following routine to foster frequent use of the Personal Thesaurus.

1. After students have read a selection or done some writing, have them turn to the Personal Thesaurus.

2. Encourage students to add new entries. Help them to understand the connection between their personal language, which might include familiar words and even slang, and the academic language of their reading and writing.

3. Call on volunteers to read a few entries aloud. Point out that writers have many choices of words when they write. Help students see that audience often determines word choice.

N

nice

admirable

friendly

agreeable

pleasant

cool

phat

A

 English Learner's Notebook

B

C

D

E

F

G

H

I

J

K

L

M

 English Learner's Notebook

N

O

P

Q

R

S

T

U

V

W

 English Learner's Notebook

X

Y

Z

(*Acknowledgments continued from page ii*)

Syracuse University Press
"The Iroquois Constitution" from *Arthur C. Parker on the Iroquois: Iroquois Uses of Maize and Other Food Plants, The Code of Handsome Lake; The Seneca Prophet; The Constitution of the Five Nations* by Arthur C. Parker, edited by William N. Fenton (Syracuse University Press, Syracuse, NY, 1981). Copyright © 1968 by Syracuse University Press.

Viking Penguin, Inc.
"The Turtle (Chapter 3)" by John Steinbeck from *The Grapes of Wrath.* Copyright © 1939, renewed copyright © 1967 by John Steinbeck.

Yale University Press
From "Sinners in the Hands of an Angry God" by Jonathan Edwards from *The Sermons of Jonathan Edwards: A Reader* published by Yale University Press. Copyright © 1999 by Yale University Press. All rights reserved.

Note: Every effort has been made to locate the copyright owner of material reproduced on this component. Omissions brought to our attention will be corrected in subsequent editions.

PHOTO AND ART CREDITS

Cover: *Flag on Orange Field,* 1957, oil on canvas, Johns, Jasper (b.1930)/Ludwig Museum, Cologne, Germany, Lauros/Giraudon;/www.bridgeman.co.uk/Cover art © Jasper Johns/Licensed by VAGA, New York, NY; **2:** Nicole Galeazzi/Omni-Photo Communications, Inc.; **4:** Corel Professional Photos CD-ROM™; **6:** Silver Burdett Ginn; **10:** *Red Jacket,* George Catlin, From the Collection of Gilcrease Museum, Tulsa; **19:** Jeff Greenberg/Photo Researchers, Inc.; **23:** *The Coming of the Mayflower,* N.C. Wyeth, from the Collection of Metropolitan Life Insurance Company, New York City, photograph by Malcolm Varon; **27:** *Anne Bradstreet, The Tenth Muse Lately Sprung Up in America,* Ladonna Gulley Warrick, Courtesy of the artist; **35:** Bettmann/CORBIS; **43:** *Patrick Henry Before the Virginia House of Burgesses 1851,* Peter F. Rothermel, Red Hill, The Patrick Henry National Memorial, Brookneal, Virginia; **48:** Bettmann/CORBIS; **54:** © Archive Photos; **61:** Liberty and Washington, New York State Historical Association, Cooperstown; **65:** David Young-Wolff/PhotoEdit; **70:** The Granger Collection, New York; **77:** The Granger Collection, New York; **81:** National Maritime Museum, London; **90:** Leonard Lee Rue III/Stock, Boston; **100:** *Seashore in Normandy,* 1893, Maximilien Luce, Erich Lessing/Art Resource, NY; **104:** New York State Historical Association, Cooperstown, New York; **108:** "I at length...," Edgar Allan Poe's Tales of Mystery and Imagination (London: George G. Harrap, 1935), Arthur Rackham, Print Collection, Miriam and Ira D. Wallach Division of Art, Prints and Photographs, The New York Public Library; Astor, Lenox and Tilden Foundations; **119:** *Moby-Dick,* 1930, pen and ink drawing, The Granger Collection, New York; **123:** Ralph Waldo Emerson (detail), Frederick Gutekunst/National Portrait Gallery, Smithsonian Institution, Washington D.C./Art Resource, NY; **125:** Tom Bean/CORBIS; **131:** © Lee Snider/CORBIS; **139:** Getty Images; **143:** istockphoto.com; **147:** eStock Photography, LLC; **151:** Courtesy of the Library of Congress; **161:** Courtesy National Archives; **169:** *Frederick Douglass* (detail), c.1844, Attributed to Elisha Hammond, The National Portrait Gallery, Smithsonian Institution, Washington, D.C./Art Resource, New York; **178:** Courtesy of the Library of Congress; **182:** CORBIS; **186:** Courtesy of the Library of Congress; **190:** Frederick Douglass—National Portrait Gallery, Smithsonian Institution/Art Resource, NY; **194:** Pearson Education/PH School Division; **202:** Annie Griffiths/DRK Photo; **206:** Corel Professional Photos CD-ROM™; **213:** Stock Montage, Inc.; **217:** Joel Greenstein/Omni-Photo Communications, Inc.; **221:** George Schreiber (1904–1977), *From Arkansas,* 1939, oil on canvas, Sheldon Swope Art Museum, Terre Haute, Indiana; **227:** Corel Professional Photos CD-ROM™; **231:** The Granger Collection, New York; **235:** Corel Professional Photos CD-ROM™; **239:** © The Stock Market/Milt/Patti Putnam; **250:** *Remember Now the Days of Thy Youth,* 1950, Paul Starrett Sample, Oil on canvas, 34 x 48 inches, Hood Museum of Art, Dartmouth College, Hanover, NH; Gift of Frank L. Harrington, class of 1954; **254:** istockphoto.com; **258:** American Red Cross; **267:** Collection of the Prentice and Paul Sack Photographic Trust of the San Francisco Museum of Modern Art; **269:** Time Life Pictures/Getty Images; **273:** © 1993 J. Fishkin. All Rights Reserved.; **277:** *Miz Emily,* Joseph Holston, 24" x16", Courtesy of Joseph Holston (www.holstonart.com); **288:** CORBIS-Bettmann; **292:** Stock Montage, Inc.; **296:** Corel Professional Photos CD-ROM™; **300:** *Girls Skipping,* 1949, Hale Woodruff, oil on canvas, 24" x 32", Private Collection. Courtesy of Michael Rosenfeld Gallery, New York; **304:** istockphoto.com; **308:** © Hulton Getty/Archive Photos; **318:** FPG International Corp.; **320:** Stock Montage, Inc.; **324:** *Deep Fork Overlook,* Joan Marron-LaRue, Courtesy of the artist; **328:** Culver Pictures, Inc.; **340:** Todd Davidson/Getty Images; **344:** istockphoto.com; **348:** © 2008 Masterfile Corporation; **352:** © Pekka Parviainen/Science Photo Library/Photo Researchers, Inc.; **356:** Dorling Kindersley, Courtesy of the Museum of the Moving Image, London; **360:** istockphoto.com; **370:** Getty Images/Walter Daran/Contributor; **379:** UPI/CORBIS-Bettmann; **383:** Photofest; **387:** James Cotier/Getty Images; **391:** The Trial of Two "Witches" at Salem,

Massachusetts, in 1662, Howard Pyle, The Granger Collection, New York; **395:** Photofest; **405:** Richard Bickel/CORBIS; **409:** Jeff Greenberg/Omni-Photo Communications, Inc.; **420:** © David Lees/CORBIS; **424:** Getty Images, Inc.; **428:** istockphoto.com; **431:** AP/Wide World Photos; **435:** Shutterstock, Inc.; **439:** © Jack Gunter/CORBIS; **447:** Warner Bros./Photofest; **451:** Reuters/CORBIS; **455:** Jim McHugh; **463:** Andrew Ward/Getty Images; **467:** Matt Lambert/Getty Images